James Belich was born in Wellington in 1956 and took his BA and MA degrees in history at Victoria University. He completed a doctorate at Oxford in 1981 while on a Rhodes Scholarship and has taught at the University of Auckland and Victoria University of Wellington. Belich is the author of numerous books, including *Making Peoples* (1996), *Paradise Reforged* (2001) and *Replenishing the Earth* (2009), and is currently Beit Professor of Imperial and Commonwealth History at Oxford University and director of the Oxford Centre for Global History.

THE
NEW ZEALAND
WARS

and the
Victorian Interpretation of Racial Conflict

James Belich

AUCKLAND
UNIVERSITY
PRESS

First published 1986
This edition 2015

Auckland University Press
University of Auckland
Private Bag 92019
Auckland 1142
New Zealand
www.press.auckland.ac.nz

ISBN 978 1 86940 827 5

A catalogue record for this book is available from
the National Library of New Zealand

Cover design: Scott Crickett
Cover photograph: Lisa Truttman

Printed in China through Asia Pacific Offset Limited

To the Memory of
Ivan Petar Anzulović

Contents

Preface   11
Introduction   15
   I The New Zealand Wars in History   15
   II The Background   17

PART ONE: THE NORTHERN WAR

1. A Limited War   29
   I Resistance and Collaboration   30
   II The Fall of Kororareka   36
   III Puketutu: the Last Open Battle   41

2. The Ohaeawai Campaign   45
   I Te Ahuahu: the Forgotten Battle   45
   II Ohaeawai and the Adaptation of *Pa* Construction   47
   III FitzRoy's Peace Effort   54

3. The Paper Victory   58
   I Ruapekapeka and the Adaptation of Maori Strategy   58
   II Peace in the North   64

PART TWO: THE TARANAKI WAR

4. A Question of Sovereignty   73
   I The Causes of War in Taranaki and Waikato   76
   II The Search for Quick Victory   81
   III The Legend of Waireka   84

5. The Intervention of the King Movement   89
   I The Kingite Decision for War   89
   II The Battle of Puketakauere   91

6. The Maori Strategy and the British Response   99
   I The Development of the Maori Strategy   99
   II The British Response: Pratt's Sapping System   108

PART THREE: THE WAIKATO WAR

7. *The Invasion of Waikato*	119
I George Grey and the Preparations for War	119
II The Opposing Armies	125
III The War Behind the Front	133
8. *Rangiriri*	142
I The Second Waikato Line	142
II The Battle of Rangiriri	145
9. *Paterangi and Orakau*	158
I The Paterangi Line	160
II The Battle of Orakau	166
10. *The Tauranga Campaign*	177
I The Battle of Gate Pa	178
II Te Ranga and the Peace in Tauranga	188
III The End of the Waikato War	196

PART FOUR: TITOKOWARU AND TE KOOTI

11. *A New Kind of War*	203
I The Conflicts of 1864–8	203
II The Escape of Te Kooti	216
III The Poverty Bay Campaign	227
12. *Titokowaru and the Brink of Victory*	235
I Titokowaru's Strategy	235
II Te Ngutu o te Manu	241
III Moturoa	248
IV The Crisis of 1868	252
13. *The Turn of the Tide*	258
I The Ngatapa Campaign	260
II The Collapse of Titokowaru's Resistance	267
III The Pursuit of Te Kooti	275

PART FIVE: CONCLUSIONS

14. *The Maori Achievement*	291
I The Modern *Pa* System	291
II The Wars and the Pattern of New Zealand Race Relations	298

15. The Victorian Interpretation of Racial Conflict   311
    I   The Dominant Interpretation   311
    II The Background of Ideas   321
    III The Problem of One-Sided Evidence   330

Glossary   337
References   338
Bibliography   375
Index   389

SKETCH MAPS

Principal locations and major tribal groups   18
Bay of Islands   31
North Taranaki   75
The Lower Waikato   121
The Central Waikato   159
Tauranga   179
Poverty Bay — Urewera   209
South Taranaki — Wanganui   237
Eastern North Island   259

Sketch maps drawn by R. M. Harris

Preface to the 2015 Edition

THIS IS A BOOK ABOUT NEW ZEALAND'S GREAT 'CIVIL WAR', the grand clash of its two peoples, Maori and Pakeha. While minor errors were corrected for the 1998 paperback edition, developments in my thinking since first publication in 1986 have not been incorporated into the book. My reasons are, first, that these developments are consistent with the main lines of *The New Zealand Wars*, and have been set out in the subsequent books *'I Shall Not Die': Titokowaru's War* (1989) and *Making Peoples: A History of the New Zealanders* (1996). Second, I do not feel that my interpretation of the wars and their myths has yet been substantially undermined by other historians or by new evidence. Third, all books are works of their time, and to pretend otherwise by comprehensively revising them is not always a good idea.

The New Zealand Wars was substantially written in 1980–84, when I was in my mid-twenties. It is, in some respects, a 'young man's book'. It was perhaps a little too eager to prove predecessors wrong, and it had over-ambitious aims: to reshape understandings of Maori–Pakeha conflict and of colonial warfare in general. It fell short of the latter objective, but it has had some impact overseas. It was published in a North American edition, and used, for example, in general works on popular imperialism and tribal warfare, and specialist works on Indian sepoys and Australian military history. I take pride in having persuaded at least a few overseas scholars to give New Zealand history its due.

I take still more pride in the fact that, in New Zealand, the book's readership has gone beyond the few—surprisingly far for an academic work which unashamedly confronts complexity. The book has not only stayed in print for almost three decades, but also provided the base for a television documentary series—an almost unimaginable fate for something which began life as a doctoral thesis. The television series may be the pudding: the book remains the proof.

Preface

THIS BOOK IS A REVISIONIST STUDY OF THE NEW ZEALAND WARS of 1845-72. It is undertaken partly for its own sake, but also in the pursuit of two themes of wider importance. The first, indicated by the 'New Zealand Wars' part of the book's title, concerns the major military events, their underlying nature, and their impact on New Zealand history. The second, 'The Victorian Interpretation of Racial Conflict', concerns the contemporary record of these events, and its implications for comparable conflicts.

The first theme stems from a widespread problem in the history of war. The problem is not simply one of neglect, but of the isolation of military history, of its separation from the mainstream of historical scholarship. This is as much the responsibility of those who have practised military history as of those who have not. The aim of the former has often been, in Michael Howard's words, 'didactic and normative',[1] and teaching people how to fight better does not necessarily make for good histories of fighting, or for historical, as against military, revisionism. The approach of 'campaign history' tends to be narrow, to implicitly deny that war is part of history as a whole, interwoven with politics and economics, society and culture, to form a single fabric. On the other hand, professional historians tend to avoid military history, partly on the principle that to study war is to advocate it. This is an ostrich-approach to the malaise of war, as irrational as it is persistent.

A number of historians have noted this, and some have also discerned a trend towards a 'new history' of warfare.[2] However, at least for those interested in resistance to European expansion, celebrating the turn of the tide may be premature. Good books have been published on warlike organizations, on the ideological and social history of war, and on the human dimension of combat. The works of Philip Mason, Paul Fussell, and John Keegan are outstanding cases in point.[3] Yet wars, in D. G. Chandler's phrase, are 'ultimately determined as a result of that nasty, messy business called *fighting*'.[4] There is, perhaps, a tendency to see the new themes in the history of war as alternatives to the study of campaigns, rather than its necessary partners. Keegan cautions us against this throwing-out of the baby with the bathwater. We still want to know who won, how, and to what degree, and, like war itself, these questions are too important to be left to generals.

Possibly, as far as some European wars are concerned, these questions have already been answered sufficiently well. The volume of research, revision, and counter-revision in the 'old' military history may be great enough, and exceptions to the rule of a narrow perspective numerous enough, to create a reliable base concerning what actually happened. A fresh generation of historians can proceed from this to explore the themes of the new military history. But, as Brian Bond, Michael Crowder, and Donald C. Gordon have observed, scholarly neglect of military history is particularly acute in cases of colonial warfare.[5] Here, a reliable and extensive base of modern conventional military histories, founded on primary research, rarely exists. In the study of colonial warfare, therefore, the re-evaluation of campaigns—a revisionist 'old' military history—must proceed hand-in-hand with an approach more akin to the new military history, one which recognizes war as an interacting part of the historical totality. To understand the social and cultural history of war—and the effect of war on social and cultural history, which is rather different—we must first know what happened, how, and why.

These considerations dictate the character and limitations of the military analysis in this book. On the one hand, like the old military history it focuses on battle, on the questions of who won, how, and to what degree—for, in many wars, winning is a matter of degree. Since the secondary literature on the New Zealand Wars often simply perpetuates inherited assumptions, even the most basic conclusions—that the British won a particular war for example—cannot be accepted merely because a dozen books draw them. Revision must proceed from the ground up. On the other hand, like the new military history, the analysis also seeks to place the events as revised in their contexts—in their military context, as part of the competition between two systems of war, and in their non-military context, as part of the broad sweep of New Zealand history, and particularly of race relations history.

But human conflict does not decline in complexity as it does in scale and, within the present limits of space, neither objective can be fully achieved. The revisionist 'old' military history approach does not produce a comprehensive narrative but concentrates on the four major wars and their major military events, to the exclusion of lesser operations. The small size of wars is too readily equated with insignificance, and it is not suggested that such operations were unimportant, but simply that they were less important. Nor does the 'new' military history approach go as far as one could wish. The anthropology of warlike organizations, the social history of war, and the human face of battle are touched on all too lightly. This book can only be a first step towards integrating the story of the most important conflict fought in New Zealand into the story of the country as a whole.

The book's second theme, the Victorian interpretation of racial conflict, arises from the fact that the history of the New Zealand Wars is essentially a situation of one-sided evidence. Broadly speaking, the British dominated the historical record. They preserved some Maori evidence, but it was a small fraction of the whole, and it was generally used to provide anecdotal curiosities rather than an alternative interpretation. The problem of one-sided evidence is familiar to historians in many fields. In innumerable cases where important historical issues involve two or more groups, the written record of all but one is lost, is inaccessible, or never existed. When the issue is some kind of conflict, and that group which dominates the historical record believes itself inherently superior to its opponents, the problem is particularly acute. Writers who are party to a conflict are likely to favour their own side, and those holding to convictions of superiority find it difficult to be fair to their 'inferiors'.

'Bias' is a convenient term for this type of subjectivity, but its pejorative connotations are not altogether appropriate. The tendency toward bias might sometimes be transcended, and it does not necessarily involve conscious distortion. It merely reflects the normal subordinacy of commentators to their intellectual context. But bias, fact of human nature though it is, obviously aggravates the problem of one-sided evidence. Historians of social conflict often face the problem in this extreme form, and so too do historians of race warfare. A great many examples of resistance to European expansion involved tribal cultures which have left no written record of their own.

Historians interested in redressing this imbalance have occasionally turned to the oral tradition of tribal societies, and one hopes that more will do so in the future. But as a solution in itself to the problem of one-sided evidence, oral tradition presents certain difficulties. If it exists, it may avoid the bitter memories of war. Unlike a document, it is not frozen in time at the point of writing, but bears the added imprint of those who passed it down through the generations. Nor is it necessarily the function of oral tradition to reflect empirical reality. Religion, genealogy, and support for claims of land ownership may be more important. The scholar who uses such data without due caution is in danger of forcing a square peg into a round hole.

Another approach to the problem of one-sided evidence, ideally a supplement rather than an alternative to oral tradition, begins by analysing the bias of the group which dominates the written record. Historians frequently refer to the bias of their sources, particularly when dealing with accounts of warfare, but all too often this is the merest lip-service—a token obeisance to the gods of subjectivity. We are told that the lens distorts, but not whether it is short-sighted or long-sighted. It is true that some types of bias are common and obvious, and that others arise from so specific a set of circumstances that they are not amenable to generalization. But perhaps another type of bias exists, based on shared preconceptions and shared conditioning, which may be subject to general rules. If a given set of cultural factors interacts in a relatively consistent way with a given type of event, then this may produce an interpretative tendency which, broadly speaking, remains constant from case to case. If such a pattern of interpretation, or misinterpretation, can be established, it may be of some use in alleviating the problem of one-sided evidence.

No historian would deny that cultural factors influence the contemporary interpretation of events. 'Cultural factors' in this sense have been variously indicated by such terms as 'intellectual context', 'total ideology', and '*mentalité*'. These terms have different shades of meaning, but they also have common ground. They imply a conceptual apparatus with which a society or group understands, and places itself in, the world around it. This conceptual apparatus should be of great interest to historians of events, because it helps determine the nature of their evidence. But there is, perhaps, a reluctance to study it as the natural adjunct of empirical revisionism. Such study is intimidating both in its practical complexity and its theoretical implications. The former makes generalization seem difficult and dangerous. The latter gives it the flavour of theoretical speculation—that wicked Siren which tempts solid scholars from the mine-face of history. In situations of one-sided evidence, we cannot afford the luxury of giving way to these doubts. They are a reason for caution, not evasion.

The second theme of this book is therefore an attempt to explore the possibility that preconceptions systematically affect interpretation, in a particular intellectual context—that of the Victorian British—and a particular racial conflict—the New Zealand Wars. We ask whether a consistent pattern of interpretation existed, how and why it worked, and whether it can be used against itself to alleviate the problem of one-sided evidence. We seek to provide an anatomy of 'bias' in a situation where biased accounts are virtually all we have. The strands of this investigation run through the whole book, but, because the findings are essentially variations on the same themes, they are discussed most fully in the Conclusion.

Introduction

I THE NEW ZEALAND WARS IN HISTORY

THE NEW ZEALAND WARS OF 1845-72 WERE A SERIES OF
conflicts involving the British, Imperial and colonial, and the Maori tribes
of the North Island. They were not, as is sometimes suggested, storms in a
teacup or gentlemanly bouts of fisticuffs, but bitter and bloody struggles, as
important to New Zealand as were the Civil Wars to England and the
United States. In proportion to New Zealand's population at the time, they
were large in scale—some 18,000 British troops were mobilized for the biggest campaign. These forces opposed a people who, for most of the war
period, did not number more than 60,000 men, women, and children:
18,000 troops were to Maori manpower what fifty million were to contemporary Indian manpower. The Maori resistance against such odds was
remarkable, and its story is worth telling in itself. But the wars were also
crucial in the development of New Zealand race relations, and they marked
a watershed in the history of the country as a whole. More than this, they
were examples of that widespread phenomenon: resistance to European expansion. Their history can tell us something about the character and interpretation of other conflicts, and about the response of non-European
peoples to the Imperial challenge.

The present state of knowledge on the New Zealand Wars presents
something of a paradox. On the one hand, a firmly entrenched and widely
disseminated received version exists almost unquestioned. It is repeated at
length by histories of the war based on secondary material and aimed at a
wide audience; more briefly by scholarly analyses to which the military
course of the wars is important but not central; and more briefly still by
general histories of New Zealand and surveys treating aspects of warfare,
race relations, and imperialism.[1] On the other hand, there has been no
substantial examination of the wars for sixty years. Good work has been
done on their causes and consequences, but not on their course. In 1966,
B. J. Dalton pinpointed this problem in a useful essay, but himself simply
resurrected a facet of the contemporary British interpretation—the defence
of the regular army from criticism—which was in abeyance.[2] In 1968, in his
book *Shadow of the Land,* Ian Wards discussed part of the conflict period in
great detail. He provided some new insights, but most of the wars occurred

15

after his chosen period, and he remained ambivalent about the result of the
most important of those he did treat: the Northern War.[3]

The most recent comprehensive examination of the wars based on
primary evidence, *The New Zealand Wars and the Pioneering Period* by
James Cowan, was published in 1922-3—closer in time to the wars
themselves than to the present day. Cowan's work has an obvious bias and
obvious weaknesses, but to castigate him for being a man of his era is a
fruitless exercise. It can even be counter-productive, because the recognition of his bias is easily mistaken for its correction. Cowan was a product of
an intensely Anglocentric, Empire-worshipping period in New Zealand's
development, and in this context his balance is quite impressive. He showed
a real sympathy for the Maoris, for example in his analysis of the Parihaka
incident of 1881, and Maori veterans trusted him enough to provide him
with accounts of their experience. These are available in Cowan's papers
and, with his published work, they help to make a re-assessment possible.[4]

But the fact remains that Cowan himself did not provide that re-
assessment. His primary objective was to rehabilitate the 'frontier period'
and 'the adventure-teeming life of the pioneer colonists', as an exciting and
instructive field of study for the young colonial patriot. Against the prevailing Anglocentric mood, Cowan looked to American rather than British
parallels.[5] He set out to show that New Zealand had a Wild West too and,
for what it is worth, he succeeded. This entailed concentrating on the
details, with a cultural mission always in mind. At one point, he helpfully
inserted a two-paragraph note on costume 'for the guidance of artists who
may some day essay to paint the historic scene at Orakau'.[6] To ensure that
justice was done to every individual's ancestors, and that every possible
locality had its heroes and its historic sites, he recorded 200 engagements
and innumerable other gallant feats and adventurous incidents. There was
little room for an overview of the British and Maori war efforts, and still
less for the substantive re-analysis of their major events. Battles are
notoriously difficult phenomena to reconstruct, and though Cowan provided
his own rich colour, he—like all other historians after him—relied for his
outlines, for the basic structures of his story, on older interpretations.
Those of Cowan's contemporaries who investigated the wars, like T.
Lindsay Buick and Sir J. W. Fortescue, though they might emphasize
different aspects of the received version, essentially did likewise.[7]

Consequently, while all around it has been re-examined, and while it has
been shorn of overt value-judgements and blatant biases, the story of the
New Zealand Wars has remained fundamentally unchanged since the nineteenth century. The Victorian interpretation is alive and well and living in
New Zealand. Conclusions about what actually happened often remain unchanged. Maori successes continue to be underestimated. British victories
continue to be exaggerated, and entirely fictional triumphs continue to be
seen as real. The degree of Maori success in all four major wars is still
underestimated—even to the point where, in the case of one war, the wrong
side is still said to have won.

As in the nineteenth century, the majority of historians emphasize British blunders as the main causes of recognized defeat. The minority revive the equally questionable contemporary hypothesis which stressed difficulties of terrain, British logistical problems, and Maori evasiveness. Both groups follow the more enlightened contemporary commentators in noting Maori courage, chivalry, and some types of skill, but they too deny the existence of strategic planning, co-ordination, and combination. 'The Maoris displayed the military weaknesses generally associated with savage races . . . he fought under no definite strategical plan and without unity of command.'[8] From W. P. Reeves— 'even their fiercest fighting leaders . . . scarcely deserved the name of generals'; through James Hight— 'they lacked enterprise, perseverence in a single line of action, and a knowledge of the broader principles of campaigning'; to Keith Sinclair— 'throughout the wars the Maoris adopted no comprehensive or co-ordinated strategy'—we hear the same story. These misconceptions persist into the *Oxford History of New Zealand*, published in 1981. 'British discipline and British artillery had proved too much for Maori warriors, and they failed to realize the dangers of continuing to meet the British on their terms, in the field. To the grenade, the rifle, and the Armstrong gun, the sap and the redoubt, they had no ultimate answer.'[9]

This received version will be challenged in this book, and an alternative interpretation offered in its place. But, as discussed in the Preface, the aims of the book go further. First, because war is only part of the historical totality, always interacting with other parts, a limited attempt will be made to explore the wider implications of the military events as revised, especially for New Zealand race relations. Second, because an understanding of the Victorian interpretation is necessary to overturn it, it too will be a subject of study. This book is not just about what happened, but about what people thought happened, and why they thought as they did.

II   THE BACKGROUND

AT THE TIME OF THE WARS, THE MAORI PEOPLE HAD LIVED IN New Zealand for a thousand years, successfully surmounting the revolutionary environmental change from tropical islands to a temperate landmass larger than Britain. The Maoris were a tribal people, with a subsistence economy based on the cultivation of root-crops, supplemented by fishing, gathering, and bird-hunting. They lived a harsh life, without metal tools or a written language. But this did not mean that their society was simple and primitive, or rigid and unchanging. Organized around a well-developed belief system, a rich oral and artistic culture, and the principle of kinship, traced through descent, Maori society was varied, complicated, and robust. It was also 'flexible, resilient, and adaptable'[10]—not ill-equipped, in some respects, to face the biggest environmental change of them all: the advent of Europeans.

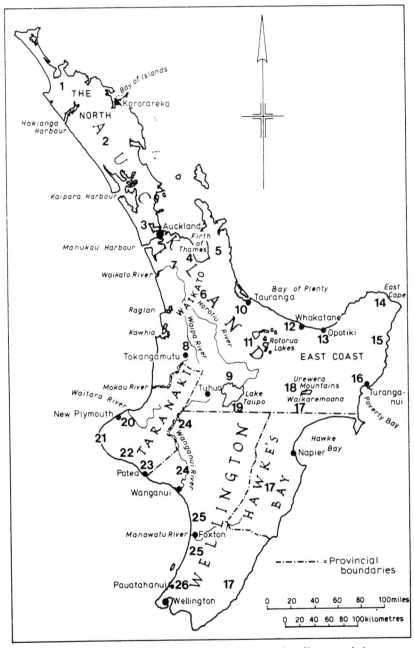

Principal locations and major tribal groups (see list opposite)

The first Maori reaction to contact with Europeans was, unambiguously enough, to kill and eat them. The Dutch explorer Abel Tasman, who visited the coast in 1642, had one of his boats attacked and four of his men killed. After contact recommenced in 1769, with the visits of Cook and de Surville, a series of similar incidents dotted the history of Maori-European relations. These made it easy to assume that uncontrolled European contact had reduced New Zealand to a state of chaos. But in relation to the sum total of contact, these incidents were exceptional. The norm was peaceful, though sometimes uneasy, co-existence and trade.

There was a simple reason for this. The Maoris wanted what the Europeans (*Pakeha*) had to offer in terms of knowledge and goods. Luxuries, particularly the musket, rapidly became necessities. All Europeans in New Zealand, both visiting and resident, were more-or-less traders—even the missionaries had to exchange goods for food, land, and protection. Consequently, they were highly valued, and carefully safeguarded. The Maoris were unlikely to eliminate the goose that laid the golden egg. But European numbers were so small, and the visits of warships so infrequent, that they could easily do so if they wished. This coercive power balanced the Maori side of the equation. If Europeans mistreated Maoris, they would be killed. If Maoris mistreated Europeans, trade would stop.

The balance was not as unequal as it seemed, because the absence of such trade goods as muskets and ammunition could be fatal for the Maoris; tribes which did not have muskets were at the mercy of those which did. For some time, few Maoris could envisage a limit to their need for European goods, and consequently a common attitude was that the more *Pakeha*, the better. The Treaty of Waitangi and British 'annexation' in 1840 did not im-

MAJOR TRIBAL GROUPS

1 Rarawa	15 Ngati Porou
2 Ngapuhi	16 Rongowhakaata and Aitanga-a-
3 Ngati Whatua	Mahaki
4 Ngati Paoa	17 Ngati Kahungunu
5 Ngati Maru	18 Tuhoe
6 Ngati Haua	19 Ngati Tuwharetoa
7 Waikato Proper	20 Te Atiawa
8 Ngati Maniapoto	21 Taranaki
9 Ngati Raukawa	22 Ngati Ruanui
10 Ngai-te-Rangi	23 Ngarauru
11 Arawa	24 Wanganui
12 Ngati Awa	25 Ngati Raukawa, Ngati Apa,
13 Whakatohea	and Muaupoko
14 Whanau-a-Apanui	26 Ngati Toa, Te Atiawa, and
	Ngati Ira.

mediately change this situation. Some chiefs did begin to have doubts about the scale of immigration, particularly the instant townships organized by the New Zealand Company on the principles of Edward Gibbon Wakefield, but over-all the basic belief in the desirability of European contact and settlement remained intact.

During the early period of contact, 1800–40, Maori society underwent certain changes and convulsions, but the destructive impact of these has been exaggerated. Some European tools and techniques were adopted in commerce and agriculture, but production was still organized and distributed for Maori ends in a Maori way. Various Christian missions had been established from 1814, and after 1830 many Maoris adopted at least the outward forms of Christianity, and were taught to write in their own language by the missionaries and their Maori acolytes. But it is possible that early Maori Christianity synthesized with, rather than replaced, the traditional belief system; and that missionary teaching was seen as a means to the end of gaining European knowledge, instead of an end in itself. The Europeans brought new infectious diseases, and these increased Maori mortality. But epidemics of some of the most lethal diseases did not occur; the Maoris may have begun to develop immunities by 1840; and overly-high estimates of the pre-European Maori population may have led to an exaggeration of the death-rate.

From 1818, parts of the North Island were convulsed by increased tribal warfare. These conflicts continued in full force until about 1833, and are known as the Musket Wars. It is sometimes suggested that they subsided because of Maori exhaustion or missionary mediation, but the restoration of the inter-tribal balance of military power seems more likely. The wars began when the Ngapuhi, of the region north of Auckland, became the first tribe to acquire significant numbers of muskets, and used them to pay off old scores and increase their wealth and prestige. Other tribes who acquired muskets early did likewise. The wars ended when all tribes had muskets. There were no more easy victories, and the balance was restored. All in all, Maori society bent but did not break under the impact of early European contact. The few hundred European missionaries, traders, and whalers who lived with the Maoris in 1838 did so on sufferance, protected by their value, not their power.[11]

Outside the points of early mass-immigration, the towns of Auckland, Wellington, Wanganui, New Plymouth, and Nelson, British annexation did not overturn the essentially Maori-dominated racial relationship. It did, however, add to pre-existing strains and create new ones. The group of Maori chiefs who signed the Treaty of Waitangi in 1840 thought they were obtaining a substantial flow of valuable *Pakeha* in return for ceding a loose and vague suzerainty. The British thought that, in return for the introduction of order and civilization, they were to get full and real sovereignty. Whether or not the different versions of the Treaty itself actually created this misunderstanding, they certainly epitomized it. In the Maori language version, the Maoris were guaranteed the free exercise of their *rangatira-*

tanga, their chiefly authority. They ceded only the newly created *kawana-tanga*—Governor's authority. In the English language version, there was no mention of chiefly authority, and the Maoris ceded both.

The historian Ruth Ross discussed this difference more than a decade ago, and the Maori wording of the Treaty is still the subject of some debate.[12] But one possible ambiguity in the English wording has received less attention. 'Sovereignty' has two relevant shades of meaning, which we can distinguish by adding the words 'nominal' and 'substantive'. Nominal sovereignty is the theoretical dominion of a sovereign—even a monarch who 'reigns but does not govern'. Substantive sovereignty is the actual dominion of a controlling power, whether a monarch or not, which exercises a decisive, though not necessarily absolute, influence over the whole of a country. There is little doubt that the British had the latter meaning in mind, but it is the former which may have come closer to the Maori understanding of the Treaty. Certainly, for many years after 1840, 'nominal sovereignty' was much closer to the reality.

This ambiguity was a source of friction. The British imagined that they were entitled to govern the Maoris in fact as well as name, although the early Governors (William Hobson and Robert FitzRoy) were sufficiently realistic to grasp that substantive sovereignty could not be applied comprehensively overnight. The Maoris resented British interference in local matters, except where they themselves invited it for a particular purpose. At the same time, they still wished to encourage trade and settlement.

These tensions, together with careless land purchasing by New Zealand Company agents, led to the first violent clash to take place after 1840: the Wairau Affray. On 17 June 1843, the local magistrate and fifty armed settlers set out from Nelson to enforce a claim to land at Wairau which they believed they had purchased. The Ngati Toa chiefs Te Rauparaha and Te Rangihaeata, great generals of the Musket Wars, believed that their people owned the land, and had not been paid for it. Similar disputes had previously been settled by compromise or set aside for subsequent adjudication, and in this case Te Rauparaha, a strong advocate of interaction with Europeans, was willing to negotiate. But the settlers attempted to arrest him—to apply British law to a Maori chief. Firing broke out, and the settlers were routed by an equal number of Maoris. The Maoris lost four killed, and the British lost twenty-two, including some slain after capture.[13] The British took no action over this incident, mainly because they lacked the military resources, and large-scale conflict was thus avoided until the Northern War broke out in 1845.

Despite Wairau, the competition between British and Maori military systems had, for the latter, an unpromising starting point. Maori tribal forces were qualitatively superior to untrained and ill-organized posses of armed settlers. But the professional military forces of the British Empire were another matter. Maori disadvantages did not lie in the area of small arms. It seems that, from 1830 if not earlier, the Maoris were able to insist on weapons of reasonable quality, avoiding the 'sham dam iron' guns made

in Birmingham and Liége for the Africa trade. Such guns cost five or six
shillings each, and 8,000 muskets exported from Sydney to New Zealand in
1830-1 had an average value of twenty-seven shillings each.[14] Particularly
in the areas of longest contact with Europeans, such as the North, the
Maoris were able to supplement their original flintlocks with double-
barrelled shotguns and percussion-lock muskets by 1845. In the Northern
War of 1845-6, they were therefore on a par with the British, who had yet
to complete the change to percussion-locks. By 1860, most Maori guns were
apparently percussion-locks, but the British had by this time switched to
Enfield rifles, firing the expanding Minie bullet. These were far superior to
muskets in range, power, and accuracy. These advantages were balanced,
however, by a lower rate of fire, and a degree of parity in small arms persisted. The Maoris had difficulty with repair, replacement, and ammunition
supply, but inferiority in small-arms weaponry remained the least of the
Maoris' problems.

The two most basic Maori disadvantages were also the simplest, though
their importance is hard to over-emphasize. Maori society had no professional warrior class, and it produced little in the way of an economic
surplus. The military force was a vital part of the labour force; economically,
it could not be spared for more than a few weeks and as a result traditional
Maori warfare had the character of sporadic raids rather than campaigns.
The Maoris therefore faced the same problem as any tribal people in conflict with a regular army: a totally inadequate capacity to sustain a war of
any length. The distinction, made throughout this book, between part-time
Maori 'warriors' and full-time British 'troops' serves as a reminder of this
crucial difference.

This compounded the second problem: inferior numbers. Maori political
entities were very small. Population figures are unreliable before 1858, but
the thirty North Island tribes averaged something over 2,000 people in
1845, and the *hapu*, or sub-tribe, was often the unit of military action. Even
when substantial combinations occurred, the need to divide the warrior's
time between the cultivations and the battlefront kept numbers low.
Though the British Empire did not commit a significant fraction of its
resources to New Zealand until 1863, the troops outnumbered the Maoris
in virtually every campaign. There was no thin red line in New Zealand,
and British numerical superiority was often very great.

Other important areas of Maori disadvantage related to the nature of their
enemy. Many writers have remarked upon the weaknesses of the nineteenth-
century British army, and one New Zealand historian has described it as a
collection of 'scum led by fools'.[15] No one labouring under this misapprehension can hope to understand the New Zealand Wars. Despite its undoubted weaknesses, the British army had a high tactical success rate
against European and non-European enemies alike. The fiasco of the
Crimean War arose primarily from logistical failings. It was not so much
that the logistic system was flawed, but that it did not exist: there was no
comprehensive supply and support organization designed to sustain an army

in the field (although some efforts in this direction were made after 1856). Logistics were organized in *ad hoc* fashion, for each particular campaign. This meant they could be either good or bad, depending on environmental conditions, the size of the force involved, and the commander's grasp of the importance of logistical planning. In New Zealand, despite persistent problems with such things as land transport, British logistics were usually reasonably good.

One of the best-known weaknesses of the Victorian army was its system of officer-selection and education. Some officers did cultivate a kind of pragmatic amateurism, emphasizing such things as sport and horsemanship as much as military knowledge, and this could create amusing foibles. Byron Farwell notes that one officer assessed a subordinate as follows: 'personally, I would not breed from this officer'.[16] But the effects of this, and of the method of promotion by purchase, can be exaggerated, at least as far as the New Zealand Wars are concerned. Officer recruitment was not exclusively from the wealthy and noble; moneyed and aristocratic families did not consist entirely of fools; and those promoted through money and influence, rather than ability, would use that money and influence to avoid being posted to New Zealand. No Guards or Cavalry units, the most fashionable regiments, served in New Zealand. Indeed, it may be that except in large wars, such as the Crimean, the dross of the Victorian officer corps graced the clubs of London rather than the battlefields of Empire. We shall see that, contrary to legend, the senior British officers in New Zealand were usually moderately competent, and a few were very able indeed.

The British rank-and-file were bullied, flogged, poorly housed and paid, and sometimes poorly fed. Yet for all this, they were extremely formidable in battle. As generations of military historians have observed, the key to this paradox was the regiment. British privates were indeed recruited from the lower classes, and liberal historians who describe them as 'scum' might care to check their philosophic consistency. But they were not drawn primarily from life-long beggars and vagabonds. They were working people who had lost their livelihoods and communities through economic recession, famine, or dispossession of land. A large proportion, even in English regiments, were Irishmen. The regiment replaced the lost community. Men fought for it, not Queen and Country. In this sense, the army was a collection of military tribes, warrior guilds comparable to the Turkish janissary corps, with their own customs, emblems, and traditions. Their high discipline involved unnecessary rigmarole, but it also provided responses automatic enough to overcome fear on the battlefield. The sudden release from discipline, in the form of an order to charge, unleashed an almost berserk ferocity. This motivation and conditioning, combined with British officers' willingness to incur higher casualties than any responsible tribal chief could contemplate, made assaulting British troops very hard to stop.

Though British officers were not the blunderers of legend, the Maori were easily able to match them in quality of leadership. A chief who derived his *mana* (authority, prestige) from inheritance or non-military achievement might be highly respected, regardless of military ability, but he would not necessarily be followed in war. Though normally well-disciplined in actual battle, warriors reserved the right to withdraw their support from a chief before or after it. An incompetent Maori warleader was therefore a contradiction in terms, since he would have no followers. But the Maoris were much less well-placed in other respects. While Maori supply organization became quite sophisticated in the Waikato War of 1863-4, their subsistence economy meant that it could never match the British. The attributes of British troops put the Maoris at a disadvantage in two important types of combat: open battle and the defence of fortifications.

The evidence on the pre-contact frequency of open battle, the clash of formed bodies of troops on open ground, is contradictory.[17] But an underlying Maori preference for open battle was apparent during the New Zealand Wars, and during the Musket Wars they seem to have been common.[18] The Maoris became skilled in the use of the musket and some of the methods associated with it, such as firing by volley. Quite well-organized bodies of warriors exchanged volleys and charges on open ground. Except for wardances which preceded them, and the cannibalism which often followed them, these battles were not dissimilar to the European norm. For the Maoris, this was by no means a fortunate coincidence. Apart from superior numbers, British regimental spirit could match the Maori tribal spirit, the British bayonet charge was as ferocious as a Maori attack, and the British were more widely experienced in this kind of combat. Societies which achieved far closer facsimiles than the Maoris of the British style of warfare, such as the Sikhs, still found difficulty in beating the British at their own game. In 1845, it was reasonable to expect that the fact that this was also the Maoris' own game would only prove a disadvantage to them—by tempting them into the very kind of combat they could not win.

Another common form of Maori battle was the attack and defence of *pa*, a term used for virtually any kind of Maori fortification. Traditional *pa* usually functioned to protect population and resources against a superior foe, either by being themselves fortified villages or by providing places of refuge to which the inhabitants of outlying villages could go with their goods in times of strife. Since they were close to centres of population, traditional *pa* were usually strategically accessible. To maximize the difficulty of attack, however, they were sited on tactically commanding points in or near these centres. This usually meant hills, or headlands on the coast.[19] In terms of warfare with Europeans, all this raised problems.

First, the local high ground on which *pa* were located could sometimes be surrounded. Though the supplies in a traditional *pa* could usually outlast those of a besieging tribal force, the same did not necessarily apply to the British. Secondly, the coastal location of many *pa* exposed them to that much underestimated land weapon, the warship. Even a relatively small sloop was a floating battery of considerable power which could—and on a couple of occasions did—reduce traditional *pa* to matchsticks very quickly.[20] Third, even where *pa* were not directly on the coast, their location near cultivated, accessible ground meant artillery could be brought up to them without great difficulty. Because traditional *pa* and buildings within them were mainly built of wood, and because their tactical location on low hills made them easy targets, they could, as Lieutenant Bennet of the Royal Engineers observed in 1843, quickly be destroyed by a couple of howitzers.[21] Finally, the capture or destruction of traditional *pa* meant the loss of the resources they contained and protected, and consequently a rapid decline in the Maori capacity to fight.

The Musket Wars resulted in a number of adjustments to the construction of *pa* to protect the garrison from musket fire, but *pa* remained vulnerable to cannon, and their function and location were not changed. Their location meant the British could easily get at them, their construction meant that the British could easily destroy them, and their function meant that their loss would be crippling.

Though it had incorporated a borrowed technology in the form of the musket, the Maori system of war in 1845 remained essentially indigenous: it was intended purely to cope with local enemies of roughly equal resources. As such, it was markedly inferior to the British system at both the quantitative and qualitative levels. Under good leaders, the Maoris could still secure isolated successes, but even in the short term they appeared to be hopelessly outmatched.

---PART ONE---

The Northern War

1

A Limited War

THE FIRST MAJOR CONFLICT BETWEEN THE BRITISH AND THE
Maoris was the Northern War, fought in the area around the Bay of Islands
between March 1845 and January 1846. The British were opposed by a
section of the Ngapuhi tribe under the chiefs Hone Heke and Kawiti. Heke
was the most prominent of the anti-government chiefs, and his name is
customarily used as shorthand for the whole political leadership. In military
terms, however, Kawiti was equally important. These chiefs fought not only
the British, but also another section of Ngapuhi. The leaders of this group
included Mohi Tawhai, Patuone, and Makoare Te Taonui, but Tamati
Waka Nene was the most notable.

The orthodox view of the Northern War, a view common to virtually all
twentieth-century works, is that the first stages were grossly mishandled by
Governor Robert FitzRoy and his military commanders. The situation was
then saved by the arrival of a new Governor, George Grey, who brought the
war to a triumphant conclusion and secured a permanent peace through
generous treatment of the defeated rebels. This interpretation will be questioned here. It will be argued that the war resulted in defeat for the British,
and limited victory for Heke and Kawiti. The argument that Maori successes arose, not from British blunders, but from radical adaptation of the
Maori military system is an integral part of this re-assessment.

Though two battles—Kororareka and Te Ahuahu—fell outside it, the
basic pattern of military operations in the Northern War was a series of
British forays into the hilly and bush-clad interior. The three major expeditions (3–12 May 1845, 16 June–15 July 1845, and 7 December 1845–16
January 1846) were so distinct from each other as to be miniature campaigns in themselves. The first expedition was planned in late January
1845, to punish Heke for his defying the Government by cutting down the
Union Jack at the important British settlement of Kororareka. At this stage,
the British may have been content to teach Heke a lesson.[1] But the expedition was not mounted until after Heke and Kawiti had captured Kororareka
on 11 March 1845, and from this point the British objective became un-
equivocal and deadly. Each expedition was intended to kill or capture Heke
or Kawiti and to destroy their forces.[2] The objectives of both the resisting
and the collaborating Ngapuhi factions, however, are less simple and they
require closer examination.

29

I RESISTANCE AND COLLABORATION

SOME UNDERSTANDING OF THE DEEPER CAUSES OF CONFLICT IS
important to the military analysis of the Northern War. If Heke was aiming
to expel the British from the North and to turn back the clock to pre-
annexation days, as is often implied, then he clearly failed. If his objective
was less comprehensive, then the question remains open. The problem of
war aims is complicated by the possibility that the Northern War was a
three-sided conflict—that Waka had different objectives from his allies the
British.

The differences between Ngapuhi resisters and collaborators were less
remarkable than their common ground. Both groups adhered to the two
great Maori principles of early race relations mentioned in the Introduction:
a determination to uphold chiefly authority against arbitrary British interference, and a desire for interaction with Europeans. The division arose,
perhaps, when measures in support of the former principle seemed to
militate against the latter—when the defence of one aspect of the *status quo*
threatened another. Thus the cleavage between resistance and collaboration
was narrow; a matter of perception and emphasis, rather than fundamental
attitudes.

The early British governors were aware that any attempt suddenly to impose substantive sovereignty was beyond their resources. But they did expect to impose ordinances, apply some laws, and take certain actions which
concerned Maoris, without necessarily consulting the chiefs. Some measures which affected the Bay of Islands were the imposition of customs
dues, restrictions on the felling of certain types of timber, and the removal
of the capital from Kororareka to Auckland.[3] All this diverted settlers from
the North and reduced economic activity, and it coincided with a downturn
in demand for New Zealand products in Australian markets. Government
interference, in itself objectionable, was also acting against the second
Maori imperative—an adequate level of interaction with Europeans. By
reacting to this, Ngapuhi resisters were pushing for more European contact,
not less.

Other government measures affecting the Bay of Islands included the execution of the minor Ngapuhi chief Maketu in 1842, for murder. The
application of British law was only possible because it happened to coincide
with Maori law, but it still created some resentment.[4] When Robert
FitzRoy, a conscientious man of some ability and more moral courage,
became Governor in December 1843, he investigated land sales and applied
the Crown's pre-emptive right to the purchase of Maori land. His police
magistrate at Kororareka, Thomas Beckham, did his best to apply British
law in the town at least with the few constables available to him. The local
settlers were naturally more reluctant to submit to chiefly arbitration and to
Maori law. For Ngapuhi, this compounded the pre-existing problem of
applying traditional law to the new range of disputes resulting from infor-

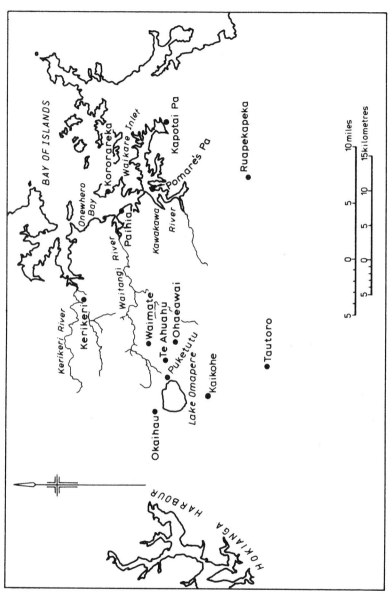

Bay of Islands, illustrating the Northern War (Chapters 1–3)

mal European settlement and contact, and of upholding chiefly authority in the face of this and other pressures.[5]

Hone Heke simply shared in the common recognition of the problem of government interference, but he was an exponent of vigorous solutions to it. One of these solutions, basically a peaceful policy, was the energetic application of Maori law and Maori local authority. Though they were hostile to his efforts, European observers could not fail to note them. One wrote that Heke 'had constituted himself a Court of Inquisition: wherever he could hear of an offence, he would come down upon the offender with a *taua* [war party], on the plea of administering justice'.[6] Comments like these have given Heke a reputation as a 'congenital busybody',[7] but his activities are open to a more favourable interpretation.

His judgement was not unfair and his approach was not biased against Europeans under his control. The term 'my pakeha' implied responsibility as well as authority. In October 1844 he took one of his *Pakehas* to task for using timber from *tapu* (sacred) ground, but added that his lieutenant 'will arrange for you to get the necessary trees on unconsecrated ground'. In general, his letter to this settler was intended: 'to search out wrongs in every portion of the country . . . interpret these words to the Europeans, also to the Maoris . . . if you the Europeans, will do [your] part, I will do mine and make amends for any wrong acts of the Maori people'.[8] Balanced as they were, Heke's efforts were not appreciated by the settlers, who believed that substantive sovereignty now rested with their race. Maori law continued to be contravened in a variety of incidents, and the settlers became increasingly reluctant to part with the customary compensation for their misdemeanours.[9]

It seemed to Heke—and to most other northern chiefs—that the bulk of their problems and prospective problems arose from government attempts to interfere in their sphere of activity. In mid-1844, Heke decided to resist the incursions closer to their source, rather than to continue to rely on *ad hoc* efforts to cope with their effects. The problem with direct measures, however, was that they could easily militate against the second of the Maori imperatives. Heke, like most other chiefs, wished to preserve the valuable Maori-European economic relationship. When war broke out, Heke's solution to this problem was to attempt to walk the fine line between conflict with the government and conflict with the Europeans as a whole. As he himself put it: 'To the soldiers only, who are enemies to our power, to our authority over the land, also to our authority over our people, let our hearts be dark.'[10]

It is generally accepted that throughout the war he made every effort to avoid harming the settlers of his area and their property. Though some settlers chose to flee, others resided behind the lines in perfect safety. It is sometimes suggested that Kawiti had a different attitude, but in fact he too sought to protect the settlers and to prevent the looting of anything other than abandoned property. 'Heki and the other chiefs declared it was never their intention to disturb the settlers, but on the contrary to protect them.'[11] Missionaries observed that the occupation of their settlements by the anti-government forces did far less damage than the occupation by the troops.[12] Other than those fighting as volunteers beside the soldiers, no civilians were intentionally killed by the Maoris in this war. Heke's forces did sack Kororareka at the beginning of the war, but it is generally agreed that this was not his intention when he attacked the troops protecting the town. Once it was abandoned, no general in the world could keep his men from plundering a town full of rum. Neutral Maoris, some of Waka's allies, and even some Europeans, are also reported to have taken part in the sack.[13] Heke went so far as to allow his desire to protect local Europeans to interfere with his war effort. He revoked his orders to destroy certain bridges when it was represented to him that these were used by civilians as well as troops.[14]

This attitude is sometimes explained in terms of Heke's chivalry or his military naivety, but in fact self-interest is a sufficient explanation. As with other Maori communities in areas of long and substantial contact, the *hapu* supporting Heke and Kawiti would suffer considerable deprivation, real and perceived, from an exodus of Europeans. The last thing the anti-government forces in the Northern War wanted was the total expulsion of the British from their area.

Heke's conduct during the war was profoundly influenced by this factor, and so were the measures he took which led to conflict. In mid-1844 he concluded that the Union Jack flying on a large flagstaff on Maiki Hill, above Kororareka, could usefully be taken as the symbol of British sovereignty in the area without causing damage to economic relations. On 8 July 1844, he cut it down. It was a repetition of this act, on 18 January 1845, which actually triggered off the war.

Again, it is sometimes assumed that Heke was being naive or disingenuous in taking a flag as the symbol of what he disliked about the new order. His fixation with 'a mere stick' can be seen as evidence of his living in a world of his own, and readers of some works on the war are left to assume that Heke's threats and depredations rather than his amputation of the flagstaff constituted the British *casus belli*. In fact the British took the incident very seriously. It is true that FitzRoy called the flagstaff 'a mere stick', and this is sometimes quoted, but he finished the sentence with: 'but as connected with the British Flag of very great importance'. The American consul at Kororareka was believed to be encouraging the anti-government group, and Magistrate Beckham wished to take a leaf out of Heke's book by cutting down the consul's flagstaff.[15] The amputation of the flagstaff had substantive implications as well as symbolic significance. If the British could not protect the flagstaff of their largest settlement north of Auckland, what could they protect? And how much credibility could their claims to substantive sovereignty retain?

It may be true that Heke was ambitious and egotistical, and it is certainly true that he sometimes used the rhetoric of a war of liberation. During the war, he referred frequently to a British desire to seize all Maori land. He berated them for their 'condemnation of the New Zealanders as slaves', and reiterated his determination to 'die for the Country provided for us by the Almighty'.[16] These statements must be treated with both respect and caution. Heke clearly did see the threat to chiefly authority, and the prospective threat to Maori land ownership, as problems which affected much more than his status alone. He was familiar with the fate of aborigines in other areas of European colonization. But his anti-British statements were very strongly worded for a man who never intentionally hurt a hair on a single British civilian's head. His resistance was in a sense designed to counter British imperialism, but only in a very limited way—so limited, in fact, that it was little more than the defence of a *status quo* of which British settlers were an integral part. He fought less to overturn the Treaty of Waitangi than to ensure the application of its Maori version. He wished to safeguard order, stability, and peace, through the energetic application of traditional law. He wished to preserve Maori local independence and the chiefly authority which protected it. He wished to regulate, not reject, European contact and settlement.

The motives of Waka and his allies in resisting Heke constitute a complex problem, and no definitive explanation can be offered here. However, two important points may be made. The first is that Waka and his allies shared Heke's concern about government interference in local affairs, and until a month before the war the level of their resentment was almost as great as his. Diplomatic measures by FitzRoy in September 1844 temporarily dampened the disaffection, but subsequent incidents rekindled it. In February 1845, the pro-government chiefs held a conference at Paihia, at which it was clear that 'Waka and other friendly chiefs were perfectly confounded as to the intention of the Government'. Waka himself was particularly irritated by an ordinance against felling *kauri* timber and 'openly declared that if the Governor had been at Hokianga he would have felled a spar in his presence to see what would happen'. Like Heke, these chiefs related current examples of government interference to the Treaty of Waitangi. 'The general reason for [the] dissatisfaction of the natives', wrote Beckham, 'appears to have been the misunderstanding [of] the Treaty of Waitangi, they conceiving that it took from them their chieftainship and lands.'[17]

The most influential missionary in the area, Archdeacon Henry Williams, was present at the meeting in February 1845. In 1840, Williams had been a major influence in inducing the Northern chiefs to sign at Waitangi, and now he found himself 'well nigh cut down for taking the part I did, relative to the Treaty'. However, by speaking at length in defence of the Treaty, and by distributing 300 copies of its Maori version, Williams was able to 'relieve their minds'. The Archdeacon wrote that 'but for the timely distribution of the Treaty I hesitate not to say that the native population to a man would have been in arms'. Williams's coup, however, meant that only Heke, Kawiti, and their immediate supporters continued to believe that the Treaty was, in Heke's phrase, 'soft soap'.[18]

FitzRoy had removed the customs taxes after an earlier meeting in September 1844 and had partly convinced the chiefs that government interference hitherto had been largely misunderstood.[19] Williams successfully asserted that these encroachments were not the tip of the iceberg and that the Treaty was not a trap. A major distinction between Waka's group and Heke's was that the former were convinced by FitzRoy and Williams, whereas the latter were not.

The second point deduces something about Waka's objectives in entering the war from his conduct during it. It is often assumed that Waka and his allies shared the British wish to capture Heke and to destroy his power, but in fact Waka's measures against Heke covered the whole range of Maori sanctions and usually stopped short of war to the death. Waka and his associates began by trying to dissuade Heke from his course.[20] Later in January, they provided guards for the flagstaff. These, however, did not use force when Heke cut the staff down for the third time. Hostilities between Heke and the British began on 3 March 1845, and were clearly in the offing for some time before this. But Waka did not take the field until late March, and then he at first simply tried to persuade Heke to go home. To verbal persuasion he added what amounted to a *taua muru* against Heke's property —a legal plundering expedition in which blood was not shed.[21]

Hostilities between Maori and Maori commenced in early April. But the fighting had the character of restrained feuding, as befitted a contest for limited objectives between *hapu* of the same tribe. 'By mutual arrangement, no ambuscades were laid, and the fighting was only in daylight.'[22] The contesting parties returned each other's prisoners, and though skirmishing continued throughout April, few men were killed.[23] After the first British punitive expedition had ended, Heke still refused to make peace and accused Waka of 'fighting for blankets'—for what he could get from the British in the most mercenary sense.[24] This exhausted Waka's considerable patience and he finally took decided measures against Heke which culminated in the Battle of Te Ahuahu on 12 June. However, Waka was supported in this engagement by only one of his allies, and Heke's main ally, Kawiti, was also absent. Both Te Ahuahu and the April skirmishes were fought without any interference by the British.

The pro-government Maoris accompanied the British on each of their three expeditions, but their conduct in these was ambivalent. They scouted for the British, skirmished fiercely with the enemy, and risked their lives to save wounded soldiers, but they did not join in the decisive clashes. This is sometimes explained in terms of their reluctance to participate in assaults which they thought would fail. But at the Battle of Puketutu on 8 May, where it was clear that an assault was likely to succeed, they hardly assisted the British in combat at all. It seems fair to suggest from all this that the feud between the two Ngapuhi factions constituted a war within a war. It was fought at a different level of intensity from the British-Maori conflict, and it seems to follow that it was fought for different ends.

Waka's group, then, shared Heke's desire to preserve Maori local independence, but came to differ from him in the perception of how acute a danger to this the government represented. Unlike their British allies, they fought a limited war against Heke and Kawiti. Exactly what their restrained operations were intended to achieve is difficult to establish with confidence. Heke's perceived ambition, and his law-giving operations, probably aroused the resentment of other chiefs. Satisfaction for traditional grievances may also have been a factor, but these may equally have acted as ceremonial justifications, like European border disputes, to cover more substantive differences. For, in defending the *status quo* from one threat, Heke created another danger to it. Heke believed that he could preserve the European-Maori economic relationship while fighting the government, whereas Waka disagreed. There was some truth in each view. The economic disruption caused by Heke's resistance was temporary, and some Europeans remained behind his lines. But others fled to Auckland, and Heke could not prevent the sack of Kororareka. Significantly, Waka did not take the field until after the loss of this valuable entrepôt, and then he would have done so whether the British liked it or not.[25] For enemies, the war-aims of Heke and Waka may have had a great deal in common. Each may have been protecting a different aspect of the same *status quo*. But whatever the precise motives of Waka and his allies, this was clearly a war of three sides in which only the British aimed for total victory through the capture or annihilation of their enemies.

II THE FALL OF KORORAREKA

BY EARLY FEBRUARY 1845, WILLIAMS'S SUCCESS IN REDUCING anti-government feeling and Heke's continued intransigence had combined to convince FitzRoy that rapid military victory was both possible and necessary. He sent to Australia for reinforcements and in the interval concentrated his resources on the defence of Kororareka. Meagre as they were, these forces appeared sufficient for the protection of one fortified settlement. A detachment of the 96th Regiment and the eighteen-gun sloop *Hazard* provided a land force of 140 soldiers, sailors, and marines. These, with about 200 armed townsmen and volunteers from the merchant vessels in the bay, manned defences consisting of two blockhouses (one protecting the flagstaff on Maiki Hill), a one-gun battery at 'Matavia Pass', and Polack's Stockade.[26] The British had four cannon on land and the *Hazard* provided additional artillery support. They wisely avoided any attempt to hold the whole of the straggling town. Polack's Stockade and the two blockhouses formed an integrated main position at the northern end of the settlement, while the one-gun battery guarded a likely Maori route of approach to the south.

At 4 a.m. on 11 March 1845, the anti-government Maoris attacked Kororareka in three groups. One, under Kawiti, surprised and took the one-gun battery. This involved a long and desperate struggle with forty-five men of the *Hazard* under Commander Robertson, but the sailors and marines were eventually forced to withdraw. The second Maori group, men of the Kapotai *hapu*, pinned the British defenders by firing from cover near the lower blockhouse. The third, under Heke, surprised and seized the flagstaff blockhouse, and severed the flagstaff for the fourth and last time. All three Maori groups then took cover and exchanged desultory fire with the defenders for several hours. At 1 p.m., the powder magazine at Polack's was accidentally blown up, but the Maoris still declined to press home their attack. Despite this, the British evacuated the town and the *Hazard* began to bombard it. Only then did the Maoris commence plundering the place. Early next day, with the plundering still in progress, the British sailed off to Auckland.

On most military criteria, the attack on Kororareka was far from typical of the battles of the New Zealand Wars. The Maoris very rarely outnumbered their opponents and, largely because of this, they seldom attacked British fortifications. Yet Kororareka set a pattern of British interpretation which, in its essentials, was to apply throughout the wars.

Despite a recent decline, Kororareka was still a major trading and ship-provisioning centre, and it remained the fifth largest town in the infant colony. Its loss was a serious blow, involving £50,000 worth of property. But the material effect was as nothing compared to the moral impact. The seizure of a British settlement, protected by the British army and Royal navy, by a force of natives was an extremely unusual event. To the British, it was as totally unexpected as it was humiliating. Before the attack a local settler, Gilbert Mair, had warned Magistrate Beckham of Maori intentions. Beckham had not so much ignored as discounted the warning, replying: 'How will the Maoris like cold steel Mr Mair?'[27] Beckham was not alone in his optimism. With armed Europeans, cannon, fortifications, and the support of the *Hazard*—'sufficient, it was thought, to keep all secure'—the town was 'full of confidence' before the attack.[28] 'Neither I nor anyone else', wrote Governor FitzRoy, 'thought of his [Heke] succeeding in an attack on our forces—small as they were.'[29] It was this shock, rather than the existence of a genuine threat to Auckland, that led the Auckland settlers to fear for their own security. They were panic-stricken at the news of Kororareka and showed 'indications of fear almost as extensive as their minds will allow'. Many sold their land and possessions for token prices and left 'as fast as ships are found to carry them'. One Auckland landlord sold his three houses for £15 before making off.[30]

In this context, the British turned to various interpretations of the battle which could palliate or acceptably explain the disaster. The explanations ranged widely. Kororareka was frequently condemned as a den of iniquity, consisting largely of grog-shops and brothels, and one interpretation of the events of 11 March was that it had shared the fate of Sodom and Gomorrah through an act of Divine Providence.[31] This was not markedly less likely than some other suggestions, but an emphasis on four factors was more common. The first and second of these were the exaggeration of Maori numbers and casualties. The forces of Heke and Kawiti were usually put at 1000 to 1200 men, and estimates went as high as 2000.[32] A maximum of 600 warriors is now generally accepted, and there is solid evidence to suggest that the actual number was 450.[33] It was sometimes asserted that the Maoris had lost 130 men or more killed and wounded, but most commentators settled on a figure of thirty-four killed and sixty-eight wounded, and this was repeated often enough to become entrenched in the historical orthodoxy. The figure for those killed may have originated with Bishop Selwyn, who made his guess on the basis of conflicting Maori stories which probably referred to total casualties. The wounded figure had no basis at all and looks very like a simple doubling of the supposed number of killed. James Kemp, who was in the Maori camp after the engagement, stated categorically that the Maoris had thirteen men killed and twenty-eight wounded, and his figure is convincing. British casualties were nineteen or twenty killed and twenty-three wounded.[34]

A third palliative was the idea that the British failures at the flagstaff blockhouse and in the defence of the town generally were offset by the rout of Kawiti's division by the *Hazard*'s party with 'tremendous slaughter'. Apart from the influence of deeper preconceptions about Maori abilities, this idea was based on two assumptions and two facts. The first assumption was that Kawiti's operations were 'completely independent' of Heke's. The second was that while Heke had directed his efforts against the flagstaff alone, Kawiti had launched a full assault on the town for the purpose of 'nothing but plunder and outrage'. This of course accorded with the perceived difference between the war aims of the two chiefs. The facts were that Kawiti had not stormed the town, and that Commander Robertson and his men had made a very determined resistance at the one-gun battery. All this led British commentators to conclude that Robertson had repelled Kawiti's assault and crippled his division. 'The repulse which the natives sustained at this point was so severe, that no serious attack was made from that quarter during the remainder of the engagement.'[35]

It seems clear, however, that the operations of the three Maori divisions were fully co-ordinated. The timing, and what we shall see was the mutually supportive character of the three attacks, provide *prima facie* indications to this effect. It is certain, moreover, that the forces of Heke and Kawiti camped together before the attack and there are strong indications that a concerted plan of action was agreed upon.[36] It is highly unlikely that this plan involved an assault upon the town. The function of Kawiti and the Kapotai was to divert and pin down the British while Heke took the flagstaff blockhouse, and in this they succeeded perfectly. Kawiti probably hoped to avoid any heavy fighting at all but, by coincidence, Robertson and forty-five men had gone up to the one-gun battery that morning to improve the entrenchments. Instead of the normal small picket therefore, Kawiti found himself opposed by a substantial party. The ensuing combat was long and fierce, and the sailors and marines did very well against superior numbers, but it is clear that they were eventually forced to retreat after losing a third of their party.[37] Having overcome this unexpected hitch, Kawiti's division reverted to its original function of pinning down the British defenders by sniping from cover.

The final feature of the British interpretation of this battle was the tendency to attribute the defeat to the exceptional incompetence or treachery of the leading figures in it. It was widely believed among the soldiers and sailors that they had somehow been betrayed by the local missionaries. Lieutenant Philpotts, who took over the naval command after Robertson fell wounded, told Henry Williams to his face that he had 'said the Natives would never come into the Town and here they are. Most traitorous conduct and you a Missionary.' His men physically threatened Williams and informed him that 'he ought to be cut in pieces and hung up'. As FitzRoy observed, the allegations were 'utterly absurd to say the very least'. But similar accusations continued to crop up throughout the Northern War, and culminated when an irate soldier 'swore to shoot [Williams] if he got a chance'.[38]

More enduring than allegations of treason, however, was the notion that the dominant cause of defeat was the utter incompetence of the officers commanding in the town—Beckham, Philpotts, and the 96th Regiment's subalterns, Barclay and Campbell. Commentators felt that the battle was characterized by 'awful blundering throughout' and FitzRoy wrote that: 'The shameful conduct of those officers whose uselessness caused the loss and destruction of Kororareka is now the subject of an enquiry —preparatory to a court martial.'[39] The unfortunate Ensign Campbell, commanding the flagstaff blockhouse, came in for particularly virulent criticism. 'I cannot conceive', wrote one officer, 'how any man with a blockhouse and guard in so commanding a position could have allowed himself to be surprised and let it be taken.'[40] The substance of the case against Campbell was that he and sixteen of his twenty men had gone a few yards from the blockhouse to observe the fighting between Robertson and Kawiti at Matavia Pass. Kawiti's objective was just such a diversion, and Campbell shared the general British belief that the Maori attack was likely to fall on Matavia, but it could still be argued that he had acted foolishly. Whether his error in leaving the blockhouse made a difference to its fall is another matter. Heke and his men had spent the night working their way, with great caution, up the flagstaff hill, which was covered with ridges 'intersected by deep hollows'.[41] The Maoris got so close to the blockhouse without being detected that when a sentry fired a single warning shot, and Campbell 'immediately turned around', they were already inside.[42] The four occupants of the blockhouse were quickly killed and 'the whole object of the native attack was gained in a moment'.[43] Heke had 150 warriors, and had Campbell and his sixteen men been with the four unfortunates inside the blockhouse, their corpses would simply have been added to the toll. Heke attacked too fast, from too close, and with too many men for there to be any other result. Campbell could have done better in terms of correct military behaviour, but he could not have saved his blockhouse.

Beckham, Philpotts, and Barclay came under criticism primarily for their decision to evacuate the town, which most commentators considered premature. The officers in question defended themselves by arguing—disingenuously—that the explosion of the magazine at Polack's Stockade had left them without ammunition with which to continue the fight.[44] Contemporary British commentators often accepted this claim, but paradoxically failed to abate their criticism. In fact the main reason for the abandonment of the town appears to have been the loss of the flagstaff blockhouse. A recent historian has suggested that this blockhouse was not vital to the defence,[45] but it is clear from maps of the fortifications that, while it did not necessarily command the town as a whole, it did command the northern end. With the exception of the one-gun battery, this was where the whole of the British defences were located. A number of contemporary accounts confirm that the blockhouse was 'the key to our position'.[46] The British leaders may have performed inadequately in varying degrees, but their mistakes were not the primary causes of defeat.

To exaggerate enemy casualties and numbers, to emphasize the part of a battle in which one's own forces were most successful, and to search out scapegoats is by no means an abnormal response to defeat. But it seems fair to suggest that in the case of Kororareka this response had two less common features. First, it disregarded logic and easily ascertainable contrary facts. The British continued to insist that the Maoris lost thirty-four killed and sixty-eight wounded despite the fact that Kemp's obviously more reliable figure became available within a few days of the battle. The garrison commanders' claim that they had abandoned the town because the gunpowder had run out was widely, though not universally, accepted. Yet this did not serve to exculpate them, nor did it take into account the well-known fact that the *Hazard* had bombarded the town after the evacuation—presumably propelling its shot with something other than powder. Most contemporaries agreed that the flagstaff blockhouse commanded the main British position at the north end of the town, yet failed to acknowledge that its loss made evacuation necessary.

The second notable feature of the contemporary British response to the loss of Kororareka is the degree to which it has endured. Historians offer a relatively reasonable figure for Maori numbers—only one-third above their real strength—and some modern writers accept that the Maori attack was skilfully planned. Others, however, uncritically perpetuate the contemporary idea that the Maoris, like their opponents, 'were remarkably inept in any form of co-ordination of their forces'. Virtually all historians echo the exaggerated Maori casualty figure, and accept that the 'routing' of Kawiti's force, said to be making 'the main Maori attack', ameliorated the British defeat. They also consistently cite the incompetence of the British leaders as the main cause of failure. 'The British authorities—civilian, military and naval—were mainly to blame for the disaster which now overtook

Kororareka.'[47] This received interpretation is inaccurate, and serves only to obscure the fact that the fall of Kororareka was neither the result of overwhelming numbers nor of British incompetence, but of precise Maori planning.

III PUKETUTU: THE LAST OPEN BATTLE

THERE WAS LITTLE FITZROY COULD DO AFTER THE FALL OF Kororareka but place Auckland in a state of defence and await further reinforcements from Australia. At last, on 22 April, these arrived in the form of 215 men of the 58th Regiment. FitzRoy felt he could waste no time in mounting a punitive expedition. Within four days a British force was sailing north towards the Bay of Islands.

The British expedition consisted of 300 regulars, about forty European volunteers, and some 120 seamen and marines. The force had no cannon, but it did have a couple of rocket tubes in the care of the grandly-named 'Rocket Brigade', eight seamen strong. The commander was Lieutenant-Colonel William Hulme, an officer of good reputation and considerable experience. The expedition's first act was to seize the neutral chief Pomare, who was thought to be supporting the enemy in secret, and destroy his coastal *pa* after his men had evacuated it.[48] Hulme then sailed further north, and landed at Onewhero Bay on 3 May 1845, and immediately marched overland towards Lake Omapere to seek out and destroy Heke. The march proved to be a difficult one. Heavy rain spoiled some provisions and ammunition and further supplies had to be ordered up from the ships. Hulme was short of transport, his men found the bush tracks difficult and, though the navy got the extra supplies up 'in an incredible short space of time', the fifteen mile march to the vicinity of Heke's *pa* took four days in all.[49]

Heke and his men had been working on a new *pa*, Puketutu, since the first intimation of a major British expedition reached them in April. They had, however, been so hampered by light but time-consuming skirmishing with the pro-government Ngapuhi that they had not been able to finish it. The place had strong double or triple palisading on three sides, but the fourth was protected only by a light fence. Moreover, one *hapu* of Heke's supporters had left him, reducing his numbers to about 200 men. However, Kawiti and 140 warriors arrived by forced march on 7 May, and the allies determined to fight, despite the weakness of Puketutu *pa*. Kawiti did not join the garrison, but remained in the bush outside the *pa*.[50]

Hulme, joined but not fully supported by the pro-government Maoris, advanced to the attack on the morning of 8 May. Though Hulme made no mention of this in his report, he had been informed that the rear of the *pa* was weak.[51] He fired off his rockets—to no effect—and sent forward a storming party of 216 of his best men towards the weak point. Just as this party was about to assault, Kawiti and his men were detected advancing from the bush to attack the stormers in the rear. Leaving sixty men to face the *pa*, the stormers hastily turned about and engaged him. A bitter struggle ensued in which an exchange of volleys was followed by close combat. The British, fighting ferociously, were gradually getting the upper hand when a small party sallied out from the *pa* and beat back the sixty soldiers facing it. The main body of the storming party were forced to turn about once more. Heke's men quickly withdrew to the *pa* but, as the British were following them up, Kawiti attacked again. He was again forced back after a fierce hand to hand fight. By this time, however, the British storming party had lost a quarter of its men and the rest were exhausted. Hulme had no alternative but to withdraw, abandoning his dead and possibly some of his wounded.[52]

Translating optimistically from Hulme's report, FitzRoy exulted in a major victory, with at least 200 Maoris killed and wounded. He reported to the Imperial Government 'with feelings of thankfulness and much satisfaction' that Hulme had 'succeeded in effectively checking the progress of the rebellion'. The rebels, he said, were 'beaten and dispersed'.[53] FitzRoy's misapprehension, which was shared by some other contemporaries, was the result of two lesser misconceptions. The first was that Hulme had never intended to attack Puketutu. Hulme claimed that he had been convinced from the outset that the *pa* was too strong to be attacked without artillery. He had sent forward the 216 men merely to loiter about speculatively in front of the palisades 'as the chances of war are many'. It is, of course, difficult to believe that Hulme could have sent his men to within fifty yards of the *pa*, where as he himself admitted they were 'exposed to a heavy and galling fire', on the off-chance that the palisade would fall down or that some other miracle would occur. Furthermore, Hulme went to special trouble to form a group of pioneers equipped with axes, whose function could only have been to cut a gap in the Maori stockade. Several observers, including two of Hulme's senior subordinates, refer unambiguously to an intended assault.[54]

The second misconception is that the operations of Heke and Kawiti were again entirely unco-ordinated. This not only contributed to the British victory claim, but also palliated an over-all defeat or turned it into a draw in the eyes of more realistic contemporaries.[55] The idea has outlived the victory claim itself. Historians accept that Kawiti 'fortuitously arrived on the scene' coincidentally at the appropriate moment, and emphasize 'Kawiti's shattered ranks' and Kawiti's 'heavy loss' as the most memorable aspect of the engagement.[56] The timing of Kawiti's two attacks and of Heke's sally should of itself be enough to invalidate this idea. Kawiti attacked first when the British were 'just on the eve of making the rush', and the garrison clearly sallied 'to the assistance' of Kawiti.[57] Kawiti actually arrived at Puketutu on the day before the battle, and consequently had ample time to co-ordinate his plans with Heke.[58] There are indications that the flags flying above the *pa* during the engagement were used to signal the need for a pre-emptive attack by Kawiti.[59]

Hulme planned to assault, and Heke and Kawiti co-ordinated their operations. The British plan foundered simply because the Maori plan worked. Though it was potentially a very strong position, Puketutu on 8 May was a 'very weak *pa*'.[60] A vigorous British assault against its unfinished side would probably have been successful. Heke and Kawiti were well aware of this, and they therefore sought to prevent an assault developing. When the British moved in to storm, Kawiti attacked them in the rear. When the British turned to deal with him, Heke relieved the pressure with a sally. The mutual support of the two Maori divisions meant that the British could deal with neither. The failure to recognize the successful implementation of a co-ordinated Maori plan precisely echoes the interpretation of the battle of Kororareka, and similar failures were to recur throughout the Wars.

Maori casualties at Puketutu were probably similar to the British loss of fifty-two killed and wounded. Official British estimates were very much greater, but it seems that Heke had five men killed, that Kawiti had twenty-three men killed, and that the number of wounded was disproportionately low because the British slew some of Kawiti's warriors as they lay injured —not an uncommon practice on either side. F. E. Maning discounted reports that the British had killed 200 of the enemy—'the fact is they killed only 28, and were forced to retreat themselves'—and the supporting evidence is strong, if less explicit.[61] It remains true that, even on these revised figures, Kawiti's casualties had been quite heavy, and that he had been forced back twice by the British in close combat. But in suffering these setbacks, he had performed his wider, battle-winning role to perfection.

Striking as it was, the earlier Maori victory at Kororareka was gained with the advantage of superior numbers and an element of surprise. The victory at Puketutu was won despite the disadvantages of a month of exhausting skirmishing with the pro-government Ngapuhi, inferior numbers, and a weak position. The anti-government Maoris had now demonstrated that the appearance of a strong force of British regulars did not spell immediate doom. This increased their support and greatly encouraged them.

Though Puketutu was a substantial and politically important Maori victory, the tactics of the battle itself did not represent any great leap forward for the Maori military system. To deal with the British as two matadors might deal with a bull was a risky business—more brilliant improvisation than a comprehensive solution to the problem of war with the British. But the Maoris did learn one great lesson from Puketutu, a lesson that was to be absolutely crucial to their powers of resistance in this and subsequent wars.

The important aspect of the battle in this respect was that in which the Maoris had been least successful. Among his other talents Kawiti counted superb tactical leadership, and the morale of his *taua* was high. They had fought with skill, determination, and courage in two clashes on open ground with a similar number of British regulars. Yet, on each occasion, they had been forced to give ground. The soldiers' combination of discipline and ferocity had proved too much. To a warrior race oriented towards open battle, this was an unpleasant conclusion. The margin had been small; it was possible to envisage a different result in slightly more favourable circumstances; and the temptation to dismiss the experience must have been great. But the Maoris faced the unpleasant problem and they accepted an equally unpleasant solution: to strike open fighting off their list of tactical options. Raids, surprise attacks, sallies from *pa* and attacks under the cover of bush were all to occur in the future, but encounter battles between organized bodies of warriors and organized bodies of troops were not. Puketutu involved the first and last major Anglo-Maori open combat in the Northern War, and virtually the last in the New Zealand Wars as a whole.

2

The Ohaeawai Campaign

FITZROY'S MISPLACED JUBILATION OVER THE FIGHT AT Puketutu soon began to wear thin. Information from various parts of the North Island indicated, so the Governor and his advisers believed, that the Colony was in a deepening state of crisis. The Chief Protector of Aborigines wrote that: 'Until a complete overthrow is given to Heke, the British possessions in New Zealand are not worth having . . . the attention of the whole Island is drawn to this struggle, and the future state of the Colony depends on the result.'[1] FitzRoy felt that the situation was in the nature of a 'peculiar and pressing emergency',[2] and when Colonel Henry Despard arrived to take over from Hulme on 1 June, he impressed this view on the Colonel. FitzRoy and Despard therefore lost no time in mounting a second expedition—this time directed against Ohaeawai, a new inland *pa* being built by Kawiti. The ensuing battle, on 1 July 1845, was the most important engagement of the war. It was, however, preceded by another significant action, one in which no British troops were involved.

I TE AHUAHU: THE FORGOTTEN BATTLE

AFTER THE BATTLE ON 8 MAY, HEKE ABANDONED PUKETUTU and returned to an old fortification of his, a small *pa* called Te Ahuahu. Some of his followers dispersed to look to their economic affairs and in early June Heke himself went off to 'kill cattle for food'.[3] In his absence, the pro-government chief, Te Taonui, seized Te Ahuahu and was quickly reinforced by Waka Nene. Heke rapidly re-assembled his warriors—though Kawiti did not join him—and attempted to recapture his *pa*. Waka and Taonui engaged him outside the *pa*, and Heke was defeated and wounded. His important new ally, Te Kahakaha, was killed.

Only one detailed account of this action exists,[4] and although the work which provides this account is by no means as fanciful as is sometimes assumed, it is not possible to reconstruct the course of the action with confidence. Perhaps partly for this reason, most historians dismiss Te Ahuahu as a minor skirmish.[5] But whatever the details of the fight, the following considerations suggest that it was a substantial battle. First, estimates of Heke's

strength at the engagement vary between 400 and 800 men and the coincidence of four separate accounts in the area of 400 to 500 men seems convincing.[6] Waka probably had about 300 men. In the context of the war's over-all
scale, these forces were considerable—in fact Heke's was probably the largest
he ever mustered without Kawiti. Secondly, the least unreliable European
estimates put Waka's casualties at twelve and Heke's at thirty. An account
derived from Maori sources clearly implies that casualties were heavier, and
the fact that the three principal leaders on Heke's side were all killed or
wounded tends to confirm this.[7]

The third consideration concerns the British reaction to the battle. It
disappeared fairly rapidly from the received version of the war—this and the
entire absence of British troops are likely to have been related—but the immediate response of British commentators was markedly different. One missionary noted that 'A sharp battle was fought on the 12th inst. between the
loyal and disaffected natives. The disaffected . . . were kept at bay all day
and ultimately driven off the field.' Another missionary confirmed this
account, and observed that Heke's men 'allow they had been severely disappointed'. An Auckland newspaper reported that 'Heke came down on Waka
quite by surprise . . . Heke beaten off, severely wounded and nearly made
prisoner, night kept Nene from pursuit.'[8] Waka Nene himself sent several
of his men with a letter to Colonel Despard at Kororareka reporting 'a most
complete victory over Heke'. Henry Williams 'corroborated the whole of
this statement, having just returned from Waimate and having seen Heke
since he received the wound. He said he was in much pain and they all
seemed much cast down by their defeat.'[9]

Te Ahuahu, then, was a major action, and it was important in several
respects. Such evidence as is available suggests that it was a clash in the
open, in the style of the Musket Wars. Waka voluntarily left his *pa* to
engage Heke's larger forces. Together with one or two subsequent engagements in other wars, this confirms that the Maoris continued to prefer open
fighting over other forms: the abandonment of open battle applied only to
counter-European warfare. Te Ahuahu was quite a substantial defeat for
Heke—the only one, as we shall see, which either he or Kawiti suffered in
the War. Through his victory at Te Ahuahu, amongst other things, Waka
was able largely to preserve himself from the fate of his allies. Furthermore,
though Heke did recover from both his wound and his defeat, the after-
effects remained with him for some time. Both FitzRoy and his successor
sought to attribute these to their own operations, and so help substantiate
the false victory claims each was compelled to make.

The final important effect of Te Ahuahu was its impact on Colonel
Despard. Waka's victory did not solve the crisis into which the Colony had
been thrown, because Heke's force remained shaken but intact and Kawiti
remained untouched at Ohaeawai. But the battle did present Despard, in his
own opinion, with a golden opportunity to quell the rebellion by rapidly
following up Waka's success. He now felt a double pressure for a quick
solution. The situation was critical, and a superb chance to save it existed,

but would rapidly slip away. It was a time, Despard wrote, for 'bold measures'.[10]

II OHAEAWAI AND THE ADAPTATION OF
PA CONSTRUCTION

SUFFERING FROM THE SAME CARTAGE PROBLEMS WHICH HAD beset Hulme, Despard struggled up to Ohaeawai. His vanguard of allied Maoris skirmished with Kawiti's scouts on 23 June, and Despard arrived before the *pa* on the next day, with 615 men and four cannon. He opened fire as soon as possible with his artillery. He had two objectives in mind. One was to create a viable breach in the palisades, and the other was to demoralize and inflict casualties on the garrison. He moved his batteries about several times to improve their firing position. Though harassed all the while by accurate sniping and irritating sallies by the garrison, the British kept up a reasonably well-directed cannonade for six days. The six-and twelve-pounder cannon failed to create a breach, and Despard ordered up a 32-pounder, the heaviest gun yet used on land in New Zealand, from the ships. As the 32-pounder fired its first shots, early on 1 July, Kawiti launched a particularly dangerous and provocative sally against one of the batteries. Despard felt he could wait no longer and launched an assault with 250 crack troops. The *pa* contained only 100 warriors at the time, but the British storming party was shattered and flung back, leaving 110 killed and wounded behind it. The impossible had occurred.[11]

If anything is a constant in the interpretation of the New Zealand Wars, it is the assumption that the British defeat at Ohaeawai was primarily caused by the monumental lunacy of Colonel Despard. This assumption took root immediately after the battle. From Despard, wrote one newspaper editor: 'We expect nothing which would be creditable to a veteran soldier. His measures show him to be ignorant of the common tactics of the field, deficient in every advantage which experience bestows, and wholly destitute of the military genius which might tend to supply the want of these qualifications.'[12] Time did not temper these opinions. At the turn of the century, W. P. Reeves wrote that the disaster at Ohaeawai was 'solely due to a commander's error of judgement'. In 1962, Edgar Holt attributed the defeat to Despard being 'stupid enough to imagine that a Maori *pa* could fall before a bayonet charge'. In the most recent book on the Northern War (1979), Michael Barthorp used a contemporary statement to entitle his chapter on Ohaeawai 'Downright Madness'. If the Northern War was historiographically as popular as the Crimean, Despard would rank with Lord Cardigan as the definitive military cretin.[13]

To some extent the attribution of the Ohaeawai disaster to Despard's blundering is founded upon the opinions of the participants in the battle.

Some of these contemporary comments have been used out of context. The contemporary reference to 'Downright Madness', for example, concerned a night escalade which was suggested but never implemented, and not the assault itself.[14] Other participants' comments were retrospective, and were influenced less by reasoned analysis than by the shock of defeat. Despite the experience of Kororareka and Puketutu, the shock was very great. 'Never did British troops pass a more dreadful night than the troops before Ohaeawai after this unsuccessful assault.'[15] The nature of their opponents naturally did not help matters. Major Cyprian Bridge recorded that after the assault he and his men were 'tired and dispirited and disgusted beyond expression at having been defeated by a mob of savages and with such fearful cost too'.[16] In this context, Despard was a natural scapegoat. Though by no means as intolerant, difficult, and immune to advice as the received picture suggests,[17] the Colonel could be tactless and irascible. His attempt —subsequently retracted—to blame members of the storming party for disobeying instructions to carry axes and ladders to cut down or scale the stockade did not endear him to the survivors. It seems fair to suggest, in sum, that the opinions of veterans like Corporal W. H. Free—in this case expressed a mere seventy-four years after the event—that Despard 'did not know his business',[18] are not quite iron-clad evidence.

While uncritically accepting the views of Despard's subordinates, contemporary commentators and historians alike ignored the opinions of his military superiors. There is admittedly a much-repeated comment allegedly made by the Duke of Wellington, the Commander-in-Chief, to the effect that Despard should have been court-martialled for launching an attack 'in the face of such hopeless difficulties'.[19] It is just possible that Wellington made some comment of this type when the first newspaper reports of the battle arrived in England, but if he did so he soon reversed his opinion. After studying the relevant reports, he wrote that 'the service has been well conducted by Colonel Despard', and that Despard should be made a Commander of the Bath, which he duly was.[20] Despard had another supporter in Governor FitzRoy, for whom Ohaeawai was an unmitigated disaster. Bravely, FitzRoy made no effort to blame his woes on the Colonel, despite the obvious temptation to do so. Nor did Despard's direct military superior, General O'Connell, commanding in Australia. O'Connell explicitly exculpated Despard from blame for the defeat and expressed continued 'great confidence in his zeal and experience as well as in his prudence'.[21]

Of course, Wellington, O'Connell, and FitzRoy could be wrong, and two major criticisms of Despard require closer examination. The first was that the assault could be seen to have no chance of success. The second, more specific, was that Despard failed to direct his attack against the point most damaged by his guns. These criticisms are unsound. Despard was no genius, but Wellington was right in concluding that he was moderately competent. The Colonel's reputation, however, is not our main concern. The crucial point is that the main causes of the Ohaeawai disaster, including the factors which deceived Despard about the effect of his bombardment and the chances of successful assault, were measures taken by the Maoris. Among these was the successful application of methods used in the Musket Wars, such as good fire discipline. The improvement of traditional features of *pa* construction—modifications rather than radical changes—were equally important. But the Maori performance at Ohaeawai also included sufficient innovations in the construction of the *pa* to make it a new kind of fortification. In terms of construction, Ohaeawai was the model for all future Maori defensive systems—the prototype of what we will call the modern *pa*.

Kawiti bore three closely related problems in mind while designing Ohaeawai: a charge by British regulars was extremely difficult to stop; any measures taken to this end had to be kept secret from the British; and the *pa* and its garrison had somehow to be protected against the new threat of artillery.

As Kawiti was now well aware, attacking British infantry were not only ferociously effective but also had a 'high breaking strain'—a large proportion of the attackers would have to be shot down before the attack would stop. When this was added to the fact that the garrison of Ohaeawai were outnumbered six to one by their opponents, it became clear that engineering measures to correct the balance were vital. To make the best of his few musketeers, Kawiti sought to ensure that they could fire and load in relative safety; that they could bring fire to bear from the maximum number of angles, and for sufficient time to do the necessary damage; and that they could be concentrated rapidly and safely at threatened points.

The two palisades of the *pa*, a strong inner fence and a lighter fence (the *pekerangi*) three feet outside it, provided some protection for the garrison. More was provided by flax matting, virtually musket-proof, which was hung on the *pekerangi* to within a foot or two of the ground. But a still more important protection for the musketeers in the firing line was the trench around the perimeter of the *pa*. This trench, located inside the inner fence, was five or six feet deep, and had firing steps cut in the side. The musketeer stood on its floor to load and stepped up to fire at ground level, shooting either through a loophole cut in contiguous timbers, or through gaps between separated timbers. To align his gun along the ground improved his aim. Even a short-range musket ball flew in a curved trajectory, and there was a tendency to fire too high. But more important was the fact that the warriors at Ohaeawai hardly needed to expose themselves at all when repelling the British attack.

Mobility within the *pa* was another problem. A single, open firing trench running right around the perimeter of the *pa* would have exposed its occupants to deadly enfilading fire—a cannon ball fired from one end could have swept a whole side clear. But if sections of trench were blocked off from each other to prevent this, safe communication would have become impossible. The storming party would have encountered only the tiny, isolated garrison of the point attacked. The solution was to 'traverse' the trench—to leave sections undug across the trench at six foot intervals along it. Each traverse had a small gap—a tiny communications trench—cut at one end to allow free passage. Alternate traverses had the gap at opposite ends. As a veteran of the garrison put it: 'You could travel right round the *pa* in the main trench, winding in and out.'[22] The garrison could be concentrated at a single point in as long as it took the furthest man to complete a zig-zagging sprint of 150 yards. Ohaeawai was probably also equipped with secondary communications trenches, giving easy access to opposite sides of the *pa* and to internal defensive features.

In the effort to bring the optimum fire to bear on a British assault force it would have been tempting to resort to the traditional fighting platform atop the stockade. The inner palisade at Ohaeawai was easily strong enough to bear such a structure, and with split timber and flax matting it could be made fairly safe from musket fire, as its use in the Musket Wars proved. But fighting platforms were easy game for artillery and Kawiti simply abandoned them. Instead he turned to salients or flanking-angles. These were the same in height and structure as the main palisade and trench, and in fact were merely projections on the main perimeter. The angles were very small, and their purpose was not really to make possible a crossfire at a distant target. They were primarily intended to provide flanking fire against an enemy standing hard against the *pekerangi*. A man shooting from a flanking angle, only a couple of yards from another shooting from the main perimeter, would cross the T of his neighbour's fire when both aimed at the same enemy. This too was crucially important because of its relationship to the function of the *pekerangi*—the outer fence. The inner fence was built of stout logs and could physically block an attacker's progress. The *pekerangi*, on the other hand, though stronger at Ohaeawai than at later modern *pa*, was not a major obstruction, particularly when damaged by artillery fire. The British storming party penetrated it at a minimum of two points on 1 July. But in struggling with the *pekerangi*, the attackers gave the defenders sufficient time to shoot them down, with the flanking fire from the salients proving particularly effective. The *pekerangi* was 'intended to delay a storm-ing party, so that while they would be pulling it down, the men behind the inner fence might have time to shoot them'.[23] It performed a function similar to that of barbed wire on more recent battlefields.

Kawiti's second major problem was to conceal his defences from the British. When first observing the Ohaeawai *pa* on 24 June, Despard could see that two 'barricades' of logs and a 'ditch' formed the perimeter. He could see a few partitions within the *pa*, but neither he nor his officers noted any significant defences in the interior.[24] This was all the information the Colonel had. At Kororareka and Puketutu, the Maoris had made no great secret of their plans and activities. Missionaries and pro-government Maoris communicating with them had been able to provide the army with reliable information. At Ohaeawai, however, the Maoris suddenly cut the normal, casual, flow of information. On 12 June, Robert Burrows and Henry Williams went to visit Kawiti at Ohaeawai—they had previously visited Heke's *pa* on several occasions. Kawiti was 'busy fortifying' the place, but he came out to see them, 'objecting to our seeing the inside of the *pa*'.

Burrows complained on 23 June that Maori proceedings 'of late have been carried on with remarkable caution and secrecy for natives, [and] it is not easy to ascertain their strength'.[25] On 2 July, when the Maoris thought British reinforcements might make a second assault possible, Henry Williams and some neutral Maoris were not allowed into the *pa* to negotiate the return of British corpses.[26]

One of the secrets Kawiti was so carefully preserving was the strength of the inner palisade. This consisted of large *puriri* logs, 'very hard wood which does not splinter much', sunk six feet in the ground and reaching ten feet above it. A six-pounder ball fired from any considerable distance merely embedded itself in these logs.[27] Though a 32-pounder ball was a different matter, only two dozen of these had been fired and the inner fence was very little damaged by the British bombardment.

Burrows and Williams had been unable to learn anything through casual spying, and Despard was in no better position to assess either the inherent strength of the inner palisade or the extent of damage done to it by the bombardment. The mat of green flax hung on the *pekerangi* completely obscured his view. Major Bridge wrote that 'owing to the elasticity and tenacity of the flax which closes up as the ball goes through, it was impossible to see what extent of damage was done to the fence'.[28] Bridge was one of those who subsequently criticized Despard for failing to direct the assault at the most damaged part of the stockade, but neither the Colonel, nor anyone else outside the *pa*, could be certain where this point was.

Kawiti's third problem was to survive the British bombardment intact. We have seen that the inner palisade was not much affected by the cannonade. This did not make entry into the *pa* impossible. The ten-foot fence was not an insuperable obstacle for active men, and the palisade could eventually be cut or pulled down, or dug up. There were also spaces of up to six feet between some of the logs, which were blocked only by much weaker split timber—main trunks in a Maori palisade were seldom completely contiguous.[29] But the strong and undamaged inner fence did make entry very difficult in the face of a hot fire, and in this respect the strength of the palisade was obviously of great importance. At least equally important, however, was the fact that the garrison survived the British bombardment unshaken and with little loss. For a hot fire to exist, there had to be men ready and able to pull the necessary triggers.

The object of the British bombardment all along had been not only to breach Ohaeawai's palisade, but also to pulverize its garrison. The gunners used grape, shell, and cannister—all primarily anti-personnel ammunition—as well as roundshot. The cannister shell of the period 'contained 54 balls and proved a most effective weapon against troops, even in fieldworks, up to the range of about 1,200 yards'. The normal (shrapnel) shell buried itself before exploding. 'It was thus particularly effective against earthworks and buildings.'[30] This, together with the accurate fire of their gunners, led the British to believe that the Maori garrison had suffered heavy losses in the week-long bombardment. On 24 June, Major Bridge wrote that 'a con-

stant fire was kept up by the guns of shell, ball and grape till dark. Many hit
and burst in the *pa* and I fancy they must have lost many men.' He made
similar reference to the 'very good practice' of the guns on 26 June, and
noted two days later that 'our guns did good execution, nearly every shot
told'. On 29 June, a new battery mounted on the nearby hill poured in a particularly accurate and heavy fire. 'This will astonish the weak minds of the
natives,' wrote Bridge.[31] During the whole bombardment, according to one
estimate, the British 'fired 400 cannon-shots into the *Pa* and through it'.[32]
By 1 July, with some rounds from the heavy 32-pounder added to the
previous bombardment, Despard was sure that the garrison's loss was 'very
severe' and that the morale of men unaccustomed to cannon fire must be all
but shattered. Major Bridge, on whose evidence historians base much of
their criticism of Despard, was of exactly the same opinion.

Despard and Bridge were not fools to have come to this conclusion, but
they were wrong. What they were unable to see, and what they could hardly
be expected to guess, was that Kawiti had independently invented the anti-
artillery bunker. These pits, or *rua* as they were called by the Maoris, were
underground compartments roofed with beams of timber. Earth, fern, and,
at Ohaeawai, possibly stones, were piled on top of the excavations to render
them shell-proof. Bunkers of this type, possibly a world first in military
engineering, can still be seen at Ruapekapeka, the site of another modern *pa*
built subsequently by Kawiti. Maori tradition describes them as follows:
'Deep *pihareinga*, or dugouts with narrow circular entrances at the top, gave
access to shelters. These caves looked like calabashes buried underground,
the narrow end uppermost. The bowl, spacious enough to accomodate 15 to
20 men, provided shelter from the weather. The occupants could sleep in
comparative safety from the firing which went on overhead.'[33] In the words
of a Maori veteran: 'we were safe below in our *ruas* when the big guns
poured shot and shell into us, therefore why should we fear the cannon of
the white troops?'[34] The bombardment cost the Maoris very few men.
Estimates of Maori casualties at Ohaeawai with any claim to reliability vary
between one and ten killed. The higher figures include men slain during the
various sorties made by the garrison before 1 July.[35] As the event proved,
Maori morale also remained high. Against the reasonable expectations of
their leaders, the British storming party found the garrison almost entirely
unharmed, and ready and willing to fight.

On the facts available to him, Despard did his best to maximize his storming party's chances of success. The best troops were selected for the task.
Two-thirds of the storming party were drawn from the flank companies of
the 58th and 99th—grenadier and light companies, the best men of the regiment. The rest were selected men and volunteers from all the British units.
Despard chose 'on or near' the north-west corner of the *pa* as his point of
attack partly because the storming party could advance under cover until
within eighty yards of the palisade. He also sought to obtain a degree of
tactical surprise by ordering his men 'to proceed in the most perfect silence
until they reach the stockade'.[36]

The attempt to obtain surprise appears to have failed, but the approach under cover did give the British some advantage. The British began their charge 'at a steady double' but, as one veteran put it, 'when we were within about fifty paces of the stockade-front we cheered and went at it with a rush, our best speed and "divil take the hindmost".'[37] The Maoris had time for only one volley before the British reached the palisades. Much therefore depended on the effectiveness of this volley. An eyewitness wrote that when the storming party was 'within twenty-five yards, they received, nearly simultaneously, a fearful volley from the enemy, which killed Captain Grant, and caused a havock in a body of nearly four hundred [sic] of the finest of troops, which threw the whole . . . into a mass of confusion. The natives continued independent firing.'[38] Another participant wrote of this devastating first volley: 'I can only describe it as the opening of the doors of a monster furnace.'[39] The precisely timed initial Maori salvo broke the momentum of the British charge, but the stormers pressed on to the palisade and spread out along the *pekerangi*, looking for weak points. They found at least two. Lieutenant Philpotts, leading the small naval component of the storming party, burst through the outer fence only to be shot down.[40] At another point, a group of soldiers: 'threw ropes over the fence, which was much shattered, and pulled it down, thus exposing themselves to a deadly fire . . . through the second fence. Not daunted, they threw their ropes over the second fence; but this, not having been so much affected by the cannon fire, resisted their attempts.'[41]

These bald words conceal a military debacle comparable in intensity and feats of courage, and not so different in scale, to the attack of the British Light Brigade at Balaclava ten years later. As they struggled with the outer fence, the British were subjected to a terrible raking fire from the flanking angles, and to equally deadly fire from the main trench to their front. The original occupants of the corner attacked were rapidly reinforced from other parts of the *pa*. The Ngapuhi warriors fired in relative safety. The inner palisade and the firing trench covered them so effectively that the British could not see them, let alone get at them. As a survivor of the storming party poignantly put it: 'Not a single Maori could we see. They were all safely hidden in their trenches and pits, poking the muzzles of their guns under the foot of the outer palisade. What could we do?'[42]

It is easy, in retrospect, to answer this question by saying that there was nothing the British could do. But the determination and almost suicidal courage with which the attack was pressed home justified every one of Kawiti's precautions. The British sustained the terrible fire at the *pekerangi* for between five and ten minutes. 'The soldiers fell on this side and that,' one of Kawiti's veterans told James Cowan, gesturing with his hands, 'they fell right and left like that, like so many sticks thrown down.'[43] Two in every five men were killed or wounded before the assault ended. Even then, the storming party did not retreat of its own accord, but was recalled by Colonel Despard. Bearing unconscious testimony to his own and his men's bravery, Major Bridge described the shattered storming party's reaction to the retreat being sounded: 'This was at first thought to be a mistake and was not attended to, for all went to work supposing the *Pa* must be taken or die in the attempt. After a little it was repeated and then all that were left prepared to obey its summons, carrying off the wounded with us.'[44]

The 100 Ngapuhi warriors at Ohaeawai had demonstrated their capacity to resist an Imperial power by defeating the best soldiers in the world, and they knew it. 'Oh sons of warrior strength,' ran the Maori victory chant after the battle:

> Behold the trophy in my hand,
> Fruit of the battle strife—
> The head of the greedy cormorant
> That haunts the ocean shore! . . .
> We shall fight, we shall fight!
> Ah! You did not remain
> In your home-land in Europe.
> [Here] you lie overwhelmed
> By the swift driving wave of the battle.[45]

III FITZROY'S PEACE EFFORT

FOR FIVE MONTHS AFTER THE GREAT MAORI VICTORY AT Ohaeawai, there was no further fighting. The most important feature of this interim period was a British campaign launched, not with the sword, but with the pen. This was an effort by FitzRoy to arrange a peace in the North which left substantive victory in Maori hands but which could be publicized as a British success in other parts of the island. Remarkably enough, one of the main elements of this propaganda operation was the claim that the Ohaeawai expedition had been a successful one.

Not surprisingly, the British troops before Ohaeawai were severely shaken by their shattering repulse on 1 July. That night some sentries, unnerved by the fate of their comrades the previous afternoon and by the loud and terrifying Maori victory celebrations going on inside the *pa*, actually left their posts and sought the comfort of the campfires—theoretically a capital offence.[46] With his men in this state, with rumours of a Maori night attack abounding, and with seventy wounded to worry about, Despard naturally took the decision to withdraw. He announced this to his Maori allies on 5 July. Waka Nene and his associates, who had taken little part in the assault on 1 July, strongly opposed the decision.[47] The next day, they changed their minds and agreed to a British retreat, but Despard had also changed his mind and decided to stay. The probable reason for this dual *volte face* was that both groups had learned that Kawiti was about to abandon Ohaeawai.[48] Waka's group now thought to occupy the *pa* without British help, and Despard saw no reason to leave them even the shabby laurels that would flow from this.

Kawiti may have been influenced by his followers' need to return to their domestic tasks and by the fact that Heke's men had just completed a new *pa*, which could replace Ohaeawai when necessary, at Hikurangi.[49] At least equally important was the fact that, for reasons outlined below, the loss of Ohaeawai was now no loss at all. Whatever his motives, on 11 July, when all serious danger had disappeared, Kawiti abandoned the scene of his great victory and retired.

Despard occupied the empty *pa* and lost no time in claiming a victory which tactically balanced the defeat on 1 July and which strategically justified the whole expedition. He claimed, first, that the 'rebels' had been so overawed by the courage shown by the troops on 1 July that they dared not face a repeat attempt. He argued that the renewal of his bombardment on 10 July convinced them that such an attempt was in the offing. 'There is no doubt', he wrote on 11 July, 'that it was the fear of another assault being made after the renewal of offensive operations yesterday that caused this retreat.'[50] In reality, Despard had neither the means nor the inclination to mount a second assault. He knew that Kawiti was about to retreat when he renewed his bombardment, and he presumably made this move to lend credibility to the victory claim he had determined on making.

FitzRoy saw fit at least to pretend to accept this claim, Despard was 'very cordially' praised for having 'almost quelled' the rebellion, and fulsome congratulations were distributed. As the weeks wore on, he supplemented the picture of a successful Ohaeawai expedition with assertions that the 'rebels' had 'suffered severely' as a result of unspecified British operations. This culminated in the claim that Heke and Kawiti had been 'sufficiently punished'.[51]

While FitzRoy's and Despard's propaganda efforts proceeded at one level, they conducted much more realistic peace negotiations at another. These involved a recognition of the hard fact that Ohaeawai was a disastrous defeat which made it difficult to continue the war, at least until a much larger force could be mustered. As early as 7 July, FitzRoy 'fully authorised' Despard 'to make such terms of temporary peace or cessation from hostilities as may be adapted to the present exigency'.[52] FitzRoy commenced serious negotiations with Heke—through Burrows, Williams, and other missionaries—and soon afterwards gave Despard orders which the Colonel declared were 'tantamount to a suspension of all active operations'.[53]

At first, FitzRoy hoped to exclude Kawiti from the peace, but as Heke refused to acquiesce in this, the Governor accepted that both would have to be included in any agreement. On 2 October, after a *de facto* truce of three months, he authorized Despard, to whom the missionary negotiators were reporting, to sign a treaty without further reference to Auckland. The Colonel was not to forget that 'a document should be written and signed in duplicate as a record'.[54]

In August, Heke responded to the first British peace initiative by stating his terms. He expressed continued suspicion of the Treaty of Waitangi and doubts about the implications of British sovereignty, but said he was ready for peace. He offered to return part of the small amount of plunder he claimed he had, and to try to induce others to return theirs. He would allow the neutral chief, Pomare, to erect a flagstaff at Kororareka as a signal for shipping 'but if it is for an Ensign of Sovereignty of the Queen I never will submit to the flag'. He defined sovereignty as 'authority over our land'.[55] These terms amounted to a limited but real Maori victory. Nevertheless, FitzRoy eventually reconciled himself to accepting them, with one exception. He demanded, and continued to demand, the cession of some Maori land.

Both Heke and Kawiti were, of course, adamantly opposed to such a concession in principle, and there was nothing about their military position which obliged them to change their view. But despite this, FitzRoy's demand was not the insuperable barrier to peace it seems at first sight. The simple reasons for this were that the block in question was very small, that very little of it belonged to Kawiti, and that none of it belonged to Heke. Heke told Henry Williams that 'not one foot of the land belonging to him was included in the terms offered'.[56] Heke therefore had no objection to the terms himself, but he was 'determined to stand by Kawiti', and Kawiti did object.[57] Kawiti, a determined opponent of the sale, let alone the cession, of land, remained adamant for two months, and it was largely his attitude which obstructed the peace effort. But he was under some pressure from his people, the area was insignificant, and Kawiti shared the rights to it with neutral and even pro-government Maoris. There are signs that, by late October, Kawiti was reconsidering his objections.[58] But by this time Fitz-Roy had received notice of his dismissal, and under his successor, Captain George Grey, the British offer lapsed.

Of course, given the fact that pro-government and neutral Maoris would suffer at least as much from the cession as would Heke and Kawiti, the measure was derisory as a punishment. Grey assumed that FitzRoy had mistakenly selected land that did not belong primarily to Heke and Kawiti, and where they refer to the matter at all, historians tend to follow this view. But Williams, Robert Burrows, and other missionaries, as well as Colonel Despard, were all fully aware of the true ownership of the land, and it is highly unlikely that they kept this knowledge from FitzRoy. It therefore seems clear that the measure was intended by FitzRoy as a token cession, a face-saving device. As such, it would constitute, with the 'capture' of Ohaeawai and the economic strains on the Maoris, the third prop of his victory claim.

There was some truth in FitzRoy's assertions that the Maoris were suffering economic hardship. The planting schedule had been severely disturbed by the war, and reserve supplies had been strained. The diversion of labour to *pa* building and defence and, to a lesser extent, the plundering activities of Waka and his group had also created hardship. Added to this, Heke was still suffering from his wound and an epidemic of 'flux' was raging in his main base at Kaikohe.[59] The effects of these problems were limited by certain strategic factors discussed below, and by the recuperative period which the peace negotiations and the victory at Ohaeawai allowed. Despard felt that the reports of economic hardship were grossly exaggerated.[60] To the extent that problems did exist, they were not the result of British initiatives, but products of Waka's operations, particularly Te Ahuahu, of disease, and of the inevitable strains of an unusually sustained warfare. But they did help to incline Heke and Kawiti towards peace.

Even at its best, FitzRoy's case for British victory was not a very good one. It was obvious to most contemporary commentators that the prospects of British success could hardly be worse. Henry Williams wrote a month after the battle that: 'Everything is uncertain around even the very existence of the Country as a Colony of Great Britain. I will be very sorry if it be relinquished as we may fear the introduction of the French with a whole train of evils consequent to such an event, yet it is evident that the troops do not relish contending this question with "these cannibals" as they are frequently termed.' When FitzRoy's assertion that 'the rebels have been sufficiently punished' became public, the *New-Zealander* was unimpressed. 'There is not a native throughout the Island but considers—and most true it is—that his countrymen have been victorious, and that the former halo of European superiority is completely dispelled.'[61]

Unsuccessful as it was, FitzRoy's effort to make the best of a bad situation was understandable in the circumstances, and it was significant in two respects. First, it demonstrated beyond doubt that Ohaeawai was a shattering blow to British hopes. The British were to mount one further expedition, and one more battle would be fought. But if any engagement in the Northern War can be called 'decisive' in the sense that it contributed most to the over-all result, it is Ohaeawai.

The second significant aspect of FitzRoy's two-pronged peace and propaganda campaign was that it constituted the prototype of a technique that was subsequently to be applied by his successor. In Grey's hands, the technique was to achieve vastly greater success.

3

The Paper Victory

IN LATE SEPTEMBER 1845, FITZROY RECEIVED NOTICE OF HIS dismissal and so joined less eminent victims like Ensign Campbell on the list of scapegoats for Heke's and Kawiti's talents. His successor Captain George Grey, an important figure in this study, arrived fresh from a successful Governorship in South Australia, on 14 November 1845. Though, in the final analysis, a more ruthless man than Heke, Grey had a considerable amount in common with the younger of his new opponents. Both were clear-thinking strategists and considerable egotists and, though here the means at Grey's disposal were vastly the greater, both were masters of propaganda with an eye on their place in history. They were about the same age, and the description of Heke as 'a man of many thoughts' applied equally to Grey.[1]

It quickly became clear to Grey that to honour the terms proposed by FitzRoy amounted to accepting defeat. 'I thought the terms offered to them [Heke and Kawiti] entirely inconsistent with the interests of the British Government.' To some extent, the new Governor was bound by the opinions of Henry Williams and Burrows that the Maoris still considered FitzRoy's offer to be open. Grey solved this problem by demanding a final reply within an unreasonably short time—five days—and, with Despard, set about organizing the third and largest British expedition inland against Kawiti's new *pa* at Ruapekapeka.[2]

I RUAPEKAPEKA AND THE ADAPTATION OF MAORI STRATEGY

THE FORCE WHICH BEGAN LANDING AT THE KAWAKAWA RIVER on 7 December 1845 was evidence of the fact that Heke and Kawiti had put the British Empire to a considerable amount of trouble. In the context of Imperial military resources, always exiguous and now further strained by the First Sikh War, it was not an insignificant force. In the context of New Zealand's isolation and of the number of men originally thought necessary to deal with the Maoris, it was a very large one. Some 1300 British were involved in all, of whom about a hundred were detached to hold the line of communication. Estimates of the pro-government Maoris, now joined by Nopera Panakaraeo and some Rarawa, went as high as 850 warriors, but the true figure was probably much lower. The British eventually included 800 regulars, sixty volunteers from Auckland, a naval brigade of nearly 400, and, interestingly enough, eighty sailors and artillerymen from the East India Company's European forces. The figure usually given is somewhat lower, but does not take account of 115 soldiers and some seamen who arrived during the expedition. This little army was supported by five warships and several transports. The artillery consisted of three 32-pounders, one eighteen-pounder, two twelve-pounder howitzers, and seven lighter pieces, including four mortars.[3] One chief of Waka's group, Makoare Te Taonui, was asked by Grey to prevent Heke, who was still at Hikurangi, from joining Kawiti. Even after this detachment, the British and their remaining Maori allies outnumbered Kawiti's Ruapekapeka garrison by about four to one.[4]

Assembling the British army at the Kawakawa was one thing, and getting it up to Ruapekapeka—appropriately enough, 'the Bat's Nest'—was another. The British had to crawl over eighteen miles of hill, bush, river, and ravine, hauling thirty tons of artillery along with them and cutting their road as they went. It took them three weeks to get the whole column up, but by Christmas the first echelon (700 men) and a couple of guns were before Ruapekapeka.

With hard experience of Kawiti's abilities, Despard proceeded with caution, despite his overwhelming force. He built strong stockades, progressively closer to the *pa*, to protect his batteries and camps. These stockades, the size of the British force, and the vigilance of Waka and his associates prevented Kawiti from interfering with the bombardment. The Colonel brought his guns into action as they came up. Hampered only by the difficulty of getting ammunition up from the coast, the British bombarded Ruapekapeka day and night for two weeks. The interior defences of the *pa* were if anything more sophisticated than those of Ohaeawai and the garrison suffered few casualties.[5] But the heavy and accurate bombardment began to have an effect on the strong palisade. On 10 January 1846—the same day that Heke, having eluded Te Taonui, arrived in the *pa* with sixty warriors[6]—three small breaches were at last formed. Fearing that the enemy would now escape, Despard considered an assault, but was dissuaded by the pro-government chiefs. On 11 January, one of Waka's men discovered that the *pa* appeared to be abandoned and the allied forces tumbled in pell-mell. Inside, they found that the place did have some occupants, in the form of Kawiti and a dozen warriors. These fired one volley and fled out of the *pa*, followed by some of the British. More of the garrison, now located in the bush outside their fortification, came to Kawiti's support and some heavy fighting occurred, with the Maoris at one stage making a move back towards the *pa*. Both sides then got under cover and exchanged a desultory fire for three hours. The Maoris then retired.

Despard and Grey lost no time in announcing a 'brilliant success'. Despard wrote that Ruapekapeka had been 'carried by assault', that a full-scale attempt to regain the *pa* had been repulsed, and that the Maoris had been driven from a further position in the bush. Grey, who was present himself and did not have to rely on Despard for information, also declared Ruapekapeka taken 'by assault' and expatiated 'on the subsequent complete defeat of the rebels Heke and Kawiti by Her Majesty's Forces outside the *pa*'.[7]

A week after the battle, Heke and Kawiti came down to the neutral Pomare's rebuilt *pa*, met Waka Nene and his associates, and agreed on peace. It was not hard for Grey to place this event in a cause-effect relationship with the engagement on 11 January. He too accepted peace, and hastened to announce that the rebels, 'beaten and dispersed' at Ruapekapeka, had gone to Pomare's 'with the intention of making their complete submission to the Government'. Magnanimous in victory, Grey soon afterwards proclaimed that, since the rebels had been so 'severely punished' in battle, 'it is not the intention of the Government to take any further proceedings' against them. Lest anyone should overlook it, the connection between Ruapekapeka and the Maori submission was hammered home.[8]

This was enough to convince contemporaries living at any distance. The Imperial Government sent its congratulations on 'the final and complete subjugation of the rebels'.[9] Settlers living in the southern settlements were likewise convinced. One Taranaki account, written in early February 1846, already had the trappings of legend: 'The troops were successful in taking the *Pah* of the Rebels Heke and Kawiti who gave themselves up to Governor Grey who shook hands with them and set them at liberty.'[10]

Most historians reject the claim that Ruapekapeka was taken by assault in favour of another contemporary version. This was that, 11 January being a Sunday, the Maoris were outside the *pa* at prayers, naively expecting that their enemies would also respect the Sabbath. Only Kawiti, 'sturdy old pagan', and a few of his fellow heathens, remained inside—'soundly sleeping while the web of fate was spun around them'.[11] Thus the British obtained the *pa* by default, although they did soundly beat the garrison in the subsequent action outside it. But whatever they think of the manner in which it was obtained, virtually all historians agree that Ruapekapeka was a Maori defeat—the decisive battle which brought the Northern War to a triumphant conclusion for the British.

The separation of Ruapekapeka from its myth is a complicated process, and it can conveniently be divided into four stages. The first relates to the emergence of the Sunday prayers story as an explanation for the Maoris' absence from the *pa*. The second concerns the validity of this story, and the real reason for the Maoris' absence. The third assesses the tactical result of the combat outside the *pa*, and the fourth discusses the strategic character of Ruapekapeka and the over-all result of the British expedition.

A substantial minority of contemporary commentators saw Ruapekapeka as something less than a decisive British victory. Henry Williams had grave doubts about the 'victory', and his biographer, Hugh Carleton, observed that 'there is some difference between taking a *pa* by assault and getting into an empty one'. The *New-Zealander* felt that the capture of Ruapekapeka was 'fortuitous' and subsequently poured scorn on the official claims. In the first published military analysis of the War, Captain Collinson of the Royal Engineers concluded that the battle was at best a draw. The Church Missionary Society's printer, John Telford, was more blunt. Despard's despatch reporting the battle, he wrote, 'could hardly have contained more positive falsehoods . . . of course, Kawiti will erect a new pah somewhere else. It were as great a folly to say that he is defeated as to say that the British were at Waterloo!!' [12]

One or two of these commentators may conceivably have been influenced by personal animosity towards Grey. But their opinions had some basis in fact. Through Maori sources, they knew that Kawiti and Heke had lost fewer men—between nine and twelve killed—than the British.[13] They deduced from this and other evidence that the action outside the *pa* had not been unequal, and they rightly dismissed the claim that the *pa* had been taken by assault. They had therefore to explain how the British had seized Ruapekapeka without defeating its garrison. Williams and other missionaries had had reason to contrast the impiety of the troops with the piety of the 'rebels', and they therefore resorted to the story of the Sunday prayers. Others, who shared the majority view of Ruapekapeka as a British victory, had also invoked this story, but to some extent the anti-sabbatarian hypothesis was an explanation of British failure and not success. The story was both intrinsically improbable and inaccurate—on a par with historical explanations in which kingdoms were lost for lack of a horse. But in the hands of those contemporaries who denied that Ruapekapeka was a British victory, it was an honest, if mistaken, answer to the real question of how the British occupied the *pa* without beating its garrison. Subsequent historians have remembered the answer and forgotten the question.

The second issue of importance is the validity of the Sunday prayers story itself. The British, as Ian Wards alone among historians has pointed out,[14] had fought the Maoris on Sundays earlier in the war—at Ohaeawai for example. But the implausibility of what is supposed to have happened is less important than what did happen. There is solid evidence to suggest that the Maoris chose to evacuate the *pa*, and that they began making preparations to do so several days before Sunday 11 January. On 8 January, a British picket saw eighty men leave Ruapekapeka. Bridge wrote: 'I fancy they are leaving the *pa* by parties and that they will shortly bolt.' The next day 'numbers of natives were observed leaving the *pa* with loads on their backs and returning for more'. On 10 January, Lieutenant Balneavis 'was sure that the natives had left or were trying an ambuscade'.[15] By this time, Waka Nene and Mohi Tawhai were certain that Ruapekapeka was being abandoned.[16] It is clear enough from this evidence that the Maoris had voluntarily decided to evacuate the *pa*. If further confirmation is needed, the fact that 'within the *pa*, no ammunition or provisions were found' seems conclusive. It is extremely improbable that the Maoris had simultaneously run out of both—particularly in the light of the fact that the 'free ingress and egress'

the bush. From there, they continued sniping in an effort to draw the troops in again, but the British would not be tempted.

Despite their lighter casualties, the partial misfire of their plan left the Maoris with what might safely be called a tactical draw. But this is less important than the fourth aspect of the battle—the strategic character of Ruapekapeka *pa*. It was this which gave the Maoris the flexibility to attempt their tactical trap and which enabled them so readily to abandon their fortification. It was this which robbed the British of any benefit from their expedition. An appreciation of this strategic factor is vital to the basic question of who won the battle, and therefore, to some extent, the Northern War. It is also vital to an understanding of the changed Maori military system.

Strategic character was more directly important at Ruapekapeka than at the two earlier Northern War *pa*—Puketutu and Ohaeawai—and it is appropriate that the discussion should centre on it. But the relevant strategic features were common to the three *pa*, and to some extent they must be examined together. In April 1845, as soon as he heard that the British were mounting an expedition against him, Hone Heke had begun building Puketutu *pa*. He had a small *pa* at Te Ahuahu, guarding some cultivations, yet he went to the trouble of building another, several miles away, from which to face the British. After the British attack failed, he abandoned Puketutu while under no pressure at all. Yet when Te Taonui and Waka Nene seized Te Ahuahu, he immediately made strenuous efforts to retake it. Kawiti also had several *pa*, but he too chose to build new ones from which to fight the British. At Ohaeawai, he applied all his energy and genius to smashing the assault on 1 July, only to abandon the *pa* on 11 July when all serious danger had passed. All three Northern War *pa* were built deep in the interior, approachable only by difficult bush tracks—quite isolated from the main areas of cultivation which *pa* were normally supposed to protect. They were surrounded by rough country, but at the same time they were relatively easy to attack once their vicinity was reached. An enemy who struggled up the miles to each *pa* would, on at least one face, find the remaining yards fairly easy to cross.

Why did the Maoris build these *pa* to face British expeditions when others were available? Why were they prepared to abandon them and not others? Why did they build them to be difficult to approach from the coast, yet easy to attack once the long haul had been completed?

Clearly one reason for the changes was that a purpose-built *pa* could be specially tailored to counter European warfare: it could incorporate the improvements and innovations in construction which had proved so effective at Ohaeawai. But this was by no means the only reason. Of the rest, the most basic was the change in the function of the *pa*. In contrast to older *pa*, the Northern War *pa* had no direct strategic or economic importance. They did not guard borders, command important routes of communication, or protect cultivations. They did not hold tribal reserves of food, ammunition, and seed crops, nor did they contain canoes, nets, tools, or other equipment. They did not act as citadels for tribal populations—their garrisons consisted mainly of warriors. In short, the new *pa* had virtually no inherent value. In contrast to traditional *pa*, they could be abandoned without a qualm.

In combination with this factor, the changes in the location of *pa* were also of crucial importance. A historian has suggested that Despard should have taken *pa* by investment, but the tactical location of the *pa* he attacked meant that they were easy to escape from, and therefore, *ipso facto*, that they were difficult or impossible to invest. The fact that an enemy, once he was within striking distance, could easily approach a *pa*, did not mean it could be surrounded. The Northern War *pa* all had thick bush and rough ground, including gullies and ravines, close to at least one of their faces. Complete encirclement was therefore very difficult, even for a large force, and escape was always possible for the garrison.

The strategic location of the new *pa* was especially significant at Ruapekapeka. We have seen that the concentration of the largest force yet seen in New Zealand was a difficult and expensive process. This force had to be shipped from Auckland to the coast, and it was only then that the major problems began. The troops with their carts and guns crawled through the bush-clad hill country at a mile a day, cutting their road as they went. They had to be fed on the way, and both men and guns had to be supplied through the eighteen days of bombardment. Against a traditional *pa*, located on the coast, near a river, or at least in a district sufficiently flat to cultivate, this huge effort would not have been required. It was the strategic location of Ruapekapeka which demanded this effort from the British, and the crucial point is that it was a very fair price for an inherently valueless *pa*.

The function of Ruapekapeka meant that Kawiti could afford to lose it, the tactical location meant that he was easily able to escape from it, and the strategic location meant that he scored a strategic success in doing so. The Maori trap was simply a bold—perhaps over-bold—attempt to add a tactical bonus to the strategic victory already assured. Of all interpreters, only Captain Collinson came close to grasping these facts.

> 1100 men were occupied a full month in advancing 15 miles and in getting possession of a *pah* from which the enemy escaped at the last moment, and escaped with the satisfaction to him of a drawn battle. The question is, was it worthwhile to go through all that laborious march to obtain such a result.[23]

II   PEACE IN THE NORTH

IT COULD BE ARGUED THAT, IF THE DECISIVE BRITISH VICTORY at Ruapekapeka is a fiction, then so too is their claim to victory in the war as a whole. But this issue is too important to turn on a debating point and as the Ngati Ruanui chief Titokowaru was subsequently to show, it was perfectly possible to lose a war without losing any of its battles. It is therefore necessary, first, to assess the British claims about the peace agreement, and to establish, as far as possible, how Heke and Kawiti saw the results of the conflict; and secondly, to examine the reasons why the anti-government Maoris accepted peace.

Official accounts presented the peace agreement of late January as an abject and total submission by both Heke and Kawiti to the British Government. This satisfies most historians, including Grey's most recent biographer, James Rutherford, who wrote that Kawiti 'showed a proper sense of the generosity extended to him' and communicated 'submissively' with Grey.[24] The whole accepted version of the peace agreement, however, is unlikely, contradictory, and inaccurate.

It was said that Heke and Kawiti gave over the whole of their lands to the Governor 'praying only that some small corner might be left them for the use of their children'.[25] If this had any basis in reality at all, it was either in the tact of Waka Nene who acted as intermediary between the 'rebels' and the government, or in Heke's sarcasm. Heke had sardonically asked Fitz-Roy if he wanted the whole of his lands and property after Ohaeawai.[26] There is, furthermore, an obvious discrepancy between the claim that the anti-government forces were forced to sue for peace by their 'defeat and dispersal', and the fact that Heke and Kawiti were accompanied to Pomare's by all their lieutenants and many of their warriors.[27] One might add that the British began their retreat from Ruapekapeka to the coast rather hastily, abandoning equipment and ammunition, and that they carried it out under constant fear of attack by their 'beaten and dispersed' enemies.[28] It seems that the British had nothing to do with the peace negotiations. The missionary Richard Davis reported the meeting at Pomare's as follows. 'News is just come that the natives have made peace among themselves, and that the loyal chief, Walker [Waka Nene], is gone to Auckland to fetch the Governor.'[29] It is certainly true that this development was not expected by Grey, who had indeed returned to Auckland. Grey did not meet either anti-government leader at this stage, though he did see Kawiti four months later. The Governor merely expressed his assent, through Waka Nene, to a *fait accompli*.

Grey's proclamation announcing the peace purported freely to grant an unconditional pardon to 'all concerned in the late rebellion' and laid down no punitive measures whatever. On the other hand, he had stated at the beginning of the Ruapekapeka expedition that it would be 'absolutely necessary to crush either Heke or Kawiti before tranquillity could be restored to the country'.[30] Like FitzRoy before him, he wisely changed his tune in practice when the military realities became apparent. In the rhetoric, however, the fact that he was unable to punish his enemies was presented as an act of considered clemency. Grey, as subsequent events were to prove, was extremely adept at making a virtue of necessity.

The opinions of the anti-government Maoris themselves indicate a clear desire for peace, but they can hardly be said to reflect a 'complete and final subjugation'. On 14 February, the *New-Zealander* reported that the anti-government Maoris 'boast very much, and they say that the Governor and the troops going away so soon was in plain English *bolting*—and they assert that many things were left behind in the camp [at Ruapekapeka]'. The same month, Kawiti was said to have informed a fellow chief:

> that, with his handful of men, he had withstood and beaten the English, with all the force they could collect from Port Jackson and other places, and that he had lost very few men. He declared that the soldiers were unable to conquer him and that peace was made not by his wish or desire but by the earnest entreaty of the Governor. As peace was made, he was willing to sit quietly and receive the white people at Kororareka but that the Flagstaff must not be erected for some time.[31]

The extent to which Heke's acceptance of peace constituted an abject submission can conveniently be illustrated by the following anecdote. Before the war, a number of minor incidents had contributed to the belief of Heke and his followers that the British were encroaching into the areas of chiefly authority and Maori local control. One of these incidents occurred when the Maori wife of a settler named Lord publicly compared Heke to a side of pork. In a society one decade away from the use of cannibalism as the final humiliation of one's enemies, this was a grave insult. Heke demanded the customary compensation, Lord demurred, and a *taua muru* became necessary. Some months later, after the second amputation of the Flagstaff, Fitz-Roy offered a £100 reward for Heke's apprehension. Heke, greatly offended, was heard to say 'Am I a pig, to be bought and sold?' In short, comparison with a pig, a purchasable piece of meat, was a mortal insult in Maori society, and Heke had special reason to be familiar with it. In October 1846, Grey despatched an emissary to Heke to effect what the Governor called a 'complete and final settlement'—thus incidentally undercutting his claim that this already existed.[32] The emissary, Edward Meurant, met Heke and though the chief warned his people that 'the Foreigners tell us many lies', Meurant was reasonably satisfied with the conference. Perhaps he was a little over-optimistic. As Meurant was leaving, Heke presented him with a gift for Grey, and 'requested that particular attention should be paid to the peace-offering . . . for the Governor'. The peace-offering, one need hardly add, was 'a large pig'.[33]

To say all this is not to deny that Heke and Kawiti wanted peace in 1846, or that the degree of their success was limited. Three major factors contributed to this. The first was that Waka and his allies persisted in opposing the anti-government forces, and that their power remained virtually intact. The 'pro-government' Ngapuhi carefully preserved themselves from the British disasters—a fact which the government diplomatically passed over, but which aroused great resentment among the troops. Waka alone had secured a substantial victory over Heke. Waka's own support appears to have diminished relative to Heke's after the war, but on the other hand he had proved himself an indispensable ally to the British. Such influence as the government had in the North between 1846 and Heke's death in 1850 was exercised primarily through Waka. In this respect, Waka owed his influence to Heke's success as well as his own. The government also sought

Waka's advice on issues affecting other parts of the colony. Waka's position was that of a respected ally rather than a loyal subject. In fact, there are signs that in his mind's eye Waka inverted the theoretical relationship. There was sometimes a proprietary air in his references to the government, and his epitaph declared him to be 'the Father of the Europeans'. In the competition for valuable *Pakeha*, Tamati Waka Nene had secured the biggest of them all: the Government.

The second factor which inclined Heke and Kawiti towards ending the war was the inevitable strain of what in Maori terms was an unusually prolonged conflict. The economic hardships and the drain of casualties were real incentives to stop the fighting. But these effects were limited in several ways. The Maoris asserted after the war that they had lost sixty killed and eighty wounded in total.[34] Heke was said to keep careful records of his casualties,[35] and this figure—as against the British official estimate of 500 killed and wounded—is a reasonable one. It may, however, have excluded lightly wounded men and 170 killed and wounded might be a fairer figure for comparison with British losses of 260 and pro-government Maori losses of between forty and sixty. Given that the total number of warriors fighting under Heke or Kawiti at some time or another was probably in the order of 1,000, it seems fair to suggest that their losses were serious but by no means crippling.

The same could be said of the economic costs of the war. The British had done some damage to the Maori economic base before and during the Puketutu expedition, as a kind of side-line to the expedition's main objective. The government's Maori allies had done more damage when, in April and early June 1845, they destroyed Heke's cultivations near Lake Omapere. A joint force had also destroyed the traditional *pa* of Kawiti's allies, the Kapotai *hapu*, on 15 May 1845. But apart from this, Kawiti's power base—his own and his allies' villages and traditional *pa* were spread over a wide area—had not been greatly affected. Heke's main base, the Kaikohe district, had also scarcely been touched. While the construction of a *pa* like Ohaeawai did involve considerable effort, it did not necessarily overstrain the Maori resources if the work was spread over a long period, and if it was followed by a temporary cessation of hostilities during which the Maoris could recuperate.

The limitations on the economic costs of the war did not arise primarily from the nature of the terrain or the dispersed character of the Maori means of production, but from the way in which these factors were used by the Maoris. The technique involved was a fundamental feature of the adapted Maori system of war, and again it centred on the strategic location of the new *pa*. In the context of a theatre of war only twenty miles long and twenty-five miles wide, each of the Northern War *pa* was isolated from the centres of cultivation and population that *pa* were normally designed to protect. Given the nature of the British war aims, this actually exchanged direct protection for more effective indirect protection. Before each British expedition, FitzRoy and Grey had informed their military commanders that their objective was to capture or destroy the rebel fighting force and its chiefs.[36] In retrospect, it is easy to suggest that attacks on Heke's and Kawiti's cultivations would have been more profitable, but to do so is to ignore the pressures on the British. Both FitzRoy and Grey felt that a prompt and clear-cut military decision was politically imperative. Problems in the south, and the reputation of the government as a force to be taken seriously, demanded a quick and emphatic decision. This pressure naturally increased after each reverse. A lengthy campaign of attrition against Maori villages appeared to be political lunacy, and the British were in any case reluctant to concede that such a course might be militarily more practicable than to seek out and destroy their savage enemy.

From the beginning of the war, the British made no secret of their intention to hunt down the 'rebels' wherever they might be. By building new *pa* in isolated locations, the Maoris could therefore channel operations into economically unimportant areas. A British force attacking a new *pa* could not simultaneously attack Maori base areas. The resources used in such an expedition could not be used against other targets. Expensive expeditions could not be mounted in a continuous series. The British therefore had a system of sporadic forays into the interior imposed on them by the location of the new *pa*. The Maoris could recuperate between these forays, and they could use the lulls to build new *pa* at an economically sustainable speed. The new *pa* acted as targets for the British and so absorbed their energy. Both factors operated indirectly to preserve the Maori sinews of war. This strategy was never entirely successful. The strain of building *pa* and of keeping forces in the field for even four months out of ten was considerable. The troops did destroy some crops and other property and the pro-government Maoris destroyed more. But the strategy was sufficiently successful to solve the seemingly insoluble problem of resisting a professional army with a tribal socio-economy.

The third factor which led the anti-government Maoris to make peace, and to keep it, was the achievement of most of their war aims. The question of the distribution of power in the north of New Zealand between 1845 and 1850 is a complicated one, and full justice cannot be done to it here. But an examination of relatively easily available evidence strongly suggests that, though Hone Heke did not rule the North after the war, he became the most powerful man in it, and that government influence remained at a low level. Though Kawiti was greatly respected, he was over seventy in this period and his profile remained lower than that of his younger colleague.

For some time after the war, Grey expatiated on the 'peace and tranquillity' that now ruled in the North and sought, in public, to present Heke as a broken man. This interpretation of the effects of the Northern War has proved historiographically influential, but in reality it was no more than a conscious artifice on Grey's part. It was designed to minimize Heke's status in the eyes of Maoris and Europeans by ignoring him and, in private, Grey explicitly said as much.[37] Furthermore, his rhetorical, high-profile, claims were contradicted by his realistic, low-profile, practice. He declined to return the troops lent for the war by the Australian colonies on the grounds that Heke and Kawiti were still dangerous.[38] He kept close watch on the independent powers in the North through his allies and a series of emissaries.[39] He sought to arrange an alliance between Heke and Kawiti and Waka and his associates, through which he might exercise some restraint on the former.[40] And Grey also tried, in September 1846, to arrange the 'complete and final' settlement he is supposed to have effected nine months earlier—thus exposing himself to Heke's little joke. Grey's reason for this move, as he himself put it, was that 'there can be no doubt that, from the general repute Heke has acquired (however unjustly), his name is the cause of constant apprehension and continual disquiet to many persons'.[41]

In late March 1846, the well-known settler F. E. Maning, in his blunt if ungrammatical way, informed his brother that:

> The govt. have proclaimed peace to be established but a more rediculous thing cannot be imagined. . . . Heke the principal boasts and indeed with truth that he never asked for peace and that the Government have left off attacking him because they were tired of getting their soldiers killed without any advantage . . . anyone to read Despard's despatches would think that we had thrashed the natives soundly whereas they really have had the best of us on several occasions. I really begin to think that it is perhaps all a mistake about us beating the french at Waterloo I shall always for the rest of my life be cautious how I believe an account of a battle

In November of the same year, Maning reiterated these points, and noted that 'the natives have consequently less respect than ever for the government'.[42]

On 4 April 1846, the *New-Zealander* noted that Heke had 600 followers and that he kept his plunder. 'So much for the "brilliant successes" at Ruapekapeka.' Five months later, Henry Williams wrote: 'it cannot be said that we have peace of a healthy character. Heke is moving from place to place exciting much sympathy . . . Heke's cause is by no means extinguished, he is at large and could command as large a force as ever.'[43]

At the end of the year, Heke visited Kororareka with a large armed force. There were few British troops in the rebuilt town, Waka had no warriors with him, and not surprisingly Richard Davis was led to remark that 'this looks bad'.[44] But Heke simply removed the remains of the men killed in the battle on 11 March 1845, and having thus asserted that he could and would do exactly what he wished, even in British Kororareka, retired peacefully. One of Grey's envoys felt that the Europeans were behaving weakly in allowing this. He was right, but they may have done so for the very good reason that they were weak.[45]

Heke's *mana* and power at this time was considerable, and he appears to have continued his law-giving operations. In August 1848 the missionary Davis wrote that 'amongst his countrymen, as a patriot, he [Heke] has raised himself to the very pinnacle of honour, and is much respected wherever he goes'. Shortly afterwards, Davis noted that 'with the exception of Walker's party, which is but small, the whole of the tribes around pay him [Heke] profound homage, and in great measure his word is their law'. [46]

In this context, the fact that the flagstaff at Kororareka remained where it had fallen on 11 March 1845 took on considerable significance. Grey may well have cared less for such symbols than FitzRoy, but if he was prepared tactfully to let the flagstaff lie to avoid offending Heke, he was hardly likely to take other measures—such as attempting to interfere in Heke's sphere of authority—which would have offended him more. The eminent settler, Hugh Carleton, had this to say about Grey's decision to acquiesce in the fate of the flagstaff. 'It is beyond dispute, that the enemy was thereby acknowledged as victorious. Governor FitzRoy could at any time have established a lasting peace, on the same terms.' Four months after Ruapekapeka, Henry Williams wrote of the situation somewhat more bitterly. 'The flag-staff in the Bay is still prostrate, and the natives here rule. These are humiliating facts to the proud Englishman, many of whom thought they could govern by a mere name.' [47]

Grey's efforts to conceal these facts should not be misunderstood. His own ego may have been involved in some degree, but to make the best in propaganda of a bad military situation was good politics. This understandable and even legitimate hoax was more successful historiographically than it was historically—we have seen that some contemporary Europeans doubted Grey's claims, and it is unlikely that many Maoris were convinced. But even at the time, Grey's propaganda did have a significant impact, and it quickly became the majority European interpretation of the Northern War. This was partly the result of Grey's own skill, but the fact that his efforts struck fertile ground in the climate of ideas was more important. The British victory claim did dampen down the island-wide effects of defeat in the North, and to this extent the British secured a kind of victory by the pen where the sword had failed.

Heke's and Kawiti's success was also limited locally, by the factors discussed above, and as we have seen, their resistance had anyway been undertaken for very limited ends. The British had at least demonstrated that their resources were great and their troops formidable, and Waka Nene and his associates held to their alliance with the Government. But the question of who won the Northern War will continue to be asked and, if a short answer is demanded, the least inaccurate is that Heke and Kawiti did. The defeat of British troops in a small war, by an inferior number of non-European enemies, was an extremely unusual event. It was a result, not of British blunders, but of the rapid and radical adaptation of the Maori military system.

PART TWO

The Taranaki War

4

A Question of Sovereignty

THE NORTHERN WAR WAS FOLLOWED BY TWO OUTBREAKS OF fighting in the south: in the Wellington region, in March-August 1846, and at Wanganui, in April-July 1847. These conflicts were complicated and interesting, but the actual fighting was very small-scale, and only a brief summary, based on secondary sources, can be attempted here.[1] The situation was similar in some respects to that of the Northern War. One cause of trouble was the hasty New Zealand Company land purchasing which had also contributed to the Wairau Affray but, as Ian Wards has shown, a good chance of compromise was lost through heavy-handed government intervention. As in the north, resistance was only one of three Maori options. Government support for settler land claims was widely resented among Maoris, but military action which might hamper economic co-operation with Europeans was held to be equally undesirable. Some believed the former danger to be the greater, and resisted; some saw the latter as the more serious threat, and actively supported the government. Most Maoris saw something in both viewpoints, and remained neutral.

The situation was further complicated by the delicate balance between the tribes of the region: Ngati Toa, who had migrated to Wellington during the Musket Wars; their allies, including parts of Te Atiawa and Ngati Raukawa, who had accompanied them; and the original inhabitants, Muaupoko, Rangitane, and Ngati Apa. Some groups were not averse to seeing their two putative overlords, Ngati Toa and the government, fight it out, and this may have reduced the support available to the resisters.

In Wellington, tension over disputed land purchases had been high since 1842. Ngati Rangitahi, a *hapu* with Wanganui connections, were particularly reluctant to part with their cultivations in the Hutt Valley, which the settlers believed they had bought. Ngati Rangitahi were backed by some of their Wanganui relatives and a section of Ngati Toa, led respectively by Topine Te Mamaku and Te Rangihaeata, both men of great ability and *mana*. Even so, the resisting forces may not have exceeded 200 warriors. The British, reinforced from the north in late February 1846, and soon joined by Governor Grey himself, numbered about 700 regulars (later 850) and 200 militia, with two warships. They also received the active help of Te Atiawa, and the less enthusiastic support of some Ngati Toa.

In February, both sides plundered or destroyed each others' property to support land claims. Shots were exchanged in March, and on 2 April some

73

Maoris killed two settlers. Te Rangihaeata probably did not instigate this act, but he declined to give up the killers, and consequently found himself the main British target. In May and June, Te Mamaku launched two surprise attacks on small British outposts, inflicting sixteen casualties and probably suffering few himself. He then apparently joined Te Rangihaeata, who had built a *pa* at Pauatahanui. Though coastal, Pauatahanui was secured from naval bombardment by mudflats. It also contained anti-artillery bunkers and may therefore have ranked as a modern *pa*. It seems, however, that it was vulnerable to an overland attack in the rear. In late July Grey mounted such an expedition, and Te Rangihaeata abandoned his *pa* without a fight. The Maoris checked the pursuing troops, under Major Last, in a successful rearguard action on 6 August, and withdrew northwards. Te Mamaku returned to Wanganui, and Te Rangihaeata built a *pa* south of the Manawatu River, from which he discouraged European penetration of the Manawatu for some years.

Grey's overland move against Pauatahanui was clever enough, but the main reason for Te Rangihaeata's withdrawal was probably his failure to obtain sufficient Maori support. He was very short of food and ammunition, as well as of warriors. The major British success was not a military event, but the seizure of the neutral chief Te Rauparaha on 23 July. Grey accused Te Rauparaha of secretly supporting Te Rangihaeata, but another motive was that the former chief could be captured, whereas the latter could not. The arrest of so important a Maori leader was a bold assertion of government power. It may have discouraged support for Te Rangihaeata, and some writers have attempted to justify it on these grounds. But, along with the seizure of Pomare in the North in 1845, it gave the British a reputation for duplicity which seriously hampered the resolution of subsequent disputes. Grey did not help matters by hanging one of Te Rangihaeata's warriors after capture.

The Wanganui conflict appears to have arisen from disputed land purchases, resentment of Grey's actions in Wellington, and the prospect of government intervention implicit in the arrival of troops at Wanganui in December 1846. Te Mamaku again played a leading role. Like Heke he stated that he would protect the Wanganui settlers, but fight the soldiers. On 18 April 1847, six Maoris brutally slew a family of outsettlers. Four of the six were captured by the Lower Wanganui Maoris, and handed over to the British, who hanged them. In early May, Te Mamaku and his Upper Wanganui warriors descended the river and blockaded the town. Despite the efforts of various historians, the connection between these incidents remains unclear. Te Mamaku maintained his blockade until 23 July, during which time the major incidents were a raid on the town on 19 May, in which seven houses were burned, and some indecisive skirmishing on 19 July, in which the British lost two killed and eleven wounded and the Maoris three killed and ten wounded. Four days later Te Mamaku and his men returned home, and the British eventually decided to leave matters as they stood.

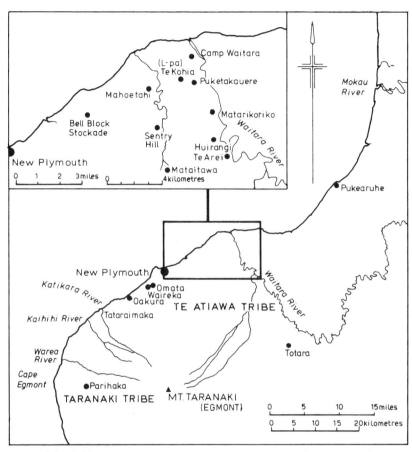

North Taranaki, illustrating the Taranaki War (Chapters 4-6)

Grey's military successes at Wellington and Wanganui were exaggerated, not least by himself. But his measures were effective enough to indicate that the British were not to be taken lightly—at least within the confines of their settlements. On the other hand, these operations re-emphasized the great lesson of the Northern War: that the coercion of the Maoris within their own areas was a difficult business. Though the British eventually forgot this lesson, the period 1848-60 was characterized as much by economic co-operation as by friction between the races.

During the 1850s, however, Maori reluctance to sell land increased throughout the island. This shift of opinion was related to the emergence of a movement for Maori confederation: the King Movement. This organization was centred on the Tainui tribes of the Waikato region, though its support was never restricted to these. The first King, Potatau Te Wherowhero, was elected in June 1858, and was succeeded by his son, Tawhiao, in July 1860. The origins and character of the King Movement are still the subjects of a debate to which no direct contribution can be made here. But the military assessment of the organization, attempted in a later chapter, indicates that its power, social efficiency, and breadth of support have been underestimated. The Movement embraced several shades of Maori opinion. The contemporary misnomers 'moderates' and 'extremists' have stuck to the two major parties, represented by Wiremu Tamehana ('The Kingmaker') and Rewi Maniapoto respectively. But all the Kingites were united in their opposition to the sale of land.

Strong opposition to the land-selling also existed outside the King Movement. In Taranaki, feuding broke out between the land-selling minority of the local Atiawa tribe, led by Ihaia, and the anti-land-selling majority, led by Wiremu Kingi, a chief who had supported the government against Te Rangihaeata when living near Wellington. In 1859, a third chief, Teira, offered to sell the British 600 acres at Waitara, and Kingi, who was generally recognized as the senior Atiawa tribal chief, vetoed the sale. Teira's offer, however, was accepted by Governor Thomas Gore Browne, who had succeeded Grey in 1855. Browne was aware that Kingi might resist, but he nevertheless felt compelled to proceed with the 'purchase' and occupation of Waitara. War consequently broke out on 17 March 1860, and lasted for one year. Te Atiawa fought unaided for a little more than a week. After this, Kingi was supported by the Ngati Ruanui and Taranaki tribes, and within a month operations were dominated by the prospect and reality of Kingite intervention.

The British were unable to achieve a military decision in Taranaki and, largely for this reason, they turned their attention to the root of the problem: Kingite military power and independence. Both Browne and Grey, who returned for his second term as Governor in September 1861, decided to invade Waikato to suppress the King Movement by force. Browne was recalled before he could implement his decision, but—after an interim period which will be examined elsewhere—Grey launched the invasion in July 1863. The subsequent operations included a little fighting in Taranaki, but were primarily confined to the Auckland Province, and the whole conflict of 1863-4 may be termed the Waikato War.

I   THE CAUSES OF WAR IN TARANAKI AND WAIKATO

THE CAUSES OF THESE WARS, IN STRIKING CONTRAST TO THEIR course, have generated more literature than any other issue in New Zealand history. Some consensus has been achieved in rejecting the old 'official' explanation that the wars resulted from Maori aggression, and this study strongly supports this conclusion. However, a convincing and comprehensive explanation for the collapse from economic co-operation to war in both Taranaki and Waikato has yet to be advanced. A substantial effort to help fill this gap would require a book in itself, but the question of causes is to some extent bound up with an appreciation of the military operations, and a very brief and limited treatment must be attempted.

It is useful to begin with one general observation. Many great historical debates concern the causes of war, and something applicable to the New Zealand case can be learned from them. The controversy over the origins of the English Civil War, for example, has indicated that mono-causal models must be treated with caution; that, on the other hand, an unweighted list of causal factors is not an explanation; and that the means available to participants must be assessed along with their motives. This debate also suggests that historians face a standing temptation to use the concept of inevitability much as medieval cartographers used the term *terra incognita*.

Tendencies of this kind can be detected in the theory that settler pressure for land inevitably brought about the Taranaki and Waikato Wars. In the definitive modern exposition of this theory, Keith Sinclair, while placing his main emphasis on the land issue, gives some weight to other factors.[2] But other writers are less cautious, and the idea that the seizure of Maori land was the main British political and military objective has been so widely adopted that the conflicts are often called 'The Land Wars'. It is true that many North Island settlers were eager to acquire Maori land, though this did not necessarily reflect real needs.[3] But, while the settlers had had responsible government since 1856, they had little in the way of military or financial resources, and the wars were actually undertaken primarily by Imperial troops. The settlers may have had the motives, but they did not have the means.

The decisions to use Imperial troops were taken by Governors Browne and Grey, with the support or acquiescence of the Imperial Government. It is sometimes suggested that Browne was a puppet in the hands of certain colonists, but B. J. Dalton has shown that Browne made his own decision for war.[4] This is certainly true of Grey. Moreover, a wide range of groups and individuals with no interest in Maori land supported the wars. These included the South Island settlers, a large section of the English and Australian press, and, in the case of the Waikato War, such clergymen as Bishops Selwyn and William Williams.[5] Selwyn and Williams make particularly unconvincing land-grabbers. Motives with a much wider appeal for the British than land-hunger must therefore be sought.

In an essay published in 1967, Alan Ward offered a whole host of alternative motives.[6] His essay was less an explanation for the outbreak of war than an unweighted list of causal factors, and these applied mainly to Waikato rather than Taranaki. But he did provide an effective critique of the mono-causal 'Land Wars' theory, and the examples he cites as evidence for several of his causal factors could be multiplied from the research undertaken for this book. In particular, the widespread desire for the imposition of British administration, law, and civilization on the Maoris was so important that it should rank with land-hunger as a cause of war.

But perhaps these factors are themselves only part of a greater whole. The wars can be seen as a series of British attempts to impose substantive, as against nominal, sovereignty on the Maoris. Ward touches on this, observing that the New Zealand governors were 'beset by a fatal tendency to believe that the Queen's government must be demonstrably exercised over all those who, since the Treaty of Waitangi, had been regarded as British subjects'.[7] But perhaps most British, not just the governors, were beset by this 'fatal tendency', and perhaps this is not simply one of a dozen equal factors, but an over-arching cause, a way of understanding the origins of the New Zealand Wars as a whole. Substantive sovereignty would allow the relatively easy purchase of Maori land, and the imposition of British administration, law, and civilization on the Maoris. But the British desire for substantive sovereignty was also influenced by less tangible factors: the complicated body of beliefs and attitudes which led them to expect to rule their new colony in practice as well as theory, and to resent the fact that they did not.

Between 1848 and 1860, the British population increased through immigration and high birth-rates, and the Maori population decreased through disease and low birth-rates, until the former considerably outnumbered the latter in the country as a whole, though not in the North Island. For the first half of the period, the British settlements expanded and government influence increased. Some Maori chiefs accepted government assistance, advice, and mediation of disputes. But these considerations should not be allowed to obscure the element of continuity between British-Maori relations before and after 1848. British sovereignty over Maori districts remained 'more nominal than real'. 'English law has always prevailed in the English settlements,' wrote Governor Browne, in 1860, 'but remains a dead letter beyond them.'[8]

The boundaries between Maori and British spheres of control were generally defined by the area of land 'sold' by the former to the latter. 'Sale' is rather a deceptive term for the most common type of alienation. By the 1860s, both races tacitly recognized that the sale of large blocks of land contiguous to British settlements involved the transfer of political and magisterial control as well as of property rights. This process had more in common with the Louisiana Purchase than the sale of a farm in England. Thus the expansion of the area of real British control was inextricably interwoven with the purchase of Maori land. Conversely, to oppose land sales was to oppose the extension of British sovereignty and to defend Maori autonomy.

In one respect, the emergence of the King Movement did not constitute a radical change in the North Island situation. It was not a declaration of Maori independence—this already existed—and it added no new territory to the Maori sphere. It sought merely to unite pre-existing independent polities. But in other ways the Movement was an important change. Together with the rise in anti-land-selling feeling generally, it raised the profile of Maori independence from a level which the British disliked but tolerated, to a level which many found entirely unacceptable.

The British were never happy about Maori control of the interior. They particularly objected to perceived Maori contempt for the government and its coercive power. Indeed, they commonly attributed the problems concerning land and law to this factor.[9] While the Maoris continued to sell land and while their independence remained inchoate, the British disliked but tolerated.it. To European eyes, Maori tribal government seemed weak and informal. British settlements and influence continued to increase and Maori autonomy could be treated as a temporary aberration, an unfortunate feature of the period of transition. The decline of land-selling and the rise of the King Movement, however, put a stop to the process by which Maori independence was being gradually and peacefully eroded. The King Movement also provided a sort of alternative government—an organization to which chiefs, including those like Wiremu Kingi who were not part of the Movement, could appeal against British sanctions. After a brief phase in which it was hoped the Movement would disappear if ignored, some of the British came to believe that a show of strength was required.

When the Waitara dispute arose, Governor Browne thought that to reject Teira's offer would be to recognize Wiremu Kingi's authority as tribal chief. The British had tacitly recognized this kind of authority in the past, but Browne now felt that British sovereignty had to be asserted by denying Kingi's autonomy, even at the risk of war. 'I must either have purchased this land or recognised a right which would have made William King virtual sovereign of this part of New Zealand.'[10]

Such factors as the particularly tense racial situation in Taranaki and the relative military weakness of Wiremu Kingi may have contributed to the location of this initial conflict, but the wars sparked off by it owed more to wider causes. The Kingites of Waikato fought less to secure Kingi in the peaceful enjoyment of his Waitara acres, than to repel a British foray across the tacitly agreed boundaries of control and so protect Maori independence, just as Heke and Kawiti had fought before them. The wide range of British opinion which supported the war did so less to expand the farms of a few hundred New Plymouth settlers, than to bring the reality of Maori control of the hinterland into conformity with the expectation of substantive British sovereignty.

This conclusion is not entirely dissimilar to what the colonial government and most settlers maintained at the time, and it could conceivably be mistaken for an endorsement of their position. Governor Browne and the colonial ministers usually argued (wrongly) that Kingi, as an individual, was not an owner of the Waitara Block, but they held that the main issue 'was one of authority and jurisdiction'. They felt that Kingi's veto of the sale as tribal chief was the assertion of a sovereign right. When one considers that Kingi, like all other chiefs, also successfully asserted the right to punish offenders, organize economic activity, and make war on other 'British subjects', it is difficult to disagree with them. But 'philo-Maori' writers such as Octavius Hadfield and William Martin expended a great deal of ingenuity in doing just that. They dismissed the sovereignty issue, and argued that 'the present is a land quarrel', wherein Kingi, a loyal British subject, justifiably resisted Browne's abuse of power.[11]

Historians have tended to follow the 'philo-Maori' tradition, itself a legacy of the myth that the Treaty of Waitangi made New Zealand British instantly, by the wave of a wand. But we can accept the colonists' assertion that they were fighting for substantive sovereignty—'to make the Maori in reality what by a legal fiction they have long been in name, British subjects'[12]—without accepting its premise: that this was a just, legitimate, and necessary act. For one thing, it can be argued that the real Treaty of Waitangi was the Maori version, and that under its provisions the Maoris retained local autonomy of the kind Kingi was exercising at Waitara. More importantly, whatever the Treaty said or did not say, the British had tacitly accepted the practical independence of Maori districts for twenty years. In effect, Wiremu Kingi was a British ally, not a subject. Perhaps the Taranaki and Waikato conflicts were more akin to classic wars of conquest than we would like to believe.

So brief an argument must remain tentative, but we can be more confident about the following conclusion. The analysis of the operations in the Taranaki and Waikato Wars will show that land was not the main British military objective. The British consistently attempted to obtain victory through decisive battle. When they failed to do so, they were sorely disappointed. In Waikato, the occupation of tracts of land was sometimes a side-effect of these attempts, but for most observers this was nothing more than a consolation prize. Of course, to seek to defeat the previous occupants does not necessarily preclude a political aim of seizing land. But the single-minded search for rapid and decisive victory accords much better with a political aim of asserting sovereignty. When the British did occupy the land supposed to be their main objective at Waitara and in central Waikato, they were not content and continued to seek to crush the Maoris in battle. In Taranaki, Browne at first hoped that a sharp local lesson would be enough to demonstrate to the Maoris that British authority was to be taken seriously, even beyond the tacitly agreed boundaries of control; that British sovereignty was to some degree substantive as well as nominal. When this effort failed, as a result of Kingite intervention, the British method became more comprehensive, though their objective remained essentially the same. In this respect, a main cause of the Waikato War was the failure of the British attempt to assert their sovereignty over the Maoris through victory in Taranaki.

In sum, it is suggested that the British sought first to check, and then to cripple, Maori independence. This was reflected in persistent efforts to defeat Maori forces in decisive battle. This view has significant implications for an understanding of the nature and results of the military operations.

II   THE SEARCH FOR QUICK VICTORY

WHATEVER ITS POLITICAL CONNECTIONS WITH ITS predecessor in the North and its successor in Waikato, the Taranaki War of March 1860 to March 1861 was militarily a separate conflict. It was fought in a different area, and there were certain differences in the strategic context. In contrast to the Northern War, the British had the advantage of interior lines and of relatively easy access to the seat of operations. The theatre of war extended north and south of the main British base at New Plymouth, and the troops were rarely called upon to march more than twenty miles from this base. Contemporary writers made a great deal of the unfavourable terrain in this area, and it is true that the interior of Taranaki province consisted principally of dense forest. But operations were restricted to the coastal strip. Part of this was Maori and European farmland, and the rest was rough but penetrable, even by convoys of carts. In contrast to the Waikato War, the main combatants on the Maori side did not have to protect their economic heartland. The Waikato Kingites fought outside their own territory, travelling to and from Taranaki when they chose. They therefore had substantially more freedom of action than in 1863-4. Despite these differences, the Taranaki War had important features in common with the other conflicts, and the two main themes of this study are equally applicable to it.

British commentators again turned to such mechanisms as the exaggeration of Maori numbers and casualties to explain or to palliate failure. Civilians specialized in emphasizing faulty military leadership. In their own defence, soldiers such as Colonel Robert Carey stressed the elusiveness of the Maoris in the 'almost impenetrable' Taranaki terrain. This, and the general reluctance to credit the Maoris with the possession of certain kinds of military talent, led writers like Carey to believe that accidents of the ground, and such things as the ability 'to burrow like rabbits through the high fern', were the essence of any Maori success. Carey wrote emphatically that 'no strategical knowledge was shewn by the Maori in his plans'.[13]

Most modern historians have tended to rely on a mix of these contemporary opinions. They agree with the settlers that one commander, Colonel Gold, was incompetent and unsuccessful. 'The incapacity of the original commander, Colonel Gold, was rightly said to be a military phenomenon in itself.' They agree with the soldiers that another commander, General Pratt, was both competent and successful. Pratt 'found the means' to beat the Maoris by 'taking *pa* with sweat not blood'. Most historians also accept that the Maoris had all the accidental advantages but failed to use them properly. 'It cannot be said that they exploited their advantages to the full.' The Maoris 'adopted no comprehensive or co-ordinated strategy'. One aim of the following analysis is to plot the emergence of these beliefs, and to assess their validity.[14]

The British reverted again and again throughout the war to their overriding military objective—rapid and decisive victory through the destruction of the main enemy warrior force. The Maoris strove to prevent this and, where possible, to take positive action of their own. Their efforts must be seen in the context of the constraints on any Maori war effort: the need to find some way of fighting full-time soldiers with part-time soldiers, and the problem of British superiority in artillery and numbers. Wiremu Kingi's Atiawa forces did not exceed 300 men and were more probably limited to 200,[15] whereas the British began the war with about 800 troops. The Taranaki and Ngati Ruanui—collectively known to the British as 'the southern tribes'—soon joined Kingi with between 400 and 500 warriors.[16] But by June 1860, the total British force touched 2,000 and by early 1861 they had 3,500 men, while the intervention of the King Movement barely doubled Maori strength.

The war can be discussed in four phases, with the last two closely inter-connected and dealt with in one chapter. The first phase, March-April 1860, was marked by the failure of Governor Browne's attempt to secure a rapid and cheap assertion of sovereignty through a quick victory, and by the British paper victory at Waireka. The second phase, May-July 1860, was dominated by the intervention of the King Movement and the crucial battle of Puketakauere. The third and fourth phases, July-December 1860 and December 1860-March 1861, saw the full development of the Maori war strategy and a sustained British attempt to solve the dilemma in which this strategy placed them.

At the beginning of March 1860, Governor Browne arrived at New Plymouth and instructed Colonel Gold to enforce the survey of Waitara. This amounted in practice to the occupation of the block. On 17 March, Kingi and seventy or eighty of his warriors threw up a *pa*, Te Kohia or the L-pa, at Waitara, and refused to evacuate it. Shots were exchanged, and the Taranaki War had begun.

In these circumstances, the British objective immediately became the decisive defeat of the enemy warrior force before the conflict could escalate. Gold's effort to secure this at the L-pa on 17–18 March was unsuccessful, and within a week Kingi's isolation had ended with the arrival of two small Taranaki war parties at Waireka to the south of New Plymouth. The Taranakis, subsequently reinforced by Ngati Ruanui, commenced vigorously to plunder the abandoned farms of the settlers and succeeded in killing half a dozen incautious colonists in the ensuing weeks. They therefore became the main focus of British attention, but Gold was able to mount no more than three movements against them by the end of April. Though as we shall see, one of these resulted in an action at Waireka, Gold was unable to achieve his object of creating in the troublesome southern tribes 'a wholesome dread of condign punishment, should they again venture to in-jure the property or persons of the European inhabitants'.[17] His efforts in this direction precluded active operations against Kingi to the north of New Plymouth, and by late April Browne had been forced by the growing threat of Kingite intervention temporarily to suspend active operations against Atiawa. The attempt to secure a rapid and cheap assertion of sovereignty had therefore failed.

It became increasingly apparent that this failure was likely to prove an expensive one, and both Browne and Gold came under considerable criticism for it. Perhaps the most galling of the several aborted initiatives seemed in retrospect to be the action at L-pa, where Kingi and his men were permitted to escape unhurt from what could have been both the beginning and end of the war. This result 'disappointed everyone', and it was recognized by some that a unique opportunity had been let slip. 'Most likely the natives will not again give our forces a similar chance.'[18] The action itself was nothing more than a minor skirmish, but the L-pa had several features that were to prove extremely significant, all arising from the fact that it was a purpose-built modern *pa*.

The first was that its anti-artillery bunkers and covered trenches effectually protected its garrison from cannon and small-arms fire. Nearly 500 troops poured in a heavy fire all day from as near as fifty yards. Two 24-pounder howitzers fired 200 rounds, 'every shot through the place', from close range, but the Maoris had no one killed. Like its precursors in the North, the L-pa was also difficult to surround and entirely expendable. Kingi and his men were able to evacuate the place easily and without a qualm on the night of 17–18 March. The 'only trophies' left to the British 'were a dog, the red [war] flag and a horn'. Equally important was the fact that the *pa* was constructed with extraordinary rapidity. It was small—about 650 square yards—but Kingi's seventy or eighty men built it in a single night. Finally, the full implications of these features continued to elude the British despite the experience of the Northern War.[19]

In 1858, when various Atiawa *hapu* were occupying *pa* built to fight each other, an artillery sergeant had been sent 'in disguise' to reconnoitre the Maori fortifications. The *pa* he found were in the old style, with large fighting platforms atop the stockade and no significant earthworks apart from ditches and open firing trenches. He observed that 'of course, when artillery is brought to bear on these defences they [would] soon give way'. He was perfectly right, just as Lieutenant Bennet had been in 1843, but this was not the kind of *pa* the Maoris chose to use against Europeans. However great the mass of evidence, the British had difficulty in retaining a grasp on this fact. They consequently found the L-pa's powers of resistance 'a cause', as the same artillery sergeant put it in 1860, 'of extreme surprise'. Colonel Gold had difficulty in recognizing anti-artillery bunkers—at L-pa ten symmetrical chambers roofed with timber and earth—for what they were. He contented himself with reporting that the inside of the *pa* was 'curiously hollowed out'.[20]

The L-pa type of fortification—easily constructed, effective, and expendable—was to re-appear a hundred times in the Taranaki War and was to be the basic building-block of the strategy with which the Maoris strove to counteract their grave military disadvantages. The British inability to

appreciate this led to an emphasis on other explanations for their failures,
and consequently in part to the failures themselves.

III   THE LEGEND OF WAIREKA

THE ONLY ENGAGEMENT OF ANY SIZE IN THIS FIRST PHASE OF
the war was the 'Battle' of Waireka on 28 March, when a British expedition
sent to rescue some settlers south of Omata clashed with Taranaki and
Ngati Ruanui raiders. Waireka owes its significance less to its military
results than to the fact that it proved to be a classic example of the construction of a paper victory. Before this can be demonstrated, however, it is
necessary to establish the outlines of the action.

The British force which marched south from New Plymouth on 28
March under Lieutenant-Colonel G. F. Murray was initially 276 strong but
was subsequently reinforced to about 360, no more than 300 of whom were
engaged at any one time.[21] The Maoris—usually assessed by contemporaries
at 460 to 600—are unlikely to have exceeded 200 warriors.[22] These were
reported to have fortified a position on the road between New Plymouth
and Omata, and Colonel Gold intended that one column under Murray
should engage them there while another column, consisting of 160 local
volunteers and militia, outflanked the fight by marching up the beach and
brought in the stranded settlers. As it happened, the position on the Omata
road did not exist. The Maoris contented themselves with sniping from
cover at both columns, and with manoeuvering between the two in an
attempt to foil what they presumably imagined to be a two-pronged effort to
surround and destroy them. Ironically, the inexperienced settlers believed
themselves to be the target of a similar attempt by the Maoris. They exchanged a heavy but hopelessly long-range fire with the well-concealed
Maori snipers, then went to ground at a nearby farmhouse and appealed to
Murray for assistance. Murray sent two small detachments, but quickly
withdrew them and, in obedience to his orders to be back by dark, left for
New Plymouth around 5.30 p.m. We are told that the militia found
themselves in dire straits, 'hotly engaged by three times their numbers of
natives, short of ammunition and all but surrounded, unable to retire
. . . without leaving their wounded to the tender mercies of savages'.[23] In
this crisis, so the story runs, a small naval brigade of sixty men from H.M.S.
Niger under Captain Peter Cracroft marched up from New Plymouth,
declined Murray's invitation to withdraw with him, and assaulted and took
the main Maori *pa*, killing anything up to 150 Maoris. Cracroft then
withdrew. He made no contact with the militia, but it was generally assumed
to be the heavy blow he dealt the Maoris which enabled the settlers to
march unmolested to New Plymouth a few hours later.

One important feature of this engagement was the impetus it gave to the
rift between the settlers and the military. The settlers believed, with some
justification, that their militia had performed well in their first battle, but

had been left in the lurch by Murray and the regulars. A letter from one of the volunteers involved which complained of 'the shameful conduct of Colonel Murray in so cruelly abandoning us' found its way into print, and volunteer Captain Harry Atkinson's assertion that there was '*no* excuse for Murray' was widely accepted. If he thought himself safe from criticism in New Plymouth, Colonel Gold was sorely disappointed. The expedition had been 'absurdly planned' by him, and Waireka was held to demonstrate 'the gross incapacity' of both Gold and Murray. In fact, there was nothing wrong with Gold's plan. Murray's behaviour was rather curious, though it is not entirely clear that the situation of the militia was really desperate. But the facts of the matter notwithstanding, the notion of the superiority of the settler-frontiersman to the incompetently led regular soldier gained ground rapidly after Waireka.[24]

Despite the belief that Murray's incompetence had robbed the battle of a decisive effect, Waireka was still seen as a great British victory. The engagement was 'the most obstinate and most successful yet fought by the British in New Zealand'. Maori losses were believed to have been 'enormous . . . fifteen to twenty carts were laden with dead and dying'. It was hoped the Maoris 'so thoroughly beaten' at Waireka would find in it 'the sanguinary lesson' so beloved of those who thought that to spare the rod was to spoil the Maori child. The foundation of this victory claim was Cracroft's storming of the Waireka *pa*. It was Cracroft's assault which 'certainly saved the militia and the volunteers from being destroyed to a man'. It was Cracroft who created the chance of decisive victory thrown away by Murray, and it was Cracroft who had made the engagement a substantial success even so.[25]

According to one account, the actual method used by the sailors in taking the *pa* was a superior form of leapfrog.

> Captain Cracroft, with his sixty bluejackets, gallantly ran up to the *pa*; they cried out, Make a back! One after the other vaulted on each other's backs, and again others on theirs, until they were level with the top of the fence, and then jumped down into the place. Before the astonished natives could recover from their surprise at this, to them, new expedient, the *pa* was taken, twelve chiefs and sixty natives were killed.[26]

Most commentators, however, were content to present Cracroft's achievement in simple if heroic terms, complete with the Nelsonian blind eye to orders. On receiving Murray's advice to withdraw, the Captain 'was merely observed to soliloquize "I purpose seeing the interior of that *pah* first".' Pausing only to address 'a few stirring words' to his men, who fought 'like tigers, quite irresistible', he 'rushed the *pah*' and 'killed everyone in it'. It was commonly stated that seventy-two Maoris were killed in the fight, and one of Cracroft's men asserted later that 'we laid out about a hundred of the Maoris'.[27] An English newspaper topped even this with a long-range estimate of 150 killed.[28] It was felt that the incident was 'perhaps the most successful attack on record against the natives'. Cracroft had hit on a recipe for taking Maori *pa* in the form of naval dash, together with that 'determination of will' which Gold and Murray were held so conspicuously to lack. 'After Captain Cracroft's exploit, a lower opinion of the strength of these places is likely to be held in future.'[29]

It is no exaggeration to say that 'the *Nigers*' became the heroes of the colony. They received a grateful and laudatory address from '180 ladies at Taranaki', and a public meeting of eminent Auckland citizens paid tribute to the 'gallant conduct and cool intrepidity . . . energy and dauntless bearing . . . promptitude, skill and courage' of this 'gallant band'.[30] The military alone were a trifle unenthusiastic, but official recognition was not lacking. Commodore Loring, Senior Naval Officer in New Zealand, had nothing but praise for 'a most dashing and judiciously timed affair'. The Admiralty responded by promoting Cracroft's First Lieutenant and Coxswain in compliment to him.[31] The fortunate Coxswain also received the Victoria Cross for his own bravery. As the war dragged on with a marked lack of 'dashing exploits', the storming of the Waireka *pa* came to be remembered as the solitary bright spot. All was 'imbecile inaction . . . save the one brilliant affair conducted by Captain Cracroft . . . at Waireka'.[32]

Historians have accepted a somewhat muted version of Cracroft's achievement and of its relationship to the battle as a whole. Most modern writers stop short of eulogy, but accept that 'the naval sortie had turned defeat into victory' and that the 'gallant and successful attack' on the strong Waireka *pa*, together with the virtual destruction of its garrison, was a notable feat.[33]

There are two weak points in the story of Waireka. Part of the case for the importance of the naval assault rests on the notion that it saved the volunteers from an absolutely desperate situation, but did such a situation exist? The militia had only one man hit before they went to ground at the farmhouse, and their total casualties were only half a dozen wounded, and one dead. Atkinson's company accounted, according to the official report, for 'at least two-thirds' of the 'not less than thirty' Maoris 'carefully estimated' to have been killed by the colonists. But Atkinson himself saw only two dead Maoris—and no live ones—during the whole day.[34] It was often asserted that the militia could not withdraw with Murray because of the need to carry their wounded. But six or seven injured men can scarcely have been a crippling encumbrance for a column which by 5.30 p.m. consisted of over 180 fit men.[35] The militia were never actually surrounded. The beach route, by which they had come from New Plymouth, remained open throughout the action.[36] The Maoris had far fewer men than the British assumed, and it seems probable that they were more interested in preventing what they believed to be an encirclement attempt, and in protecting the plunder they had collected at another nearby farmhouse, than in pressing home a costly attack against the militia over open ground. The militia were unaware of this last factor, and it was perfectly natural for them to over-estimate the seriousness of the situation in what was after all their first action, but the regular who defined this action as 'a great deal of noise . . . and very little harm done' may have come close to the truth.[37] There is therefore no real need to look for a decisive event which rescued the militia.

The second *prima-facie* weak point in the story of Cracroft's success is that his only casualties were four men slightly wounded. Cracroft himself attributed this to his attack completely surprising the Maoris, and this was the generally accepted explanation. But Cracroft also reported that he had fired several 24-pound rockets into the *pa* a few moments before he attacked.[38] Surely this would have been enough to alert even the most unwary of garrisons.

These considerations suggest that there is something wrong with the received version, and in fact this version was not universally accepted. Colonel Carey felt that the battle had been 'very exaggerated',[39] and there is substantial evidence to indicate that the '*pa*' Cracroft attacked was little more than a camp, and that it was virtually unmanned. According to army surgeon Morgan Grace's compendium of evidence from the soldiers of Murray's column, some of the retreating troops met Cracroft's sailors as they marched up and informed them that:

> there was an empty *pa* just near the high road, full of curios and pigs . . . and they rushed on. When the sailors got out of the bush they saw the stockade in the open [and] . . . rushed right at it. A few old Maori seeing us retire, had returned to the *pa*—which was a land title and not a fighting *pa*—to cook some potatoes. These fired a volley on the sailors and then ran away. One or two Maori were killed and several sailors wounded.[40]

Though he vouched for the reliability of his eyewitnesses' account, Grace sometimes paid considerable attention to dramatic effect, and his soldier-informants were interested parties. His version, however, does not lack corroboration. The Waikato Maoris considered the British account to be a fabrication, and one contemporary writer referred to Cracroft's target as merely a 'temporary *pah*'.[41] But the decisive supporting evidence consists in three accounts given to A. S. Atkinson some weeks after the action, and in the account of the Reverend Thomas Gilbert who watched part of the battle from the Maori side of the field. Atkinson wrote:

> Parris . . . tells me that the two Ngapuhi boys lately sent home had a long conversation with him about the war. According to them there were *no men killed in the Pa* at Waireka (when Captn. Cracroft stormed it). Old Paora Kukutai was shot (I believe by E. Messenger) running away from the *Pa*. . . . This account agrees perfectly with two others from independent sources—1st Riemenschneider who met the Taranakis at Warea after they retired—& 2nd, Edd. Messenger who went up to the *pa* with the storming party & when inside 'couldn't see any one to stick or shoot'.[42]

Gilbert and his family, with the missionary Brown and several other settlers, were the people the Waireka expedition had set out to rescue. In fact, the group had never been in any danger, having been 'made *tapu*' by the southern tribes. They watched what they could of the battle from Brown's house under Maori protection. Gilbert 'had no idea that the *pah* was actually stormed and taken'. Maoris passing to and from the house towards evening told the Europeans about the progress of the action 'but [said] not a word of the *pah* being taken'. 'Thus', wrote Gilbert, at the end of the day 'we were still ignorant of the success of the battle.' Maori reports were 'anything but cheering'. When Gilbert learned on his return next day to New Plymouth that he had witnessed a great British victory, he assumed that the Maoris had simply sought to deceive him, even to the extent of attributing the 'complacent grin' of one chief to his escaping the fate of his brethren.[43]

The chief's good humour was more probably the result of his participation in what he saw as a fairly successful little action. It is difficult to avoid the conclusion that Cracroft's exploit amounted to the over-running of a lightly fortified camp occupied by a very few Maoris, and that the 70–150 warriors said to be killed in fact numbered about one. Given the centrality of Cracroft's fictional triumph to both contemporary and historical interpretations of the battle, these interpretations must be dismissed. The Waikato Maoris told a local missionary that the British victory claims for Waireka were 'all fudge', and it seems we must accept their conclusion.[44]

The customary British partiality to the Senior Service, the firm belief in the dash and unorthodoxy of sailors ashore, the idea that the militia were in grave danger from which something must have saved them, and other factors peculiar to Waireka clearly made their contribution to the legend of Cracroft's triumph. Cracroft himself—who to his credit gave a relatively low figure for Maoris killed—could hardly be expected to look a gift horse in the mouth. To have informed the admiring '180 ladies of Taranaki' that they had got the wrong man would have required an almost superhuman commitment to truth. But it seems fair to suggest that more general factors again played a part. The conviction that British fighting men were inherently superior to Maori warriors, and that this superiority need only be recognized by confident leadership to come into play, created a fertile ground for the Waireka myth and was in turn reinforced by it.

5

The Intervention of the King Movement

THE SECOND PHASE OF THE TARANAKI WAR (MAY-JULY 1860) was notable for the intervention of the King Movement and the Battle of Puketakauere. These events marked a major departure in New Zealand history—the first clash between the British and a substantial combination of Maori tribes fighting as a single, supra-tribal entity. Though some young men may have been primarily interested in plunder and excitement, the Kingites as a whole entered the war reluctantly, cautiously, and with essentially defensive objectives in mind. It was not until the Battle of Puketakauere on 27 June 1860 that substantial Kingite involvement became a reality. The possibility of intervention, however, had a considerable effect on British strategy prior to this.

I THE KINGITE DECISION FOR WAR

FROM THE OUTBREAK OF THE WAR, SOME SETTLERS FACED THE prospect of Kingite intervention with equanimity, seeming almost to see it as a chance to gather all the dissident elements of the Maori population in Taranaki—'the more the merrier'—and to destroy them there without disturbing the rest of the country. It was believed that 'the battlefield in Taranaki will be quite sufficient to prove to the natives that they cannot cope with the Europeans'. Decisive victory in that province would enable the government 'to require the Waikatos to abandon their foolish movement'. The King Movement, in short, could be destroyed outside New Plymouth.[1]

Once intervention appeared unavoidable, Browne and his advisers seemed to come around to something like this position. Because the very existence of the Movement 'could not fail to bring about a collision between the races' anyway, it was 'fortunate' and 'on the whole [a] matter of reasonable congratulation' that the government 'should have come openly to an issue with the King party before the preparations of the enemy were complete'. To an extent, this was making the best on paper of a bad situation, primarily for the benefit of the Imperial Government. Browne did believe that a victory which convinced the Maoris 'that success on their part was hopeless' would greatly discourage the Kingites, and perhaps even lead to the collapse of the Movement. But the firm assertion of sovereignty did not necessarily have to be comprehensive to be effectual. A sharp check to Kingi before the Movement intervened or, failing that, a sharp check before it intervened very much, might be enough. The Governor was sufficiently realistic to grasp that early victory would anyway be cheaper and more practicable than the defeat of a greatly reinforced Maori army. From the outset, therefore, Browne and his advisers rightly saw the Kingite intervention less as an opportunity of killing two birds with one stone, than as a grave danger to be avoided.[2]

There were two possible means to this end. One was to destroy Kingi and such support as he already had, and so leave the King Movement nothing in which it could further involve itself. The other was to keep the Kingites at home by diplomacy, and the government bent considerable efforts in this direction. The problem, however, was that the two methods could become mutually exclusive. With great political meetings in Waikato in April and May considering intervention, Browne was forced to conclude that any further attack on Kingi without renewed provocation 'would enlist the sympathy of the whole Maori population in his favour'. He therefore ordered Gold to suspend hostilities against Kingi on 20 April 1860, and renewed the instructions on 17 May. The 'southern tribes' were still fair game, but Kingi was the more accessible target, and the need to keep him isolated thus operated to protect him. This was the King Movement's first impact on British strategy, and it occurred more than two months before the first exchange of shots between Kingite warriors and British troops.[3]

The prospect of intervention also made itself felt before the reality in another sphere. This involved the possibility of a Kingite attack upon Auckland. Undoubtedly this possibility was played up by the government to strengthen the case for Imperial reinforcements—something that Governor Grey was to make a familiar tactic—and both the mass of evidence and the inherent likelihood suggests that no real threat existed.[4] But Browne genuinely believed that there was a chance of an attack, and on several occasions, beginning in May 1860, withdrew troops or withheld reinforcements from Taranaki to guard against it. The numbers involved were seldom large, but this was another instance of the baneful effect of Kingite intervention—even as an abstract possibility—on British freedom of action.

The suspension of hostilities against Kingi lasted from 20 April to 23 June 1860, and during this period the competition between the government and the tribes in arms for the ear of the King Movement was a diplomatic extension of the Taranaki battlefield. On the government side, documents were circulated among the Waikato chiefs putting the case against Kingi, and agents attended the April-May meetings, assiduously reporting the speeches and sometimes speaking themselves.[5] The missionaries acted as a permanent lobby against intervention. Even those who believed the government in the wrong over Waitara were still opposed to any escalation of the conflict. Browne also organized a large Maori conference of his own for early July, directed less at converting confirmed Kingite chiefs than at consolidating the support of pro-government chiefs, and at convincing waverers.

On Kingi's side, three diplomatic measures taken were the dispatch of letters presenting his case and appealing for help, the reception of Kingite envoys in Taranaki, and the effort of his own delegation—including representatives from the three combatant tribes—in Waikato.[6] The details are obscure, but by mid-April, despite the adverse conclusion of one Kingite investigator,[7] a substantial body of Waikato opinion appeared convinced of the justice of Wiremu Kingi's case. The Taranaki delegation, furthermore, had formally tendered the allegiance of their three tribes to King Potatau on 10 April.

Clearly these were major steps in the direction of intervention, but they did not make it certain. Remaining doubts appear to have centred on the questions of whether Waitara had come under the aegis of the King before the purchase was completed, and of whether the organization of the King Movement was sufficiently complete for it to take a firm stand. We may assume that general doubts about the viability of a struggle with the British, and about the economic consequences of a collision, were also factors. The Taranaki delegation was unable to overcome these doubts entirely but, when they returned home in early May, they were accompanied by a mainly Ngati Maniapoto *taua* under the able war chief Epiha Tokohihi. Epiha and his men went to Taranaki as nothing more than a peaceful escort for the returning envoys, but at some stage between mid-May and mid-June 1860, they decided to fight the British. Even this did not make substantial Kingite intervention inevitable. It may have been Epiha's personal decision—there is some indication that only part of his *taua* consented to it—or it may have been the result of instructions from Waikato to offer Kingi token support, or to test the viability of resistance without commitment.[8] Whatever the case with this point, the decision resulted in an engagement which led to much greater Kingite involvement, and this in turn provided the Maoris with a chance of victory in the war as a whole.

II THE BATTLE OF PUKETAKAUERE

FOR TE ATIAWA, THE PRESENCE OF THE NGATI MANIAPOTO *TAUA* was an opportunity that could not be let slip. With its help, they might win a battle against the British which would both improve their position in Taranaki and, by involving Epiha and demonstrating the viability of resistance, lead to really substantial Kingite support. The problem was to bring about an action in favourable circumstances. To do this they resorted to a stratagem which was subsequently to be used quite often by the Maoris—the construction of a *pa* in unacceptable proximity to a British position. In early June the Atiawa and Ngati Maniapoto began building a *pa* at Puketakauere, a mile from the British field base at Camp Waitara and in full sight of it.[9]

This move was both a challenge and a military threat to the British. It restricted their freedom of movement to and from the camp, and endangered its supply and even its security. The Maori initiative, moreover, found fertile ground in the British attitude. Widespread criticism of the troops' performance at Waireka, and of their inactivity generally, had had its effect, and officers and men were chafing at Browne's restriction on operations against Kingi. On 23 June a British reconnaissance party approached the Maori *pa*-builders, and was fired on. This clearly constituted the 'further provocation' Browne had specified as a pre-requisite for the resumption of offensive operations against Te Atiawa. It is possible that the incident was manufactured by the British. Browne knew before it occurred that Kingi was 'likely to remove all cause for forbearance on my part by recommencing hostilities against us', and one local settler believed that the reconnaissance party was 'sent out really as a bait'. Whatever the truth of this the British Commander at Waitara, the capable, vigorous, and popular Major Thomas Nelson, sent immediately to Gold at New Plymouth for reinforcements and permission to attack. On 26 June Gold obligingly forwarded 180 men and the hope that Nelson would 'teach the troublesome Natives a lesson they will not easily forget'. At 5 a.m. on 27 June, Nelson marched out with 350 men and two howitzers to do just that.[10]

The ensuing engagement, the Battle of Puketakauere, was the most important action of the Taranaki War, with profound strategic and political effects on its course. Despite the relatively small scale of the forces involved it was one of the three most clear-cut and disastrous defeats suffered by Imperial troops in New Zealand.

The Maori position lay between two swampy gullies forming a V-shape pointing north toward the Waitara River. Its two principal features were the low hills of Puketakauere and Onukukaitara. The latter hill was actually the site of the newly built stockade which took its name from the former. Onukukaitara, the south-easterly hill, appeared 'easily approachable even by heavy guns' through the mouth of the V formed by the gullies, and was 'apparently without entrenchments'.[11] Puketakauere proper, in the north-west, was an ancient *pa* site but seems to have had no stockade, and Nelson believed its defences to be light or non-existent. Though at least part of Epiha's *taua* was present, many Atiawa were inland at the Mataitawa cultivations with Wiremu Kingi himself, and the Maori garrison was small. The one contemporary account with solid claims to reliability put it at 'not two hundred' men, though some Atiawa reinforcements may have come up from Mataitawa in the later stages.[12] The general command appears to have been held, not by Epiha, but by the Atiawa war-chief Hapurona, 'a little, fiery man with a jealous temper and great military talent'.[13] Subsequent European estimates were greatly to inflate Maori numbers, but these were motivated by retrospective considerations other than accuracy, and a rough knowledge of the relative weakness of the garrison may well have been a factor in inducing Nelson to attack with confidence.

The British force was largely made up of élite troops. A naval brigade sixty-eight strong, usually considered the perfect unit for assault, and the flank companies of the 40th comprised about two-thirds of the force. Nelson divided his men into three divisions. He himself, with Captain Seymour

R. N., retained command of the main body, nearly 180 strong. The two 24-pounder howitzers accompanied this division, which was intended to breach the stockade on Onukukaitara and attack across the open ground in front. Part of the Light Company and 'the fine grenadiers of the 40th' were formed into a second division, 125 strong, under Captain Messenger. The plan was for Messenger to 'get possession of Puketakauere mound' as the main division commenced its assault, cut off one Maori route of retreat, and support Nelson's efforts against Onukukaitara. The remaining division—fifty or sixty men under Captain Bowdler—was to take up a position between the *pa* and Camp Waitara which would cut another Maori route of retreat or reinforcement. The *pa* would be 'thus surrounded so that none coming out could escape from one force or another'. It is important to note that there is absolutely no indication from these dispositions that Nelson expected any support from New Plymouth. On the contrary, they indicate that he was confident of success with the force in hand.[14]

Messenger's division had the greatest distance to travel, and his night march across partly bush-covered ground was a difficult exercise. It was primarily this difficulty which later gave rise to the accusation that Nelson had planned his operation in total ignorance of the ground. In fact the area, which was after all in full sight of Camp Waitara, had been closely reconnoitred on 23 June, and had been visited on 24 June by a missionary who reported his findings to the military.[15] Furthermore, Messenger was guided by Ihaia, chief of the Atiawa landsellers—a fact which Nelson's critics failed to note. Ihaia was ill at the time, and Messenger's march was certainly trying for his men, but Ihaia 'did his duty' and got the troops into position on schedule.[16]

The other divisions also got into position without mishap, and at about 7 a.m. the howitzers opened fire. 'Great secrecy' had been preserved regarding British movements, and although the Maoris hoped for an attack at some stage, Nelson may have succeeded in obtaining tactical surprise.[17] The artillery created a small breach in the Onukukaitara Stockade and Nelson advanced to the attack. Messenger, having arrived in position only moments before, was resting his tired men, but on hearing Nelson's musketry he too moved forward. Thus far, all had gone according to plan, but from this point the British part in the action dissolved into two distinct combats—Nelson's operation in front of Onukukaitara and Messenger's efforts against Puketakauere.

Nelson's men were crossing the open ground towards the south-west face of the stockade 'when they were fired upon by the Maories, a great many of whom were in a deep trench outside the *pa* which they [the British] did not know of '.[18] The 'deep trench' was in fact a small natural gully in which the Maoris had dug rifle pits, but the crucial fact was that the advancing British did not know that it was fortified. They advanced with their attention focused on the stockade, which in practice was 'only a draw' to divert British attention from the real danger in the gully.[19] In effect, the British were ambushed during their advance on what they assumed to be the key to the

Onukukaitara defences. 'The natives, lying down with loaded guns, started up when the [British] line was within a few yards; their numbers were great, their guns were double-barrels and they fairly shook the advancing party.'[20]

Nelson's men recoiled from this unexpected and 'most destructive' fire.[21] The Major ordered a renewed advance, and his men responded bravely. But more Maoris moved out of the stockade to the advanced entrenchments—a movement which some contemporaries mistook for the arrival of Maori reinforcements—until 'the *pah* was probably almost empty'.[22] Consequently, despite their best efforts, the British could make no progress. Nelson, a very determined officer, maintained his position for some time in the hope that Messenger's diversion would enable him to renew his attack. Eventually, however, with his force continuing to suffer casualties with parties of Maoris now moving up through the bush on to his flank, and with no sign of relief from Messenger, he had no alternative but to retreat, picking up Bowdler's men on the way back to camp. Nelson himself claimed that the withdrawal was made in good order, but his men had been through a trying experience, and according to other accounts ammunition wagons were abandoned and 'great disorder' prevailed.[23]

It is more difficult to discover what happened to Messenger's division. He was operating on less favourable terrain than Nelson, his force was eventually broken up, and it was evidently hard enough for the men on the spot to know what was happening. One thing is clear however. Though Messenger joined Nelson's retreating force just as it got back to camp, he did so with only a remnant of his command. Another party came in later in the day, as did a number of individual stragglers, but Messenger's division had been comprehensively shattered. The Grenadier Company alone reportedly lost thirty-three men, and total casualties probably amounted to a third of the force.[24] Most of these men were killed outright or wounded, left on the ground, and slain without mercy by the Maoris.

The repulse of Nelson's division paled before this disaster, and the course of events that led to it can tentatively be reconstructed as follows. Messenger apparently advanced to attack Onukukaitara in the rear *via* Puketakauere Hill. But he found his immediate objective entrenched and 'full of the enemy'. Despite this he pushed on, and 'for a time it seemed as if the attack in the rear would succeed'.[25] But the Maoris probably transferred men from the combat with Nelson, and Messenger soon came under a very heavy flanking fire. It is unclear whether this fire came from more concealed rifle-pits or from parties of the garrison moving into the bush, but whatever the mechanism it seems to have developed into a counter-attack. This was probably the hardest fighting of the entire battle, and Ngati Maniapoto figured prominently.[26] The Maoris did not have the numbers to press home attacks over open ground, but the British were broken up into three groups. Messenger managed to get 'about thirty men together', pass around the eastern side of the Maori position, and over the ground originally occupied by Nelson's division to Camp Waitara.[27] Lieutenant Jackson, leading a second party, wisely lost himself in the bush and struggled back to the camp some hours later. The third party, under Lieutenant Brooke, was driven on to some swampy ground and annihilated.

The British reaction to the disaster at Puketakauere displayed many of the characteristics apparent in the interpretation of the Northern War. Some individuals had difficulty in recognizing the defeat for what it was. Nelson's report disingenuously played down the action, and an official proclamation labelled it 'a skirmish', and made no mention of any repulse.[28] Some settlers initially accepted that the battle was indecisive, and were so frustrated by the failure to effect anything in the war hitherto that they were prepared to welcome any sign of activity. Puketakauere, though 'bloody and indecisive is still a break in the cloudy view'.[29] Others simply found the news hard to believe. J. C. Richmond dismissed the first report as 'a foolish attempt at a hoax'.[30]

But the myth of Puketakauere as an indecisive skirmish was still-born. Certain facts—particularly the abandonment of the wounded—were all too clear, and by 6 July the 'skirmish' had become 'the worst reverse we have ever suffered in all our engagements with the natives'.[31] Memories of the Northern War had dimmed. It had generally been taken for granted that all the troops required for victory was a brave and energetic leader and a willingness on the part of the Maoris to stand and fight. When these ingredients failed so signally to produce the expected result, the shock was naturally considerable. Once it was recognized, the defeat had therefore to be acceptably explained and the shock somehow softened. The process of bringing perceived events as nearly as possible into conformity with expectations again followed the Northern War pattern. A hypothetical European renegade leading the Maoris to victory put in an appearance,[32] but the main emphasis was on enormous Maori casualties as a palliative for defeat, and on overwhelming Maori numbers and faulty British leadership as an explanation of it.

From the first, British reports, both official and unofficial, stressed the 'very great' losses of the Maoris. 'The dead were lying in heaps on the ground and the execution by grape and cannister was immense.'[33] The most common figure—originating with Nelson himself[34]—was 130 to 150 Maoris killed, but reports were found which improved even on this. The actual Maori loss can be established with an unusual degree of confidence. No less than five reports from independent Maori sources, two of which actually named the killed, put the Maoris loss at five dead.[35]

Several of the reports asserting that five Maoris had been killed became available to the British immediately after the battle. They, however, preferred their own conjectures. The *Taranaki Herald* of 7 July quoted two accurate reports from Maori sources only to comment 'but the probable truth is . . . that their total loss in killed and wounded is upwards of 200'. The exaggeration of enemy casualties is a common enough occurrence in war, but by any criterion this was an extreme case. Despite the ready availability of reliable figures, the British continued to multiply the number of Maoris killed by a factor of 25 or 30. It seems reasonable to assume that the tendency arose from the idea that the Maoris simply must have paid an enormous price for their victory over British troops. Facts were immaterial to this conviction.

The exaggeration of the number of Maoris engaged in the battle took a similar form, though it functioned as an explanation rather than a palliative. It was well known that relatively few Waikatos had joined Kingi, that most Taranaki and Ngati Ruanui were away to the south, and that the Atiawa forces were small. Puketakauere, however, brought about a dramatic upturn in appreciations of Maori strength. The Maoris suddenly became 'a large army'. A common estimate was 1,000, and accounts emphasized the 'overwhelming numbers' of the Maoris as an explanation of defeat. 'The great numerical superiority of the natives alone made it necessary for our troops to retire.'[36] But it was rare for this factor to be presented as the only cause of defeat. Even at odds of two to five, British troops should still have triumphed according to contemporary theory. 'When 400 Englishmen have not proved more than a match for 1000 Maoris' something more of an explanation than mere odds was required.[37] To many it was clear from the outset that human error also lay at the root of the trouble. 'That blame must attach somewhere is only too apparent.'[38] The only point in question was the name of the scapegoat.

There were three possible candidates for this unwelcome distinction —Messenger, Nelson, and Gold. Before the retreat on 27 June was properly over, Nelson showed signs of attributing the most humiliating aspect of the defeat, the abandonment of the wounded, to Messenger. He ordered the exhausted Captain back out to look for stragglers as soon as the force reached camp, and he significantly omitted his senior subordinate from a list of commendations which included all six other unit commanders.[39] Fortunately for Messenger's reputation, this broad hint was not taken up, either by contemporaries or historians, and the main subjects of criticism were Nelson and Gold.

As commander of the troops in the battle, Nelson was the most plausible scapegoat on the face of things. He did come in for some criticism, particularly from soldier-authors such as Carey, who defended Gold.[40] Some of the objections to Nelson's conduct were that he did not have an adequate knowledge of the ground, that he attacked with a hopelessly inferior force, and that he divided up even this. These criticisms are dealt with elsewhere, and it is unnecessary to enter into a lengthy defence of Nelson to suggest that they were substantially unfounded. The one criticism that is in any sense appropriate is that Nelson was unduly confident of his force's ability to beat the Maoris because he failed to appreciate the nature of their tactical approach. This failure was common to the great majority of Nelson's countrymen at the time—his subordinates were even more confident than he.

Nelson was extremely popular with his men, was respected by them for his talents, and he also impressed the settlers with his courage and energy. Indeed, it appears from contemporary comments that he was considered the most capable and vigorous officer to serve in the Taranaki War.[41] Commentators retained their high opinion of Nelson after Puketakauere, and to a certain extent this is to their credit. But this did not end the scapegoat hunt, which simply shifted in the direction of the already unpopular Gold —inherently a less likely candidate than Nelson who actually directed the battle. A scapegoat was necessary. It could not be Nelson. It must therefore be Gold.

The criticism of Gold, expressed especially but by no means exclusively by the New Zealand settlers, reached new heights of vituperation after Puketakauere. He was accused of cowardice, there was an attempt to persuade the senior militia officer to arrest him, and he was replaced by Major-General T. S. Pratt in early August as a direct result of the battle on 27 June. The nicest thing said about him was that 'there is something so touchingly dense in his stupidity that you can view him as a gigantic baby.'[42] The basis of the attack on Gold was, first, that he had ordered Nelson to attack with a hopelessly small force and, secondly, that he had arranged to bring up a column from New Plymouth to Nelson's support but failed to do so. In fact, Nelson needed no encouragement to attack and pressured Gold to give permission. Gold reinforced Nelson to an extent that not only the Major but everybody else considered sufficient, and it is true that lack of numbers was not the main British problem in the battle. Gold approved of the intention to engage the Maoris but made no stipulation as to how this should be done. As Gold himself put it: 'everything was left to the Major's own discretion, from his personal observation'.[43] As for the pre-arranged plan for support from New Plymouth, it seems clear that no such thing existed. Gold did march out to within two or three miles of Camp Waitara, and some critics actually suggested that he sat out the battle there. But in fact he left only when he heard the fight had commenced and arrived well after the fighting had ended.[44] His message to Nelson of 26 June made no reference to any concerted operation, and Nelson evidently made his dispositions on the assumption that he would be acting independently. According to M. S. Grace, 'the general impression in both camps was that Major Nelson had neither expected nor much desired Colonel Gold's co-operation', and Gold himself categorically denied promising it.[45] Contemporary debate followed a logic of its own whereby the only question was whether Gold or Nelson was to blame. The defence of one was an attack on the other, and the possibility that neither officer was responsible for the defeat apparently occurred to no one.

Modern historians have exercised a commendable discretion in accepting that Maori casualties were light, but on the whole they perpetuate the notion that the main cause of defeat was the incompetence of the British leaders involved. J. W. Fortescue distributed unfounded criticism with an even hand, stating that 'the whole proceeding was one of almost criminal folly'. Most writers, however, emphasize the rather more plausible idea that

Nelson attempted 'a naive and optimistic plan'. This continued stress on the failure of British leadership, understandable though it is in the light of contemporary emphasis on the same factor, leaves us with an utterly inadequate explanation of the Maori victory at Puketakauere.[46]

The Maori tactics and engineering techniques which were the real cause of the British defeat, utilized the basic attributes of the modern *pa*, apparent in the Northern War and at the L-pa, but with a greater emphasis on deception and concealment. One ploy was the fortification of Puketakauere Hill. Nelson had not divided his force into two main parts with the intention that they should act independently, but in the hope that they would supplement each other's efforts against the same objective: Onukukaitara. This was a perfectly good plan, but because the Maoris had interposed a strongpoint unknown to the British, on Puketakauere Hill, Messenger could not perform the task allocated to him, and the British effort dissolved into two autonomous actions. This fragmentation was the result, not of any error by Nelson, but of Hapurona's skill, and it applied only to the British. The Maoris were able to switch warriors to and from each focus of action. In short, the British were forced to fight two battles, while the Maoris fought one.

The most prominent feature of the Maori defence was the simple stockade on Onukukaitara, and the *pa* therefore appeared to be a relatively straightforward fortification. An engineer officer wrote that 'the pah certainly looked innocent enough as seen from the camp'.[47] But in effect, the stockade was a false target, containing few warriors. It drew the fire of the British artillery, engaged the attention of commander and troops, and was the object of their attack, while the Maoris won the battle from entirely different positions. These positions, on and around Puketakauere Hill, along the flanks and in the middle of Nelson's route of advance, were all well-concealed, and some had safe communication with each other, being 'connected by underground galleries about three feet high'. Most of the concealed positions, in the words of a naval officer who inspected the *pa* after the Maoris abandoned it two months later, were 'riflepits of a ingenious and novel construction, so made that it is impossible to fire into them from outside'.[48] The rifle pit—sometimes a simple short trench, sometimes a tiny *pa* in itself—was to become a characteristic of Maori earthworks, and so too was the emphasis on concealment, deception, and surprise.

6

The Maori Strategy
and the British Response

I THE DEVELOPMENT OF THE MAORI STRATEGY

THE THIRD PHASE OF THE WAR BEGAN IN JULY WITH A PERIOD OF
Maori ascendancy arising from the Battle of Puketakauere and the arrival of
substantial numbers of Kingite warriors to join Epiha's vanguard. The
most important feature of this phase was the final formulation of a Maori
strategic approach which, in embryo, had already exerted a profound influence on the conflict. This strategy continued to frustrate the British in
their search for a decisive victory.

The Battle of Puketakauere created a local crisis in which the British were
thrown on to the defensive and an attack on New Plymouth itself was widely
feared. But what alarmed Governor Browne most was the danger that the
Maori success would lead to a general rising while the bulk of the troops in
the country were concentrated at Taranaki. He appealed urgently for reinforcements to Britain and Australia to protect the other settlements, but it
seemed clear to him that the best prospect of preventing escalation lay in a
decisive victory at Taranaki. 'Some decided and indisputable success at
Taranaki is absolutely necessary to prevent other tribes joining those now in
arms against us.'[1] Thus the 'quick victory' imperative of the opening phase
of the war took on a new lease of life, with Browne and the naval commander, Commodore Loring, mercilessly pressuring Gold and his successor, General Pratt, who took over on 3 August, into seeking a decisive
success.

On 16 July, Browne noted that Gold had 2,000 effectives and that he
would therefore 'be able to strike a vigorous and effective blow on the rebel
forces either on the north or south of New Plymouth'. On taking command,
Pratt was informed that 'every day's delay will give increased confidence
and add to the strength of the enemy' and that 'prompt and vigorous offensive operations are absolutely necessary'. Browne stressed that these operations must have so clear cut a result 'that even the Maoris will be constrained
to admit that it has been successful; and I must add, that they invariably
construe escape into victory'.[2] With Puketakauere in mind, Browne also ad-

jured his military commanders to remember 'that another reverse would be attended with disastrous consequences to the whole of the settlements in this island'.[3] Browne thus indulged in a cliché familiar to subordinate officers in most wars, whereby he instructed his General immediately to effect everything without risking anything. But it remains true that throughout the rest of the war he provided his commanders with one clear and reasonable objective—the decisive defeat of the enemy in battle—and that he offered them every support toward this end. And, though they did so more cautiously than Browne may have liked, it was this that they strove to achieve throughout the year.

But as the repetition of Browne's demand indicates, the British were unable to gain their objective. On the contrary, July and August were the worst months of the war for them. The Maori tide lapped to the gates of New Plymouth until the town, together with the British posts in the countryside, were said to be 'in a state of siege'. 'The natives have come close up to the town, murdering every soul who is fool enough to go half a mile outside the ramparts.'[4] Disease, a result of extreme over-crowding, was rife and the devastation of property continued while various British initiatives proved ineffective. The settlers were 'bordering on despair' and one regular soldier wrote that he had never 'lived through such a state of apprehension as at present'.[5] At the end of August the pressure decreased when many of the Maoris returned to their homes, abandoning their most advanced positions, including Puketakauere which had now served its purpose. Commodore Loring attributed their withdrawal to 'the usual instability of savage nature', but in fact they had gone home to plant.[6] This gave the British more freedom of action, and as commentators were quick to point out, improved the chances of success even if it made 'decisive' action more difficult by providing fewer Maoris to kill. Despite this, September was marked not by a great victory but by two minor clashes in which the British were generally believed to have been humiliated.

The first occurred at Huirangi where Pratt destroyed some *pa* after they had been vacated on 11 September. His vanguard entered a copse beyond a *pa*, was ambushed by a small Maori force, and the whole British column withdrew with insignificant casualties. There are signs that by retreating rather than attacking Pratt avoided one of the concealed-position traps which the Maoris were beginning to favour.[7] But the settlers preferred to interpret it as 1,500 troops 'put to flight by a volley from forty-one Maories'. The settlers were 'quite disgusted' with this 'disgraceful' incident. 'Only imagine a force of nearly 1500 strong with large guns retiring, or rather running away from *30* savages, and a general in command.'[8] A broadly similar incident occurred on 29 September when 500 troops under Colonel Leslie were ambushed while destroying an empty *pa* by about 100 Maoris and lost five men wounded. This was denounced as 'one of the most disgraceful affairs that ever cast discredit on British arms'.[9] These comments were probably unjustified, but it is clear that the British were unable to take advantage of the Maori planting season to strike any heavy blow. By mid-October the chance had been lost as the Kingites reinforced their contingent to full strength, and another expedition, to Kaihihi on 11-12 October, yielded only empty *pa*. Public disenchantment with the war was considerable.

It looks as if the day of hopefulness has passed away, and the dark night of despondency has set in . . . we have been pushed back, and back, and back until it has become clear that we have been plunged into a wasting and dishonouring war which there is neither the enterprise to carry out, or the energy to prosecute to a successful and manly result.[10]

Even the first taste of British victory did not lift the gloom appreciably. A party of Ngati Haua Kingites began entrenching on an old *pa* site at Mahoetahi on the morning of 6 November. Intended as the first echelon of a larger force, this party was between fifty and 150 strong.[11] By an extraordinary but well-documented coincidence, Pratt was planning to occupy Mahoetahi with a strong column that very day.[12] His force was ready to move when he received news that the Maoris had forestalled him. He was therefore able to surprise them with 1,000 men. He stormed the incipient fortifications, which were 'in many places open',[13] and routed the Ngati Haua defenders. An attempt was made to inflate this into a great and decisive victory—'the hottest engagement ever fought in New Zealand or anywhere else'.[14] But the disproportion of numbers was so great and so obvious that the initial British euphoria rapidly waned. 'There is nothing connected with the engagement of which we can boast . . . still, we have, during the course of this war become so accustomed to ignominious defeats that even this small victory is welcome.'[15] A wide range of contemporary commentators, including General Pratt, soon accepted that Mahoetahi had had neither strategic significance nor moral effect, and that it had brought victory no closer.[16] By the end of 1860 the British efforts to break the deadlock had still to bear fruit.

Contemporaries put forward two alternative explanations for this lack of success. Again, the colonists stressed weak leadership—'the wretched imbecility of those in command'. Pratt had, by September, already proved himself to be 'not the right man in the right place'. The settlers 'did hope that on the arrival of General Pratt a new state of things would have been observed; but he is merely following in the steps of his predecessor'. A few commentators even felt that Pratt was performing worse than that 'absolute unredeemed fool', Colonel Gold. 'Contrasted with the present our late Commander-in-Chief derives considerable lustre.'[17]

The military responded by suggesting that decisive victory was unobtainable simply because the Maoris were impossible to catch. Before Puketakauere, Gold reported that though he had 'every anxiety to strike a decisive blow' against the southern tribes there was 'hardly any chance of catching them'. As late as 10 December, Pratt felt 'as if I were fighting a "will o' wisp"'.[18] This notion of a war primarily characterized by Maori elusiveness aided by inaccessible terrain has generally been accepted by historians, and it is largely on this basis that the Taranaki struggle is considered a guerilla conflict.

These two explanations of the British lack of success may have some elements of truth, but neither is anything like satisfactory. It seems likely that the real explanation was the existence of a coherent Maori strategy. The local manifestation of this strategy in Taranaki was based on two broader techniques. One, the expendable, effective, and easily built modern *pa*, has been examined above. The Taranaki-style modern *pa* went some way towards counteracting British superiority in armaments and numbers. The other technique addressed the problem of fighting full-time soldiers with part-time soldiers throughout a virtually continuous campaign. The key to this was the nature and extent of the King Movement's involvement in the Taranaki War.

There is no question that, throughout the war, the Kingites were concerned to limit the scope of the conflict. They were careful to prevent the extension of fighting to other provinces, and their warriors in Taranaki were never more than a minority of the total number available. Together with the equally unquestionable fact that many Kingites were very reluctant to go to war with the British at all, this has led to the assumption that only a relatively small group of extremists fought in Taranaki, and even that the Movement as such could not really be considered a combatant. Such thinking is unsound, first because the Kingite commitment to the Taranaki War was not so limited, and second because there were very good military reasons for the limits which did exist.

As is often the case with Maori numbers, it is difficult to establish just how many men came down from Waikato to fight in Taranaki. Parties were constantly coming and going, and the British frequently exaggerated the numbers concerned. Nevertheless, it is possible to establish the general pattern of warrior movements, and make some estimate of the numbers involved. Much of the evidence comes from John Morgan, a missionary living in the Waikato, who regularly passed on estimates of Kingite strength to Governor Browne. Epiha and his men went home in late August, returned in mid-October, 1860, and possibly went home again in December.[19] Epiha was reinforced soon after the Battle of Puketakauere. Various parties arrived in July and by August there may have been something in the order of 500 Kingites in Taranaki.[20] Most of these warriors went home to do their planting at the end of August, but by mid-October more parties were arriving, and at the beginning of November the number was probably about 600.[21] Further parties set out in late November, on 18 December, and in early January, and these known movements are probably only a sample of actual departures. In January 1861 there were probably 800 Kingites with Wiremu Kingi.[22] Many, perhaps most, of these returned home in February, but they were replaced, and the Kingite presence did not drop below 400, probably rising again to another peak when the war ended in March.[23] A few of these men came from Tauranga, Rotorua, and Taupo, but most were from the Tainui tribes of the Waikato area. In sum, though 800 was the probable peak at the scene of action at any one time, it is difficult to believe that less than 1,200 different Waikato warriors fought in Taranaki, at one time or another, and 1,500 seems more likely. This probably represented between a third and a half of the total strength of the Waikato or 'core' Kingite tribes.

Clearly, Kingite commitment to the war was by no means so circumscribed as is sometimes supposed, but there were limits. The two principal ones were that no more than a quarter of the available warriors fought in Taranaki at one time, and that care was taken to restrict the war to that province. These restrictions seemed strange to some British commentators. They observed that for Waikato the war was almost a seasonal sport. 'It became the fashion for all the adventurous men to spend a month or two in the year in Taranaki.' They noted with some irritation that warriors walking the streets of Auckland had been killing Englishmen the preceding month. 'Rifles and tomahawks at Taranaki and fraternization in Shortland Crescent'.[24] But only a few Europeans realized that this tacit neutrality pact combined with the circulation of warriors between Waikato and Taranaki to form the very foundation of the Maori war effort. It was only by operating a sort of shift system that the Kingites were able to keep a substantial number of warriors in Taranaki, and so partly overcome the great disadvantage of a tribal socio-economy in conflict with a professional army. As that perceptive missionary Robert Burrows put it towards the end of the war: 'The present mode of warfare can be carried on for almost any length of time by the natives; small parties are constantly joining those at Taranaki; who take the place of others that have been for some time fighting; and thus give them an opportunity of withdrawing for a time for the purpose of cultivation, and then to return and resume their hostile position.'[25]

The same economic problem was further minimized by the continued availability of markets in Auckland Province. This was particularly important as regards ammunition. The war had led Browne to tighten restrictions on the sale of ammunition and arms to the Maoris, but peace in Auckland made it far easier to circumvent these and to obtain the ready cash necessary for illegal purchases. Transactions on the coast with visiting ships were a source of ammunition, and these were probably not entirely cut off even during the Waikato War, but some of the rare hard evidence on the blackmarket in arms indicates that important purchases were made on European land to the south of Auckland.[26] Money for such purchases came largely from trade with Auckland Province. This diminished during the Taranaki War, but it did not end, and it is quite possible that the diminution was exaggerated by the transfer of trade from Auckland Town itself to markets at Waiuku and Kawhia, and by an increased use of pro-British Maoris as middlemen.[27] European traders and missionaries, moreover, remained in the Waikato throughout the war. Another missionary, John Morgan, described the situation as follows:

At present the Auckland Province is neutral and a strange state of affairs exists.

The very natives who have been in arms against the Gov[ernment] at Taranaki, return home to reap the crops they left growing when they went to fight, and are now taking down their wheat for sale at the English settlement of Waiuku and there and at Auckland purchase the supplies they require and then return home, many of them to return to the war. The Gov[ernment] know this to be the case, but wisely they allow it to pass not wishing to extend the war by seizing the offenders.[28]

It is true that the government was aware of the plain facts, and that until the arrival of large reinforcements from December 1860, it was not much better able to sustain a war on the two fronts than the Maoris. But it is clear that the British did not fully grasp the significance of the neutrality of Auckland. On several occasions troops were removed and reinforcements withheld from Taranaki for fear of an attack on Auckland, whereas in fact the best protection for the province was its vital role in the Maori war economy.

Thus there is no need to over-emphasize political divisions, or lack of widespread commitment, within the King Movement to explain the limited nature of its war against the British. Nor should these limits be exaggerated. A third or a half of the warriors of Waikato can scarcely be considered an extremist minority, and the rest did not necessarily remain at home because they were unwilling to fight. They may equally well have done so because greater numbers could not be maintained. The restriction of the war to Taranaki and the circulating warrior force did not completely overcome the great constraints on a tribal society's war effort. Waikato strength significantly diminished during the planting season in September 1860 and there are signs that ammunition and food shortages did occur towards the end of the war.[29] But in comparison with the logistically impossible situation which must otherwise have occurred, and to the actual economic and manpower strains of the larger-scale, strategically different Waikato War, these problems were minor. These basic Kingite methods alone could not win the war, and they could not provide the means of matching the British in resources. But they could and did provide sufficient men and supplies to make possible a local strategy in Taranaki which stood a chance of preventing British success.

Aspects of this had begun to emerge before Kingite intervention, but the strategy became fully developed only after Puketakauere. It consisted of three main elements. The first was the maintenance by the Maoris of a war on two fronts, together with a credible threat to New Plymouth. Whenever the British moved against the tribes south of New Plymouth, a threat to the town from Te Atiawa (and later the Waikatos) in the north could draw the troops back to its defence and *vice versa*. This was more or less the technique applied by Heke and Kawiti at the Battle of Puketutu in 1845, but in a strategic rather than a tactical form. There is an indication that the process originated as a planned strategem,[30] but even if it developed naturally it was very effective. As early as 24 March, Gold was forced to break off his operations against Kingi by the advance of Taranaki raiders towards New

Plymouth from the south. Murray's strict orders to return from Waireka arose from the need to protect the town. Even during the suspension of hostilities against Kingi the need to keep a strong force at Camp Waitara in case he took the initiative hampered operations against the southern tribes. One of Gold's main reasons for remaining on the defensive after Puketakauere, despite the pressure from Browne and Loring, was the 'absolute necessity' of protecting New Plymouth. As soon as he arrived Pratt complained that his troops were inadequate to protect 'this scattered and irregularly built town' from Maoris on one side while attacking Maoris on the other.[31] In October, Pratt's expeditions were prematurely recalled two or three times by threats to the town.

Robert Ward doubted that an attack on New Plymouth 'was ever seriously planned' by the Maoris, and it is true that they never had the numbers to contemplate anything much more than a night raid on a fortified settlement usually containing over 1,000 men. But all that was required was that the threat be credible, and this it certainly was. Despite attempts to reduce the perimeter, the town did not lend itself to defence, and Colonel Carey doubted its capacity to withstand a determined attack.[32] Alarms were frequent throughout the war, particularly during August 1860 when the Maoris built strong *pa* within two miles of the town—potential bases for an attack which could not easily be captured. In this month the Maoris looted houses just outside the perimeter and set fire to some temporary barracks within it. They fired on the trenches from twenty yards and killed a settler on the town's racecourse.[33]

The threatened attack never eventuated, but it did have a deadly effect on the Taranaki colonists. The need to contract the perimeter of the defences led to overcrowding, and consequently to disease. According to one account, no fewer than 121 settlers died from disease during the war, as against a peace-time death rate of twelve or thirteen per annum.[34] New Plymouth thus functioned as a liability as well as a vital base. It did so, not for any inherent reason, but because the Maoris maintained the credibility of the threat of attack.

The second element of the Maori strategy consisted simply of an offensive against settler property—raids to remove or destroy houses and household goods, stock, crops, and agricultural equipment. The southern tribes commenced looting in the first week of the war, though it may be noted that the Maoris claimed that the British had begun the chain of destruction by destroying Kingi's property on the Waitara block. The removal of crops and cattle deprived the British of supplies and forced them into greater dependence on the New Plymouth roadstead. It also went some way towards solving the Maoris' own acute supply problems, and so enabled them to remain in the fields for longer periods. Ngati Ruanui at least did not consume all the stock they captured. In 1865, British commissariat officers in their territory noted the thriving herds of thoroughbred horses and cattle. A little-known effect of the War of 1860–61 was the creation of a pastoral boom amongst the South Taranaki Maoris.[35]

But more important than all this was the fact that the removal or destruction of settler property was the main means available to the Maoris of taking the war to the enemy. Through it, they could inflict costs on the colonists which might undermine the will to fight and discourage a repetition of the conflict. On 21 February 1860, when war seemed imminent, the Superintendent of Taranaki wrote:

> There is in most parts of the settlement a desire among the settlers to remain in their districts, organised as volunteers and militia, for the protection of their property. That this is practicable is the view of some persons of experience here, and if practicable it is surely highly desirable. The natives will make little resistance in the open field but they look to intimidate and punish the Europeans through their large stake in the undefended country districts. It will be to take from them their hope of a successful resistance if we are prepared to meet them in this.[36]

Some attempt was made to implement this policy. Posts at Omata, the Bell Block, Waireka, and Tataraimaka were garrisoned, partly by local militia, in the hope that they would provide some protection for the surrounding districts. This, of course, meant that the troops involved (from 500 to 1,000 men)[37] were unavailable for other operations, but this heavy price bought nothing. Property losses were already substantial before Puketakauere. By August, despite efforts by detachments of troops to collect cattle and grain, and the fact that no stock was kept for breeding lest it be driven off, New Plymouth was reduced to salt rations and cattle had to be imported along with everything else. '"The garden of New Zealand" is turned into a howling waste.' By the end of October a settler could write: 'Little remains of the settlement of Taranaki outside the 50 acre section to which the town is reduced.'[38] By the end of the war some 200 farms had been destroyed or ruined. Property losses exceeded £200,000 in value, without counting lost production. New Plymouth survived on the troops' business, militia pay, and other central government hand-outs, and it is fair to say that the British Province of Taranaki had ceased to exist as an economic entity.

The effectiveness of Maori raiding operations was greatly increased by the availability of modern *pa*. *Pa* provided depots where plunder could be collected, and safe bases to which raiders could retreat if threatened. *Pa* could be located very close to the raiders' target areas and could be built very quickly. In this bandit-style war within a war, British problems were greatly compounded by the fact that the bandits they faced had what amounted to portable lairs. Collectively, the Taranaki modern *pa* also constituted the third element of the Maori strategy. In effect, they formed a flexible cordon around the British positions. When the Maoris were able to adopt an aggressive approach, as they did after Puketakauere, the cordon could be expanded towards the British. From these advanced positions, the Maoris could apply their other two techniques more intensively. When Maori strength was reduced, as it was during the planting season in September, the cordon of *pa* could be contracted. Even in this form, it served to keep the British penned in a restricted area. This minimized the damage the British could do, and the effects of the supply and manpower constraints on the Maori war effort, by protecting the cultivations and base areas.

In either case the cordon continued to hold, even if individual *pa* or groups of them were abandoned before a British initiative. A British force might be too strong, the garrison too weak, or supplies inadequate for a particular *pa* to hold out. But there were always more *pa*—on 29 July 1860, a settler counted ten from Camp Waitara[39]—and the effort of mounting an expedition and of destroying the *pa* that were evacuated was enough to blunt the British foray. In these cases the British drive was not stopped or repulsed so much as absorbed, as if it had been striking a cushion. Gold's expedition against the Warea *pa* (24-30 April) and Pratt's expeditions against the Huirangi (11-12 September) and Kaihihi River (12 October) positions were examples of this.

Alternatively, if the Maori garrisons were sufficiently strong, and supplies adequate, they could maintain their positions and invite attack. If the attack eventuated, the Maoris had the advantage of strong fortifications and a carefully prepared battleground to give them a good chance of inflicting a costly defeat on their enemy—as they did at Puketakauere. If the British declined to attack, the Maoris had a secure position from which to implement the other elements of their strategy.

In July and August 1860, the Maoris expanded their cordon of *pa* and built strong positions within one or two miles of each of the British main bases—Camp Waireka, Camp Waitara, and New Plymouth itself. It is this in particular which invalidates the idea that inaccessible terrain allowed the Maoris to avoid combat. At this time, the British had only to cross a mile or two of 'inaccessible terrain' to come to grips with their 'elusive enemy'. They did not do so because, though they had yet to appreciate fully the defensive qualities of the modern *pa*, Puketakauere had indicated that they could not attack a strong position successfully at an acceptable cost. That they should reach this conclusion was understandable, but it eliminated the chance of a decisive victory over an insultingly accessible foe who was plundering the very streets of New Plymouth.

The three elements of this strategic approach supplemented each other to form a seemingly intractable barrier to British hopes. The British were naturally reluctant to assault a strong *pa* and the Maoris would simply abandon relatively weak, poorly supplied, or poorly garrisoned *pa*. There appeared to be no simple method of achieving the British objective of decisive victory. Yet if they did nothing the Maoris would continue to destroy the economy of Taranaki Province and to threaten New Plymouth. These factors, together with the grave danger of escalation, made inactivity seem as dangerous as activity. But the British were not bereft of ideas, and by the end of 1860 they had begun to formulate a new solution to their dilemma.

II THE BRITISH RESPONSE: PRATT'S SAPPING SYSTEM

THE METHOD TO WHICH THE BRITISH TURNED IN AN EFFORT to solve their strategic dilemma was a classic technique of siege warfare—attack by an approach-trench dug towards the enemy lines until they were rendered untenable. This technique was called sapping, after the approach-trench or sap. In Taranaki, the construction of redoubts of various size along the line of operations was an integral part of the sapping system. The redoubts were built to consolidate gains made by the sap, to provide bases for the sapping parties, and to create protected batteries for close range cannon-fire. Throughout, a major problem was effectually to protect the men pushing on the sap from Maori fire. Apart from as heavy as possible a covering fire of musketry and artillery, there were three main protective devices: gabions, or packs of bullet-proof material such as earth and fern, which collectively acted as a portable parapet; sap-rollers or mantelets —large wicker-work screens mounted at the head of the sap; and traverses, or sections of the sap left undug to prevent Maori fire raking its length.

The possibility of taking Maori *pa* by sapping had been noted, and on one occasion briefly tried, earlier in the war, but Pratt first began systematically to apply the technique on 29 December 1860. From then until the final cease-fire on 18 March 1861, sapping dominated the British operations. The sapping system was directed against a series of *pa* extending east up the Waitara River. The most important were Matarikoriko, Huirangi (re-occupied by the Maoris after Pratt's September expedition had come and gone), and Te Arei. No less than eight redoubts were built in sequence by the British to act as bases for sapping operations against these Maori positions. The first pa attacked was Matarikoriko, approached on 29 December by means of the first of the eight redoubts, and evacuated by the Maoris on the night of 30 December.

Some British observers saw the occupation of Matarikoriko as a great victory. They reasoned that the Maoris had been forced from a valuable position with heavy losses.[40] In fact Matarikoriko was not particularly valuable—the main *pa* had taken no more than two days to build—and Maori losses were trivial.[41] The real reason for its evacuation was probably that the position had been intended only as a trap for the British if they assaulted. The British at first thought that the *pa* was fairly weak but the troops subsequently discovered that a very formidable collection of concealed rifle pits flanked the route any storming party would have to take.[42] When it became clear that the British had no intention of assaulting, Matarikoriko lost its usefulness and the Maoris abandoned it. Before doing so they used some of their concealed pits to ambush skirmishers, to obtain some sort of consolation prize. They killed three and wounded twenty-two soldiers, and could therefore claim Matarikoriko as a minor victory for themselves.

After Matarikoriko, Pratt continued his series of redoubts eastward towards the Maori lines at Huirangi, beginning a double sap towards the pa itself on 22 January. The Maoris evacuated Huirangi a week later. The outstanding event of these operations was an assault by 140 Kingite and Atiawa volunteers against the third in the series of British redoubts. The attack was pressed home with great courage and vigour, but was repulsed with heavy loss. As at Mahoetahi, bad luck was partly to blame for the defeat. The garrison had been reinforced to 400 men only the night before the attack, and some evidence suggests that the Maori plan was leaked to the British.[43] But the attack remained an unnecessary gamble, with high costs and small profit likely even if successful, and the action must be seen as the Maoris' one major blunder of the Taranaki War. That this blunder should elicit the greatest outburst of contemporary British praise for Maori skill and courage was hardly a coincidence. Naturally enough, the British were more generous—and perceptive—in victory than in defeat.

The last and most important of the sapping operations began on 10 February 1861, against the immensely strong defensive lines of Te Arei. This long and costly operation was the main test of the sapping policy and its details will be treated in the analysis below. While the fighting continued at Te Arei, the peacefully inclined Kingite chief Wiremu Tamehana arrived from Waikato. He obtained the agreement of the fighting chiefs to an attempt to stop the conflict on the basis of the *status quo*. A truce was arranged on 12 March, but Pratt found the Maori terms unacceptable, and the fighting recommenced on 15 March. Browne, however, was of a different mind to Pratt and he despatched an envoy, the Native Secretary Donald McLean, to effect a cease-fire. Hostilities accordingly stopped on 18 March. The British and the Maoris did not explicitly accept each others' terms in the ensuing negotiations, and Browne fully intended to renew the struggle elsewhere, but the effective result was the end of the Taranaki War.

There were two main kinds of contemporary opinion on the sapping system. The colonists, true to form, heaped opprobrium on Pratt and his 'totally useless' sapping policy, this 'lazy *dilettante* style of playing at war'.[44] The unsuccessful Maori attack against Number Three Redoubt did very little to vindicate Pratt's approach. On 8 February, J. C. Richmond wrote that 'the face of the war can hardly be more unsatisfactory than now. . . . General Pratt and his "sappy" procedure would absorb 10,000 men at Waitara and look for more.' Richmond's friend and ally, Captain Harry Atkinson, was even more vehement. 'If that old muff [Pratt] does not soon alter his tactics we shall be in a jolly mess for the winter.' These views were widely shared among the colonists.[45]

The second contemporary viewpoint, the case for sapping, was put primarily by its architects—General Pratt, his chief engineer Colonel T. R. Mould, and his adjutant-general Colonel Carey. Since they expressed their views mainly after 18 March, they argued not only that sapping appeared to be an effective method which might win the war, but also that it had actually done so. Carey wrote that the new policy had achieved 'repeated and unvarying success', through which the conflict had been 'brought to a successful termination'. Pratt himself claimed that the 'continuing success' of his sapping system had left the Maoris 'thoroughly sickened' of the war and induced them to submit. Sapping, wrote Colonel Mould in the detailed engineering report of 30 March 1861 on which Pratt and Carey also based most of their arguments, had been 'the real cause of the present cessation of hostilities'.[46] Was the sapping system so effective and did it really lead to a clear-cut victory in the Taranaki War? Was Pratt's new approach the solution to the dilemma in which the Maori strategy placed the British?

The defence of the sapping policy was hampered by its antecedents. As practised by Vauban, Cohorn, and their successors, sapping had been essentially a siege method: a technique which, when coupled with close encirclement, could bring about the relatively rapid capture of a valuable fortress together with the surrender or destruction of its garrison. In Taranaki, Maori *pa* had little value in themselves, and they were never surrounded. When a sap eventually placed the British in a position to storm at low cost, the Maoris were both able to leave and could afford to do so. Here, therefore, sapping was a siege method without a siege. To their credit, the defenders of sapping recognized this factor. Carey, in particular, came to realize that *pa* had nothing to make their seizure inherently significant. 'None of the positions taken up by the natives were of the slightest importance to them or us. . . . The abandonment of the *pahs* after they had served their purpose was part of their system of war.'[47] The usual arguments for sapping were clearly inapplicable to Taranaki, and Carey and his associates had therefore to rest their case on three less conventional assertions.

The first of these was that the sapping operations cost the Maoris vastly more casualties than the British. Pratt and his associates may sincerely have held this belief, but it was totally unsupported by both the probabilities and the evidence. Two specific examples will suffice to demonstrate this. The figure of 220—precisely broken down into killed, wounded, and missing—emerged from nowhere to be accepted by many British as the Maori loss at Matarikoriko.[48] It was inherently unlikely that the Maoris should suffer major losses in this or any other sapping operation. Despite the various protective devices, it was extremely rare for troops pushing forward a sap to lose fewer men than the defenders. Observers repeatedly emphasized that the Maoris were very well protected in their entrenchments and that they took great care not to show themselves out of them.[49] Not a single corpse or wounded warrior was seen by the British during or after the engagement, and the hackneyed allusion to 'blood-stained trenches' was resorted to as proof of the assertion that Maori losses had been heavy. Such reliable evidence as is available indicates that the Maoris lost about six killed at Matarikoriko.[50]

The fighting in the last days of the war, at Te Arei, provides a second example. In the period between the two truces (15-18 March) the British lost a dozen men killed and wounded and claimed that the Maoris had suffered 'a heavy loss'. The Maoris on the other hand informed McLean a few days later that they had had only one man wounded in this period, and this was subsequently confirmed by the Waikato Kingites.[51] Overall, it may be that the Maoris lost no more than thirty men killed and wounded in resisting the sapping operations of 29 December to 18 March, against a British casualty list of about seventy men.

The second element of the case for sapping was the assertion that the system wore down the Maoris by attrition. The process of attrition had a moral as well as a material effect. Pratt claimed that sapping, more than any other form of warfare, was 'inexpressibly galling' to the Maoris, wearing down both their will and their capacity to resist. The reasoning behind the claim of a psychological effect was best outlined by Colonel Mould. In the case of spasmodic British initiatives such as occasional assaults on *pa*, argued the Colonel, the Maoris had time to use customary devices such as *haka* and war speeches to 'inflame their passions and excite their courage' for battle. In the face of a 'patient though determined advance' by sapping, on the other hand, 'this excitement they cannot sustain'. The Maoris, continued Mould, 'lose heart in proportion as they lose ground and men ... they become wearied and depressed, are confounded by a mode of attack so novel and so pertinaciously persisted in, and desirous of peace and rest.'[52] This almost amounted to saying that sapping had bored the Maoris into submission. Clearly, if implicitly, the argument owed something to racial stereotypes. The 'patient though determined advance' of dogged John Bull had been too much for the real but ephemeral courage of the excitable natives.

The best evidence for the assertion that sapping had a baneful psychological effect on the Maoris was their unsuccessful assault on Number Three Redoubt at Huirangi. It could be argued that, bored to frustration by the new British approach, the Maoris had attempted an unnecessary and desperate deed and had suffered the consequences. The attack certainly was a gamble, and it is probably also true that it was partly motivated by boredom. Many of the warriors in Taranaki, nurtured on stories of open combat and fierce assaults in tribal wars, had seen little real action, and were no doubt eager for it. But this had nothing to do with sapping. In December 1860, before Pratt had initiated his new policy, speakers at a great meeting of the Maori forces had strongly advocated aggressive and reckless action. 'The tribes were rashly exhorted to abandon the rifle pits, and throw themselves headlong on the military—"to act as their fathers had done".'[53]

The British could have fanned these flames as effectively by sitting quietly in New Plymouth and their outposts as by applying the costly sapping system. As J. C. Richmond put it, in a perceptive memorandum to the Secretary of State for War: 'It must be observed that the repulse of an attack on the advanced redoubt on January 23rd was not due to the [British] mode of operations. . . . Such an attempt will not be renewed.'[54] Richmond's prophecy proved accurate. The Maoris rarely needed more than one lesson in what not to do, and there were no more wholesale reversions to traditional tactics in this war or the next.

Attacks like that on Number Three Redoubt were not an inevitable consequence of sapping, but it was less unreasonable to suggest that such continuous operations placed a much greater strain on Maori material resources than did the sporadic expeditions of 1860. Yet the Maoris were able to alleviate it, and place the British in turn under strain, by the continued application of their own strategy. The movement of men and supplies from Waikato to Taranaki continued in 1861. The circulation of warriors from their homes to the front involved, if anything, greater numbers than in 1860.[55] This, of course, ameliorated both the material and psychological effects of attrition by sap—if the latter existed at all.

Maori marauding continued unabated in January-March 1861. Property was looted and destroyed, and settlers were killed when trying to bring in their stock. In February a settler wrote: 'At no period have the limits of safety around the town been so circumscribed as at present.'[56] Lack of space and fresh food meant that disease in the town increased. No fewer than fifty-one settlers died of disease in New Plymouth while the sapping operations were in progress.[57] The southern tribes, prompted by the Kingite leaders, mounted further convincing threats against New Plymouth from the south 'in the hope of diverting the General's attention from the north'.[58] To an extent, they succeeded in doing this. The need to protect New Plymouth and to combat Maori marauding robbed Pratt of at least 1,000 effectives, who might otherwise have been used to make the advance of his saps truly unremitting. As it was, shortages of men and supplies forced him to suspend sapping operations for two periods of two weeks each, allowing the Maoris some breathing space.

All this meant that the Maori war-machine was able to bear the strain of the British sapping operations—a fact confirmed by the events at Te Arei. The continued application of the Maori strategy also meant that the war placed a considerable strain on the British in their turn. Attrition worked both ways, and despite their inferior resources it was by no means a foregone conclusion that the Maoris would be the first to succumb to it.

Pratt's new approach was neither a means of bleeding the Maoris dry nor an effective form of attrition in any other sense, but there was rather more substance to the third element of the case for sapping. Though lulls did exist, British operations of early 1861 kept up a much more concentrated and sustained pressure on the Maori *pa* cordon than those of 1860. Previously, occasional British expeditions had occupied *pa* in scattered parts of the district, and then usually abandoned them. Under the sapping system, *pa* were occupied progressively at a single point on the Maori defensive belt—the series of *pa* along the Waitara River—and the ground gained was retained through the construction of redoubts. The cumulative effect of this process threatened to breach the *pa* cordon and to expose such Atiawa bases as Mataitawa to British seizure. This was the real danger of the sapping policy and by the beginning of February 1861 the Maoris had clearly recognized it as such. Matarikoriko had been abandoned after two days of attack and Huirangi after a week. In contrast, Te Arei was defended with the greatest possible tenacity. The Maoris 'spared neither labor or ingenuity' to turn the place into 'the strongest and best defended *pah* in the country'.[59]

The entrenchments, 'covered over and quite invisible', extended about a mile from north to south, and hidden rifle pits were located up to 800 yards in front (west) of the main position.[60] The Maoris used regimental bugle calls to confuse the troops, dummies to draw their fire, and made every effort to impede their work on the sap, as well as 'amusing themselves by calling out in excellent English the various military commands such as to the right incline fix bayonets now my lads charge'.[61] On the night of 26 February the Maoris raided the sap-head, destroyed hundreds of yards of trench and carried off fifty gabions and three sap-rollers.[62] On 5 March, they launched a feint attack against the British right and then fired on the sap-head at twenty-five yards range from concealed rifle-pits, shooting thirteen men.[63] The British responded with extremely heavy musketry to minimize Maori activity—some soldiers fired off 120 rounds before breakfast. But they rarely fired at specific targets. The troops, wrote J. C. Richmond, 'keep loading and firing without any aim the whole day'. Maori fire was also quite heavy but it was carefully controlled. 'They did not fire at random but each time selected some group to shoot at.'[64] British losses mounted slowly but steadily until they exceeded forty men, while Maori casualties remained light.[65] In the end it was the British, not the Maoris, who were led to remark that 'our men are dribbled off daily'.[66]

By 18 March, after five weeks of intensive effort, the British sap-head was still ninety yards from the first main line of Te Arei entrenchments, and the troops had been forced to abandon the latest of their redoubts by heavy enfilading Maori fire. On this, the last day of the war, J. C. Richmond wrote: 'We are all, I think, more depressed and hopeless than ever. General Pratt's conduct looks more and more idiotic.'[67] This extremely determined resistance at Te Arei was not the only Maori response to the threat to their *pa* cordon. A British observer noticed on 9 March that the Maoris were in the process of constructing yet another line of defence behind Te Arei.[68] Even if Pratt had eventually taken Te Arei, the *pa* cordon would have remained unbreached. At great cost in effort and considerable cost in blood, Pratt was merely pushing his way further and further into a series of defences that was in practice infinite.

It was not military success but the lack of it that made the British willing to accept peace in Taranaki. The continued failure of the troops to achieve anything of significance contributed, first, to the growth of a substantial peace party among the colonists and, second, to the conviction that a favourable decision would never be achieved in that theatre of operations.

At the outbreak of the War the majority of settlers had wholeheartedly supported Browne's stance, but by the end of 1860 opinion had become more evenly divided. Doubts about the justice of the Waitara purchase—the factor which had influenced the small group of missionaries and philanthropists who had opposed the war from the outset—contributed less to this change than did the military situation. In November 1860 a colonist wrote:

> It is now becoming apparent that the natives have it in their power to protract this
> unhappy war as long as they please. . . . [they] are too clever tactitians to meet us
> on open ground. . . . All the advantages are on their side. They have comparatively
> little, we everything, to loose by a continuation of the war. These considerations
> incline a very large portion of the population of the colony—especially of the Nor-
> thern Island . . . to desire peace.[69]

The economic implications of military failure in Taranaki were an important factor. Emigration, that crucial source of fresh labour and capital, was
'suddenly checked' by the arrival of news of the war in England in May.
The colonists' friends in London strove to overcome this problem by declar-
ing in July 1860 that 'all well-informed persons must know that long before
a person leaving England now can find himself landed in New Zealand the
rebellion will necessarily be at an end'. But as it became clear that this was
nonsense, the problem increased. Emigration through London to New
Zealand dropped from 5,198 in 1859 to 2,051 in 1860. British merchants
held back consignments to New Zealand, necessitating more expensive
replacement purchases in Australia. The general lack of confidence combined
with these factors to produce a recession in the North Island at least.[70] The
very existence of a de-stabilizing war may originally have contributed to
this, but it was lack of success that rapidly became the crucial factor. A
newspaper correspondent argued in September 1860 that the cause of the
depression in Auckland was 'the very vacillating and tedious manner' in
which the war was being conducted. 'The exhibition of anything like decision' at the front would 'at once' bring about an economic upturn. A
Wellington correspondent wrote along the same lines. 'Were the current of
events to take a decided turn in favour of the Europeans in the military
operations at Taranaki, there is no doubt that the commercial horizon
would very soon brighten.'[71] The tide did not turn, the horizon did not
brighten, and public disillusionment with the war grew.

The loss of public support for the war as it was being conducted could not
help but affect Browne and the Stafford Government. 'Want of success at
Taranaki has produced the usual effect on the public mind', wrote Browne
bitterly in a private letter. 'Those who were most clamourous for war have
altered their opinions and consider war under any circumstances wicked
and unholy.' But in official circles, public opinion and economic factors
were less important than the growing conviction that the war could not be
won in Taranaki. Though he was subsequently to portray his sapping
system as the master-stroke of a victorious war, General Pratt himself expressed doubts on 10 January 1861. If the war were to remain confined to
Taranaki, he wrote, 'it is difficult to foresee when it may be brought to a termination with any force I am likely to have at my disposal.' Pratt maintained
that the only answer was 'not to confine the war to this province, but to
make aggressive movements into the Waikato's own country'. Others had
arrived at this conclusion. John Morgan, for example, had been advocating

an invasion of Waikato since September 1860 on the grounds that operations in Taranaki had become hopelessly bogged down. By early 1861, Governor Browne had come around to this opinion. A British force eventually exceeding 3,500 men had striven for an entire year to no great effect, and the conclusion that success in Taranaki was beyond the British was becoming unavoidable.[72]

It could be claimed that the decision to abandon Taranaki in favour of Waikato was no more than a re-direction of effort—that it did not end the war, but simply changed the venue. But in practice the decision amounted to an acceptance of peace on terms which fell far short of Browne's original objectives. The theoretical conditions of peace were as follows. The Taranaki Maoris were to hand over their plunder and those of their tribesmen who had killed unarmed civilians, and formally submit to the Queen's authority. The southern tribes were to provide compensation for their systematic destruction of property. But possession of the Waitara block was to depend on an investigation, no land was annexed—though the British kept their redoubts—and there was no hint of any practical guarantee of Maori submission to British law.[73]

Even these terms constituted a considerable climb-down by Browne, and they were enough to enrage the New Plymouth settlers.[74] But in reality the situation was far less favourable to the British. As B. J. Dalton puts it, 'from the first these terms were almost wholly nugatory'. Only a fraction of the Atiawa—forty men, twenty-three women, and one child—formally accepted the terms.[75] The remaining combatants did not even make a verbal submission to British authority. No plunder, no 'murderers', and no compensation was given up. On the contrary, the southern tribes added a further 1,000 head of stock to their already extensive expatriate herds after the cease-fire of 18 March. These tribes added insult to injury by banning the passage of travellers and mail through their territory—the very opposite of acceptance of British rule.[76] The Taranakis and Ngati Ruanui also seized the 4,000-acre Tataraimaka block—part of the European settlement of Taranaki for fifteen years—as hostage for the 600 acres at Waitara. The Taranaki settlement was thus not only crippled by Maori depredations, but also reduced in size by some six per cent—a curious result for what is sometimes portrayed as a successful war of British expansion.

To say that the British did not win the Taranaki War is by no means an original conclusion. In 1861, it was widely accepted in New Zealand that the war had ended unfavourably—even humiliatingly—for the British. 'A year's war is a joke', wrote the editor of the *Southern Cross* bitterly. With more equanimity, a settler informed an English friend that she was 'amused at your newspapers talking of the Waikatos as being completely defeated'.[77] When Colonel Carey's book reached New Zealand in 1864, its reviewers were shocked by the assertion that Pratt had led an ever-victorious army.[78] Once the original sense of outrage had died down, however, preconceptions about the likely results of European–non-European conflict made it easy to forget that the failure had ever existed. One would expect that this movement of opinion would have involved a wholesale endorsement of the case for sapping, which was also the only case for British victory with any claim to credibility. Pratt, Mould, and Carey had always stressed the close connection between the sapping system and British victory even to the point of circularity. The British were victorious because sapping was effective. Sapping was effective because the British were victorious. One was not possible without the other. Historians have failed to realize this. Some early writers echoed the bitter settler criticism of Pratt and his sapping policy, but accepted the victory claim. Recent historians have commented favourably on the sapping system, but have been more cautious about the victory claim. Each of these views is paradoxical as a whole and inaccurate in its parts. The case for sapping and the case for British victory are mutually dependent. The fact that each is utterly unconvincing doubly disproves both.

To say this is not to suggest that clear-cut victory went instead to the Maoris. The Maoris could not be wholly satisfied with the results of the war. They may have suffered something like 200 killed and wounded, against a British casualty list of 238. The Maori loss, though less in total than the British, included a much higher proportion of killed, and the Maoris were less able than their enemies to afford such a toll. Accumulated reserves of ammunition were reduced, and economic resources were strained. Browne showed no sign of implementing his commitment to investigate the Waitara sale, and the block remained in British hands for some time to come. From Wiremu Kingi's viewpoint, though not that of the Maori cause generally, the southern tribes' possession of Tataraimaka was poor compensation for the loss of his home. But whereas the British war aims—the imposition of substantive sovereignty by decisive military victory—were aggressive and positive, the Maori objective was defensive and negative —simply to thwart the British effort. The military stalemate of 18 March therefore amounted to a British failure and a Maori success. The King Movement was the major contributor to this success, and it had fought in a cause which enlisted the sympathy of the majority of the Maori race. Its support increased greatly as a consequence. The King Movement was strengthened rather than weakened by the Taranaki War.

The Kingite warriors had demonstrated that they could block British moves across what before 1860 had been the tacitly agreed boundaries of control. While Kingite power remained intact, there could be no more seizures of land like that at Waitara, and no more *ad hoc* attempts to impose British law beyond the borders of their settlements. It was the British recognition of this fact that made the Taranaki War, in retrospect, something of a hollow success for the Maoris. Browne, and eventually his successor, George Grey, realized that the imposition of the type of sovereignty they and most of their compatriots considered appropriate in a British colony demanded one essential pre-requisite: the destruction of Kingite power by an invasion of Waikato.

PART THREE

The Waikato War

7

The Invasion of Waikato

I GEORGE GREY AND THE PREPARATIONS FOR WAR

AFTER THE TARANAKI WAR, IT SEEMED CLEAR TO BROWNE that the Kingites had to be compelled to submit to British rule. He sent an ultimatum to the Movement's leaders, and when it was rejected, he decided to invade the Waikato.[1] Though many settlers agreed that this was necessary, the more perceptive among them felt that the resources were not available. Browne remained determined. Then, like FitzRoy and for similar reasons, he was dismissed and replaced by Grey.

Grey arrived in September 1861, and promptly suspended Browne's invasion plan. For the next year and a half, it seemed as if a new war might be avoided. Then in March 1863, Grey went to Taranaki and re-occupied the Tataraimaka block, held by the Maoris as a hostage for Waitara. There was no resistance. During April Grey made preparations to return Waitara to the Maoris, but, on 4 May, thirty Taranaki and Ngati Ruanui ambushed and killed nine soldiers at Oakura, near Tataraimaka. Despite this, the Waitara purchase was renounced on 11 May. On 4 June, the new British commander, Lieutenant-General Duncan Cameron, with 870 troops, attacked and defeated a party of Maoris at Katikara, on the Tataraimaka block, killing twenty-four. Like Mahoetahi this British victory was grossly exaggerated. The Maori force was only fifty strong, and its defeat was therefore not major.[2] More as a result of other factors than of this engagement, the Taranaki theatre then became virtually dormant. The bulk of the troops were shifted to Auckland and the scene changed to Waikato. On 11 July, alleging Kingite instigation of the Oakura ambush and a 'determined and bloodthirsty' plot to attack Auckland, Grey ordered the invasion of Kingite territory. The ensuing conflict lasted for fifteen months, and was the largest and most important of the New Zealand Wars.

Grey's conduct in the period between the Taranaki and Waikato Wars is as confusing to historians as it was to his superiors at the Colonial Office. However, two main strands are discernible: a 'peace policy' and a 'war policy'. The first is sometimes seen as an effort to solve the problems bequeathed by Browne through peaceful measures. The second consisted in active preparations for an effective invasion of Waikato.

Grey's peace policy included a scheme for Maori local administration—known as the 'new institutions'—and the return of the Waitara block.

Introduced in November 1861, the former measure was based on Maori co-operation, and it was hoped that the Maoris would welcome it. Some did, using it as a supplement to traditional forms of local government, and rejecting aspects they did not like. The 'new institutions' scheme has been variously described as a mere blind to conceal preparations for war; as a token attempt to implement Colonial Office policy, to which Grey 'never attached any real importance'; and as a genuine effort to secure the submission of the King Movement—an effort which, as late as April 1863, Grey was convinced would succeed.[3] It may be that Grey sincerely hoped the scheme would wean Maoris away from the King Movement by providing an alternative local administration in which they could participate. But the 'new institutions' may also have been an integral part of his preparations for war. As Grey was well aware, a major problem facing a successful invasion of Waikato was that hostilities in other districts could divert troops. The risk could be reduced by attaching uncommitted Maoris to the government through such things as the new institutions scheme. From the outset, Grey acknowledged to his superiors at the Colonial Office that this was his aim, at least in part. The new institutions would utilize 'the present intermission in military operations' to 'reduce the number of our enemies'.[4]

Perhaps the return of Waitara was intended to have a similar effect. There are signs that Grey arranged with the local Maoris to trade Waitara for Tataraimaka, thus liquidating the Taranaki liability, and freeing his resources for Waikato.[5] But he delayed fulfilling his part of the bargain, while trying to persuade the Colonial Ministry to take joint responsibility for the move. Some Maoris assumed that he had reneged on the deal, and mounted the Oakura ambush. Yet, by returning Waitara anyway, Grey partially achieved his aim. After Katikara, the Taranaki theatre became quiescent. The British garrison, soon reduced to less than 700 men, mounted a few expeditions, and their commander sometimes attempted to elevate these into significant successes. But there was very little fighting, and for much of the time until April 1864, the local Maoris were 'perfectly quiet'.[6] It seems inappropriate to describe these sporadic operations as 'The Second Taranaki War', and their low intensity might be credited to Grey's 'peace policy'.

All this casts Grey's activities in a very poor light, implying that he planned the Waikato War well in advance. Yet this conclusion seems difficult to avoid, and it does not necessarily mean that Grey was some kind of in-human warmonger—though he could certainly have taught Machiavelli a trick or two in methodology. Grey had some real empathy with the Maoris, and he deplored vulgar racial prejudice directed against them. But he also believed them to be 'a semi-barbarous race, puffed up with the pride of an imagined equality'.[7] Like many of his contemporaries, he considered that the Maoris' only chance of advancement, even of survival, lay in submission to substantive British sovereignty, and amalgamation with the settlers. During his first governorship, he felt that this was indeed happening, slowly but surely. During his second, the King Movement presented a solid obstacle

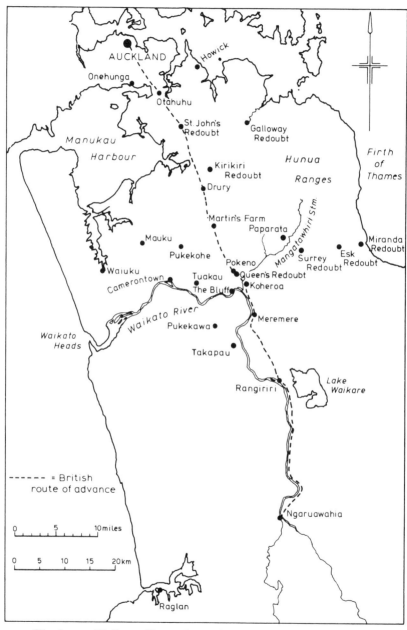

The Lower Waikato, illustrating early phases of the Waikato War
(Chapters 7–8)

which had to be removed. No doubt Grey would have preferred to remove it by peaceful means, but it is very hard to believe that he considered this realistic after about the middle of 1862.[8] Grey's 'peace policy' might better be described as his indirect preparations for war.

Grey's war policy, his direct preparations for war, is of considerable importance to the following chapters. His perception of the resources required for an effective invasion of Waikato, and his success in acquiring them, was to have a profound effect on the course of the war and on the development of race relations in New Zealand.

An invasion of Waikato was clearly the logical way to go about destroying Kingite power. The economic bases of the core Kingite tribes were located in the Upper Waikato, around Matamata, Hangatiki, and Rangiaowhia. It was reasonable to assume that the Maoris would feel compelled to fight for these, and so expose themselves to decisive defeat. Though the British sometimes played up the difficulty of the terrain, for the same reasons that had applied in Taranaki, the Waikato basin was perhaps the best district in the North Island for European-style military operations. In comparison to the scene of some Victorian campaigns it was 'as level as a bowling green and as smooth as a drawing room floor'.[9] This meant that the British might catch the Maoris in the open even before the invading army reached the Upper Waikato, and so achieve the quick decision which was universally preferred. The existence of the navigable Waikato River was equally important. Water carriage had a far greater capacity than land carriage, and for a substantial part of the route into the Waikato the British could use the river for supply and, to some extent, for the transport of troops.

These geographical factors meant that an advance into Waikato, in contrast to the sporadic British forays of earlier wars, could actually be an invasion proper: a continuous offensive. Moreover, it would be directed against a target of great value to the Maoris, and it would be large in scale. The 'shift-system' which kept a Maori force semi-permanently in the field in Taranaki would therefore be extremely difficult to repeat, and great pressure would be placed on tribal economies and manpower.

But the geographical situation could only be exploited with the appropriate resources. These consisted, first, in a logistical system which could supply an invading army without pause. In practice, this subdivided into a commissariat organization, a road from Auckland to the Waikato, and vessels for the river. For large-scale transport against the current some of these vessels had to be steamers, which could tow supplementary barges. The second crucial resource was manpower. A sufficient force had to be available from the outset to operate and protect the supply system, and to provide a striking force, or 'column of attack'. Beyond this, a continuing inflow of reinforcements would be required to hold the ground gained, and to provide extra logistical support as the line of communications lengthened. The larger the force, the greater the chance of quick victory.

Grey's measures in the period September 1861–July 1863 prove that he rapidly grasped the need for these prerequisites of successful invasion. This,

rather than his much over-rated combat achievements, provides the best
evidence of his military abilities. But to realize what was needed was one
thing; to obtain it was another. Most of the men and much of the money and
equipment had to come from the Imperial Government, and it is difficult to
imagine a government more reluctant to part with such resources than that
of Britain in the early 1860s.

Outside Britain and India, the Imperial Government had about 41,000
troops. This was insufficient to fulfill its responsibilities in any coherent
way, and Imperial defence 'policy' essentially consisted in 'fire-fighting':
sending reinforcements to trouble-spots once war had broken out. Browne
had acquired his troops for the Taranaki War on this basis: he got his army
by beginning his war. Grey, on the other hand, wanted his army before his
war commenced; and however rational this may sound, it was an extremely
ambitious aspiration in the context of Imperial defence in the 1860s. It was
made more so by strong pressure in England for colonial self-defence, by
the French, American, and Russian war-scares of the period, and by the
extreme sensitivity of the Imperial Parliament to military expenditure.

Influenced largely by these factors, and perhaps also by humanitarian
considerations, the Imperial Government opposed invading the Waikato to
force the Kingites to submit. Grey had been appointed to effect 'peace and
good understanding between the two races'. The 'armed forces should not
be used for the mere purpose of extracting from the Maoris a verbal renun-
ciation of the so-called Maori King'. Far from being willing to increase the
forces in New Zealand, the Secretary of State for the Colonies expected 'a
speedy and considerable diminution' in those already there.[10] In sum, Grey
had the will to invade, or at least to place himself in a position to do so effectively, but he did not have the means. The Imperial Government had the
means, but it did not have the will. This happy dilemma might have continued to protect the Maoris indefinitely. But Grey succeeded in retaining
the Taranaki army, in guaranteeing its rapid increase, and in acquiring the
necessary logistical system.

Grey did not so much overcome as circumvent Imperial objections. The
campaign of misinformation involved was extremely complicated, and it is
impossible to go into the details here. The basic tool at Grey's command
was a near monopoly of the flow of information to the Colonial Office. This
was used to create a picture of a tense situation in which Maori aggression
was possible at any time, but which was amenable to a peaceful solution if,
and only if, a sufficient force was provided to act as a defence and a deter-
rent. The Empire was constantly invited to save the pound that renewed
war would cost by spending a penny on prevention. Whenever a reduction
in the existing force in New Zealand was threatened, Grey blocked it by
asserting that it would lead to 'some great disaster', namely renewed war.
To give one of many possible examples, in March 1862, the Australian
governors asked that some of their troops lent for the Taranaki War be
returned. Grey replied that this withdrawal of 300 men from a force of
6,000 'would most probably result in the renewal of hostilities'.[11]

Grey used this argument not only to retain the resources he had, but also to increase them. The most important augmentation was a logistical system. This began with the construction of a road from Drury, just south of Auckland, to the Kingite border in December 1861. A natural corollary was the establishment of a 'Commissariat Transport Corps' to supply the troops working on the road, and steamers to supplement the system were ordered in 1862. Grey argued that the road and its protective redoubts constituted a 'defensible frontier' or 'military front' which would defend the Auckland out-settlers against Maori attack.[12] A number of factors indicate that this was completely untrue, but it is enough to observe that the 'defensible frontier' pointed the wrong way—it ran north-south instead of east-west. It had no defensive function, but on the contrary absorbed resources which could otherwise have been used to provide the Auckland settlements with real protection.

Of course, Grey could still claim that the road, and the body of troops he stationed at the end of it, deterred the Maoris from aggressive action. Allegations of hostile Maori intent were the major element of Grey's misinformation campaign. They functioned both to justify an invasion and to help retain or acquire the resources for it. Historians have concentrated on a particular group of letters forwarded to the Colonial Office immediately before the invasion. Grey offered these as conclusive proof of the Maori intention to attack. Dalton has convincingly discounted this assertion, and one might add that it was only a part of a series dating back to December 1861.[13]

Perhaps the best evidence against Grey's case was the reluctance of the colonists to contribute to their own defence. In 1861-2, the colonial defence vote was £8,031, of which £500 remained unspent, as against an Imperial expenditure of about £400,000 in that year.[14] It was not that the settlers were so mean as to prefer death to expenditure, but that they believed no threat of Maori attack existed. Even after the Oakura ambush, an incident which lent some credibility to Grey's allegations, the Colonial Ministry refused to call out the militia on the grounds that Auckland and Wellington were in no danger.[15] It was not until late June, when Grey convincingly revealed his intention to invade Waikato, that ministers provided their full support.

The refusal to embody the militia after the Oakura ambush almost proved fatal to Grey's attempt to manipulate the Imperial Government. As usual, Grey suppressed the relevant correspondence, but General Cameron forwarded it to London—a rare breach of the Governor's monopoly of information. Grey had applied for three regiments after the outbreak in Taranaki, largely on the basis of an alleged Maori threat to Auckland.[16] The troops had been ordered out, but Cameron's information indicated that the threat did not exist. In a memorandum which has been overlooked by historians, the Duke of Newcastle, Secretary of State for the Colonies, wrote: 'This important and most unsatisfactory correspondence ought clearly to have been sent to the Secretary of State for the Colonies by Sir

George Grey. He did not do so, for fear he should prevent compliance with his applications for more troops. . . . I must say, I think if he had sent it, the reinforcements ought to have been refused. The question—a very difficult one—now is whether the order should be recalled by next mail.'[17] Newcastle decided that the die was now cast and the troops—who were to prove a vital reinforcement—were not recalled. But though he did nothing about it his conclusion was essentially the right one: that the Imperial Government had been tricked into providing 3,000 men for the invasion of Waikato. Grey retained the Taranaki army and acquired his logistical system in much the same way.

Grey's success in obtaining an army from the Imperial Government is a notable example of the influence of the periphery of Empire on the metropolis. In May 1864, the Imperial forces in New Zealand amounted to 12,000 men—more than were available for the defence of England at the time. The decision to commit these troops was taken, not in London, but in Government House, Auckland. Such a situation was by no means unique in the history of the Victorian Empire. It could be argued that Bulwer Lytton with Afghanistan in 1879 and Milner with the Transvaal in 1899, matched Grey's success in manipulating his masters. But for the Maoris, Grey's achievement created a military problem which dwarfed their disadvantages in earlier wars. It remains to examine the character and extent of the disparity in resources.

II THE OPPOSING ARMIES

THE NUMBER OF IMPERIAL TROOPS IN THE WAIKATO WAR IS generally put at 10,000 and it is sometimes suggested that these were supported by a similar number of colonial troops. Many writers give the impression that these forces were available for most of the war. This view has been questioned by B. J. Dalton, who suggests that the number of regulars in New Zealand did not reach 10,000 until 1866, and that with the exception of a brief period in mid-1863, only a few hundred colonial troops were useful to General Cameron.[18] This difference of opinion reflects a contemporary debate which also influenced many other aspects of the interpretation of the war. The colonists liked to supplement their criticism of the military by alleging the misuse of large resources. Defenders of the military leadership, on the other hand, tended to 'round down' the numbers available in an effort to maximize the army's achievements.

Both sets of figures are misleading. On 11 July 1863, there were less than 4,000 troops in Auckland Province available for the invasion. But Grey's measures and the endeavours of the colonial government ensured a continuous and rapid increase until an Auckland peak of about 14,000 effective troops was reached in March 1864. Of these, over 4,000 were colonial, 9,000 were Imperial, and a few hundred were pro-British Maoris, or

'Queenites' in contemporary parlance. The magic number of 10,000 Imperial regulars in New Zealand as a whole was reached in January 1864, when the last of ten regiments arrived.[19] Drafts for these units, a third battery of artillery, and a battalion of the Military Train brought the total for New Zealand to 11,355 by 1 May 1864.[20] The naval brigade, which often acted as an élite infantry unit, should be included in any assessment of Imperial strength. The peak Imperial commitment was therefore nearly 12,000 men, of whom three-quarters were effective and serving in Waikato. The total mobilization—men who served in the British forces at some time or another—was in the order of 18,000 men.

The colonial forces fell into three categories: two small permanent corps, the Colonial Defence Force (cavalry) and the Forest Rangers; the Waikato Militia or 'Military Settlers'; and the Auckland Militia and Volunteers. The Forest Rangers and Colonial Defence Force rarely had more than 200 men serving in Waikato between them although, once trained, their specialist character made them more useful than their numbers imply. The Waikato Militia were recruited largely from the Australian and Otago goldfields and paid by the colonial government. After a period of full-time service, they were to be additionally rewarded from the confiscation of Kingite land—a measure which the government optimistically hoped would make the war pay for itself. The total number of Waikato Militia rose rapidly from about 300 in early September 1863 to 4,000 early in 1864. Colonial returns tended to exaggerate the number effective, but the remarks of Imperial officers show that the number useful for some kind of service rose from over 1,000 in October 1863 to perhaps 3,600 in April 1864.[21] There was a similar colonial tendency to inflate the effective strength of the Auckland Militia and Volunteers, but in August 1863 there were 1,650 on active and useful service (from a paper strength of over 3,000).[22] Thereafter the number declined steadily as more Waikato Militia became available.

With one or two exceptions, the Queenite contribution to the British war-effort was negligible. For most of the war the British were supported only by a small minority of Waikato proper, and this was reduced by the defection of the Ngati Whauroa *hapu* to the Kingites on 7 September 1863. From March 1864, to the east of Waikato, a majority of the Arawa confederation supported the British, for the particular purpose of denying their Ngati Porou neighbours free passage over their territory.

The British forces performed three basic roles during the Waikato War. All three functions involved some danger and all were shared by Imperial infantry, whom no one could deny were 'effectives'. The first was the transport of supplies through the war zone. This task was undertaken by the Commissariat Transport Corps assisted by sailors and the Waikato Queenites. The second role was the protection of the communications system. The number of troops devoted to this depended on Maori action. The third role, forming the column of attack, may seem the most important but in a sense it had the lowest priority. The supply system had to be manned and protected before the column of attack could exist.

The commander of these forces, Lieutenant-General Duncan Cameron, fared very badly at the hands of contemporary writers, and his competence, though not his moral character, has made an equally unfavourable impression on most historians. Cameron shared the preconceptions of his peers, and he fitted some of the stereotypes of his profession, but in reality he was an unusually able commander. He was thorough and cautious, yet capable of bold initiatives when the situation warranted them. He showed more flexibility and willingness to learn than other British commanders in New Zealand. General Colin Campbell, Lord Clyde, reportedly considered him to be 'the finest soldier in England' and in other circumstances he might well have ranked with Wolseley and Roberts among Victorian generals. The parallel is reinforced by the calibre of Cameron's staff. D. J. Gamble, the quartermaster-general, H. Stanley Jones, the commissary-general, Robert Carey, the adjutant-general, James Mouat, the Principal Medical Officer, and such staff officers as W. H. St. Hill and G. R. Greaves, were all capable and energetic men. Gamble, in particular, was 'a most zealous officer and one of rare business abilities'.[23]

Cameron and most of his staff had served in the Crimean War, and they were determined to avoid a repetition of that logistical fiasco. The ordinary supply difficulties of a campaign in Waikato were not inconsiderable, despite the advantages offered by the river and the relatively favourable terrain. As Martin van Creveld has pointed out, armies lacking railways generally relied on the war zone for their supplies, more often through local contracts than plunder, and the *ad hoc* character of commissariat organization reflected this.[24] But Auckland settlement could supply only a fraction of the army's needs and the Waikato district could supply less. Most requisites had to be imported from England and Australia, and then transported up to 100 miles into the interior—a process which sometimes required a dozen changes in types of carriage.[25] These basic problems of supply—difficulties which did not involve Maori action—were tackled by the British with complete success. Men complained about the size of the pickle ration, and at one point some Waikato Militia were reportedly left 'in a shameful state of semi-nudity', but no soldier ever starved in Waikato, and the sick-rate never exceeded five per cent.[26] The efforts of Cameron and his staff were one key to this, and their success makes it clear that the British learned something from the Crimea. The other key consisted in Grey's preparations. The transport services were greatly expanded during the war, but the corps created in 1862 to supply the road building was the vital kernel. As one senior commissariat officer put it: 'To the previously existing nucleus of the Commissariat Transport Corps I attribute in a marked degree, the success which has attended all the arrangements of this campaign. It was the foundation of the whole service.'[27] Grey's preparations and the talents of Cameron and his staff ensured that as far as natural obstacles were concerned the British invasion ran like a well-oiled machine. The campaign was one of the best-prepared and best-organized ever undertaken by the British army.

The estimate of Kingite military strength now accepted by historians is an integral part of a generally unfavourable assessment of the efficiency of both the King Movement and the Maori war effort in Waikato. The Movement, it is said, derived such unity as it had from traditional alliances. It 'had little real political coherence and no effective institutions for co-operative action'. Maori courage and fort-building skill 'were not matched by strategic sense . . . the tribes fought for the most part each in defence of its own territory with little co-operation from others'. Historians frequently imply that no great fraction of Maori manpower was mobilized. 'At the highest, a total of about 2000 Maoris were prepared to take up arms.'[28]

The Maori war effort is very difficult to assess with any degree of precision. The questions involved are complicated in themselves, and are closely connected with wider questions about Maori society which cannot be dealt with here. The paucity of Maori evidence is also a problem. Yet it is possible to demonstrate that the received version misrepresents such facts as are available.

Of about twenty-six major North Island tribal groups, no less than fifteen are known to have sent contingents to Waikato. Apart from the Ngati Maniapoto, Ngati Haua, and Waikato proper tribes, these included Ngati Paoa, Ngati Kahungunu, Tuhoe, Ngati Tuwharetoa and Ngati Raukawa (of the North Taupo region). They also included Ngati Porou, Ngai-te-Rangi, Whakatohea, Ngati Maru, Taranaki, Wanganui, and one or two sub-tribes of the Arawa confederation. In addition to these fifteen, Whanau-a-Apanui, Ngati Awa, and Rongowhakaata were involved in the Tauranga Campaign, and probably also sent men to Waikato. Some Atiawa and Ngati Ruanui probably also served, under the general heading of the Taranaki tribes, and a few certainly did. Only six tribal groups—Rarawa, Ngapuhi, Ngati Whatua, Ngarauru, and the mixed tribes of the Wellington and Manawatu regions—had little or no known involvement, and at least a few Ngati Raukawa of the last-named region did join their relatives in Waikato.[29] Since operations were primarily confined to two tribal districts in Waikato and Tauranga, it is clear that most Maoris fought for something other than the direct defence of their own territory. It is equally clear that the breadth of Kingite support has been grossly under-rated.

The great majority of tribes contributed to the Waikato war effort in one way or another, but the implications of this should not be exaggerated. Tribal support was always qualified in one or more ways. The tribal entity itself was seldom politically cohesive. The decision to fight might be taken by a single *hapu* and did not necessarily reflect the feelings of the tribe as a whole. Waikato proper and the Arawa confederation each had some *hapu* supporting the British, while others were fully committed to the Maori King. But this extreme division was less common than the situation in which a proportion of warriors went off to fight for the King while the rest remained at home and fought no one. Though there were exceptions, such as Ngati Porou, the active proportion generally decreased as the distance from the front increased. No doubt the degree of commitment to the Kingite cause contributed to this, as did a sense of the immediacy of the threat presented by the invasion of Waikato.

But there were other factors. To despatch warriors to Waikato from afar increased supply difficulties, multiplied the loss of labour to the tribal economy, and was believed to expose the tribal homeland to British attack. Some tribes restricted the size of their contingents for these reasons, rather than from any lack of commitment to the Kingite cause. One Thames chief, in denying that he had sent warriors to fight in Waikato, expressed his feelings with a song about 'a married lady accused of a liaison with her lover, she acknowledges the inclination but denies the act'.[30] Moreover, neutrality at home and hostility at the front had certain advantages for the Maori war effort, just as it had had in Taranaki. One of the few Europeans to realize this was John Gorst, author of a contemporary analysis of the King Movement. 'All the tribes of New Zealand either supported or sympathised with the Waikatos. That all have not actually risen in arms against us is no proof to the contrary; for one Maori tribe can carry on the war better, if other tribes remain neutral and furnish supplies.'[31] 'Neutrality' is not an entirely appropriate term because most of the tribes supporting the King Movement sent fighting contingents. But it is quite true that a filter of 'neutral' tribes around the war zone not only improved the capacity of the neutrals to support their own contingents, but also provided a vital source of supplies, particularly ammunition, for the tribes within the war zone.[32] With their own trade with Auckland at a standstill, the Waikatos must have relied heavily on this source. The system of neutral areas feeding the war zone did not work as well as in Taranaki, because the Waikato War was much larger in scale, but it did help to prolong the Maori resistance.

The most basic limitations on the size and duration of tribal contributions in men were shared by tribes both within and without the war zone. All tribes were subject to the same economic and social constraints. Except for the briefest of periods, many warriors had to remain at home to help sustain the tribal economy, and individuals had to return to look to their domestic affairs after a spell at the front. The general pattern was therefore the familiar one of a constant turnover of personnel—small groups came and went all the time. But to have any chance of opposing the huge British army effectively, the Maoris had to over-extend the Taranaki shift system. On three occasions the Maoris assembled armies of between 1,000 and 2,000 men and maintained them for three months: at Meremere (August-October 1863), at Paterangi (December 1863-February 1864) and at Hangatiki and Maungatautari (April-June 1864). The strains of supply and lost labour were so great that each of these concentrations had to be followed by dispersal, and these cycles had an important effect on operations.

These two patterns—the constant departure and replacement of small groups and the cycles of concentration and dispersal—meant that Maori strength at any one time substantially understated the total mobilization. It is quite true that the peak Maori strength at one time and place was about

2,000 warriors (Paterangi, January 1864), but of course this number reflected a higher turnover. An overlap in personnel between the three armies certainly existed—it was this which made the strain so great—but it was far from complete. Each army included warriors who had not served in either of the others. Furthermore, some hundreds of warriors who had not served in any of the great armies fought in the Tauranga Campaign, which was an integral part of the Waikato War. It is therefore safe to conclude that the total Maori mobilization was not 2,000 but at least 4,000 warriors. This excludes the men involved in the sporadic and muted operations in Taranaki. If one in four of the total Maori population of the North Island was a warrior, then 4,000 men represents something like one-third of the total available manpower.

Methods of supply, recruitment, and command are more difficult to assess than numbers. It is true that Maori organization was informal and unstructured. But the absence of European forms of organization does not mean that organization *per se* was absent. A Maori conference had no chairman, no agenda, and no vote, but it could reach a consensus and act on it. All that can be said about Maori logistics here is that large numbers of men were clearly fed for substantial periods during which they produced very little themselves. At Paterangi, the Maori army was supplied from the rich agricultural district nearby, but even here the collection, distribution, and transport of provisions required some degree of organization. There is no way in which the Meremere army could have been supplied from the locality, and we can be certain that this concentration demanded the transport of hundreds of tons of food and ammunition over long distances. These goods were probably carried by canoe, and in this sphere the Waikato River was as important to the Maoris as it was to the British.

Recruits often set off for the front on their own initiative, and were replaced on an *ad hoc* basis. On some occasions a tribal meeting decided who should go and who should stay.[33] But there was some attempt to encourage and regulate recruitment by the Kingite leadership. Senior Kingite chiefs wrote to, or visited, tribes outside the war zone in an effort to spur recruitment. On 3 October 1863, the King's Council issued a circular 'to all the tribes' requesting that one-fifth of all warriors should come to Waikato.[34] This rare surviving document may indicate the existence of others, and it is by no means impossible that the request was complied with by some tribes.

As for leadership, examination of the Battle of Orakau will show that the Maoris did suffer from some of the problems associated with unstructured and divided command. But as a general rule, they followed a coherent and consistent strategic plan. This involved the construction of a series of defensive lines sited to obstruct the British advance. These shared most of the technical characteristics of other modern *pa*, but they were far larger than their predecessors. Except for Rangiriri they were groups of fortifications rather than single *pa*. The Paterangi Line dwarfed even Te Arei, the largest *pa* of the Taranaki War, and the Pukekawa-Meremere-Paparata Line was fourteen miles long. Clearly, the construction of such fortifications required a united and well-organized effort, and this, together with the consistency of the Maori strategy, indicates that some sort of central command existed.

It is not easy to say what form this took, or how the relevant command decisions were reached. Some Europeans felt that such minimal central leadership as they could discern emanated from councils—perhaps the King's Council, drawn from the King's own tribe and visiting chiefs. It is equally likely, however, that one or two respected chiefs informally persuaded others to consent to their plans. All sources give the impression that two Maori leaders were particularly influential during the war: Wiremu Tamehana and Rewi Maniapoto. Tamehana is rightly considered the outstanding figure of his time in terms of personal ethics and statesman-like qualities. He was also a respected and competent general, but his deep Christian antipathy to violence may sometimes have affected his military judgement.

Rewi, leader of the so-called 'extremist' Kingites, was a more realistic individual. At an early point in Grey's governorship, Rewi had concluded that the British intended to invade Waikato in any circumstances short of a voluntary abandonment of the King Movement. It is possible that he was quite right. He advocated defensive preparations but was able to carry out very few in the face of Tamehana's opposition. Whatever the vagaries of his subsequent political career, in 1863-4 the Maoris had enormous respect for Rewi's military talents. He was too young to have established a general's reputation in the Musket Wars, and it is therefore reasonable to assume that he did so in the Taranaki War. It may be that Rewi played a leading role in formulating the Maori strategy in both Taranaki and Waikato. Like Cameron, Rewi could be both cautious and bold, but he showed a deeper understanding of the enemy military system than any of his opponents. It seems that there was a third, less well-known, leading Kingite general: Tikaokao of Ngati Maniopoto. Tikaokao apparently had a very impressive record in the Taranaki War, and in October 1863 he was 'elected general' of the Kingite army. There is no evidence of friction between Rewi and Tikaokao, and it may be that the latter acted as a kind of chief of staff.[35]

The Maori war effort in Waikato must be judged on two separate but compatible criteria: first, in relation to earlier levels of Maori social efficiency in its military application and, second, in relation to the task in hand—opposing the British. In the first context, the Maori war effort was nothing short of a staggering achievement. The mobilization of one-third of the available warriors, and the maintenance of an average of perhaps one-ninth in the field, was comparable to some European mobilizations. It is probable that a higher proportion of Maoris fought for the King in Waikato than did Americans for the Revolution in the War of Independence. In relation to previous Maori war efforts and to traditions of tribal disunity and individual independence, this was a remarkable performance.

Traditional factors had some influence on the degree of unity achieved. Some warriors of the Taupo and Tauranga districts may have come to fight in Waikato partly because of links of kinship with Rewi and Tamehana.

The four Waikato tribes were connected through legends of shared descent from the crew of one immigrant canoe. But an alliance in which two-thirds of the tribes were represented cannot be explained by traditional factors alone. Kingite tribes had fought bitter wars amongst themselves before 1835, and the Maoris traditionally retained old grievances to the point where eternal feuds were common. Even among the Waikato tribes, at the highest level, good traditional grounds for feud existed. In his pagan youth, Tamehana had led a war party which killed a near relation of Kings Potatau and Tawhiao.[36] Thus in terms of Maori custom, the King could well have been at war with the Kingmaker. From this level down, traditional enmities were transcended more often than traditional alliances were invoked. Bishop William Williams noted this factor with surprise when referring to the participation of several East Coast tribes in the war.

> The fact that the East Cape natives have joined in this war is not to be accounted for upon any ordinary practice of the New Zealanders. There is no recognized connexion between them and the Waikato, but the reverse. The natives of this coast used to say two years ago, when first asked to join the Waikatos 'Have we forgotten how Waikato treated us years ago? According to our custom, should we not rather rejoice to hear that they were killed by the white people?' But now, not only have they been stirred up to go, but some too have gone, whom I should least have expected to take such a step.[37]

In relation to the traditional scene, the Maori war effort in Waikato was characterized by efficiency rather than inefficiency and by unity rather than disunity. It may be that our understanding of the King Movement and of the question of Maori nationalism needs to be re-examined in the light of this.

On the second criterion—comparison with the opposing forces—Kingite power was much less impressive. The total British mobilization was about 18,000 men, or 150 per cent of the number of Maori warriors in the whole North Island. Against 18,000 men, even 4,000 did not amount to much, and to compare mobilization figures is to understate the real disparity. The Maoris' sole advantage was that they were able to approach their peak field strength more rapidly than the British. For the first two months of the war they were outnumbered only four to one. After this, the disparity mounted until it reached ten to one, and the superior British capacity to keep troops in the field also came into play. The Maoris came remarkably close to maintaining a substantial force permanently in the field—roughly nine months out of twelve—but they did not come close enough. With their ability to mount a continuous offensive, the British were able to take advantage of the periods when the Maori armies dispersed. The Kingites succeeded in mobilizing an unpredecented proportion of their resources, but these did not compare with those available to the British. It may be that Maori disadvantages were as much a result of hard demographic fact as of inferior social efficiency. There were simply a lot more British than there were Maoris. But whatever the explanation may have been, the most fundamental feature of the Waikato War was the vast British superiority in numbers.

Against this background, the Waikato War of 1863-4 can best be understood as a rhythm of British initiative and Maori response, which was repeated four times. Each British initiative involved one or more attempts to bring the Maoris to battle and to crush them decisively. On three occasions, the British sought to do this by advancing up the Waikato and forcing the Maoris to fight in defence of their homes. The Kingites sought to check them by building great lines of defence—at Meremere in August 1863, at Rangiriri in November 1863, and at Paterangi in January 1864. The fourth cycle of the war, in Tauranga on the east coast of Waikato, also involved a British effort to secure decisive victory, but otherwise it followed a strategic pattern of its own.

III THE WAR BEHIND THE FRONT

ON 9 JULY 1863, GOVERNOR GREY ORDERED THAT ALL MAORIS living between the Waikato and Auckland should be expelled south of the river unless they took an oath of allegiance to Queen Victoria. Three days later, General Cameron and the first echelon of the invading army crossed the Mangatawhiri stream—the tributary of the Waikato which marked the northern Kingite border. On 17 July, Cameron moved a short distance south from his advanced camp and attacked and defeated a Maori force at Koheroa. Though this action was greatly over-rated by the British, it could realistically be seen as a promising beginning to the vigorous advance up the Waikato which was intended to destroy the main Kingite forces and so finish the war quickly. Yet it was not until 31 October—no less than three and a half months later—that the British renewed their southward march. The colonists attributed 'this most serious, and, as it seemed to us, almost fatal delay' to the incompetence and lack of foresight of the General and to the tendency to pamper the troops. William Fox quoted an Imperial officer as instructing a patrol commander 'to be sure [to] have his men back to tea, for the evenings were getting cool'. Cameron and his supporters blamed the delay on ordinary logistical problems, the difficult nature of the terrain, and the government's mishandling of the expulsion of the Lower Waikato Maoris.[38]

A basic assumption behind both these views, and an important part of the generally unfavourable assessment of the Maori war effort in Waikato, was the notion that the Kingites made little attempt to hamper British communications in this period. Such Maori activity as there was between Auckland and 'the Front' was commonly seen as unco-ordinated and strategically pointless revenge raiding by young Maoris living north of Waikato, who had been expelled from their homes after 9 July. This assumption has been accepted by some historians. The Kingites, writes B. J. Dalton, made 'no serious attempt to use their superior mobility in order to interfere with the troops' highly vulnerable communications'.[39] The evidence points to a different conclusion.

The British advance was held up before it had properly begun by Maori strategic action, based partly on a defensive line centred on Meremere. The Meremere Line included positions at Pukekawa in the west and Paparata in the east as well as Meremere proper. The Line was manned by the first of the great concentrations of warriors. This provided a force fluctuating certainly between 900 and 2,000 men and probably between 1,100 and 1,500.[40] The Line was not completed until late August. Once complete, it was strong but not impregnable. A sufficiently large force, sufficiently well-equipped with boats, could be split into two independently powerful divisions. One could outflank Meremere by the river and attack it from the rear, while the other held the Maoris in front. It did not take long for this possibility to occur to Cameron, and by early August he had the resources to attempt it. Two crucial questions obviously arise from this. Why did Cameron allow the Maoris to complete the Meremere Line, and why did he fail to move against it until 31 October?

The events of 17 July set both the historiographical and historical patterns for the opening phase of the Waikato invasion. In the first of the two actions fought on that day, Cameron with 553 men attacked a Maori force which had just begun to entrench at Koheroa. The British were checked by the Maori fire and began to falter. Cameron rushed twenty yards in front of his men and urged them on. They rallied, renewed their advance, and carried the 'partly formed' rifle pits. The Maoris withdrew slowly until they reached a ravine, then fled. The British hailed the engagement as a great victory. They claimed that the Maoris numbered 300 to 400 men or even more, and casualty estimates went as high as 150, against twelve British killed and wounded.[41] In fact there were no more than 150 Maoris, and there may have been as few as 100.[42] These men were drawn from local tribes, and may simply have been intended as an observation patrol. Five Maori sources confirm that only fourteen or fifteen warriors were killed.[43]

Cameron deserves credit for his promptitude and courage, but this was clearly a minor action. The emphasis on it obscured the far greater strategic significance of a tactically comparable Maori victory which occurred the same day, well behind the British lines. A *taua* of Ngati Paoa warriors attacked a convoy and its escort at Martin's Farm, about halfway between Drury and Queen's Redoubt on the Great South Road. The British were 'overpowered by numbers' and pursued down the road towards Drury. The convoy and escort were eventually rescued by other British units but not before they had lost some horses, several carts and sixteen men killed and wounded—one-third of the escort's strength.[44] The Maoris lost one or two men killed.[45] In terms of Kingite morale, this victory counter-balanced the defeat at Koheroa—a parallel which the received version fails to recognize—but this was as nothing compared to the strategic effect. The attack indicated that the Maoris intended 'to hover in the long belt of bush which covers the Hunua and Pokeno Ranges, and so threaten the General's communications between the Queen's Redoubt and Auckland'. This necessitated increased protection for the British supply route 'and to effect this a chain of military posts was formed along the Great South Road'. These five new redoubts were garrisoned by 510 men. The cost of Martin's Farm to the British was not sixteen men to the total effective strength but 510 men to the column of attack.[46]

Furthermore, this action was only the first of a series. Settlers were killed and wounded in four attacks in July, and each of these raids necessitated a British rescue patrol. On one occasion, near Kirikiri on 22 July, one of these patrols was ambushed in turn, and the rescuers themselves had to be rescued.[47] The total of six Maori attacks between 17 and 30 July involved twenty-seven British casualties, two of whom were harmless old people. The six attacks in which blood was shed were only the tip of the iceberg. Shots were exchanged on other occasions, and even reports of Maori raiders had to be investigated by British patrols. As one British staff officer put it: 'From this day [17 July] the enemy set to work in characteristic fashion. They attacked all weakly defended posts, the convoys on the road, murdered isolated settlers and infested the bush like so many wild animals. Calls for military assistance came from all parts.'[48]

The net effect was to tie up most of Cameron's manpower. On 30 July, the general wrote: 'the bush is now so infested with these natives that I have been obliged to establish strong posts along our line of communication, which absorbs so large a portion of the force that until I receive reinforcements it is impossible for me to advance further up the Waikato.'[49] Cameron's forces were not sufficiently increased until late August and it was this delay which enabled the Maoris to suspend their raiding operations and concentrate their energies on completing the Meremere Line.

By late August the British army had been increased from the initial 4,000 to 6,000 effective men. Cameron now had the armoured steamer *Avon* and enough boats, barges, and canoes to take a force up the Waikato and land it south of Meremere. He was therefore in a position to think of renewing the invasion, despite the now considerable strength of the Meremere Line. But the Kingites had constructed the Line with the renewal of their own aggressive raiding campaign in mind. The central position at Meremere was flanked by Pukekawa in the west and Paparata in the east. Originally simple camps for the July raiding parties, these two *pa* did more than simply strengthen Meremere proper.

Pukekawa. . . . and the line of country it secured . . . enabled them [the Maoris] to cross the Waikato where and when they chose, effecting diversions in our rear, and carrying war into the settled districts near Auckland. . . . Nor was the Paparata *pa* of less consequence to the enemy. If Pukekawa protected his left flank and nullified the effects of our posts on the river, Paparata protected the right flank of his central position at Meremere, and gave him the run of the extensive tract of country lying between the Thames and Wairoa.[50]

From one of these bases, on 25 August, the Maoris renewed the war behind the front with 'a determined and unexpected attack' on a party of troops, again near Martin's Farm.[51] This action inaugurated a renewal of the raiding campaign which continued throughout September and October and dwarfed the July offensive. Again, the British were paralysed. The dozens of small actions fought in these months were principally important in their collective effect, but one operation, occurring on 7 September, requires more detailed treatment.

In mid-August, the British had established a supplementary line of supply utilizing the Waikato River. Provisions were brought from Onehunga to the Waikato Heads by steamer, then transferred to canoes and paddled upriver to Queen's Redoubt by the pro-British warriors of chiefs Te Wheoro and Waata Kukutai. A protective redoubt at Tuakau, garrisoned by a detachment of Imperial regulars, and an intermediate depot at Camerontown, guarded by more pro-British Maoris, formed vital parts of the system. The whole operation was directed by James Armitage, the resident magistrate of Lower Waikato. This system cut out fifteen miles of difficult overland cartage from Drury to Queen's Redoubt, it utilized the greater carrying capacity of water transport, and because the pro-British Maoris were prepared to provide most of the labour, it made few inroads into Cameron's own strained manpower resources. In all it was vastly preferable to the alternative route, and may well have become the main British line of supply. Cameron and his staff were well aware of these advantages and they greatly appreciated the services of the Queenites.[52]

Once it became apparent that the route was to be a major part of the British system of supply, the Kingites decided to destroy it. From their base at Pukekawa, a party of about 100 warriors, mostly Ngati Maniapoto, launched a surprise attack on Camerontown on the morning of 7 September. Armitage was returning downriver with a convoy on that day, and he co-incidentally decided to go on ahead himself to borrow an extra canoe. Around 8 a.m. he stopped at Camerontown. The Ngati Maniapoto *taua* were hidden in the bush near the river-bank, perhaps waiting for the convoy to arrive and augment their catch, but when Armitage and four of his assistants began to re-embark, they sprang their ambush. They killed the five men, and then attacked the depot and its protecting *pa*. As their subsequent defection proved, the garrison of Camerontown, men of the Ngati Whauroa *hapu*, were rather luke-warm Queenites and they put up little resistance. Colonist writers saw this as confirmation of their suspicion that the 'so-called friendly natives' were all Kingites at heart, and it was generally believed that the Ngati Maniapoto took Camerontown without much of a fight.[53] But it seems clear that more Queenites, probably the men of Armitage's convoy, came up after the flight of Ngati Whauroa and engaged Ngati Maniapoto. The course and casualties of this second action are unknown, but it involved a quarter-hour of heavy firing, and it is clear that Ngati Maniapoto had the better of it. They burned the depot and its protecting *pa* together with over forty tons of commissariat stores.[54]

These events attracted far less public attention than their sequel. The troops at Tuakau were informed of the attack by escaping Queenites and a detachment of fifty men moved out to the rescue. They overheard the Ngati Maniapoto 'laughing and chattering' in the bush near Camerontown, and concluded 'that they were all drunk' on captured rum. The British commander ordered a charge, expecting to surprise and rout his intoxicated foes. Instead the British were themselves surprised. The Captain's order to charge 'had scarcely passed his lips when, as if by enchantment, the whole bush was lighted up with a terrific volley'.[55] Both officers and several men fell and the rest of the troops beat a hasty retreat. Ngati Maniapoto had been feigning drunkenness, and were 'in reality on the qui vive'.[56] The British were hunted through the bush until nightfall, but they were competently led by Colour-Sergeant McKenna, and Ngati Maniapoto, fighting their third action of the day, wished to minimize their losses and did not press home their attacks. Consequently the troops escaped with only nine casualties.[57]

To the extent that these events made any impact on the interpretation of the war, the last action was seen as by far the most important episode. Of this in turn, the most significant feature appeared to be that after both officers had fallen, a mere sergeant had led the men to safety. There is no doubt that Sergeant McKenna behaved well, but the over-riding emphasis on his deeds was misplaced. For one thing, the Ngati Maniapoto feat in winning three victories in one day—let alone in demonstrating considerable acting ability—surely matches McKenna's judicious flight. The fair distribution of laurels, however, is less important than the recognition of the real importance of the events of 7 September. This, of course, was the destruction of the Waikato Heads supply system. After noting how cheap and effective the system was, a British commissariat officer regretfully observed that the attack on Camerontown had 'put a stop to this arrangement'.[58] Though it is impossible to deduce from the history books, this surgical severance of a major British supply route was easily the most important single action of the first phase of the war.

Camerontown was the outstanding incident, but the range of Maori activities in September and October was great. Bands of from twenty to 200 warriors roamed north through the bush from Pukekawa and Paparata, covering an area of about 800 square miles. They often remained at temporary camps deep in the bush during the day, and travelled at night, sometimes attacking at dawn. They ambushed messengers, sentries, and other individuals. They drew small parties of troops into the bush and inflicted casualties on them. They launched, but rarely pressed home, attacks on strong patrols and redoubts. The British lost about fifty troops killed and wounded, a dozen settlers—some armed and some not—and an unknown number of Queenite Maoris. The Kingites tried to keep their own casualties light, and they usually succeeded, but by no means all these actions were tactically Maori victories. An attack on a small militia stockade at Pukekohe East on 8 September, for example, was repelled with quite heavy losses. But tactical results were of little relevance to the strategic impact, which was to press the British into reducing their striking force to the level of ineffectiveness.

Cameron did not sit supinely by and allow this to happen. He tried several measures which he hoped might deal with Maori raiding without absorbing too many men. These included a bold night march on 1–2 August by the whole column of attack, whereby Cameron hoped to surprise the raiding base of Paparata. But the Maoris were too strongly posted and too wary, and Cameron was forced to withdraw without result. A longer-term measure was the 'Moveable Column', organized in early September and made up of picked regulars and the newly formed Colonial 'bush fighting' unit, the Forest Rangers. The Moveable Column was intended to hunt down Maori raiding parties in the bush and destroy them. But at this stage the Maoris were out to raid, not to fight strong pursuit groups, and for once the label 'elusive' was appropriate. Despite its best efforts the Moveable Column was unable to catch the enemy, and it saw virtually no action. Raiding continued unabated. The Maoris, cried one settler on 17 October, 'have been permitted to roam about with impunity, inflicting the most cruel barbarities, murdering and tomahawking our neighbours. What has become of the "flying column"? Where are the "forest rangers"?'[59]

Cameron's effort to secure his communications on the cheap had failed. He was therefore forced to depend on the system of escorts, patrols, and redoubts, and this was expensive in men. Cameron divided the area behind the front into three district commands.[60] A substantial force had to be kept at the headquarters of each to succour the small parties and posts which regularly came under attack. The striking force itself often became involved in this rescue duty. Stockades and redoubts, manned by anything from twenty-five to 500 men, were built all over the district, not only to protect the line of supply directly, but also to cut Maori access to the British rear areas. By late October there were about twenty redoubts, and they increased the logistical difficulties disproportionately to the number of men in their garrisons. Each group of posts off the Great South Road had to have its own line of supply, and the Maori raids precluded the use of much civilian labour. 'The country was infested by guerilla bands of the enemy, and contractors could not be induced to undertake deliveries [to] the various posts.'[61] The Commissariat Transport Corps consequently had to be increased beyond the level required to supply the army if it had been concentrated at the front. The destruction of the Queenite-manned Waikato Heads supply route of course greatly increased the pressure on the Great South Road route, and this in turn necessitated increases in the Transport Corps. Each convoy had to have a strong escort.

All this meant that during September and October, the Maori raiding offensive robbed Cameron of three-quarters of his effective force and so paralysed him. But the British army was constantly growing, and there was an eventual threshold. By late October the supply protection system had absorbed nearly 6,000 men. A point of acceptable, though not total, anti-raiding effectiveness had been reached, and any further reinforcements would go to the column of attack. Between 20 and 30 October several hundred Waikato Militia replaced regulars at the outposts and in the Transport Corps, and so augmented the striking force. By 28 October, a second river steamer, the *Pioneer*, and 500 Imperial troops, brought from Australia by H. M. S. *Curacoa*, had also arrived at the front.[62] The resulting British freedom to move is sometimes attributed to the arrival of the *Pioneer*, but the *Avon* and other boats and canoes had been available since early August, and the extra troops were the crucial factor. Cameron now had nearly 2,000 men in his striking force, and he lost no time in using them to implement his long-matured plan of out-flanking Meremere by river.

On 31 October, the river flotilla landed 600 men at Takapau nine miles in rear of Meremere. Cameron ordered them to entrench while he and the flotilla went back for a second echelon of 600 men. Cameron intended to use the balance of his force to hold the Maoris in front, while the 1,200 men at Takapau attacked the less well-protected rear of Meremere and destroyed the Kingite army. As the Maoris were aware, he would probably have succeeded, and on 1 November they decided to evacuate. The British blocked the north and south and the Waikato blocked the west, but the route to the east was still open—'a Maori position is never without its means of escape'[63]—and the Kingites got clear without losing a man.

Meremere was more valuable than most earlier modern *pa* because it had a specific obstructive purpose, but its loss was not in itself of great importance to the Maoris. In theory, the Meremere Line could easily be replaced by other lines further up the Waikato. As we shall see, the Maoris' real problem after 1 November arose from the fact that they had temporarily exhausted their resources in building and manning Meremere, and in conducting operations behind the front. Nevertheless, up to this point in the war, the British had had the worst of it. They had sought quick victory, and when that failed, they had sought to offset fourteen weeks of enforced immobility with the annihilation of the Kingite army at Meremere. This attempt had also failed, and the main British response to the escape of the Maoris was not satisfaction at the 'bloodless victory' of the official portrayal, but 'great disappointment'.[64]

On 8 July, having had two years in which to study the country and build up what seemed an appropriate and adequately defended supply system, Cameron had concluded that commissariat transport and protection would absorb about forty per cent of his effectives.[65] Without the benefit of hindsight, this was a reasonable estimate. It catered for patrols to deal with a small amount of raiding, for small escorts, for the garrisons of the original military posts at Drury, Queen's Redoubt, and 'the Bluff', and still left sixty per cent of the troops. As it happened only fifteen to twenty per cent of the effective force proved to be available for the column of attack. Of the remainder, only a part of the Transport Corps, perhaps five per cent of the whole force, could properly be said to be dealing with ordinary logistical difficulties. The balance of seventy-five to eighty per cent were absorbed,

not by problems of terrain or by British inertia, but by Maori action: the
raiding offensives of July and September-October.

General Cameron argued that the Maoris responsible for these raids were
the young men of lower Waikato who had been expelled from their villages
under the proclamation of 12 July. He blamed the government for disregarding his advice and allowing these men to depart with their guns, and consequently for the suspension of his southward advance.[66] This attempt at self-
defence against unjust allegations of procrastination has lent support to the
notion that the Maoris made little effort to hamper Cameron's communications, and that they fought without coherence and without any strategic
over-view. It is true that some dispossessed Lower Waikatos were among
the raiders, and there is little direct evidence about Maori command decisions in this period. But the case against this assumption seems overwhelming. The scale of the campaign alone surely makes the notion of sporadic,
unorganized revenge raiding appear highly improbable —analogous, one
might say, to finding a fully-equipped climber at the top of a mountain and
assuming he had arrived there by accident. Other factors also indicate that
the raiding was part of a Maori strategy.

When the dispossessed Lower Waikatos conducted raids, they rarely did
so independently. They sometimes used Paparata and Pukekawa bases, and
they were frequently accompanied by other tribes. It is probable that most
or all the tribes garrisoning the Meremere Line took part in the raiding at
one stage or another. Ngati Maniapoto, Ngati Haua, Ngati Raukawa,
Taranaki, Ngai-te-Rangi, and Ngati Paoa certainly did.[67] The brother of
Rewi Maniapoto and young sons of Wiremu Tamehana, the two leading
Maori generals, were involved in various raids. Tamehana and Rewi
themselves took part in at least one attack, and Rewi was widely believed to
have instigated the raiding.[68] There is also an indication that Tikaokao called
in the raiding parties in late October 'as he suspects that the troops will soon
make an advance movement [on Meremere]; and it is desirable that they
should have the whole of their force together'.[69] Another relevant consideration is the suspension of the raiding campaign between 1 and 25 August. If
the local Maoris were simply venting their ire over the loss of their homes,
why should they stop their activities so soon, and why should the suspension coincide so precisely with what all observers agree was a very intensive
effort to complete the Meremere Line?

It seems reasonable to conclude that the war behind the front was not a
scattering of revenge raids, but a co-ordinated part of a well-planned and
effective Maori strategy, carried out under the auspices of the Kingite 'high
command'. Like one subordinate element of the Taranaki War strategy, and
unlike most Maori operations, the raiding campaign had the character of a
guerilla war. The Maoris made good use of the bush and they did prove extremely elusive. Causing the enemy heavy casualties in close combat was
less important than forcing him to spend more men on protecting his communications. These guerilla operations were only a part of the Maori
strategy. The other, more 'conventional' part, was the Meremere Line. The

two elements were inter-dependent. The Line provided secure bases for the raiding campaign, and the raiding campaign prevented the concentration of a large force against the Line. As a whole this strategy was enough to stop an army which grew from 4,000 to 8,000 men, for fourteen weeks—despite the careful British preparations for war. The Maori army which achieved this feat is not likely to have exceeded 1,500 men.

The effects of the raiding campaign did not end with the fall of Mere-mere. The Maoris had conclusively shown that they could seriously threaten British communications, and whether they actually mounted such threats or not, Cameron could not afford to relax his hold on the area behind his front. Isolated Maori operations behind the lines during the suc-ceeding months served to remind him of this. In mid-November, Cameron sent 800 men to the Thames to form a line of redoubts westwards to Queen's Redoubt, so as to hamper Maori access to the east of Lower Waikato. The following month, a 700-man expedition to Raglan performed the same function for the west, and throughout the war Cameron devoted the majority of his men to the protection of his supply lines. The General was not jumping at shadows. That the Maoris should raid infrequently when the rear areas were well protected was no proof that they would con-tinue to do so if the protection was removed. Another loss of provisions on the scale of Camerontown might well have compelled the British to pick up their skirts and scuttle back to Auckland. Cameron could not take this risk, and so his very large army was transformed into a much smaller striking force for each battle. The failure of historians to appreciate the reasons for this transformation has led to the fundamental misunderstanding of both the British and Maori performances in the Waikato War.

8

Rangiriri

THREE WEEKS AFTER THE FALL OF MEREMERE, GENERAL Cameron and 1,400 men advanced thirteen miles southwards and attacked a new Maori position at Rangiriri. The ensuing battle cost both sides more men than any other engagement of the wars, and it warrants close attention. Rangiriri was not an enclosed fortress, but another line of defence. It was much smaller than Meremere, but it too blocked the British advance and so constituted the second Waikato Line. Before turning to the battle itself, it is necessary to examine the problems facing the Maoris in building and manning a new defensive system so soon after their efforts at Meremere.

I THE SECOND WAIKATO LINE

THE MAORI OFFENSIVE-DEFENSIVE OPERATIONS BASED ON THE Meremere Line were remarkably effective. The cost in dead warriors was light, and if the Maoris had had a permanent army with the economy and social organization to sustain it, the strategic consequences of the abandonment might not have been great. Rangiriri was only one of several potentially strong positions further up the Waikato, and the Maoris could simply have held one of these and attempted to reproduce the Meremere effect. But the facts that the Maoris did not have a full-time army and that Cameron, unlike his predecessors, had the resources and logistical organization for what amounted to a continuous offensive presented the Maoris with two related problems—lack of time and lack of men.

The real price that the Maoris paid for their success at Meremere and in the war behind the front was not in ground or lives, but in less tangible resources. For more than three months, they had kept a very large force in the field. The usual circulation of warriors between their homes and the front certainly helped, but the strain of such sustained effort remained immense, and the Maoris temporarily exhausted their war-making capacity. It was therefore inevitable that the Meremere army should break up. The Kingites were prepared to make unprecedented efforts to resist the British, and the process of re-assembling began almost immediately. But it was clear that General Cameron would not halt his advance to suit Maori convenience, and the question was whether the Kingites would have sufficient time both to create a suitable defensive line and to muster an adequate garrison for it.

These considerations dictated the selection of the position at Rangiriri, as the second Waikato Line. A certain amount of work had been carried out at Rangiriri before the fall of Meremere. Even before the war broke out, a long ditch had been dug there between the Waikato River and the neighbouring Lake Waikare.[1] Since the beginning of the war men and women had been working on the Rangiriri defences whenever they could be spared from building, manning, and supplying the Meremere system. So when concentrated work began on Rangiriri in early November, the Kingites had at least a chance of making it defensible, despite a circumscribed work-force drawn mainly from local tribes.

Rangiriri was a defensive line rather than a fort. Though for some reason contemporary accounts usually give 500 yards for the length of the front, the actual length was at least 1,000 yards, spanning the whole distance between the Waikato and Lake Waikare.[2] The front line, running east-west, consisted of 'a double ditch and parapet'—a long trench in front, then a parapet of banked-up earth, then another trench. The trenches varied from nine to fourteen feet in depth and were so wide that they 'could not be leaped'.[3] They were equipped with 'excavated holes or casemates in which they [the garrison] might shelter themselves from the fire of an attacking force'.[4] These of course were the Maori bunkers, and from them the defenders could move to firing-steps cut in the sides of the trench after a bombardment. The parapet was fourteen to twenty-one feet high from the bottom of the trench. The front line had one or two small salients to provide enfilading fire. Another line of defences ran south from the left-centre of the main line at a right angle to it. This line faced the river and was intended to guard against a river-borne force attacking directly from its boats.

A low ridge ran north-south down the centre of the works, and on one or two of its southern hillocks further defences had been begun, but these were incomplete when the British attacked on 20 November. It was possible to assume from these unfinished defences that Rangiriri was extremely vulnerable from the south or rear, and such an assumption was to affect the interpretation of the battle on 20 November. In fact, the main line and its supporting works were almost as defensible against attack from the south as from the north, and the ground in the south was too swampy and broken to be suitable for a full assault. The unfinished defences in the south, though presumably intended to provide supplementary cover for the rear of the main line when complete, were, on 20 November: 'likewise so far detached from the main works and from each other that, from their isolated positions, they would have been as much a source of weakness to the defenders as an annoyance to the attacking force had they been manned to oppose our landing'. They were therefore guarded at most by pickets and were more probably not manned at all.[5]

Like a number of other modern *pa*, Rangiriri had an innovative tactical feature which might surprise an attacker. The creation of this may be credited to Te Wharepu—a leading chief of Waikato proper who acted as the supervizing engineer in the construction of Rangiriri. It consisted in a small but extremely strong redoubt, with attached works, located near the centre of the main line. The redoubt had a bastion on the north-west corner, and lines of rifle-pits extended to the south to cover the approach from the rear, where a gap formed an entrance. This entrance was covered by a number of concealed firing positions, so that for attackers it was less a gate into the redoubt than a trap. Most modern accounts imply that the redoubt was detached, but in fact it was integrated into the main line, and the two works probably shared a parapet. The redoubt's bastion actually protruded north of the main line and formed one of its salients. On all sides other than the north, the redoubt had its own wide and deep ditch and a high parapet, with individually fortified *whare* and deep bunkers inside. Its firing positions 'were in many places arranged in terraces, so there was often a double line of fire and sometimes a triple line of fire, on the principal lines of approach'.[6] The redoubt was very strong indeed, but its strength as such was not its most significant characteristic.

After the battle General Cameron wrote: 'the strength of this work [the central redoubt] was not known before the attack as its profile could not be seen either from the river or from the ground in front'.[7] This is confirmed by a number of other accounts, and it was not simply a retrospective excuse. As we shall see, Cameron and his staff reached the same conclusions before their attack. The redoubt was very small in area, it had a low silhouette and it effectively blended into the other works. It was very strong, it was 'the real key of the position',[8] and neither of these things were known to the British in advance. These facts were to dominate the course of the battle.

The unfinished state of the defences in the south of Rangiriri did not constitute a major weakness, and the fortifications did have real strength at other points. The Maoris had therefore solved the problem of creating a viable line of defence with circumscribed resources and in a short time. But could they find the men to man it? The short answer to this question is that they could not. The main burden of the completion and manning of Rangiriri appears to have fallen on Ngati Mahuta—who provided about 150 warriors of the garrison—and on certain other sub-tribes of Waikato proper, such as Ngatiteata, Ngatihine, and Patupou. Ngati Mahuta were King Tawhiao's own people, and the other tribes were close relations, but this was less important than the fact that it was these people who happened to live near Rangiriri. The process of concentrating afresh began almost as soon as the Meremere army dispersed, and by 20 November the Waikatos had received some non-local support. This included a group of forty or fifty Kawhia Ngati Mahuta (a section living on the west coast), a few Ngati Paoa and, above all, a force of Ngati Haua under Wiremu Tamehana and Tioriori, more than 100 strong. These reinforcements brought the garrison of Rangiriri to about 500 men.[9]

The small size of the Maori garrison, and the fact that it was primarily drawn from only two tribes, has sometimes been treated as an example of the supposed Maori incapacity to combine. The absence of Ngati Maniapoto in particular is noted and attributed to a quarrel between that tribe and Waikato due, according to one modern account, to 'a breach of Maori etiquette' by the garrison of Rangiriri.[10] There may have been some ill-feeling between Waikato and Ngati Maniapoto—after the battle it would be natural for those who had suffered to resent the fact that others had not. It is also true the Ngati Maniapoto and the Rangiriri garrison belonged to different political schools of thought within the King Movement. But it is highly unlikely that these factors explain Rangiriri's weakness in men. The difficulty of concentrating anew after the supreme effort at Meremere is, *prima facie*, a far more probable explanation and it is supported by the following considerations.

Ngati Maniapoto were the colonists' favourite bogeymen. They were paradoxically accused of both cowardice—some asserted that it was this which kept them away from Rangiriri—and of an intransigent determination to kill all Europeans and to fight to the death.[11] Derogatory British comments about the behaviour of this tribe must therefore be treated with suspicion. Furthermore, Ngati Maniapoto were by no means the only tribe present during the Meremere operations and absent at Rangiriri. Most other Kingite tribes were also absent for the reasons outlined above. Several sub-tribes of Waikato proper which lived some distance from Rangiriri, such as Ngati Apakura, were among the absentees. Ngati Apakura were relations of the garrison of Rangiriri, the King was their high chief, and they are unlikely to have stayed away through choice. Finally, the evidence suggests that many warriors were actually on their way to Rangiriri at the time of the battle. A large body of warriors (400 according to British estimates), probably representing the balance of Waikato and Ngati Haua strength, arrived just after the battle.[12] Te Heuheu Horonuku and his Ngati Tuwharetoa were on their way back from Taupo, further parties of Ngati Paoa had reached Lake Waikare by 21 November, and various other groups appear to have been in the area. At least some Ngati Maniapoto were also nearby.[13]

It seems clear that the Maoris were doing all they could to strengthen their forces at Rangiriri, but this does not affect the fact that they had not yet done enough. It was simply not possible properly to man extensive defences with 500 musket-armed men. The real weakness of Rangiriri was not inadequate fortifications, but a woefully inadequate garrison.

II THE BATTLE OF RANGIRIRI

AGAINST THESE THINLY MANNED DEFENCES, CAMERON launched his attack on the afternoon of 20 November. The received account of this important battle is deceptively simple. Cameron, we are told, planned to take advantage of his river flotilla 'to land a force in the rear [of Rangiriri]; and to attack simultaneously from front and rear'. Despite problems with the rear attack, due to wind and current preventing the boats from getting into position on schedule, the frontal attack was launched after a bombardment. The British 'charging with fixed bayonets, captured the two outer defence lines'. The river-borne force finally landed 'and drove the Maoris out of another set of entrenchments'. The Maoris found themselves 'rapidly driven out of the whole position except for a high redoubt in the centre'. The British had so far suffered little loss and—it is either expressly stated or implied—the Maoris were now surrounded. Though Rutherford says the whole Maori position was 'surrounded and stormed', historians generally give the impression that there was then a pause, after which Cameron launched three attacks on the central redoubt. One of these attacks was made by artillerymen armed with revolvers, and two were mounted by seamen of the naval brigade. These attacks, which for convenience we will call the R.A./R.N. assaults, are usually presented as the outstanding tactical feature of the battle. Though they failed and the Maoris retained possession of the redoubt throughout the night, we are informed that they were forced to surrender at discretion the next morning.[14]

Where they subject these events to analysis of any kind, historians generally make one or both of two points. The first is that the British victory at Rangiriri was the natural result of qualitatively superior British resources. The battle showed that Maori methods 'were in the long run no match for gunboats, howitzers, Enfield rifles and hand-grenades'. Occasionally, Cameron's skilful application of these resources is seen as a crucial contributor to the victory, but in either form this view involves one crucial proposition: that the British had developed, or stumbled upon, a real solution to the tactical problem of the modern *pa* system.[15]

The second major point made by historians relates more directly to Cameron's personal performance. Much more common than any allusion to the General's skill is a heavy emphasis on his blunder in launching the R.A./R.N. assaults against the central redoubt. Most writers join Holt in designating these attacks 'a futile waste of life'.[16] In one of the few modern assessments of colonial 'small wars', Brian Bond uses this very incident to illustrate 'the inflexibility of British tactics'. 'Cameron at Rangiriri ... ordered three successive frontal assaults which resulted in nothing but futile loss of life.'[17] Though Rangiriri was the most important combat victory in which Cameron held personal command, it also marks the absolute nadir of his reputation as a tactician.

One basis of this assessment is the assumption that the heavy British casualties in the battle were a result of the R.A./R.N. assaults. A simple preliminary point must be made here. The British casualty returns show that only twenty-one of the 132 men killed or wounded at Rangiriri came from the two corps which alone launched the three assaults.[18] In other words, the attacks which are often portrayed as the main tactical events of the battle accounted for less than one-sixth of the total British loss. Of how the other 111 men met their fate, of how and where the real crisis of the battle occurred, the received version tells us little.

The historical orthodoxy on Rangiriri descends from the common stock of contemporary interpretation, but it has almost no basis in fact. Since the battle is also important and complicated, there is no alternative but to attempt to reconstruct its course piece by piece. This can best be done by dividing the action into three stages. The first consists of the initial British attacks, and the analysis of it is preceded by a brief explanation of Cameron's tactical thinking. The second stage, artificially but conveniently distinguished from the first, includes both a number of events overlooked in the received version, and the three assaults upon which so much emphasis is placed. The third stage covers the night of 20 November and the morning of 21 November. The analysis of this period shows how the British obtained their victory.

General Cameron began planning his attack on Rangiriri immediately after the fall of Meremere. His thinking was dominated by two considerations. The first was the belief that the Maori position was not strong. This conclusion was based on careful reconnaissance. On 30 October, while searching for a landing place in the rear of Meremere, Cameron and his staff examined Rangiriri from the river. The place, wrote Colonel Gamble, 'is situated very low; and the entrenchment . . . appeared to be open to enfilade from the river, besides seeming to be otherwise not formidable. It is just a common embankment with a trench cut in front of it also'.[19] When Cameron re-examined the position from the river on 18 November, and for a third time from the ground in front on the day of the battle, he saw nothing to affect this assessment.[20] He therefore concluded that Rangiriri could be taken by a well-mounted frontal assault.

The belief that a successful assault was possible was coupled with a conviction that it was necessary—a conviction which the experience of Meremere operated to encourage. The escape of the Maoris from Meremere had created a wave of disappointment, and the British, including General Cameron, greatly feared a repeat performance at Rangiriri. 'Many were the speculations as to whether the Maoris would stand, or whether they would run at the mere approach of danger as at Meremere, and the general feeling was one of anticipation of disappointment at the waste of so much force.'[21] Cameron's main concern, therefore, was to prevent the escape of the enemy. Every effort had to be made to cut his routes of retreat but, barring complete encirclement (impossible at Rangiriri because of Lake Waikare), the close contact and close pursuit bound to result from a successful assault was the best guarantee of real damage to the Maori force.

Accordingly, when advancing south from Meremere on the morning of 20 November, Cameron divided his army into two divisions.[22] His own, 900 strong, advanced up the bank of the Waikato to make the frontal assault. The other, consisting of 320 of the 40th Regiment under Colonel Leslie, with 200 seamen and marines available if necessary, was transported south by the river flotilla with the aim, in Cameron's own words, of 'gaining possession of a ridge 500 yards behind the main entrenchment, and thus intercepting the escape of the enemy'.[23] Clearly, the assumption that simultaneous attacks were planned from front and rear is mistaken. Leslie's task was purely to cut off the Maori retreat. The frontal assault by Cameron's division was also aimed at preventing escape, though by different means. Cameron's objective was less the capture of Rangiriri than the destruction of its garrison.

The two British divisions arrived on schedule at Rangiriri at about 3 p.m. Cameron deployed his division and began bombarding the enemy works with three field pieces and the armament of two out of four gunboats. But an adverse wind and a strong current created unexpected difficulties for the riverborne division under Leslie. At 4.45 p.m., Leslie had still to land. With darkness approaching and the evacuation of Meremere in his mind, Cameron felt he could wait no longer and launched his frontal attack. He had 320 men of the 65th under Colonel Wyatt on his right (the river side), with 290 men of the 1/12th and 2/14th under Colonel Austen prolonging the line to the left. Wyatt's 65th carried some scaling-ladders and were accompanied by a dozen Royal Engineers. A company each of the 65th and 40th, together some 185 men, were in reserve.

Historians give the impression that the whole main line of the Maori works was carried in the first rush, but the clear consensus of the contemporary accounts is that the Maori front was penetrated only on its left—the river side. From this point, the eyewitnesses begin to contradict each other. Some official reports state that, despite a 'sharp quick and heavy fire', the 65th advanced over the 600 yards from their original position and stormed the left of the Maori lines without a check.[24] The function of the British left (12th and 14th) was to approach the enemy position and 'keep down the fire in the centre'[25] and these reports leave us to assume that they succeeded in doing so. The problem with this official version is that the 65th, who with their ladder-carrying detachment and accompanying engineers were obviously intended as the storming party, seem to have crossed their part of the line 'without any difficulty' and to have lost very few men in doing so.[26] On the other hand, we are invited to believe that the 12th and 14th suffered heavy casualties in *not* attempting to storm their section of the line.

The 14th, after losing Colonel Austen early in the advance, approached very close to the centre-right of the Maori line, the point where Te Wharepu's redoubt was located. 'It was here that the principal casualties in that corps took place, and Captain Phelps received his death wound within 30 yards of the parapet.' Captain Strange, who succeeded to the command of the 14th, reported that his men advanced to within twenty-five yards of the Maori line, and even commended a certain Ensign Green 'who ran along the parapet desiring the men to follow him'. Some men did follow him into the ditch, but they could get no further in the face of murderous fire, and the extremely lucky young Green was soon forced to join them. Two officers of the 12th recorded a 'desperate attempt to climb the earthwork'. Led by Lieutenant Murphy, some of the men of this unit 'scrambled on to the parapet, only to be shot down'. Murphy was killed, and in fact the 12th, whose part in the battle is rarely referred to by historians, suffered higher proportionate losses than any other unit involved.[27]

It seems clear that, contrary to plan, the British left wing did launch a heavy though unsuccessful assault on the centre of the Maori line. How did Cameron's plan go so substantially awry? A possible answer was given by W. G. Mair, a soldier-settler attached to the regular force who observed the battle.

> When the advance was sounded the 65th descended to the tea-tree [*manuka* scrub] on their left, and, cowed by the heavy fire, lay down, while the 14th went on, three of their officers, Austin, Phelps and Murphy, falling before they got near the great ditch. St. Hill then went to his regiment, and said: 'I'm ashamed of you, 65th; close to your right and charge,' and told Colonel Austin to do the same with the [12th] and 14th.[28]

St Hill was only a Lieutenant, but he was also Cameron's A.D.C., and it is perfectly possible that he was sent forward to speak with the General's authority in an effort to put the attack back on its pre-concerted lines. It is also quite possible for even the best regiments momentarily to lose their nerve, and it is hardly surprising that military eyewitnesses should fail to mention such an occurrence. In fact one or two civilian accounts do mention a 'slight hesitation' in the 65th's advance, and a rumour subsequently emerged to the effect that the men had refused to obey their officers at some point in the battle.[29] Furthermore, the officers of the 12th refer to several ladders which were with their unit.[30] At the beginning of the British attack, all ladders were with the 65th. The discrepancy can only be explained if the 65th inclined to their left to the extent that the extreme left of their line became intermingled with the 12th.

These considerations suggest the following hypothesis. Contrary to plan, the 65th appears to have inclined to the left, perhaps to take advantage of the cover of some scrub. Whether or not they actually 'lay down' as Mair asserted, this movement seems both to have upset their momentum and to have caused their extreme left, including a few ladder-bearers, to fuse with the 12th's right. Perhaps these men caught up their new neighbours in their own appointed task, because the 12th and 14th then pressed home an unscheduled attack against the Maori centre-right. It should be borne in mind that these two units had previously been deprived of their commander, Colonel Austen, to whom Cameron had presumably confided his plan in most detail. Despite the massive ditch and parapet this attack was made with great vigour. But heavy Maori frontal volleys, apparently reserved until the enemy were very close, and a galling flanking fire from a salient, repelled it.[31] The degree of British determination is illustrated by the fact that, despite this fire, several men got on to the Maori parapet where with the exception of Ensign Green they were all killed. Casualties may have been as high as forty men killed and wounded.[32] The 14th and 12th thus became the first victims of the unexpected strength of Rangiriri's central redoubt. The story of their attack has disappeared from the received version, and it is as well to add that their efforts were no less brave for being both unsuccessful and unsung.

After their 'slight hesitation', the 65th rallied and continued their advance against the Maori left. Cameron had planned that this part of the Maori line should be the sole point of attack because it could be enfiladed by cannon fire from the river flotilla.[33] Perhaps stung by their officer's comments on their initial loss of nerve, the regiment now advanced with considerable *élan*, the trenches were bridged with planks, and the left of the Maori main line was carried. As we have seen, this was done fairly easily and with light casualties. It seems fair to assume that the explanation for this was bound up with the attack of the 12th and 14th against the centre-right of the Maori line. It is clear enough that this attack had begun before the 65th made their rush at the river end of the line. We know that, for the size of the position, the Maori garrison was very small. With their right about to come under attack, and with no evidence of an equally immediate threat to their left, it would have been natural for the Maoris to concentrate their attention and their manpower at the point of greatest danger. The Maoris simply did not have the men for a more cautious policy. With a front of over 1,000 yards, and with the 12th's and 14th's attack still in full swing, rapidly adjusting this distribution to cope with the 65th's assault would have been impossible. Consequently, while the Maori right was able to smash the attack on their position, the weakened Maori left, which held a somewhat weaker position anyway, not only gave way at the extreme left of the main line, but also abandoned the river-facing line of trenches to the 65th's attack. The unplanned and unsuccessful attack of the 12th and 14th thus constituted a costly but text-book perfect feint which enabled the 65th to roll up the Maori left.

For the historian, this point marks the end of the first stage of the battle, but there was no such breathing space in the engagement itself. To observers watching from the river, the action through the first and second stages appeared to consist of a continuous and entirely successful British attack. The repulse of the 12th and 14th on the far side of the field was not visible to them.[34] They therefore celebrated the accuracy of the brief preliminary bombardment and the success of the 65th's attack with clapping and cheering, one witness reportedly crying 'that's a stinker for you my adjective niggers . . . that was into his ivories by jingo'.[35] They watched the 65th penetrate the extreme left of the Maori main line. They saw them swing inland, carry the river-facing line, and rush on towards the central redoubt. During this process, Cameron committed his two companies of reserves to exploit in full what seemed to be the decisive break-through. One company was sent south to pursue some of the defenders of the Maori left who had not been able to join their comrades on the right, and to co-operate with Colonel Leslie's division which was only now beginning to land. The need to prevent the Maoris escaping clearly remained uppermost in Cameron's mind. The other company of the reserves joined the 65th as they moved to assault the central redoubt. So too did the 12th after their own abortive attempt on the redoubt, while the 14th reverted to its intended role of providing covering fire.

The Maori defence seemed completely broken and the final assault appeared to be a formality. 'Now we in the boats thought the work was done, and the place taken. . . . Presently, to our great surprise we saw there was a check.'[36] The reinforced British right, about 500 strong, assaulted the central redoubt only to meet the same fate as the left. The Maori fire from the redoubt and its adjacent works was very heavy, and probably took the form of at least one carefully timed volley from the terraced firing positions, followed by independent fire. The British 'were reluctantly compelled to fall back under cover of the captured earthworks, after losing many brave men'.[37]

During or immediately after this major attack, several groups of soldiers worked their way to the rear of the redoubt where the small gateway seemed to offer a better chance of forcing an entrance. This was deceptive. At least three small-scale assaults—spin-offs of the British right wing's main attack—were launched against 'this gate of death'. One was led by the Adjutant of the 65th, Lieutenant Lewis, and two by the ubiquitous St. Hill. Each was smashed by 'a volley from fourteen to twenty muskets' aimed from the firing positions that had been so carefully prepared to cover the gap. 'We could not drive out the Maories partly owing to their bravery, but mainly owing to the consummate skill with which they had arranged their defensive works.' Again, losses were heavy and they were increased by the fact that some of the men involved in these attacks found themselves cut off in a corner formed by the angle of two trenches and exposed to fire from the gap. At one time, four British corpses, seven wounded men and seven unhurt men were crammed into this corner. More men were killed while trying to go to their aid.[38]

The British had inflicted quite heavy casualties on the Maoris—probably something in the order of thirty killed, though with a disproportionately small number of wounded.[39] The bulk of these people had fallen on the left of the Rangiriri defences, where the British had seized substantial sectors of the entrenchments. The troops now had the Maoris enveloped on three sides—the 14th in the north, the main body of the right wing (65th, 12th, and reserves) in the west, and detachments of the right wing, by now supported by Leslie's division, in the south. On the other hand, the British had failed completely in two major and at least three minor attacks on the central redoubt at a cost of about 110 men in all. In addition to casualties, some of the defenders of the Maori left wing had been unable to withdraw to the central redoubt and had therefore fled. But it is unlikely that the total reduction in the garrison exceeded 100, which left about 400 to defend a position more proportionate to their strength. Though smaller than the original fortification, this position included more works than the redoubt proper. The Maoris seemed to have continued to hold, or at least to control, some lines of rifle pits to the south and east of the central redoubt. More importantly, they still held the right of their main line. This meant, first, that their position was tenable against further attack, and second, that they still had a good route of retreat by canoe across Lake Waikare. In essence, then, Cameron's problem remained unchanged. He still had a strong position to take before he could march on south, and he had yet to destroy the enemy warrior force. He had, however, 110 fewer men with which to do it.

This situation was to remain constant until the fighting ended at nightfall. Both the Maoris and the British had suffered the great bulk of their total casualties, and in fact the tactical crisis of the battle was over. But historians generally give the impression that the most important events of the battle begin at this point. Cameron indulged in his 'futile waste of life' by launching the R.A./R.N. assaults. As we shall see, the suggestion that no further assaults were necessary because the Maoris were surrounded is incorrect, and only the allegation that one of the assault parties was stupidly selected need concern us here. Two of the three attacks were made by a group of ninety sailors under Commander Mayne, and blue-jackets were considered to be élite assault troops. The third attack was launched by Captain H. A. Mercer and thirty-six Royal Artillerymen. Why, some commentators asked, were artillerymen used when 'over 600 British infantry were lying under cover'?[40]

Cameron was probably influenced by the fact that all the infantry of his division had been involved in hard fighting, which left the artillerymen as the only fresh troops immediately at hand. Further, the artillerymen were armed with revolvers, which impeded men less than rifles when scrambling over obstacles. The previous attacks had been launched in quick succession, and the pause between the last of these and Mercer's attack was very short. Mercer's attack was simply part of a series, and like the two naval attacks— which also failed—it was launched when it seemed that just a little more effort would bring about the fall of the weak-looking redoubt. But the rights and wrongs of Cameron's decision are less important than the fact that only six artillerymen were killed and wounded—and at least two of these were hit while attempting to rescue the wounded Mercer after the assault had failed. In launching this attack Cameron committed at most a minor mistake, and one which contributed very little to the toll of killed and wounded. The R.A./R.N. assaults were merely minor incidents in the second phase of the battle—a phase which involved a total of at least eight unsuccessful attacks on the Maoris' central redoubt.

The final stage of the battle involved little or no fighting. The British spent the night 'bivouacked on the wet ground, disgusted and disheartened'.[41] Some attempt was made to mine the enemy parapet but the ground proved too sandy, and the Maoris retained their positions throughout the night. At dawn they hoisted a white flag, and a little later the 183 occupants of the redoubt and its adjacent works, including a few women, became prisoners.

Most contemporary interpreters, including some eyewitnesses, and all historians, present this last event as an unconditional surrender forced on the Maoris by the British. This is one of the firmest elements of the received version. Two specific explanations for the Maori decision are offered. The first is based on information given to James Cowan by a Ngati Tamaoho veteran of the garrison.[42] This warrior claimed that the Maoris surrendered primarily because they had exhausted their ammunition. This assertion is contradicted by the bulk of evidence, including a collective account by the Rangiriri prisoners which is quoted below. Several British eyewitnesses refer to a steady fire having been kept up by the Maoris during the night, and a number state categorically that 'a plentiful supply of ammunition' was found in the redoubt after the battle.[43] This explanation should therefore be dismissed.

The second, more widely accepted, explanation rests primarily on the assumption that the Maoris were surrounded. This belief survived despite universal acceptance of the fact that many Maoris escaped during the night. Contemporaries made the two beliefs compatible in some degree by assuming that the Maoris slipped through the British cordon in ones and twos 'as they are such slippery devils'.[44] The trouble with this idea of an unorganized flight by individuals is that two very specific groups were among the escapees. The first consisted of the principal chiefs among the garrison —Wiremu Tamehana and, possibly, King Tawhiao, whose loss would have been a crippling blow to the King Movement, and Te Wharepu, who was very severely wounded. These leaders left at different times.[45] Tamehana was accompanied by thirty-six warriors, and the King and Te Wharepu are certain to have had substantial escorts as well.[46] The second group was the wounded. Reports of the number of wounded among the prisoners vary from none to thirteen, and all agree that the number was surprisingly small. The 65th may have killed some Maori wounded during the storming of the left flank, but a number greater than those found by the British in the redoubt certainly survived. These men are unlikely to have escaped without help, and in fact a party of Maori reinforcements arriving too late for the battle met whole canoe-loads of wounded crossing the lake. Clearly, an organized evacuation, in about four echelons, was carried out by the Maoris. This, of course, accords with the assertion made above that the Maoris retained a route to the lake. Though a few of the 14th got into the outer ditch of the Maori right-wing entrenchments, there is no record at all of the British ever seizing it, whereas several eyewitness accounts state or imply that the Maoris retained it. In other words, the Maoris were never surrounded, and could have left at any time.

If the Maoris were not surrounded, why did they 'surrender unconditionally'? The Maori answer to this question was that they did not intend to surrender at all, still less unconditionally, but that they were 'humbugged' by the British during an attempt to negotiate. This claim was made by the Rangiriri prisoners in conversation with a newspaper correspondent some months after the battle. In the correspondent's paraphrase:

At Rangiriri, the prisoners strongly affirm, they had discussed in the night whether they should decamp as had done Thompson [Tamehana], Wharepu . . . and others. They affirm that they were not surrounded. Some of the Chiefs, however, said that the pakeha had always respected the white flag in the war in Taranaki, and that it would be better to hoist it in the morning and treat. At daylight it was hoisted, in tumbled the soldiers . . . [who] shook hands with them and got completely intermixed with them. After about twenty minutes, up came the General, and his first step was to command them to deliver up their arms. 'Halloo!' said they 'we did not bargain for this. We hoisted the white flag with a view to treating.' 'It is too late now' said some of the chiefs, 'we must give in.'[47]

This explanation derives some support from certain British accounts which, in contrast to the official reports, note that ten or twenty minutes elapsed between the hoisting of the flag and the surrender of arms; from the elimination of other alternatives; and from the comment of W. G. Mair that in a subsequent battle he 'did not like to show a white handkerchief on account of the misunderstanding about it at Rangiriri'.[48] But the decisive confirmation consists in two British eyewitness accounts of the incident. Given the importance and the controversial nature of the issue, it is necessary to quote these in full. The first account was given to Archdeacon Maunsell by Lieutenant Pennefather who was one of the men who 'tumbled' into the Maori redoubt.

The Maoris then (at 5.00 a.m.) hoisted the white flag. He [Pennefather] at once scrambled into their redoubt, and with his men mingled amongst them, shaking hands, and the General came up about ten minutes afterwards complimented them on their bravery and demanded their arms. To this they demurred: but the chiefs felt that to resist now was out of the question and decided upon delivering up the arms as required having first said that the reason of hoisting the white flag was that *they might ask what terms they might expect.*[49]

The correspondent of the *New-Zealander* also observed the incident.

[At dawn] a native appeared on the parapet showing a white flag and was very much annoyed to find that no white flag was shown on our side, but that the troops gradually closed in, and lastly got inside, while he was calling out for an interpreter and waving the soldiers back, evidently wishing to make terms for himself and his party. They were all very much surprised when they found they must give up their arms and be considered as prisoners.[50]

The white flag was no mere vestige of the age of chivalry, but a prerequisite of communication between combatants without which it would be impossible to negotiate an end to hostilities. Both the British and (since 1860) the Maoris were perfectly well aware that showing a white flag did not necessarily mean surrender. Both sides had used it for other purposes in the past. On their own criteria, the British took unscrupulous advantage of one of the most practically valuable and widely accepted laws of war. It is ironic that the hand-shaking between troops and warriors at Rangiriri, of which much is made in New Zealand legend, should be bound up with such an incident.

Despite this, the degree of British duplicity at Rangiriri should not be overstated. The finer points of the conventions of warfare were not necessarily always uppermost in the minds of privates and subalterns, and the action of Pennefather and his men appears from the above accounts to have been spontaneous. Cameron's decision a few minutes later to utilize this action to disarm the Maoris despite the flag of truce was more conscious, and it was not exactly honourable. But Cameron had had eight assaults on the central redoubt bloodily repulsed, and it was not surprising that he should seize his chance rather than risk more of his men, particularly in the case of what he perceived as a 'savage' enemy.

But what concerns us most here is that the capture of Rangiriri was not the result of assault or encirclement, but of the British misuse of a flag of truce. The Maoris might conceivably have eventually decided to surrender unconditionally anyway, but they might also have repelled further assaults and escaped across the lake intact. The question of what the Maori intentions really were when they raised the white flag is scarcely less hypothetical. The Maoris may have been trying to begin over-all peace negotiations from what they perceived as a position of some strength. They may have been attempting to gain time for the arrival of reinforcements. According to one writer, the Maoris 'could easily have escaped if they had chosen, but they had waited on in the hope of being reinforced'. And it is true that Maori reinforcements were on the way.[51] But whatever the Maoris may have been doing with their white flag, they were certainly not trying to surrender unconditionally.

Forty-one Maori corpses were found after the battle, including five women and children.[52] It was frequently suggested that many more had been lost in the swamps, but this is unlikely. The British searched the area thoroughly for two days, and at least four bodies were found in the swamps and included in the above total.[53] The number of adult male corpses found—thirty-six—accords very well with two Maori estimates of thirty-five men killed.[54] Most of these men were slain when the 65th carried the left of the main line, and in the heat of battle the troops as usual made sure of their victims. The number of wounded was therefore disproportionately low. All accounts agree that few were found among the prisoners. Several canoe loads of injured, however, were evacuated before the 'surrender'—possibly as many as thirty or forty people.[55] We may conclude that the Maoris lost thirty-five or thirty-six men killed, and perhaps a similar number of wounded.

The historical tradition outlined at the beginning of this examination of Rangiriri descends from two lines of British contemporary interpretation. After the battle, some commentators celebrated a major, clear-cut success, arising directly from the superiority of British arms. Nature was back on its pre-destined course, and the Maoris were invited to despair at the 'resistlessness' of the British. 'The vaunting savage who had threatened to sweep the Pakehas into the sea, and raise up a Maori nationality on the ruins of British dominion, has retired before the over-whelming advance of the Anglo-Saxon.' In the language of Carlyle's 'beneficent whip', one newspaper editor piously hoped that 'the fall of Rangiriri may mark an epoch in the advance of the Maori people towards a higher civilization'.[56]

These commentators adjusted the facts to fit the pre-conceived pattern. The enemy, wrote an eyewitness, 'were numerically superior to our troops'. Estimates of Maori casualties, apart from the prisoners, went as high as 280 killed and wounded, or even 200 killed outright. 'The Maoris', wrote Surgeon Andrew Carberry, 'were confronted with an equal number in the strongest position they could select [and] were routed.' As we have seen, the Maoris were outnumbered almost three to one by the British and their loss in killed and wounded was in fact moderate. The troops lying 'disgusted and disheartened' outside the central redoubt on the evening of 20 November after the last blood in the battle had been shed, would no doubt have been interested to learn that they had just 'routed' the enemy.[57] Despite all facts to the contrary, however, many interpreters persisted in this line of thinking. Even observers who were fully familiar with the true character of the white flag incident chose to see Rangiriri as the kind of victory the British army was expected to win in conflict with non-Europeans. It was attributed to Cameron's 'skilfull measures' and decisive results were confidently anticipated.[58]

The second type of contemporary reaction was very different. According to this view, the results of the battle did not justify the price paid. The return on 130 British casualties was seen as both qualitatively and quantitatively inadequate. Some writers observed that the Maori prisoners were 'lean, hungry-looking kine', the 'Maori scum of the whole island'.[59] Disregarding the fact that men were hardly likely to look their best after a desperate battle, William Morgan wrote 'it is extremely annoying, in fact it is galling, to think of our losing so many fine officers and men by such savages as those we had a sight of yesterday.'[60]

The numerical rate of exchange was also unacceptably low. Morgan was surprised that 'not more than 50 natives have been found killed'. Archdeacon Maunsell expressed similar sentiments after inspecting the Rangiriri position at the end of the battle. 'I was surprised to find so few dead and so few wounded. Though we have up to this time lost 44 [dead] they have lost as far as we can ascertain only 41 [dead] of whom 4 were women and one a boy.'[61] Most commentators comforted themselves with the thought that many Maori bodies had been lost in the swamp. But perhaps some were not entirely convinced of this, for they continued to dwell on the 'immense loss' suffered by the British, rather than the 'great victory'. For this group, the heavy British casualties not only cast a pall over the victory, but also reduced its effect on the Maoris almost to the point where it ceased to be a victory at all. 'The heavy loss of officers on our side affords no slight encouragement and compensation to rebel vengence.' The Kingites were still 'very far' from being vanquished. 'From what I can learn', observed Morgan, 'the Rangiriri affair has had anything but a subjugating tendency; indeed the effects are just the reverse.'[62]

It was this kind of opinion that led an English writer to state that the colonists were 'furious at the failure at Rangiriri'.[63] Their fury was directed at

Cameron. Together with some English interpreters, a number of settlers latched on to the R.A./R.N. assaults as the main events of the battle. They assumed that these assaults were blunders, and that they had caused the heavy British casualties which some commentators found so galling. We have seen that the former assumption is questionable, and that the latter is entirely gratuitous.[64] Though Rangiriri was by no means his best performance, Cameron showed considerable skill and determination. He seized his opportunities promptly, if unscrupulously. The Maoris were not surrounded, and in terms of his objectives his decision to continue his assaults on the weak-looking central redoubt is understandable. The real responsibility for the high British losses rests not with Cameron but with Te Wharepu. Unlike the rifle pits at Puketakauere, Te Wharepu's redoubt was not concealed. It was simply a great deal stronger than it was made to look. This not only tempted Cameron into launching his assaults, but also ensured their failure.

The uncritical perpetuation of these two lines of thought has left us with a fundamentally inaccurate picture of Rangiriri. Whether the emphasis is on Cameron's skill or on Cameron's blunders, the white flag incident, the effect of the central redoubt and of the Maori weakness in men, and indeed the main events of the battle, are all overlooked. As for the real implications of the battle, the commentators who saw it as a virtual British failure were wrong. Rangiriri did cost the Maoris some ground and some lives. The penetration of the Maori left early in the action highlighted the vast disparity between Maori and British resources in gross manpower, and in the capacity to keep this manpower continuously in the field. For the Kingites, this was a depressing consideration, but even more depressing was the loss of 180 prisoners. The number of killed and wounded was not great, but when the prisoners were added Rangiriri became the most costly defeat in terms of men which the Maoris ever suffered at British hands. The more perceptive British commentators realized that it was the capture of the prisoners which made Rangiriri a major blow to the Maoris. 'A loss which they have been not only unaccustomed to but must regard as a serious misfortune.'[65]

On the other hand, the prisoners remained alive, and this 'serious misfortune' was therefore not necessarily irrevocable. Ten months after Rangiriri, in the dying days of the Waikato War, virtually all the prisoners escaped and eventually found their way home. This did not help the Maoris at the time of the battle, but in some respects it did reduce it to an ephemeral British success. In November 1863, Rangiriri seemed a serious defeat, but the white flag incident meant that the Maoris were less impressed by the 'resistlessness' of the British than by their duplicity. Rangiriri clearly did not represent a solution to the tactical problem of the modern pa. On the contrary, the repulse of no less than eight assaults on Te Wharepu's central redoubt was a telling demonstration of how great the problem was, and this had significant effects on Cameron's thinking and so on the result of the Waikato War. Heavy British losses did provide some 'compensation to rebel vengence', and the battle did not undermine the Maori will to resist.

9

Paterangi and Orakau

THE BELIEF THAT RANGIRIRI HAD BEEN WON BY SUPERIOR British military skills as well as resources involved both the tacit assumption that it was a blueprint for future victories, and the explicit assumption that it would demonstrate to the Kingites the hopelessness of further resistance. This led naturally to the expectation that it would prove politically decisive. Events immediately after the battle served to reinforce this expectation. Tamehana sent his personal *mere* to Cameron, and this action was seen by some as a 'token of submission'. Te Wharepu and other Waikato and Ngati Haua chiefs, together with the Rangiriri prisoners, expressed a willingness to negotiate. Then, on 8 December, the Maoris allowed Cameron to occupy the King's capital at Ngaruawahia. Grey informed Newcastle that: 'there can, I think, be no doubt that the neck of this unhappy rebellion is now broken'.[1]

Historians agree that the 'extreme' Kingites were determined to fight on, but they frequently follow a section of contemporary British opinion in assuming that the 'moderates' were now ready to submit. They therefore conclude that the British forsook a real chance of peace after Rangiriri, and discussion centres on whether Grey or the colonial ministry were responsible for this.[2]

It is true that the 'moderates' wished for peace after Rangiriri—they had never wanted war—and it is possible that they were prepared to accept the loss of the thirty mile stretch of territory up to Ngaruawahia.[3] But it is clear that they were not prepared to accept anything like the terms which the British continued to demand: submission to the Queen and the surrender of all arms and all land except for reservations allocated at the government's discretion. Even before the end of November, they began building further defences to the south of Ngaruawahia. The first of these *pa* to be completed, at Maungatautari, belonged to Tamehana, the most pacifically-inclined of the 'moderate' chiefs. Tamehana informed the Queenite chief Wiremu Nera that he would remain at Maungatautari. 'If the Governor follows me here, I shall fight. If not I shall remain quiet. . . . But if the General goes to Waipa (to attack) the Ngati Maniapoto I shall be there.'[4] Ngaruawahia was not a major economic centre, and Grey's emphasis on its importance in December 1863 contrasted markedly with his dismissal of it as a significant military target before the war.[5] Tamehana's gift of his *mere* and the evacuation of Ngaruawahia arose either from a willingness to negotiate a com-

158

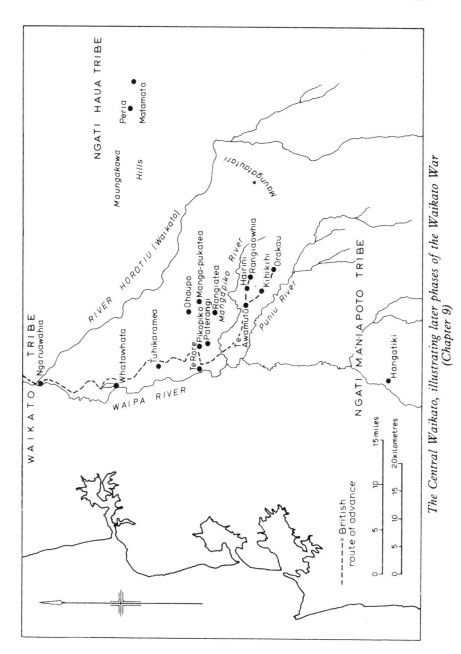

The Central Waikato, illustrating later phases of the Waikato War
(Chapter 9)

promise peace, or from the need for time to construct a new line of defence. Neither action reflected a willingness to surrender unconditionally. Despite Rangiriri, even the most moderate chiefs were still prepared to fight for their remaining land, their independence, and their King.

To achieve his objectives, Cameron therefore had no alternative but to press on with his invasion. The remaining operations in the Waikato basin consisted of two further British attempts to end the war with a decisive battle. The first of these occurred at Paterangi in late February 1864, and the second at Orakau at the end of March.

I THE PATERANGI LINE

SOON AFTER THE FALL OF RANGIRIRI THE KINGITES BEGAN work on their third line for the defence of Waikato. This ambitious complex of fortifications was located about twenty-five miles south of Ngaruawahia, and for convenience we may call it the Paterangi Line, after its largest *pa*. The purpose of the Line was, in general, to stop the British advance and, in particular, to protect the agriculturally rich Rangiaowhia district. Rangiao-whia ranked with the Hangatiki and Matamata-Peria districts as a major economic base for the core Kingite tribes, and its loss would be a con-siderable blow. 'So long . . . as these pas remained in the hands of the natives, so long were they free of any serious mishap, for the country from which they had been expelled was of slight value compared to the fertile territory the possession of which they were then disputing.'[6]

The strength of the Paterangi Line directly reflected the value of the area it protected. It was the largest system of fortifications that the Maoris ever built. There were at least four large *pa* within five or six miles of each other, covering all the main routes to Rangiaowhia and sited to provide mutual support. Each of these positions was in itself a complex set of entrench-ments. Paterangi proper had three substantial redoubts on one face alone. This *pa*, which blocked the most likely British route of advance, had a pro-tected water supply, two old cannon ready for action, and a particularly large 'shell-proof *whare*' which probably acted as a headquarters bunker for Rewi Maniapoto. It also had all the usual defensive features. The other three main *pa*—Pikopiko (or Puketoke), Rangiatea, and Manga-pukatea were equally strong and almost as extensive. Contemporary maps indicate that there may have been three or four other substantial fortifications in the area.[7]

This system was constructed by a Maori concentration comparable to that at Meremere, and perhaps even larger. The Paterangi army was in a sense the re-mobilized Meremere force, though with a proportion of different per-sonnel. Rangiriri interrupted the process of re-assembly but by early December enough men had gathered to undertake the massive task of building the Paterangi Line. By the end of the month, the basis of the Line was in existence and by late January 1864 it was complete. Though precision is impossible, it is fair to assume that the garrison was between 1,200 and 2,000 strong. The more reasonable European estimates vary from 1,200 to 3,000, an estimate based on Maori evidence gives a peak of 2,000 men, and it is very difficult to believe that many fewer could have built the works in the time available, even with considerable help from women.[8] As usual, however, there was a turnover of personnel and the number fluctuated. By 20 February, the strength had probably dropped from its peak, and a total of 1,500 warriors is a reasonable guess. All the major Kingite leaders were present, and the army was drawn from more than a dozen tribes. Large as it was in the context of Maori resources, this force was barely adequate to man the vast Paterangi defences. This meant that the Kingites were unable to guard the less likely paths to Rangiaowhia.

While the Maoris were fortifying the Paterangi Line, the British were crawling towards them from Ngaruawahia. Cameron occupied the Kingite capital on 9 December, but he did not move south to Whatawhata until two weeks later. On 1 January 1864, he moved on a further five miles to Tuhi-Karamea. He did not continue on up the Waipa River towards the Maoris until 27 January. He then marched to Te Rore, facing the Paterangi Line, but it was not until 20 February that he made any aggressive move. As they had done before and after the fall of Meremere, the colonist press complained loudly about the delays,[9] but there were good reasons for them. The first was simple logistics. By January 1864, the British had 7,000 men south of Ngaruawahia,[10] and the difficulty of supply naturally increased proportionally with numbers and distance. The second reason was bad luck. On 8 February the *Avon* struck a submerged tree in the Waipa and sank. With the *Pioneer*, this steamer was the centrepiece of the transport system. It not only carried twenty-five or thirty tons of supplies itself on each trip, but also towed several barges carrying more stores. For a few days, the fate of the Waikato invasion hung in the balance while desperate efforts were made to complete the fitting-out of a third steamer, the *Koheroa*, which had just arrived in Auckland. The supply situation 'was so urgent that it was decided to launch her as she was, a mere shell', and matters became even more critical when the vessel burst several plates in her hull at the Waikato Heads. It was only when the vessel arrived at Te Rore on 18 February, with thirty tons of supplies, that Cameron was able to proceed against Paterangi. 'Had a delay of another few days occurred [the British] would have been compelled to fall back.'[11] The *Koheroa* had been ordered a year before from the Sydney shipyards, and the importance of the British preparations for invasion could hardly be more clearly underlined.

The third factor behind the slow British advance was essentially the aftereffect of the Maori campaign against enemy communications of July-October 1863. 'Every precaution was taken . . . to secure the advance up the Waikato country, and to prevent the supplies being intercepted.'[12] Cameron's striking force in January 1864 was nearly 3,000 strong and not many more than 500 men would normally have been needed to supply this force, so half the 7,000 men south of Ngaruawahia were devoted to protecting the line of supply. The need to protect communications greatly compounded the other two problems behind the slow advance. Twice as many men had to be supplied, and the margin for such accidents as the sinking of the *Avon* was gravely reduced.

The slow British advance did not relieve the pressure on Maori resources completely. The distance between Ngaruawahia and Paterangi was short, and the Line had to be manned and supplied against a sudden British thrust. But the delays did provide a chance to complete the works, and by the end of January they were formidable. Inevitably, given the size and function of the Line, it was not possible to conceal their strength as had been done at Rangiriri. It was clear to the British from the outset that each *pa* 'would be a fearful place to storm'. Pikopiko, for example, was 'no despicable object even to the greatest ignoramus on works of defence'. After their advance from Tuhi-Karamea, the British had ample opportunity to reconnoitre and they were impressed with what they saw. 'The engineering skill displayed by the natives in the construction of their works was of the highest order, and was a matter of much wonder to General Cameron and his officers, who could scarcely believe that a savage race without any education in military tactics could have designed and so thoroughly carried out the details of such a complete system of defence.'[13] Fortunately for the British, Cameron did accept the fact that the works were strong, whoever he thought planned them. By 4 February the General had concluded that the Line 'cannot be taken by *coup de main*'. As Bishop Selwyn wryly remarked, 'the popular idea of "rushing" seems to have been abandoned since Rangiriri'.[14]

Cameron therefore decided to attempt to outflank the Maori defences. A Maori Ephialtes was essential to this plan, and one was available in the form of the half-caste James Edwards, or Himi Manuao. Edwards had lived in Rangiaowhia before the war, and he undertook to guide the British to it by a route which passed around the southern flank of Paterangi proper and through Te Awamutu. Despite Edwards's knowledge of the ground, the proposed operation was both difficult and risky. The major difficulty was that the British would have to pass within 1,500 yards of Paterangi *pa* without being detected. To do this Cameron's outflanking column would have to march over a very rough bush track at night and in silence—a tall order for the best irregulars, let alone for regular troops. To make the task easier, Cameron gave orders that his men should travel lightly equipped. This was wise, but it necessitated a division of force. A supplementary column would have to bring up artillery and supplies after the initial penetration had been made. The principal risks were that the outflanking column's own communications might be cut, and that if it was detected it might be attacked while carrying out its difficult night march. To guard against the first danger, by leaving a strong force before Paterangi to watch the Maoris, increased the second, by weakening the outflanking column.

Cameron's plan was a finely calculated gamble, but it was justified by the prize at stake. Historians imply that the British simply aimed to seize the

Rangiaowhia district, and indeed this area was sufficiently important to be an object of attack in itself. But Cameron's primary objective was nothing less than the destruction of the Kingite army. By outflanking the Line, he hoped he could force the Maoris to fight a pitched battle for Rangiaowhia. In daylight, on open ground, and with his men prepared, Cameron was understandably convinced that he could win such a battle so decisively as to end the war. As Grey cautiously explained to Newcastle, after outlining Cameron's plan: 'If the natives continue to hold their ground until these movements are completed, it is possible that General Cameron may succeed in striking so decisive a blow that it will bring this unhappy combat to a close.'[15]

Cameron probably decided on the outflanking plan at some time in January, but was delayed by the problems outlined earlier. When the arrival of the *Koheroa* ended the latest supply crisis, Cameron moved swiftly. On the night of 20 February, with a column of 1,230 men, he set off along the rough track under Edwards's guidance. A masking force of about the same strength was left in front of Paterangi, and 600 men of the supply column held themselves ready to move. The night was pitch black and Cameron's column passed so close to Paterangi that they could clearly hear the sentries shouting their watch-cries. 'The men marched in perfect silence which is the hardest thing a British soldier can do.' Cameron reached Te Awamutu at day break and immediately pushed on to Rangiaowhia. He found the town 'nearly deserted'.[16] The few people in the place were mainly women and children, but a dozen warriors put up a gallant fight—in which Colonel Nixon was mortally wounded—before being overwhelmed. Having made his presence felt, Cameron withdrew to Te Awamutu to await the Maori reaction. The supply column, escorted by 650 men, joined him that afternoon. The significance of Cameron's withdrawal from Rangiaowhia is generally overlooked. It confirms that the British objective was less the town itself than the Kingite army.

As Cameron had hoped, a Maori force left Paterangi and reoccupied Rangiaowhia early on the morning of 22 February. With Paterangi virtually emptied, Cameron ordered up strong reinforcements from the masking force. But before these could arrive, his scouts reported that the Maoris had begun entrenching a position—Hairini Ridge—between the British and Rangiaowhia. Cameron decided to attack before the defensive works could progress too far, and at 1.30 p.m. he did so.[17]

The Maoris made no real effort to hold their embryonic trenches against the vigorous assault of the 50th Regiment and its supports. The few warriors who made up the front line 'fell hurriedly back before the leading files of the 50th could reach them'. Cameron launched his cavalry (forty Colonial Defence Force and thirty-five men seconded from the artillery) in pursuit. These were checked by the disciplined volleys of the Maori reserve, under Wiremu Tamehana. The Maoris then withdrew.[18] Though some British commentators tried to make a notable victory of it, the 'Battle' of Hairini was an anti-climax. Cameron himself estimated the Maori strength at only 400 men, and a Kingite veteran's account confirms this figure. Even the British assessments of Maori casualties rarely exceed thirty killed, and Tamehana, a reliable source, stated that the Kingites 'lost' nine men in all, at least one of whom was wounded and taken prisoner. The British had twenty-two casualties, of whom only two were killed.[19]

It seems clear that in entrenching at Hairini the Maoris simply intended to delay the British, while Rangiaowhia and the Paterangi Line were evacuated with all supplies that could be carried. The Maori stand at Hairini was basically a bluff, and once Cameron called it, the aim of the small Maori force was to escape intact. The front-line was only a hundred strong and the reserves—300 men—were positioned to cover the retreat. As Tamehana put it: 'I preferred that there should be but few to advance in front, to be light, so as not to be eager to fight.'[20] Some warriors advocated a more valiant and less rational course, and there was apparently considerable debate, but it is clear from the Maori conduct of the engagement that realistic councils prevailed.

The respite earned at Hairini enabled the Maoris to get all their people, guns, and ammunition out of the Rangiaowhia district and its now-useless defensive line, although a quantity of food supplies had to be left behind. The Paterangi army broke up, but the Maori resistance did not lose its coherence. Apart from various smaller fragments, scattered about the country for supply reasons, there were two main divisions. Rewi Maniapoto and one division withdrew south of the Puniu River to cover the Ngati Maniapoto bases in the Hangatiki valley. Tamehana and the other retreated to Maungatautari, which blocked a British advance up the Horotiu into Ngati Raukawa territory and lay on the flank of the route to the Ngati Haua economic centres at Matamata and Peria. Cameron occupied the Rangiaowhia district and prepared to move against Tamehana.

The first point to be made about these events relates to the well-known Maori belief that Rangiaowhia was the victim of a treacherous British attack. According to this, Bishop Selwyn and General Cameron sent a message to the Kingites agreeing to set Rangiaowhia aside as a place of safety for the women and children. Convincing Maori evidence indicates that some such message was in fact sent.[21] On the other hand, it is extremely improbable that Cameron would have committed himself to not attacking so important an economic target, the very hub of the Kingite supply system. Further, if the Maoris genuinely believed that Rangiaowhia had been declared immune from attack, why did they go to such enormous trouble to block all major routes to it, building no less than four large *pa* for the purpose? The answer may be that Selwyn and Cameron, concerned at the killing of non-combatants at Rangiriri, intimated to the Maoris that women and children would be safeguarded where possible, and that they should be kept out of the firing lines—without specifying any sacrosanct ground. Subsequently, the Maoris misunderstood this, or raised the issue in response to one-sided aspersions cast on their own actions. Non-combatants may have been intentionally killed at Rangiaowhia, and some certainly were at the later engagement of Orakau, but accusations of British duplicity might be better directed at their conduct at Rangiriri.

As far as the military results are concerned, Cameron did not achieve his primary objective of destroying the Kingite army. The Maoris, though apparently with considerable reluctance, had come to the hard-headed decision to abandon the Paterangi Line and the rich district it protected. By doing so, they saved their army. It was less a question of exchanging the district for the army than of losing one rather than both. An all-out pitched battle was almost certain to result in a crushing Maori defeat at the hands of the large British force. The Rangiaowhia district would then have fallen anyway. As it was, the raid on Rangiaowhia and the 'Battle' of Hairini—in reality a carefully limited rearguard action—together cost the Maoris only twenty warriors killed.

The British were disappointed in their hopes of decisive success, as some of them admitted. 'It will be seen', wrote one newspaper correspondent 'that the success of today's engagement has not been so decided as might have been wished.' A colonial officer observed that 'most of us felt dissatisfied with the day's work'. Grey and the colonial government were also reported to be very disappointed. As at Meremere, and to a lesser extent at Rangiriri, the Maoris had escaped from the closing jaws of the British trap.[22] Nevertheless, unlike Meremere, Cameron's Paterangi manoeuvre did constitute a substantial success for the British. At a cost of less than thirty British casualties, the Maoris had been forced out of their strongest system of fortifications and consequently out of one of their richest economic centres. The loss of the Rangiaowhia district severely and permanently weakened the King Movement, and the blow to Maori morale was considerable. Paterangi, though close to bloodless, was in reality the greatest British victory of the Waikato War.

The victory was partly the result of inferior Maori resources. With a few hundred more men, the Maoris could have blocked the Te Awamutu route as they had blocked the others. The chance that made James Edwards available was also important. As Cameron himself admitted, 'without his [Edwards's] assistance to guide the column, the night march of the 20th could not have been undertaken'.[23] But at Paterangi, in contrast to Rangiriri, the balance between luck and generalship favoured generalship. Unlike many of his contemporaries, Cameron had learned some lessons from Rangiriri. Despite pressure from Grey and the colonial government, he refused to assault the Paterangi Line, and instead turned to his outflanking manoeuvre. In retrospect, this may seem an obvious alternative, but it involved great risks and difficulties. Cameron calculated and minimized the risks and overcame the difficulties. The conception and implementation of the Paterangi manoeuvre were little short of brilliant. One may guess that, in another war, Cameron's achievement would have earned him a permanent reputation as a general of the first order. But the grim realism of the Maoris in cutting their losses meant that decisive victory continued to elude the British.

II THE BATTLE OF ORAKAU

THE BATTLE OF ORAKAU (31 MARCH TO 2 APRIL 1864) IS PERHAPS the best-known engagement of the New Zealand Wars. It is Orakau which is usually selected by writers to provide an anecdote illustrative of the conflict. As *Rewi's Last Stand*, the battle has even inspired a feature film. This relative fame stems from two widely held assumptions about the significance of the engagement. The first is the belief that it was the heroism displayed by the Maoris, at Orakau above all, which created an enduring respect for their enemies in the minds of the British regulars, resulting in an increasing reluctance to fight in New Zealand. The battle is therefore seen to mark the apex of the Maori military achievement. Yet it is also seen as the nadir of Maori fortunes in terms of success, for the second general assumption about Orakau is that it was the decisive British victory which brought the campaign in the Waikato basin to a triumphant end.

The interest generated by Orakau as an heroic and decisive event led researchers—notably James Cowan—to seek out and record a uniquely large number of Maori accounts. This lends an analysis of the battle special importance because of the light that is thrown on the strengths and weaknesses of Maori organization, discipline, and leadership.

After the fall of the Paterangi Line, Ngati Maniapoto and their allies met at Wharepapa village, just south of the Puniu River, to discuss their prospects. Despite the recent reverse 'the decision to continue the war was unanimous'.[24] Because most of the troops which the British could spare from guarding the land they had occupied were concentrated against Tamehana at Maungatautari, Ngati Maniapoto had a lull in which to decide how to proceed. The two principal options were to adopt Tamehana's strategy of guarding the hinterland with large *pa* on its fringes, or to seek battle with the occupying forces north of the Puniu by building a *pa* under their noses. Rewi suggested that the decision should be postponed until he had consulted Tamehana. The bulk of the Kingite western wing accordingly remained south of the Puniu while Rewi travelled towards Maungatautari in the east.

Along the way, Rewi came upon another segment of the dispersed Paterangi army—a fateful accident. These warriors were mainly Tuhoe and Ngati Raukawa, and they were led by a set of fire-brand chiefs including Piripi Te Heuheu, Te Whenua-nui (Tuhoe) and Te Paerata (Ngati te Koheroa *hapu* of Ngati Raukawa). The Tuhoe had come a long way to fight the *pakeha* and they wished to do so immediately. Te Whenua-nui proposed to Rewi 'that you give us Orakau as a place to use our guns and ammunition. They are too heavy to carry all this way for nothing.'[25] Orakau was a pleasant village north of the Puniu and within three miles of British-occupied Kihikihi, so this in effect was the rasher option proposed at Wharepapa. Rewi spoke very strongly against the idea. 'Only by not fighting [at present] may I retain my lands. . . . Do not fight at Orakau. If you must fight, then do so at [Maungatautari, under Tamehana] . . . If you Tuhoe persist in your desire for battle, I alone will be the survivor.'[26]

Tuhoe and Ngati Raukawa decided to disregard his advice and march to Orakau. Rewi had done all he could to shake their determination, and he could simply have left them to their fate. But these men had originally come to fight at his particular request, and he had links of kinship with some of them. Some of his own tribesmen were also keen to adopt an aggressive policy and fight north of the Puniu.[27] It is also possible that some European aspersions cast on his personal courage had percolated through to the Kingites,[28] and although these were totally unjustified, they may conceivably have influenced him. For whatever reasons, Rewi cast in his lot with his allies and accompanied them to Orakau, probably arriving late on 28 March 1864.

The Orakau site suited the Tuhoe and Ngati Raukawa purpose in that the ground was fairly flat and easily worked, and because it offered the prospect of immediate battle from its proximity to the British. But Rewi's objections to fighting at Orakau were sound. The site had no integral water supply and it could easily be encircled. The former weakness, of course, was unimportant without the latter. In the words of one of the garrison, 'it was not a suitable place at all'.[29] However, having bravely but rashly selected an unsound position, the Maoris proceeded to make the best they could of its tactical possibilities. By working day and night (in shifts because there were not enough spades) they succeeded in making the *pa* viable—though not complete—by the time the British attacked. Limitations of time and tools meant the *pa* was both fairly simple and only moderately strong, but it was tenable against assault if skilfully defended.[30] It consisted of an oblong redoubt with two small bastions and one large but unfinished outwork. The whole was about 4,000 square feet in area. The *pa* had interior bunkers, traversed trenches, firing apertures, and a post and rail fence around it acting as a *pekerangi*. Its most notable feature was that it was very low indeed. The top of the main parapet was only four feet above ground. Together with the fact that the *pa* was sited among some peach trees, this meant that its strength was difficult to assess. It is even possible that it was not immediately apparent that the place was fortified at all.

The Maori force collected to defend this position included representatives of at least nine tribes, but the two units which made up its core were the Tuhoe and Ngati Raukawa. Tuhoe were sixty or more strong and were accompanied by twenty Ngati Kahungunu from Hawke's Bay. Ngati Raukawa, mainly of Ngati te Kohera *hapu*, supported by some of their Ngati Tuwharetoa neighbours were in similar or slightly greater strength. Only a fraction of Ngati Maniapoto were present. This contingent was probably Rewi's own bodyguard and was variously put at from fifteen to fifty strong. There were no other substantial tribal contingents, but most of the Waikato tribes were represented—including Ngati Mahuta, Ngati Mahanga, Ngati Hinetu, and at least two others. Some Ngati Porou, Whakatohea, and Whanau-a-Apanui, and perhaps others as well were also probably pre-

sent under the general heading of 'the East Coast Natives'. One or two
Arawa of Ngati Manawa and at least two warriors from the Manawatu
district were also among the garrison.[31]

Accounts generally agree that these contingents totalled about 300
people,[32] but the fighting strength is more difficult to fix because this figure
included a considerable number of women (who do not appear to have been
involved in actual combat) and a few children. Cowan gives 310 people, including about twenty women, but he seems to have overestimated one contingent by about forty men, and perhaps to have understated the number of
women.[33] The account of some Maori prisoners recorded immediately after
the battle gave 200 men and 100 women.[34] Before the Maoris had suffered
many casualties, two European eyewitnesses put the garrison at 200 to 250
people.[35] Roughly 200 to 250 warriors and something like fifty non-
combatants may be a reasonable estimate.

There were occasions, such as at Puketakauere in 1860, where the construction of a modern *pa* so close to a British force as to provoke a prompt
attack was perfectly justified by strategic necessity and the tactical suitability
of the site. Orakau was not one of these. The site was convenient in the
sense that it could be fortified fairly rapidly, but this advantage was negated
by the absence of an integral water supply and the ease with which it could
be surrounded. The lack of an escape route transgressed a fundamental
principle of the modern *pa* system, and Orakau is the only case of the
Maoris making such an error when facing Imperial troops. A viable alternative strategy was available: protecting Ngati Maniapoto and Ngati Haua
economic bases with flexible defensive lines. Tamehana was applying this
strategy at Maungatautari, Ngati Maniapoto had considered beginning a
parallel defensive line south of the Puniu,[36] and it was this policy that the
Kingites as a whole were soon to adopt.

It seems clear that Rewi was fully aware of these factors. But against his
better judgement he decided to join his allies. There are two ironies here. It
was a bond between disparate tribes—unity rather than disunity—which involved the Kingites' leading general in a potential disaster. And it was Rewi
Maniapoto, of all the generals of the wars the least inclined towards irrational if valiant gestures, who found himself committed to the 'last stand'
that was to bear his name in the popular mythology.

On the morning of 30 March, the Maoris fortifying Orakau were spotted by
a surveyor, and the news was reported to Brigadier General G. J. Carey at
Te Awamutu by midday.[37] Though Cameron himself, with 1,000 men, lay
facing Tamehana, Carey was able to muster 1,120 men for immediate service from the local garrisons. Carey correctly surmised that the Maoris were
unaware they had been detected, and that their *pa* was incomplete. But
Orakau looked deceptively weak, and Carey's information led him to
underestimate the strength of the defences already completed. He therefore
decided to attack as soon as possible. His men were to march in three

separate columns—the main force, under Carey himself, of 730 men and two smaller columns totalling 390. Carey intended that they should arrive together at Orakau at about dawn of 31 March. It is sometimes implied that this bold manoeuvre was aimed solely at encircling the Maoris, and it is true that the role of the two smaller columns was to prevent a Maori escape. But Carey believed that the Maoris' works scarcely existed as yet, and he planned that his main force would assault Orakau on arrival and destroy its garrison.

Assisted by half-caste guides, the three columns completed their difficult night march virtually on schedule. The vanguard of the main column, about 240 men under Captain Ring, saw nothing to disabuse them of the opinion that the *pa* was weak, and 'rushed immediately to assault the apparently open position of the enemy'.[38]

Though the Maoris had seen the enemy only moments before, they reacted calmly. Despite the previous divisions among the leadership, there was no dispute about Rewi's command in actual combat. Rewi placed most of his warriors in the outer line of the trench, with a reserve of forty veterans in the centre of the *pa*. Rewi rejected a suggestion that the Maori fire be reserved for a range of a couple of yards. 'The whites of their eyes' maxim was all very well, but at that range a single volley might not be enough to break the British momentum. Instead, Rewi decided to open fire at about fifty yards range just as the British began to scramble over and through the post-and-rail fence. Men with *tupara* were ordered to reserve their second barrel.[39] These dispositions were sufficient to halt Ring's attack. The message that the *pa* was unexpectedly strong had yet to sink in, however, and reinforced by one company Ring renewed the assault. Again, the Maoris 'fired in disciplined volleys under the direction of the chief Rewi'.[40] The men fired in two sections to give a platoon-fire effect which minimized the pause for loading. Again the British were repelled, with two captains, including Ring, among the casualties. A third, less well-organized attack led by Captain Baker met with a similar fate. Carey's attempt at *coup de main* had been decisively defeated, and Maori morale was high. 'Each of these unsuccessful assaults was complimented by derisive cheers from the natives, accompanied by the encouraging cries of "Come on, Jack, come on!"'[41]

Having discovered the 'immense strength' of Orakau the hard way, Carey now 'decided on surrounding the place' and the second and longest phase of the battle began. With the two smaller British columns now in position, the *pa* was quickly encircled and its access to water cut. The ease with which this was done proves beyond doubt that the Orakau site was really a weak one, however strong the fortifications. Carey now realized that he had an unparalleled opportunity to deal the Kingites a crushing blow, and he sent Cameron an 'urgent appeal' for reinforcements so as to be absolutely sure of his prey.[42] The implications were immediately clear to Cameron, and his response was prompt. A reinforcement of 150 men arrived that afternoon, followed by 220 at dawn on 1 April, and Cameron himself with further troops early on 2 April. Orakau became the focus of attention for the very good reason that it represented a chance to end the war at a stroke with that clear-cut victory over a significant Kingite force which had hitherto proved so elusive. The Orakau garrison was not a large fraction of Kingite strength, but it was reasonable to believe that the moral effect of its total annihilation, together with the death or capture of Rewi, would prove a mortal blow to the Maori cause. As more troops arrived to tighten the British cordon around Orakau, and 'every possible precaution [was] taken, by the proper distributing of the force, to prevent the escape of the enemy', the possibility seemed to develop into a certainty.[43] The Auckland public were informed that 'the Maories cannot escape as they are wholly surrounded', and a triumphant end to the Waikato War seemed imminent.[44]

Though the destruction of the Maoris seemed to be only a matter of time, Carey was eager to hasten the process. We may guess—perhaps ungenerously—that he wished to secure the victory he had earned before Cameron arrived to take the credit. He positioned his men very close to the pa, to be ready to grasp any chance of a successful assault. The Maoris, however, produced 'some very good shooting', which forced the British to withdraw to a safer distance, and themselves indulge in a little entrenching, scraping out shallow rifle pits 'with their bayonets and hands'.[45] Despite this, men continued to be hit, and the three days in the trenches were to prove almost as trying for the besiegers as for the besieged.[46] Carey also attempted to breach the pa with a bombardment, but the three six-pounder Armstrongs available to him could make little impression on the earthworks. A third measure looked more promising. This was a 'flying sap', dug as rapidly as possible towards the pa. Begun soon after the encirclement on the morning of 31 March, in a protected hollow about 150 yards from the Maori defences, the sap was expected to be 'under the pa by midnight'.[47] The British had reckoned without their enemies. The Maoris concentrated an accurate fire on the sap-head, launched a couple of small sallies at it, and according to one account, even ran out a counter-sap.[48] They succeeded in killing or wounding several of the working party and in putting the sap thirty-six hours behind schedule, but the British persisted in their efforts.

As early as the night of 31 March, the garrison of Orakau ..ad begun to run short of essentials. A Ngati Maniapoto chief, Te Winitana Tupotahi, who appears to have acted as Rewi's adjutant, inspected the stocks and found that little water remained, and that ammunition was running short, despite the most careful control of its use.[49] Tupotahi reported this to Rewi, and suggested a breakout attempt that night. A conference was called, and Tuhoe and Ngati Raukawa opposed the idea. According to two Maori sources, Rewi himself was also opposed. He may have guessed—correctly— that the British considered an escape attempt a 'certainty' on the first night, and were therefore ready for it. He may have wished to co-ordinate the attempt with a taua of reinforcements which had been seen during the day. For whatever reason, Tupotahi's suggestion was rejected.[50]

The reinforcements which may have influenced the Maori decision had appeared about a mile to the south-east of Orakau around midday, 31

March. They were warriors from Maungatautari of Ngati Haua, Ngati Raukawa, and Ngati Tuwharetoa and they were led by Te Heuheu of the last-named tribe and perhaps by Tamehana himself. They were eager to come to the help of the beleaguered garrison but they arrived a little too late. The British cordon was now tight, they had been seen by the troops, and would have to cross hundreds of yards of open ground in the face of massed rifle and artillery fire, and according to European estimates they numbered no more than 150 men. It seemed impossible to break into or out of Orakau. As a member of the garrison put it: 'Te Heuheu . . . and a small party came as near to us as they could, but were fired at by the big guns. They sat on the hill and wept their farewell, for they thought that we would none of us escape.'[51] By the night of 1 April the water was exhausted and some men were firing peachstones instead of bullets—though each warrior kept a couple of rounds as an ultimate reserve. It was now clear that the Maungatautari *taua* was unable to help, and perhaps in the hope that the British would be off their guard, Rewi now advocated an escape attempt by the garrison on its own. But the Tuhoe and Ngati Raukawa remained adamant, and the siege moved into its third day.[52]

About noon that day (2 April) General Cameron, who had arrived a little earlier, invited the Maoris to surrender. Perhaps with Rangiriri in mind, the garrison rejected the offer with only one dissenting voice. Cameron, who sincerely admired the Maoris' courage, suggested that the women should be sent to safety, but they preferred to stay and die with the men.[53] The end of these negotiations brought the impatience of the tired and tense British troops around the *pa* to a fever pitch. There was also 'a large con- sumption of ration rum and some of the men were very reckless'. Two assaults, probably unauthorized, were launched by groups of twenty or thirty men. They failed with a heavy proportion of casualties. This ended the second phase of the battle.[54]

Orakau had resisted a total of five assaults but the situation inside the *pa* was now hopeless. The water was gone and the ammunition was very nearly exhausted. It was clear to even the most diehard of the chiefs that their fifty- six hours of continuous resistance could not be prolonged. This made the refusal to surrender all the more remarkable because the single remaining alternative—a breakout in daylight—scarcely seemed a realistic option at all. The Maoris may have hoped that the rejection of terms would be followed by an all-out assault, in which they would go down fighting. According to some sources, Carey was willing to oblige, the sap having reached the *pa*'s outwork; but Cameron wisely vetoed the idea.[55] Thirst could be expected to do the work more cheaply. The Maoris resolved to attempt the seemingly impossible, and at 3.30 p.m. the whole garrison went over to the attack in an effort to cut its way out.

It says a great deal for the nerve of Rewi and his associates that they did not allow even this desperate expedient to become uncontrolled. 'Every- thing was as properly planned as if they had forgotten that hordes of their enemies were at that moment undermining their last prop of support.'[56] In the last extremity, the Maoris still tried to maximize their slim chance of success by good management. The Maori attack was launched simultaneously by the whole garrison from the south-east angle of the *pa* while British attention was focused on the sap, now in the last stages of completion, at the opposite corner. The Maoris advanced in a compact body with the women and children in the centre and the best warriors in front. Most men had reserved a few rounds for such an eventuality, but the column at first withheld its fire and advanced in perfect silence. The British had been expecting action of some kind but the nature and timing of the Maori move momentarily disconcerted them. The Maoris were able to reach the top of the ridge perhaps 200 yards from the *pa* with little loss.

They had not yet broken through the cordon, however, which at this point consisted of men of the 40th Regiment. These were stationed behind the ridge, and the first they saw of the Maoris was the whole column charging down the slope towards them, firing as they came. The numbers and behaviour of the 40th were the subject of some contemporary controversy, as we shall see, but they were unlikely to have been less than 150 strong, and they stood their ground and got in one heavy volley. Despite this, the Maori column broke the British line. To record the experience of one Tuhoe member of the Maori vanguard, prominent in this remarkable event:

A fence, over-grown with fern, stood in front. As we scrambled over it, we saw more soldiers before us, a long double line of them. We rushed that line. They shot us and stabbed us with bayonets. We strove to break that line. As we reached it a soldier tried to bayonet me. I parried the point and shot that soldier. He fell against the next man who shook him off, as a man from the rear line stepped forward into the vacant space. I shot that man with my second barrel and darted through the line.[57]

The Maoris thus broke through the British cordon intact, and reached a clump of *manuka* bush where they broke up into smaller parties to confuse pursuit. But their ordeal was by no means over. The British, enraged at losing their prey at the last moment, followed the fugitives with all possible energy. Though they had split up, the Maoris continued to resist in an organized fashion. Rewi's own party, firing at his command, shot several pursuers.[58] But the British—particularly the small force of cavalry and the fast-moving Forest Rangers—did considerable execution. The Maoris suffered most of their losses during this pursuit.

British losses in the Battle of Orakau were sixteen killed, and fifty-three wounded, some mortally.[59] Maori casualties in this engagement are particularly difficult to estimate, but it is clear that, as a result of the vigorous pursuit, they were high. A day or two after the battle, the British began claiming that 150 to 200 Maoris had been killed, and this figure is still generally accepted.[60] However, a surprising number of earlier British reports gave fifty for the number of Maori bodies counted. It seems likely that, for once, this was an underestimate. Rewi was reported to have stated that eighty Maoris were killed, and this appears to be a reasonable figure.

The British brought in twenty-six Maori wounded alive, and perhaps a dozen or so more may have been carried off by their friends. Eighty Maoris killed and forty wounded may not be far wrong.[61]

It must be said that, in striking contrast to the legend, this disproportion of killed and wounded suggests that the Orakau pursuit involved a large-scale massacre of wounded non-combatants. Other evidence strongly supports this conclusion, and indicates that women and possibly children were amongst the killed. Even the colonial press—an institution not noted for philanthropy—regretted that 'women—many women—slaughtered . . . are amongst the trophies of Orakau'.[62] Despite this, the notion that Orakau marked an immediate step towards mutual respect between the races in New Zealand has combined with the undeniable heroism displayed by the Maoris to make the battle a kind of symbol of the wars. It is sometimes assumed that the battle was not only symbolic, but typical. As far as the Maoris' strategic decision to fight at Orakau is concerned, nothing could be more false.

Some writers have deduced from the Orakau experience that the classic weakness of Maori *pa* was their lack of an integral water supply, and this notion has made its contribution to the characterization of Maori resistance as brave, and clever, but essentially incoherent. A number of Maori *pa* did lack a water supply, but this was a trivial disadvantage if the Maoris could leave at any time they chose. It was the lack of an escape route which made the decision to fight at Orakau such a blunder, and it was an exceptional blunder. In this sense, the outstanding feature of Orakau was not that it was typical, but that it was unique.

In other respects, however, something can be learned from Orakau about Maori military methods in general. In council, before and during the battle, with Rewi only one voice among several, the Maori leadership made faulty decisions. The Maoris should have attempted a breakout on the night of 1 April, and they should never have fought at Orakau in the first place. Rewi was overruled despite the fact that he was generally acknowledged to be the best war leader and was held in great respect. Several warriors—including one of the Ngati Raukawa chiefs who consistently opposed his decisions in council—died shielding Rewi from enemy fire.[63] The first concern of wounded warriors when picked up by the British during the pursuit was to ask what had happened to Rewi. So many did so that the British initially believed that they were lamenting Rewi's death or wounding. Gustavus Von Tempsky, a Captain in the Forest Rangers, noted one such incident, and observed 'the word on the dying lips of the two other wounded Maoris had also been "Rewi-Rewi"'.[64] The Maoris would die for Rewi but they would not always obey him. This is exactly what we would expect from Maori social organization, where a chief's authority extended as far as he could persuade his people to follow him.

But whatever the divisions in council, in actual combat the Maoris applied a unified tactical scheme, and they showed a high degree of battle discipline. Organization was tight and efficient. Ammunition, for example, was distributed by the women from a central armoury where six men worked permanently as cartridge-makers. Men used their bullets sparingly—one warrior fired only thirty-six rounds in three days of battle.[65] In combat Rewi was in undisputed command. 'Only one man was in high command, and that was Rewi.'[66] Volleys and even individual shots were fired on the leader's order, and this principle continued to apply during the pursuit. During these last stages of the battle, according to his own account, Rewi instructed his men as follows: 'I called out to some of my people who were a little ahead of me . . . "Come here; one of you fire there" to another, "Fire over there"; to one who was standing close to me I said "You fire right in here."' He continued to direct his men until the pursuit ended, telling them 'Don't run; go easily' the better to keep the British at a distance.[67] It appears that, in actual combat, the Maoris were prepared to suspend their individual independence in the interests of fighting more effectively.

Another striking feature of the Maori performance at Orakau was the success of their column in breaking the line of the 40th. This feat was largely attributable to the determination and disciplined cohesion of the Maori phalanx, and deserves to rank as one of the most remarkable incidents of the wars. But it was an exceptional incident—the 40th had been surprised and outnumbered—and could hardly be said to undermine the Maoris' own basic premise: that open battle with British troops was to be avoided.

The defeat of the 40th gave rise to vituperative criticism of the regiment and its commander, Colonel Leslie. One commentator labelled these allegations 'a tissue of the grossest calumnies', and based his defence on the assertions that most of the 40th had been sent to make more gabions for the sap or been removed to give some cannon a clear line of fire, and that General Cameron had commended the regiment.[68] In fact, only a minority of the men were making gabions, and there was a hill between the 40th and the *pa* through which cannon clearly could not fire. Moreover, Cameron himself was among the regiment's fiercest critics. 'General Cameron got in a temper and slanged Colonel Leslie ("Gentle Arthur" as he is called) for letting the enemy pass.'[69] But it was less the mechanics of the 40th's failure—there were mitigating circumstances—than its results that lent force to this criticism. Leslie's inability to stop the Maori escape had done nothing less than rob Orakau of its fruits. For once Cameron and his implacable opponent, William Fox, were in full agreement. The General informed Grey that: 'But for the want of vigilance on the part of the 40th Regiment, who were stationed at that part of the cordon to which they [the Maoris] directed their flight, not a man of them would have escaped.' And Fox later wrote of the 40th incident: 'had this not unfortunately happened, Rewi, the most influential chief in the war party, must have fallen into our hands.' The *Southern Cross* went further, and wrote of 'the transaction which snatched a crowning victory from our hands and turned it into a humiliating defeat'.[70]

'Humiliating defeat' is a strange term for what is conventionally seen as the decisive British victory of the Waikato War. It appears that both labels are extreme. The Maoris suffered heavy casualties and they themselves saw the battle as a substantial defeat. On the other hand, Orakau was for the British the cruellest disappointment of the entire war. From the afternoon of 31 March to the moment the Maoris broke out two days later their fate had seemed irrevocably sealed, and the final crushing British victory simply a matter of time. Eighty Maori corpses were a poor second prize to the power of the King Movement and a victorious end to the war.

Bitter defeat though it was for the Maoris, Orakau had virtually no strategic results. The core tribes of the King Movement lost fewer men there than at Koheroa. Casualties among other tribes were fairly evenly distributed, so Orakau did not compare even to Rangiriri in terms of crippling a single tribe's warrior force. The battle cost the Kingites no land, and as we shall see it did not affect their will to resist further invasion. Orakau was the lost chance of decisive British victory in the Waikato War. It was not that victory itself.

After Orakau, the Maoris resorted to their old strategy by manning a set of fortifications which functioned as a fourth line for the defence of Waikato, though it had two widely-separated flanks. In the east, a series of *pa* bordering the Maungatautari and Mangakawa ranges, protected Ngati Haua and Ngati Raukawa base areas. The western flank, consisting of three strong *pa* south of the Puniu River, covered the Ngati Maniapoto base area of Hangatiki. From April, the Line was manned by the third of the great Maori concentrations. Though the Maoris acknowledged the loss of the British occupied territory, the limits of which they already referred to as 'the boundary' (*aukati*), they were determined to resist continued invasion. Rewi and Tamehana informed two British envoys that 'if the *pakehas* attempted to carry on the war in any district beyond the boundary, they would fight again.'[71] Contrary to the general belief, the Maoris were still both willing and able to resist effectively if attacked.[72]

Cameron had been preparing for operations against the eastern flank of the Line before the unexpected engagement at Orakau. With the interruption over, he advanced to attack one of the Maungatautari *pa*—Te Tiki o te Ihingarangi. Tamehana had completed this *pa* in December 1863, and it was extremely strong. The Maoris awaited attack, justifiably confident that they could repel any assault. Fortunately for the British, this was also apparent to Cameron. He concluded that, like Paterangi, Te Tiki was 'too strong to be taken by *coup de main*'. Unlike Paterangi, however, it could not be outflanked and the British simply settled down in front of it. On 5 April, after waiting for three days, the Maoris evacuated Te Tiki, probably because they had exhausted its supplies. This did not affect the general argument, because Te Tiki was only one of a group of *pa*, and Cameron's problem remained intact.[73]

After ten months campaigning, the General was growing disenchanted with his search for decisive battle in Waikato. The reasons for this will be discussed below, but the fact itself is sufficiently proved by his subsequent movements. After the Maori evacuation of Te Tiki, Cameron left the bulk of his troops holding their conquests in central Waikato and withdrew the core of his striking force to Auckland. Though it was not apparent to anyone at the time, this ended the active war in the Waikato basin.

At Auckland, Cameron considered sending reinforcements to Taranaki, where the intensity of operations showed signs of increasing. Then important information arrived from a new theatre—Tauranga, on the east coast of Waikato. In January 1864, a small expedition had been despatched to Tauranga under Colonel G. J. Carey, who was soon replaced by Colonel Greer. Greer had remained on the defensive, holding 'Camp Te Papa' on the Tauranga Harbour, but the local Maoris, Ngai-te-Rangi, had begun making aggressive movements. These culminated on 3 April, when Ngai-te-Rangi began building a *pa* within three miles of Camp Te Papa. The proximity of this *pa* to a good harbour meant that, if he chose, Cameron could concentrate as many men and guns against it as he thought necessary—without the problems of transport and supply that had bedevilled him in Waikato. It was an unprecedented opportunity, and Cameron lost no time in seizing it. By 21 April he himself was at Te Papa and by 26 April his striking force had joined him. The focus of the war now switched to Tauranga.

The Tauranga Campaign

THE ORIGINAL BRITISH EXPEDITION TO TAURANGA WAS designed, not to seize more land as is sometimes suggested, but to disrupt the system whereby 'neutral' tribes supplied the Waikato front with provisions and warriors while cultivating in peace at home.[1] The expeditionary force landed on 21 January 1864, and was soon ordered by Grey to act on the defensive, to avoid involving those Tauranga Maoris who appeared genuinely to be neutral. Cameron was displeased by Grey's interference, but in reality it was unimportant. Colonel Greer and the British expedition controlled Tauranga Harbour even while acting defensively, and so blocked the conduit through which the Waikato front had received warriors from the East Cape, and possibly ammunition from illicit traders.[2] Moreover, the local Maoris could hardly rely on Grey's instructions. They had to assume that Greer planned to attack when it suited him.

This posed serious problems because the terrain in Tauranga precluded obstructive lines on the Waikato model, and because the Maoris could not maintain their warrior force in the field indefinitely. As usual, the Maoris were heavily outnumbered, so they could not launch a substantial attack on the British camp. Ngai-te-Rangi at first simply dispersed to protect their scattered villages, but when their contingents in Waikato returned home they adopted a strategy designed to induce Greer to attack a carefully prepared position while their warrior force remained intact.[3] This policy, tactically defensive but strategically offensive, had been applied by Hapurona at Puketakauere, in 1860, and was to be perfected by the Ngati Ruanui chief Titokowaru in 1868.

At one level, the strategy took the form of propaganda. Beginning in March, Ngai-te-Rangi sent Greer a series of challenges, offering to come and have breakfast in his camp, and even to build a road for him to the *pa* they wished him to attack. Other challenges were less frivolous. 'Do you hearken. A challenge for a fight between us is declared. The day of fighting: Friday, the first day of April. This is a fixed challenge from all the tribes.'[4] The heroic character of these challenges has so impressed historians that they overlook the strategy behind them. The Ngai-te-Rangi war chief, Rawiri Puhirake, 'was experiencing the greatest difficulty in keeping his young men together during such a long period of inactivity'. He hoped to provoke Greer into making the necessary attack. As Major Nelson showed at Puketakauere, the British were by no means immune to this kind of challenge, but in this case Greer stayed in his camp. The Maoris therefore stepped up their campaign of provocation, 'becoming daily more daring'. They raided Camp Te Papa one night, and finally built a *pa* within three miles of it: Pukehinahina, or the Gate Pa. This exposed Greer to further raids, interfered with his control of Tauranga Harbour, and hampered his freedom of action. It was an unacceptable threat, but Greer cautiously applied for reinforcements before attacking it. Coincidentally, Cameron had returned to Auckland just before these requests arrived. He saw that the location of the Gate Pa offered unusual prospects for a successful assault, and instead of sending a few reinforcements, went to Tauranga himself with his whole strategic reserve.[5]

Cameron's prompt and intelligent decision gave him an enormous superiority of force at a battle-site conveniently close to his shipping. Rawiri could not have predicted Cameron's move, and he had been expecting reinforcements from the East Coast tribes. These had been turned back by the Queenite Arawa on 22 April, and subsequently defeated in an open battle at Matata, south of Maketu.[6] Consequently, Rawiri had only 230 warriors at the Gate Pa when the British marched out to attack on 28 April.[7] Against this, Cameron had 1,700 effective men after garrisoning the camp. The great majority of these were élite light infantry and naval brigade. Cameron also had by far the most powerful artillery train ever used in New Zealand.

The Maoris had at last induced the British to attack them on ground of their own choosing, but they could be forgiven for thinking that they had caught a Tartar. As one Gate Pa warrior put it: 'When we gazed at those sons of thunder, launched forward in their might, can you wonder that the cooked potatoes seemed to have lost their sweetness and many a one of us seemed to forget his hunger?'[8]

I   THE BATTLE OF GATE PA

THE GATE PA WAS SITED ON A NECK OF LAND 300 YARDS WIDE flanked by the tidal swamps of Tauranga Harbour. It consisted of two redoubts. The major work, ninety by thirty yards in size, was manned by about 200 Ngai-te-Rangi warriors at the time of the British attack. The lesser redoubt—about twenty-five yards square—was garrisoned by thirty-five warriors, mainly Ngati Koheriki. Rawiri Puhirake was in overall command. On 27 April, General Cameron made a 'close reconnaissance' of the Maori position and began moving up his troops from Camp Te Papa. By the afternoon of 29 April he had concentrated his men and guns around the *pa*. His artillery had created a practicable breach in the parapet of the main redoubt, and it was at this breach that Cameron launched a strong and well-supported assault column at about 4 p.m. This column, consisting of part of the élite 43rd Regiment and a naval brigade, succeeded in entering the *pa* through the breach, but within ten minutes it was streaming back in absolute rout, leaving a hundred dead and wounded behind it. Nothing fur-

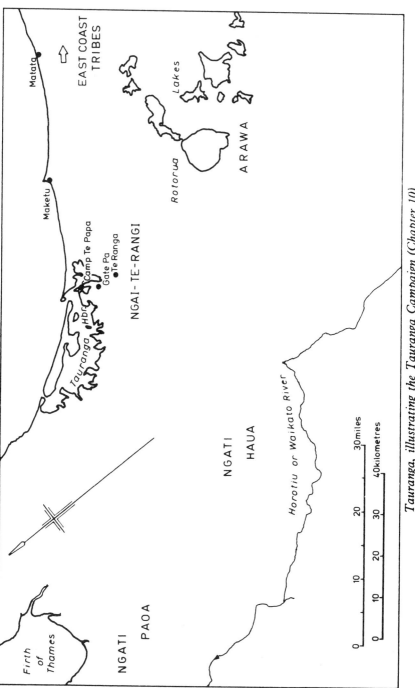

Tauranga, illustrating the Tauranga Campaign (Chapter 10)

ther happened until nightfall, when the Maoris evacuated the *pa*, taking many abandoned British weapons with them, and suffering little loss while making their escape.

The Battle of Gate Pa was arguably the most important battle of the New Zealand Wars, in terms of both its political effects and its wider implications for military technology. Historians have failed to appreciate its full significance because the contemporary British interpretations, on which they rely, were dominated by the shock of defeat and the need to palliate it. This analysis will first outline the contemporary reaction, and then test the explanations offered against the events of the battle itself.

One or two twentieth-century historians have dismissed the action at Gate Pa as 'only a minor tactical set-back', but to contemporaries it seemed a defeat 'perhaps unparalleled in the British military annals'.[9] An army of 1,700 good British troops, equipped with a strong artillery train, had been defeated by less than one-seventh their number of Maoris. With good reason, observers had stated before the battle that they expected the Maoris to flee as soon as they became aware of the strength of the force brought against them.[10] If they did stand, 'an awful day of vengence for these infatuated rebels' was anticipated. 'No doubt was entertained of our ultimate success.' The way in which these expectations were shattered shocked everyone. The 'feelings of sorrow and surprise' with which the 'disastrous' news was received in Australia and England was exceeded only by its impact in New Zealand.[11]

> The night of the 29th April was, in the British camp at Tauranga, a night of deep humiliation and mutual reproach. The men were disgraced in their own eyes, and what would the people of England say? There is not a more gallant regiment in the service than the 43rd. . . . But now where were all the laurels they had won in the Peninsula and India? Soiled and trampled in the dust, and by whom? Not by forces equal to them in arms and discipline; not by foemen worthy of their steel; but by a horde of half-naked, half-armed savages, whom they had been taught to despise.[12]

Melodramatic though they were, these words accurately reflected the sentiments of the troops in New Zealand. Von Tempsky wrote that 'the consternation amongst the officers in the Waikato district at the Tauranga news, was something I have never witnessed before. . . . Everyone was mad —gloomy—and brooding over the prospect of an endless campaign, over the chances of revenge.'[13] Cameron himself, a man with a reputation for stoicism, was reportedly not immune to the prevailing mood. At the sight of the storming party recoiling in rout, 'the general dashed his field-glass on the ground, turned his back on the fugitives, and retired to his tent to conceal his emotion'.[14]

In contemporary British eyes, the action at Gate Pa was a traumatic event and commentators lost no time in offering a wide variety of explanations for the disaster. Most prominent was the charge that the men of the assault party had displayed indiscipline and, still worse, cowardice during the attack. 'There can be no doubt', wrote Archdeacon Octavius Hadfield, 'that the

men of the assaulting party were a lot of arrant cowards.'[15] This accusation
was most strongly endorsed by civilian writers but was lent tacit support by
Cameron himself. The General declined to visit, or even enquire after, the
wounded officers of the 43rd, inducing one of them to describe him as an
'ungrateful beast'.[16] Members of the assault column tended to blame their
colleagues. The officers alleged that 'our men ran like redshanks'. The 43rd
insisted that the fault lay with the navy, and the defeat entered the annals of
the regiment as 'this disastrous retreat, commenced by the Naval Brigade'.
The seamen completed the circle by blaming the officers. They threw in an
allusion to 'a mistake' of the totally uninvolved 68th Regiment for good
measure.[17]

A parallel or alternative explanation was to accuse Cameron of 'incapacity,
mismanagement and the reckless sacrifice of valuable lives'.[18] At first,
critics did not feel the need to resort to specifics but were content paradoxically to couple charges of bull-headed rashness with what they perceived at
other times as Cameron's tendency to over-caution. Though they were by
no means alone in blaming Cameron for the defeat, the New Zealand colonists developed the accusation in most detail. It was said that Cameron had
mishandled the bombardment to the extent that it did 'fully as much harm
to the soldiers of our own force . . . as to the natives in the *pa*'. He had also
bungled the assault—launching it in near darkness, failing to make a diver-
sionary attack, and needlessly using two different corps in the assault
column which resulted in fatal confusion. Furthermore, it was argued, there
was no need to assault at all. The *pa* could easily be surrounded, therefore
the Maoris 'might easily have been forced into surrender or compelled to
fight outside'.[19]

A third school of thought attributed the repulse to accident. The official
explanations fell into this category. Cameron admitted himself 'at a loss to
explain' the rout of the assault group. He could only tentatively suggest that
the 'intricate nature' of the works and the loss of so many officers had confused the men—two points echoed faithfully by the other official accounts.[20]
But more popular than this was the idea that the Maoris had actually fled at
the first impact of the assault, only to be driven back into the *pa* by the 68th.
The storming party assumed these were fresh Maori warriors counter-
attacking, someone raised a cry of 'Good God! They are coming in
thousands', and panic ensued.[21] This idea is convincingly circumstantial,
and is the explanation most twentieth-century historians tend to stress.[22]

To assess these diverse explanations it is necessary to examine the
preparations made by Cameron for his attack. Despite retrospective allusions to the 'great strength' of Gate Pa, on the day before the battle it seemed
unimposing. Ensign Nicholl of the 43rd wrote: 'The Pah from the outside
looks the most insignificant place.'[23] But after the experience of Rangiriri
and Orakau, Cameron treated it with caution, mustering the maximum
number of men and guns, and making the most careful preparations.

As usual, Cameron's objective was to destroy the Maori force, and not to
capture an inherently valueless *pa*. Accordingly, on 28 April, he despatched

Colonel Greer and 730 men of the 68th Regiment around the Maori flank to cut off their retreat. This was a dangerous operation. Greer had to cross nearly a mile of tidal mud-flats, and the route was vulnerable to fire from the outskirts of the Maori position. Cameron assisted Greer by making a 'feigned attack' on the front of the *pa*, rightly assuming that Rawiri had pickets covering Greer's route. The chief could not count on the frontal demonstration being a feint, and his shortage of men forced him to call in his pickets. Greer was thus able to get to the Maori rear unhindered, and he correctly attributed his success to the perfect timing of Cameron's diversion.[24] The General was well aware that, strong as it was, Greer's force could form no more than a loose cordon across the broken and bush-covered ground at the rear of Gate Pa. This made the enemy's 'retreat in daylight impossible, but was necessarily too extended to prevent his escape by night'.[25] Like most Maori positions, the Gate Pa was impossible to besiege properly. Since he wished to destroy the garrison, Cameron had therefore to attack.

To maximize his chances of successful assault, Cameron laid down an artillery bombardment of unprecedented intensity. The guns available to him included eight mortars, two howitzers, two naval cannon, and five Armstrong guns.[26] Mortars and howitzers were the classic shell-throwing siege ordnance of the period, generally considered to be effective against earthworks, as well as against common masonry defences. The two heaviest mortars threw a 46-pound shell, the naval cannon were 32-pounders, and the howitzers were 24-pounders. Powerful as they were, these weapons were conventional, single-cast and muzzle-loading, but the British were also equipped with the latest science could provide: the Armstrong gun. This gun was both rifled and breech-loading, and a new process was used to cast it which made possible the use of a huge weight of shell without a corresponding increase in the weight of the gun. Invented in 1854, the Armstrong had first been used at the attack on the Taku forts in China in 1860. These were tremendously strong masonry fortifications of the conventional type and the Armstrongs used were only twelve-pounders. Nevertheless, according to Garnet Wolseley their shells succeeded in 'actually knocking the wall about'.[27] At Gate Pa, apart from two six-pounder Armstrongs, there were two 40-pounders and one enormous 110-pounder—'probably the heaviest gun ever used on shore against tribesmen'.[28] It is scarcely surprising that the naval crew of this early Big Bertha maintained that they were 'going to blow the Pah to the devil'.[29]

The concentration of British artillery was of considerable power even in absolute terms. When it is considered that these guns fired unhampered by enemy artillery from a distance of 350 to 800 yards at a target of less than 3,000 square yards, their power appears awesome. Gate Pa was the ultimate test of strength between British and Maori military technologies, between modern artillery and the modern *pa*. In a wider sense, it was to be the first of many contests between breech-loading, rifled, composite-cast heavy artillery and trench-and-bunker earthworks.

The British guns were positioned in four main batteries, 350 to 800 yards distant from the *pa*. On the afternoon of the 28th, they opened fire and continued shooting for about an hour. Just after dawn the next day, they opened again and kept firing until about 4 p.m. Two factors slightly reduced the effect of this long bombardment. First, the Maoris had cunningly placed their red war flag some sixty yards behind their actual position. It is possible that they had also thrown up some mock fortifications at this point.[30] This induced some of the British gunners initially to believe that the centre of the Maori position was marked by the flag, and to direct their fire at it. This ruse did not fool all the gunners, and those it did deceive were not deceived for long. The second factor which hampered the bombardment was the somewhat erratic performance of the Armstrong guns. For all their weight, range, and technical sophistication these weapons still had teething problems, and several writers allude to Armstrong shells overshooting the *pa* or failing to explode. While it was perfectly true to say that this occasionally happened—one shell was found unexploded in 1983[31]—the legend quickly developed that the Armstrongs were next to useless. This is quite false. The very first shot from the 110-pounder Armstrong exploded only ten yards behind the *pa*, killing two Maoris on its way.[32] Even at short range, this was good practice. According to Commodore William Wiseman, the officer with ultimate responsibility for the Armstrongs: 'the fire from the Armstrong guns and the 24 pounder howitzers was extremely good. [D]uring the day 100 rounds were fired from each of the Armstrongs to great effect and without a single thing going wrong.'[33]

Some shots were aimed at the false target of the Maori war flag, some Armstrong shells did over-shoot the *pa*—which was after all only thirty yards wide—and some did fail to explode. But most of the British fire was accurate. Few eyewitness accounts fail to stress the excellence of the gunners' practice. Certainly, the average rate of fire—about 100 rounds per gun[34]—was outstanding. In all, perhaps thirty tons of shot and shell were dropped on or near the Maori position—some 300 pounds for every member of the garrison. By 4 p.m. on 29 April, a large breach had been made in the main Maori redoubt, the paling fence and other above-ground defences had been flattened, and, perhaps most important of all, the garrison had been subjected to a pounding of shocking intensity. Moreover, the Maoris had scarcely fired a single shot in reply to the bombardment. Most of the British thought that the garrison had either evacuated the place somehow, or been wiped out. A few Maoris were observed moving about by some staff officers 'but the general impression was, that the shot and shell had done their work so effectually as to leave few of them alive'.[35] The time to assault had arrived.

The assault was organized with the care that characterized the rest of Cameron's dispositions. The assault party itself was 300 strong—half naval brigade under Commander Hay and half 43rd Regiment under Colonel Booth. The mixed composition of the force was retrospectively criticized, but sailors and marines were generally considered assault troops *par ex-*

cellence. The 43rd Light Infantry was unquestionably an élite unit, and the
mixture of troops and sailors had never posed a problem before. The assault
party advanced in column, four abreast, while the fire-power of the line formation was provided by 180 men of the 'Moveable Column' under Major
Ryan, who extended as close as possible to the enemy parapet to keep down
the fire of any who had survived the bombardment. A further 300 men from
the naval brigade and the 43rd followed in close support. Excluding the
68th in the rear, 800 men were involved in the attack, but the assault
column had the crucial role.

It is clear that General Cameron made the most thorough and careful
preparations for his attack—in fact they seemed to some to exceed the
demands of the task in hand. He concentrated as many men and guns as
possible for the operation—going so far as to supplement his already large
batteries with two ships-guns during the bombardment. His encirclement
manoeuvre was both necessary in terms of his aims and well-conducted. He
ensured that his bombardment was intensive and effective, and did not
order an assault before a practicable breach had been made. His storming
party was carefully selected and well supported. His one error, if it can be so
called, was to assume that the bombardment had crippled the Maori garrison. He was by no means alone in this assumption. In fact it could be said
that what distinguished Cameron from his contemporaries was his greater
respect, not his undue contempt, for Maori defensive capacities. His failure
still further to transcend contemporary preconceptions is poor ground for
indictment. Yet despite Cameron's meticulous preparations, the attack was
repulsed. This is the central mystery of the battle.

While the contemporary accounts are contradictory on many issues, they
generally agree that at some point in the engagement there was a lull during
which the assault party or most of it remained inside the *pa*, apparently
victorious. 'The pa seemed in the hands of our soldiers.' Captain G. R.
Greaves who was with the leading files of the assault party, wrote that he
actually left the *pa* and reported to Cameron that the place was taken. As he
was speaking, the supposedly victorious assault party came streaming back
in rout.[36] It is primarily this factor which makes the notion of escaping
Maoris, driven back into the *pa* by the 68th and panicking the assault party,
seem the most plausible of the contemporary explanations. But according to
the original version of this story, put forward by the seamen of the *Esk* in
defence of their own conduct, it was actually an attack by the 68th on the
rear of the *pa* which was the cause of the panic. The 68th, they claimed,
were mistaken for Maori reinforcements.[37] It is unlikely in itself that fully
accoutred British troops should be mistaken for Maori warriors stripped for
battle, and the commander of the 68th categorically denied that his men
made any such attack.[38] The sailors' story was simply one of the many unjustified recriminations exchanged by the members of the assault party. The
form into which this story was subsequently distorted is as unlikely as the
original. A few Maoris had found the bombardment too much for them, and
had tried to slip away, but it seems clear that these attempts took place

before or after the assault. The one member of the garrison of the main redoubt who left accounts of his experience specified only three warriors who had returned to the *pa* after failing in such an attempt. Even if these three had returned during the assault, they were hardly enough to stampede 300 British troops.[39]

But something did happen, after the lull, to turn the battle from victory into defeat for the British. Several contemporary British observers provided full descriptions of this decisive, battle-winning event—descriptions which were forgotten or ignored by interpreters. These observers, together with two Maori eyewitnesses, confirmed that the bulk of the garrison did not at any stage evacuate the *pa*. A few did,

> but the majority had concealed themselves in chambers dug out in the ground, and covered with boughs of trees and earth. . . . When the defenders of the walls retreated before the impetuous onset of the storming party . . . the others remained in their hiding places and bided their time. . . . [then suddenly] they opened a destructive fire upon them. The effect was much the same as if a volcano had suddenly opened beneath their feet, and began to pour forth volumes of smoke and flame; many of our men were killed and wounded at the first discharge. . . mere courage could avail nothing against this invisible foe.[40]

This version is corroborated by four other British accounts and derives further confirmation from the following considerations. First, it appears that the assault party penetrated the breach easily at the outset and suffered few casualties in the process because the Maori fire was 'very feeble'.[41] In normal circumstances, defenders would inflict their heaviest casualties on attackers at this early stage of the attack. The Maoris had time after the end of the bombardment to man their firing positions on the outer parapet. That they did not do so in any numbers may indicate that they wished to tempt the British into the main redoubt. Secondly, according to the legend, the first period of the assault was characterized by fierce hand to hand combat. 'Navy cutlass met long-handled tomahawk—*tupara* was clubbed to counter bayonet and rifle. Skulls were cloven—Maoris were bayoneted—Ngai-te-Rangi tomahawks bit into *pakeha* limbs.' But according to the British casualty lists, only three men received anything other than gun shot wounds.[42] Thirdly, 'the roofs of the pits were loop-holed' to allow for direct overhead fire.[43] It is hard to see what purpose this could serve unless the Maoris expected the British to enter the redoubt.

The main redoubt at Gate Pa was used as a trap for the British. The assault party charged gallantly, entered the breach, and scattered the token force of Maoris holding the front line of trench and parapet. This light resistance came as no surprise. The British believed that their massive bombardment had crippled the garrison, and this belief was reinforced by the Maoris firing 'only occasionally, by a single shot' before the attack—a restraint enforced by Rawiri's strict instructions.[44] It seems that fighting between the garrison of the small redoubt and a few files of troops who had over-lapped the breach was continuous,[45] but in the main redoubt there was a lull and the place seemed taken. Suddenly the main British force was struck by heavy volleys. These volleys took the British completely by surprise, they were fired at close range, and they came from all directions. Some men were even shot from beneath their feet as they stood on the roofs of covered trenches and bunkers—a horrible fate.[46] The soldiers and sailors could not retaliate effectively against their hidden enemies. They withstood this deadly fire for perhaps five minutes—a long time in the circumstances—and then, despite the desperate efforts of their officers, they broke and ran. Cameron promptly committed the support group in an effort to retrieve the situation, but these men were caught up in the flight of the assault party. The bulk of the British forces in front of Gate Pa were thus involved in the rout. They were subjected to a galling crossfire from the two redoubts, and Cameron reportedly had difficulty in rallying them.[47] It is therefore worth making the hypothetical but significant point that if the Maoris had anything like the numbers necessary for a pursuit, the British army could well have been comprehensively crushed.

The maze-like character of the inside of the main redoubt, the mixing of soldiers and sailors, and even the return of a few Maoris from attempts to escape through the 68th may have contributed to the British repulse. But these factors were essentially secondary if they had any influence at all. Confusion, panic, and the deaths of many leaders did occur, but they were the results and not the causes of defeat. The dominant cause of the repulse was a well executed Maori plan. That the trap this plan involved was enough to rout a superior number of élite British troops is not really surprising. We have seen that the assault party was unexpectedly assailed from all directions by heavy volleys fired at very close range by hidden warriors. What troops in the world could have sustained this situation for long? The aspersions cast on the 43rd and the naval brigade, like those directed at Cameron, appear to be totally unwarranted.

The one thing contemporary explanations of the British defeat had in common was the lack of emphasis on the role of Maori skill and forethought. This is not to say that the courage and chivalry demonstrated by Ngai-te-Rangi were ignored. These aspects of the Maori performance received generous treatment. Cameron himself made reference to the fact that wounded soldiers had not been mistreated. One Maori, the *wahine toa* (woman warrior) Heni Te Kiri-Karamu, gave water to wounded men at considerable risk to herself. Like the Maori defiance at Orakau, this incident gave rise to a romantic legend of Gate Pa as the epitome of the spirit of Christian chivalry in which the war was allegedly fought. Complimentary as this was to the Maoris, it operated to obscure their other achievements.

For one thing, the trap into which the British assault party fell was surely a remarkable tactical ploy. The use of concealed or deceptively weak-looking fortifications to ambush attackers was, as we have seen, a major element of the tactical repertoire made possible by the flexible modern *pa*. Rawiri's trap at the Gate Pa was perhaps the ultimate refinement of this technique. It amounted to using the enemy's overwhelming strength against him and it involved the fearsome risk of allowing the assault-party, which alone heavily outnumbered the garrison, into the main redoubt. Inside, the redoubt was less a fortification than a killing ground, as soldiers who inspected the redoubt after the battle attested. 'Those who were in this morning for the first time say that they never saw such a place in their life, and that you might as well drive a lot of men into a sheep pen and shoot them down as let them assault a place like that.'[48]

The Maori trap was brilliantly implemented as well as brilliantly conceived. In proportion to the size of the *pa* and its garrison, the bombardment was comparable to some in the First World War. Anyone familiar with the literature of that conflict will know that for defenders promptly to take up their firing positions and fight, after their senses had been racked by heavy shelling and when every instinct urged them to stay at the bottom of their bunkers, was no mean feat. Commentators frequently remark with admiration on the German capacity to recover promptly from the psychological effects of bombardment. The Maori recovery at the Gate Pa required equivalent nerve, commitment, and discipline. Indeed, discipline characterized the Maori proceedings throughout the battle. When Heni Te Kiri-Karamu arrived with the Ngati Koheriki *taua*, Rawiri explained 'the plan of campaign' to them and they accepted it. Not a shot was fired except on Rawiri's explicit command. According to Hori Ngatai, the chief 'ordered us not to utter a word or fire a shot till the proper time came for the order'.[49]

Brilliantly conceived and implemented as it was, the trap itself was perhaps less remarkable than the fact that the Maoris survived to attempt it. No more than fifteen of the garrison were killed by the massive bombardment. The Maoris had from 3 to 28 April to perfect the main redoubt and they made the best of their time. This redoubt had most of the features described in the analyses of earlier actions, and there seems to have been particular emphasis on one or two protective devices. Ngai-te-Rangi opted for numerous small anti-artillery bunkers rather than a few large ones. The main redoubt was 'like ratholes everywhere, with covered ways and underground chambers'. This meant that if a shell did penetrate a bunker only its few occupants would be killed. In the compressed space the explosion would tend to kill not wound, and this contributed to the low proportion of Maoris wounded. A British commentator inspecting the main redoubt noted that 'some of their hiding places twist, so that you cannot see the further end.' Again, this minimized the effects of a shell-blast. Communication between bunkers was by 'underground passages'. We have seen that the Maoris remained protected when they opened a massed fire— through gaps in the roofs of firing-galleries and from under the eaves of sunken *whares* or 'underground houses with beams', as one Englishman described them. It seems that the special requirements of Gate Pa necessitated two types of underground construction: relatively shallow covered firing positions, and deeper bunkers in which the garrison could sit out the bombardment.[50]

Clearly, the Maori victory at Gate Pa owed a great deal to Rawiri Puhirake's inspired tactical leadership. But it seems that, as at Rangiriri, the main responsibility for the design of the defences rested with a specialist engineer, in this case Pene Taka.[51] If this is true, then Pene Taka deserves to rank as an innovative master of field-fortification in the tradition of Kawiti. Over-all, his defences successfully protected their occupants from the massive bombardment, confounding British expectations and making possible the Maori victory. Their effectiveness suggested a conclusion about the competition between earthworks and artillery which the British, fascinated by their own artifact technology, found very difficult to accept: the bigger the gun, the deeper the hole.

II TE RANGA AND THE PEACE IN TAURANGA

THE DEFEAT AT GATE PA GAVE RISE TO GREAT PESSIMISM ABOUT British prospects. Grey was horrified by the disaster, writing privately that 'we are all here plunged into a sorrow and grief that I cannot describe'.[52] British terms for an end to the war were under discussion, and from early May Grey 'suddenly' began to express doubts about their harshness in regard to the extensive confiscation of land. B. J. Dalton, who dismisses the Gate Pa as 'a minor tactical setback', is at a loss to account for this change, but it was probably the result of the recent military disaster. The colonial ministry strongly resisted Grey's new-found moderation, but they too were sufficiently impressed by the Gate Pa to assent to an attempt by Grey to secure a local peace in Tauranga.[53]

On 12 May Grey arrived at Te Papa and conferred with Cameron. Shortly afterwards he met some neutral Maoris who agreed to act as intermediaries with the Kingites. Grey 'expressed a desire for the two races to be at peace, and promised generous treatment to the natives in arms in the case of surrender'.[54] We can only be certain of this guarantee of 'generous treatment', but subsequent events suggest Grey offered terms that were considerably more explicit and tempting. Ngai-te-Rangi had been campaigning for four continuous months, as yet without any substantial help from other tribes, and despite their victory they were not averse to peace. On 20 May the neutrals met the Kingites—though Rawiri himself was absent—and discussed peace. The Maori mediators reported to Civil Commissioner T. H. Smith that the Kingites expressed themselves 'willing to give up their arms and cease fighting if they can have full claims over their lands, and the Governor will promise to see that no harm befalls them'.[55] By 26 May a couple of Ngai-te-Rangi warriors had come in with their guns, and a British observer noted that peace seemed near. By the beginning of June, Commodore Wiseman could speak of 'the cessation of hostilities' in Tauranga as an accomplished fact.[56]

Government pessimism about the situation in Tauranga was influenced by General Cameron's view of the defeat of Gate Pa. On 15 May Cameron informed Grey that he had decided to abandon aggressive operations in Tauranga and withdraw his striking force to Auckland, leaving Greer, strictly on the defensive, to hold Te Papa. Grey entirely concurred in this decision, and Cameron lost no time in implementing it. On 16 May he left for Auckland with 700 men leaving instructions for more troops to follow.[57] Cameron sought to explain this strategic *volte face* in terms of the inaccessible terrain to which he said Ngai-te-Rangi had withdrawn, and of increasingly unfavourable weather.[58] This was nonsense. Far from being inaccessible, the new Kingite positions were only twelve miles from Te Papa—in an area which, according to a British officer's report, 'appears to be an easy one to operate in'.[59] The weather, as the event proved, would be suitable for campaigning for another two months. It seems clear that the real cause of Cameron's decision was the disaster at Gate Pa. Cameron had seized his strategic chance to concentrate overwhelmingly superior forces at an enemy weak point. He had made meticulous preparations for his assault. Yet he had failed, and as he himself admitted, he did not know why.[60] He was therefore in no position to guard against a repetition of the disaster, and consequently he had 'no intention of carrying on further aggressive operations at Tauranga'.[61] There were wider implications to this decision. Though unfinished defences were subsequently assaulted on Cameron's orders, the Gate Pa was the last completed modern *pa* he ever attacked.

The attitudes of the British leadership, and the peace negotiations after the Battle of the Gate Pa are important in two respects. First, by removing his striking force to Auckland, Cameron acknowledged that his effort to win the Waikato War in Tauranga had been blocked, and blocked permanently. Tauranga again became a secondary theatre. Secondly, it was clear that the British were compelled to face the prospect of a moderate peace settlement in Tauranga, and that the Ngai-te-Rangi Kingites were also ready for peace. The terms the two sides were prepared to accept were separated by a margin that was distinct but not great, and peace was nearly achieved—a factor of great significance for the assessment of the Tauranga campaign.

But Commodore Wiseman was wrong: hostilities in Tauranga had not yet ceased. On 21 June, a strong British patrol came upon a Maori force at Te Ranga and through the ensuing battle the British were able to salvage a considerable amount from the campaign.

The engagement at Te Ranga was in itself a relatively straightforward affair.[62] On the morning of 21 June, Greer marched out of Te Papa on a reconnaissance in strength. Four miles beyond the Gate Pa he unexpectedly came upon Rawiri's forces fortifying a potentially strong position. Rawiri had about 500 men. Greer's force numbered 600—mainly 43rd and 68th Light Infantry, but including a detachment of the 1st Waikato Militia. It was clear that the Maori position was far from complete. In fact, it was nothing more than a line of unfinished rifle-pits and was therefore very vulnerable. Nevertheless, Greer did not attack immediately. He deployed his men, opened fire, and sent to Camp Te Papa for reinforcements. When these—220 men including a few cavalry and one Armstrong gun—were sufficiently close to provide support, Greer ordered a charge. The Maoris resisted vigorously, but the British were scarcely hampered at all by the incipient earthworks and, after an initial volley, the defenders had no time to reload. In contrast to the Gate Pa, therefore, most of the fighting was hand to hand. All accounts agree that the Maoris fought with desperate determination, but they were forced from their line of pits by the fierce British attack—the 43rd in particular were 'mad for revenge'. Apparently, Rawiri succeeded in rallying his men, and more bitter fighting ensued. Then Rawiri himself was killed. The Maoris may have been slowly withdrawing prior to this, but it was not until Rawiri fell that they broke and fled. The cavalry pursued but the nature of the ground was such that the pursuit was not very effective.[63]

As far as the course of the battle is concerned, the British interpretation of Te Ranga presents no problems comparable to the interpretation of other major engagements. The British claimed it as a clear-cut victory, marked by the competence of their officers and the courage and élan of their troops. On this occasion they were perfectly right. But the contemporary assessment of the strategic and political importance of Te Ranga is a different matter.

The campaigns analysed above show that a Maori commander, caught as Rawiri was at a disadvantage, would normally have abandoned his position. Exceptionally, a *pa* such as Rangiriri might have a strategic value which might make it worth defending at a disadvantage, but Te Ranga had no such importance. Why then did Rawiri stand his ground in the two hours between the British arrival and the attack? The hope of a timely reinforcement may have influenced him. In the later part of the battle, a second Maori force was seen approaching, and when Rawiri was killed and his men broke, this force was only 500 yards away.[64] The possibility that Rawiri had little choice but to stand may have been equally important. Greer sought to take advantage of the terrain to ensure that 'the troops were so disposed in front, and on both flanks, that retreat without heavy loss seemed impossible for the Maoris.'[65] In fact, the Maoris did not lose many men in the pursuit, and if they had scattered and run at the first sight of the British, they might have escaped with little loss. Still, it may well have seemed to Rawiri that the British were so distributed that to stand was only marginally less safe than to flee. That the victor of Gate Pa declined flight in the hope that his friends would arrive was probably the extent of his error. It seems fairer to credit Greer with making the Maori retreat difficult by the judicious deployment of his troops, than to criticize Rawiri for not assuming the worst would happen.

Greer's dispositions were not the only contribution good British leadership made to the victory at Te Ranga. Greer's patrol in strength of 21 June was not an isolated incident but part of a policy developed, as Greer himself admitted, by General Cameron.

The principal ingredient of the British success at Te Ranga was shared by their three other clear-cut victories—the minor actions of Mahoetahi in November 1860, and Katikara and Koheroa in June and July 1863. In each case the Maoris were attacked in incomplete fortifications. Cameron had commanded in two of these actions. It was, of course, conventional military wisdom to attack an enemy unprepared if the chance arose, but Cameron's thinking seems to show a gradual progression from this adage to the conviction that the only positive way to deal with modern *pa* was to attack them before completion. The shattering lesson at the Gate Pa was final confirmation. After it, Cameron ordered Greer to adopt a policy of patrolling in strength with a view to attacking any Maori force in the vicinity of the British posts before it could entrench. He reiterated these orders in a letter to Greer on 18 June, and it was to Cameron's 'foresight' that Greer attributed his victory.[66] At Tauranga, this policy was essentially defensive, in that it was designed to prevent the Maoris building *pa* in the immediate neighbourhood of the British posts from which they might threaten the troops. It was not an effort to secure decisive victory through an offensive strategy, but it did bring about a substantial success. Acceptance of the basic maxim of attacking an enemy before he could prepare was common enough. But it seems that the only officer to come close to seeing this approach as a partial answer to Maori military methods, and therefore close to recognizing the systematic nature of these methods, was the much-maligned General Cameron.

But did Cameron's policy of spoiling attacks offer a comprehensive solution to the modern *pa* problem? The General himself did not think so. He refused to follow up the success at Te Ranga, despite pressure from the colonial government, and he acted with great caution during the rest of his operations in New Zealand. This suggests that he did not think Te Ranga could be repeated at will. He was right for the following reasons. For engagements like Te Ranga to occur, strong British patrols had to come upon the Maoris not only at the right place but also at the right time. Wiremu Kingi and seventy men had built the L-pa in a night, and though larger and more complex *pa* such as Meremere required much more time, the period between the commencement of a *pa* and its becoming defensively viable, if not complete, was always limited. The British had to catch the Maoris in this period. This was difficult enough even when patrols had to cover a relatively small area around a British base. Rewi had managed to make Orakau defensible before being discovered, though it was only three miles from a British camp. If spoiling attacks were to be used on the strategic offensive, deep in Maori territory, the difficulty was greatly compounded. As the area of operations increased, the chances of coming upon a *pa* in its vulnerable stage naturally decreased. Furthermore, it was, as we have seen, very unusual for the Maoris to stand in a *pa* that was unfinished or unsatisfactory in some other way. For every Koheroa or Te Ranga, there were several instances of Maori garrisons simply leaving if caught at a disadvantage. In short, good British leadership was only one ingredient of success at Te Ranga. The other was a great deal of luck.

In comparison to Mahoetahi, Katikara, and Koheroa, the British numerical advantage at Te Ranga was minor, and this battle therefore came much closer to proving that on an open field British troops were superior to Maori warriors. The Maoris at Te Ranga fought well and bravely and the margin was narrow, but it was crucial. That the troops would win, given 'a fair field and no favour',[67] was of course a notion very close to British hearts, but it was also the assumption on which the Maori tactical thinking behind the modern *pa* was based. The Maoris were not in the business of putting up gallant fights, but of winning battles. In the modern *pa* they had invented a system which could often do just that for them by minimizing their numerous disadvantages. It was only when battle occurred before the system could be put into operation that the Maoris suffered clear-cut and comprehensive defeats. In this sense, Mahoetahi, Katikara, Koheroa, and Te Ranga were the exceptions that proved the rules of the modern *pa* system.

Te Ranga was unquestionably a substantial victory for the British. It was celebrated by them—with some justice—as 'by far the most brilliant achievement obtained throughout the whole war'. The relationship of Te Ranga with the disaster at Gate Pa gave special satisfaction. The similarity of the terrain of the two battle sites received great emphasis. The ground at Te Ranga, wrote Fox, was 'almost exactly similar to that which they had occupied at the Gate Pa'. Colonel Gamble echoed his words with the qualification 'only that of course they [the Maoris] had not had time to strengthen it to any extent with entrenchments'. One might be forgiven for thinking that this was no minor difference. But, however false, this comparison highlights the importance of Te Ranga to the British as the perfect salve for the wounds of Gate Pa. Te Ranga could be taken to prove that Gate Pa was the result of an exceptional failure of leadership, or of the troops' courage and discipline, or that it was simply an unfortunate accident. The role of the 43rd at Te Ranga both reinforced this perception, and seemed particularly appropriate in itself. Colonel J. E. Alexander noted that: 'It was a matter of special satisfaction that the 43rd had an opportunity, at Te Rangi, of recovering from any depression they may have felt on account of the unlooked-for repulse at the Gate *pah*.' Te Ranga, according to Von Tempsky, ensured that 'the stain on the honour of the 43rd began to fade into a mere shadowy hue.' The Gate Pa had been shown to be an accident; the Maoris had got their deserts; the 43rd had got its revenge.[68]

This satisfying pattern was completed by the third major event of the Tauranga campaign. On 24 July, 133 Ngai-te-Rangi warriors came into the British camp and made their peace. By 29 August, the whole of the tribe—except one *hapu* (Piri Rakau) of three dozen warriors—had followed suit.[69] A total of 230 warriors accepted peace, and some guns and some land were surrendered. The British saw this as total victory—'unconditional submission'—and they believed it to be solely the result of Te Ranga. The Maoris, committing hubris with their brave but fortuitous victory at the Gate Pa, had met their inevitable nemesis at Te Ranga and in the submission it brought about. Te Ranga slipped easily into the mould of the British winning the last, decisive, battle. The Ango-Saxons, aroused by an admonitory check, had gone on to win in a battle which did not merely restore parity but gave total victory. Musing on the Tauranga campaign, and in particular on the Battle of Te Ranga, Von Tempsky wrote: 'I would rather face the victor of a hundred fights, than a brave man who is still smarting from a thrashing that he has accidentally received. . . . I think all Ango-Saxon races require a certain amount of beating before they begin to do their best.'[70]

In this way, a simple over-view of the Tauranga campaign was formed, centred on the close connection of the three major events. Though this over-view owed as much to contemporary preconceptions as to the events themselves, its essentials have been accepted by historians and it still constitutes the received version of the Tauranga campaign. This interpretation contains several weaknesses, one of which—that it underestimates the impact of the Gate Pa—has already been outlined. Another weakness is the overestimate of Te Ranga, for in fact this engagement was less than decisive.

As usual, Maori casualties appear to have been exaggerated by the British. Contemporary commentators gave figures as high as 200 for the Maori killed at Te Ranga, and historians accept that 120 warriors were slain, but the original official figure was 105 killed. This precisely equalled the sum of the number of Maoris found dead in the trenches—sixty-eight—and the number taken prisoner—thirty-seven.[71] This is rather too much of a coincidence, and it suggests that the prisoners were counted twice. Furthermore, only sixty-eight guns were captured by the British, which conformed to the number of bodies found in the trenches but not to the number claimed as killed.[72] The fleeing warriors were highly unlikely to have burdened themselves with other men's guns. By the same token, few wounded men would have been able to escape. There were twenty-seven wounded men among the prisoners—only ten Maoris surrendered unhurt—and we must assume that part of the expected proportion of wounded were killed by the British. Few Maoris asked for mercy, some continued fighting after being injured, and it was difficult to restrain troops unleashed in a ferocious attack like that at Te Ranga. We may therefore conclude that Maori casualties at Te Ranga, apart from the ten unhurt prisoners, were in the order of 100—sixty-eight killed, twenty-seven wounded and captured (of whom fifteen subsequently died) and perhaps a few wounded but escaped. The British lost fifty-two men killed and wounded.[73]

Though lower than the generally accepted figure, the Maori losses were heavy enough, and it was less the scale of casualties than their distribution that ameliorated the disaster. British commentators assumed that the Maori force at Te Ranga, commanded as it was by Rawiri Puhirake, consisted of the garrison of Gate Pa reinforced by more Ngai-te-Rangi warriors and a few allies. On this basis, and on the basis of inflated casualty figures, it was possible to conclude that the battle had broken Ngai-te-Rangi military power. It seems, however, that not many of Rawiri's Gate Pa force were with him at Te Ranga. The Maoris at Gate Pa captured dozens of Enfield rifles, together with ammunition, and they would probably have used these weapons rather than their own. Only two of the sixty-eight guns captured at Te Ranga were Enfields.[74] The turnover of warriors this suggests is exactly what we would expect from a tribe struggling to sustain five months of active campaigning—and many Ngai-te-Rangi had been fighting in Waikato for months prior to this. Indeed, Ngai-te-Rangi's contingent at Te Ranga may have been fewer than 100 strong. Substantial East Coast forces had finally succeeded in crossing Arawa territory and linking up with the men of Tauranga. Ngati Porou and Whakatohea contingents were certainly present at Te Ranga, and it is probable that they were also supported by their allies of the March and April expeditions against the Queenite Arawa—Whanau-a-Apanui and Ngati Awa. A third component of the Te Ranga force were the Kingite Arawa, men of Ngati Pikiao and Ngati Rangiwewehi.[75] Some evidence suggests that these Arawa and the Ngati Porou contingent, actually bore the brunt of the battle. In short, the Maori force at Te Ranga was a composite one, and the tribes contributing to it consequently shared the burden of casualties. No tribe lost more than thirty men, and therefore no tribe could be considered crippled.[76]

These factors seem to have been appreciated in British official circles immediately after the battle. Te Ranga was welcomed as a significant triumph, but decisive results were not expected from it. Colonel Gamble anticipated very modest strategic advantages: 'its result will probably be that the enemy will not again venture near our posts at Tauranga'.[77] The colonial government strongly urged that the success be followed up with all possible vigour, in an effort to achieve decisive victory.[78] Clearly they did not believe that Te Ranga had already achieved such a victory: it was a beginning rather than an end. Cameron's convictions about British prospects in Tauranga were in no way shaken by Te Ranga. He refused the government's request on the grounds that decisive victory was impossible, not because he thought it had already occurred on 21 June. 'There is no reason to hope that any such decisive result as that anticipated by Ministers, or that any real advantages whatever, would be obtained by following them [the Tauranga Kingites] into the interior.'[79] As far as the British leaders were concerned, it was not until the 'unconditional submission' of July and August that Te Ranga was retrospectively endowed with its war-winning character.

A further weakness of the received version is that the evidence does not support the idea that the peace agreements of July and August constituted an unconditional surrender. For one thing, Grey guaranteed to annex no more than one quarter of Ngai-te-Rangi land.[80] As it happened, much less than this—a mere 50,000 acres—was eventually confiscated.[81] Ngai-te-Rangi thus emerged from the war rather better off in terms of land than some of the pro-British Maoris caught up in the confiscations in the Waikato.

The surrender of arms was also little more than a token. The 230 warriors who came in between 24 July and 29 August handed over only eighty-one guns. Given the casualties at Gate Pa and Te Ranga and the capture of

British rifles at the former action, Ngai-te-Rangi probably had more guns than they had live warriors. Moreover, the quality of the weapons surrendered was poor—only seven or eight first-line guns (rifles and *tupara*) out of eighty-one.[82] It was common knowledge that most of the guns were Ngai-te-Rangis' grandfathers' weapons rather than their own: 'the rusty muskets were accepted as a figure of speech for submission.'[83] It is highly likely that the Tauranga Maoris remained fully armed, and that the British knew this to be so. A third important consideration is that the British actually agreed to provide the Ngai-te-Rangi with food and seed crops to tide them over the after-effects of their long campaign. The government paid £2,312 for this purpose to one contractor alone, and the total cost is likely to have been considerably greater.[84]

In relation to the original British objectives and to the attitude of the colonial government, these were very mild terms. Indeed, they were embarrassingly mild and Governor Grey and the officials who assisted him with the negotiations did their best to minimize the appearance of leniency. The symbolic character of the cession of land and the surrender of arms, and the fact that the colonial taxpayers were to feed their erstwhile enemies, were passed over as lightly as possible. There may even have been some tampering with the official translations of the negotiations to support the announcement of 'unconditional submission'.[85] Some appearance of leniency remained however, and typically Grey sought to explain it as a freely-given recognition of the chivalry with which the Ngai-te-Rangi had fought. These merciful measures were taken purely out of the goodness of the government's heart, and after the Maoris had surrendered unconditionally.[86] Not quite everybody accepted this claim. Grey's political enemies among the colonists preferred to attribute his moderation to the influence of an amorous encounter with a Ngai-te-Rangi woman, and indulged in a little slanderous satire to this effect. 'Some liking for our race he still retains/Our dusky sisters lead the Chief in chains'.[87] Grey's sexual exploits and his desire to be merciful to the clean-fighting Ngai-te-Rangi may have existed, but it is highly improbable that either factor had any effect on the Tauranga peace terms.

We have seen that the Battle of Te Ranga was less than decisive, and that Cameron was not inclined to make a further attempt at decisive victory. It is also clear, from the negotiations following Gate Pa, that the British were prepared to consider a compromise peace if the military situation warranted it. Furthermore, it has been shown that the terms agreed in July and August were in fact moderate, and it is unlikely that Grey would voluntarily have made such concessions, however saintly the Ngai-te-Rangi code of war. It therefore seems probable that, far from surrendering unconditionally, the Maoris accepted peace on the basis of terms previously offered them; and there is explicit evidence to support this view.

In mid-July, Archdeacon A. N. Brown, a Tauranga missionary, had discussions with some Ngai-te-Rangi. He concluded that, if unconditional surrender were insisted upon, Ngai-te-Rangi would continue to resist, and he wrote as much to Governor Grey.[88] Soon after this, Grey sent an agent, H. E. Rice, to see the main body of the Ngai-te-Rangi. The nature of Rice's activity is apparent from a speech of commendation made by the Maoris at the peace conference of 25 July. The Maoris said that 'they felt highly pleased with Mr Rice in going to see them, as it had a most beneficial effect upon them . . . and has caused them to come foreward and accept the terms of peace the Governor has offered them . . . '. According to another translation, they were more blunt, stating that 'if Mr Rice had not come there would have been no peace'.[89]

The Thames Civil Commissioner, James Mackay, was also involved in the proceedings. He believed that Rice had taken 'too much upon himself' in the negotiations before 25 July, and that according to official policy the Maoris 'should come in of their own accord and give up their Arms, powder, Land etc *unconditionally*'. Mackay attempted to intervene, informing some Maoris that 'You must give your land to the Governor—He will give you a small portion of it . . . the greater part of the land is for the Governor.' According to the Maoris, 'this had a tendency to harden their hearts', and if Mackay had been the official negotiator, 'not one of them would have come in'. But Colonel Greer, who consistently supported Rice, arrested Mackay and confined him 'to the neighbourhood of his tent'.[90] Much remains to be learnt about these occurrences—regarding the attitude of the colonial ministry for example—but it seems reasonable to conclude that Rice, probably acting on secret instructions from Grey, negotiated moderate terms with Ngai-te-Rangi. The Tauranga peace was not an unconditional submission followed by an act of mercy, but a compromise agreement.

None of this should be taken to mean that Te Ranga had no impact on the Maoris, or that the peace was entirely satisfactory to them. Even a relatively small cession of land was a grave loss, and it was undoubtedly Te Ranga that brought Ngai-te-Rangi to accept it. The battle therefore helped to close the gap that had existed in May between the terms that the two protagonists were prepared to accept. Another factor was simple exhaustion. This had existed before Te Ranga, and it was this which made the British provision of food particularly important. But the factor which induced the British to make this and other concessions, and which forced them to the negotiating table without achieving decisive victory, was the Battle of Gate Pa. Neither economic exhaustion nor defeat at Te Ranga was enough to expunge this great Ngai-te-Rangi victory. Not one but two battles in conjunction decided the issue of the Tauranga Campaign—Te Ranga and the Gate Pa.

III THE END OF THE WAIKATO WAR

TE RANGA WAS THE LAST BATTLE, NOT ONLY OF THE TAURANGA Campaign, but also of the Waikato War as a whole. Historians consistently assert that, with 'the final and decisive blow' in the Waikato basin at

Orakau, Te Ranga brought about complete victory for the British. 'This was the end of any real concerted resistance. The King Movement was broken: The King's followers were scattered, imprisoned or dead, and the lands of their fathers were gone to the Pakeha.'[91] The British, we are told, had conquered the Waikato, destroyed Kingite power, and so achieved all their objectives.

It is true that, on balance, the British won the Waikato War, and that this helped to ensure European dominance in New Zealand. One Kingite tribe, Waikato proper, lost virtually the whole of its land; an area which, at over one million acres, dwarfed the annexation in Tauranga. No single engagement was an annihilating blow, but the cumulative effect was considerable: some 500 Kingite warriors were killed or wounded. The process of attrition was even more important in another respect. The economy of the core Kingite tribes was heavily strained, and had perhaps even collapsed temporarily. Reserves of food and ammunition were nearing exhaustion, and military demands on the labour force reduced production. The European trade had virtually ceased, and most of the inhabitants of British-occupied territory had withdrawn south to the unconquered land.[92] Consequently, the loss of extensive cultivations—particularly at Rangiaowhia—had not been coupled with a proportionate reduction in the number of mouths to be fed. Increased disease went hand in hand with food shortages. Less tangible, but equally important, were the moral effects of constant retreat, and of the loss of materially and culturally valuable ancestral homes. Some tribes outside the Waikato became disenchanted with the King Movement, and the Waikato tribes themselves were less willing and able to involve themselves in quarrels outside their territory. In the conflicts after 1864, Maori resistance therefore lost much of its coherence and most of its unity.

Yet despite all this the degree of British success was distinctly limited. It was less clear to contemporaries than it is to historians that the Waikato War had ended in complete triumph, and that the British objectives had been achieved. Many observers felt that, despite Orakau, much remained to be done in the Waikato basin. 'The supremacy of British arms has not yet been established.' On the contrary 'the rebels seem in excellent spirits and determined to fight'.[93] Neither Te Ranga nor the 'unconditional submission' in Tauranga materially affected this situation. On 28 July 1864, the *New Zealand Herald* reported that the Kingites 'are far from being sufficiently humbled to offer any terms that can possibly be received'. The missionary John Morgan wrote: 'little real progress has been made during the year towards the settlement of the difficulty, for although the Waikato Country is partly occupied by our troops, it is the opinion of many best acquainted with maori matters that the country is now in really a worse position than it was a year ago. . . . The natives do not feel that they have been subdued. . . . To say the least the war party are as defiant as ever.'[94]

Then on 10 September an event occurred which reinforced the impression that the war was far from over. Some 200 Maori prisoners of war, including virtually all those captured at Rangiriri, escaped from Kawau

Island, north of Auckland, and began building a *pa* on the coast opposite. They were supplied with arms, food, and the promise of military protection by the powerful Ngapuhi tribe, which had hitherto been neutral. The involvement of the Ngapuhi—Heke's and Kawiti's people—greatly compounded the problem presented by the escape of the prisoners, which in itself went some way towards neutralizing the Maori defeat at Rangiriri.[95] At the time, the end of the war seemed further away than ever. Robert Burrows observed that 'upon the whole the colonists are full of gloomy foreboding'. In November, the Provincial Council of Otago petitioned the Colonial Office for the separation of the South Island, on the grounds that

> after sixteen months warfare, a deplorable loss of life, and the expediture of a vast sum of money . . . no appreciable results have been attained. . . . It appears to this Council that the objects proposed to be secured . . . have not been attained, and the sacrifices the people of this Province were called upon to make have hitherto been made in vain. . . . The Council declares its conviction that the Province is unable to endure a burden *imposed for unattainable ends*.[96]

The colonial ministry agreed that further operations were required to win the war in the Waikato—and so, initially, did Governor Grey. Both the Governor and the ministers had committed themselves to a policy of extensive confiscation of Maori land. This was designed to help finance the war—by sale and as requital for the services of the Waikato Militia—and to ensure that the subjugation of the King Movement was permanent. Nothing like the amount of land required—variously estimated at between three and eight million acres—had yet been conquered. Furthermore, such tribes as the Ngati Maniapoto, 'perhaps the most deserving of punishment', had lost virtually no land at all, and retained complete independence. This particular fact disturbed Grey as much as it did the ministry. The Ngati Maniapoto, wrote Grey, 'have escaped untouched in every engagement —they never fight, and do nothing but murder and pillage, having escaped hitherto without punishment, they are as unsubdued as ever'.[97] In general, the colonial government felt that Maori independence had yet to be broken, and that even the simple fact of British victory had not been sufficiently demonstrated. After Te Ranga, ministers stated that the rebellion was still 'far from being suppressed', and the situation remained the same in late September. 'In the opinion of the Ministers the position of the Maoris as defeated rebels had yet to be unequivocally exhibited.' Grey's position on the broad issue was less explicit, but he joined the colonial ministers in pressing Cameron to undertake further operations in Waikato. Grey urged that the occupying army should take any chance to strike a blow beyond the present limits of conquest, and that the Maoris should be constantly harassed so as to induce them to submit. Ministers also recommended 'harassing the enemy', and specifically advocated a move into Ngati Maniapoto territory, and an attack on the Ngati Haua base at Matamata 'as soon as possible'.[98] As the year progressed, however, first Grey and then the ministers were forced to accept that further operations would not be forthcoming. As far as military measures were concerned, the war was over. Factors such as the increasing reluctance of the Imperial Government to bear its share of the financial burden contributed to this, but the crucial factors were the military realities.

Early in the war, Cameron had learned that the occupation of a Maori *pa* meant little in itself. As he later expressed it, 'I considered it perfectly useless to undertake operations against a *pah*, without a chance of taking prisoners, or inflicting some loss on the enemy.'[99] Cameron also knew that *pa* could very rarely be surrounded. At Orakau, a unique opportunity had been lost. This left assault as the only means of destroying the garrison of a modern *pa*. If a *pa* was substantially incomplete, it could be stormed. But, as we have seen, catching the Maoris in such a position depended heavily upon chance. Catching the Maoris in a complete *pa*, on the other hand, was an easy matter. But Cameron's experience with assaults on completed *pa* was decidedly discouraging. His troops had launched no less than fifteen assaults, large and small, on complete *pa*. Of these only one—against the left of the Rangiriri trenches—had succeeded. Even this success owed something to accident, and it had secured only an inessential part of a fortification. Opportunities that had seemed highly promising, like the attacks on the weak-looking Rangiriri redoubt, had resulted only in repulse. Finally, the attack on Gate Pa—the perfect prospect for a successful assault—had led to disaster. After Gate Pa, Cameron decided that the successful assault of completed *pa* was beyond him: that he had no solution to the tactical problem of the modern *pa*. Decisive victory was therefore not possible, and Cameron refused to make further vain attempts in Tauranga or Waikato. Grey and the colonial government had no practical alternative to acquiescing in this decision.

Cameron reluctantly agreed to undertake another campaign, briefly discussed in the next chapter, in the less important Wanganui theatre, early in 1865. But he wrote that a 'decisive blow' was not possible here either, 'and if Her Majesty's troops are to be detained in the colony until one is struck, I confess I see no prospect of their leaving New Zealand'.[100] This meant that the situation in Waikato remained as it had been in April 1864. Te Ranga was a blow to morale, even for the Kingites of the Waikato basin, who had not been involved in that battle. But it was balanced by the escape of prisoners from Kawau, which substantially reduced the Waikato loss in warriors. The Kingites accepted the loss of the land already conquered, but as we have seen they were quite ready to resist any further offensives, and they had the means to do so in the fourth Waikato Line. It was the Line which actually delineated the area of British conquest, and this area was by no means as great or as satisfactory to the conquerors as has sometimes been assumed.

This misunderstanding arises partly from a curious ambivalence in the use of the term 'Waikato'. The word has two pairs of meanings. The first is the sense in which it has been used here: the four Waikato tribes and their territory. The second, here 'Waikato proper' and 'central Waikato', is the tribe of Te Wherowhero—itself actually a confederation of small tribes —and its territory. Some writers fail to make a consistent distinction and we find the British attacking 'Waikato', in the first sense, and conquering the whole 'Waikato' in the second sense. In fact, the British conquered less than one-third of the territory of the four Waikato tribes, and these four only constituted a part of Kingite support. The British confiscated what they conquered—no more, and no less. Beyond the border, the independent King Movement remained; battered, weakened, but intact.

The King Movement survived the Waikato War not because the British had acquired as much land as they wished to, nor because the Movement was so crippled that the British were unconcerned about the remnant. It survived because the British were militarily unable to destroy it. Fainthearts, cried the editor of the *Wellington Independent* after the Battle of Orakau 'would have us depart from the original objects for which we commenced the War. . . . What is this but a tacit admission that we are unable to compel submission under the original terms?' [101]

As is usually the case in war, victory in Waikato was a matter of degree. Overwhelmingly superior resources, efficiently acquired and applied by Grey and Cameron, secured a limited victory for the British. They seized a million acres, and, more importantly, they severely damaged the power and morale of the King Movement. In the long term, this facilitated the peaceful process by which the Kingites were eventually parted from most of their land, and by which they eventually became subject to British law. This became clear only in retrospect, and the British commentators quoted above consequently underestimated their success to some extent. But their opinions are more accurate that the historical orthodoxy. The modern *pa* system secured for the Maoris a degree of success which circumscribed the British victory. This too may have had long-term implications for New Zealand race relations.

PART FOUR

Titokowaru and Te Kooti

A New Kind of War

BY THE END OF 1864, THOUGH KINGITES AND BRITISH TROOPS still tensely confronted each other across the *aukati*, the Waikato War had ground to a halt. But in other parts of the island, a new kind of war had already emerged. In April-May, 1864, fighting unconnected to the Waikato War occurred in Taranaki and Wanganui. During 1865 and 1866, a profusion of other campaigns were fought across the country. Two of these involved Imperial troops, but most of the fighting was carried on by colonial forces, and various groups of Maoris. More limited fighting occurred in 1867 and early 1868, in the Bay of Plenty. These campaigns were small in scale, British objectives were localized, and Maori resistance was greatly fragmented. Then, in mid-1868, came a resurgence of Maori resistance under two great generals and prophets: Riwha Titokowaru of Ngati Ruanui, and Te Kooti Rikirangi Te Turuki of Rongowhakaata. Part IV of this book is primarily devoted to the main campaigns of these two Maori leaders, which together can be seen as the fourth major New Zealand War. But the operations of 1864-8 make up the background to this war, and they have considerable importance in themselves.

I THE CONFLICTS OF 1864-8

THE FIGHTING IN THIS PERIOD CONSISTED OF A DOZEN distinct campaigns and major expeditions in as many districts, spanning the whole breadth of the North Island. Over seventy engagements were fought, most of them very small, and there were also scores of raids on farms and villages. Local factors were important, and operations in the same month or in the same district often had little in common. A full treatment of this period cannot be attempted here. The approach adopted is, first, to look at the general causes of conflict, and then to provide a brief outline of the various campaigns. The reader should note that this summary relies on secondary sources to a much greater extent than the rest of the book, and is therefore provisional in character. Finally, in an attempt to explain the outcome of these conflicts, it is suggested that the period saw major changes in the Maori and British military systems. This part of the discussion, in particular, serves as an introduction to the wars of Titokowaru and Te Kooti.

During 1864-8, local rivalries were often important in deciding the make-up of the various Maori factions, but the influence of local and traditional factors can be exaggerated. A dozen separate campaigns did not suddenly break out as some kind of island-wide coincidence. There appear to have been two general causes of conflict: confiscation and *Pai Marire*.

In 1864 and 1865, the colonial government declared vast areas of land on the east and west coasts to be confiscated. The acreage involved was often estimated on the basis of rough sketch maps. The area actually occupied, or even surveyed, was much smaller, and the local Maoris probably believed these initial boundaries to be final. They accepted peace on this basis, reconciling themselves to the loss of a limited acreage. While financial stringencies and other considerations prevented the government from extending confiscations, the local peace remained intact. But as resources became available, and the risk of resistance seemed to diminish, the government would proceed to survey and occupy more land. The Maoris viewed this as renewed aggression, and fought back. This process of creeping confiscation was probably the major cause of several conflicts in the 1864–8 period, and of Titokowaru's War.[1]

A brief assessment of the influence of *Pai Marire* is more difficult. *Pai Marire*—'The Good and the Peaceful', also known as 'Hauhauism'—was a syncretic religion originated by the prophet Te Ua Haumene, of the Taranaki tribe, in 1862. It had messianic and millenarian aspects, and theologically combined traditional Maori religion and the Maori versions of Christianity with Te Ua's own innovations. The time and place of its origin tend to contradict the common assumption that it arose from despair at defeat in war: the Taranaki tribe had not been defeated in the 1860–1 conflict, nor, indeed, in the Waikato War. Little is known of the development of *Pai Marire* before April 1864, but from that date it spread rapidly across the country, with King Tawhiao becoming a convert in November 1864. The original form of *Pai Marire* may have died out as early as 1866, with the death of its founder, but related or similar cults developed around leaders such as Hakaraia, Te Whiti O Rongomai, Titokowaru, Te Kooti, and Tawhiao himself. Just how revolutionary an ideological change the new religions represented remains open to question, as does their precise relationship to the wars. Similar cults had emerged before the wars, and early Maori Christianity itself can arguably be understood as a syncretic religion, even an adjustment cult.

Until fairly recently, *Pai Marire* has been viewed as a bloodthirsty and militaristic belief which gave a new savagery to Maori resistance. On this basis, some of the campaigns of 1864–8 can be seen simply as a product of the new anti-*Pakeha* fanaticism. Two incidents lend some support to this view. In April-May 1864, *Pai Marire* adherents launched three sudden attacks in Taranaki and Wanganui—areas which had hitherto been quiescent. On 2 March 1865, two weeks after *Pai Marire* evangelists had arrived at Opotiki on the East Coast, the local missionary C. S. Volkner was killed by Maoris among whom he had lived for four years. However Paul Clark has shown that both incidents involved subordinate prophets acting against

Te Ua's wishes, and against the basic precepts of *Pai Marire*. Volkner's killing was also influenced by the fact that he acted as a government spy. Clark
argues from this, and from a range of other evidence, that the religion was a
peace-oriented adjustment cult, though strongly opposed to the alienation
of land, and eager to strengthen Maori identity.[2]

Clark's argument is reasonably convincing, at least as far as Te Ua's own
philosophy is concerned, and it seems that the contribution of *Pai Marire* to
the outbreak of conflict was generally indirect. From late 1864, Te Ua and
his Waikato converts sent emissaries to other parts of the island, particularly
the East Coast. These made converts rapidly, and some chiefs saw this as a
threat to the existing distribution of power within their tribe. They
therefore attacked *Pai Marire* adherents in a conservative attempt to maintain the *status quo*. In other cases, attacks occurred for the opposite reason.
Chiefs saw opposition to *Pai Marire* as a means of increasing their power, or
gaining some advantage in a local dispute. The civil wars within Ngati
Porou and Ngati Kahungunu arose largely from these factors. Other
violence was produced by the colonists' hostile reaction to the new religion.
Several expeditions were launched against the 'murderers' of Volkner, who
were very broadly defined. Several *Pai Marire* groups which did not want to
fight were attacked by the colonists. It is sometimes assumed that those
groups which had actively supported the Maori King also supported *Pai
Marire*, and after Tawhiao's conversion there was certainly a strong connection between the two. But the division was far from clear-cut: Kingites or
ex-Kingites fought both for and against *Pai Marire*.[3]

All this made for a diverse and complicated series of conflicts, but an
attempt must now be made to summarize them. Fighting on the West Coast
can be divided into four campaigns. The first consisted of the *Pai Marire* initiatives of April-May 1864. On 6 April, a small Taranaki party attacked and
routed a British patrol on open ground near Oakura.[4] On 30 April, a larger
Pai Marire force frontally attacked a British redoubt at Sentry Hill and was
repulsed with heavy loss. The crude Maori tactics were attributed to the
religious fanaticism of the *Pai Marire* prophet in charge, but were in fact
imposed on him by his secular subordinates.[5] Six weeks later, 300 *Pai
Marire* converts from the Upper Wanganui *hapu* advanced south towards
the British settlement of Wanganui Town, led by another Taranaki prophet. Their way was successfully barred by their Lower Wanganui
relatives, in a fierce but ritualized front-to-front battle at Moutoa on 14
May.[6] For our purposes, these engagements are principally interesting for
the unusual Maori tactics involved: an emphasis on frontal attack and a
tendency to revert to other traditional forms of fighting in purely Maori
encounters.

The second West Coast campaign was very much larger in scale—an
offensive launched northwards from Wanganui in January 1865 by Imperial
troops, eventually more than 3,000 strong. This operation was reluctantly

undertaken by Cameron at the behest of Grey and the colonial government. Since they could not persuade the General to mount a further campaign in Waikato, they wished to crush a secondary bastion of Maori independence —the South Taranaki tribes—while they still had the use of Imperial troops. On 24 January, the British field force, about 1,200 strong, advanced from the outskirts of Wanganui to Nukumaru, about fifteen miles north, accompanied by Cameron but under the operational command of Brigadier-General Waddy. That day and the next, between 400 and 600 South Taranaki warriors, perhaps supported by individuals from Waikato, attacked them from the surrounding bush. Both attacks were repelled after fierce and confused skirmishing. The British lost fourteen killed, and the Maoris at least twenty-three.[7] This action is sometimes presented as the finest example of Maori military prowess, and it is true that they attacked with great courage and some tactical skill. But the attack had little chance of success, better options were available, and it was therefore an uncharacteristic waste of lives.

After Nukumaru, the Maoris adopted a more promising course of action. They concentrated in a strong, newly-built *pa* at Weraroa and invited Cameron to attack. Despite pressure from Grey, Cameron declined to oblige, on the very good grounds that an assault was likely to fail, and that any other form of attack with the forces available would permit the Maoris to escape and would therefore be useless. Instead, the General masked Weraroa with a strong force, secured his communications by building several redoubts, and proceeded north. On 13 March, some 200 Ngati Ruanui opposed him in the open at Te Ngaio, and were heavily defeated. On 31 March, Cameron reached the Waingongoro River, sixty miles north of Wanganui, and halted his advance.[8]

Cameron was subjected to extremely severe criticism for his tardiness in the Wanganui campaign, and it is true that he moved circumspectly. This has been variously attributed to his incompetence and lethargy; to his fear of the bush after the Maoris used it to launch the surprise attack at Nukumaru; and to moral doubts about the campaign arising from reports received about the injustice of an earlier colonist purchase of land at Waitotara. Several writers add Cameron's disgust at a bitter controversy with Grey during March-May 1865, mainly over the General's refusal to attack Weraroa. The notion that Cameron was simply a bad commander can be dismissed out of hand, and the other claims are scarcely more plausible. In standing orders issued to the Wanganui expeditionary force on 17 December 1864, well before Nukumaru, the first reports about the Waitotara purchase, and the controversy with Grey, Cameron instructed his commanders to proceed cautiously at Wanganui and forbade attacks on *pa*. He also sent his resignation to the War Office on 7 February 1865, when the Wanganui campaign was only two weeks old, and when the Weraroa controversy had yet to develop.[9]

Cameron disliked the Wanganui campaign, and decided to conduct it very cautiously, well before it began. His attitude clearly arose less from moral or political considerations than from his experience of the Waikato War. As we have seen, a year of hard and frustrating warfare had taught him respect for the Maori capacity to threaten his communications, and a still greater respect for, though not a full understanding of, the modern *pa*. 'Experience has shown me', he informed Grey, 'that it is not generally desirable to attack such positions as the Weraroa Pa.' He therefore felt that the Wanganui campaign could not produce the 'decisive blow' which might induce the Maoris to submit.[10] Though unpredictable Maori errors exposed them to two unnecessary defeats at Nukumaru and Te Ngaio, neither was crushing, and, overall, Cameron may have been right. The General himself conducted no further operations, and left the colony in August 1865.

As a kind of postscript to the Wanganui campaign, colonial forces conducted two operations in July 1865. Under Grey's personal direction, and without Cameron's knowledge, a small force captured a Maori supply depot in rear of Weraroa on 20 July. The remaining Weraroa garrison—many warriors had already left—evacuated the *pa* next day. Grey and others publicized this as a great victory, demonstrating Grey's brilliance as a tactician, and the superiority of colonial over Imperial troops. But, as B. J. Dalton has shown, the 'great victory' was a non-event.[11] Weraroa had lost its strategic importance long before, when Cameron outflanked it and moved north. Grey could only have gained a substantive success by destroying the garrison, and this he certainly did not do. The Weraroa legend is simply another example of Grey's ability as a self-propagandist; of the colonists' readiness to believe the worst of the regulars; and of the British capacity to create a paper victory out of almost nothing.

The other colonial operation of July 1865 consisted in two weeks skirmishing with the Upper Wanganuis around Pipiriki, a redoubt built by the colonists fifty miles up the Wanganui River. The skirmishing, elevated in colonial legend into a 'siege', involved an incident where the colonist commander, Major W. Brassey, floated Latin messages asking for relief down the river in a bottle. In fact the colonists had no men killed, and Maori casualties were probably also light. The 'siege' ended when Brassey gave up on his bottled request and, in William Fox's immortal phrase, 'relieved himself'.[12]

The third and fourth West Coast campaigns can be dealt with more briefly. Between 3 January and 6 February 1866, Cameron's replacement, Major-General W. C. T. Chute, devastated the territory of the South Taranaki tribes between the Waitotara River and Mount Egmont. Maori resistance was brave but decentralized, and small local forces were repeatedly driven out of unfortified villages and traditional *pa* by vigorous assaults. The most notable action occurred on 14 January, when the British stormed the traditional *pa* of Otapawa at the cost of about seven killed.[13] Chute then marched a mixed Imperial, colonial, and *kupapa* (pro-government Maori) force through the bush inland of Egmont to New Plymouth.

This brief operation was the last of any importance involving Imperial troops and was Chute's only New Zealand campaign. But he was highly praised for his performance by Grey and the colonists, particularly for the march around Mount Egmont. The reputation this has given him may be undeserved. Those who praised Chute were largely interested in high-lighting, by contrast, the supposed incompetence of General Cameron. Chute was a bold and vigorous commander, but his unvarying recipe for taking enemy positions with a frontal assault, preceded by little in the way of reconnaissance or bombardment, would certainly have brought him to grief against a well-manned modern *pa*. Further, his vaunted expedition around Mount Egmont, which was not opposed by the Maoris, got lost and ran out of supplies. A commissariat officer 'became so exhausted that he was obliged to be left in a blanket at the foot of a large tree, and Captain Leach gave him his last wet biscuit to keep him alive'.[14] Chute's force had to eat its pack-horses, and was saved from starvation only by the arrival of a supply party from North Taranaki. Thus Chute narrowly escaped becoming one of the few generals to lose an army without the presence of an enemy to excuse him.[15]

The remaining campaign was conducted by colonists and *kupapa* under Major Thomas McDonnell, in June-November 1866. Fought in the same area, against the same enemy, McDonnell's campaign followed a pattern similar to Chute's. Villages and cultivations were attacked, and when their owners sought to defend them, they usually did so without outside help and from unprepared or hastily-prepared positions. McDonnell had fewer troops than Chute, but he was an able—and ruthless—commander. Both campaigns succeeded in intimidating and weakening the local Maoris, and an uneasy peace prevailed on the West Coast from November 1866 to June 1868.[16]

Most of the fighting on the East Coast occurred between June 1865 and October 1866. It is sometimes known as the East Coast War, but was in fact a complicated series of intersecting conflicts.[17] Hostilities were triggered by the arrival of *Pai Marire* emissaries in various parts of the East Coast in early 1865, and by the killing of Volkner. The first major outbreak was the Ngati Porou civil war of June-October 1865. After initial defeats—notably Tiki-tiki on 20 June—the anti-*Pai Marire* faction, led by such chiefs as Ropata Wahawaha, overcame their opponents with the help of colonial troops and arms. Meanwhile, the colonial government launched a series of expeditions against the 'murderers' of Volkner, and anyone associated with them. Some were mounted by the 'East Coast Expedition'—colonial units and Wanga-nui *kupapa* from Taranaki—which landed at Opotiki in September.[18] Others were mounted by the pro-government Arawa. These expeditions tended to follow the pattern of Chute's and McDonnell's West Coast cam-paigns, with the Whakatohea tribe, *Pai Marire* sympathizers, suffering par-ticularly severe economic damage.

In November 1865, once *Pai Marire* adherents in the northern East Coast had been scattered or induced to submit, government forces attacked

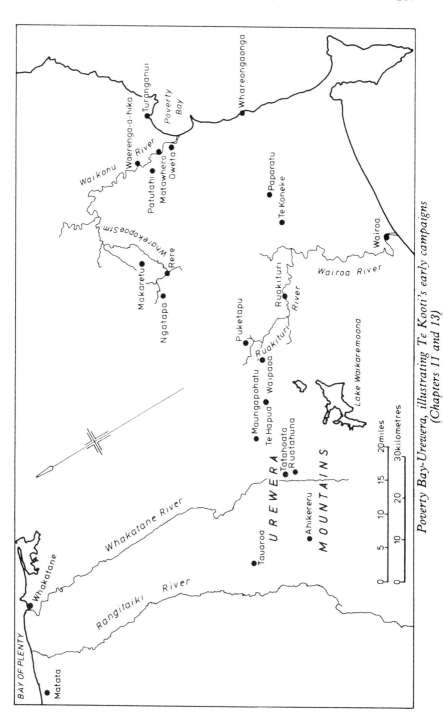

Poverty Bay-Urewera, illustrating Te Kooti's early campaigns (Chapters 11 and 13)

'Hauhau rebels' of the Rongowhakaata and Aitanga-a-Mahaki tribes of Poverty Bay. The Maoris assembled at Waerenga-a-Hika, a large *pa* seven miles from Turanganui (now Gisborne). Fighting between them and colonial units, actively assisted by *kupapa* Ngati Porou, was initially quite severe, but the Maori resistance seems to have become half-hearted. On 22 November 1865, they surrendered their strong and well-manned *pa*, and became prisoners. We are invited to believe that they did so because the colonists' only cannon, a six-pounder without proper ammunition, fired two salmon-tins filled with shrapnel into the *pa*.[19] This is clearly inadequate, and the surrender of Waerenga-a-Hika remains to be explained through further research.

In December 1865-January 1866, another civil war was fought, this time among the Ngati Kahungunu of the Wairoa or Northern Hawke's Bay region. The *Pai Marire* faction, led by Te Waru Tamatea, an Orakau veteran, fought a small *kupapa* faction under Kopu Parapara and Ihaka Whanga. Most Ngati Kahungunu remained neutral, or wavered between one side and the other. The *kupapa* faction won because they called in colonial and Ngati Porou help. A sequel to this brief campaign occurred nine months later, when *Pai Marire* adherents of Ngati Hineuru—a *hapu* living between Ngati Kahungunu and Ngati Tuwharetoa territory, related to both tribes—travelled into the Napier district. Under the instructions of their prophet, Panapa, 'they remained quiet and refrained from any act of violence', at the 'fenced village' of Omaranui. Maori evidence indicates that this 'rebel army' was only eighty strong. They were, however, attacked and crushed by colonial forces under Colonel G. S. Whitmore, supported by the influential Ngati Kahungunu chief Tareha te Moananui.[20]

The period November 1866 to July 1868 was relatively peaceful but small-scale fighting occurred in the Tauranga, Rotorua, and Opotiki districts. In Tauranga, while most Maoris held to the peace agreement of 1864, the tiny Piri Rakau *hapu*, led by the prophet Hakaraia, opposed the extension of confiscation into their territory. At first, they did so by turning back surveyors unharmed, but when the government sought to arrest them, fighting broke out and continued from 18 January to 3 March 1867. Though their villages and crops were destroyed, Piri Rakau managed to evade several colonist and Arawa expeditions: 'the enemy did not muster above 50 to 60 and they harassed fully 800 men for months.'[21] Later in March, Hakaraia and some of his men, reinforced from Waikato, sought revenge against the Arawa by raiding their homes at Rotorua. The Arawa suffered considerable economic damage in their turn, before colonial reinforcements forced Hakaraia and his allies to withdraw. Hakaraia, a leader who deserves more attention from historians, retired to Kingite territory and joined Te Kooti in 1869.

Similarly, in Opotiki, the Tuhoe proved reluctant to accept confiscations on their northern border, and from early 1866 to May 1868 they made occasional raids on the military settlers farming the disputed land. Several punitive expeditions were mounted by the colonists, but met with little success. The young Ngai-Tama chief Eru Tamaikowha was prominent in these sporadic operations. Though the government forces never seem to have suffered more than two casualties in any engagement with Tamaikowha, he gained a considerable reputation for ferocity and guerilla skill.

The British and their Maori allies were by no means uniformly successful in the conflicts of 1864–8. Many expeditions were fruitless, and Imperials, colonials, and *kupapa* are all known to have suffered occasional tactical defeats. If British interpetative tendencies held true, further research may reveal such defeats were more frequent. Moreover, the British failed to secure anything like a complete political victory. A few Maori groups were actually conquered, more were weakened and intimidated, but most Maoris remained independent in practice.

It was partly this lack of decisive success which led to the downfall of Governor Grey. By 1865, the Imperial Government had at last decided that Grey's effort to crush Maori independence could drag on for ever, and that Imperial troops must be withdrawn. Grey procrastinated as only he could, but against his will the troops were first disengaged from active operations, then removed entirely from the Governor's control, and finally, by May 1867, withdrawn. One regiment remained, under strict instructions to take no part in active operations. Grey's resistance to the withdrawal of troops, compounded by other incidents, finally exhausted the Colonial Office's patience with his manipulation of it. In 1867, after a turgid exchange of recriminations, he was dismissed and replaced by Sir G. F. Bowen. George Grey, the last governor to hold substantial executive power, was the most eminent of many scapegoats for Maori military skill and tenacity. If the Waikato War had ended quickly, as Grey intended, or if subsequent operations had led to complete success, he might have been able to give his second New Zealand governorship the appearance of another pro-consular triumph.

Despite all this, it remains true that the Maori war effort in this period was much less successful than in earlier or later wars: 1864–8 was the nadir of Maori resistance. Why was this so? The explanation offered here, as a hypothesis rather than a definitive solution, emphasizes three inter-related developments: the *kupapa* phenomenon; the emergence of a new British military method; and certain changes for the worse in Maori military methods.

The *kupapa*, Maoris fighting on the British side, were variously known as 'loyalists', 'Queenites', and 'the friendly natives'. During the Taranaki and Waikato Wars, with the exception of Arawa opposition to the East Coast Kingites, they were not an important military factor—perhaps because of the wide Maori consensus in favour of the King Movement. Subsequently the situation became more like that of the Northern War, with *kupapa* acting as the third side in a multi-faceted conflict. Collaboration became much more complicated, however, since many tribes and regions were involved rather than one. The motives of *kupapa* groups varied enormously, as did their degree of commitment to the British cause. The one common factor was that this commitment was never complete. The *kupapa* did not share British aims; they had their own, which seemed to them to be honourable and in their best interests. It was a matter of their aims intersecting with the British at certain points.

At one end of the scale were *kupapa* groups whose support for the British was relatively whole-hearted. These included the bulk of the Arawa, who had become estranged from their Maori neighbours, and needed their alliance with the government to survive in isolation. There were also one or two regular colonial units recruited from *kupapa* tribes, and subjected to European military discipline, or 'de-tribalized', to use the colonial phrase. Another, more important, group in this category of commitment, were the bands of warriors collected around an able chief whose power within the tribe had been created or greatly increased by his *kupapa* activities. Ropata of Ngati Porou and Kepa te Rangihiwinui of Wanganui are the best-known examples. The majority of each tribe, outside Ropata's and Kepa's immediate followings, were less committed to the colonist cause. The colonists found these groups fairly reliable allies, but even they would sometimes refuse to co-operate. Ropata, the colonists' favourite *kupapa*, drove his paymasters to distraction during the Ngatapa campaign by taking the field at his own pace. Arawa and Ngati Porou regular units suddenly threw off military discipline in early 1869, and refused to enter a new theatre of war for tribal political reasons.[22]

A second category included groups who fought hard in the British cause, but only for a particular and limited reason of their own. Close economic connections with the settlers were probably important here. The Lower Wanganuis may have fought their kin at Moutoa in 1864 to protect their valuable entrepôt of Wanganui Town. Ngati Kahungunu of the Napier district would fight anyone, including *Pai Marire* evangelists, who appeared to threaten their economic relationship with the settlers of Napier. Others might seize the opportunity of a British campaign to gain an advantage over local rivals.

Towards the bottom of the scale of commitment, *kupapa* groups gave only superficial support to the British; they mobilized and accompanied colonial expeditions, but declined to do much fighting. These Maoris might have mixed sympathies, but the proximity of colonial forces to their homes made a *kupapa* role expedient. Others might join up simply for pay. The Wanganui tribe called out its *levée en masse* to oppose Titokowaru in 1868—every old man and boy who could carry a gun.[23] Most of these people did little fighting, but they did collect four shillings a day. This may seem mercenary, but it did the resisting Maoris little harm, and provided the Wanganuis with a valuable cash industry. *Kupapa* groups often changed their category of commitment. Rongowhakaata and some Ngati Kahungunu were half-hearted in operations against Te Kooti until he killed their relatives. They then pursued him more vigorously than the colonists.

The British rarely recognized this scale of commitment, and they frequently accused *kupapa* of treachery, cowardice, lethargy, and incompetence. But variations in the intensity of the *kupapa* war effort were usually attributable to tribal political factors. When they chose to be, *kupapa* were normally good soldiers. Their efficiency was further improved by government economic support, which enabled them to muster larger forces and maintain them for longer than Maori resisters. In this sense, the *kupapa* war effort was not 'tribal', but had the same economic advantage as European troops. Despite their qualified commitment, *kupapa* were vital to the colonists after the withdrawal of Imperial troops. Without them, the colonial operations of 1864–8 would have been far less successful, and the wars against Titokowaru and Te Kooti might have been lost.

The second development which reduced the effectiveness of Maori resistance was the emergence of a new British system of war. To some extent, this system was the product of a theory advocated repeatedly by New Zealand settlers since the beginning of the Taranaki War in March 1860. The colonists argued that the solution to the difficulties of war with the Maori was an approach which combined inherent British military virtues and European technological advantages with the irregular skills of the Maoris themselves. Beginning as a criticism of Imperial troops, who were supposed to be crippled by tradition, rigid discipline, and conservative commanders, this argument, under labels varying from 'guerilla warfare' to 'bush-scouring', became an act of faith with many commentators. Indeed, it was a theme of most colonist discussions of the wars.[24]

At its fullest, the 'bush-scouring' theory entailed a 'flying column' of a few hundred men, untrammelled by a large supply train, hunting down the Maoris in the bush, and forcing them to fight by attacking their villages and cultivations. The columns might include some picked Imperial regulars, selected for their fitness and adaptability, but they would largely consist of settler-frontiersmen, supposedly natural 'Indian-fighters'. These 'irregulars' were to be supported by native auxilaries, preferably under European officers, and they were to be led by vigorous and unorthodox commanders, unimpressed by the rules of conventional warfare. They were also to be appropriately armed for bush-fighting, which ideally required weapons which could be loaded and handled in a restricted space, and which produced high short-range firepower. The 1860s saw the emergence of progressively more reliable breech-loading rifles and carbines, and proponents of bush-scouring maintained that advantage should be taken of this technological development.

Many of the colonial operations of 1864–8 can legitimately be seen as an application of the bush-scouring theory. Broadly speaking, they fitted its four basic criteria of composition, weaponry, leadership, and strategic approach. During 1866, the government's European forces on active service numbered about 2,000 men.[25] They were drawn largely from the military settlers recruited since 1863 to occupy the confiscated lands (in Waikato, Taranaki, and elsewhere) after a period as full-time soldiers. Their backgrounds were varied, and sometimes disreputable, but they were generally tough characters who made good soldiers in the right circumstances. Most units were in effect regular troops: the Patea and Wanganui Rangers, the reconstituted Forest Rangers, and the 1st Waikato Militia, which had been kept on pay after the other three Waikato regiments had been discharged to take up their confiscated farms. The 1st Waikato was still armed with muzzle-loading Enfield rifles, but other units had Terry and Calisher carbines and five-shot revolvers—breech-loading and repeating weapons suitable for bush-fighting. In 1867, this miscellany of units was greatly reduced in numbers and formed into a colonial regular army, euphemistically named 'the Armed Constabulary'. The constabulary was formed too late to participate significantly in the campaigns of 1864-8, and its quality will be discussed in the next chapter. But throughout the period colonial units did, as we have seen, have the support of 'native auxiliaries'—the *kupapa*.

The colonial military leaders were usually bold and active, and were sometimes very able. Some were British regular officers who had resigned their commissions to settle in New Zealand, such as Whitmore, J. Fraser, and J. H. H. St John. But many were young middle-class settlers. The McDonnell brothers, the Mair brothers, R. Biggs, F. Y. Goring, and G. A. Preece are examples. There were also a few adventurers of various nationalities—such as Captain Davis, an American, and two Prussian officers who had fought in Latin America as mercenaries: Von Tempsky and C. H. Weber. These officers frequently applied the bush-scouring theory, and they did so successfully. Colonial columns entered the bush, and threatened targets highly valued by the local Maoris: crops, villages, and sometimes non-combatants. The Maoris would either not fight for these, and suffer a heavy moral and economic blow, or fight for them in *ad hoc* fashion, with small local forces and from unsuitable positions. Not unnaturally, the colonists assumed that their long-advocated theory had been borne out in its entirety, and indulged in a chorus of 'I told you so'.

In fact, contrary to the belief of some of its advocates, bush-scouring was not simply a matter of letting tough pioneer frontiersmen fight the Maoris in their own way. Few New Zealand settlers actually fitted this legendary type, and Imperial troops were capable of bush-scouring, as Chute's 1866 campaign showed. Bush-scouring was not a panacea for all circumstances, based on the inherent abilities of settler-frontiersmen, but a military method appropriate only in a certain context—when the enemy were divided and disorganized, and fought without a strategic overview. During 1864-8, this context existed; in earlier and later wars, it did not. The third crucial development of 1864-8 was this temporary change in the Maori military system.

One assumption behind the bush-scouring theory was that the Maoris were evasive guerilla fighters, who preferred to avoid British forces of any strength. They could only be pinned down by attacking their valuable villages, which were sometimes deep in the bush. As far as the Taranaki and

Waikato Wars were concerned, this assumption was false. The Maoris spent much of the former and most of the latter in modern *pa*, accessible to a regular army. The British objective was quick victory through the decisive defeat of the main Maori force, and they could only achieve this by attacking the *pa*. Masking the *pa*, and bush-scouring against the Maori base areas in a war of economic attrition would be a long and slow process, and anyway the *pa* cordons and lines of Taranaki and Waikato often physically blocked such a move. Moreover, the Maoris used the modern *pa* as a springboard for their own depredations against vulnerable settler farms and the army's lines of communication. The British had either to devote large resources to protecting these—resources which were then unavailable for bush-scouring—or, again, attack the raiders' base: a modern *pa*. Pursuing the raiders in those bush areas which did not contain vital villages and cultivations did little good, since the Maoris could evade their pursuers, as they did Cameron's flying column in 1863. Thus when the Maoris were united in following a firm strategic plan, when they vigorously disputed the initiative with the British and consistently applied the modern *pa* system, 'bush-scouring' did not work. The analysis of Titokowaru's War, in the next chapter, strongly supports this conclusion. But in 1864–8, Maori resistance rarely had these characteristics, and bush-scouring was therefore effective.

One reason for the incoherence of Maori resistance was the diminished influence of the King Movement. The effective Maori strategies of the Taranaki and Waikato Wars had been largely based on Kingite leadership, organization, and resources. In the absence of this support, local Maori resistance efforts lacked cohesion as well as numbers. In the Northern War and Titokowaru's War, brilliant, influential, and pragmatic individual leaders supplied this lack, and imposed a hard-headed strategic approach on their followers. In 1864–8, for whatever reason, such leaders did not emerge. This meant that Maori resistance took on a hand-to-mouth character, with people fighting only for their own village and from hastily selected, hastily prepared positions. Another result was the tendency to revert to traditional tactics. Attacks, open battles, and the defence of traditional *pa* were far more frequent in 1864–8 than in the rest of the New Zealand Wars. An underlying preference for these types of fighting, so much more satisfying to the warrior ethos than a circumspect approach, always existed among the Maoris. When faced solely by other Maoris, they indulged it, and even against the British it occasionally rose to the surface, as at No. 3 Redoubt in 1860. But normally the Maoris held this preference in check when fighting the British. With rigorous realism, Maori generals set aside their favoured type of fighting and opted for the most effective method. With less able, influential, or pragmatic leadership, this restraint did not occur, and actions like Nukumaru and Te Ngaio took place —courageous and tactically well-handled, but fundamentally misconceived.

There were, no doubt, other factors behind increased British success in 1864–8. The peaceful orientation of some *Pai Marire* prophets seems to have hampered the war effort of certain Maori groups—a curious reversal of the old view of *Pai Marire* as a militant creed. The highly localized objectives of most British expeditions may also have contributed—they did not present the kind of threat likely to unite large bodies of Maoris. But the main reason for increased British success was that the decline in the coherence and pragmatism of Maori resistance created an opportunity which the British were able to exploit through their valuable *kupapa* allies and their bush-scouring system. At the cold-blooded analytical level, the British deserve credit for this, but the human cost should not be forgotten. Across half the North Island, this new kind of war spread like a lethal blight, leaving violent death, starvation, and misery in its wake.

II   THE ESCAPE OF TE KOOTI

FROM THE BEGINNING OF 1867 TO THE MIDDLE OF 1868, APART from skirmishing on the Urewera border and the brief campaign in the Bay of Plenty, the North Island was in a state of uneasy peace. Then in June 1868, Titokowaru's War broke out in South Taranaki. Fierce fighting spread into the Wanganui region, the north-west of Wellington Province, later that year. Meanwhile, on the opposite coast, a band of Maori prisoners of war escaped from the Chathams, an isolated island group 400 miles east of New Zealand, to which they had been exiled in 1866. They landed near Poverty Bay on 10 July 1868. They were led by Te Kooti, and for the next four years, in over thirty expeditions, the government hunted them across Northern Hawke's Bay, the Urewera, Taupo, East Cape, and the Bay of Plenty.

Titokowaru and Te Kooti gave each other little or no direct support, they did not co-ordinate their plans, and their operations took place in entirely different areas. In these respects their campaigns can legitimately be seen as separate conflicts: Titokowaru's War and Te Kooti's War. On the other hand, the two wars were fought at much the same time and against a common enemy: the colonial government. Events on one coast therefore affected events on the other, and the colonists always had to consider the two wars as a whole. A compromise between these considerations is attempted here. The remaining sections of this chapter trace the early campaigns of Te Kooti, to the peak of his success in late 1868. The next chapter takes Titokowaru's War to the same point, and then discusses the position in which the victories of both leaders placed the colony. Chapter Thirteen discusses the turn of the tide against the Maoris, and outlines the way in which both resistance efforts petered out.

A sub-theme of these chapters, supplementing the two main themes of the book, is an attempt to compare Titokowaru and Te Kooti. Ranking military leaders in order of excellence is better avoided in most circumstances, but in this case such an evaluation already exists and is firmly entrenched in the historical orthodoxy. Many writers dismiss Titokowaru in a few lines, if they mention him at all, and some explicitly inform us that 'Te Kooti proved a more formidable and skilful opponent'. Explicitly or implicitly, the comparison is often extended to other Maori war-leaders, and we get the impression that Te Kooti was the only Maori general worthy of the name.[26] It will be argued that this assessment is false in itself, and that it helps to perpetuate a false picture of the wars as a whole. But the purpose is not to denigrate Te Kooti. To say that his generalship was flawed and his military importance exaggerated, is not to deny that he was skilful and important. Nor should it detract from his still greater significance as a spiritual leader of his people.

Te Kooti was born about 1830, into the Rongowhakaata tribe of Poverty Bay.[27] He began his military career as a *kupapa*, and was among the government forces at the siege of Waerenga-a-Hika in November 1865. By his own account, he shot two *Pai Marire* adherents during the fighting, but he was arrested by his own side for firing blanks. He was soon released for lack of evidence, but was re-arrested in March 1866, for spying, and deported without trial to the Chathams. The charges were probably trumped up by the established leaders of Poverty Bay, both Maori and *Pakeha*, who seem to have seen Te Kooti as a rival for local influence.

Over 160 of Te Kooti's erstwhile *Pai Marire* enemies were also prisoners at the Chathams. They included Rongowhakaata and Aitanga-a-Mahaki warriors captured at Waerenga-a-Hika, and the Ngati Hineuru captured at Omaranui in 1866, together with individuals of various other tribes. By the end of 1867, Te Kooti was recognized as leader by these men, achieving his ascendancy in a manner described below. Government treatment of the prisoners was mixed. Their families were permitted to join them, and some of the guards were kind. Others beat the men and molested the women, and promises of release after two years' good behaviour were not kept. On 4 July 1868 the prisoners took matters into their own hands.

On that day, the schooner *Rifleman* sailed into Waitangi, the township of the main Chatham island of Wharekauri, where the prisoners were kept under control by a redoubt, a resident magistrate, and sixteen armed guards. The *Rifleman* brought supplies from the mainland, but unloading was postponed because of heavy rain. During the early afternoon, Te Kooti and fifty of the prisoners entered the guardhouse of the redoubt on the pretext of sheltering from the rain. At Te Kooti's signal, the prisoners suddenly tackled and overpowered the guards on duty. The rest of the redoubt was quickly occupied, and the off-duty guards seized and bound with the others. The armoury was broken open, and rifles distributed and loaded. The prisoners then set off to perform previously appointed tasks. One party ensured that no word of the rising reached settlers outside Waitangi, or the *Rifleman* in the bay. Another party went out to the ship by boat, posing as workers sent to unload, and quickly took control of it from the crew. Nothing was forgotten. A second vessel at anchor off Waitangi was beached

to prevent word being sent to the mainland. Messengers collected those
prisoners working outside the town. Arms, ammunition, money, and water
were gathered and taken aboard the *Rifleman*, as were the Maori women
and children. That same day, carrying virtually all the prisoners—163 men,
64 women, and 71 children—the *Rifleman* set sail for New Zealand.

This remarkable escape was carried out with little violence and great efficiency. The prisoners had good reason to desire revenge against their cap-
tors, and one guard was killed, against Te Kooti's orders, by a prisoner who
had a personal grudge against him. But there were no other fatalities. Most
of the guards were treated 'very gently', and even the unpopular Captain
Thomas, the Resident Magistrate, had his painfully tight bonds replaced at
his request by handcuffs, and had his personal cash returned to him.[28] The
escape was clearly the product of a comprehensive, pre-arranged plan,
designed around the arrival of a large ship. Despite its complexity, and the
need to operate in many small groups, it was implemented perfectly. As the
government official who reported on the incident remarked: 'it is difficult to
say whether one's wonder is excited more by the precision, rapidity and
completeness with which the enterprise was planned and executed or by the
moderation shown in the hour of victory by a gang of barbarous fanatics.'[29]

After a difficult voyage, the *Rifleman* reached Whareongaonga, on the
East Coast fifteen miles south of Poverty Bay, on 10 July. The prisoners remained there for several days, recuperating and unloading supplies. They
released the *Rifleman* and its crew unharmed, reportedly with a gift of
£150.[30] During this time, government emissaries visited them and demanded
their surrender. Te Kooti refused, but strongly re-affirmed the peaceful intentions demonstrated at the Chathams. He and his people then moved off
inland, having indicated that 'they had no wish to fight unless attacked'.[31]
But the government decided against leaving them alone, and soon dispatched
strong forces to intercept them. Before examining the resulting campaign, it
is necessary to consider the nature of Te Kooti's leadership, and the composition and command of the forces opposed to him.

Te Kooti was not a chief, he had no tribal basis of support, and his *mana*
did not depend upon military success. Yet his authority over his followers
was very great—indeed it was more absolute than that of any Maori leader
before or after him. His power arose from his religion, *Ringatu*, the Upraised
Hand. *Ringatu* is a syncretic millenarian belief similar in some respects to
Pai Marire. Te Kooti originated the religion in 1867 at the Chathams, and
soon converted most of his fellow prisoners. Te Kooti and his followers
believed that he was the infallible mouthpiece of God. He formulated a
beautiful set of church services, and laid down a code of conduct which
governed his people's daily lives—this conformed to most Maori customary
practices, but contravened a few.[32]

Ringatu was arguably the most comprehensive, sophisticated, and
resilient of the new Maori religions. Te Kooti developed it fully in the years
from the end of his war in 1872 to his death in 1893, but it was already
remarkably mature when he returned to New Zealand in 1868. The all-

embracing, complete nature of *Ringatu*, and the utter security of Te Kooti's place in it, gave him important advantages as a military leader. The loyalty of his followers was virtually immutable, he was able to gain fresh adherents readily, and his resistance acquired an enormous resilience—again and again, Te Kooti rose phoenix-like from the ashes of defeat. In fact, the military-religious link was so strong that, in the absence of a better alternative, '*Ringatu*' is not an inappropriate label for Te Kooti's warriors.

Te Kooti was also able to control a group of powerful and independent-minded lieutenants, some of whom had far greater hereditary *mana* than their leader. Among the Chatham Island exiles, with whom Te Kooti always retained a special bond, were Ngati Hineuru leaders captured at Omaranui: Nikora, Petera Kahuroa, and Te Rangitahau (actually of Ngati Tuwharetoa). The most notable of the prisoners taken at Waerenga-a-Hika was Eru Peka Makarini (Edward Baker McLean), reputedly the illegitimate son of a colonist official, 'the greatest of ruffians and Te Kooti's best fighting man'.[33] This formidable group was later supplemented by Te Waru Tamatea and Nama, chiefs of the Upper Wairoa Ngati Kahungunu who joined Te Kooti in October 1868. Te Waru was a widely respected chief, and some colonists believed him to be the actual leader of the *Ringatu* band, but in fact, like all his colleagues, he was a loyal subordinate of Te Kooti's.

Te Kooti was able to dominate these men and their warriors through what is sometimes described as 'charisma', but this was not the ephemeral magnetism of the hysterical evangelist or soap-box orator. Te Kooti's powerful personality always worked in concert with his well-developed belief system, which reconciled the temporal and spiritual worlds in a way many Maoris found intellectually convincing as well as emotionally satisfying. In 1869, Hakaraia—*Pai Marire* leader in the Bay of Plenty campaign of 1867, and himself a very influential prophet—joined Te Kooti at Taupo. Hakaraia said, 'Te Kooti is a true man. I thought I knew a good deal, but this man's knowledge is much greater than mine. I shall have to succumb to him.'[34] Hakaraia's decision was reasoned as well as emotional, and he did not 'succumb' entirely: 'No-one ever dares to contradict him [Te Kooti] except old Hakaraia, who generally gets his own way.'[35] But Hakaraia's mountain came to Te Kooti's Mohammed, and stayed to the death.

The religious element was most important, but there were other notable aspects of Te Kooti's leadership. His early life as a small trader and coastal sailor bequeathed skills useful to a guerilla captain: horsemanship, boat-handling, navigation, and a knowledge of the terrain around Poverty Bay. More useful still was his unusually deep knowledge of Europeans. He had business contacts with the settlers of Poverty Bay, and he is reported to have had a mission school education and to have visited Auckland. There is even an indication that he could read English.[36] If true, this was a very rare skill indeed. Many Maoris were literate, but most only in their own language. However he acquired his knowledge, Te Kooti was very adept at predicting and manipulating *Pakeha* responses.

The war against Te Kooti was fought by local militia and volunteers, and Armed Constabulary—who contributed decisively to the crucial Ngatapa campaign. But much of the fighting was done by *kupapa*—Rongowhakaata (Te Kooti's own tribe), Ngati Kahungunu, and Ngati Porou, later joined by Arawa and other tribes. The degree of commitment of these tribes varied in the ways outlined above, and there were sometimes rivalries between various *kupapa* groups. British commentators frequently referred to the baneful effect of these divisions, as well as other supposed *kupapa* weaknesses. Factionalism among the colonists received much less emphasis, but in reality it hampered operations more. The problem was the feud between the Stafford Government, in office since 1866, and Donald McLean.

After a long and influential career as Native Secretary and Chief Land Purchase Commissioner, McLean had settled down in Hawke's Bay. By 1868, he was uncrowned king of the province. His formal powers included the offices of Agent for the General Government on the East Coast, Superintendent of Hawke's Bay, and Member of the House of Representatives for Napier. His informal power was based on a wide network of clients and allies, both Maori and *Pakeha*. Contrary to the impression he and his friends chose to give, he did not actually control any Maori group, but his influence over some chiefs, particularly of Ngati Kahungunu and Ngati Porou, was greater than that of any other European. The Stafford Government, whose important members for our purposes were E. W. Stafford himself, T. M. Haultain (Defence Minister), and J. C. Richmond (*de facto* Native Minister), had to balance the needs of the wars on both coasts. They felt that the situation on the West Coast was the more dangerous, and accordingly concentrated the vast majority of the colonial army there. McLean felt that insufficient resources were being devoted to his district. This was natural enough, but he often took high-handed action in support of his claims, organizing his own expeditions in competition with those of the government.

The most important government military commander in the war against Te Kooti was Colonel G. S. Whitmore. Whitmore was perhaps the most able British leader of the wars next to Cameron, though he never acquired the same respect for Maori abilities. A British regular officer who topped the Staff College in 1860, he also had considerable experience of irregular warfare—against Bantu and Boers in South Africa. He came to New Zealand in 1861 as Cameron's Military Secretary, and though he resigned his commission in 1862 and bought an estate in Hawke's Bay, he served as a volunteer on the staff through much of the Waikato War. He had a very rare mix of military qualities: an excellent theoretical knowledge, particularly of strategy and logistics, combined with energy, resolution, and the willingness and capacity to conduct operations on a shoe-string in the worst of terrain. He was also cursed with the personal charm of a rattlesnake. Like his New Zealand-bred rival, Thomas McDonnell, he was touchy and egotistical. Unlike the popular McDonnell, he was also tactless and élitist.

'I go on a totally different principle to McDonnell', wrote Whitmore privately, 'I keep my distance from . . . all the Force. I am never "hail fellow well met" with anybody. I live at my own establishment with Mr Foster (who is a gentleman and suits me very well).'[37]

Not surprisingly, Whitmore was extremely unpopular in many quarters. He was variously described as 'the great tyrant', 'that chip of the Devil', a 'diminutive beast', and 'a little conceited, egotistical, self-sufficient ass'.[38] Among the many who loathed Whitmore was McLean, though he addressed the Colonel as 'My Dear Whitmore' in correspondence. Whitmore heartily reciprocated this dislike, informing a government minister that 'McLean has got the end of your money bag and if he does not empty it I shall be surprised. It was all he wanted.'[39] This attitude exacerbated the feud between the government and McLean.

Whitmore was clearly a prime target for the usual scapegoat hunt in cases of military failure, but antipathy towards him also added a peculiar twist to general trends of British interpretation. Another important government commander in Te Kooti's War was Ropata Wahawaha of Ngati Porou. Ropata was determined, fearless, and able. He was also ruthless, playing a prominent part in several killings of helpless captives, sometimes with his own hand. These characteristics combined to make him the colonists' favourite *kupapa*. Normally, the colonists under-stated the *kupapa* contribution and over-stated their weaknesses. But, when the unusually popular Ropata and the unusually unpopular Whitmore took the field together, the situation was reversed. Thus Whitmore's greatest success, the capture of Ngatapa, was sometimes wrongly credited to Ropata.

Te Kooti's initial campaign lasted about one month after 15 July 1868, and included three engagements: Paparatu (20 July), Te Koneke (24 July), and Ruakituri (8 August). Like the two most important of Te Kooti's other campaigns, Poverty Bay and Ngatapa, it consisted of colonist attempts to catch him as he marched from the alluvial plains of Poverty Bay to the relative safety of the high country bordering the Urewera Mountains and Lake Waikaremoana. The two colonist bases in this area were the coastal settlements of Wairoa and Turanganui, with the main base at Napier, eighty miles to the south. On 15 July, Te Kooti left Whareongaonga for the ancient stronghold of Puketapu, near Waikaremoana. His aim was to get his 300 men, women, and children, with their supplies from the *Rifleman*, to refuge at Puketapu with the least possible fighting. But the weather was bad, his much-encumbered band moved very slowly, and there was only one viable route—a fact well-known to the government forces.[40]

British estimates put Te Kooti's effective strength on this long march at 130, 150, or 200 warriors, and historians have accepted the higher of these figures. They were not too far from the total number of men in Te Kooti's following (160), but they grossly exaggerate the number of armed men. We know that Te Kooti took thirty-two rifles, eight shotguns, and one carbine, with about 100 rounds per gun, from the Chathams. Maori accounts show that he obtained a further six guns from local Maoris at Whareongaonga. His effective strength at Paparatu was therefore forty-seven, and he captured ten rifles there. Thus at Te Koneke he had about fifty-seven armed men—a figure confirmed by two British reports based on Maori sources. A further fifteen or twenty armed Ngati Kowhatu (a *hapu* of Ngati Kahungunu) may have joined him just before Ruakituri.[41]

Against these, the government hastily organized three pursuit columns. The first, from Poverty Bay, consisted of sixty-six European volunteers and twenty-two *kupapa*, under Major R. N. Biggs, Captain Charles Westrupp, and Lieutenant J. Wilson. The second, from Wairoa, included twenty-five Europeans and 100 *kupapa*, under Captain W. A. Richardson. The third, thirty European and forty Maori volunteers from Napier, was led by Colonel Whitmore, who held the over-all command. Whitmore and his men arrived at Turanganui by sea on 20 July, and were later joined by fifty-two Armed Constabulary under Major James Fraser, shipped down from Opotiki.

The Poverty Bay column was the first to make contact. Biggs heard of Te Kooti's departure from Whareongaonga on 15 July, discovered that he planned to make for Puketapu, and marched immediately to intercept him. On 18 July he took up a position at Paparatu, blocking the route. Biggs himself then left to arrange supplies and reinforcements, handing over command to Westrupp. On the morning of 20 July, the government scouts sighted Te Kooti, and Westrupp with fifty men and Wilson with forty occupied two hills above their camp, commanding the track.

The colonist positions were too strong for frontal attack, and Te Kooti had little more than half their effective force, but the only route to safety lay through them. Te Kooti therefore split his band into two. A few riflemen, under Te Kooti himself, attempted to hold the enemy's attention in front, while most of the armed men—between thirty and forty Ngati Hineuru under Nikora and Te Rangitahau—took a four-mile detour over very rough country and attacked Westrupp's position in the rear. From about 8.30 a.m., Te Kooti's party, supplemented by unarmed men and perhaps women to give the impression of greater numbers, began exchanging fire with the colonists. This continued for several hours. 'All the while they kept up a great shouting and hallooing.' On several occasions, they made as if to charge, and some entered the colonists' camp and seized untouched and urgently required rations which had arrived just before the action commenced. Peka Makarini, who had learned to play the bugle in the Chathams, added insult to injury by playing mess-calls to the hungry colonists. As the afternoon wore on, the Maoris began making 'a series of small charges'—rushes from cover to cover similar to modern infantry tactics—towards Westrupp's men, fixing their attention all the more firmly on the front. At about 4 p.m., Nikora and his men at last came up behind Westrupp and opened fire, hitting a quarter of Westrupp's men with their first volleys. The colonists' position was now hopeless. They fled, Maori and *Pakeha* alike. Exhausted and hungry, with their aim of clearing a path to safety achieved, Te Kooti's forces did not pursue. Westrupp's casualties were not great—two killed and ten wounded—but Te Kooti gained guns, supplies, and eighty horses, and his losses were light.[42]

Westrupp's retreating force came upon Whitmore's advancing column at Te Arai on 21 July. Whitmore, who as yet had only his seventy Napier men with him, attempted to persuade the Poverty Bay men to accompany him to renew the attack on Te Kooti. Exhausted by their recent efforts, bereft of equipment and horses, and shaken by their defeat, they refused. Deeply frustrated, Whitmore lost his temper, calling them 'cowards and curs', but to no avail.[43] The Poverty Bay men returned home to recuperate, and Whitmore had perforce to await their return or the arrival of Fraser's constabulary. In the meantime, he ordered Captain Richardson and the Wairoa column to delay Te Kooti's march.

Richardson made the attempt at Te Koneke on 24 July. Accounts of this minor action are sparse and contradictory, but it appears that half of Richardson's 100 *kupapa* declined to fight. With his remaining seventy or eighty men, 'rounded down' to twenty in his report, Richardson exchanged a desultory fire with Te Kooti. *Ringatu* warriors then began working their way up the bush-clad gullies on Richardson's flank, and he withdrew and returned to Wairoa. Richardson lost one *kupapa* killed and another accidentally wounded. Despite his claims to the contrary, his opponent's casualties were probably also slight.[44]

With all three pursuing columns temporarily withdrawn or halted, Te Kooti now had an opportunity to complete his escape. But the weather intervened against him. Even in good weather, travelling over very rough country with children and supplies, Te Kooti could not 'make above three or four miles a day'. And from 25 July it began to rain very heavily, flooding streams and rivers. The rain later turned to snow. 'A foot of snow fell last night,' remarked Whitmore laconically. In these conditions, both sides had to seek shelter where they were, and the campaign was suspended for a week.[45]

On 31 July, joined at last by Fraser's constabulary and a reorganized Poverty Bay column, Whitmore renewed his advance, in slightly improved weather, with a total of 230 men. The Poverty Bay men had not forgotten his insults, however, and on 5 August they 'struck', refusing to cross the boundary of the district in which they had volunteered to serve. After a colourful confrontation in which Whitmore had graves dug for the miscreants preparatory to execution, he accepted the inevitable. The Poverty Bay *kupapa* saw no reason to fight if their *Pakeha* did not, and they went home too. Whitmore's force was now reduced to 130 men, but with typical determination, he pressed on, closing with Te Kooti by the hour.

On 8 August, realizing that he would soon be caught, Te Kooti took up a very strong position in the gorge of the Ruakituri River and waited. That afternoon, he was sighted by Whitmore's scouts and the colonists moved in to the attack. As Whitmore's column struggled in single file up the boulder-filled gorge, Te Kooti opened fire on their front and right, from positions including a small island in the river. Whitmore pushed on, trying to find an open space where he could form up and charge. 'The enemy had however so carefully selected the field that no such spot could be found.'[46] Whitmore then asked the Napier *kupapa*, as yet unengaged at the rear of the column, to cross the river downstream and take Te Kooti in the flank, but no ford could be found nearby. Suddenly, the *Ringatu* forces rushed the colonist van and drove it back with heavy loss. For a few moments, Whitmore's position was extremely precarious. Then the Napier *kupapa*, theoretically commanded by Captain Herrick but more probably led by their able young chief, Henare Tomoana, at last managed to cross the river. Their fire soon forced Te Kooti to abandon the river island. This, and the continued steadiness of Whitmore's Europeans, prevented Te Kooti from pressing home his advantage. Whitmore drew off, leaving five dead and carrying six wounded with him, three of whom died that night. Te Kooti continued his march, and reached Puketapu within a few days.

A few British commentators made spirited attempts to present Ruakituri as a victory: 'to say that we were defeated is puerile'.[47] Whitmore devoted several paragraphs of his report and several subsequent letters to showing, through a curious process of deduction, that the Maoris had 'at least twenty or thirty casualties and probably more'.[48] In fact, Maori losses were two killed, one mortally wounded, and eight wounded, including Te Kooti, hit in the ankle.[49] The large anti-Whitmore faction, on the other hand, risked puerility by seeing Ruakituri as a terrible defeat caused by Whitmore's cowardice and incompetence. 'Whitmore came back on Friday after getting what everybody but himself calls a thrashing.'[50] Ruakituri was certainly not a 'thrashing' for the colonists, and the performance of Whitmore and his men was impressive. But it was a British defeat, in that Te Kooti had slightly the better of the hard-fought tactical contest and entirely achieved his strategic objective: escape to Puketapu.

The British interpretation of Ruakituri and the other actions of Te Kooti's opening campaign exhibits the usual characteristics, with one important variation: the use of *kupapa* as scapegoats for defeat. In the case of Ruakituri, criticism was muted. Whitmore, usually a ready critic of *kupapa*, grudgingly acknowledged that Ngati Kahungunu 'behaved very well for Maoris'. But the defeats at Paparatu and Te Koneke were attributed to *kupapa* 'apathy—call it by no worse a name'. T. W. Gudgeon, a colonial soldier and historian, sarcastically noted that one Maori 'deserter' told a European officer that he was going for a drink of water; 'he must have gone a long way for he was absent four years'. The false implication that cowardice, rather than a conflict of loyalties, explained the *kupapa*'s action was typical of the colonist attitude.[51]

The *Ringatu* band remained at Puketapu for over two months from mid-August. The people fortified the naturally strong old *pa* site, while their leader recovered from his wound. During this period, something occurred which could easily have made Te Kooti's first campaign his last. On 7

September, the colonial forces on the West Coast met disaster at Te Ngutu o te Manu. The government immediately withdrew all constabulary from the East Coast, and made a serious attempt to come to terms with Te Kooti, and so free further resources for the struggle against Titokowaru. The government peace offer, which reveals the primacy of the western theatre in colonial thinking, has been overlooked by historians. But the Defence Office archives show that in mid-September Father Reignier, a local Catholic missionary, was sent as a secret emissary to negotiate peace with Te Kooti. Defence Minister Haultain eventually authorized the following terms in a letter to Whitmore. 'What the government requires from the escaped prisoners is that they shall surrender themselves and give up their arms. No further proceedings will in that case be taken against them. Land will be found for them to live on. You may communicate with Father Reignier and authorise him to say so much.'[52]

Reignier made some kind of contact with Te Kooti, and passed on the gist of the government offer, but it is not clear whether he was able to deliver Haultain's final proposal. If he did, Te Kooti rejected it. The surrender of arms would mean trusting to the government's good faith, and the British in New Zealand had a poor record in this respect. Te Kooti was probably aware that government scouts had been inspecting Puketapu, and he was informed of a colonial plan to attack the place.[53] By mid-October, it had become clear to Reignier that Te Kooti's intentions were now definitely hostile.

That Te Kooti should suspect the government's sincerity was understandable but, ironically, the peace offer was almost certainly genuine. As we shall see in the next chapter, colonial fortunes on the West Coast had reached so low an ebb that peace and land for 300 escaped prisoners who had defeated government forces three times was an acceptable humiliation. Mistrust, the legacy of Te Kooti's unjust imprisonment, of broken promises on the Chathams, and of various events earlier in the New Zealand Wars, blocked a real chance of compromise peace on the East Coast, and sentenced hundreds of Maoris and Europeans to their deaths.

Having abandoned hope of peace, Te Kooti began an intensive political campaign for Maori support. With no tribal base and little arable land around Puketapu, the *Ringatu* band desperately needed food and ammunition from the local tribes. They also needed arms and, above all, men, for a full-scale war against the *Pakeha* which would secure their own position and reverse the decision of the East Coast conflicts of 1865–6. Te Kooti's messengers travelled far and wide. He is known to have communicated with the Opotiki and Taupo tribes, and with the King Movement, as well as with the nearby Tuhoe, Rongowhakaata, and Ngati Kahungunu.[54]

Considerable sympathy and passive support was expressed, but these people had had enough of warfare. The material results of Te Kooti's drive for support were bitterly disappointing. He was joined by small minorities of only two tribes. The Tuhoe people of the Urewera Mountains were generally sympathetic, and apparently planned meetings for early 1869 to decide on large-scale support, but by the end of 1868 only thirty Tuhoe war-riors had joined. Te Kooti's main allies were the Upper Wairoa Ngati Kahungunu: fifteen Ngati Kowhatu, a small number of Ngati Mihi, and Te Waru and Nama with about fifty men. The last-named killed four of their *kupapa* relatives from Lower Wairoa before leaving their homes for Puketapu—an action of which Te Kooti disapproved. These men proved to be brave and loyal supporters, but they numbered little more than 100 altogether. With his Chatham Islanders, and taking account of a few casualties, Te Kooti now had about 250 men, of whom perhaps fifty were still unarmed.[55]

In the three engagements of July and August 1868, Te Kooti and his men displayed the mastery of guerilla warfare that was to characterize all their operations. The leader laid his plans carefully and comprehensively, taking full account of likely enemy reactions and showing a good eye for terrain and a great aptitude for manoeuvre. His men were brave, skilled with their weapons, and very well-disciplined, but were also capable of operating in small independent groups. The three engagements were important in that they enabled Te Kooti to complete his escape, and survive to fight another day. But for all this, too much has been made of them. Many writers exag-gerated their military significance and endowed them with a mysterious quality. In a book published in 1902, Whitmore wrote of Te Kooti at Paparatu: 'Undoubtedly the extraordinary prestige this remarkable man afterwards acquired sprang from this brilliant, and to the Maori mind inex-plicable success.' Later writers quote this with approval, and extend the comment to cover Te Koneke and Ruakituri as well.[56]

Te Kooti is believed to have had very few other clear-cut combat vic-tories, and these authors presumably seek to explain his great military reputation. But in reality Te Koneke was an insignificant engagement, and Paparatu and Ruakituri were small and limited. All three were rearguard actions, designed to enable Te Kooti to continue his march rather than to damage or destroy the enemy. The government lost more than twice as many men at Te Ngutu o te Manu as it did at all three. The miraculous feat, 'inexplicable to the Maori mind', which could be taken to prove Te Kooti's divine backing was not Paparatu, but the escape from the Chathams. Exiled across 400 miles of stormy sea, given up for dead by their people, 300 prisoners, men, women, and children, had suddenly been transported back to their homes, despite armed guards, storms, and distance. As the London *Times* of 2 October 1868 put it, 'the tale is worthy of Captain Marryat'. *Ringatu* now had its myth of passage, and 'the Maori mind' could be forgiven for seeing the hand of God in it. The South Pacific did not part, but the escape compared favourably to the multiplication of a few loaves and fishes. As for the great victory which established Te Kooti's military reputation among the Maori, this was not Paparatu or Ruakituri, but a brilliant raid on Poverty Bay in November 1868. For Te Kooti had had enough of being the hunted.

III   THE POVERTY BAY CAMPAIGN

IN EARLY NOVEMBER 1868, TE KOOTI ABANDONED HIS BASE AT Puketapu and with it his role as a hunted fugitive. Suddenly taking the initiative, he descended on the British and Maori settlements at Poverty Bay and destroyed them. He then succeeded in withdrawing his forces to a new base at Ngatapa, in the teeth of a prompt and vigorous counter-offensive. Te Kooti's retreat from Poverty Bay to Ngatapa is often treated as part of a subsequent campaign against the latter place, but it properly belongs with the attack on the former. Te Kooti not only delivered his raid on Poverty Bay, he also got away with it, and these two operations constitute phases of the same campaign.

In mid-October 1868, the colonial authorities at Napier received information that Te Kooti was about to attack Wairoa. They concluded that 'there could be no doubt' that Wairoa was in 'imminent danger', and they responded promptly.[57] By 25 October the Wairoa garrison had been reinforced from 200 to about 700 men, mainly *kupapa*. By this time, however, it had been discovered that the emergency was a 'hoax'—a 'false alarm'—and that Te Kooti had in fact remained well inland.[58] Some 500 men of the force mustered for the defence of Wairoa were dispatched with Major Charles Lambert to seek him out, leaving on 27 October. But Lambert found nothing. He established that Te Kooti had left Puketapu, and the expedition returned to Wairoa on 6 November, 'like the troops of a certain famous British duke'.[59]

While the Wairoa expedition was busy chasing his shadow, Te Kooti and his followers were marching north from Puketapu towards Rere. With few supplies and many women and children, the march was a difficult one, and some people are said to have died of exhaustion and starvation along the way.[60] But on about 6 November, the *Ringatu* forces reached Rere and turned eastwards. Two days later, they reached the neutral Maori village of Patutahi in the hills overlooking Poverty Bay. The inhabitants were secured to ensure that no warning reached the settlements on the plain below. On the night of 9 November, Te Kooti left his women, children, and some warriors at Patutahi, and quietly moved down to Poverty Bay with one hundred men.[61]

The government had considered an attack on Poverty Bay possible for some time, and certain precautions had been taken. A redoubt had been completed at Turanganui and a screen of scouts stationed on the outskirts of the district. Almost all of the fifty adult male settlers were members or ex-members of colonial military units, and they had recently been reinforced by 100 Ngati Porou *kupapa* under Henare Potae.[62] The local Maoris, perhaps 150 men, were neutrals or passive supporters of one side or another, and most were unarmed. The colonist commander, Major R. N. Biggs, had received several warnings of an imminent attack but previous false alarms, particularly the recent embarrassing panic at Wairoa, made him wary of over-reaction. If an attack did eventuate, Biggs was convinced it would come from the south and he positioned his scouts accordingly. The scouts were certain to give ample warning of an attack from that direction, and Biggs therefore postponed calling the inhabitants into the Turanganui redoubt.[63]

But Te Kooti was well informed of Biggs's dispositions and he made his approach from the west. He was therefore able to avoid the colonist scouts and take Poverty Bay completely by surprise.[64] He split his force into small parties, and at about midnight on 9/10 November struck Matawhero and other Bay settlements simultaneously. Within a few hours fifty of the inhabitants—men, women, and children—had been killed, and the district was in Te Kooti's hands. The defenders outnumbered the attackers, and they slept with their arms by them, but they had no chance to utilize these advantages. Tactical surprise was total, Biggs and his subordinate commanders were sought out and killed early in the action, and the concurrent multiple attacks bred panic and paralysis. Survivors from the settlements in the plain fled to the Turanganui redoubt, where they and the garrison stayed put, imagining that the enemy had anything up to 700 men. Their state of mind is illustrated by the fact that Mrs James and her eight children were mistaken for 'hundreds of Hauhaus'.[65] The *Ringatu* forces did not lose a man.

The attack on Poverty Bay was no hit-and-run raid. The shock to the government forces was such that Te Kooti retained unchallenged control of the district for a week, despite the arrival of 180 reinforcements at Turanganui between 13 and 16 November.[66] During this time, Te Kooti remained based at Patutahi but his patrols roamed the district collecting large quantities of horses, cattle, and supplies and taking some 300 local Maoris prisoner. Some of these prisoners, again including both sexes and all ages, were picked out from among their fellows and executed. The number killed was probably between twenty and forty—in addition to the thirty-four Europeans and twenty Maoris killed early in the raid.[67] Perhaps 100 more of the unfortunate prisoners later starved to death or were killed by government troops in mistake for Te Kooti's followers.[68] One of the most crucial, and most frequently overlooked, facts about the attack on Poverty Bay is that the victims were principally Maori.

The Wairoa scare of mid-October may well have been intentionally created by Te Kooti to divert attention from his real target. There was some suggestion that the Wairoa 'bubble' was fabricated by 'two notorious schemers' among the locals for the sake of additional military expenditure.[69] But the original false notification of a planned attack had come from one of Te Kooti's men, couched as a warning to neutral Maoris to stay clear of Wairoa.[70] The concentration of the government forces there looks very like the result of a carefully planted piece of misinformation. Te Kooti probably effected a similar espionage coup at Poverty Bay itself. It seems likely that Biggs's assumption that an attacking force would use the southern route was based on information from spies in Te Kooti's following. Biggs was fully aware that the western track existed, but his conviction that the enemy would not use it was absolute. It is certain the government did operate some

secret agents, and Biggs told Lieutenant Gascoyne that 'he was kept well informed by spies of the rebels' doings'.[71] But Biggs's spies were in fact double
agents or were themselves deceived.

It seems the ground for the Poverty Bay raid was prepared by a two-
pronged misinformation campaign. At the strategic level, this ensured that
government resources and attention were primarily concentrated on the
wrong place, and at the tactical level it meant that such defenders as Poverty
Bay did have confidently expected any attack to come from the wrong direction. This remarkable feat of deception, with the tactics of 10 November,
made Te Kooti's Poverty Bay operation one of the most cleverly planned
guerilla raids ever launched.

Though the investigation of 'atrocities' is not a primary purpose of this
study, some further reference must be made to Te Kooti's actions in killing
so many civilians. Predictably, the colonists had few doubts about this matter.
The 'Poverty Bay Massacre' was a barbaric deed of the worst kind; proof of
the unregenerate character of the savage to be flung in the faces of Exeter
Hall humanitarians along with the Cawnpore Massacre and the Jamaica
Rebellion.[72] This interpretation still persists in some quarters, but a view
more favourable to Te Kooti has also emerged. The 'Matawhero Raid' was
an understandable act of war, explicable in terms of atrocities committed by
the British, of Maori custom, and of Te Kooti's desire for revenge on those
who had unjustly imprisoned him.[73]

The events of Poverty Bay were of two kinds. The first occurred mainly
on the night of 10 November. The *Ringatu* forces attacked the houses of
armed settlers. They killed civilians in the process but their objectives were
primarily military: to dislocate the enemy defence. Up to this point, the killings were no better and no worse than the bloody aftermath of Orakau. In
each case, the dead civilians were 'flying fish crossing the prow of the war-
canoe' and 'unfortunate victims of the heat of battle' in the respective
platitudes of Maoris and British. But the killings did not stop there. Three
Maori eyewitness accounts leave no doubt that in the days after 10
November at least twenty of the Maori prisoners, ranging from infant boys
to old women, were killed in cold blood on Te Kooti's direct orders. In one
incident, according to two of Te Kooti's prisoners, 'Piripi, his wife, and five
children, and Pera, were set apart, and then shot and sworded.' Pera's wife
heard Te Kooti give the order: 'God has told me to kill women and
children, now fire on them.'[74]

The first type of event fits easily within the 'Matawhero Raid' interpretation. The government had pursued Te Kooti for months, its field forces
were too large for him to attack, and he could hardly be expected not to
retaliate in the only way open to him. But it is hard to see how 'Matawhero
Raid' can embrace the second type of event. Maori traditions of collective
responsibility, whereby your kin benefited from your virtues and answered
for your vices; colonist executions of captured warriors during the campaigns of 1865–6; Te Kooti's resentment of his unjust imprisonment, and
of the failure of his tribe to aid him in his time of need; his desire to in-

timidate *kupapa* enemies into inaction; the mysterious dictates of his God—all this can help explain, but not justify, the later events at Poverty Bay. Like biographers of Cromwell, students of Te Kooti will have to reconcile his great and essentially constructive contribution to the history of his people with the unnecessary killing of harmless non-combatants.

The second phase of the Poverty Bay Campaign began about 17 November, when Te Kooti commenced his withdrawal from Poverty Bay. With children, prisoners, and plunder hampering his march, he did not go far, but took up a position at Makaretu on the Wharekopae Stream about thirty miles from Turanganui. On 19 November, 200 Ngati Kahungunu from the Napier area arrived at Turanganui under Tareha Te Moananui, Henare Tomoana, Hamuora Tairoa, and other chiefs. Losing no time, these men moved off in pursuit of Te Kooti on 20 November, accompanied by 140 Ngati Kahungunu already at Turanganui, by 100 local Rongowhakaata, and by Lieutenant Gascoyne and eight Europeans. On 23 November, the expedition came upon Te Kooti at Makaretu and prepared to attack.

Te Kooti was outnumbered by two to one, and he was burdened with at least 400 non-combatants, and a great deal of plunder, including sheep and cattle. The spoils of Poverty Bay did not include much ammunition, however, and Te Kooti was very short of this. His position was not strong—less a fortification than a camp of tents on a small flat next to the high banks of the Wharekopae.[75] When the *kupapa* advanced promptly and vigorously to the attack, therefore, the destruction of the *Ringatu* force seemed imminent. But Te Kooti did not wait for the *kupapa*. Instead, he sent his men out to engage in the open. A heavy firefight ensued. Some Ngati Kahungunu under Hamuora Tairoa charged the *Ringatu* centre. They were repelled, and Hamuora was killed. The *kupapa* were gradually driven back by *Ringatu* warriors skirmishing from cover. Several *kupapa* attempts to stand failed when Te Kooti's men threatened their flanks and set fire to the adjacent bush. The *kupapa* lost about twenty men and their situation became critical, but they continued to resist doggedly. Eventually, by digging firebreaks and hastily entrenching themselves, they managed to hold their ground on a ridge one mile from Makaretu.[76]

In the succeeding days, the situation at Makaretu remained static, with both sides now short of ammunition and busy entrenching. Despite their repulse, the *kupapa* remained determined, and they only awaited the arrival of more ammunition to renew their assault. They knew supplies were on the way from a commissariat depot which had been formed at Patutahi. Unfortunately for them, this was also known to Te Kooti.

On 26 November Te Kooti dispatched twenty picked cavalry to raid the Patutahi depot.[77] The appearance of this party may provide an interesting corrective to our expectations. All the men were well mounted and well armed with modern rifles and carbines. They were probably dressed in new suits or European uniforms, taken at Poverty Bay and the Chathams; and they were commanded by Edward Baker McLean. Peka Makarini's leadership constituted the most constructive European contribution to the Poverty Bay Campaign. He led his men around the *kupapa* front, by a circuitous southward route to avoid detection, and attacked the Patutahi depot at 8 a.m. on 27 November. The totally unexpected appearance of charging 'Hauhau' cavalry was enough to rout the garrison of eleven Europeans and fourteen *kupapa*. The *Ringatu* troop destroyed the depot and such supplies as they could not carry, and returned to Makaretu with 16,100 rounds of ammunition.[78]

The success of this raid provided Te Kooti with much-needed ammunition and, even more importantly, it paralysed Tareha and his associates. With their superior numbers, the *kupapa* could still hold their positions but they could not renew their offensive unless reinforced and re-supplied. This stalemate continued into December.

Meanwhile a new government force had taken the field. Superintendent McLean had been trying to organize a *kupapa* expedition from Wairoa, either to reinforce Tareha directly or to co-operate with him in a pincer movement. Te Kooti's position at Makaretu was too far inland for a movement on his rear to be an easy matter, but the prompt addition of the Wairoa forces (200 more Ngati Kahungunu and 158 Ngati Porou) to the enemy in his front would probably have been fatal to him. But for once, Te Kooti received a reprieve that was not of his own making. McLean considered Lambert, the commander at Wairoa, to be a fool and, still worse, a Ministry man. He therefore sought to arrange the expedition through his own man, F. E. Hamlin, who arrived at Wairoa on 21 November. Lambert heartily reciprocated McLean's dislike and he blocked Hamlin's efforts. By the time the government intervened, reprimanding McLean for failing to go through the proper channel but endorsing his plan, five days had been lost.[79]

Nevertheless, on 26 November the Wairoa expedition at last set out, 370 strong including the ruthless and redoubtable Ropata. On 2 December, after a difficult march, they arrived before Makaretu. Again, the *Ringatu* forces appeared doomed. Field engineering was never Te Kooti's strong point, and despite his efforts of the past week his fortifications were not very formidable.[80] The *kupapa* had received fresh ammunition, brought up from Turanganui under heavy escort, and they were now 800 strong. On 3 December, they launched a full-scale attack, with Ngati Porou in the centre and the Napier and Wairoa Ngati Kahungunu on either flank. After a brief struggle, Makaretu was taken.[81]

But to their dismay, the triumphant *kupapa* found that they had missed their quarry. A few days before their attack, Te Kooti had taken his women, children, prisoners, and plunder, together with two-thirds of his warriors, three miles further inland to a new position at Ngatapa. He left only a rearguard of fifty to eighty men.[82] Though they fought bravely these few could not resist the *kupapa* onslaught, and they lost at least fourteen men killed.[83] But by holding Makaretu until 5 December, they had enabled Te Kooti to thwart his enemies yet again.

The *kupapa* found their barren success enormously frustrating. They decided that 'no quarter should be given'. Some of the *Ringatu* casualties were wounded, captured, then killed. Quarrelling broke out among the *kupapa* force. Ngati Porou wished to kill two surviving prisoners whom Tareha had taken under his protection. Tareha refused to allow this, and Ngati Porou therefore declined to proceed with the pursuit. They soon changed their minds, but by then Tareha in his turn had had enough, and he returned to Turanganui with most of his men. The rest of the force, still at least 450 strong, marched on towards Ngatapa.[84]

Ngatapa *pa* was far from complete, and as we shall see in a later chapter, it had grave strategic weaknesses. But its position was tactically very strong— on the crest of a steep range of hills, almost impossible to attack on three sides and difficult on the other. Despite this, the *kupapa* attacked promptly, expecting to find shaken fugitives gone to ground. Instead, they struck a prepared *Ringatu* force, entrenched and under tight control. Their van met with murderous volleys and was routed. Further shaken by a *Ringatu* sortie, the bulk of the *kupapa* broke and ran, and complete disaster was only prevented by the courage and determination of Ropata. With only thirty men, later increased to about 120, Ropata seized an unfinished outwork of the *pa* and held out tenaciously, despite heavy casualties. But the rest of the force were too discouraged by their initial repulse to support him, and he eventually had to give up his position. All the *kupapa* then withdrew, moving off fast to avoid a counter-attack. The sustained attempt to gain revenge for Poverty Bay had failed.[85]

Though the contemporary British interpretation of these operations has been faithfully followed by historians, it presents an instructive amalgam of contradiction and inaccuracy. We are given the impression that the government force was a sepoy army, organized and officered by a few Britons who also found time to set 'a bright example of courage and daring'.[86] Tareha's expedition was said to have been launched by McLean and led by Gascoyne or even Westrupp. To the extent that the results were less than perfect, this was mainly attributable to *kupapa* weaknesses which even British leadership could not erase. Ngati Porou were sometimes excepted from criticism, but as for Ngati Kahungunu: 'the greater number of these fat and well-to-do Maoris from Hawkes Bay would rather run than fight'.[87] The tribal squabbles of these lazy savages were also subjected to contemptuous comment. Despite this, the operation was presented as a major government victory. Each of the three major engagements (Ngatapa and the two actions at Makaretu) was a tactical success, though the over-all result was not entirely satisfactory because Te Kooti escaped. In short, the second phase of the Poverty Bay campaign was seen as a qualified government success. The British were responsible for the success, and the *kupapa* were responsible for the qualifications.

As the above account indicates, this view is inaccurate. Far from being organized by the British, Tareha's expedition left Turanganui despite the decision of Westrupp, McLean, and the Ministry to remain on the defensive until European or Ngati Porou reinforcements arrived. Gascoyne's command, as he himself admitted, was 'merely nominal' and, apart from organizing the supply, Westrupp's contribution was confined to wishing the expedition luck from Turanganui, and 'hoping to heaven it may turn out well'.[88] In fact, the expedition was initiated and led by the Ngati Kahungunu and Rongowhakaata chiefs. Most of these had not made war vigorously before Poverty Bay. After it, they pursued and fought Te Kooti for two weeks with the greatest determination, despite difficult terrain, inadequate supplies, and the demoralizing genius of their enemy.

Even so, only one of the three main engagements—the second attack on Makaretu—was even a tactical government victory. Some 800 *kupapa* overwhelmed the fifty to eighty men of the *Ringatu* rearguard. The disparity in numbers made this result virtually inevitable, and it was foreseen by Te Kooti. His earlier withdrawal with all his non-combatants and plunder, and most of his warriors, meant his enemies gained an empty victory if ever there was one. The fact of this early retreat is clear from some of the primary sources,[89] but it is impossible to deduce from most of the official accounts and subsequent histories.

The other two engagements were clear-cut tactical victories for Te Kooti. The first attack on Makaretu was portrayed as a limited government success which cost Te Kooti twenty or thirty dead as against a dozen *kupapa* casualties. But Gascoyne, who provides the only first-hand British report, speaks of desperate defence rather than successful attack. 'The Hauhaus immediately attacked us on all sides, but we stubbornly held the ridge.'[90] 'The ridge' was 1,600 yards from the *Ringatu* camp, so the *kupapa* actually lost a great deal of ground during the battle. They also lost about six killed and twelve wounded, while Te Kooti had two killed and ten wounded.[91] No wonder that a few British commentators were forced to concede that 'success was only partial' and to celebrate an attack that 'had almost proved successful'. In fact, it was a complete failure. Similarly, Peka Makarini's brilliant raid appeared as 'a slight turn of affairs in favour of the enemy', and only Archdeacon W. L. Williams acknowledged 'this disaster (for such it really is)'.[92]

The story of the attack on Ngatapa of 5 December was also rapidly laundered to exclude the initial panic in which 'every man retreated with the utmost expedition for nearly half a mile'. The eventual *kupapa* withdrawal, it was claimed, was the result of lack of ammunition, or lack of food. But Westrupp, with supporting evidence from Gascoyne and Tuke, denied that the force lacked supplies.[93] British estimates of *Ringatu* casualties for the whole operation (20 November-5 December) went as high as 150 killed, but the real figure could not have been higher than the *kupapa* loss of between forty and fifty killed and wounded.[94]

The British view of these operations owed as much to local factors as to the general trend of their interpretation. Discounting the contribution of both the Ministry and some of the *kupapa*, the McLean faction claimed the credit. They had therefore to establish that there was credit to be claimed, and they 'rejoiced' in their fictional 'splendid victory'. Expectations of success were high throughout the campaign. 'The enemy are in a trap, plunder and all.' 'There is now every probability of Te Kooti's capture.' Given the disparity of force, these high hopes were understandable, but they made the British all the more reluctant to admit disappointment.[95] This received version is both false and paradoxical, with the colonists using the *kupapa* as scapegoats for what they maintained was a series of victories. In fact, the operations enabled Te Kooti to escape scot-free with the fruits of his Poverty Bay raid, in the teeth of vastly superior enemy forces. The primary reason for this was not *kupapa* inadequacy, but Te Kooti's skill.

Titokowaru and the Brink of Victory

WHILE TE KOOTI WAS FIGHTING HIS EARLY CAMPAIGNS ON THE
East Coast, a still more formidable Maori resistance leader emerged in the
West. Titokowaru of Ngati Ruanui was both the greatest and the least-
known of the Maori generals. In keeping with the overall pattern of the
British interpretation, his enemies found his victories so stunning and so
humiliating that they paid him the ultimate compliment of forgetting him,
as a child does a nightmare. Titokowaru was not just a general. Like Te
Kooti, he was a spiritual leader—whose impact on the Taranaki Maoris has
yet to be determined—and, unlike Te Kooti, he was also a pioneer of passive
resistance. He opposed, by peaceful means, the extension of confiscation
before his war broke out on 9 June 1868; he joined the Prophet Te Whiti O
Rongomai at Parihaka long after it; and his last political act was a hunger-
strike in a colonist gaol.

The combination of passive resister and fierce war-chief, who used
ceremonial cannibalism to intimidate his enemies, is a curious one, and
clearly Titokowaru was a remarkable and complicated man. But, while his
importance is recognized, full justice cannot be done to him here. His
biography is a task for someone with a deeper knowledge of Maoridom than
the present writer. This chapter concentrates simply on his major campaigns, in the context of the military and interpretative trends of the New
Zealand Wars as a whole. It turns, first, to the problem facing Ngati Ruanui
in their new attempt at resistance and to the strategy developed to solve it;
then to the two battles which were the acid test of this strategy; and finally
to the crisis into which they, together with Te Kooti's Poverty Bay campaign, plunged the colony.

I TITOKOWARU'S STRATEGY

TITOKOWARU'S WAR WAS PRECEDED BY TITOKOWARU'S PEACE—
the eighteen-month period between the campaigns of 1865–6, which were
so disastrous for the South Taranaki Maoris, and the outbreak of renewed
fighting in June 1868. In this period, Titokowaru came to British attention
as leader of the Ngaruahine *hapu* of Ngati Ruanui, and a peacemaker of
great importance in Taranaki as a whole. He declared 1867 'the year of the
daughters . . . the year of the lamb', and visited the colonist garrisons for

ceremonies of reconciliation. He travelled among the local tribes persuading them to accept that the fighting was at an end. Though the colonists were subsequently to portray these endeavours as disguised preparations for war, at the time they commended them. 'Ever since Titokowaru made the first overtures towards establishing friendly relations with us, he has shown the most untiring energy in his efforts to bring other tribes to make peace.'[1]

Until the end of 1867, Titokowaru's efforts were largely successful. But from that time he and his people were faced with the problem of 'creeping confiscation'. In 1865-6, the British had confiscated and occupied some land in South Taranaki, and subsequently the local Maoris had brought themselves to accept this. But the area theoretically confiscated was much greater. The colonists seemed to believe that when Maoris reluctantly acquiesced in confiscations, they meant the land marked on maps in Wellington, rather than that actually occupied. Accordingly, in early 1868, they proceeded to survey and settle more Ngati Ruanui land. This placed the *hapu* affected in a very difficult position. The campaigns of 1866, when Chute and McDonnell had destroyed many villages and cultivations, had damaged their economies to the point where they could not afford to lose more land. But these campaigns had involved enough defeats to make resistance seem no longer viable. Some *hapu*, including Titokowaru's Ngaruahine, were thus faced with the options of starving or fighting an apparently hopeless war.

At first, Ngaruahine attempted various forms of passive resistance. They protested against surveying and land clearance, then physically but non-violently opposed it—dismantling surveying equipment and huts, and burning fences. They warned the new settlers to quit and, when they did not, harassed them with small robberies. But, backed by the colonial forces, the new settlers stayed on. Finally, on 9 June, after six months of attempting peaceful solutions, Ngaruahine killed three settlers near Ketemarae. Titokowaru's Peace was over, and Tikokowaru's War had begun.[2]

The scene of this conflict was the area between Wanganui and Mount Egmont. At about seventy miles north-south and perhaps thirty miles east-west, it was larger than the Taranaki theatre of 1860-1. The terrain of the coastal strip was mixed—scrub, thick bush, and open country, with hills and dense bush inland. The area south of the Waitotara River, especially the long-held district south of the Kai-iwi Stream, was, by 1868, part of the valuable farming hinterland of the large British settlement of Wanganui. The land further north, between the Waitotara and Waingongoro Rivers, was also under partial British control, though the Ngarauru tribe and the Pakakohe and Tangahoe *hapu* of Ngati Ruanui continued to live on the remnants of their land. Most of this district had been confiscated, and much of it occupied and farmed by the British after 1865. The main colonist strongpoints were Wairoa (present-day Waverley), Waihi, and Patea. The main base area of the Ngaruahine *hapu* was the district north of the Waingongoro, which included dense *rata* forest, also known indiscriminately as bush, and Titokowaru's major settlement of Te Ngutu o te Manu, 'The

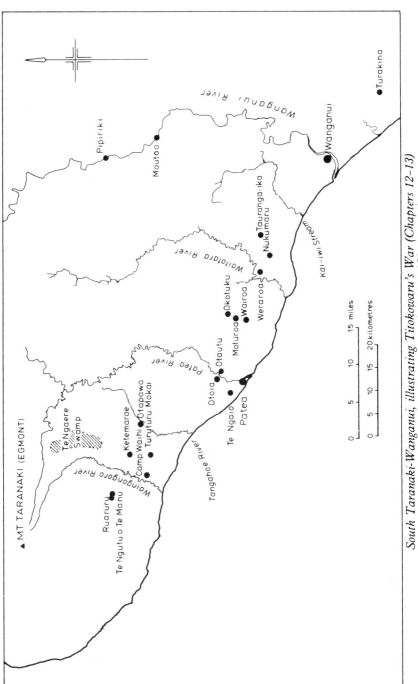

South Taranaki-Wanganui, illustrating Titokowaru's War (Chapters 12–13) and the West Coast Campaigns of 1865–6 (Chapter 11)

Beak of the Bird'. Though the colonial authorities were permitted to enter
this district before the war, and even occasionally to arrest individuals when
Ngaruahine wished to avoid conflict, it was not under real British control.
    The war which began with the killings on 9 June posed an apparently in-
superable problem for Titokowaru and his people. This stemmed partly
from the new colonist 'bush-scouring' method of warfare, and partly from
the good quality and greatly superior numbers of their troops. In late
August 1868, before the first major engagement with Titokowaru, the
'Patea Field Force' consisted of 770 Europeans and 150 Wanganui *kupapa*.[3]
The hard core of this force were Armed Constabulary, the new permanent
force created in 1867. The constabulary was included in subsequent
widespread criticism of the colonial forces, and it did have some problems.
Despite screening of recruits for fit, experienced men 'of character', there
were cases of insubordination, knife-fights, and drunkenness—one man 'cut
his [own] throat in a fit of delirium tremens'.[4] But such peccadilloes do not
necessarily preclude military efficiency in a force as a whole. Reports of indiscipline and inefficiency in the constabulary, as in other colonial corps,
were either grossly exaggerated or reflected the result—not the cause—of
demoralizing military disaster. Generally speaking, the constabulary were
very good soldiers. They included men from disbanded colonial units such
as the Forest Rangers, discharged Imperial regulars, and miscellaneous but
tough recruits, among them British and American goldminers, sailors, and
adventurers, and the odd Greek, Gurkha, and Frenchman. Organized in
small units ('divisions') capable of acting independently, they were equipped
for bush-fighting with revolvers and breech-loading carbines.
    With one or two Patea militia units of similar quality, drawn from soldiers
recently discharged to become military settlers, the constabulary made up
about a third of the Field Force's Europeans. The remainder were 'Wellington Rifles' and 'Wellington Rangers', and other newly-recruited
volunteer units from Nelson, New Plymouth, and Wanganui. The calibre
of these troops will be discussed below. They were certainly inferior to the
constabulary, but the best of them rapidly improved in efficiency, and the
first-class portion of the Patea Field Force was therefore constantly
growing.
    The *kupapa* part of the Field Force was 150 men in August 1868, but rose
to 457 in early November.[5] As usual the motives of these pro-government
Maoris were mixed, and only a minority of the 457 were thoroughly committed to the colonist cause. This minority, however, consisted of about 110
experienced Wanganui warriors under Kepa te Rangihiwinui ('Major
Kemp'), and they were an important addition to colonist strength.
    The colonial officers came in for the same type of adverse criticism as
their men, and again this contained a small element of truth. In Colonel
Whitmore's opinion, one constabulary sub-inspector 'is a big girl and
should not be ever made an inspector'.[6] Other officers, often as a result of
nerve-wracking experiences in battle, had problems with drink and cowardice. But, broadly speaking, the quality was again high. Junior officers such

as Goring, Swindley, Morrison, Northcroft and, in particular, J. M. Roberts, earned praise even from so hard a taskmaster as Whitmore. Their seniors, Majors (or constabulary 'Inspectors') Von Tempsky and Hunter were equally capable. The abilities of the two commanders-in-chief, McDonnell (until October 1868) and Whitmore, are treated elsewhere, and it is enough to say here that the former had a deserved reputation for ruthlessness and success, while the latter combined an unattractive character with military knowledge and ability of the first order.

The strategic aspect of the 'bush-scouring' method consisted of attacking economic targets such as villages and crops. This either destroyed the Maoris' war-making capacity, or induced small groups to defend their own livelihoods piecemeal from unsuitable positions such as unfortified villages or traditional *pa*. The strategy had worked well in South Taranaki in 1866, and there is every indication that McDonnell, who had then been one of its principal architects, intended to apply it again once he had trained his new units. Titokowaru was thus faced with good troops, good commanders, and a proven enemy strategy. How was he to oppose them?

Titokowaru's original force was miniscule. Two of the three main Ngati Ruanui *hapu*, Tangahoe and Pakakohe, did not support him during his first campaign. Until mid-September 1868, Ngaruahine fought virtually alone.[7] Calculations based on colonial population figures, the more reasonable British head-counts from the field, and the evidence of three followers of Tikokowaru indicate that Ngaruahine mustered less than eighty men, including a few individuals from other tribes and *hapu*.[8] These warriors were experienced, disciplined, and tough; they were well supplied with ammunition and their chiefs—Haowhenua, Toi Whakataka and, later, Katene Tuwhakaruru—were able men, but they were pitifully few. Titokowaru fought his first campaign at odds of nearly twelve to one.

The superficially obvious answer to the colonial strategy of attacking economic targets was for Titokowaru to take the initiative himself and force the war into enemy territory. But he clearly did not have the numbers for this. Eighty men could not attack settlements or major redoubts, still less the Field Force itself. This placed him in a dilemma. Tangahoe and Pakakohe, together with other potential supporters like the Ngarauru tribe, understandably feared a repetition of the disasters of 1866. In the words of one chief, 'I came out of fire, now I have no wish to return to it.'[9] They would not join Titokowaru until he gave them some evidence, in the form of military success, that a return to 'the fire' could be avoided. Thus, to get more warriors, he needed to win, and to win, he needed more warriors.

There was one solution, and Titokowaru seized upon it. He could not take the direct initiative, but what he could do was try to channel the eventual colonist offensive on to the point most favourable to himself. If he could somehow induce the colonists to ignore his cultivations and attack him before they were ready, on prepared ground of his own choosing, he might stand a chance of success. No one was privy to Titokowaru's thoughts at this time, but the circumstantial evidence indicates overwhelm-

ingly that to do just this was his initial strategic objective. From the outbreak of the war to 7 September, all his efforts were directed towards forcing the enemy to attack him at his bush stronghold of Te Ngutu o te Manu,
ten miles north of the Waingongoro.

His method can be defined as a strategy of controlled provocation. It
affected the colonists on two levels: the psychological and the material. On
the former level, Titokowaru made use of propaganda in the form of letters
and messages passed to the colonists through unaligned Maoris. He is said
to have responded to Governor Bowen's offer of £1,000 for his capture,
dead or alive, by putting a reward of two shillings and sixpence on the head
of the Governor—an assessment of relative values which could hardly fail to
provoke.[10] More importantly, he flaunted his location at Te Ngutu. He left
the colonists in no doubt of his intention to stand there, and challenged
them to come and get him. In one of his 'laws' communicated to the colonists on 30 June, he stated (in the third person): 'Although a thousand
should go he will be found at Te Ngutu-o-te-Manu; should even the whole
island rise against him, he will stay at Te Ngutu-o-te-Manu, with his
women and children.'[11]

On the material level, the strategy of controlled provocation was more
prosaic but no less effective. From 12 June, Titokowaru instituted an intensive campaign of raid and ambush. Supply columns, woodcutting parties,
and stragglers were attacked. This led the settlers between the Waitotara
and Waingongoro Rivers to abandon their homes, which were then
plundered and burned. Fences and crops were destroyed, and a great deal of
stock was driven off. This naturally incensed the settlers, who were soon
'chafing at the vexatious delays that are taking place in following up the
murderers'. Directly and through the press, they placed pressure on both
the government and McDonnell to put a stop to the depredations by attacking that 'devil of a place rejoicing in the name of Tengutatamana'.[12]

There were other pressures. The civil authorities in South Taranaki
believed that the longer Titokowaru was left unpunished, the greater the
chance of other *hapu* joining him. The Resident Magistrate, James Booth,
wrote that 'only if a blow sudden and effective is struck at the root of the
evil', which he specified was Te Ngutu, could the situation be controlled.[13]
From 10 July, when Te Kooti landed at Poverty Bay, the government also
had to consider a new theatre of war. Though determined to concentrate on
Titokowaru, they could hardly allow their main army to remain inactive in
South Taranaki while there were constant calls for troops on the East Coast.
For over a month, McDonnell resisted these pressures. He intended first to
complete the training of the new volunteer units, then to apply his own
strategy.[14] But his natural predilections were against him. Fiery and
volatile, and aware of the fact if not the extent of Titokowaru's numerical
weakness, the Colonel was not the man to take provocation lightly. His
determination to persist in his own plans was gradually undermined.

McDonnell's resistance was finally broken on 12 July, when Ngaruahine
made a carefully planned attack on a small constabulary redoubt at

Turuturu-Mokai, three miles from the main colonist camp at Waihi. This was a remarkable little action in that the Maoris under Haowhenua's operational command, killed ten and wounded six of the twenty-one man garrison without entering the redoubt. Turuturu-Mokai was subsequently enshrined by James Cowan as 'the Rorke's Drift of the New Zealand Wars', though in this case the 'Zulus' lost only three men while being 'beaten off again and again by the little garrison'.[15] Since the vast majority of contemporary commentators rightly saw the action as a striking colonist defeat, this is a rare case in which an historian has led, rather than followed, the myth-making process. But the engagement's major significance was its strategic effect. The close proximity of Turuturu-Mokai to the strong force at Waihi made the Maori success a particularly embarrassing one for the government—a painful singeing of the colonist beard. McDonnell arrived at the redoubt soon after the action, viewed the carnage, and walked outside with Captain Roberts. 'When they had gone a short distance he said, "Sit down." Drawing his sword, he extended the blade, gleaming brightly in the winter moonlight, and brought it back up to his lips, kissed it, and said dramatically, "Roberts, I shall have revenge for this."'[16] Titokowaru had won the strategic contest. From this point, McDonnell was intent on attacking Te Ngutu as soon as possible. Consequently, though the Maori disadvantage in numbers remained very great, it was reduced by the fact that an attack would be made only by those troops sufficiently trained for bushfighting. Still more important, Titokowaru could fight on ground of his own choosing.

McDonnell's first two attempts on Te Ngutu proved anti-climactic. The first expedition (10–11 August) was aborted because of bad guides and adverse weather. The second, on 21 August, was cleverly launched by McDonnell after heavy rains had rendered the Waingongoro River apparently impassable. The colonists reached Te Ngutu, found that Ngaruahine were out gathering food, and succeeded in burning part of the village. However, the Ngaruahine counter-attacked rapidly with heavy fire from the bush. The colonists withdrew, and were pursued back to the river. Ngaruahine lost only one or two men killed to the colonists' four killed and nine wounded, and there were some indications that the affair was intended as a trap by Tikokowaru. Whatever the case with this, and despite McDonnell's claims to the contrary, it was a Maori success—if a very minor one.[17] It was not until 7 September, on their third attempt, that the colonists succeeded in fighting a full-scale battle at Te Ngutu.

II TE NGUTU O TE MANU

MCDONNELL LEFT CAMP WAIHI ON HIS THIRD EXPEDITION against Te Ngutu soon after 3 a.m. on 7 September. He had 360 men, the cream of the Patea Field Force, in three groups: Von Tempsky's (142 Europeans), Hunter's (108 Europeans), and Kepa's (110 *kupapa*).[18] He crossed the Waingongoro at about 5 a.m. and skirted the river for three hours before striking north into the dense *rata* forest. McDonnell did his best to keep his movements secret, passing a neutral village in darkness 'so as not to be seen', and revealing his plan to his men 'only after the Waingongoro had been crossed'. The plan was to attack Te Ngutu through the neighbouring village of Ruaruru, one mile to the east.[19] As it happened, the colonists missed Ruaruru, backtracked, and approached Te Ngutu from the north. A little after 1 p.m., *kupapa* scouts located the *pa*. Soon the force came upon some outlying huts, whose occupants fled to raise the alarm and were fired on. With surprise now lost, McDonnell pressed on with all speed and entered Te Ngutu clearing.

At the southern end of the large clearing, which included scattered clumps of scrub, was the enemy *pa*, bounded on the north and west by the shallow Mangotahi Stream and on the east by the bush. The visible defences consisted of a low earth rampart encircled by a wooden stockade and a trench. These fortifications did not seem particularly strong, and the moment's warning given Ngati Ruanui was hardly enough to organize an adequate defence. McDonnell therefore prepared to assault. He apparently sent Kepa and most of his men on a wide flanking move into the bush on the left (east), with orders to 'work round the pah on that side'.[20] Von Tempsky was sent forward across the clearing and began extending to the left, close to the *pa*.

Despite McDonnell's best efforts, Titokowaru was aware of the colonist expedition. He had sent the women and children to safety, and told his warriors to be ready for battle about midday.[21] His followers later attributed his prescience to divine inspiration, but there is an alternative explanation: Titokowaru is known to have had a secret lookout post near Camp Waihi.[22] When the shots at the outlying huts established the precise direction of the attack, he immediately sent most of his men out into the bush with the order '*Whakawhiria*'—'encircle them, twist them round and round'. He remained in the *pa* himself with about twenty men. The other forty, split into tiny groups, opened fire from positions round the edge of the clearing and possibly in the clumps of cover within it. Some of these positions had been prepared beforehand. The hollow trunk of a large *rata* tree had been loopholed, but hidden rifle pits were probably more common. Almost as soon as they entered the clearing, therefore, the whole colonist force came under fire.[23]

Ngati Ruanui were adept at getting the fastest possible rates of fire from their weapons, and they fired from carefully chosen and concealed positions at ranges as close as ten yards. They therefore caused heavy casualties despite their low numbers. One group of eight warriors shot ten men in a couple of minutes, hitting several more than once.[24] According to eye-witnesses the Maori fire was 'terrific', 'fearful', 'something awful'; 'men were being knocked over like ninepins'.[25] The colonists sought cover where they could, units and sub-units were quickly isolated, and no uncommitted reserve remained with which to regain the initiative. McDonnell found that he was 'under fire from front, right and rear, but except within the palisading in the clearing to our front, we could see no enemy'. He therefore continued to concentrate his attention on the *pa* stockade. Major Hunter and No.3 Division of the constabulary were sent to assault it, but before they had moved far so many men were shot that McDonnell cancelled the order.[26] Von Tempsky, close to the *pa* on McDonnell's left, was also anxious to attack, but several of his men were shot and soon he himself fell dead.

So little time had passed that Kepa's flanking movement had yet to take effect, but it was already clear that the situation was hopeless. If the colonists took to the inadequate cover available to them, they could do nothing decisive and were picked off gradually. If they sought a decision by deploying in the open preparatory to an assault, they were picked off fast. McDonnell therefore made the inevitable decision to retreat. The evidence conflicts on the precise timing of this decision, but it seems that the colonists suffered most of their casualties before it was made.[27]

The colonists withdrew eastwards, the only direction open to them, but retreat did not end their trial. Titokowaru sent most of his men after them under Katene Tu-whakaruru. Katene was no doubt personally inclined towards a reckless attempt to annihilate the beaten enemy—his young child was brutally killed by the *kupapa* during the battle—but Titokowaru's injunctions prevailed. The pursuit was at once vigorous and tightly controlled. The colonists were actively harried all the way to the Waingongoro, but Ngati Ruanui made no attacks over open ground and confined themselves to sniping from cover. So, while they added at least a dozen casualties to the colonists' toll, they suffered little or no loss themselves. Indeed, Ngati Ruanui lost no more than three men killed in the battle as a whole.[28]

The government force was split into several groups during the retreat, and these reached Waihi at different times. One group, seventy men under Captain Roberts, arrived well after the others. Some commentators implied that McDonnell, intent on making his own escape, had abandoned this group to the full fury of the victorious enemy. In fact, except for one brief period which Roberts handled well, the Maori pursuit concentrated on eighty men under McDonnell, who were acting as rearguard to Major Hunter and a larger party carrying wounded. Most evidence indicates that McDonnell conducted the rearguard with skill and courage. The contrary allegation was just one of many slanders exchanged after the battle.[29]

Despite the gallantry of McDonnell and Roberts, eight hours of being hunted through the bush after a terrible defeat completed the demoralization of the government troops. Fifty Europeans were listed killed and wounded, and total casualties may have been greater—the general belief that no *kupapa* were hit is probably untrue.[30] This loss was bad enough of itself, but it was soon dwarfed by the disintegration of the Patea Field Force. Hundreds of men deserted, refused to re-enlist for a further term of service, or became 'worse than useless'. The *kupapa*, 'strongly impressed by Titokowaru's *mana*', went home; Von Tempsky's crack constabulary division mutinied; and six out of eight European units involved in the defeat ceased to exist. The government, left with 'a miserable excuse for a military force', had no choice but to abandon its main base at Waihi, together with several lesser posts and many farms, and withdraw to Patea. The Battle of Te Ngutu o te Manu was thus no mere repulse of an assault party, with ample reserves to fall back on, but the comprehensive destruction of the colony's only striking force.[31]

The British response to this disaster is an important illustration of the interpretative process at work during the New Zealand Wars. McDonnell and his men began their expedition with high reputations, largely deserved, and ended it in recrimination and obloquy, largely undeserved. The commander blamed the troops and the troops blamed the commander. The press and public blamed both.

There is evidence to suggest that McDonnell was not a well-balanced character, and at first sight this might seem to support the explanations of the defeat based on his shortcomings. But unfortunately psychological instability does not always preclude good generalship. The great Prussian marshal, Blücher, believed himself to be pregnant with a white elephant, and he helped defeat Napoleon. McDonnell was never in this psychiatric league, and he was in fact an able irregular leader—cunning, ruthless, and vigorous. To this he added great personal prowess with weapons and bushcraft, a flamboyant style, and a knowledge of the Maoris that was almost as great as he thought it was. This was enough to make him the colony's favourite commander—'a host in himself' and 'a terror to the rebels'.[32] Until 7 September 1868, New Zealand's Davy Crockett was not Von Tempsky, whom posterity has treated more kindly, but McDonnell. If Te Ngutu cost Von Tempsky his life, it cost McDonnell his reputation. Within twenty-four hours 'excessive adulation' had become 'a storm of abuse'. 'McDonnell, from being the pet of everyone, was suddenly declared unfit for his position.' After three weeks of this, McDonnell wrote pathetically of 'the combination of troubles both domestic and public' which were 'nigh sending me distracted and I am far from strong'. He was encouraged to leave his command soon afterwards.[33]

The reputation of McDonnell's men suffered the same abrupt reversal of fortune, not least at the hands of the Colonel himself. Some commentators criticized the whole force, but most concentrated on the newly recruited Wellington units—the 'Rangers' and the 'Rifles'. Before the battle on 7 September, observers noted that many of these 'recruits' had actually seen service before, and that they responded remarkably well to training. They were highly praised for their performance on the two earlier expeditions against Te Ngutu. The press and the government were pleased that they had 'preserved untarnished the reputation of the British settler', and McDonnell wrote that the Wellington men had displayed 'all the fine qualities of tried veterans'. The Rangers, he reported two days before the battle, were 'one of the most efficient and best conducted' units in the Field Force.[34]

Retrospect changed all this. After the battle, McDonnell suddenly remembered that his 'tried veterans' were 'drunken useless vagabonds'. Other commentators now recalled that the Wellington volunteers were 'easily panic-stricken', 'a rabble of half mutinous and altogether drunken cowards'. They were in fact 'real brutes, thoroughly funked'. It was suggested in Wellington that publicans should refuse them service, and all citizens were advised to shun them. This treatment apparently induced one volunteer to commit suicide on his return.[35]

The interpretation of the events of 9 September 1868 began as this shocked reaction, more notable for vehemence than coherence. But it rapidly developed into a dual explanation for the defeat which became almost universally accepted. The battle was lost primarily through McDonnell's errors and the failings of his men. This tradition has been uncritically perpetuated by twentieth-century writers, including a few who examine the battle in some detail.[36] But how much substance do the twin explanations really have?

One specific criticism of McDonnell was that he should have attacked at night. When the enemy *pa* was first located, about 1 p.m., Kepa te Rangihiwinui reportedly advised the Colonel to take this course—'but nothing would do but he must attack at once'.[37] Yet it seems obvious that McDonnell was right in this. To wait for five or six hours would only increase the chances of detection, and place his men at a disadvantage in darkness against an enemy more familiar with the ground. It is hard to believe that Kepa actually made this suggestion.

Another, more pervasive, criticism of McDonnell was that he retreated prematurely instead of charging the *pa*. 'A Com[mandin]g Officer never made a worse mistake.'[38] McDonnell did decide to retreat soon after the battle commenced, but not before the situation had become hopeless and most of his casualties had occurred. He tried to organize an assault, but could not do so because the enemy dominated the area in which the assault group had to deploy. What the Colonel's critics were advocating was that he should have massed his already shaken units in an area dominated by a triple Maori cross-fire, then launched the survivors frontally over open ground at an undamaged palisade. This could only have added a miniature Ohaeawai to his already considerable troubles. Strategically, McDonnell made the mistake of bowing to Titokowaru's will, but tactically he played a losing hand well. He did his best to obtain surprise, he cut his losses once it became clear the situation was hopeless, and he conducted a difficult retreat with determination and courage. The colonists were fortunate that McDonnell, and not one of his critics, held the command.

The second explanation for the defeat stressed the ill-discipline, inexperience, and cowardice of the colonial troops. Our sympathy for McDonnell is tempered by the fact that he subscribed to this view. It was alleged that many men had fled the field, and that they had also tended to bunch together during the battle, so presenting easy targets to the enemy, whereas they should have sought cover individually. These failings were, and still are, supposed to have been a main cause of defeat. This explanation is ridden with contradiction. McDonnell clearly intended it as an alternative to that based on his own incompetence, but others used the two in concert. The battle was lost because McDonnell failed to attack with troops that were already in full flight for Waihi. These men not only fled at the first shot, but also suffered unnecessary casualties by bunching up on the battlefield. A few days before the action, they were described as splendid soldiers, but they lost because they were a cowardly rabble. Historians did not originate this explanation, but their failure to recognize the obvious inconsistencies cannot entirely be excused.

Virtually no specific allegations were made against the constabulary and *kupapa* who made up two-thirds of McDonnell's force. On the contrary these men were rightly praised for their conduct, and they alone outnumbered Ngati Ruanui four to one. Most criticism, as we have seen, was directed at the Wellington 'Rifles' and 'Rangers'. These two units were chosen for the striking force in preference to several others, and their least fit men—a quarter of the whole—were weeded out before the expedition commenced. The idea that they bunched up on the battlefield, and therefore suffered disproportionate losses, is not borne out by the casualty list.[39] Most of the Wellington men took part in the organized retreat with one or other of the three main groups. A minority of about forty did flee the field without orders, but not before the general retreat had commenced.[40] The 'Rifles' and 'Rangers' disintegrated after the battle, but so too did veteran units. In sum, great demoralization and a degree of disorganized flight did occur at Te Ngutu, but as a consequence of disaster, not as a cause of it.

The emphasis on the failings of McDonnell and his troops is largely unfair as an assessment of the colonist performance, and utterly inadequate as an explanation of defeat. As usual, it also functions to conceal the true explanation: good Maori strategy and tactics. This is not to say that the qualities of Titokowaru and Ngati Ruanui did not receive some acknowledgement. Contemporary and modern accounts agree on the chief's cunning and vigour, and the warriors' courage and bushcraft. But this recognition is superficial, and it is not presented as the decisive cause of the colonist defeat. Moreover, even in the hands of twentieth-century historians, it stresses the less impressive and more primitive aspects of the Maori achievement. 'The ferocious one-eyed Titokowaru breathed more fire to his warriors.' 'Amongst these trees, their naked brown skins nearly blending in colour with the trunks . . . [Ngati Ruanui] darted from one cover to another with the quickness of monkeys.'[41] These factors may have existed; they may even have been of some help in winning the battle; but as an explanation of a brilliant victory they are pitiful.

For Te Ngutu o te Manu deserves to rank as a brilliant victory, despite its small scale. It was created partly by the qualities of the Ngati Ruanui warriors: courage, bushcraft, and the less widely recognized attributes of tight discipline and good marksmanship. But the main key to success, the main direct cause of the colonist defeat, was Titokowaru's tactical approach. The core of this was the interaction of two features of the battlefield: the *pa* at the end of the Te Ngutu clearing, and the concealed firing positions on the perimeter. The *pa* was in reality a mere diversion, a straw man. The colonists did not actually assault it, but they thought in terms of doing so, and all their movements were made in relation to it. The firing positions outside dominated the clearing and they were occupied by the Maoris as the battle commenced. The colonists were thus invited to take up as their battle-lines an area already controlled by the enemy. With their attention focused on the *pa*, which they believed to be the decisive point, the colonists did not threaten the firing positions, which were in fact the decisive points. These positions in turn prevented any substantial attack on the *pa*, since the areas in which an assault party would have to assemble were within their field of fire. Caught in this cleft stick, the colonists had no real choice but to accept their defeat and withdraw. Titokowaru then introduced an offensive element into his battle plan by launching the vigorous but economical pursuit which completed the enemy's discomfiture.

This small tactical masterpiece exploited the opportunity created by the strategy of controlled provocation. The strategy forced McDonnell to abandon the 'bush-scouring' policy of attacking economic targets, which would probably have led to success. It compelled him to attack prematurely, with only the best-trained portion of his Field Force, and so reduced the odds in his favour. And it led him to direct his efforts against a position selected and painstakingly prepared by the enemy.

Titokowaru's strategy and tactics in the Te Ngutu campaign together made up an integrated military method. At first sight, it seems rather different from the system used by earlier Maori generals, and in some ways it did bear his characteristic stamp. His use of the bush and the strong offensive element in his operations, which will appear more clearly below, were unusual if not unique. But some differences are more apparent than real, especially in the light of his subsequent campaigns. Te Ngutu was a *kainga* or village rather than a purpose-built *pa*, but its economic importance was reduced by the removal of non-combatants and livestock before battle. All Titokowaru's later *pa* were purpose-built modern *pa* proper. The insignificance of anti-artillery defences arose simply from the fact that the colonists were not expected to bring big guns deep into the bush. Titokowaru showed his ability in this area with Tauranga-ika, a *pa* built in December 1868, which was as cannon-proof as any.

In other respects, the similarity between Te Ngutu and earlier campaigns is obvious and striking. Tactically, the Battle of Te Ngutu resembled that at Puketakauere on 27 June 1860, with which Titokowaru was certainly familiar. In both actions, the Maoris used their *pa* as a false target which engaged British attention while the battle was won from concealed rifle pits. In both cases the location of these firing positions at the edge of the bush enabled the Maoris to occupy them and move from one to the other unseen and unhampered. Strategically, the Ngutu campaign was similar to the operations leading up to the Battle of Gate Pa. Both Ngai-te-Rangi and

Ngati Ruanui wished to force the British to attack them at a time and place of their own choosing. Both succeeded in doing so through provocation: propaganda coupled with pin-prick raids launched from the position they wanted the British to attack. Titokowaru's military method was a form—arguably the highest form—of the flexible modern *pa* system.

III MOTUROA

TITOKOWARU'S VICTORY AT TE NGUTU NOT ONLY PREVENTED the conquest of his base area north of the Waingongoro, but also gained him the district between that river and Patea. As the colonists left their camps, redoubts, and farms, these were occupied by triumphant Ngaruahine warriors, in the first substantial reconquest of Maori land since the Taranaki War. During September, the men of Pakakohe and Tangahoe, some Ngarauru, and perhaps a few individuals from other tribes, joined Titokowaru's force. In early October, Titokowaru marched south to Otoia, a little north-east of Patea, and built a *pa* there. But, for seven weeks after Te Ngutu, he made no substantial offensive moves—no attempt to exploit his victory by destroying the colonist forces.

Titokowaru's next victory was followed by a similar period of inaction, and in both cases the colonists were mystified by his lethargy, though they thanked God for it. Colonel Whitmore, who replaced the unfortunate McDonnell on 18 October, wrote: 'the inexplicable inaction of the enemy so close to our front lost him his golden opportunity to complete his already unequalled triumphs by stamping out the small force opposed to him.'[42] This reflects the persistent British failure to recognize the constraints under which their Maori enemies fought. For one thing, Ngati Ruanui had waged war for four months. They now needed time to recuperate—to repair their weapons, collect food and ammunition, and plant their crops. Secondly, though Titokowaru's force had increased and his enemies diminished, numerical parity was still very far away. Titokowaru's followers now included much of the Ngati Ruanui and some of the Ngarauru warrior force, but they still numbered no more than 200, and 150 is more likely. This was a far cry from the colonist estimates of 400 to 1,000 warriors.[43]

As for the government forces, Whitmore claimed that he had barely 200 effective men, whereas his returns show 632 Europeans and 457 Wanganui *kupapa*. The discrepancy is partly explained by Whitmore's tendency to understate his own numbers, and so play up his difficulties, but the question of effectiveness is more important. About 120 of the Europeans were totally ineffective, and over 200 more were doubtful—a legacy of the Ngutu disaster. A third of the 300 utterly reliable men had to be left in key redoubts to steady other units. The Wanganuis, as we have seen, had different objectives from their allies, and Whitmore could count on only 100—Kepa's immediate followers. But the rest would certainly fight hard if the war entered their territory, and would probably do so if their entrepôt of

Wanganui Town was threatened. Similarly, the 200 doubtful Europeans, though inadequate for offensive operations, were perfectly capable of defending fortified posts. So Whitmore's army had a defensive strength of 600 men, or 950 if the Wanganuis as a whole were involved, and an offensive strength of 300. The offensive force alone outnumbered Ngati Ruanui by two to one, had greater firepower, and included 100 mounted constabulary who could act as infantry or cavalry. It was therefore more than a match for Ngati Ruanui in open country.[44]

Thus Titokowaru's problem, though less in degree, remained essentially similar to that which had existed before Te Ngutu. He no longer needed to fear a colonist offensive against his villages and cultivations, and he had conquered the land for which he had gone to war. But, to keep it, he had to inflict further punishment on the colonists before the impact of Te Ngutu wore off, and before the major recruitment drive instituted by the government could take effect. He could not do so by attacking strongly garrisoned redoubts, or by fighting in the open. Again, he had to force the enemy to attack him in a position which would compensate for his inferior numbers.

Titokowaru at first sought to induce Whitmore to attack Otoia by raiding the area between Patea and the Waitotara River. But, by mid-October, the area had been largely evacuated and Whitmore proved impervious to this pressure. The only remaining possibility was to threaten the agriculturally rich area south of the Waitotara, an important part of the Wanganui hinterland. Whitmore considered the protection of this district his primary task.[45] But Otoia was an unsuitable position for this purpose, and Titokowaru had therefore to outflank Whitmore at Patea and move south to a base which presented a credible threat to the Waitotara district. The movement had to be made without being caught in the open by Whitmore and his cavalry. Accordingly, Titokowaru contrived to give the false impression that he planned to march direct on Wanganui by the coastal route.[46] The colonists soon began to suspect that they were 'being humbugged',[47] but their need to watch the coastal route enabled Titokowaru to depart unnoticed from Otoia at the beginning of November, outflank Whitmore at Patea, and march south to Moturoa, a position in the bush near Wairoa.

The Waitotara district now lay open to the south, and to pound the point home Titokowaru sent a raiding party into it. This raid actually occurred while the Moturoa move was still in progress, but it seemed to confirm that the Wanganui hinterland could easily be devastated from the new Maori position. The colonist commander at Wanganui, Lieutenant-Colonel Gorton, concluded that 'Titokowaru's intentions are to harass the district on this side of the Waitotara'. Whitmore immediately left Patea and marched south to Wairoa. He concentrated his offensive force, including 100 constabulary newly arrived from Auckland, and prepared to attack Moturoa. 'I felt', he wrote, 'that I must do something at once or Titokowaru would neglect my force and invade the settled districts.' Once again, Titokowaru had imposed his will on his opponent, and the colonist forces advanced to battle on terms of their enemy's choosing.[48]

On the morning of 7 November 1868, Whitmore marched out of Wairoa to attack Moturoa with over 600 men. Of these, 200 Wanganui *kupapa* refused to enter the bush, and a militia unit was left on the track to guard the reserve ammunition. Whitmore therefore launched his attack with four divisions of constabulary, two small Patea volunteer units, and some *kupapa* under Kepa. Because Whitmore did not provide the normal statistics in his report, the strength of each of these units is difficult to fix, but they totalled between 350 and 400 men, mainly constabulary.[49] Like Te Ngutu, Moturoa was sited in a clearing in the midst of the bush, but it was only four miles from the colonist base at Wairoa, and Whitmore's guides knew the ground well. The short march was therefore completed quietly and without difficulty.

Whitmore's observation of the *pa* and the reports of his scouts led him to conclude that 'the enemy had not discovered our approach'. It was also clear that the *pa* was far from complete. The Maori right was guarded by a steep gully but the left was apparently vulnerable to a turning movement. The fortifications that did exist seemed weak. Whitmore could detect no entrenchments, and 'the palisade appeared to me to give no protection to its defenders except concealment'. Nor did it seem much of an obstacle to a storming party. 'The palings were miserable affairs', wrote Whitmore, 'I could easily have cut the lot with my clasp knife.'[50] Whitmore's plan, formulated jointly with Kepa, was that the chief and his *kupapa*, with No. 1 constabulary, should outflank the *pa* to its left and fire into its open rear. Once Kepa was in position, Major Hunter with the 'select veterans' of No. 3 and the Patea volunteers was to storm the left of the *pa*. No. 2 division was to cover the colonist left, and No. 6—a large division of 106 men—was to remain in reserve in the centre. These two units were to empty their breechloaders as fast as possible into the fragile stockade. With this support from the front, and Kepa's fire from the rear, Hunter was expected to have no difficulty in carrying the place.

As it happened, Ngati Ruanui were not surprised, their left flank was not vulnerable, and their fortifications protected them very well indeed. Kepa never got into position, Hunter's assault was shot flat, and he himself killed. The colonists recoiled from Titokowaru's counter-attack and were hotly pursued back to Wairoa. Thus Whitmore, like McDonnell before him, was utterly defeated, losing between fifty and sixty killed and wounded to the Maoris' one dead and a few wounded.[51]

Virtually all accounts agree that the colonial troops fought well at Moturoa, but apart from this, British explanations of the defeat had all the variety and inaccuracy we have come to expect. According to some of his subordinates, Whitmore's stupidity was to blame—not because he had launched an assault, but because he had failed to do so again, and retreated instead.[52] Historians repeat the litany. Moturoa was Whitmore's 'one great blunder', his 'foolish but disastrous mistake'.[53] The contemporary comments from which these opinions derive were merely reflexive slanders with no basis in fact, but, like McDonnell, Whitmore forfeited sympathy with a singularly unedifying defence. The problem, he argued, was Titokowaru's superiority in numbers. 'He could not have brought up less than 500 or 600 men against us.' The real Ngati Ruanui strength could hardly have been above 150 men, and Maori accounts give 100.[54] But, so the story ran, the colonists had depended for parity on the 200 *kupapa* who had refused to enter the bush. According to Whitmore, these 'traitors or arrant cowards' were 'the real delinquents', as their desertion had left him with a hopelessly inadequate force. Remarkably enough, Whitmore nowhere informed his superiors of the actual numbers he had taken into battle, contenting himself with a passing reference to 'two hundred rifles'.[55] Exaggerating Maori numbers was a very common feature of the interpretation of the wars, but most British generals stopped short of halving their own. Whitmore was fully aware, two weeks before the engagement, that he could not rely on the majority of the Wanganuis for this kind of operation.[56]

Lack of numbers was clearly not the colonist problem, and the only area where Whitmore's generalship seems genuinely questionable is his underestimation of the Maori fortifications. But this was a very common British tendency, arising from preconceptions about Maori abilities rather than stupidity. Furthermore, the Moturoa defences were in fact very deceptive. Kepa had also believed them to be weak.[57] Whitmore was simply unfortunate enough to be a good general matched against an excellent one.

Titokowaru's tactics in the Battle of Moturoa fall into three categories: the selection of the optimal location for his *pa*, the use of deceptive fortifications, and the exercise of tight control over his men. To force the colonists into battle at Moturoa, Titokowaru had had to risk building his *pa* in a short time—four days, as it turned out. His selection of site minimized this problem, and also provides a good example of the difference between modern and traditional *pa*. A high hill—Okotuku—rises behind Moturoa and it seems the obvious place to fortify. But this hill was the site of a traditional *pa* easily stormed by Chute in January 1866 with a force of similar size to Whitmore's. Titokowaru avoided it, and opted for a position on flat ground south of Okotuku Hill, at the northern end of the Moturoa clearing. The site formed a narrow waist between a steep gully on the west (the Maori right), and an area of very thick bush and broken ground on the east. With a few supplementary defences in the latter area, these two features protected the flanks of the position and meant that the *pa* need not be fully enclosed. In fact, it consisted simply of a single south-facing line. Four days of hard work were enough to make this very strong.

The main defence consisted of a firing-trench six feet deep, with traverses and firing-steps. The earth from the trench was banked up behind it to form a second firing line, a few feet above the first. The palisade, which was indeed fairly flimsy, served merely to conceal these lines. Men in the trench fired through a gap left between the lighter palings and the ground. Men behind the earth bank fired through gaps left between the palings. The double line of fire this created was supplemented by three *taumaihi*—squat towers ten to twelve feet high and fifteen feet around, built of packed earth and fern.[58] These must have blended into the adjoining palisade, because, though Maori evidence makes it quite clear that they existed, they are not mentioned in the colonist accounts. All the important Maori defences were therefore effectively concealed or disguised, and the *pa* was 'supposed at first to be a simple palisade' by the colonists. Thus Hunter's assault party unexpectedly met a three-level barrage of bullets 'flying like hail', and was decimated. One survivor wrote, 'I never saw the like of that sheet of fire.'[59]

Though the main *pa* this time had a crucial physical purpose, like Te Ngutu it also functioned to divert enemy attention from the bush on the flanks. Again the bush acted as a safe Maori pathway around the battlefield, and again it seems to have included some concealed rifle-pits, especially in the dense foliage east of the *pa*. From these positions, a small party was able to block Kepa's flanking movement quite easily. Ngati Ruanui also demonstrated an extraordinary degree of discipline. The colonist advance was expected at some time, and when the sentries reported it, the men went to their posts silently, leading the colonists to believe that they retained surprise. The *pa* line was divided into three sections, each with one *taumaihi*, and each held by one of the main Ngati Ruanui *hapu*. The section attacked by Hunter was actually held by the newly joined Pakakohe, but these men were already integrated into Titokowaru's system.[60]

Once they had repulsed Hunter's attack, Titokowaru ordered most of the garrison into the bush flanking the clearing. The bush concealed but did not prevent movement, and small groups of Ngati Ruanui were therefore able to attack much larger enemy formations. East of the *pa*, these warriors 'threatened to outflank No. 1 division A.C. and the *kupapa* under Kemp [Kepa]'. These units were pressed in upon the remains of Hunter's force, and the whole was only saved by the advance of part of the reserve. West of the *pa*, No. 2 division of constabulary was also threatened. Had Whitmore continued to hold his ground, as his critics suggested he should, this unit would have been destroyed, exposing Whitmore's whole left flank. William Wallace, a veteran of No. 2, wrote: 'If we had remained a little while longer . . . our small unit would have been done for as the Maoris were nearly all around us.' Thus Whitmore was in danger on both flanks, and it was this threat of encirclement—not the simple repulse of his assault —which forced him to withdraw. While successful defence prevented a colonist victory, it was successful attack which gave it to the Maoris.[61]

IV   THE CRISIS OF 1868

IN MID-1868 IT HAD SEEMED AS IF THE NEW ZEALAND WARS were over. The colonists entertained reasonable hopes of digesting the confiscated lands at their leisure, and of entering a long-anticipated but long-delayed period of rapid progress. The renewed outbreak of expensive warfare on both coasts was thus a severe blow in itself, and the five minor victories won by Titokowaru and Te Kooti in July and August made the situation still more frustrating. Then, by 10 November, the successive heavy blows of Te Ngutu, Moturoa, and Poverty Bay converted an irritating drain on colonial resources into a serious threat to European dominance. During November and early December, Te Kooti brilliantly evaded his pursuers and escaped unscathed with the spoils of his raid. On the West Coast, the colonists recoiled from the victorious Titokowaru and withdrew to Nukumaru. When news of Poverty Bay reached them, they pulled back still further—for reasons discussed in the next chapter. As he had done after Te Ngutu, Titokowaru followed them up. Further Ngati Ruanui and Ngarauru warriors, together with individual recruits from other tribes, mainly Taranaki and Te Atiawa, brought his strength up to 400 men. In mid-November, he built a new *pa*, Tauranga-ika, fifteen miles north of Wanganui, and his raiding parties reached the town's very outskirts. Except for the fortified settlements of Patea and Wairoa, Titokowaru now controlled virtually the whole area between Mount Egmont and Wanganui. During this period, the only good news received by defence officials in Wellington was that one of their number, C.E. Haughton, had won a yacht in a raffle.[62]

It is important to appreciate the severity of the crisis in which these events placed the Colony. Contemporaries considered the Battle of Te Ngutu o te Manu to be 'absolutely disastrous': 'the most serious and complete defeat ever experienced by the colonial forces', 'the most disastrous affair that ever took place in New Zealand'. It alone created a 'grave crisis'. On 24 September, a newspaper correspondent reported from Patea that 'the small and utterly disorganised force here might any night be cut up and cooked by Tito Kowaru'. With an unfortunate turn of phrase, this writer continued: 'it is useless mincing matters. . . . Unless something is done and done quickly we had all better clear out.'[63]

The government tried to 'do something'. It desperately sought men for the constabulary from all over New Zealand, and sent recruiting officers to Australia, stretching its financial resources to the limit. Governor Bowen risked Imperial displeasure by transferring two companies of the 18th regiment from Wellington to Wanganui; though these troops' strict orders not to fight outside the towns continued to apply.[64] The colonial government also transferred virtually all the constabulary on the East Coast (fifty-seven men) to Wanganui. Despite their vehement objections, the East Coast settlers and their *kupapa* allies were thus left to face Te Kooti alone. As we have seen, the government also swallowed its pride and secretly attempted to open peace negotiations with the escaped prisoners.

These efforts did not prevent the Wanganui settlers from blaming the government for the loss of their farms and the crippling of the local economy. 'Thanks to Colonel Haultain and the Government for the ruined misery brought upon this district.' Dissatisfaction with the Stafford Ministry's handling of the war was widespread, and in late September it survived a motion of no confidence by a single vote. News of the second military disaster, at Moturoa on 7 November, had one beneficial effect in that these political rivalries were temporarily set aside. 'However much people might disagree on many public questions', said Dr Featherston,

Superintendent of Wellington and one of the Stafford Ministry's most bitter opponents, 'they must all be unanimous in the opinion that never since the foundation of the colony have they been called upon to meet such an emergency as that which has now arisen.'[65]

For Moturoa in its turn changed a grave situation into an acute national emergency. It seemed that, whoever led them, the colonial forces were unable to stop Titokowaru. Far from the seat of conflict, the editor of the *Otago Witness* wrote: 'The conviction is universal throughout the Colony that at no time in its history has greater danger been imminent. The Colonists are left to themselves and they have suddenly discovered that they are unable to protect themselves.'[66] This view may not have been quite universal, but it was certainly widely shared. Petitions and public meetings appealed to Governor Bowen for Imperial help 'to avert the extinction of those dearest to us'. In the interim, settlers living north of Wanganui abandoned their farms and fled to the town—some even left the colony. The influx of refugees created great economic hardship. In the week after Moturoa, during a visit optimistically designed to boost morale, Governor Bowen noted the 'piteous sight which the streets of this town now present almost hourly, destitute women and children flocking in for food and shelter'. Business was at a standstill, many people had lost their means of support, and one settler sent a letter to Australia requesting 'bread for the most destitute'.[67] The prevailing sense of insecurity did not stop at Wanganui. As far south as Foxton settlers fled their homes. The government did not dismiss this as unreasoning panic. On the contrary, it advised settlers to withdraw to centres of population and made active efforts to fortify these. The militias of Rangitikei, Manawatu, Wellington, and the Hutt Valley were called out and placed on active service.[68]

While the victories of Titokowaru gave the crisis of 1868 its substance, Te Kooti's Poverty Bay raid lent it a touch of terror. A horrified shudder ran through the colony at the news from the East Coast. 'The wildest imagination could hardly have conceived of a more terrible calamity. In all the annals of the struggles of civilization against man in his natural savage state, nothing more appalling in degree if not in extent has ever been recorded.'[69] Newspaper reports such as this dwelt on the gory details of the raid, and often exaggerated them. This natural response to a terrible event subsequently functioned to focus attention on the Poverty Bay campaign at the expense of the Te Ngutu and Moturoa operations. At the time, Te Kooti was seen as a lesser threat than Titokowaru, for all the horror the former's deeds aroused. Settlers left Wanganui, not Napier, and until December the vast majority of the colonial forces were concentrated on the West Coast. But Poverty Bay materially increased the government's problems and greatly increased the sense of crisis, exciting emotions ranging from cries for vengeance to utter terror, and sometimes combining the two.

The contemporary reaction to the colonist defeats of 1868 was no mere exercise in newspaper panic-mongering. The sense of crisis was too widely shared, too closely reflected in actions as well as words, to leave any doubt that it was genuine. But were the sincere fears of the colonists soundly based? Did the small forces led by Te Kooti and Titikowaru really threaten British control of the North Island?

In late 1868, the settlers and soldiers in Wanganui believed that a full-scale attack on the town by Titokowaru was possible at any time. To this extent, they misunderstood the nature of the danger they were in. Titokowaru's numbers grew rapidly after Moturoa, but only to a peak of about 400 warriors.[70] Wanganui was garrisoned by at least 600 effective troops, and was therefore secure against direct attack. But the threat to the town was still real enough. From his new base at Tauranga-ika, Titokowaru could devastate the whole Wanganui hinterland, both north and south of the town. Land communication would eventually become impossible for anything except a large armed force. Like New Plymouth before it, Wanganui would soon cease to be a viable economic entity. But the Imperial ships, men, supplies, and money which had sustained New Plymouth through 1860 were not available to Wanganui in 1868. After each of his victories, Titokowaru had taken control of the areas evacuated by the colonists, leaving their larger strongpoints behind him to wither harmlessly on the vine. He had done it with Patea, he had done it with Wairoa, and he could do it with Wanganui.

European control of the West Coast between New Plymouth and Wellington was thus genuinely threatened by Titokowaru. The danger presented by Te Kooti was not so severe. Essentially, he was a guerilla fighter, unable to defeat the main colonist field force in battle. He was a brilliant raider, whereas Titokowaru was a conqueror. Moreover, in some areas he had not gained that vital prerequisite of success in guerilla warfare—the support of the local population. But, while the colonial forces were concentrated at Wanganui, there was little chance of his being caught. Te Kooti could therefore be expected to keep the East Coast in a turmoil indefinitely.

In this context, one colonist observer wrote: 'The self-reliant policy has failed, and the only hope left for the Colony is to sue for protection to the Mother Country.'[71] But, as some colonists acknowledged, this 'only hope' was not realistic. The Imperial Government was heartily sick of its New Zealand entanglement. A substantial British army had failed to achieve decisive victory in the Waikato War, and London was still wrangling with Wellington over the costs. Had a large town fallen with the loss of thousands of European lives, public outcry in Britain might have forced renewed intervention, but such an event was never likely, and the mere threat of it was not enough. The colonists believed that such a threat existed, and that the military situation could hardly be more dire. They appealed for help on this basis, and the Imperial Government bluntly refused.[72] The colony was on its own, and this state of affairs was made all the more alarming by one further possibility: the outbreak of a general war through the involvement of the King Movement.

Kingite intentions in this period require further research, and it is impossible to be definite about them here. Before November 1868, relations between the King Movement and Titokowaru had not been good. In 1867, as part of his peace campaign, Titokowaru had rejected the authority of King Tawhiao.[73] Perhaps influenced by this, and by the continued war-weariness of Waikato, a Kingite emissary to Ngati Ruanui had advised against intervention in August 1868. In his frustration, Titokowaru reportedly responded by cursing Tawhiao.[74] But Titokowaru's great victories in September and November, together with Poverty Bay, changed the situation. A real chance of reversing the decision of the Waikato War emerged. It would have been strange if the Kingites had not seriously considered taking this chance, and the evidence indicates that they did. They placed pressure on the Wanganui *kupapa* to cease supporting the government against Titokowaru—'leave him alone to do his work'. The Waikato tribes began preparing for war, many Maoris and settlers believed that a large-scale Kingite offensive was imminent, and a small Ngati Maniapoto war party actually did raid North Taranaki in February 1869, killing nine people.[75]

Intelligent observers among the colonists were in no doubt about the likelihood of Kingite intervention, nor about its próbable outcome. J. C. Firth, a careful student of Kingite sentiment for his own purposes, wrote: 'Waikato, the heart of the island, though full of excitement and preparation, is still at peace. Until a blow has been struck there, the war will not have become general; and there is yet hope, though I confess a small one, that the final and terrible catastrophe may by God's blessing be averted.'[76] In the context of the time, Firth's remarks passed for optimism. David Monro, Speaker of the House of Representatives, wrote: 'If there be a general rising of hostile Maories throughout the North [Island] as appears to be threatened at the present moment, I do not think that the colony is capable of grappling successfully with the difficulty.'[77]

A fundamental British assumption during the New Zealand Wars was that ultimate victory was certain. The successive disasters of 1868 brought matters to such a pass that some colonists were induced to overcome this deeply entrenched preconception, and face the prospect of defeat. This prospect was not one of European extermination or expulsion, but of a return to the race-relations situation of 1859: a British periphery co-operating economically with a much larger Maori hinterland. Peace on this basis would involve the return of the confiscated land. In British eyes, such a course of action was almost inconceivable—a humiliating admission of failure and a mortal blow to the colony's future. Yet there is evidence to suggest that some colonists, including members of the General Assembly, were actually considering it.[78] Others spoke openly of the likelihood of Maori victory. On 30 November, Bishop Williams wrote:

> The number of reverses we have received during the last six months is truly astonishing. There have been a great number of them and not a single success to put on the other side. What does this seem to indicate, but that God's hand has been turned against us. As a community and as a government we have been puffed up first with the idea that we were in the right; and secondly that we are able to

put down the natives by our own strength. We have been trying for a very long time to stem the torrent, but we are carried away from day to day further from the object we wished to attain. . . . All this speaks plainly enough. Unless it should please God to check the progress of the natives . . . there will be no settlers living in the country except in the towns.[79]

Though white New Zealand survived it, the crisis of 1868 was sharp and severe; its effects are likely to have been profound and its implications certainly were. However much they mistook the nature of their danger, many colonists recognized the crisis for what it was and, at the time, said so emphatically. Yet the extent of the emergency, and sometimes even its existence, is not apparent in the historical orthodoxy. In 1868, the government desperately began to fortify settlements in the Manawatu and called out the militia as far south as Wellington. Colonel Whitmore urgently advised settlers south of the Wanganui to leave their farms for the nearest redoubt. Ten years later, T. W. Gudgeon, in his history of the wars, dismissed the settlers' reaction to Titokowaru's victories as 'the usual panic' and called their insistence on fortifications south of Wanganui 'absurd'. In his memoirs, published in 1902, Whitmore wrote sarcastically 'that in Wellington itself there were some who expected from day to day to see the advance of Titokowaru's band . . . taking possession of the suburbs of the city'. Thus the crisis of 1868 was retrospectively played down.[80]

Historians have accepted the distorted version of events. They place their main emphasis on Poverty Bay, emotionally the most terrible, but militarily the least serious of the three great Maori victories of 1868. Titokowaru's achievements were gradually watered down to the point where his name does not feature at all in New Zealand's two most widely read general histories.[81] As a result, the military crisis of which he was the principal architect—perhaps the greatest threat to European dominance in the history of New Zealand—has all but disappeared from the received version.

13

The Turn of the Tide

NOVEMBER 1868 MARKED THE NADIR OF THE COLONY'S MILI-
tary fortunes, but within three months the situation had changed entirely.
Te Kooti had been severely defeated, Titokowaru had ceased to be a threat,
and the risk of Kingite intervention had therefore receded. The first episode
in this reversal of fortune was an expedition of 24 December–5 January
against Te Kooti at Ngatapa—the *pa* unsuccessfully attacked by Ropata on
5 December, at the end of the Poverty Bay campaign. The expedition was a
product of what we will call the East Coast strategy. The implementation of
this strategy began on 2 December, when Colonel Whitmore and 220 men
embarked at Wanganui for Poverty Bay, arriving two days later. Though
small, this detachment included the four best divisions of the Armed Constabulary. In practice, it was the colony's sole effective field force. Its
transfer therefore constituted an abrupt shift in the focus of the colonist war
effort from the West Coast to the East. Understandably, this sudden switch
of emphasis has led to the assumption that the colonists saw Poverty Bay as
a much greater disaster than Moturoa and reacted accordingly. This con-
forms to the legend that 'Te Kooti was a much more dangerous opponent
that Titokowaru'.[1] But, like the legend it serves, the assumption is false.

The East Coast strategy originated with Whitmore. On 24 November, in
an important memorandum, the Colonel offered his reflections on the
critical military situation to the Defence Minister.[2] He noted that disaster in
east and west, and various signs that the Kingites might take a hand, created
a multiplicity of threats. Against this was the hard fact that 'we can only
maintain one Field Force'. Consequently, 'nothing general in the way of an
offensive movement is possible'. On the other hand, while farmlands could
not be protected from marauders, towns and redoubts could be defended by
local forces. It followed that the proper policy was for threatened regions to
stand on the defensive 'until successively the Field Force can come to their
relief'. Rather than attack everywhere and succeed nowhere, the colony
should concentrate a decisive superiority at a single point. Whitmore might
be no match for the genius of Titokowaru, but this simple strategic insight
was to help turn the tide of war. The most unpopular colonist commander
was also the most competent.

Whitmore was convinced that the West Coast was the wrong place for the
first application of his strategy—not because the problem there was less than
in the East, but because it was greater. 'I feel strongly that the district from

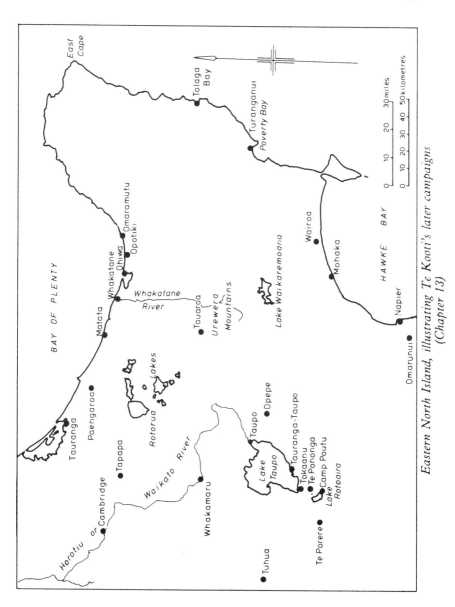

Eastern North Island, illustrating Te Kooti's later campaigns (Chapter 13)

Wanganui to Patea is far from being one in which a rapid success is probable. The force required needs more discipline and more training, and perhaps more numbers, than anywhere else.' While the necessary troops were assembled and trained, Wanganui Town and its outposts could be strongly garrisoned and the 200–300 veterans surplus to this requirement could be shipped east. This force would be 'amply strong enough to overcome Koti without aid'. It could then return to Wanganui to join the growing army facing Titokowaru. Here, Whitmore underestimated Te Kooti, but his basic premiss was sound. Defeating Te Kooti would not be easy, but it would be easier than defeating Titokowaru.

Despite the widespread panic in Wellington Province over the danger presented by Titokowaru, the government took its courage in both hands and assented to Whitmore's bold plan. It did so with great trepidation, however. Whitmore was ordered to leave Wanganui as secure as possible against attack. He complied by withdrawing to the Kai-iwi Stream, ten miles north of Wanganui Town, thus adding another tract of country to the area abandoned to Titokowaru after Moturoa. A defensive system was set up, based on the fortifications of Wanganui Town and several redoubts along the Kai-iwi. This was garrisoned by 180 Imperial troops, at least 200 good militia and volunteers, and 240 armed constabulary. New recruits tripled the number of constabulary by the end of December. Reserves of 700 further militia and up to 500 Wanganui *kupapa* completed the defending force.[3]

The government remained nervous despite these measures. Haultain informed Whitmore that 'if you cannot settle affairs there [on the East Coast] and be back at Wanganui . . . within a month, I shall say you have failed in your promises, and have no right to expect me to believe you again.' Only days after Whitmore had actually departed, Haultain's doubts grew into a virtual change of heart. The Colonel was 'urgently required at Wanganui'. 'The sooner Whitmore gets back the better as the people are in great alarm.' Under this heavy responsibility, with his own reputation as well as the fate of the colony clearly at stake, Whitmore set off for the East Coast.[4]

I THE NGATAPA CAMPAIGN

THE IMMEDIATE OBJECTIVE OF WHITMORE'S EAST COAST strategy was Te Kooti's stronghold of Ngatapa. The fortress was situated on a high hill in the midst of mountain country, about fifteen miles northwest of the modern locality of Ngatapa and thirty-five miles from Poverty Bay. The hill rose 800 feet above a ridge at its base. A lower hill, subsequently called 'the Crow's Nest', protruded from the same ridge about half a mile to the east. Ngatapa hilltop was triangular—the colonists compared its shape to a tadpole or an open fan.[5] A narrow 'razor-backed' ridge, extending west from the apex of the triangle, formed the tail or handle. The only reasonable approach was along the main ridge from the Crow's Nest to the base of the triangle. On the south flank, the sides of the bush-clad hill dropped away steeply and the north side was 'nearly perpendicular'.[6]

The Ngatapa defences were progressively improved by Te Kooti throughout December. The main fortifications were three straight lines of trench and high earth parapet. The outermost line covered, but did not enclose, two small springs, the garrison's main water supply. All these lines faced east, and the extremely difficult approaches from other directions were covered by a single line of entrenchment. Bunkers and rifle pits in the interior of the *pa* completed the defences.

Ngatapa had a number of theoretical tactical deficiencies. The water supply was not secure, and the parapets were too wide to allow guns to be depressed to cover the ground immediately outside them.[7] The bunkers apparently lacked the depth or twisted entrance necessary to block a shell or divert its blast. Little thought had been given to the creation of traps and diversions, used in the past to destroy British assaults. The garrison was much weaker than is generally supposed. There were at least 500 people in the *pa* at the time of Whitmore's attack, but most of these were *Ringatu* women and children and Poverty Bay prisoners. Several estimates, based on head-counts and inside information, show that the effective garrison was small—between 115 and 200 men.[8] But the natural strength of the position, together with the courage and excellent discipline of its defenders, meant that these weaknesses were minor in themselves. Ngatapa was all but impossible to take by assault. 'The bare idea of taking it by storm is utterly inadmissible.'[9]

The real weakness of the *pa* was as much strategic as tactical: it could be virtually surrounded. The process of investment would not be easy, nor would it be complete. On the south face, and on the razor-backed ridge, the besiegers would have to scramble round from the east and cling precariously to the steep slopes. Without the enormous numbers necessary to cordon off the bush at the bottom of the hill, they could not cover the north face at all, and escape down this might be possible for the desperate. But what the modern *pa* system demanded was not a perilous exit for the disorganized flight of individuals, but an adequate route of retreat. This should permit the removal of wounded and equipment, and prevent close pursuit either by allowing effective rearguard action, or the lapse of considerable time between the evacuation and its discovery. Ngatapa had no such route of retreat. It was this which gave the weakness of the water supply its significance, and it was this which made the place more a traditional than a modern *pa*. That Ngatapa was an ancient Tuhoe stronghold serves merely to confirm this fact.

Soon after he arrived at Poverty Bay, Whitmore learned from those involved in the attack of 5 December that Ngatapa could be invested, and from the outset he intended to take advantage of this weakness. Whitmore's transfer to the East Coast was therefore a potentially decisive act of grand strategy. Using their monopoly of steam transport, the only European technical advantage which the Maoris could not counter, the colonists sud-

denly placed the core of an effective field force on the East Coast for the
first time. Unlike tribal levies and local militia, this force was capable of
conducting a siege. This, with the inherent weakness of Ngatapa, created a
theoretical opportunity for the colonists to destroy one of their two enemies.
But the opportunity had still to be grasped in practice, and this depended
upon three variables: whether Te Kooti would wait to be besieged; whether
Whitmore could muster enough men for the task; and whether he could
supply them for long enough. The interplay of these three factors is the
story of the Ngatapa campaign.

The first variable, the continued presence of Te Kooti at Ngatapa, came
close to ending the campaign before it had properly begun. Between 5 and
11 December, Whitmore received reports that the *Ringatu* forces had abandoned the *pa* and retired inland. These reports were false, and Whitmore
was later hypocritically mocked for believing them. Lieutenant Gascoyne,
for example, poured retrospective scorn on those who accepted the 'foolish
rumour'—presumably forgetting that he himself had been an author of it.[10]
But at the time, the information seemed convincing and, with the crisis on
the West Coast in mind, Whitmore acted on it. He announced that the
operation was over, and on 12 December began embarking his men on the
colonial steamer *Sturt* for Wanganui. Fortunately for the colonists, 'the
Sturt objected' by holing itself, and the troops were landed while the vessel
was repaired.[11]

Te Kooti chose this moment to make a second descent on Poverty Bay.
On 13 December, in a lightning foray, he killed three incautious Europeans
and had the better of a skirmish with *kupapa* at Oweta. Whitmore pursued
him 'but was fairly outmarched', losing two men to Te Kooti's sharpshooters in the process.[12] Ironically, this brilliant, pin-prick raid, brought
off in the teeth of greatly superior government forces, kept Whitmore's East
Coast strategy alive. For there was now no doubt that Te Kooti remained
based at Ngatapa.

Having discovered that, for the moment at least, his target remained in
place, Whitmore had to assemble sufficient men for a siege. He was soon
compelled to admit that his initial optimism had been misplaced, and that
his West Coast veterans would have to be supplemented by at least 300 men
from local sources. Despite the presence of the Native Minister, J. C. Richmond, who acted both as government legate and Whitmore's Commissary-
General, this presented problems. The local settlers held the government
responsible for the Poverty Bay disaster; McLean, their uncrowned king,
was disinclined to co-operate; and Whitmore's unpopularity among the East
Coast settlers was barely exceeded by Te Kooti's. The Colonel was welcomed
at Poverty Bay with placards stating 'The Gravedigger has arrived'. The
local press was so unhelpful that one of Whitmore's few friends was led to
remark: 'it would have been a great saving of life and property if a few
newspaper "editors" and "own correspondents" had been hanged before
the campaign commenced.' Whitmore believed that the local settlers were
purposely obstructing him, and only twenty volunteers or militia eventually

accompanied his expedition. He reportedly tolerated their presence 'only for the purpose of having them still to growl at and insult'.[13]

The attitude of McLean and his network of clients and allies was still more damaging. Ever since Te Kooti's escape from the Chathams, the Superintendent had been bombarding Wellington with appeals for reinforcements. When informed on 28 November that his prayers were to be answered in the form of Colonel Whitmore, he decided that the cure was worse than the disease. He wrote privately that nothing could be 'more offensive' to East Coast settlers than the Colonel's presence, and that *kupapa* antagonism to Whitmore was 'a deep-rooted prejudice . . . amounting to a superstitious belief'. If Whitmore came, he prophesied, 'the colony will lose the services of upwards of 1500 natives'. Finally, he bluntly asked the government to 'take Whitmore back', and organized a petition to the same effect, reportedly paying agents to collect signatures.[14] But McLean's efforts failed, and Whitmore lost no time in giving fresh cause for offence. He superseded and ignored Captain Westrupp, the commander at Poverty Bay and a client of McLean. Westrupp poured out his resentment of 'the great tyrant' in letters to his chief. In case McLean should waver in his dislike, he was informed that Whitmore 'states that you sold yourself for £5,000'—an obscure reference, but by no means an improbable example of Whitmore's tact.[15]

The end result was that McLean withdrew his support from the general government war effort. Some elements of this internecine feud were harmless enough. McLean sent back an official whose services had been rejected by Richmond, noting that 'he is really a good man but is unfortunately liable at times to mental derangement'. Richmond complained that the Napier band seemed to be reserved for the triumphal entry of 'pet Maoris', whereas 'when he or Col. Whitmore came here they never had the band'.[16] But other consequences of the feud were less farcical. McLean's antipathy cost Whitmore the services, not only of the Napier band, but also of 700 Ngati Kahungunu.

When Whitmore arrived at Poverty Bay on 4 December, he found nearly 600 local troops there—sixty European volunteers, 330 Ngati Kahungunu and 192 Ngati Porou.[17] The problems with the volunteers have already been noted, and within two weeks the Ngati Kahungunu had been transferred to Wairoa. From there, joined by 400 fellow tribesmen, they mounted their own expedition against Te Kooti. McLean pursuaded the Ngati Kahungunu to make this expedition despite a government veto, and it split the campaign into two. Its leaders assumed that Te Kooti would leave Ngatapa as soon as Whitmore approached, and they hoped to catch him inland. They were wrong, and the Wairoa expedition consequently proved useless. Indeed it was worse than useless, since it left Whitmore without enough men to besiege Ngatapa.[18]

The only alternative source of men was Ngati Porou. Their leader, Ropata, was determined to return home to Waiapu to refit after the effort of the Poverty Bay Campaign. Whitmore argued that the real reason for their departure was hatred of Ngati Kahungunu; McLean and the local settlers argued that it was hatred of Whitmore.[19] Whatever his motives, Ropata left with most of his men on 16 December. The campaign now turned on whether he would be back in time. Thus Whitmore's arrival at Poverty Bay had been greeted by a mass exodus of *kupapa*. McLean had managed to make his prophecy self-fulfilling.

While Whitmore waited for Ngati Porou, he made active preparations for his advance. He massed supplies at Poverty Bay and reconnoitred his route. Tension mounted over whether Te Kooti would remain at Ngatapa. Richmond frankly doubted it, and McLean's party, of course, were pessimistic. Westrupp wrote: 'Whitmore [is] as usual fretting and fuming getting up large stores of food and ammunition ready for an expidition against the enemy stronghold—I don't think he will find him at home.'[20] However, in the week after Ropata's departure, Whitmore was joined by recruits from the south and a fresh constabulary division—sixty 'de-tribalised' Arawa —from Tauranga, bringing his strength to 320 constabulary.[21] This did not solve his manpower problem, but it did ameliorate it, and he decided to proceed on the assumption that Ngati Porou would join him shortly. On Christmas Eve, the Ngatapa expedition at last began, and on 27 December Whitmore took up a position three miles from the fortress.

Until Ngati Porou arrived, Whitmore could do no more, because without them he did not have enough men to encircle Ngatapa. The manpower shortage also precluded a convoy system to bring up supplies. Instead, Whitmore planned that his force should carry its supplies with it, lightening the load progressively by forming depots along the route from Poverty Bay. Four depots were accordingly set up: Forts Fraser, St. John, Arawa, and Richmond—the last at Whitmore's position of 27 December, close to Ngatapa. Under this system, the amount of supplies was fixed on the assumption that investment operations would begin on 27 December, and that Ropata would bring his own supplies. As the crucial date passed by, with no sign of Ngati Porou, Whitmore's resources wasted away fruitlessly. Furthermore, if Te Kooti had ever had any doubts about the government's intention to attack, he now had none, and could leave as he chose. Thus Whitmore sat before Ngatapa, with the three pre-requisites of victory—reinforcements, guaranteed supply, and the presence of the enemy—still uncertain.

Meanwhile, Ngati Porou had in fact arrived at Poverty Bay on 26 December, but were delaying their march because Ropata was ill. Richmond tried to hurry them up, but even this most 'loyal' of *kupapa* tribes was not subject to orders. 'I am much put out by these Ngati Poro fellows', wrote Richmond, 'it is terribly frustrating to have to do with such allies.' On 29 December, they were still only half-way to Ngatapa, and a desperate Whitmore rode back to urge them on. This created a fresh problem: Whitmore's normal manner with those he believed to be his subordinates was unlikely to impress Ropata. But Whitmore was warned 'not to bounce Rapata', and he managed to contain himself. Ropata agreed to hasten his advance and on the morning of 30 December, Ngati Porou arrived at Fort Richmond.[22]

But just as one problem appeared solved, another made itself felt. The delays, combined with the fact that Ngati Porou had brought little ammunition with them, upset the supply system based on the depots. More food and ammunition had somehow to be brought up. On 30 December, a steamer arrived at Poverty Bay with seven tons of biscuit and 10,000 rounds. Richmond had these brought up by cart to Fort Arawa, then by packhorse to Fort Richmond. From there to the Crow's Nest, where Whitmore had decided to begin his siegelines, they had to be carried by a fatigue party of thirty men—all that could be spared. These men, mostly members of the much-maligned Poverty Bay militia, made several trips a day with huge loads over ground so rough that ponies fell over when attempting it. Richmond, unable to find enough drivers for his carts, drove at least one up himself. By such desperate expedients, the besiegers of Ngatapa were supplied day by day.[23]

The difficult process of encircling Ngatapa now began. On 31 December, the whole force moved to the Crow's Nest and fortified it. Detachments then advanced towards the *pa* and began digging in. Snipers exchanged long-range fire and the government troops pushed forward their approach-trenches until the best exit from the *pa*, along the main ridge, was blocked. At least five adequate paths, however, remained open when night fell.

The steep and broken ground about Ngatapa, together with the accurate fire of Te Kooti's sharpshooters, meant that the siegelines had to be built up step by step. At 5 a.m. on 1 January Major Fraser with 100 constabulary, and Ropata's co-chief Hotene, with 100 Ngati Porou, scrambled along the south slope of Ngatapa hill to block the razor-backed ridge in rear of the *pa*. Their advanced guard took up a precarious position across the ridge and clung there. At 7 a.m. Ropata, with eighty Ngati Porou and the Arawa constabulary, began extending left from the siegelines on the main ridge, supported by Whitmore and the main body. This process continued all day. Though the garrison were already trying to conserve ammunition, Ropata lost two men killed. But he succeeded in sealing off the base of the Ngatapa triangle, and it was subsequently discovered that he had cut off the garrison from the two small springs—its main water supply. The final encirclement move was carried out the same day. Major Roberts and his division followed Fraser and Hotene's route halfway around the south side of the *pa*, and dug into the slope below Te Kooti's entrenchments. Though the garrison rolled boulders down on them, they maintained their position, blocking the last three paths out of the *pa*. Thus, after many trials and tribulations, the investment of Ngatapa was completed.

Most of the actual fighting occurred on 2–4 January, after the result of the campaign had practically been decided. The garrison made belated attempts to break through the siegelines. Small groups made several sorties, all of which were repelled. A counter-sap was dug, probably designed to cover a large-scale sortie. Efforts were made to dislodge Fraser's men from the razor-backed ridge, but the constabulary clung bravely to their position. Two small government attacks were made, and these were subsequently interpreted as the first steps in an all-out assault. In fact they were reactions to the garrison's escape attempts; one took the counter-sap, the other was designed to relieve the pressure on Fraser. There was a minor scare when Ngati Porou ran out of ammunition, but the constabulary made over some of theirs, and on the night of 4 January the government noose seemed tight. Then, early the next morning, Te Kooti and his people lowered themselves by ropes over the precipice on the north side of Ngatapa and escaped.[24]

It might be assumed that, as so often before, the Maoris had snatched victory from the jaws of defeat, and it is true that the almost miraculous escape prevented complete disaster for Te Kooti. But it did not prevent severe defeat. The escape route used was so poor that no effective rearguard action could be organized, and the flight was quickly discovered. Ngati Porou and the Arawa constabulary were unleashed in pursuit—European troops were not used because the *kupapa* feared they might mistake allies for enemies. For two days, the *Ringatu* fugitives were hunted through the bush and most, weak from lack of food and water and with little ammunition to defend themselves, were caught. About 135 women and children and 140 men were taken prisoner.

Some 120 of the male prisoners were then killed. This was not done in the heat of battle. The men were collected and executed in batches 'after a few questions'.[25] The killings were carried out primarily by Ngati Porou, but the colonists must bear a large share of the responsibility. Ropata was praised for the killings and, though this was generally glossed over, the Arawa— colonial regulars—also took part in them. Whitmore and Richmond forbade the slaying of women and children, with mixed success, but they endorsed the slaughter of the men. Richmond reported: 'Ngati Porou are off on a long chase today, intent upon exterminating "Iwi Kohura" [*Ringatu*], and I thought it right, and in accordance with the wishes of the Government and country, not to with-hold their hands.'[26]

The Ngatapa Massacre was perpetrated in revenge for Poverty Bay, but this served only to compound the tragedy. The occupants of Ngatapa included many Maori prisoners from Poverty Bay and, since scarce food and water had mostly been reserved for the fighting men, these people were the weakest of all. There can be no doubt that many were caught and killed by the government forces. Poverty Bay was 'avenged' partly on its victims.

Ngatapa did not destroy Te Kooti and it did not end his resistance. The prophet's magnetism and determination were such that he was eventually able to reconstruct a dangerous guerilla band, and to use it. It could be argued from this that, like Rewi at Orakau, Te Kooti left the British with an empty victory. But there were several differences between the two Maori defeats. Orakau had no strategic effect, whereas Ngatapa crippled Te Kooti for three months and freed Whitmore to concentrate the growing colonial army against Titokowaru. Orakau cost Rewi perhaps one-third of his garrison, whereas Te Kooti lost two-thirds at Ngatapa. The Orakau garrison was only a fraction of the Kingite army, whereas the Ngatapa garrison was the whole of Te Kooti's. Orakau was a comprehensive disappointment for the British, whereas Ngatapa ended an unbroken succession of defeat. But, in the long run, perhaps the most important difference was that Orakau was an exceptional Kingite error, whereas Ngatapa manifested an enduring flaw in Te Kooti's generalship. Despite inadequate supplies and the clear possibility that the British would invest, Te Kooti had refused repeated opportunities to retire with his forces intact. His reasons were a mystery to his followers and they are a mystery to this writer, but the decision itself was clearly a major error of generalship. Ngatapa had every chance of resisting an assault, but little chance of resisting a siege. With the lesser inadequacies of the Ngatapa defences, and the evidence of subsequent stands in *pa*, this error indicates that Te Kooti, the master of guerilla warfare, was not a master of the modern *pa* system.

II THE COLLAPSE OF TITOKOWARU'S RESISTANCE

IF TITOKOWARU'S EARLY OPERATIONS MAKE AN EPIC STORY OF success against the odds, his last campaign is a strange tragedy. On 3 February 1869, in the face of a renewed colonist advance, the seemingly invincible Maori general abandoned his finest *pa* without a fight. Most of his warriors then left him, and his conquests were re-occupied by the colonists. Though Titokowaru himself remained uncaught and independent, in effect he had lost his war. This section begins with a brief narrative of these events, then addresses the central problem of why Titokowaru's resistance collapsed in the way it did. Finally, some comments are made on Titokowaru's historical reputation.

While Colonel Whitmore was absent on the East Coast (2 December 1868 to 16 January 1869), the colonial forces at Wanganui built up into a small army, eventually approaching 2,000 men. Titokowaru now faced more enemies than Heke and Kawiti in the Northern War, but the government attempted no major offensive moves against him until Whitmore and his battle-hardened constabulary returned to Wanganui from the Ngatapa campaign.

As they had done before Moturoa, Whitmore and others wondered at Titokowaru's failure to take the offensive himself in this period. But of course 400 men could not attack 2,000. Titokowaru did not remain inactive, however. He improved his fortifications at Tauranga-ika until it became one of the most formidable modern *pa* ever built. He devastated the Wanganui hinterland, burning farms and abandoned military posts, and driving off horses and cattle. His raiding parties occasionally clashed with enemy patrols, but as they themselves acknowledged, the colonists could do little to stop the destruction except attack the raiders' base at Tauranga-ika. Thus, for the third time, Titokowaru sought to force the colonists to attack him in a carefully prepared position. Despite the result of the two earlier campaigns, public outcry over Maori depredations, a vast numerical advantage, and the new confidence born of Ngatapa ensured that Whitmore was willing to oblige.

The Colonel returned to Wanganui on 16 January, and set up his head-quarters at Kai-iwi four days later. His field forces numbered 1,753 men, including 405 *kupapa*.[27] His lieutenants included Kepa te Rangihiwinui and Lieutenant-Colonels St. John and Lyon—as well as McDonnell, who had returned to the front in a subordinate capacity. On 21 January, the colonial army began a cautious and methodical advance towards Tauranga-ika, cutting a road and sending out reconnaissance parties as it went. Mounted Maori patrols were seen on the 23rd, and the colonist van lost three men in skirmishes on the 26th. Early on 2 February, Whitmore finally arrived before Tauranga-ika. His artillery opened up, and he began entrenching in front of the *pa*, pushing his trenches to within fifty yards by nightfall.

Whitmore reported that his men 'all seemed very anxious to close with the enemy and were apparently in excellent spirits'. That evening, they sang ballads in their trenches, and were applauded and encouraged to continue by the opposing garrison. The fraternization was somewhat spoiled by one Maori wit, who shouted: 'Come on Pakeha and be food for the Maori, we are waiting to eat you, send all the fat ones in front.' The press corps accompanying the army left the colonial public in no doubt that a great and hard-fought battle was imminent. 'The fate of Wanganui and surrounding districts for many years to come depends upon the success or failure of Colonel Whitmore's force in the engagement now daily expected.' The colonists greatly outnumbered the Maoris and they included many veterans, but 'the enemy is strongly posted, enthusiastic; united and determined'. Everyone waited with bated breath for the decisive clash. Then, on the morning of 3 February, the colonists discovered that Tauranga-ika had been evacuated during the night.[28]

Though it was not apparent to the colonists for six weeks, the abandonment of Tauranga-ika marked the beginning of the end of Titokowaru's resistance. His army immediately began to disperse, 'whole hapus were breaking away'. With forty loyal warriors, Titokowaru covered the retreat of his erstwhile allies in a series of fierce rearguard actions.[29] On 3 February, the leading government pursuers had four men shot in ambushes, and lost Titokowaru's trail. Numerous patrols were sent out, and contact was restored two weeks later, but the colonists were again checked by an ambush in which seven constabulary were killed.

These ambushes hampered Whitmore's 600-man pursuit force, and they might have disheartened troops of lesser calibre, but the picked Europeans and *kupapa* involved had reached a high pitch of efficiency, and they pushed on with a terrible eagerness. They were encouraged by the desire for revenge, and by the offer of head-money for enemy corpses—some *kupapa* and at least one European took this literally and brought Whitmore the smoke-cured heads of several Maori stragglers.[30] On 13 March, after several frustrating near-misses, they came upon Titokowaru with his Ngaruahine warriors and their women and children at Otautu. The government troops moved in to attack the unfortified camp, but were held by a thin line of Maori riflemen, helped by a heavy fog. First the non-combatants, then Titokowaru and his men, escaped almost unscathed. In this the last of Titokowaru's victories, the government lost six men killed and twelve wounded, while the Maoris lost only two or three stragglers, 'old cripples probably', caught and killed.[31]

The government troops continued the hunt. One colonist wrote: 'I do not see how they can escape from us, hampered as they . . . are with women, children, and wounded.'[32] On 24 March, Titokowaru was indeed nearly caught at Te Ngaere swamp, but again managed to escape. He made his way to Totara, in the Upper Waitara area of North Taranaki. After a despairing appeal for the help of Australian aboriginal trackers, Whitmore finally admitted defeat in a private letter to the Defence Minister, mixing his metaphors in frustration. 'It is with the greatest regret and vexation that I have to report that after a bush campaign such as there has not yet been in this country for distance traversed and fatigue undergone, I believe Titokowaru has slipped through my fingers under my nose.'[33]

During the pursuit of Titokowaru from Tauranga-ika, the Kingite attack on Taranaki, mentioned in the last chapter, occurred. On 13 February, about fifteen Ngati Maniapoto warriors attacked the Pukearuhe Redoubt at Whitecliffs, the northern-most European outpost in Taranaki. Though the redoubt was theoretically a military post, the inhabitants were off their guard, and one woman, four children, and the missionary J. Whitely were killed, in addition to three military settlers.[34] The incident is generally dismissed as the isolated act of a few individuals, but there are indications that the raid itself, though not the killing of harmless civilians, was sanctioned by the Kingite leadership.[35] The raid might therefore be seen as a declaration of war by the King Movement. At the time, the colonists certainly saw it as such, and placed New Plymouth on a war footing, strongly reinforcing the local volunteers and militia. During March, a force of Kingite warriors assembled at Mokau, just north of the Taranaki frontier. It was persistently rumoured that they were about to invade the province, and on 5 April Whitmore's field force marched round Mount Egmont to New Plymouth.

Though the King Movement probably hoped to restrict hostilities to Taranaki, the situation was extremely tense. What the colonial government feared, of course, was that the Kingites would combine with Titokowaru. This would divide the colonial forces, multiply their enemies, and severely reduce *kupapa* support. The Arawa constabulary, together with a recently arrived Ngati Porou division, would hunt Titokowaru for ever, but they were not prepared to fight the King Movement. Even the fearless Major Kepa, an advocate of war with almost anybody, 'seems startled at the idea of 600 Ngati Maniapoto being at Taranaki'.[36] Titokowaru was in communication with the King—and apparently also with Te Kooti.[37] His position at Totara was less than two days' march from Mokau, and he no doubt wanted an alliance. But by early April, the collapse of his support was clearly apparent, and he lost his value as an ally. The Kingites made no further moves and the colonists, wisely curbing their rage at the Pukearuhe raid, did likewise. Had the raid occurred two weeks earlier, the government would have faced a two-front war on the West Coast, and Whitmore would have had to suspend his advance on Tauranga-ika and reinforce Taranaki. But, for Titokowaru, the raid occurred too late. Perhaps, in the long run, it also occurred too late for the King Movement.

From April 1869, there was no more fighting on the West Coast. Whitmore again transferred the core of his field force to the East Coast, leaving from New Plymouth mid-April. About 160 constabulary, backed by 350 other first-line troops, were left at Taranaki. Some 1,600 men—still substantially more than the force operating against Te Kooti—remained on active service south of the Waingongoro, guarding against Titokowaru's return to the area, and hunting down his erstwhile allies of Ngarauru, and the Ngati Ruanui *hapu* of Pakakohe and Tangahoe. A few of these people, including at least one old woman, were killed and many were induced to surrender.[38]

Titokowaru himself was left alone at Totara, and it is important to note that the colonists' forbearance was not voluntary. The chief's location was no secret, and the terrain around Totara was no more difficult than that traversed in the pursuit from Tauranga-ika. There were no further attacks partly because the government did not feel able to risk hostilities with the neighbouring tribes, and partly because Titokowaru was still dangerous. It seems that he began to regain some of his influence in late 1869: some of his people rejoined him, he collected ammunition, and he is said to have sent thirty men to join Te Kooti. He may at this stage have formed some kind of alliance with the influential religious leader Te Whiti O Rongomai of Parihaka. Te Whiti was a pacifist, but Titokowaru left the government in no doubt that he would fight if attacked. On 17 September 1869, a government spy reported that 'Titiko says that if the Pakeha comes to attack him he will turn round and fight them. . . . I told you before that Titiko will not give in.' A year later, Titokowaru was reported to have said 'that he and the Government were carrying their guns upright, one watched the other—and when the government bring their guns to the "present" he would also bring his to the present.' Titokowaru's downfall was not complete. Throughout the 1870s, his armed presence helped protect the area between the Warea and Waingongoro as a bastion of Maori independence.[39]

On 2 February 1869, Titokowaru was at the peak of his success. He had an unbroken series of victories behind him, and he faced his foes from a *pa* which he had spent eleven weeks turning into an engineering masterpiece. His force was stronger than ever—five times the number with which he had begun the war—and, as we have seen, it was full of confidence. On 3 February he abandoned Tauranga-ika and his force began to break up.

Within two months South Taranaki had changed hands yet again, and the war was lost. Why did Titokowaru's resistance collapse so suddenly and completely? The evacuation of Tauranga-ika was clearly the turning point, and the reason for this is the key to the larger question.

The official explanation for the events of 3 February was that Titokowaru abandoned his *pa* because he feared that the colonist attack would succeed. Whitmore wrote that 'as Titokowaru must have had plentiful supplies, it is difficult to imagine any reason, except fear, for his abandoning it.'[40] The claim that Titokowaru was frightened out of Tauranga-ika by the colonists was widely accepted, and became a vital part of the interpretation of the war. In fact, three forms of attack were open to Whitmore on 2 February: bombardment, assault, and encirclement. Only the first was actually tried, and this could not have forced the Maori evacuation. The colonist artillery was weak—two light Armstrong guns and a few small Cohorn mortars. Except for a high watch-tower which the look-outs probably left once firing commenced, Tauranga-ika had excellent anti-artillery defences, including deep bunkers roofed with timber, earth, and galvanised iron taken from settler houses. As we would therefore expect, the bombardment of 2 February was almost harmless—only one person was wounded.[41]

The notion that fear of an assault led the Maoris to leave is equally improbable. Tauranga-ika was not simply impervious to shellfire, it was immensely strong in other respects. Once the enemy bombardment was over, the garrison would leave their bunkers and occupy two firing lines, one above the other. These were protected by a double palisade, a deep firing trench, and an earth parapet. A third level of fire would come from the low *taumaihi* located in the bastions at each angle of the *pa*. The bastions also enfiladed every possible approach for an assault party. Communication trenches ensured that the garrison could concentrate in safety at threatened points. No wonder that, after inspecting the *pa*, experienced colonial observers considered it impregnable to assault. 'It is more than doubtful if we should have taken it by storm'; 'In all my experience in the last war I have never seen a more formidable position.'[42] Rather inconsistently, Colonel Whitmore himself agreed. 'No troops in the world could have hewn their way through a double row of strong palisades, backed by rifle pits and flanked by two-storied erections, such as are constructed in this fortification, defended by excellent shots and desperate men.'[43] Having reached this conclusion after inspecting the *pa*, Whitmore naturally denied that he had ever intended an assault. But there were signs that on 2 February he was planning to launch one the next morning.[44] Had he done so, he would have suffered a terrible defeat. The prospect of an assault which he was certain to repel is unlikely to have frightened Titokowaru out of Tauranga-ika.

At first sight, encirclement might seem to have been a better prospect for the colonists. Unlike Te Ngutu and Moturoa, Tauranga-ika was not actually inside the bush. But it was within easy musket range on two flanks. An attempt at complete investment would therefore have involved entering the bush. In the light of Titokowaru's earlier battles, we would expect him to have catered for this by constructing hidden positions in the bush. Whitmore later denied that the Maoris had any intention of fighting outside the *pa*, and claimed that he planned to make a complete encirclement on 3 February. But, in a report of 2 December, Whitmore himself noted the existence of 'further defences' in the bush outside Tauranga-ika, and Titokowaru had had two months in which to improve these to his satisfaction. A newspaper correspondent also referred, on 2 February, to a Maori 'position further back in the bush'.[45] Whitmore could easily have begun an encircling move on 2 February, and we may guess that, whatever he said subsequently, his tardiness stemmed from a reluctance to encounter hidden bush positions. His claim to the contrary was presumably made to support the suggestion that he had never intended to assault.

The abandonment of Tauranga-ika was not the result of any direct colonist threat. Another explanation, put forward by a recent writer, is that the Maoris left because they were short of food. This is unconvincing. Whitmore's belief that Titokowaru 'must have had plentiful supplies' has already been quoted. The *pa* had good communication with the area that supplied its garrison in normal times; a great deal of plundered food, especially livestock, had been collected from settler farms; and several large caches of potatoes were later discovered nearby.[46] A further possibility is that the Maoris had run out of ammunition. According to a government spy, Titokowaru himself later claimed that this was the case.[47] Despite his reported imprimatur, the claim is very hard to accept. Throughout the war Titokowaru had received adequate ammunition supplies through neutral tribes, and from captured enemy stocks.[48] There was no major expenditure of ammunition before 3 February, and the Maori rearguard fired off rounds freely afterwards. And why should Titokowaru put so much effort into fortifying Tauranga-ika and inducing the colonists to advance on it if he did not have the ammunition to resist the lightest attack?

There is one consideration which militates against all these explanations: most of Titokowaru's force left him as a result of events at Tauranga-ika. Neither a temporary problem such as food or ammunition shortage, nor a withdrawal to avoid a powerful colonist attack, is likely to have had this effect. Strategic withdrawals were a characteristic of the modern *pa* system, and were not seen as defeats by the Maoris. The only explanation which accommodates this factor was put forward by Kimble Bent, a deserter from the British army who followed Titokowaru throughout the war. In his memoirs, dictated to James Cowan, Bent stated that Titokowaru was having a sexual liaison with the wife of an allied chief. This became known to the people in Tauranga-ika, presumably on the night of 2 February, and they concluded that this destroyed their leader's sacred prestige—'*mana-tapu*' in Bent's phrase. The garrison felt that 'it would be disastrous to make a stand there after their *tohunga*, their spiritual head and their warleader, had lost his *mana-tapu*'. A council of chiefs decided on immediate evacuation.[49]

This explanation may seem far-fetched, but Bent's account of the incident, though brief and given fifty years after the event, is fairly convincing, and his recollections are reliable at other points.[50] Being inside Tauranga-ika at the time, he was in a good position to know, and had no obvious reason to distort the truth. His story is supported by an independent and contemporary source. On 4 March 1869, R. Parris, the Taranaki Civil Commissioner, passed on information from neutral Maoris who had been in contact with Titokowaru. 'Ahitana's Natives report that Titokowaru's followers are leaving him, in consequence of his intriguing with their women.'[51] Further, it seems that the dispersal of Titokowaru's followers resulted from his very sudden loss of prestige and authority—whether through an illicit liaison, or from some other cause. The confidence of the Tauranga-ika garrison on 2 February included a continued trust in Titokowaru's supernatural powers. A Maori story, dating from that day, attributed the ineffectiveness of the colonist bombardment to these. 'Titokowaru's god and his great priestly mana prevented the shells from entering the pa. He stayed them just outside the palisade wall, just as if he had put out his hand and so they fell short, all outside the stockade.'[52] But after Tauranga-ika 'great dissension prevailed' amongst the Maoris, and prisoners reported that disillusionment with Titokowaru caused the numerous desertions. Titokowaru's subordinate chiefs were 'very dissatisfied with him and intend to leave him'. The Maori army melted away, not for military, economic, or general political reasons, but because the bond which united them, their leader's *mana-tapu*, had broken.[53]

Kimble Bent's explanation fits the facts better than any other, and a few further points are worth mentioning. First, Titokowaru's secular authority and his special connection with the supernatural world were closely interwoven in the minds of his followers. A blow to one was a blow to the other. Secondly, at a more mundane level, an affair would have cost Titokowaru the support of his partner's husband—and his kith and kin. Finally, according to Bent, another *tohunga* partly restored Titokowaru's sanctity in a religious ceremony in late 1869, and the fact that the partial renewal of the chief's influence dates from that time supports the rest of Bent's account.[54] All the same, it seems strange that Titokowaru's great *mana* should prove so fragile, and Bent's explanation does not fully satisfy this writer. An element of mystery remains, and its elimination must be left to a student of the oral history of the South Taranaki people.

Titokowaru often appears in nineteenth-century writings as an inhuman monster. He and his followers were labelled 'fiends in human shape' and a species of 'wild beasts'. His 'ultra-barbarity' and even his appearance—'the ugliest and most villainous-looking Maori I ever saw'—were remarked upon,[55] but most emphasis was put on his cannibalism. The Auckland *Punch* placed this advertisement on his behalf, though the subject was rarely a joking matter.

TITO-KAWARU & CO.,
BUTCHERS AND DRYSALTERS
The Gorge — Patea — West Coast

> Families waited on in Town or Country at
> surprising short notice. A large supply
> of Cured Constable, Potted Pakeha, and
> Dried Militiamen always on hand.[56]

Titokowaru's followers did indulge in acts of ceremonial cannibalism, and
the chief made use of this to inspire terror among his enemies, and ritually
cement alliances among his friends. These acts were rare, they occurred as
strictly regulated religious ceremony involving the bodies of slain enemies,
and Titokowaru did not partake himself.[57] One might add that, as with the
headhunting initiated by Whitmore, the victims were already dead. This is
not to suggest that cannibalism was an acceptable activity, and still less that
Titokowaru was more merciful than other generals of the wars. When his
warriors met unarmed civilians, they sometimes killed them, and wounded
enemies were always slain. But 'atrocities' on the government side were as
horrifying. At Handley's Farm on 30 November 1868, volunteer cavalry
killed Maori boys aged ten and twelve.[58] In another, less well-known, incident on 15 December 1868, the cavalry 'murdered two old Maoris, a man
and a woman, burnt their bodies and did other atrocities which if done by
the Maoris on us would create a great sensation'.[59] When, during May-July
1869, some of Titokowaru's one-time allies came in and surrendered on the
promise that they would not be harmed, the men were suddenly shipped to
prison with hard labour in Otago, where many of them died.[60]

Titokowaru no more deserves to be remembered solely for his 'atrocities'
than does Whitmore, and his reputation for savagery served to shift attention from his military achievements. Another kind of alternative emphasis
worked similarly. After the war, the colonists began to stress the deeds and
misdeeds of Te Kooti, at the expense of Titokowaru. Te Kooti was in fact
less dangerous to the colonists, and this was widely acknowledged at the
time, but he was also less dangerous to remember. As anyone at all familiar
with the received version will admit, this trend continues into the modern
literature. In some books Titokowaru does not figure at all, or lurks in the
background. In others, Titokowaru's achievements are partially recognized,
but the reader is left in no doubt that Te Kooti was the more important warleader of the two.

A more direct tendency to downplay Titokowaru's achievement can also
be discerned, though it never entirely succeeded. After Tauranga-ika, Whitmore was heavily criticized for 'allowing' Titokowaru to escape—'a greater
blunder than to allow Titoko to escape never was committed'. Initially the
colonists believed that the chief's evacuation of Tauranga-ika was some
deep stratagem, and that his power was as great as ever.[61] When it became
clear that Titokowaru's support had melted away, they concluded that his
downfall was due to some act of theirs. They had therefore to find it. The
official claim was that the occupation of Tauranga-ika was the necessary
'great success', and one modern historian accepts that 'Whitmore frightened
the Hauhaus out of it'.[62] But some contemporaries preferred to attribute

Titokowaru's collapse to Otautu, where he 'suffered a terrible defeat'.[63]
Thus there were two competing candidates for the position of decisive
British victory in Titokowaru's War, and in the subsequent years colonial
writers fell back on asserting that Titokowaru had been 'utterly defeated' or
'completely beaten' without being specific.[64] It is still very easy to conclude,
from more recent literature, that the colonists defeated Titokowaru.

False victory claims and alternative emphases which obscured the reality
do not exhaust the list of colonist responses to Titokowaru's War. Another,
less tangible, reaction was simply to play it down, to portray it as a minor
police action, a storm in a teacup, and even to forget about it. The deeper
reasons for this will be discussed in the Conclusion, but one factor is plain
enough. The humiliating defeats which Titokowaru inflicted on the colonists were not compensated for by any crushing victory. The attempts to
promote Tauranga-ika and Otautu to this status were too paradoxical to be
entirely satisfactory. Titokowaru lost his war, but the colonists did not win
it. If anything can be called an historical accident, it is the fall of
Titokowaru.

III   THE PURSUIT OF TE KOOTI

THE LAST PHASE OF THE NEW ZEALAND WARS CONSISTED IN A
variety of campaigns against Te Kooti, fought over a period of no less than
three years. The government forces, Maori and European, sought repeatedly
to catch and kill their elusive foe. Their determination arose partly from the
fact that Te Kooti alone kept alive the fire in the fern, which might easily
spread again, but largely from their desire for revenge on the perpetrator of
massacres. They failed, at a cost of hundreds of lives and hundreds of
thousands of pounds. On the other hand, Te Kooti's military power,
though repeatedly revived after defeat, was renewed in ever smaller
measure, and he made his last escape with only six followers to his name.
His final and permanent resurgence after 1872 was not a military
phenomenon.

After Ngatapa, Te Kooti remained quiet in the Northern Urewera, and
the colonists began to think that they had heard the last of him. Defeat had
left him with less than 100 followers, including sixty men and some women
of the original Chatham Island exiles.[65] Other women and those of the
children who had survived were probably apportioned among the Tuhoe, in
an ill-fated attempt to save them from the rigours of campaigning. This
force was too small to do much itself, and despair at the Ngatapa disaster
must have been great, but Te Kooti now displayed his remarkable powers
of recuperation. He planned a new raid, on Whakatane in the Bay of Plenty,
to obtain ammunition, of which he was desperately short, and to secure
recruits from the Ngati Awa and Whakatohea tribes, among whom he
already had sympathizers. Eight Whakatohea joined him early in February
1869, and another small section were persuaded to do likewise, possibly by

threats, when Te Kooti visited their *pa* of Ohiwa on 2 March.[66] Several
Tuhoe chiefs and their men also agreed to join the raid. One notable exception was Eru Tamaikowha, who at no stage supported Te Kooti. The
resulting force, though later assessed at 400–500 by the colonists, was given
as 160 men by Maori sources and this is by far the more likely figure.[67]

On 9 March 1869, these warriors moved down from the Urewera Mountains. A detachment of sixty men was sent to recruit among the Ngati
Manawa, and perhaps to establish a base at Tauaroa, while Te Kooti and
the remaining 100 men marched to the Ngati Pukeko *pa* of Raupora, three
miles from Whakatane. Te Kooti began by attempting to negotiate, but the
garrison apparently suspected him of treachery and opened fire. He then
besieged the *pa*, while detachments looted and burned Whakatane village
and Te Poronu mill, killing the French miller and two Maori women. But
there was no wholesale slaughter of civilians, and after a gallant resistance
the garrison of Raupora 'made a sort of treaty with Te Kooti', and
evacuated their *pa*. Some 200 militia and *kupapa* came up from Opotiki on
12 March, under Major W. G. Mair, but Mair considered Te Kooti too
strong to attack. By 15 March, when Arawa reinforcements increased
Mair's force to 450, Te Kooti had begun his retreat. Mair made contact
again, and followed the raiders to Tauaroa, but was unable to encircle them,
and, after standing his ground and defying the enemy for a day and a night,
Te Kooti slipped away. The colonists blamed Te Kooti's escape on Arawa
timidity, but the boldness of the raid seems to have disconcerted both
Europeans and Maoris.[68]

Te Kooti retired into the Urewera in late March. Though well-conceived
and handled, the raid had been disappointing. He had not lost the forty-five
killed of colonist estimates, but he had lost thirteen men, mainly in the
fighting at Raupora, and he had gained few recruits and little or no ammunition. A way of recouping the situation then presented itself. Te Kooti
learned that the Ngati Kahungunu of Wairoa and Mohaka had mounted an
expedition to Waikaremoana, presumably acting on reports that he was
camped there. This left Mohaka undefended. The place was the home of
the Ngati Pahauwera *hapu*, actively hostile to Te Kooti since his landing
from the Chathams, and a large supply of government ammunition was
known to be stored there. Te Kooti traversed the Urewera, crossed Waikaremoana by canoe, detached Te Waru to divert the Ngati Kahungunu and
prevent their premature return, and descended on Mohaka in a lightning
march. Te Kooti's accurate intelligence, instant decision, and capacity to inspire his tired men to rapid movement across the mountains, spelled doom
for the people of Mohaka.

Te Kooti's force again seems to have consisted of only 100 men, but
Mohaka contained barely a dozen warriors. These, supported by women
and old men, held out with great bravery in a stockade called Hiruhama
when the *Ringatu* warriors attacked on 10 April. A second stockade was captured—by Te Kooti's treachery according to most accounts, though the
occupants fired first, and a *Ringatu* warrior 'of great strength' lifted the gate

off its hinges. Unlike Whakatane, no mercy or restraint was shown to Mohaka. Some fifty-seven Maoris and seven Europeans, mostly women and children, were slaughtered, and the surrounding settlements were looted and burned. A great deal of plunder was taken, including horses, some ammunition (the rest was hidden or blown up by Ngati Pahauwera), and a great deal of rum from the Mohaka Hotel. 'Some of our men got very drunk', said Peita Kotuku, a veteran of the raid, 'and when they joined in the attack on [Hiruhama] . . . they behaved so recklessly, heedless of cover that they were shot dead. Te Kooti was very angry at his men getting drunk while they were fighting.' Te Kooti lost most of his twelve killed in this way. The government relieving forces had no better luck than at Poverty Bay or Whakatane. On 11 April, 100 Ngati Kahungunu under Ihaka Whanga came up, but fell into a prepared ambush and retreated. Other government forces arrived too late, or pursued too cautiously. Te Kooti left Mohaka on 12 April and retreated in leisurely fashion, pausing 'to enjoy the liquor from the hotel', before crossing the Lake into the Urewera.[69] These raids went some way towards replacing the men and *mana* lost at Ngatapa.

On the West Coast, in early April 1869, Whitmore had given up the pursuit of Titokowaru, and moved north to New Plymouth. Here, he and J. C. Richmond wisely decided against embroiling the government in a war with the King Movement. At about the same time, news of the Whakatane Raid reached New Plymouth. Whitmore and Richmond determined again to shift the main colonial striking force to the opposite coast, to deal with the resurgent Te Kooti. By 20 April, Whitmore and some 600 constabulary had been transferred by steamer to Opotiki.

A key aspect of both the Whakatane and Mohaka raids had been the use of the Urewera Mountains as a safe base. These mountains, varying from 2,000 to 5,000 feet above sea level, were the ancient home of the Tuhoe, a small but warlike tribe which had had little direct contact with Europeans. Their main centres of population were the small mountain valleys of Ahikereru and Ruatahuna, and their sacred mountain was Maungapohatu, the inner sanctum of the Urewera. The Tuhoe country had a great reputation among the neighbouring tribes as a graveyard for invading forces. While the mountains remained inviolate, Te Kooti would always have a sanctuary in which he could rebuild his strength after defeat.

Whitmore concluded that, to put an end to Te Kooti, the government had to grasp the nettle and invade the Urewera. Despite the doubts of the Defence Minister, he rapidly set about organizing a three-pronged invasion. Whitmore planned that one column, under Lieutenant-Colonel Herrick, would advance from Wairoa and enter the Urewera from the south by crossing Waikaremoana. Another column, under Lieutenant-Colonel St. John, was to leave Opotiki and invade from the north, up the Whakatane River. The third, under Whitmore himself, would also start from Opotiki, construct a chain of forts between the roadstead of Matata and Tauaroa, and enter the Urewera from the west, following Te Kooti's route after the Whakatane raid. The three columns were to meet at Ruatahuna. In all, about 1,300 government troops were involved—620 constabulary, 95 militia, and 560 *kupapa*—evenly divided between the three columns.[70]

Herrick's expedition proved to be a bloodless but expensive fiasco. Herrick and J. C. Richmond, who again acted as the colonial Carnot, decided to cross Waikaremoana in large boats, some carried up in pieces from Wairoa, some built on the spot. This plan was not so wild as was later supposed. The boats were eventually brought up and built, and if maintained would have facilitated an invasion and permanently reduced the utility of the Urewera as a refuge for Te Kooti. But creating a fleet on an isolated lake in mountain country proved to be no easy matter, and by the time it was finished, both Te Kooti and Whitmore had left the Urewera and the campaign was long over. This expedition cost between £40,000 and £60,000, a waste which proved to be politically damaging to the Stafford Ministry.[71]

The other columns were more successful. Both entered the Urewera on 4 May and reached the Ruatahuna Valley on 8 May. On the way, each column destroyed one or two Tuhoe settlements and lost a few men in an ambush. The only heavy fighting occurred at Orangakiwa, a *pa* protecting Tatahoata village, where St. John's column lost a dozen men before the Tuhoe evacuated. The combined columns remained at Ruatahuna for several days, systematically destroying crops and villages. Meanwhile, Te Kooti remained on the northern shore of Waikaremoana, probably awaiting an attack by Herrick's column. Once it become clear that Herrick would be occupied for some time, Te Kooti moved to the aid of his Tuhoe allies. On 12 May his van, under Peka Makarini, ran into a strong government reconnaissance party and skirmished with it, losing three killed. Te Kooti then took up a naturally strong position in a gorge, and awaited Whitmore's attack. The attack never came, and on 14 May the government forces began their withdrawal from the Urewera, completing it on 18 May.[72]

As usual, the colonists blamed the need to withdraw on the timidity of the *kupapa*—in this case, the Arawa, 'this braggart and useless tribe'.[73] It is true that the Arawa refused to advance beyond Ruatahuna, but there was good reason for their caution. The line of supply stopped at the edge of the mountains, and from that point the troops had only as much food and ammunition as they could carry with them. By 12 May, this was running short. Sickness was increasing. At least twenty-four Europeans were incapacitated by dysentery. Whitmore himself was 'purging and vomiting the whole day', and had to be carried on a litter.[74] The Arawa also rightly believed that Te Kooti awaited them in a strong position. To some extent, Whitmore acknowledged these factors. 'I confess that . . . I had many doubts as to the advisability of pressing much further into an unknown region, even with willing troops.'[75] This did not stop him from blaming the Arawa nor, to complete the circularity, from claiming that the invasion was a brilliant success.

Whitmore retrospectively asserted that the invasion was intended to force Te Kooti into open country, where he could easily be defeated, by destroying the food supplies of his Tuhoe hosts. In early June, Te Kooti did indeed leave the Urewera for Taupo, where he was later defeated. It followed that Whitmore's plan, which he modestly described as 'the true strategical policy', was entirely successful. This claim was based on a dubious use of hindsight. The real aim of the invasion was to destroy Te Kooti. Whitmore's criticism of the Arawa indicates disappointment with the results of the operation, and before it began he wrote: 'Te Kooti is said to be at Ruatahuna and I trust to bail him up there.' Whitmore did not succeed in this, and his invasion may not even have been the decisive factor in inducing Te Kooti to go to Taupo. Taupo was better able to supply the *Ringatu* band during winter than was the Urewera, and it was closer to its main prospective ally, the King Movement. A section of the local people (Ngati Tuwharetoa) sympathized with Te Kooti and had invited him to join them in February 1869—before the Urewera invasion was even conceived.[76]

The invasion was therefore no outright success but Whitmore and his men did have reason to be proud of themselves. The Armed Constabulary did most of the fighting, losing fourteen men killed and wounded, while the *kupapa* lost four. They attacked with verve and skill, they remained steady in ambushes, and they performed remarkable feats of endurance—St. John's column crossed and recrossed the Whakatane River twenty-eight times in one day, carrying seventy-pound packs.[77] Bludgeoned into shape by the 'great tyrant' (Whitmore), inspired by victory at Ngatapa, and toughened during the pursuit of Titokowaru, the constabulary had become light infantry as good as any. Tuhoe resisted bravely, but on a piecemeal basis, defending their own villages with little discernible co-ordination. They paid the price that usually attended this type of warfare—at least twenty people killed, including women and children, about fifty captured, and crops and villages destroyed. This permanently weakened Tuhoe and it was probably one of the factors which persuaded Te Kooti to move to Taupo.

Te Kooti's next campaign consisted of operations to the north and south of Lake Taupo. The campaign began when Te Kooti left the Urewera in early June, with perhaps 150 men and a smaller number of women. Te Kooti's *mana*, already partially restored by the Whakatane and Mohaka raids, was further increased by an action on 7 June at Opepe, fifteen miles from Lake Taupo. Te Kooti's vanguard on the march from the Urewera, commanded by Te Rangitahau, received information that a small party of colonist cavalry was camped at Opepe, expecting to be joined by some *kupapa*. Posing as the *kupapa*, some of Te Rangitahau's men entered the camp peacefully. The colonists were volunteers, not constabulary, and they incautiously accepted the visitors at face value. The *Ringatu* warriors killed nine without loss to themselves—the largest number of European combat troops ever killed by Te Kooti's forces in a single action. Five troopers escaped.[78]

The effect of the Opepe affair was increased by the strange colonial decision to abandon the forts built by Whitmore on the western fringe of the Urewera. Whitmore had planned to use these as bases from which to pursue Te Kooti to Taupo, but the Colonel himself had had to go to Auckland to recuperate from the rigours of the Urewera campaign. In his absence, the temporary commanding officer, Lieutenant-Colonel Harington, withdrew the garrisons and other units in the area to the East Coast—apparently for further drill. This, combined with confusion arising from a change of government on 28 June and the onset of winter, gave Te Kooti and his people a welcome respite of three months.

The change of government had other effects on military operations. Fox and McLean replaced Stafford and Haultain as Premier and Defence Minister. There was a marked increase in the degree of civilian control of operations. The new administration was committed to cutting back expenditure, and future expeditions were conducted on a shoe-string. The Armed Constabulary, which had just reached its peak of efficiency, was reduced, and the process of converting it into a police force began. And, as one would expect with McLean at the Defence Office, Whitmore's temporary absence from the field became permanent. In one respect, however, the attitude of the Fox Government was similar to that of its predecessor. It was very keen to catch Te Kooti, despite its financial worries, but it was not prepared to catch him at the price of war with the King Movement. At the very outset of the South Taupo campaign, the official controlling the government forces informed the military commander that: 'McLean keeps impressing upon me that I must not allow anything to be done to make difficulties with the Waikatos, so bear that in mind.'[79] This political constraint was to have an important effect on operations.

The lull in operations between June and September 1869 was also a period of political activity for Te Kooti. Leaving most of his people at Tokaanu, on the southern shore of Lake Taupo, he travelled north to the King's capital at Tokangamutu in July to visit Tawhiao. His purpose was to persuade the King Movement to enter the war. The Movement's response to Te Kooti's overtures is difficult to establish precisely, partly because the evidence is limited, and partly because that which does exist shows strong differences of opinion among the Kingite leadership.

One section, including Tamati Ngapora, was suspicious of Te Kooti's motives and did not wish to support him. It is often assumed that this reflected the attitude of the Movement as a whole, but two Maori accounts indicate that another section, at least equally influential, was much more favourably inclined. This section included Rewi Maniapoto and King Tawhiao himself. It seems that a compromise was eventually reached whereby the Kingites gave Te Kooti every support short of actual hostilities. Hakaraia, who was now closely associated with the Movement, joined Te Kooti with thirty warriors. About fifty of Te Kooti's people, probably women, children, and injured men, were taken in and protected by Ngati Maniapoto, and some ammunition may have changed hands. Above all, a military legation went with Te Kooti to observe the fighting at Taupo. This certainly included Rewi and, according to one account, it also included Tikaokao—the two leading Kingite generals.[80]

Te Kooti eventually found permanent sanctuary in the King Country,

and it seems reasonable to suggest that the Kingites always deeply sympathized with those in arms against the government. This was reflected in
the raid on North Taranaki of February 1869, and the fairly consistent
policy of benevolent neutrality towards Te Kooti. But the Kingite chiefs, as
responsible leaders of a people who had recently suffered much in war, had
to take into account their chances of success. With Titokowaru, they waited
too long, and their intervention was aborted once his collapse became
known. With Te Kooti, their military legation was to decide that the
Ringatu forces had no prospect of victory in the Taupo campaign, and that
there was little point in fully committing themselves to a lost cause.

Te Kooti returned to Tokaanu in August, and government moves against
him began in September 1869. The colonist offensive was supplied and
organized from Napier by J. D. Ormond, an associate of McLean who had
been appointed agent for the general government on the East Coast.
Ormond ran the campaign in a vigorous and business-like manner, but with
a very tight budget and a limited grasp of the needs of an army in the field.
The military commander was Thomas McDonnell, whose relations with
the Fox Government were initially much better than Whitmore's. *Kupapa*
made up the majority of the force involved, and their chiefs obeyed
McDonnell only when it suited them, though 'Fighting Mac' usually contrived to give the impression that his control was greater than was in fact the
case. The force eventually assembled numbered between 600 and 700 men,
of whom only 100 were Europeans. A section of Ngati Tuwharetoa had
decided to oppose Te Kooti, and in August these men (about 130) assembled
near the present site of Taupo township, at the north-east corner of the
Lake. Here they were joined by fifty Arawa *kupapa* and two European
officers: Captain J. St. George and Lieutenant G. A. Preece. In early September, two parties of Ngati Kahungunu, totalling about 230 men, and the
100 European constabulary under McDonnell, arrived at the southern end
of the Lake and formed a camp at Poutu, about a day's march from
Tokaanu. On 1 October, a contingent of the Wanganui tribe, under Kepa te
Rangihiwinui, arrived to complete the force. The Wanganuis were variously
estimated at from 112 to 160 men.[81]

It is impossible to be definite about Te Kooti's numbers. On the one
hand, the original 150 men brought from the Urewera were joined by at
least 100 Ngati Tuwharetoa under their great chief, Te Heuheu Horonuku.
On the other hand, some of these new adherents were not fully committed
to Te Kooti's cause, and some of the *Ringatu* force, including Te
Rangitahau, remained camped to the north and did not take part in the campaign. A total of 200 warriors, of whom as few as 100 may have been entirely
reliable, is therefore a reasonable guess for Te Kooti's strength in the
following operations.[82]

Given the disparity in numbers, Te Kooti decided that his best hope lay
in attacking the government forces separately, before they could concentrate. His first opportunity came on 12 September, when one party of Ngati
Kahungunu, 120 mounted men under Henare Tomoana, pushed forward

and took up a position at Tauranga-Taupo, on the shores of the Lake. Te Kooti attacked Ngati Kahungunu with his whole force. Tomoana hastily but effectively entrenched his position and proved too strong to assault. About 100 of Tomoana's horses were captured, but he lost only three wounded to Te Kooti's three killed and several wounded, and his force remained intact.[83] Te Kooti tried again two weeks later at Te Pononga. He engaged Ngati Kahungunu, now reinforced to over 200 men and supported by the fifty Arawa, who had by this time arrived from the north. After heavy skirmishing, he was again repulsed, losing five killed and proportionate wounded to the *kupapa* two killed and four wounded.[84]

The colonists, particularly McDonnell, were somewhat scornful of these *kupapa* successes and attributed them to European leadership or the threat of European troops coming up in Te Kooti's rear. But it seems clear that the credit properly belongs to Henare Tomoana and Ngati Kahungunu. In terms of ability, Tomoana should rank with Kepa and Ropata among the *kupapa* commanders. The engagements at Tauranga-Taupo and Te Pononga, though minor in themselves, were important because they marked the failure of Te Kooti's attempt to defeat the government army in detail and therefore eliminated his sole chance of victory in the campaign. Recognizing this, Rewi and Tikaokao returned home after Te Pononga, taking with them Te Kooti's prospects of support from a Kingite army. These two actions, rather than the subsequent larger battle of Te Porere, spelled the beginning of the end for Te Kooti.

At the end of September, Te Kooti moved a little south of Tokaanu and built a *pa* at Te Porere—an oblong redoubt with ditch, parapet and flanking bastions and two small detached works, on a low rise at the edge of the bush west of Lake Rotoaira. Once joined by Kepa, McDonnell advanced with most of his men (about 540) and attacked on 3 October. McDonnell sighted the *pa* at mid-morning, and split his force into two roughly equal parts. One, theoretically commanded by Lieutenant-Colonel Herrick, but actually by Kepa, included Wanganui, most of the constabulary, and 100 Ngati Kahungunu. This force advanced towards the left of Te Porere and engaged Te Kooti's skirmishers, compelling them to abandon one small outwork and fall back on the main position. Te Heuheu and some Ngati Tuwharetoa warriors were posted in the bush flanking Kepa's advance, and a party was detached to deal with them. According to Kepa, Te Heuheu did not resist, but withdrew immediately. Kepa and all his men moved in on the main *pa*, and took up a position very close to it. Some men were able to occupy the ditch itself, because the loopholes did not permit the defenders to depress their guns sufficiently to fire into it, and because the two flanking bastions were so poorly sited that they did not cover the ditch.[85]

Meanwhile, the other government force (Arawa, Ngati Tuwharetoa, and 120 Ngati Kahungunu, with McDonnell and some constabulary) also advanced and drove in the enemy's skirmishers, easily capturing the other detached outwork. They then rushed forward towards the main *pa*. They too found the ditch unexpectedly safe, and linked up with Kepa. Both forces now occupied the ditch on two, possibly even three, sides of the main *pa*. According to some accounts, the *pa* was then stormed outright, but it seems more probable that the garrison, seeing that their position was hopeless, began to flee before the government assault. Whatever the precise sequence of events, the government troops scrambled into the *pa* from the ditch and took it, killing all the men they found and wounding several women. A total of thirty-seven of Te Kooti's people were killed, including ten or twelve Ngati Tuwharetoa, and thirty women and children were captured. Government casualties were four killed and four wounded.[86]

Te Porere is historiographically exceptional, in that a good modern account exists in the form of Ormond Wilson's booklet on the battle,[87] but historically it follows the pattern set at Ngatapa. The poorly designed loopholes and bastions at Te Porere were only symptoms of a more fundamental malaise: Te Kooti's imperfect tactical understanding of the modern *pa*, and his reluctance to accept the strategic limitations this imposed on his operations. Te Porere cost Te Kooti fewer casualties than Ngatapa, but in a sense its baneful consequences were more permanent. Te Porere was his last stand in a prepared position, and his last attempt at anything other than raid, ambush, and the evasion of pursuit.

After Te Porere, Te Kooti fled westwards towards present-day Taumarunui in the southern King Country. McDonnell, who seems to have run short of money and supplies, temporarily lost contact with him. However Kepa, now joined by more Wanganuis under Topia Turoa, followed him up. Te Kooti went to ground at Tuhua, and remained there at least until the end of November. The government became aware of his location, but he was not attacked for one reason alone: Tuhua was inside Kingite territory. The Wanganui force included several chiefs, Topia among them, who were sympathetic towards the King Movement. Their antagonism to Te Kooti arose from his having killed one of their kin during the Te Porere operations. When King Tawhiao vetoed their pursuit, through the agency of another Wanganui chief, the 1840s resistance leader Topine Te Mamaku, they obeyed, and Kepa had perforce to follow suit. The government could still have attacked with McDonnell's Europeans and the East Coast *kupapa*, but they decided not to do so, 'it not being considered advisable to risk an embroglio with Waikato'.[88] There can be little doubt that Kingite protection saved Te Kooti at this time.

But Te Kooti did not remain at Tuhua. His departure may have stemmed from a Kingite desire to be rid of a dangerous guest, but there are indications that the Movement had already decided to offer him permanent sanctuary if he agreed to remain peaceful.[89] It may be that Te Kooti simply wished to join Hakaraia—which is what he actually did—or that he hoped for renewed support from the East Coast tribes. Whatever his reasons, he left Tuhua and took up residence at Hakaraia's village of Tapapa, in Ngati Raukawa territory about fifty miles north of Taupo, in early January 1870.

While at Tapapa, Te Kooti offered to meet the Auckland land baron, J. C. Firth, at Matamata. Much to the ire of the government, Firth agreed. At the interview, Te Kooti made it clear that he wanted peace, on the condition that he was left alone. But the colonists were not yet prepared to give up their vengeance, and, by mid-January, substantial forces began closing in on Tapapa. McDonnell and 250 men marched north from Tokaanu up the eastern side of Lake Taupo, while Kepa, Topia, and 370 Wanganuis moved up the west side. Lieutenant-Colonel Moule, and 135 of the constabulary and militia guarding the confiscated land in Central Waikato, came south from Cambridge. Lieutenant-Colonel Fraser with ninety constabulary and 150 Arawa, moved to cut off Te Kooti's retreat to the Urewera, and a further 210 Arawa marched to join McDonnell. In all 1,200 men converged on Tapapa.[90] To oppose them, Te Kooti may have had as many as 200 men, but there are strong indications that he had about 100—sixty of his own warriors, and thirty or forty new adherents, mainly followers of Hakaraia.[91] It is no wonder that the government was confident. On 19 January, Ormond wrote 'one days advance will close the road to the Urewera country and then if we do not get Kooti we never deserve to'.[92]

On 20 January, McDonnell was joined at Whakamaru by the Wanganuis, and the combined force of over 620 men advanced on Tapapa. When he learned of their approach, Te Kooti moved out, and the government forces seized the empty village. On 24 January, McDonnell decided to establish a base camp at Tapapa, send Kepa and 200 Wanganuis to locate the enemy, and join him with the main force early next morning. On 25 January, just as the main force was about to depart Tapapa, they received a surprise visit from Te Kooti. Instead of fleeing as fast as he could, Te Kooti had doubled back on his tracks and attacked his pursuers under cover of a heavy fog. Tactically, honours were evenly divided in the confused bush skirmishing which followed. Te Kooti routed a section of *kupapa*, but did not have the numbers to press home his attack, and was eventually forced back in his turn, while Kepa came upon his bush camp and captured 100 horses. Each side lost four killed and about the same number wounded. But Te Kooti's bold counter-attack disconcerted the government forces, and in the confusion they lost his trail.[93]

Te Kooti now moved north in the direction of present-day Te Puke, probably hoping to find a way round the north of the Rotorua lakes towards the Urewera. But he ran into Fraser's force, and though his van, under Makarini, successfully ambushed Fraser's scouts at Paengaroa, killing four for no loss, he seems to have concluded that this route was blocked.[94] He then marched south towards Lake Rotorua, the heart of Arawa territory, with the government again in ignorance of his location. On or before 7 February 1870, he opened peace negotiations with the Arawa elders near the present site of Rotorua City. This is usually seen as a treacherous tactic designed to facilitate a massacre of Arawa non-combatants while their warriors were away, but this is by no means proven, and there can be little doubt that Te Kooti had had enough of fighting. Unfortunately for him, the 210 Arawa warriors who had gone to join McDonnell, finding that the Colonel had lost Te Kooti after Tapapa, returned home. They were accompanied by Lieutenant Gilbert Mair, an officer with an ususual degree of influence over the younger Arawa warriors.

Mair reached Rotorua on 7 February, and found some Arawa elders going under flag of truce to negotiate with Te Kooti. Mair threw down the white flag and immediately attacked Te Kooti's band, which was awaiting the envoys nearby. Mair was supported by some of the 210 warriors, and a running fight ensued. Mair and the Arawa pursued with great determination and courage, but the *Ringatu* rearguard under Makarini and Te Kooti himself managed to hold them up sufficiently for the whole band to escape. The Arawa had one man killed and seven wounded, while the *Ringatu* band lost several warriors killed. Among the slain was Peka Makarini—Edward Baker McLean. Portrayed by the colonists as a fiend in human shape, Makarini was a brave, loyal, and able soldier. His unusual career reportedly began with European legal training. It ended with a rearguard action which enabled Te Kooti and his people to escape to the Urewera.[95]

The final phase of Te Kooti's later campaigns lasted from March 1870 to May 1872. After escaping from Mair and the Arawa, Te Kooti again took refuge in the Urewera. But the mountains were no longer sacrosanct, and over a dozen expeditions rampaged through Tuhoe territory in search of the dwindling *Ringatu* band. The 'Arawa Flying Column'—200 young Arawa separated from their chiefs and trained and commanded by Preece and Gilbert Mair—carried out several of these expeditions, but most were mounted under a new system instituted by McLean. These columns consisted entirely of *kupapa*, under their own chiefs, serving without pay in the hope of a reward of £5,000 for the capture of Te Kooti, and lesser sums for his followers. 'This', thought T. W. Gudgeon, was a 'very wholesome change [which], if looked into closely, amounted to this: according to numbers killed, so will be your pay'.[96]

The *kupapa* approved of the change in command structure. 'The Maoris', wrote Ropata, 'are very impatient and incapable of obeying and carrying out the instructions or commands of European officers.'[97] They were less impressed with the change in payment. Gudgeon might think it 'very wholesome', but one chief thought it 'very foolish'. In May 1870, Ngati Kahungunu mounted a large but fruitless expedition to Waikaremoana, but thereafter operations were left to the Arawa Flying Column, and Kepa and Ropata and their men. These forces partly made up for the absence of wages by plundering Tuhoe and the neighbouring tribes, some of whom were also victims of Te Kooti. Some Whakatohea chiefs informed the government that 'we have been sufferers at the hands of two parties, viz., Te Kooti, and Whanganui—I mean Major Kemp'.[98]

As *kupapa* columns crossed and re-crossed the Urewera in search of Te Kooti, pillaging as they went, active *Ringatu* support dropped away through sheer exhaustion, though Tuhoe continued to provide tacit assistance, sometimes helpfully guiding government columns in the wrong direction. By late 1870, several Tuhoe chiefs had made their peace with the government, and Te Waru of the Upper Wairoa Ngati Kahungunu, for so long Te Kooti's loyal supporter, had surrendered. Te Kooti made two minor forays to the coast (to Tolaga Bay and Omaramutu) in March and July 1870, but neither did much to recoup his fortunes. He was eventually forced to avoid even the villages of his Tuhoe friends; food and ammunition shortages became acute; and more and more of his followers left him, were killed, or died of starvation. By March 1871, he had twenty-five men left to him [99]

In these circumstances, under almost continuous pressure from a vastly more numerous enemy, Te Kooti's withdrawals inevitably lost their deliberation and became flights. He was simply hunted from pillar to post, and all the *kupapa* had to do to take his camps was to find them. This happened on three occasions. On 23 March 1870, Kepa and 400 Wanganuis found the *Ringatu* camp at Maraetahi and stormed it, killing nineteen people including some prisoners executed. 'Hakaraia son of satan', in Kepa's phrase, was amongst the killed.[100] On 15 August 1871, Mair and his Arawa took another camp at Waipaoa, and on 1 September the same year Ngati Porou took Te Hapua, killing eleven people. Te Kooti was present on each occasion, but escaped by a hair's breadth.[101] On 14 February 1872, Preece and his company of the Arawa Flying Column, scouting to the west of Waikaremoana, sighted Te Kooti and his few surviving followers and opened fire at 400 yards range. The fugitives scrambled up a cliff and escaped. As they did so, an Arawa private, Nikora te Tuhi, levelled his carbine and fired the last shot of the New Zealand Wars.

Further expeditions were mounted in April and May 1872, but found no trace of their prey. With five men and one woman, Te Kooti had finally succeeded in evading the government posts and columns, and making his way to the King Country. There he remained, still bitterly hated and feared by colonists and *kupapa*, and still with a price of £5,000 on his head, but securely protected by the King Movement. In 1883, he was finally pardoned as part of a government attempt to open up the King Country by peaceful means. He died in 1893.

Before leaving the operations of Te Kooti, it is necessary to attempt some overall assessment of his generalship. This was always related to his religious leadership, and here the comparison with Titokowaru is useful. Like other prophet-generals before them, the two derived both strengths and weaknesses from the fusion of military and religious authority. On the positive side, it greatly increased their followers' confidence in them, and their control over their followers. Maori forces usually exhibited good discipline when in actual battle, but that shown by the soldiers of Titokowaru and Te Kooti was extraordinary. Small groups, out of communication with each other, operated with perfect precision according to a pre-conceived plan. Complicated manoeuvres and an otherwise dangerous division of already-small forces became possible, and this in effect multiplied Maori numbers. This discipline was not of the type that destroyed a subordinate's initiative. It was based, rather, on faith in the leader. The lieutenants of the two generals were unswervingly loyal, but they could use their own judgement when necessary, and adjust the master-plan according to changed circumstances.

Another shared characteristic of the two generals was their remarkable understanding of their enemies. Te Kooti certainly had, and Titokowaru may have had, unusually close experience of the *Pakeha*, and both were profound students of *Pakeha* psychology. They were better able to predict a colonist commander's responses than he was able to predict theirs. Other Maori generals, such as Rewi Maniapoto, had similar abilities, but they had much greater difficulty in getting their prognoses of likely enemy action accepted by their followers. Here, Te Kooti's and Titokowaru's religious authority was crucial. A prediction about enemy movements presented as a rational deduction from the evidence was open to debate; an authoritative prophecy was not.

These attributes enabled Te Kooti to develop a mastery of the lightning raid rarely equalled anywhere. His major raids all followed a similar pattern. The target was carefully selected and struck suddenly, perhaps after the enemy had been thrown off balance by some kind of diversion. An easily controlled force of 100 picked men was split into smaller parties to attack various points simultaneously, thus spreading the maximum confusion among the enemy. The parties would rendezvous at an advanced base, established before the raid, collect their plunder and re-organize. The retreat would be carried out in a deliberate and controlled manner, with rearguard actions preferably taking the form of skirmishes, manoeuvres, or sudden counter-attacks. This type of operation occurred not only after the Poverty Bay, Whakatane, and Mohaka raids, but also after the landing from the Chathams and during the North Taupo campaign of early 1870.

But success as a raider was not enough for Te Kooti. Like all other Maori generals, he sometimes needed to block an enemy initiative, to stand his ground and protect an area of land, to defeat a substantial enemy force in battle. When other generals sought to do this, they sometimes succeeded by using modern *pa*. When Te Kooti tried, he failed. His major *pa*, Ngatapa and Te Porere, had grave tactical weaknesses, and the former was poorly located as well. Te Kooti was thus deprived of the strategic benefits of the modern *pa* system, and was forced to rely solely on guerilla techniques for his successes. He is the only Maori general who can usefully be described as a guerilla leader.

Titokowaru was also adept at guerilla methods, though his skill in this area was not as prominent as Te Kooti's. The Ngati Ruanui chief used raids as a part of his over-all strategy, and his handling of his only retreat (after Tauranga-ika) was masterly, despite the most adverse circumstances. But his guerilla operations were only a supplement to the modern *pa* system. It was the latter which enabled him to stop a colonist offensive in its tracks, and to reconquer and hold the land for which he fought. It was the effective use of the modern *pa* which distinguished Titokowaru from Te Kooti, and it was this which made him the more dangerous of the two to the colonists.

Yet Te Kooti proved to be more resilient than Titokowaru, and here the religious factor may provide some kind of explanation. Titokowaru's religion appears to have been less original than Te Kooti's; it depended more on traditional Maori beliefs and on *Pai Marire*. The rules of Titokowaru's religion were external to him. He broke them and was himself broken. Te Kooti made his own rules, and therefore could not break them. To some extent, he was *Ringatu*. So Titokowaru won his battles and lost his support. Te Kooti lost his battles and kept his support. Indeed, in the form of the living *Ringatu* religion, he still has it.

PART FIVE

Conclusions

14

The Maori Achievement

AT THE BEGINNING OF THE NEW ZEALAND WARS, THE MAORIS seemed impossibly outmatched by the British in military technology, organization for war, and simple numbers. In the end, it required 18,000 British troops, together with careful preparation and logistical organization, to defeat them—and even then they were able to delay and limit the enemy victory. After Imperial troops were withdrawn, Titokowaru came within an ace of success against vastly superior colonial forces, a result which might have reversed the decision of the Waikato War. Prior to this, the Maoris blocked the British in two wars, and regularly defeated forces several times their own numbers—forces which were not trapped or surprised, but which actually chose to give battle. On the extant record—an important qualification—this was a unique feat of resistance to nineteenth-century European expansion. Abd el-Kadr, Shamil, and Sitting Bull; the Afghans, the Sudanese, and the Ethiopians—all were either more decisively defeated or had the advantage of superior numbers. Even the Boers, during their most successful phase in the Second South African War, suffered from less of a disparity in artillery and numbers. The Maoris were not supermen, and they did not receive the secrets of success in a flash of divine inspiration. How then is the effectiveness of their resistance to be explained?

I   THE MODERN *PA* SYSTEM

BROADLY SPEAKING, IT CAN BE SAID THAT THREE TYPES OF military resistance to European expansion were possible. First, indigenous methods of warfare could be used. These were generally ancient and traditional, but could include new local inventions. The heavy Zulu stabbing *assegai*, and the tactics associated with it, originated by Shaka as an improvement on throwing spears, was a new but indigenous development. Imported weapons could be incorporated into an indigenous system of war without necessarily revolutionizing it. The second type was imitative, the comprehensive copying of the European system. The third type can be described as adaptive innovation: a system which ideally transcended the stratifications of both others, and which was specifically designed to cope with European methods—not as a copy of them, fighting fire with fire, but as an antidote to them, fighting fire with water.

The indigenous Maori system of war could not cope with British war-ships, artillery, and numbers, through open battle or the defence of traditional *pa*. But guerilla techniques can be seen as a further indigenous alternative, and the Maoris were quite capable of using these systematically. They sometimes did so, but (with the exception of Te Kooti's operations) only as a supplement to other forms. We have seen that the mainstream of Maori operations fall outside any useful definition of guerilla war. The axiom that guerilla methods are the only effective way in which the weak can fight the strong is often parroted regardless of its applicability. Guerillas usually pay a heavy price for their mode of war in social and economic dislocation and in the occupation of their more accessible centres of population. It is not normally a method of preventing conquest, but of making it expensive to the conqueror. Leaders from Vercengetorix to Mao have therefore turned to it only as a last resort. The Maoris had a system with which they could hope to protect their land, and they were wise to prefer it to guerilla methods.

The Maoris also rejected imitative methods. Evidence suggests that this was not simply because they could not imitate. As early as 1845, the Maoris had cannon, and there are signs that the King Movement began developing a regular army between 1861 and 1863. In 1862, the Waikato missionary, B. Y. Ashwell, saw fifty uniformed Kingite troops who were 'apparently equal to an English regiment as regards order and discipline'. John Gorst knew of four similar companies, and was told that the men received rations and were paid three pence a day—not a great deal less than a British infantryman's pay after stoppages.[1] There is no indication that this tiny standing force—New Zealand's first regular army—was ever employed as such in the Waikato War, and the Maoris were wise to avoid the temptation. Their regulars were clearly too few to meet the British force in the kind of front-to-front combat for which they had been drilled.

As for artillery, the Maoris had cannon at Ohaeawai and Ruapekapeka in 1845-6 and at Meremere and Paterangi in 1863-4. The Maoris also had competent gunlayers among them—men trained on whalers and other vessels—and they sometimes had a limited amount of gunpowder to spare. But their cannon were old, with bores made irregular by corrosion, and with makeshift carriages which made them difficult to aim and dangerous in the recoil. More importantly, the available projectiles—stones and pieces of scrap metal—were totally inadequate. These missiles made accurate and powerful fire all but impossible. Such weapons were of little use in open battle or even in the defence of *pa*. In the latter case, they were almost a liability because the essence of Maori strategy was the preparedness to abandon *pa*. A European-style reluctance to lose their guns might have proved fatal, and on the few occasions that they used cannon, the Maoris derived little benefit, and readily abandoned them.

There was one occasion on which Maori artillery could have been very useful. This was at Meremere, where an effective bombardment could have sunk the British steamers and delayed Cameron's invasion for yet more weeks. The Maoris did their best to seize this chance by acquiring the largest gun they ever used—a 24-pounder—and by siting it perfectly. When the *Pioneer* came upriver to reconnoitre on 30 October, the Maoris made good practice despite the limitations of their equipment. One superb shot actually hulled the steamer. Had the projectile been adequate this shot might have sent the ship to the bottom. But, unfortunately for the Maoris, the missile was a seven-pound grocer's weight, and with an unerring homing instinct, it lodged harmlessly in a cask of beef in the *Pioneer*'s hold.[2]

The Maoris could have opposed Cameron's invasion with a small, well-drilled regular battalion equipped with cannon, but to do so would have meant defeat and they knew it. With inferior numbers and faulty equipment there was simply no point in imitating the British military system and playing the Europeans at their own game.

The method to which the Maoris actually turned was essentially innovative: it differed from both their traditional system and the British system. It was applied in a variety of ways, according to the needs of a particular campaign, and it was progressively improved, but it was based on the same principles throughout the wars. What was the underlying character of this system? How did the Maoris come to create it, and why was it so successful?

A hypothesis recently put forward by Daniel R. Headrick could be taken to provide a technological explanation for the relative success of Maori resistance. Headrick argues that a decisive contributor to the increased speed and facility with which Europeans were able to subdue non-Europeans was the 'fire-arms revolution of the mid-century'.[3] The development of the breech-loading and repeating weapons greatly increased the range, power, and firing-rate of small arms. Imperial warfare in the nineteenth century can thus be divided into two phases. In the first six decades of the century, small arms, whether rifles or muskets, were all muzzle-loaders with a slow rate of fire and a relatively short range. These weapons did not necessarily dominate a battlefield, and a wide range of tactics remained possible for those who opposed European forces. Furthermore, some non-European peoples already possessed the musket, and others could fairly easily acquire them through trade. Most European guns and ammunition in this period were hand-made, and could therefore be repaired or copied locally. The similarity of weapon types over the years meant that guns could be accumulated over a long period and remain roughly on a par with European weapons. After the firearms revolution, however, weapons were factory-made and they could not easily be repaired or supplied with ammunition from local manufacture in pre-industrial societies. They also underwent constant improvement and models therefore became obsolete very rapidly. High firepower also made most forms of the tactical offensive almost impossible, and military systems in which attack was a staple were unable to adapt with sufficient rapidity.

A rough parity in weapons therefore gave way to a decisive imbalance. In the first period, Europeans were able to overcome vigorous and well-led non-European resistance only after fighting long and hard. The wars against Abd el-Kadr, Shamil, and the Sikhs are cases in point. In the second period, conquest was easier and cheaper because of decisively superior European firepower. Headrick cites the African examples of Ashanti, Senegal, Sokoto, Chad, and the Sudan. The Maoris were rarely as well-armed as the British, but as we have seen the difference in small arms was far from decisive. The Maoris were adequately supplied with muskets, and it was not until 1865, when three of the four major wars were over, that breech-loaders became the staple weapon of the British forces. One could therefore suggest that Maori resistance belonged mainly to the first phase of Imperial warfare, and to attribute its relative effectiveness primarily to rough parity in small arms.

It will become clear that this argument is inappropriate in the New Zealand case, but it does provide a framework which illuminates the true explanation of Maori success. In reality, the Maoris faced a comparable problem to the people who fought Europeans after the firearms revolution. Few historians dealing with the theme fail to note that the norm in Imperial warfare was European numerical inferiority. In New Zealand, this situation was completely reversed. This meant that an attacking Maori force in 1845 would meet with the same fate as attacking Sudanese in 1898: destruction by overwhelmingly superior firepower. An attack by 100 men on 1,000 musket-armed men was comparable to an attack by 1,000 men on 100 troops equipped with breech-loaders. From the first, therefore, the tactical problem the Maoris were struggling to solve in their wars with the British was that of the second phase of Imperial warfare: overwhelming enemy firepower.

The Maori solution was to strike attack and open battle off their list of tactical options. Instead, they developed a new kind of fortification: the modern *pa*. To achieve their objectives the British had to attack these positions. Originally, *pa* included a considerable amount of timber palisading, and it was often this that caught the observer's eye. But in fact it was the earthworks which were always the most important, and some *pa* in Taranaki and Waikato included no timber at all. The crucial parts of the earthworks were those below ground level; tactically, modern *pa* were trench systems. As such, they were not an uncommon response to the situation in which high enemy firepower rendered the open battlefield almost untenable. In Europe, entrenchment was as old as gunpowder, and it was traditionally the resort of a numerically weak force. But primitive earthworks such as those used in Europe before the Russo-Turkish War of 1878 were found to be 'a good deal less of a problem' to an attacker than normal forts.[4] It was only as a result of the firepower revolution that entrenchment began, in the American Civil War, to be used frequently and systematically. Boer methods in the Second South African War paralleled the Maori system more closely, because they too not only entrenched for defence but also eschewed attack.

The Maoris, however, did not find rifle trenches enough in themselves.

There were two main problems: the protection of the garrison from heavy bombardment, and the actual repulse of the assault. In terms of artillery, the Maoris were unlucky enough to be on the wrong side of the firearms revolution, even from a purely technical point of view. The British army was the first to be equipped with breech-loading, composite-cast artillery. From 1860 to 1871—when, largely for economic reasons, they reverted to muzzleloaders—the British had the Armstrong gun. They used these, in concert with conventional cannon, in Taranaki and Waikato. Te Arei, in March 1861, was probably the first trench system to be bombarded by modern heavy artillery.

The problems this created for the Maoris were greater in degree than those faced by the Americans and the Boers. The Maoris had no effective long-range weapons to keep enemy artillery at a respectful distance, and their *pa* were often so small that the British were able to lay down bombardments that were enormous in relation to the target. The British fired roughly twenty times the weight of shell per square yard at Gate Pa, on 29 April 1864, as they did into the Somme battlefield during the initial bombardment of 24 June-1 July 1916.[5] Even if generous allowance is made for the increased effectiveness of explosives, and for the fact that some shots fired at the Gate Pa missed their target, it is clear that the Maoris underwent a heavier bombardment in one day than the Germans did in seven.

One method of counteracting the threat of heavy bombardment was applied by both the Maoris and the Boers. Traditional Maori *pa* and the first Boer entrenchments of 1899—at Belmont and Graspan—were sited on tactically commanding ground. At the Modder River, De La Rey switched his entrenchments to the foot of *kopjes* whose crowns were the obvious targets for the British guns. Just as it had done in New Zealand forty years earlier, this provided a false target for the enemy. The Maoris took the technique further. At Puketakauere, they placed their main firing trenches well in front of virtually unmanned stockades, and the British shells passed harmlessly overhead. They actually constructed false targets, instead of relying on natural features.

But a more important protection from heavy bombardment was the antiartillery bunker. In contrast to most American and Boer trench systems, these were an integral feature of the modern *pa* because the Maoris often had to face much heavier bombardments per square yard of ground and per man of the garrison. They would sit out the cannonade in their bunkers and then move, through communication trenches or passages, to their firing positions. This, of course, is strikingly similar to the pattern on the Western Front in 1914-18, where static battle lines made possible concentrations of artillery so large that trenches alone were inadequate.

The second major tactical problem with the defence of modern *pa* was the repulse of the assault. The ferocity, élan, and self-confidence of British troops made them extremely formidable in the attack—the conviction that they could not be beaten by inferior numbers of natives added an element that almost amounted to fanaticism. At Ohaeawai and the Gate Pa, forty per cent of the assault party had to be shot down before the rest retreated. Added to this, modern *pa* often had to be relatively modest fortifications: low enough to avoid undue attention from artillery, and small enough to be built quickly. The notion of British assault parties being hurled against massive ramparts or stockades built on precipitous crags is therefore entirely inappropriate. Orakau, which repelled five assaults, stood on a low rise and was only four feet high.

An even more important aspect of the problem of repelling assaults again related to rapid small-arms fire, or rather, to the lack of it. The attackers' possession of rapid-fire small arms did not make a great deal of difference in assaulting trench-and-bunker systems. Much lighter defences than were necessary to stop a shell could also stop a bullet. This remained true whether the bullet was fired by a musket, a breech-loader, a repeater, or a machine gun. Even without the examples of Te Ngutu and Moturoa, it would be clear that British possession of rapid-fire weapons could have made no difference to attacks on *pa*. The important point is not that the British eventually got rapid-fire weapons, but that the Maoris rarely had them. The 'killing ground' outside a Maori position was limited by the effective range of the musket—about eighty yards. At best, each warrior could fire three shots a minute, and even at eighty yards muskets were notoriously inaccurate. The Maoris therefore lacked what is generally considered to be a vital ingredient of trench warfare: the capacity to produce rapid long-range fire. They had to seek ways of repelling a determined and numerically superior foe without the benefit of obstructive defences or modern weapons.

Contrary to legend, the Maoris were usually reasonable marksmen, in so far as good shooting was possible with a musket. This, together with good fire discipline, was important in the repulse of assaults, but the decisive factors concerned the construction of *pa* and the preparation of the surrounding battlefield. Carefully sited firing positions and salients for enfilading fire were regular features of *pa*. So too were light defences, like the *pekerangi*, which impeded an attacker and allowed time to shoot him. These devices were common in *pa* of the Musket War era, but the heavy dependence on features which might surprise an attacker was a new development.

In some cases, such as Ohaeawai and the Gate Pa, the very survival of the garrison after a heavy bombardment had an important shock effect. In the former case, the lack of damage to the physical defences was also an unpleasant surprise for the British. Hidden rifle trenches, like those at Puketakauere, and deceptively weak-looking fortifications like those of Rangiriri and Orakau, might also prove decisive. False targets might distract assault parties as well as artillery. At Puketakauere, and at Titokowaru's *pa* in 1868, the whole central position was a false target which fixed British attention and enabled the Maoris to pick them off from rifle pits on the flanks. At Gate Pa, the interior of the *pa* was in fact a trap—a maze-like confusion of trenches dominated by hidden firing positions. The British were allowed in and shot down. In terms of protecting the garrison, modern *pa* were trench and bunker systems; in terms of repelling assault, they were carefully prepared killing grounds. These traps and deceptions, together with the basic features of *pa* construction, were functionally analogous to the defender's rapid-fire small arms of later trench warfare.

Modern *pa* can be seen as an early trench and bunker system, comparable to those of the American Civil War, the Russo-Turkish War of 1877-8, the Second South African War, the Russo-Japanese War of 1904-5 and, especially, those of the Western Front in 1914-18. The vast difference in scale may make one balk at this last comparison, but the fact is that the Gate Pa would have done very well indeed as a tiny section of the Ypres Salient. Modern *pa* had wooden *pekerangi* instead of barbed wire and flax baskets of earth instead of sand bags, but the trenches and bunkers were essentially the same. In the long-occupied bunkers of Te Arei in 1861, the comparison extended to graffiti and the comforts of home.

The fact that the Maoris were the first to develop this system of war may be dramatic, but it is unimportant in itself. A Leif Eriksson can be found for every Columbus, and there is no evidence of any transference of knowledge—on the contrary the British rapidly forgot what they had learned. But to fit the Maori achievement into the broad pattern of military developments is important because it helps explain how and why they created so effective and innovative a system. A rational response to high firepower was to entrench. A rational response to massive bombardment was to make bunkers. The Maoris faced a more difficult problem than their successors in the need to repel assaults with inadequate weapons; and here their solution was ingenious and perhaps unique. But in other respects the Maori system was an intelligent but not uncommon reaction to the problem of high enemy firepower.

Of course, there was somewhat more to the modern *pa* system than common sense, and the preceding argument does not explain why other peoples, such as the Africans and the Europeans, either failed to adopt trench systems or persisted in believing they could be taken by bombardment and frontal attack. This is obviously a large question, and here we can barely touch on it. Perhaps tradition gave the Maoris some advantage. Traditional and modern *pa* had little more in common than Camelot and the Maginot Line, but traditions of fortification at least provided serviceable construction principles. Efficient techniques of collective labour, and a flexible leadership system whereby one chief could hold the main command while an expert engineer designed the *pa*, were clearly useful. Individual innovators may also have been important. Models of Kawiti's Ohaeawai were carried all around the country by Maori messengers in 1845.[6] But perhaps the most important feature distinguishing Maori resistance can be discerned in the almost complete Maori avoidance of attack. Other peoples, such as the Sudanese in 1885-98 and the Europeans in 1914-18, found it hard to believe that the problem of attack against high firepower was not amenable to a quantitative solution. Whether or not they themselves used trench warfare in defence, they persisted in hoping that more men, more guns, or more determination would turn the scale in attack. The Maoris never made this mistake—perhaps partly for the simply reason that quantitive solutions were not open to them. Their inferiority in numbers and artillery was obvious and immutable from the very first.

Maori resistance had its weaknesses and limitations. Tribal differences often led Maori groups to act against their own long-term interests, and the fact that parochialism was sometimes transcended shows that it was not necessarily inevitable. Maori leaders sometimes made mistakes, and their followers sometimes forced them into error. Successful Maori generalship required not only skill and vision, but also influence great enough to overcome the underlying preference for attack and open battle, and men's natural desire to fight for their own homes to the detriment of a co-ordinated strategy. The modern *pa* system was mainly defensive. Only Titokowaru was able to use it consistently to seize and hold the strategic initiative, and no leader was able to mount a really substantial tactical offensive, and so annihilate a British army. The modern *pa* enabled the Maoris to repel British assault parties, but these usually had ample reserves to fall back on, while the Maoris never had the numbers for counter-attack and pursuit. This explains why casualties on both sides were disproportionately low for the intensity of the conflict. It is counter-attack and all-out pursuit, the follow-up of victory, that causes really heavy casualties and destroys armies. In the New Zealand Wars, it rarely occurred. The British had the numbers, but not the opportunities. The Maoris had the opportunities, but not the numbers. Finally, while sustained by a tribal socio-economy, the modern *pa* system's capacity to thwart superior forces was not infinite. Using it, the Maoris could block continuous offensives by twice their own numbers, or sporadic offensives by six times their strength. But they could not block the continuous offensive of an army six times as great as their own, and so they lost the Waikato War.

In military terms, the most remarkable thing about the New Zealand Wars was not the eventual Maori defeat, but the degree of their success along the way. This success was not fruitless, and the benefits of the Maori achievement for the Maori people will be discussed in the next section. The key to Maori success was the modern *pa* system; an innovative military method designed as an antidote to the British system, a form of counter-European warfare. The modern *pa* system meant that the British did not win the New Zealand Wars through superior technology, superior methods, or indeed through any kind of qualitative superiority at all. In the final analysis, they won for the same reason that the Goths beat the Romans: overwhelming numbers.

II THE WARS AND THE PATTERN OF NEW ZEALAND RACE RELATIONS

THE CONTEMPORARY BRITISH INTERPRETATION OF THE NEW Zealand Wars, discussed as a whole in the next chapter, presents a very distorted picture of the Maori achievement. With some partial exceptions, modern historians have failed to correct this. They select a mixture of contemporary views, eliminate the overt value-judgements, and make minor adjustments, but they perpetuate the main lines of older interpretations—and so, to some extent, endorse them through repetition.

This defective picture of the Wars is a *received* version. Historians have inherited it, not created it. But the fact remains that it is the merest travesty of one of the most efficient and effective resistance efforts ever mounted by a tribal people against European expansion. This situation is serious enough of itself. It deprives New Zealanders of a terrible but important element of their history, obscures the true capacities of the Maori people, and helps conceal the grimmer realities of New Zealand race relations. But a misunderstanding of the course of the Wars may also have implications for connected fields of study. This section briefly explores some possibilities, and seeks to set the revised picture of the Wars in the context of the broad sweep of New Zealand race-relations history. This involves a classic historian's dilemma: the choice between the devil of pretending that parts of a whole are discrete phenomena, and the deep blue sea of trespassing outside one's speciality. Here, as elsewhere in this book, the latter danger is preferred, but it should be noted that the intention is less to provide answers than to ask questions.

The legend of the New Zealand Wars assumes that, despite a relatively enlightened race-relations policy, the outbreak of war was inevitable because of a fundamental material conflict: the competition for land between Maori and settler. Though some historians are ambivalent about Taranaki, there is still a strong tendency to see the British as having been inevitably victorious in each war. But the courage and chivalry of the Maori in their hopeless struggle is said to have created an enduring esteem for them in the minds of their enemies. With the older humanitarian strand in British policy, this respect survived various trials and tribulations to form the basis of modern, model, New Zealand race relations—so much better than those of settlement colonies in Australia, America, and Africa.

In the past, this legend has reinforced, and been reinforced by, two other myths. The first, discussed more fully in the next chapter, was the belief that the Maori was inevitably dying out as a result of contact with Europeans. The idea of 'Fatal Impact' was influential in New Zealand as early as the 1830s, when perceived evidence of Maori depopulation seemed to indicate that they would soon share the fate of other aboriginal victims of European contact. From 1860, the belief received a fresh impetus from the imported compound of ideas conveniently known as Social Darwinism, and between 1870 and 1900 it was quite prevalent. In 1881, A. K. Newman said what many others thought about the Maori: 'Taking all things into consideration, the disappearance of the race is scarcely subject for much regret. They are dying out in a quick, easy way, and are being supplanted by a superior race.'[7]

Within a few years of Newman's epitaph for the 'dying Maori', various factors, including evidence of an increase in the Maori population, led the legend, in its extreme form, into decline. But a moderated version exerted a persistent influence. The Maoris may not have been dying out before 1840, but they were in a state of social and cultural collapse. They may not have been dying out in 1870-1900, but they were in a state of despair, demoralization, and sullen apathy. In each case, the dire Maori situation facilitated their rapid assimilation into the British polity, and their less rapid social amalgamation. Maori independence, except for isolated post-war pockets so irrelevant that they were left alone by the colonists, quickly disappeared.

In 1885, a more benign alternative myth emerged in the form of Edward Tregear's book *The Aryan Maori*. Deriving his ideas from contemporary anthropology and philology, Tregear argued that Maori and European were descended from the same Aryan ancestors. Despite criticism and even ridicule, Tregear's idea caught on. In the first decades of the twentieth century, it was supported by writers such as S. P. Smith and J. Macmillan Brown, and it found its way into the popular ideology.[8]

To some extent, the legend of the Aryan Maori acted as an antidote to the legend of the Dying Maori: the Maori was not a congenital inferior doomed to extinction, but a wayward younger brother who could be saved. But, like the moderate version of the earlier legend, it encouraged an assimilationist view of the Maori past and the Maori future, and it fused with the myth of the New Zealand Wars. Like the courage and chivalry displayed by the Maori during the wars, an Aryan origin indicated that the Maori was both worthy and capable of assimilation into British civilization. 'The ordinary European', wrote Tregear, 'need not blush to own his brotherhood with . . . the heroes of Orakau.'[9]

The myths of the New Zealand Wars, of the Dying Maori, and of the Aryan Maori, are the component parts of a greater myth: the legend of New Zealand race relations. This emphasizes inevitability, minimizes the importance of conflict and Maori success in it, and presents a pattern of nineteenth-century race relations which is like a simple slope—short, straight, and for the Maori, downward. From this nadir the Maori are said to have been hauled by more enlightened Pakeha policy and a modern organization of their own—'the Young Maori Party'—which itself apparently advocated Maori-European amalgamation. The origin and underlying nature of part of this legend is discussed, in another context, in the next chapter. But what of the reality?

In the last generation, aspects of the race-relations legend have been subjected to historical revision. Recently, in a fine essay, J. M. R. Owens has cast what must surely be enduring doubt on the Fatal Impact thesis as applied to Maori society before 1840. In 1967, Alan Ward expressed dissatisfaction with the emphasis on European land-hunger as the predominant cause of war. In his subsequent book, Ward emphasized Maori initiatives in the 1840-90 period, together with the positive aspects of their engagement with British law and administration. Ann Parsonson has challenged the assumption that Maori society after 1840 was dominated by European influences. In the present writer's opinion, she underestimates the effectiveness of the King Movement, the Maori war effort, and the Maori capacity sometimes to transcend the parochial concerns that were admittedly the bread and butter of existence. But she paints a compelling picture of a competitive, robust, and autonomous Maori society which, while it incorporated some European methods, concentrated primarily on traditional and local issues. Though from an entirely different angle, Ward's work supports her thesis to some extent, and Ward certainly supports John A. Williams, M. P. K. Sorrenson, and others, who have questioned the concept of the post-war period as one of Maori withdrawal and sullen apathy.[10]

This trend towards revision is to be welcomed. But there is, perhaps, still cause for disquiet. For one thing, the fact that the received version is partly an ideological problem is not always grasped. The race-relations legend is an aspect of the New Zealand *mentalité*, with certain functions and a certain unity. Purely empirical revisionism addresses only the symptoms of the disease. The Hydra's heads are lopped off right and left, but the body remains unthreatened—even unrecognized. Secondly, revision had not extended to the wars, which were arguably the fulcrum of the entire race-relations process. Historians may know that they were important, but not exactly how or why. There is a missing piece, a very large one, in the jigsaw puzzle of race relations history.

H. M. Wright's hypothesis, published in 1959, was a step forward. Wright suggested that a period of Maori cultural assertiveness was followed, from 1830, by a mass adoption of Christianity, resulting from social dislocation and a loss of confidence in traditional beliefs. But this model has largely been rejected, on empirical grounds, without being effectively replaced. Moreover, it applies primarily to the years before 1850, and it does not eliminate the old idea of Fatal Impact, but simply adjusts the timing.[11] Apart from Wright, scholars chip away at the race-relations legend, but they cannot entirely destroy it without advancing some alternative model, which is similarly clear, comprehensive, and connected. The model might simply be less wrong than the legend but, without it, there is no focus for debate, no tangible format to facilitate the percolation of scholarly revision through to the wider public.

We are in danger of lapsing into the hackneyed catch-cry of the revisionist historian: 'in reality, things were much more complicated'. The catch-cry, of course, is perfectly true of race relations in nineteenth-century New Zealand. But this does not mean that there was no pattern; no general shape which, when elucidated, assists understanding more than it risks inaccuracy. In tentatively suggesting the following pattern, the present writer seeks to place the revised picture of the New Zealand Wars in its context and to emphasize three things: British aspirations as the agent of change; durable Maori independence, protected by military power, as the agent of stability; and the possible connections between this and Maori social and cultural resilience in the twentieth century. There is, of course, a danger of swinging the pendulum too far. Maori demoralization and social dislocation did occur at various times and in various areas. In a sense, the key difference in this approach is one of perspective. We do not ask how Maori society was damaged; we ask how it survived.

New Zealand race relations in the nineteenth century can be understood as the growth, contraction, and interaction of two zones. Broadly speaking, the zones were the geographical areas predominantly controlled by one people or the other, but this territorial definition is not absolute. Power could be divided according to kinds of issue as well as geographical areas. The rulers of a part of one zone might have great influence over part of the other. They might even exercise a kind of *suzerainty*—the right of general control over a semi-independent or autonomous entity. But they did not *rule*; they did not exercise a decisive internal influence, they did not impose the major social constraints, and they rarely supplied the main coercive power which backed them. The zones were not totally independent of each other, but they were autonomous.

The relationship of the two zones can be seen as passing through three phases, though these are essentially divisions of convenience, reference points marked out on a greater continuity. In the first, from the emergence of the European zone to 1863, Maori independence predominated. In the second, 1863-9, the tide of Maori autonomy began to turn, and in the third, from 1869 to some point early this century, it gradually ran out.

The European zone originated around 1820, when the first tiny mission and trading communities began tentatively to organize some of their own affairs, under the watchful suzerainty of the local Maori chief. Generally, the zone tended to expand, though it occasionally contracted, as with the destruction of the Whangaroa mission in 1827. Great expansion occurred from 1839, with the prospect and reality of official British intervention, and the advent of organized immigration, but it is important to emphasize the continuity. In some respects, the Treaty of Waitangi of 1840 is an artificial watershed. It changed the material race-relations situation in degree, but not in kind. Maori independence persisted, and in the North Island the situation until 1863 continued to be one of Maori predominance. They controlled most of the land and—at least until 1861—most of the people in the North Island. Some historians acknowledge this, but it has not been fully incorporated into the orthodoxy. New Zealand historiography has yet to recover from the fact that, in 1840, a few London map-makers coloured the North Island British red.

As suggested in a previous chapter, the British zone grew through the alienation of Maori land. Maoris sold for many reasons: to attract *Pakeha*, to meet debts, to gain capital for the development of remaining land or for arms and ammunition. One owner of a block might also sell to revenge himself on a rival co-owner, or make the ultimate assertion of owernship in the case of a disputed claim. Willingness to sell land did not necessarily indicate naivety, demoralization, or social dislocation. A preference for short-term over long-term benefits is human nature, and group-owned assets in many societies are subject to the same tendency. There is usually someone willing to sell. This gradual, natural, leakage of Maori land, and the consequent diminution of the Maori zone, could be stopped by asserting the authority of tribes to veto land sales—by asserting what amounted to a sovereign power. The King Movement was partly designed to reinforce this authority. Maori autonomy and the capacity to constrain land sales were thus inextricably linked.

The zones were politically independent of each other, but their relationship was close. Some kinds of social and cultural interaction were common, and legal and administrative interaction did occur. The apparatus of British law made an early appearance in the Maori zone. From 1846, Resident Magistrates worked in some Maori districts, under varying legislation, and they appointed Maori subordinates such as Wardens and Assessors. Alan Ward has shown that some Maoris were very willing to use this legal apparatus, and even requested that it be applied more energetically. With reference to Grey's 'New Institutions' scheme of 1861, Ward writes that in some Maori districts 'the coming of "the law" was hailed as enthusiastically as the coming of the gospel twenty years earlier'.[12] But like Christianity before it, the law was an invited guest whose attributes supplemented, but did not replace, those of its host. The introduction of even the most skeletal British legal apparatus into the Maori zone was very far from comprehensive. Where it did exist, it generally lacked coercive backing and worked only when the Maoris let it—a discretion they exercised very selectively. The positive response of some Maori groups in some periods may indicate the emergence of a fascinating syncretic system of social constraint, but it did not indicate real British control.

Economic interaction was vital to both zones. There were recessions and fluctuations, but generally Maori markets, primary production, and coastal and river transport under-pinned the economy of the European settlements. These settlements in turn provided the Maori with markets for their own goods, and trading-centres for the distribution of European goods. These activities were less competitive than complementary: the Maori zone was the European hinterland, the European zone was the Maori entrepôt. Economically, the two were mutually dependent. Even the most staunch Maori opponents of British expansion, in the midst of the war period, found this situation satisfactory. In March 1863, a Ngati Ruanui spokesman noted that, as a result of the Taranaki War, 'the only land in European hands was the town'—New Plymouth. 'As for the town,' he informed Governor Grey, 'let it be; it was very right that there should be a market for their produce.'[13]

The Maori-European relationship can be described as a collaborative association, and as such it fits the general theory of collaborative imperialism put forward by Ronald Robinson. 'Empire' depended on the consent of the 'governed', and this in turn depended on the extent to which Empire served the interests of the governed, or some of them.[14] But there is, perhaps, a residual implication of non-European subordinacy which is not entirely appropriate for New Zealand. It is true that cultural and technological borrowing was primarily from European to Maori and that, in the broadest sense, this may have involved a kind of subordinacy. But this type of equation can be taken too far. The original borrowing of Christianity, the potato, and the gun, did not make Europe subordinate to Palestine, Haiti, or the Islamic Empire, any more than the borrowing of the Welsh longbow made late medieval England subordinate to Wales. In most respects, the Maori-European relationship was a two-way process; each zone was dependent upon the other, and the term 'symbiosis' may be preferable to 'collaboration'. Certainly before 1840, and arguably before 1863, Europeans in Maori society were less the dominating agents of Empire than something akin to Jewish communities in some European societies, their power more commercial than political. Indeed, we could go further and compare the early *Pakeha* to Indians in Fiji or even Asians in modern Britain. The Maoris were by no means the last people to live to regret a policy of uncontrolled immigration.

The great threat to the Maori-European symbiosis was less a material conflict of interest than a conflict of aspirations. A situation of parity with, or inferiority to, peoples like the Maori simply did not accord with British expectations. The British were not satisfied with part of the land, part of the economy, or part of the government. But the persistent stereotype of the fat and greedy settler has always been a scapegoat for less tangible factors. British expectations arose, less from individual greed, than from the racial and national attitudes that were part of the Victorian ethos.

The tension between expectation and reality was, perhaps, the most fundamental cause of the New Zealand Wars. But it existed long before them. Even before 1820, the isolated European individuals living with the Maoris would, no doubt, have preferred to control their hosts. They did not try, because of the obvious Maori monopoly of armed might. From 1840, large-scale European immigration made Maori military superiority less obvious, and the theoretical British assumption of sovereignty increased the expectation that they would rule in practice. There followed a series of British attempts to bring the reality into conformity with the expectation; to convert nominal sovereignty into substantive sovereignty. In 1843, a posse of armed settlers set out to teach Te Rauparaha that he was subject to British sovereignty in fact. At Wairau, it was routed. As historians have observed, this was the first and last settler commando ever mounted in New Zealand, and this fact in itself was significant for race relations. With all due respect to British humanitarianism, one reason why New Zealand settlers did not treat the Maoris as their Australian counterparts did the Aborigines was that, when they tried, they got killed.

The Northern War was the next British initiative, or rather a Maori response to FitzRoy's hesitant attempts to assert British authority. Once Heke and Kawiti had called FitzRoy's bluff, with the sack of Kororareka, the British applied substantial coercive power for the first time: an expeditionary force which eventually grew to 1,300 Imperial troops. But they applied it in vain, and their forces were thwarted three successive times. In the smaller conflicts at Wellington and Wanganui, the Maoris were less successful. But they did not suffer defeat in battle, and their resistance seems to have slowed the alienation of land in Wanganui and the Manawatu.

The 1840s have been described as a time of testing, and this is true, but British power did not emerge very well from it. The conflicts of this period, particularly the Northern War, helped establish the limits of the two zones, and of the relationship between them. The British showed themselves to be far from helpless, and henceforth their zone, too, was protected by military power, though the Maori belief that Europeans were valuable continued to be important. But Heke and Kawiti had successfully defended their autonomy against government encroachment, and in the succeeding decade the government consequently did less encroaching. Other chiefs in other districts did not fight their own 'Northern Wars' because they did not have to.

Thus checked, and believing Maori independence was fading naturally, the British were more circumspect between 1848 and 1860—the heyday of New Zealand race relations. But the pressure of expectation was too great, and in Taranaki in 1860 the British again sought to assert their sovereignty within the Maori zone. This time, their forces grew into a small army of 3,500 Imperial and colonial troops, but again they were blocked. Eventually, in the Waikato War of 1863-4, a large British army, in which perhaps 18,000 men served at one time or another, achieved victory over the King Movement. But British success was qualified in two senses. Since the King Movement survived, the British victory was limited in itself. Secondly, after the withdrawal of Imperial troops, Titokowaru and Te Kooti created a second chance for the Maori people—an opportunity to reverse the decision of 1864. But this second chance just failed of fruition, and from 1869 the tide had definitely turned.

The Maoris lost in the end, and this had grave consequences for them, of which casualties, economic damage, and some demoralization were only the most obvious. Defeat reduced the political cohesion of some tribes, as it did the power and influence of the main supra-tribal organization: the King Movement. This in turn reduced the capacity of the Maori to control social and cultural assimilation, the application of coercive British law, and the alienation of land. Confiscation was not so important. It fell mainly on three or four tribes, and of the 3.5 million acres theoretically confiscated, only 1.6 million were actually occupied.[15] But the diminution of Maori power and political cohesion enabled the British, with the help of the Native Land Court machinery established in 1865, to inaugurate a new spasm of land-selling similar in scale to that of 1840-55. By 1891 the Maoris retained only eleven million of the North Island's twenty-eight million acres. Moreover, land owned by the Maoris was no longer a broadly accurate definition of the extent of their autonomous zone. A substantial minority of Maori land was leased, or held in small blocks scattered through *Pakeha* territory, and was therefore under British control.

But the autonomous Maori zone did not suddenly disappear in 1869. The period 1863-9 was the point where the tide of Maori independence began to turn, but that tide ran out very slowly. Maori autonomy persisted long after the wars, and perhaps the reason for this was less Pakeha benevolence than latent Maori military power, and the after-effects of formidable resistance. More speculatively, it is suggested that this durable autonomy was linked to the movements and organizations which helped preserve Maori vigour and identity—*Maoritanga*—in the twentieth century. After the wars, Maori autonomy was protected in two apparently very different ways: through centres of resistance, and through centres of 'collaboration', used here in the narrower sense of alliance with the government.

The largest centre of resistance was the King Movement, whose territory came to be known as the King Country. At least until the mid-1880s, this area was an independent state, making and enforcing its own laws, conducting its own affairs, sheltering fugitives from *Pakeha* justice, and killing Europeans who crossed its borders without permission. As Sorrenson has shown, it was not a centre of 'sullen isolation', but of economic and cultural activity, involving many Maoris outside its borders.[16]

There is no doubt of the King Movement's independence for many years after the war which was supposed to have subjugated it, but we have a great deal still to learn about it. We do not know precisely when its autonomy came to an end. The conventional cut-off point, King Tawhiao's visit to the confiscated Waikato in 1881, is unsatisfactory,[17] and 1890 may be more realistic. We do not even know how big the King Country was. Ngati Haua were soon tempted away from it, and it is generally assumed that it was restricted to Ngati Maniapoto territory. But this is not proven. Some Ngati Haua returned to the Kingite fold, and it may be that some Ngati Raukawa, Ngati Tuwharetoa, and even Wanganui territory was in practice part of the King Country. A survey in 1884 indicates that it encompassed 7,000 square miles, nearly one-sixth of the North Island—quite a large 'isolated pocket'.[18] Thus, in the late nineteenth century, an independent Maori state nearly two-thirds the size of Belgium existed in the middle of the North Island. Not all historians have noticed it.

There were other centres of resistance, notably the Urewera district and South Taranaki. Significant European penetration did not occur in the former until the twentieth century. In the latter, the prophet Te Whiti O Rongomai prevented the sale or occupation of land, harboured fugitives, and provided a major focus of cultural activity. South Taranaki independence probably ended in 1881, when a government expedition raided the central community of Parihaka.

Where it is recognized, the survival of these parts of the Maori zone is attributed to *Pakeha* benevolence or disinterest, or to the wise policy of non-intervention instituted by Donald McLean (Native Minister 1869-76). But voluntary restraint of this type was not a marked settler characteristic, particularly after such incidents as the Kingite killing of nine Europeans (including women and children) at Pukearuhe in 1869, and the slaying of trespassers in 1870, 1873, and 1880. After the 1870 incident, McLean—to whose forbearance Kingite survival is often credited—wrote: 'I consider that at no time has there been a better *casus belli*.' But Cameron's army had not been able to crush the King Movement, and the force available to the colony was very much smaller. A Kingite leader told McLean: 'Do not think that I have forgotten how to use my weapon. It is sheathed by Tawhiao's orders, but still I have hold of the handle of it.' McLean was no benevolent philanthropist, but he was a realist, and making a virtue of necessity was a well-tried government tactic in New Zealand.[19]

Kingite independence was an after-effect of the formidable Maori resistance of the wars period, and so too, perhaps, was that of the Tuhoe in the Urewera. As the operations of 1869–72 showed, the Urewera Mountains were not inaccessible, but campaigning in them, against tough Tuhoe warriors, was a difficult and expensive business. An expedition mounted in 1895 to enforce a survey expected to meet resistance, and perhaps it did not do so only because a negotiated compromise was reached, which involved some legislative recognition of Urewera autonomy.[20]

At first sight, it is more difficult to ascribe the autonomy of South Taranaki to the same cause, because Te Whiti was firmly committed to pacificism. But the government took the threat of resistance very seriously. Te Whiti gave sanctuary to a Maori who shot a surveyor in 1878, but the government did not act until 1881. When it did move against Parihaka, the Native Minister, John Bryce, took no less than 1,600 troops on the expedition.[21] Bryce may well have failed to comprehend Te Whiti's movement, and his mobilization of so large a force against a small group of pacifists has occasioned sarcastic comment, but to some extent his fear was understandable. For a close ally of Te Whiti's was Titokowaru and, unlike historians, Bryce had not forgotten the disastrous campaign of 1868, in which he himself had been a young officer.

The survival of these autonomous areas may be much more than an interesting anachronism. For one thing, they saved Maori lives. The decline of the Maori population, which continued generally until about 1890, was less severe in these areas.[22] They preserved land which would otherwise have been alienated much earlier. They may also have encouraged a degree of residual autonomy, even after resistance ceased to be realistic. The King Movement was still collecting taxes, administering justice, and discouraging land-sales in the 1890s.[23] And organizations and movements based on the centres of resistance exerted an important influence long after this. The King Movement created the *Kauhanganui* (Great Council) in 1894, provided a platform for the great twentieth-century Maori leader Te Puea Herangi, and continued to be 'a bulwark for Maori ideals and values'.[24] Would any of this have occurred if Cameron had wholly achieved his aim in the Waikato War?

Tuhoe provided some of the support for Te Kooti's *Ringatu* religion, and a new prophet, Rua Kenana, emerged from the tribe in 1905, and remained influential until his death in 1937. The Parihaka community continued to be active until Te Whiti's death in 1907, and there may be a link between South Taranaki autonomy in the nineteenth century and the Ratana Movement which began in 1921. T. W. Ratana, a Maori religious and political leader of great importance, came from a pro-government tradition on his father's side, but both his mother and his wife were South Taranaki Maoris by birth and inclination, and much of his early support came from that region.[25]

The second bastion of Maori autonomy was collaboration. The *kupapa* position can no longer be automatically judged with approval for its foresight in seeing the futility of resistance. Resistance was not futile, and there is a possibility, hypothetical but harsh, that greater support for Titokowaru would have brought him victory. But the Maori had an age-old tradition of tribal division, and to criticize them for not transcending this still more than they did would be an unreasonable use of hindsight—like disparaging an early four-minute miler for not breaking 3.50. And collaboration did yield important benefits for the Maori people.

The colonial government ended the wars in alliance with a number of Maori tribes, notably Ngati Porou, Ngati Kahungunu, Wanganui, and Arawa. In the post-war period, these *kupapa* found that *Pakeha* friendship could be as damaging as hostility. Some engaged in land-selling with the enthusiasm of the 1840s, and for similar reasons. They found themselves caught up in the Native Land Court machinery and suffered the consequences. Much of the land sold between 1870 and 1891 came from *kupapa* tribes. But fighting for the government could protect tribal cohesion and power as much as fighting against it. The *kupapa* retained their military power, and were not always averse to using it. In 1879 an armed party of Arawa occupied the local Land Court, there was some resistance to land purchase among Ngati Kahungunu, and in 1880 the Wanganui tribe prevented a government survey by armed force and blocked the Wanganui River to *Pakeha* traffic.[26] The Wanganui leader was none other than Major Kepa te Rangihiwinui.

In the North, the autonomy of Ngapuhi was shored up by their history of both resistance and collaboration. In 1864, twenty years after Grey was supposed to have imposed British authority, F. E. Maning wrote: 'Here in the north there is no more hope of establishing the supremacy of the law than there is of flying in the air. Without a successful war of absolute conquest there is no more sign of the natives having any inclination to submit to British law than there was twenty years ago *not so much* indeed.'[27] This remained the situation. Between 1866 and 1888, without successful interference from the government, Ngapuhi *hapu* indulged in at least five feuds, with the loss of a score of lives—a salutary reminder of the unattractive side of Maori autonomy, which also included customary killings for sorcery and adultery. Ngapuhi also withheld offenders from the police, and retained the willingness and capacity to resist government encroachment until the end of the century—when people did begin 'flying in the air'.[28]

Ngapuhi and the *kupapa* tribes, including Wanganui, Arawa, and Ngati

Kahungunu, were also the originators of a new and important movement: *Kotahitanga*, the Maori Unity Movement. Beginning about 1880, this movement held parliamentary assemblies throughout the 1890s, encouraging *Maoritanga* through its activities, edicts, and publications, and agitating for recognition from the colonial government. *Kotahitanga* eventually obtained some support from the King Movement, and its general principles, if not the original organization, exerted considerable influence in the twentieth century. In 1893, *Kotahitanga* claimed that if 'these loyal Natives had not fought in [the] wars, [British] authority and sovereignty of and over New Zealand would have ceased long ago'.[29] Few Europeans would willingly have acknowledged this, but it was probably true, and post-war *kupapa* autonomy and the limited government recognition of their contribution during the wars were arguably part of the basis of *Kotahitanga*.

The *kupapa* had been vital to the colonist war efforts in 1865-72, and they could not be denied some share in the post-war settlement. The four Maori seats in the House of Representatives, established in 1867, were a case in point. This measure was rendered acceptable to colonial politicians largely by the need to cement *kupapa* alliances, and it was to *kupapa* chiefs that the seats went.[30] The appointment of *kupapa* leaders to the Legislative Council fulfilled the same purpose, as did pensions, medals, assessorships, and other tokens of government esteem. Not all these measures were immediately useful to the Maori, but they did create a foothold in the *Pakeha* machinery of government. This was later utilized by a new kind of *kupapa*: bi-cultural politicians such as James Carroll and Peter Buck, and organizations such as the Young Maori Party. The foothold was subsequently also used by Kingite, Ratana, and independent politicians.[31]

During the wars, the colonists had never liked relying on *kupapa* help. They did so because they had to, and they had to because of the strength of Maori resistance. The *kupapa* share in the post-war settlement was an indirect result of the war effort of the resisting Maoris.

The autonomous Maori zone persisted long after the wars, but the date of its demise is difficult to fix. Further research is required, but various considerations lead one to speculate about a twentieth-century ending. To give two examples, the last case of armed Maori resistance occurred in 1916, when the Tuhoe prophet Rua Kenana was arrested, on dubious charges, after a gun-battle in the Urewera in which ten people were killed or wounded. The police expedition was 'conducted like a military operation' entering alien territory.[32] Secondly, a recent statistical analysis of crime rates reveals that the rate of Maori assault convictions (a key indicator in the study of social cohesion) did not match the European rate until the decade 1908-17, being previously very much lower.[33] This suggests that, until 1908-17, Maori social constraints operated so effectively that there was little violent crime, or that Maoris punished their own violent crime, or that it was punished by no one. None of these possibilities implies a high degree of government control.

Thus it may be that the process by which the British zone absorbed the

Maori was very slow, lasting for a century after 1820. The main reason for the gradual pace of change was Maori military power: the prospect, reality, and after-effect of formidable resistance. Before the 1863–9 turning point, resistance had already had substantial benefits for the Maori. They ceased to be the senior partner in the racial relationship in that period, not 1840, 1843, 1845, or 1860. The slow pace of change also meant that subjugation, when it came, was less complete, as with the Saxon conquest of the Celtic Britons subsequently known as Welsh. Language, culture, and identity were preserved. This was beneficial in itself, and provided a springboard for subsequent social and political resurgence. The preservation of identity does not, of course, mean the absence of change. Maori society has always been capable of adaptation without losing its fundamentally Maori character.

The New Zealand race-relations legend, like most myths, has its element of truth. British humanitarianism, attempts at understanding, and generous recognition of Maori qualities such as courage and chivalry, did exist. This created some freely-given respect for the Maori in British minds, with positive effects on subsequent race relations. Partly due to this, Maori culture and society survived the New Zealand Wars and their aftermath. But a more important cause of Maori durability was the limit their resistance imposed on British victory. Such things as the King Movement and the Maori seats in parliament are only the most obvious fruits of this. The Maoris owe something to British wisdom and tolerance, but they owe more to the strength of their own right arm.

The race-relations legend is dangerously inaccurate, but it cannot be dismissed as a mere colonialist trick, an oppressor's sleight-of-hand. It is a complex social, political, and cultural phenomenon of enormous power, one of New Zealand's founding myths, a part of the national ideology. In the form determined by the myths of the New Zealand Wars and the Aryan Maori, it can arguably be seen as progressive and beneficent—an antidote to 'hard racism', a balm for the wounds of conflict, a successful exercise in hypnotherapy. But even if this were accepted, the legend has had its day. It is time for New Zealanders to face the facts of their history, and seek to solve, rather than conceal, the problem it has bequeathed to them.

—————15—————

The Victorian Interpretation of Racial Conflict

THROUGHOUT THIS BOOK, THE CONTEMPORARY BRITISH interpretation of the battles and campaigns of the New Zealand Wars has been investigated in as much detail as the events themselves. The purpose of this has been to go beyond the mere detection of 'bias' in the British writings which dominate the historical record, and seek to understand how that bias worked. This concluding chapter summarizes the results of the investigation, and offers an explanation for the pattern of interpretation which emerges. It then suggests that these findings have a wider application: that they can be used, at least in cases of racial warfare, to alleviate the problem of one-sided evidence.

I THE DOMINANT INTERPRETATION

CONTEMPORARY BRITISH OPINIONS ABOUT THE NEW Zealand Wars can be discussed as a single 'dominant interpretation' in two senses. Firstly, the British interpretation dominated the Maori as far as the written record was concerned. Whatever their historical success, historiographically the British won the New Zealand Wars hands down. The second sense is perhaps less obvious. Throughout the Wars, there were some British commentators who doubted their compatriots' victory claims, and even gave the Maoris some of the credit due to them. Their opinions help make revision possible. But, normally, these commentators did not put their pieces of information together to form an idea of the Maori military system. Those few who did were overwhelmed, ignored, set aside, or forgotten. The more objective or generous British interpreters form an important minority in recognizing the existence and impact of specific Maori victories, but they tended to rejoin the mainstream of interpretation in incorrectly explaining them, in ascribing them to particular rather than general causes. Moreover, it was the mainstream of interpretation which was the more widely received and accepted. It was endorsed, repeated, and amplified until it became the dominant interpretation; the general rule which absorbed, replaced, or *dominated* the exceptions.

The dominant interpretation rarely involved overt hypocrisy or conscious

311

distortion—indeed, it was compatible with real respect for some Maori qualities, and with a humanitarian 'philo-Maori' position. It was not a culpable act of deception for which its authors should be chastised, but it did produce a fundamentally and systematically false picture of the New Zealand Wars.

In different respects, the dominant interpretation can be understood as a system and as a framework. It was not systematic in the sense of an artifice or conspiracy; there was no collective and methodical censorship, no conscious plot to deceive. But it was systematic in the sense that it operated according to a discernible pattern which, broadly speaking, remained constant from case to case. It was also systematic in that its component parts formed an integrated whole. The components were numerous, diverse, and sometimes logically contradictory, but they addressed connected problems, maximized each other's strengths, and compensated for each other's weaknesses. Their relationship can be understood as that of a succession of safety nets, each filtering out a further share of the unacceptable facts and implications which had escaped those above it.

In other respects, the dominant interpretation had the character of a framework: a collection of limits containing within it considerable room for variation. Interpreters of the New Zealand Wars shared a British heritage, but otherwise they were a diverse lot, ranging from privates to generals, missionaries to settler politicians, Wanganui newspaper correspondents to London newspaper editors. Their accounts naturally varied substantially; there were great differences in emphasis, and sometimes intense conflicts between opposing schools of thought. But, in the final analysis, the British interpretation was more remarkable for its consistency than its diversity. The set of options was large, but it was limited by pressures to which virtually all interpreters were subject. They could select varying combinations of options, but they could not extend the set. Occurrences such as defeat evoked responses drawn from the same restricted range. Diversity and internecine debate was contained within a greater unity, a framework flexible but strong.

The functioning of the dominant interpretation can be summarized as follows. The dynamic force behind it was the expectation of victory. This sometimes led to the exaggeration of real British victories and the creation of fictional ones. Where defeat was recognized, the jarring disjuncture between event and expectation created a traumatic shock, which then had to be alleviated, mainly through the development of acceptable explanations for the disaster. British stereotypes of their own and of Maori military abilities determined what was acceptable and what was not. Unacceptable implications which survived this part of the process were subsequently downplayed, obscured, or forgotten.

The enormously powerful British expectation of victory pervades the interpretation of the Wars. Sometimes, it proved so strong that it simply overshot the evidence—given one element of an equation, commentators would deduce the second from the principle that the British always won battles against savages. In 1864, one writer referred to the Maori victory of Puketutu during the Northern War as follows: 'Engaged on both sides here, the rear rank of the soldiers faced round and charged with the bayonet. Further description is superfluous.'[1] At Cracroft's *pa* at Waireka in 1860, the presence of the enemy was also superfluous, and the expectation of victory created a fictional triumph.

This tendency often acted in concert with a reluctance to credit the Maoris with strategic finesse and the ability to co-ordinate the movements of two or more groups, and with the propensity to exaggerate Maori numbers and casualties. As we have seen, the combined effect was the frequent creation of fictional victories, and the still more frequent exaggeration of real ones. The expectation of victory also meant that when defeats were recognized, they created a massive shock. British responses to defeat basically consisted in an effort to absorb this shock; through some kind of palliative, which counter-balanced the disaster; through a satisfying explanation which softened the blow by providing acceptable reasons for it; or through a suppressive reflex, whereby the defeat was played down, ignored, or forgotten.

One kind of palliative involved taking that aspect of a lost battle in which the British had been least unsuccessful, and treating it as an autonomous operation. This ameliorated or even nullified the disastrous aspects. Another common palliative was the exaggeration of Maori casualties. The thin red line may have been worsted, but not before it had piled the ground high with Maori corpses. High Maori casualties might be deduced from 'bloodstained trenches' observed after a battle or from the number 'seen to fall'. British accounts were liberally peppered with both phrases. The former made a corpse from a cut finger, while the latter ignored Maori combat practice: when you were fired at, or about to be fired at, you instantly dropped to the ground. The British knew of this practice—some colonial units adopted it—but its implication for estimates of Maori losses were rarely acknowledged.[2]

Hard evidence of Maori casualties was often manipulated. When Maori estimates of their own casualties were received, the British dismissed or discounted them, or assumed that they referred only to chiefs. When Maori bodies were counted after a battle, it was assumed that many more had been carried off. This assumption was sometimes true, but more often it was both gratuitous and false. On one occasion, it was too much even for the colonial press. 'It is generally supposed that the Hau Haus have been exterminated to the extent of something under 10,000, but with the usual tact and consideration that distinguishes these playful creatures, they have done their own undertaking and removed the entire lot.'[3] British exaggeration of Maori casualties was also important in the manipulation of victory, but it had its greatest impact as a palliative for defeat. The more damaging or embarrassing the defeat, the greater the tendency to inflate Maori losses. On some occasions high estimates of Maori casualties lacked even a frail basis in fact, and were created purely by the need for them. 'Their wounded are not more than 8', wrote one British commentator, 'our wounded come to near

100. From this it will be seen that a large number of them must have been lost in the lagoon.'[4]

Palliatives were important, but the main way of ameliorating the shock of defeat was to offer acceptable explanations for it. The first and most simple acceptable explanation was overwhelming Maori numbers. There was a tendency to exaggerate Maori numbers at all times, but immediately after British defeats it suddenly became acute. The interpretation of the Battle of Puketakauere provides a good example of this. As with the exaggeration of Maori casualties, slender favourable evidence was accepted, strong contrary evidence was rejected and, on occasion, no evidence at all was required. The British were outnumbered because they were beaten, and they were beaten because they were outnumbered. The exaggeration of enemy strength is very common in war, and emphasis on it may seem to belabour the obvious. But the tendency was pervasive, influential, and persistent. The Maori achieved what they did with a quarter as many fighting men as most contemporary British believed, and half as many as most historians believe.

A still more important acceptable explanation was to attribute defeat to the deficiencies of the military forces. Englishmen were not unaccustomed to criticizing their generals. The emphasis on the responsibility of the leader, as with the hero-worship of Nelson and Wellington, could apply to defeat as well as victory, as the Crimean War showed. But it seems fair to suggest that the New Zealand scapegoat hunt was unusual in degree if not in kind. Of the thirteen Imperial and colonial officers who held independent commands of any importance during the Wars, not one escaped severe criticism. Other theatres of war have been the graveyard of reputations, but the death rate was rarely quite this high.

If attacks on the leadership in New Zealand were unusual in degree, the other aspect of the criticism of the military was extremely unusual in kind. This was the series of aspersions cast on the quality of the rank and file. The 96th, 40th, and 43rd regiments were heavily criticized for their performances at Kororareka, Orakau, and the Gate Pa respectively. The 43rd, which had one of the highest reputations of any active regiment, and their naval partners at the Gate Pa, Britain's favourite fighting men, appeared as 'arrant cowards'. Even the frontiersmen-soldiers of the colonial forces, so highly praised for their prospective deeds before they took the field, found themselves subjected to terrible abuse after their defeats in 1868.

Both failed leaders and failed troops could be seen as exceptions to the rule of British military excellence, rather than evidence that the rule itself was questionable. In 1860, the New-Zealander was 'driven to a very painful contrast between our commanders who imperil New Zealand, and those who saved our Indian Empire two years ago'. Similarly, failures by the troops cast doubt, not on the over-all reputation of British soldiers, but on the failure of particular units to live up to it. 'If the 96th is a specimen of the [new] army, the sooner the Horse Guards incorporates the pensioners, the Old Peninsula and Waterloo men, the better.' Colonial soldiers, as 'troops of British lineage', were victims of the same high expectations.[5]

When British commentators acknowledged the failure of their officers and men, but could not bring themselves to ascribe it to cowardice or incompetence, they did not shrink from offering mysterious or even ridiculous explanations. In 1868, a colonial writer regretted that 'some fatality appears to hang over our colonial forces, for, let them be commanded and officered in as seemingly efficient a manner as possible, still they are doomed to discomfiture.' In 1860, the *Times* of London offered the following explanation for British failures in the Taranaki War: 'Can it be that the very insignificance coupled with the boastful insolence of the enemy unsteadies our men and puzzles our commanders, just as at chess a bad and reckless player is sometimes more formidable than a master of the game?' There was something strangely desperate about the great New Zealand scapegoat hunt.[6]

A third favoured explanation for British difficulties was sometimes used in concert with assertions of military incompetence, but it appeared most often as the counter to such allegations. This was the argument that British problems were primarily the result of the New Zealand terrain, in combination with various Maori 'natural advantages'. We have seen that problems of terrain were sometimes exaggerated. Rough country was common, but the Maoris often selected fairly accessible positions and waited to be attacked in them. Still more questionable was the concept of special abilities: advantages which were very useful, but of a distinctly 'lower' type. The capacity to 'burrow like rabbits through the high fern' was one. 'Anyone who knows what it is to shoot a snipe or a rat when running, can form some idea of the motion of a native in the bush.' The Maoris were also blessed with inborn aquatic skills. 'Amphibious in their habits, they are as much at home in the water as on land.' Innate Maori bushcraft, whereby they 'appeared and disappeared in the most marvellous way', was stressed time and time again by British writers. These abilities made possible the characteristically evasive Maori tactics.[7]

The kernel of truth was deceptive. The Maoris were skilled in bushcraft, and some were good swimmers and boat-handlers, but these talents were of limited use in constructing and utilizing the modern *pa* that were the main British problem and the major cause of their defeats. The emphasis on 'natural advantages' not only provided false but acceptable explanations of defeat, but also helped to create a false picture of the wars as guerilla conflicts where the problem was not beating the enemy but finding him.

The fourth common explanation was to attribute Maori success to imitation. After inspecting some Maori entrenchments, one British officer suggested that perhaps 'the most studious of them have been reading our works published on fortification.'[8] Few commentators were happy to attribute successful imitation to Maori scholarship, however, and allusions to European renegades acting as the medium of information were more common. After inspecting the scene of his defeat at Ohaeawai *pa* in 1845, Colonel Despard wrote: 'The strength of the place has struck me with surprise, and I cannot help feeling convinced that the Natives could not have constructed

it without some European assistance.'[9] Six months later, white men were
rumoured to have shown the Maoris how to make breastworks at
Ruapekapeka, and allusions to renegades imparting European knowledge
were to recur throughout the wars.[10]

The Europeans supposedly responsible for Maori military education were
usually British army deserters, but the range included Australian convicts,
American traders, Irish Fenians, and French missionaries. Colonel H. J.
Warre breathlessly informed his superiors that there could be 'very little
doubt that the Maori insurrection has been encouraged and fostered by
Foreign Priests'.[11] There are indications that a few Europeans did help the
Maoris, and this may be worth further study, but their aid usually took the
form of arms and ammunition.[12] A few British deserters actually lived and
fought with the Maoris, but their status was low. Moreover, the private
soldiers involved were hardly in a position to give instruction on a system of
fortification which was a mystery to their generals—'our works published
on fortification' would have been of little help to the Maoris even if they
had access to them. Normally, however, these questions did not arise,
because there were no deserters with the particular Maori groups referred
to. Their presence was simply deduced from the quality of the Maori
entrenchments.

These explanations had two things in common: they were acceptable to
the British, and they were inaccurate. What defined acceptability and
precluded accuracy was a British stereotype of Maori military abilities.
British commentators were quite capable of recognizing some Maori
qualities: courage, chivalry, dexterity at guerilla methods, and intuitive or
traditional fort-building skill. But there were others that they were reluctant
to acknowledge. For some commentators, these included good marksmanship, discipline, and the capacity for sustained and well-organized physical
labour. We have seen that these features of the dominant interpretation properly belong in the dustbin of historical apocrypha. Collectively, they could
result in quite serious distortion: some Maori victories could not be explained
without reference to good shooting, battle discipline, and high work-rates.
But a still more important aspect of the stereotype was the reluctance to
credit the Maori with the higher military talents: the capacity to co-
ordinate, to think strategically, and to innovate tactically and technically.

Occasionally, the British belief that the Maori lacked these talents was explicit, though it was usually coupled with a reference to their possession of
other qualities. The Maori were 'clever at building stockades and fighting in
the bush', according to the *Nelson Examiner,* but 'incapable of combination'.
Colonel Carey freely acknowledged Maori bush-fighting ability, but stated
categorically that 'no strategical knowledge was shewn by the Maori in his
plans'. 'With all their cleverness', wrote Von Tempsky, the Maoris 'have
not the true military sagacity.'[13] But the decisive evidence for the existence
of this belief is implicit, though clear and overwhelming. The British consistently sought to avoid the conclusion that the Maori possessed the higher
military talents, despite the fact that a major manifestation of these talents,

the modern *pa*, was constantly before them. Instead, they searched widely and desperately for alternative explanations for their defeats and difficulties.

This tendency was more complicated than simply not seeing what one did not wish to see. For some British interpreters, it was less a failure to perceive than a reluctance to recognize. In 1869, Colonel Whitmore, in commenting on a minor ambush set by Titokowaru, noted that individual scouts had been permitted to pass unmolested. He suspected that the chief had done this intentionally, to avoid springing the trap prematurely, but he expressed this conclusion very tentatively: 'If this surmise is too civilised a motive for his [Titokowaru's] movements, it is very difficult to understand why he permitted so many individuals travelling almost alone to pass . . . and reserved his attack for the strongest party likely to pass.'[14] Whitmore was no fool; he had recent hard experience of Titokowaru's abilities, yet he still hesitated to credit him with so simple a trick.

Good enemy tactics and strategy were relatively easy to overlook or avoid, but sophisticated Maori field engineering was more tangible and, consequently, less easily ignored. The British often occupied abandoned modern *pa*, and the facts of construction stared them in the face. The more able and open-minded of them were not always content to attribute the quality of these fortifications to Maori tradition, instinct, or mimicry. But their recognition of Maori ability was incomplete or short-lived. In early 1846, the newly-arrived Governor Grey—a trained army officer—produced a relatively enlightened memorandum on war against the Maori. Like most other analysts, he unduly emphasized Maori guerilla skills, but he acknowledged that their *pa* were formidable, impregnable to light artillery. But he concluded: 'there is, however, no doubt that a battery of 18-pounders, of 24-pounders, or of 32-pounders, would in hours knock these stockades to pieces.'[15] Grey's insight was real but partial. He recognized that Maori anti-artillery defences created a problem, but assumed that it was amenable to a simple quantitative solution.

A few British officers, including General Cameron, had a more comprehensive understanding of the modern *pa* than Grey. After leaving New Zealand, Cameron became Governor of Sandhurst, the institution in which British army officers were trained. He was succeeded by General Frederick Middleton who, as an Ensign in the 58th regiment, had seen service in New Zealand.[16] From 1866 to 1884, the military education of British officers was controlled by men who had first-hand knowledge of the effectiveness of sophisticated earthworks. Cameron in particular knew as much about modern *pa* as any European and the Waikato War was the major active command of his career. Cameron took his training job seriously, and his tenure was marked by persistent attempts at reform in the face of great difficulties, but neither he nor Middleton, as the British performance in later wars made clear, passed on any of their knowledge of trench and bunker systems.

Another officer, George Greaves, later a full general and prominent member of the 'Wolseley Ring', actually described modern *pa* as 'perfect examples of field-fortification'. In 1920, in the preface to Greaves's *Memoirs*,

Field-Marshal Earl Haig wrote: 'I cannot name any other general from whom I learnt more practical soldiering.'[17] Haig, of course, was the Commander-in-Chief of British armies on the Western Front in 1915-18. We can perhaps gather from this how much the 'perfect examples of field-fortification' taught Greaves about the tactical limitations of offensives against earthworks.

Military thinking is often glacial in its rate of change, and these examples are merely suggestive anecdotes. But the officers concerned came closer than their fellows to understanding the Maori military system, and the fact that they came so far and no further is illuminating. Their knowledge was set aside, or held at arms length. It was not taken on board, not fully incorporated into their understanding of warfare. They failed to grasp that Maori methods formed an original and innovative military system—a system which cast doubt on the conventional axioms of European warfare. Most British interpreters, believing that Maoris could not possess the higher military talents, neither heard not listened to the lessons of the Maori system. The relatively enlightened minority heard, but they did not listen.

The British stereotype of Maori military abilities created the limits within which their interpretation had to operate. According to the stereotype, certain Maori abilities did not exist, and consequently could not be used to explain British defeats and difficulties. In particular, Maori strategic skill and field-engineering innovation, products of the higher military talents, were the last explanation to occur to the British observer. Since they were also the true explanation, the whole British interpretation was reduced to something like an attempt to explain a football game without reference to the ball.

Acceptable explanations were the most pervasive feature of the dominant interpretation. But, constrained as they were by the British stereotype of Maori abilities, explanations alone were not always found to be sufficient. A residue of unpleasant implications remained, and this was dealt with by what might be described as a suppressive reflex: a tendency to play down, obscure, or forget the unacceptable. Such tendencies existed during the war period, but their main effect was retrospective. As the years passed by, they became the point where the contemporary interpretation of the wars merged imperceptibly into historiography.

Those writers who discussed the wars in the years after 1872 sometimes scoffed at contemporary panic, and implied that the whole struggle was a storm in a tea-cup. We have seen how this tendency worked in the case of Titokowaru and the crisis of 1868. Its persistence is reflected in the statement of the respected historian James Hight, made in 1933 in the *Cambridge History of the British Empire*, to introduce the chapter on the wars. 'The wars have no claim to any great importance except for the political and sociological questions involved. They were small in scale, taught few, if any, striking lessons in the art of war, and are scarcely entitled to be classed in the category of "war" as recognised by international law.'[18] This assertion was a legacy of earlier interpretations, rather than a deduction for which Hight was wholly responsible, but for all that it could hardly be less true.

A more subtle but equally persistent form of suppression was to obscure Maori success, and the problem of how it was achieved; to distract attention from it by emphasizing other aspects of the Maori performance. Praise for Maori courage and chivalry, one of the more attractive elements of the dominant interpretation, was unfortunately a case in point. Contemporary British recognition of Maori courage and chivalry did occur, it was sincere, and soldiers and settlers deserve full credit for it. But it did not reflect a British capacity objectively to assess the Maori military performance as a whole. Indeed, it helped conceal their failure to do so.

Maori heroism at Orakau, in particular, was widely admired. Cameron and Gamble, the Deputy Quartermaster-General, praised the garrison's bravery, and they are much quoted. Similar praise from colonial writers is now less well known, but even authors very hostile to the Maori cause, such as Fox and Featon, commended their courage at Orakau. During the battle, Rewi or one of his subordinates had responded to a British call for surrender with the words: '*kaore e mau te rongo—ake ake*' ('Peace shall never be made—never, never'). Various versions of this became compulsory quoting in discussions of the wars; perhaps the most famous phrase in New Zealand history, with an entry all of its own in the national *Encyclopaedia* of 1965. As the Orakau legend burgeoned, the reality languished. The tactical brilliance of the counter-attack which led to the Maori escape, their strategic blunder in fighting at Orakau, the British massacre of women and wounded, and the fact that the battle had little over-all effect, were all obscured by the emphasis on romantic heroism, and on the British recognition of it. But British generosity, though real, was deceptive. Gamble wrote lyrically of the garrison's escape from Orakau 'calmly, in the face of death' in a 'silent and compact body', but he also believed Maoris to be 'incapable of prompt and organised action on emergencies'.[19] Admiration for some Maori qualities, such as courage and chivalry, gave British accounts the appearance of objectivity, not the reality.

The emphasis on Maori courage and chivalry began during the wars, but it increased greatly soon after them, growing almost to the point where it subsumed all else. Through histories, novels, poems, school texts, paintings, and film it perpetuated the notion of the wars as a limited fight with gloves on, a breeding-ground of mutual respect. The effects of this largely false picture on the race-relations legend have already been noted, and it also functioned to conceal the need for revision and obscure other aspects of the Maori performance—aspects ultimately more important than courage and chivalry. For to describe the Maori war effort primarily as brave and chivalrous is to offer a deceptive fraction of the truth, rather like describing Napoleon Bonaparte simply as a good brother. Yet it is this aspect of the Maori performance on which most attention has been focused. Pitifully enough, the closest thing to a historical debate on the wars is over precisely which member of the Orakau garrison said '*ake ake*'.

The stress on courage and chivalry was the most important way in which British defeats and their cause were obscured by an alternative emphasis, but it was not the only one. Colonial writers emphasized Maori 'atrocities' as much as their courage and this performed a similar function. The cannibalism of Titokowaru's followers received more attention than his brilliance as a general. The tendency to portray Te Kooti as the most able and formidable of Maori military leaders had the same effect. The least successful of the Maori generals, in the strictly military sense, Te Kooti became the best known.

The suppressive reflex had a direct effect on particularly embarrassing events which were difficult to accommodate in other ways, and perhaps it also exerted a less tangible influence. The half century after 1872 was in some respects an assertive phase of white New Zealand culture, though it remained Anglocentric. Proud references were made to the progress of the country, and to the peacetime achievements of the colonial pioneers. The colony—a titular 'Dominion' from 1908—happily shouldered more than its share of the South African and First World Wars. This was a time when one might have expected more use to be made of the budding nation's warlike past. After all, the colony had been at war for more than half of its first thirty years and, in proportion to the population, the conflict was large in scale. Instead of contenting themselves with imported military glory, patriotic writers could have dwelt upon the deeds of their own expeditions, colourful units, and heroes. Suitably interpreted, the wars could provide a rich harvest in these respects; stories of Ngatapa and the Urewera Campaign, 'Buck's Bravos' and 'The Young Brigade', 'Fighting Mac' and the Mair brothers, were not inherently inferior to imported martial legends.

A few writers did attempt to use the wars in this way, including T. W. Gudgeon in *Reminiscences of the Maori Wars* and *Defenders of New Zealand* and G. Hamilton-Browne in his works on the Armed Constabulary. To some extent, James Cowan belongs in this category. But these writers self-confessedly wrote to fill a gap, to rescue an exciting and instructive past from a present which for some reason neglected it. They sought to lead, not follow, public opinion. Gudgeon wrote to save his comrades in arms from the oblivion which already threatened them by 1879, Hamilton-Browne called his Armed Constabulary 'the Lost Legion', and, in 1922, Cowan wrote that 'in testing the historical knowledge of the average New Zealander the fact is too apparent that the young generation would be better for a more systematic schooling in the facts of national pioneer life and achievements which are a necessary foundation for the larger patriotism'. His books on the wars were designed to help correct 'this deficiency in the popular mentality'.[20] But these writers failed in their efforts. As the basis of 'the larger patriotism', the New Zealand Wars did not capture the people's imagination. The children played old-world soldiers at Waterloo, not Rangiriri, and new-world soldiers at the Wagon Box, not Ngatapa.

Why? A certain lack of cultural independence and of a New Zealand historical sense may have contributed. But one suspects that this was as much an effect as a cause. Disguising reality is difficult, and the efficiency of the mechanisms outlined above was not absolute. The story of the wars had been rendered more palatable by scapegoat hunting, by neglecting Maori innovation, by emphasizing their chivalry or their barbarism. It had been laundered time and time again, but stubborn stains still remained. There were just too many Little Big Horns in New Zealand's Wild West. So Gudgeon, Hamilton-Browne, and even Cowan, pushed their barrow uphill. The suppressive reflex was the fail-safe device of the dominant interpretation. The final safety-net was to forget.

II THE BACKGROUND OF IDEAS

SOME ASPECTS OF THE BRITISH INTERPRETATION OF THE NEW Zealand Wars will be very familiar to readers of military history. Contemporary accounts of most wars tend to be biased towards the writer's own party. But the natural predilection for reports favouring one's own side is not enough to explain the interpretative phenomenon outlined above. Unacceptable facts and implications were suppressed almost to the point of overkill, and the real explanation of British defeats was avoided with a desperation that might be described as psychotic in an individual. In the search for alternative explanations, the British did not stop short of verbally crucifying their own generals, nor of stretching credibility to its limits. Why did this dominant interpretation exist, and why did it have these characteristics?

The explanation offered here is that the dominant interpretation was the product of a dialectic between events and preconceptions. Some preconceptions were so widely shared and so highly valued that most British commentators protected them from threatening evidence. Protection took the form of converting the realities into the least unpalatable shape possible, through the various mechanisms outlined above. It was a two-way struggle, and preconceptions did not always win; sometimes the evidence was simply too blatant to be suppressed or acceptably explained. But there was always a pressure to bring events into conformity with expectations.

Most of the relevant preconceptions were related to the body of thought known as Victorian ideas of race. An extensive literature exists on this subject, and no attempt at a full examination is possible here, but it should be noted that Victorian racial thought was older, more complicated, and less intentionally malign than is sometimes implied. The purpose here is not retrospectively to apply current criteria to these ideas, but to assess their effects on an influential historical interpretation. The nineteenth-century British were neither the first nor the last group of people to see their success as evidence of their inherent superiority, and to look to racial and other hypotheses to rationalize this belief. Our society, no doubt, has its own ethnocentric preconceptions, and we should therefore curb our self-righteousness in discussing those of others. But this is no good reason for acquiescing in the addition of their problems to our own.

One effect of British racial attitudes was the totally unselfconscious use of an ethnocentric system of measurement; a culture-specific frame of reference. European styles of military organization and generalship were wrongly assumed to be the only effective forms. Te Kooti was believed to be the most able Maori leader partly because he adopted some of the accoutrements of European generalship. On horseback, 'attired in a red shirt with boots and breeches, a sword suspended from his side', communicating with his subordinates by orderly, Te Kooti seemed to control his forces in a way the British understood.[21] A more traditional Maori command system was not so easily recognizable. Similarly, it was difficult for the British to accept that the King Movement was an effective military organization. Where was the chain of command, the staff, and the commissariat? Equally hard to accept was the way in which sophisticated artifact technology, the European hallmark, was neutralized by superficially less impressive techniques. It was almost impossible for a Victorian to acknowledge that a wonderful scientific achievement such as the Armstrong gun was functionally inferior to an anti-artillery bunker, a mere hole in the ground.

This ethnocentric frame of reference formed a passive backdrop to the interpretation of the Wars, limiting the British ability to recognize Maori military achievements for what they were. But there were three other groups of ideas which played a more active role, joining the events themselves as the positive determinants of interpretation. The first was the conviction of British military superiority *per se*; the second was the notion that British victory over such people as the Maori was, by a law of nature, inevitable; and the third was the belief that most non-European peoples, including the Maori, lacked the intellectual qualities known as 'the higher mental faculties'.

Military achievement was one sphere in which British convictions of superiority were particularly strong. Recent historians stress the undoubted weaknesses of the Victorian army, and it is easy to forget that, on the extant record, this army won four-fifths of its battles before the Second South African War. Given this record, a belief in the superiority of British arms did not have to be based on anything other than empirical observation, and it seems probable that it was both derived from, and reinforced by, actual events. But the line of reasoning normally used went further than this. Military excellence was seen, not as an acquired attribute of the British regular soldier, but as a characteristic innate in all Britons. The typical qualities of the British soldier were also those of Carlyle's John Bull: 'Sheer obstinate toughness of muscle; but much more, what we call toughness of heart, which will mean persistence hopeful and even desperate, unsub-duable patience, composed candid openness, clearness of mind.'[22] Not only was military excellence a constant; it was also a defining feature of the Briton. Consequently, though the notion of military superiority predated the nineteenth-century upsurge of interest in race, it lent itself easily to fusion with ideas of racial superiority.

The conviction of British military superiority might be quietly stated or unspoken, but it was very widely shared amongst interpreters of the New Zealand Wars, and it applied whether the troops were Imperial or colonial, regulars or militia. The emphasis was not on one particular military virtue, but on a mixture of them all. 'Heroic courage and hardihood, skilful strategem and brilliant manoeuvring' were among 'the well-known characteristics of the British fighting man', but so was 'moral resolution . . . determination of will', otherwise known as 'ordinary British spirit'.[23] The stress on 'ordinary British spirit' as both the distinguishing attribute of the Briton armed, and a virtue common to all Britons, meant that defeat by a smaller number of natives was fraught with peculiarly unattractive connotations. It could be considered 'un-British' in the sense that it indicated a lack of mental and moral fibre, one of the essential characteristics by which the British defined themselves.

The second group of ideas concerned the inevitability of British victory over the Maori. This belief was closely associated with the idea of Fatal Impact, discussed in a different context in the previous chapter. It was not derived simply from the fact that the British had more men and more guns, or indeed from the conviction that they were superior soldiers, but from what was widely perceived as a law of nature. A basic axiom of nineteenth century racial thought was that Europeans in contact with lesser races would inevitably exterminate, absorb, or, at the very least, subordinate them. As with the conviction of military superiority, this belief arose from an amalgam of experience and theory. By the early part of the century, the decline of aboriginal populations in many areas seemed to indicate that 'uncivilised man melts "as snows in the sunshine" before "superior" capacities'.[24] In an age without knowledge of bacterial and viral infection and immunity, there was a strong tendency to attribute this, not merely to practical factors such as disease and alcohol, but also to more mysterious causes.

Two schools of racial thought, in particular, came to be used as a theoretical justification for this widespread perception. From 1840, racial determinists of a polygenist* tendency, such as Robert Knox and the American J. C. Nott, argued that race was the key determinant of history, that racial antagonism was inherent, and the inferior state of the dark races was unchangeable. From 1850, the evolutionist theorists Herbert Spencer, Charles Darwin, A. R. Wallace, and their disciples made possible the assumption that the fittest races, namely the Europeans, survived at the expense of others through the inevitable struggle for existence. The difference between these views were profound, but for our purposes the similarities are more important. Both held that the dark races would inevitably die out, at least in the temperate zone, as a result of contact with whites—though Knox had doubts about the long-term viability of European colonization.[25] Both schools, while acknowledging that armed conflict was not an absolutely

---

* The belief in multiple creation, in several original Adams and Eves, sometimes involving a view of human races as separate species of the *genus homo*.

necessary part of the process of extermination, tended to use warlike imagery, and to see warfare as a common instrument of nature. Both argued that the process would occur whether one liked it or not, but tended to see it as ultimately beneficent and progresssive.

The application of this concept of Fatal Impact to New Zealand was widespread,[26] but it was not universal and it was rarely unqualified. Extermination was often watered down to read assimilation or subordination. It was sometimes argued that Europeans had no role at all to play in the fading away of the Maori; that the process was well advanced before Europeans arrived. Many writers hoped that the process was reversible, and deeply regretted perceived indications that it was not. Though many believed this natural law made race conflict inevitable, few—except in newspaper rhetoric—used it to advocate war. But whether or not one believed aboriginal extinction to be absolutely inevitable, or that war was a necessary or desirable part of the process, the slightest degree of commitment to the Fatal Impact concept made one thing perfectly clear. Once war did break out, the Europeans would certainly win.

The assumption that British victory was inevitable naturally reinforced expectations of success in individual engagements, but it also added a certain flexibility to the dominant interpretation. Through the concept of the decisive 'last battle', it could incorporate early defeat. The legendary John Bull had always been terrible when roused, but slow to wrath, and the Prussian Von Tempsky was happy to extend this principle to all 'the Anglo-Saxon races'. Sometimes, observers found the British habit of losing the first engagements in a particular war intensely frustrating. 'How is it that Englishmen will NEVER learn to strike first blows that need no repetition? Why DO they never make their first means equal to the emergency and ensure success without passing through failure?' But it was a habit, an irritating but acceptable inconvenience. 'It seems as if it were passing into something like a law that British fighting men, whether in quarrels great or small, must get a taste of discomfiture at the outset to rouse them thoroughly to vigilance and activity.'[27] Here was a pattern which rendered early defeat more or less acceptable and as such it was regularly applied in New Zealand. Overall, it arguably had a certain validity, but in practice it was applied to each individual war regardless of fact. The greater the initial 'taste of discomfiture', the more decisive the last battle had to be. The Northern War was the extreme example, but there were also clear applications in Taranaki, Waikato, Tauranga, and Titokowaru's War.

These two groups of preconceptions combined to create the enormously powerful expectation of victory—and its inverse, the shocked reaction to defeat—that was the dynamic force behind the British interpretation. But it was the third group of ideas that set the limits within which this force could work. Though they might select the most favourable elements available, interpreters drew their particular stereotype of Maori abilities from a general stereotype of the savage. A dislike of steady labour and the 'excitability' that led to poor marksmanship were aspects of this, as were some 'natural advantages'. But the most important feature of the stereotype was the absence of the intellectual qualities of scientific curiosity, inventiveness, and high reasoning ability. These were collectively known as the 'higher mental faculties', and their warlike manifestation was the higher military talents.

The most obvious proponents of the belief that non-Europeans lacked the higher faculties were polygenists and near-polygenists such as Knox, Nott, and Frederic William Farrar. Farrar wrote that: 'The grand qualities which secure the continuous advance of mankind, the generalising power of pure reason, the love of perfectibility, the desire to know the unknown, and, last and greatest, the ability to observe new phenomena and new relations, —these mental faculties seem to be deficient in all the dark races.'[28] Nott and others promoted this widespread perception into scientific fact, proven by phrenological experiment.

The polygenists were most explicit, but beliefs of this kind were not restricted to their extreme of the range of racial thought. Evolutionists, including Darwin and Spencer themselves, and others such as Wallace and Francis Galton, accepted what, for our purposes, was a milder version of the same concept. Wallace argued that, after a certain point in time, natural selection in humans applied mainly to mental and moral, rather than physical, characteristics; and so 'in conjunction with scarcely perceptible modifications of form, has developed the wonderful intellect of the Germanic races'. It was this that enabled these races, 'when in contact with savage man, to conquer in the struggle for existence'.[29] The Christian degenerationist, Archbishop Richard Whately, who believed that retrogression explained the savage state, wrote that 'savages never seem to discover or invent anything'. Even the early nineteenth-century monogenist writers J. C. Prichard and William Lawrence, founding figures in British anthropology and biology, and strong proponents of the unity of man, shared this belief to some extent. For these writers, black equality was prospective, not actual, and it was a distant prospect. Later anthropologists, notably John Lubbock, Lord Avebury, who saw the savage state as the lowest stage on the progression to civilization, tended to agree. Lubbock wrote that the savage mind was 'easily fatigued', their languages 'very poor in abstract terms', and that indeed some abstract ideas were 'entirely beyond the mental range of the lower savages, whose extreme mental inferiority we have much difficulty in realising'.[30]

The absence, poor development, or disuse of the higher mental faculties was held to explain the stasis, or 'conservatism' of non-European peoples. This was not an eccentric minority position, but a point where several otherwise diverse theories intersected. Victorian anthropologists, wrote Christine Bolt, 'were generally agreed on the conservatism of primitive peoples'.[31]

The soldiers and settlers who left opinions about the New Zealand Wars did not have to be familiar with the theories involved to accept the basic principle, and sometimes they did so explicitly. 'Those best acquainted with the natives', stated the *Otago Witness*, 'confirm that they are deficient in the higher qualities of the human mind.' Such bluntness was rare; it was widely acknowledged that the Maoris had many good qualities, and comments on their deficiencies were usually coupled with references to these. The Maoris are 'very apt to learn', wrote William Colenso, but 'barren of originality'. 'Naturally a noble race', wrote Richard Taylor, 'bodily and mentally superior to most of the Polynesians, their fine intelligent countenances present the exterior of a fair-built house, which only requires to be suitably furnished.' His son, B. K. Taylor, was firmly of the view that the Maoris could eventually be raised to equality, but in the interim it was 'observable that the Maori cannot entertain two separate subjects at the same time'. The influential ethnographer A. S. Thomson, an army surgeon, felt that the Maoris were advancing up the scale of civilization, but believed that his crude craniometry tests proved them to be 'inferior to the English in mental capacity'. 'The faculty of imagination is not strongly developed among them . . .', wrote Thomson, 'not one good example of invention, the highest function of this faculty, can be quoted from among their works.'[32]

When Europeans, including those in New Zealand, compared themselves to tribal societies they perceived an enormous gulf. One of the ways in which they sought to explain the difference was by reference to the higher mental faculties, the 'grand qualities which secure that continuous advance of mankind'. Thus the higher faculties were not simply a criterion on which to build racial hierarchies, but the very engine of progress and evolution—the processes which gave Europeans their pre-eminence. The conviction did not have to be absolute. As with the Fatal Impact, there were more moderate fall-back positions—the higher faculties had atrophied through disuse, or were simply under-developed. An underlying, unstated belief that the Maori had not invented guns and a written language because they could not was compatible with a great deal of respect for other Maori virtues. The Maoris could be beautiful, strong, heroic, and chivalrous; they could display intelligence of various kinds; but they could not invent or theorize. At the very least, they could not invent or theorize to the same level as Europeans.

The European monopoly of the higher mental faculties was the inner tabernacle of Victorian racial attitudes. To question it was to question a whole world view. When events did indeed cast doubt on it, as with evidence of Maori possession of the higher military talents, Victorian commentators avoided, misinterpreted, or suppressed them. Thus the real explanation for British defeats and difficulties in the New Zealand Wars was banished from the realm of the acceptable.

The groups of ideas outlined above manifested only the simplest and most popular aspects of scientific theories. To accept Spencer's metaphor of the struggle for existence, you did not have to understand his theory of the dynamics of matter, or even know who he was, any more than a small capitalist needs to be familiar with Adam Smith to advocate free enterprise. Moreover, scientific theory was only one of several contributors. Non-scientific schools of racial thought such as Romantic Anglo-Saxonism; con-

cepts such as Progress and philanthropy which were only indirectly connected to racial issues; and the parochial chauvinism sometimes called 'folk
racism': all played their part. Above all, experience or perceived experience
had its influence, causing and being caused by theory like the proverbial
chicken and egg. Victorian attitudes to race were a web spun from many
starting points. Literate Victorians were caught at the intersections; the
junctions where many otherwise diverse strands over-lapped.[33]

That some Victorian racial preconceptions were widely shared does not
prove that they were cherished—valued so highly that they had to be protected from adverse reality. Here, one can do little more than refer the
reader to the work of J. W. Burrow, Leon Poliakov, and D. A. Lorimer
—each of whom, in very different ways, argues that race-related ideas fulfilled an important social or ideological function for the Victorians—and
make the following observation.[34] Racial ideas are not just images of others,
but of one's self and one's own society. Superiority and inferiority, inevitable victory and inevitable defeat, higher faculties or the lack of them;
each are two sides of the same coin. To question the one is to question the
other, and thereby cast doubt on an individual and collective self-image.
Victorians, like other people, were not eager to ask such questions.

To those familiar with early European literature on New Zealand, the
notion that unfavourable racial preconceptions were widely applied to the
Maori may seem surprising. Early published references to the Maori, with
an Enlightenment objectivity, ensured that their less attractive customs did
not obscure their virtues. European writers usually ranked the Maori high
on their various racial hierarchies, and remarked favourably on their capacity
for improvement. Monogenist, Christian philanthropist, and humanitarian
notions of Maori equality influenced colonial legislation. Missionary
authors lauded the Maori adoption of Christianity, books on colonization
made much of their eagerness for European contact and settlement, and
various writers praised their martial qualities of courage and chivalry. But it
is all too easy to exaggerate the extent and implications of this favourable
publicity.

Much of the early literature on New Zealand was in fact part of two great
advertising campaigns: the effort to obtain support for missionary activity
and to cast its achievements in the best possible light, and the effort to
attract settlers to a young and distant colony in competition with better-
known fields of immigration such as North America where land was
cheaper and the voyage out shorter. These objectives required an appropriate portrait of the Maori. For the former they should be 'neither too
ignorant or too savage to be made the subject of the saving and sanctifying
influence of the Gospel'.[35] For the latter, they were best seen as harmless
and useful collaborators in the work of colonization, providing a market and
labour force and adding 'a freshness and piquancy to the country'—
altogether 'a principal inducement which should lead intending emigrants

to make the choice of New Zealand'.[36] Neither portrait necessarily reflected the view of settlers who had actually made 'the choice of New Zealand'.

Furthermore, favourable images of the Maori did not always survive the wars. The case for Maori 'salvageability' was based partly on their readiness selectively to adopt European ways in commerce, agriculture, literacy, and religion. Maori resistance was seen as a reversal of this trend; evidence that the civilizing mission had failed, or even that it had always been doomed to failure. From the first killings of civilians in March 1860, Maori 'atrocities' reinforced this tendency—a tendency which closely parallels the Victorian response to the Jamaica Rebellion of 1865. For those who had always doubted 'bungling and theoretical philanthropy', Maori 'atrocities' and the fact of war itself were proof of their fundamentally unregenerate character.

> We have dealt with the natives of this country upon a principle radically wrong. We have conceded them rights and privileges which nature has refused to ratify. . . . We have pampered ignorance and misrule, and we now experience their hatred of intelligence and order. The bubble is burst. The Maori is now known to us as what he is, and not as missionaries and philanthropists were willing to believe him. [In reality, the Maori is] a man ignorant and savage, loving darkness and anarchy, hating light and order; a man of fierce, and ungoverned passions, bloodthirsty, cruel, ungrateful, treacherous.[37]

The 'missionaries and philanthropists' themselves were not immune to this tendency. As the Maoris turned away from conventional Christianity towards overtly syncretic religions, the missionaries became disillusioned. Many who had fearlessly argued the justice of the Maori cause in the Taranaki War of 1860, and consequently looked more sympathetically on Maori military endeavours, felt that the Waikato War of 1863 was the 'sharp lesson' which, sadly, the Maoris both needed and deserved. This group included such notable 'philo-Maoris' as Bishops Selwyn and William Williams, R. Burrows, R. Maunsell, and B. Y. Ashwell. By 1864, the Church Missionary Society in New Zealand was supporting, in principle, the confiscation of Maori land.[38] The civilizing mission was not abandoned, but gentle persuasion based on the conviction that the Maori knew what was good for them gave way to language more like Carlyle's 'beneficient whip' and W. P. Andrews's 'great civiliser, the sword'. Like the liberal parent whose promising adolescent has committed some nasty crime, the Maoris' self-appointed mentors regretted that they had spared the rod and spoiled the child, and they did not intend to make the same mistake again. In many ways, the 1860s—the decade of war—marked the nadir of the Maoris' racial reputation in the eyes of their white neighbours, and the interpretation of the wars could not help but reflect this.

It is equally important to note that favourable images of the Maori were often qualified in various ways. Like Prichard and Lawrence, humanitarian New Zealand writers usually saw Maori equality as prospective rather than actual. The notion of a civilizing mission involved assumptions of cultural superiority, and the image of the Maori that served the missionary purpose necessarily contained both favourable and unfavourable elements. The savage could not be so degraded as to be beyond redemption, but he had to be degraded enough to urgently require it. The rejection of one group of racial preconceptions was sometimes qualified by the acceptance of another. James Mouat, Cameron's Surgeon-General, believed that 'in point of mental endowment, it is questionable if, with equal cultivation [the Maori] capacity for intellectual achievement would fall short of those of the average European'. But the possibility was unlikely to be tested, since 'it requires no great sagacity to foresee that in a generation or two the race must become extinct'.[39]

British respect for the Maori military virtues of courage and chivalry was also qualified. We have seen that it did not indicate a real objectivity. It did not necessarily imply that the Maoris were the equals of the British—'daring and courageous though they be, they are no match for the British'. 'The New Zealanders', wrote F. E. Maning, 'are not to be despised when they have numbers on their side.' William Swainson chastised his compatriots for believing that no coloured race could stand against them, but 'disproved' this assumption by stating that: 'our troops were driven from the field, to the astonishment of the insurgents themselves, by a Maori force not more than double the number of our own troops.'[40] The Maori might outrank the Hindu and the Hottentot on the scale of martial races, but he was only a non-commissioned officer after all.

Historians still perpetuate the old notion of the wars as a breeding-ground of mutual respect between troops and warriors, leading to 'a warm comradeship between victor and vanquished'. We are even told that this had an effect on operations. The 40th regiment, 'lost in admiration at their heroism', actually allowed the Maoris to escape from Orakau, and Cameron and his men's regard for the Maoris and their cause is sometimes said to have hastened the army's withdrawal from New Zealand.[41] This is a hybrid of fact and fairy-tale, in which the latter predominates. In Cameron's case, doubts about the justice of his cause were a suspiciously late development; his disillusionment with the war predated them, and stemmed instead from the impossibility of decisive victory. As for his subordinates, Von Tempsky justly doubted that the British soldier 'has ever distinguished himself by prying into the causes of the war he was engaged in'. The later Waikato operations were unpopular with the troops, but because of the absence of glory, excitement, loot, and fun—'the town of Auckland has no provision for public amusements'. 'Draught colonial beer is so bad it is hardly fit to drink.'[42] A casual kind of contempt for the Maori was more common than respect. 'Nigger', even then a pejorative term, was apparently in general use, and pyrrhic Maori tactics could arouse disgust as easily as esteem—the former could even involve a marginally better appreciation of the Maori military system than the latter. The Maoris, wrote Sergeant William White, 'like other vermin, were partial to underground holes, and once concealed in these could not possibly be ferreted out. Now all this puzzles an English soldier; he is a match for an army of men, but he feels at a loss with an army of *rats*.'[43]

This is not to say that positive attitudes to the Maori had no mitigating effect on the British interpretation of the wars. To some extent, they did. Humanitarian, philo-Maori, or unusually objective observers often transcended one set of preconceptions, although they normally fell victim to another. On the other hand, local factors could also exacerbate the situation. Some colonists believed that New Zealand was 'the Britain of the South', a colony with a very great future. Its settler-frontiersmen, who were a cut above their neighbours across the Tasman, were natural Indian fighters. The Colony, an 'infant Hercules' to use a contemporary phrase, would soon strangle the Maori serpents surrounding it—if the hidebound Imperial regulars ever gave the settler volunteers their head. These views did not make Titokowaru's humiliating defeats of the adolescent Hercules any easier to swallow.[44]

To prove empirically that racial preconceptions were in fact a part of the general Victorian consciousness, and that they were not substantially modified in New Zealand, would require a whole series of investigations into the dissemination of ideas among the Victorians in general, and in New Zealand in particular. In the absence of such studies, this argument has dealt in probabilities, in impressionistic evidence, and in 'defences in the alternative', to borrow the legal phrase. But the argument is not totally reliant on such considerations. Hard evidence for it, of both a positive and a negative kind, exists in the preceding chapters. Time and time again, in case after case after case, Victorian interpreters of the wars distorted the facts and their implications, and they did so in an unconscious but systematic way. On the positive side, the links between these distortions and racial preconceptions were often quite obvious. On the negative side, if shared racial preconceptions did not create this collective and systematic distortion, what did?

III   THE PROBLEM OF ONE-SIDED EVIDENCE

NEW ZEALAND INFLUENCES HAD A CONSIDERABLE IMPACT ON the interpretation of the wars. Some exacerbated the tendency to force events into conformity with racial preconceptions, some ameliorated it. Some appeared to ameliorate it, but did not. Yet, in the final analysis, these were local variations upon a more general theme. Interpreters of the wars owed their convictions of superiority, their belief in the inevitability of victory, and their ultimately derogatory stereotype of the native Maori, not to the New Zealand periphery, but to the metropolis: Victorian Britain. It was not a New Zealand colonial interpretation of racial conflict, but a Victorian one.

In New Zealand, this interpretation has endured largely for the simple reason that it monopolized contemporary literature on the wars. No substantial and well-developed competing body of literature, produced by the Maoris or some third party, existed to provide an alternative interpretation. This situation of one-side evidence is far from unique. The problem of the enduring dominant interpretation may be general, not particular. To a greater or lesser extent, it may occur in most of Victorian Britain's colonial wars. If other European empires had similar racial preconceptions—and recent studies suggest that, for this purpose, French and American attitudes were not decisively dissimilar—then the problem may extend to their colonial wars as well.[45]

To be sure, the Maori military system was probably an unusually effective form of counter-European warfare, and events therefore clashed with cherished preconceptions with uncommon force and frequency. Consequently, misapprehensions on the scale of the British interpretation of the Northern War may be rare. But this was an extreme case. Milder adjustments of reality may be more common, and these may be important only cumulatively. Their influence will not necessarily affect the issue of who won or lost. But one does not have to be entirely convinced by hypotheses like that of T. O. Ranger to accept that the character and intensity of resistance, the ways in which people won or lost, can have a profound effect on a society or a colonial relationship.[46]

The possibility that the enduring dominant interpretation is a widespread problem cannot, of course, be tested here. But it does seem that the few Victorian books which discussed colonial warfare in general exhibited some of the characteristics of the interpretation of the New Zealand Wars. In the most notable of such works, C. E. Calwell stressed exceptional leadership errors and inaccessible terrain as the main causes of occasional disasters and more frequent difficulties. Small wars 'are often campaigns rather against nature than against hostile armies'. 'The enemy', Calwell advised, 'must be made to feel a moral inferiority throughout. The lower races are impressionable. They are greatly influenced by a resolute bearing and a determined course of action.' There is a touch of this legacy in some more recent works. 'Any hint of anxiety', writes Cyril Falls, 'acts as a sort of tonic to primitive peoples.' In colonial warfare, 'a bold confident bearing counted almost as much as straight shooting'. 'The Europeans', writes Lewis H. Gann, 'enjoyed complete moral ascendancy over their opponents, whose resistance was perhaps born of despair more than any belief in ultimate victory.'[47] Successful resistance to Imperial expansion is often explained in terms of exceptional European leadership failures, and of non-European imitation, or 'natural advantages'. Unsuccessful resistance is sometimes attributed to non-European's 'fatalistic acceptance of the inevitable', and to the fact that their military methods were 'usually of the most primitive kind, deficient in leadership, direction and endurance'.[48]

One specific case in which the New Zealand effect may have been duplicated is that of the Anglo-Zulu war of 1879. In a recent analysis of this conflict and its effects, Jeff Guy argues that the decisiveness of the Battle of Ulundi has been over-estimated.

The conventional view, which equates the end of Zulu power and independence with the British military victory at Ulundi in July 1879, is a misleading over-simplification. It . . . ignores the fact that, by the time the battle was fought, the intensity of Zulu resistance had already persuaded London that the cost of ending Zulu independence by force of arms would be too high . . . and that orders had been given that Zululand should not be annexed. Neverthless, Isandlawhna could not go unavenged . . . the 'stain' on Britain's honour had to be wiped out. To achieve this . . . Ulundi was promoted to the rank of a major military victory. Peace was in fact attained in the weeks that followed Ulundi by promising the Zulu people that they would retain possession of their land if they laid down their arms.[49]

Guy does not attempt a substantive military re-analysis, and his Ulundi case is too perfunctory to be entirely convincing, but he is right to point out that remarkably few rounds were fired by the British in repelling a supposedly fierce and sustained assault on their square.[50] If he is correct, then this is the very kind of interpretative phenomenon that occurred several times in the New Zealand Wars. It is especially similar to the received version of the Tauranga campaign of 1864. A humiliating defeat, followed by a real but exaggerated victory, which is not only made to lay the ghost of the earlier disaster, but which also becomes the necessary 'last battle' when peace is made and falsely presented as complete submission. Once suitably roused, the Anglo-Saxons proceed to the inevitable decisive victory.

The problem may be widespread, but what of the solution? If all or most of the evidence on a conflict comes from one side, and if it is subject to the distorting influence of shared preconceptions, how is revision possible? Must we not register our doubts about the received interpretation and acknowledge that, since it is all we have to work with, we can reject but not replace it? Perhaps the answer is no. Perhaps the problem of systematic bias in cases of one-sided evidence contains the seeds of its own solution. The solution has to do with the way in which a society forms its interpretation of traumatic and complicated events such as battle.

The complexity of battle is a truism of military historiography. 'Write the history of a battle? As well write the history of a ball.' The chaos of action and interaction generates a profusion of evidence on aspects of itself, but little on the whole of itself. Initially, no one, not even the general, has an over-view: diaries, letters, unit reports, and recorded comments reflect only the immediate concerns of small groups or individuals.

This evidence preserves only a fraction of the complexity of actual events; but it is still an enormous morass, confused and confusing. People feel the need to render it comprehensible, to impose some structure on it, to make sense of it, to *interpret* it. As the interpretations form, as they become more and more widely accepted as the authorized versions, so it becomes more and more necessary for them to accommodate the cherished preconceptions of the day. Thus the dominant interpretation comes into being, an accep-table compromise between fact and preconception. During the process of formation, non-interpretative evidence, partial interpretations, and minority interpretations are replaced, absorbed, or demoted to curiosity status by the dominant interpretation. In trying to describe this process, one inevitably gives the impression of separate compartments, and a neat, one-way, chronological sequence. This, of course, is false. The borders of the compartments are jagged, not neat; some may even occur simultaneously; and the whole process can take a day, a year, or a decade—sometimes all three. But the central point is this: the dominant interpretation does not necessarily form instantaneously, and evidence from the time before it forms, is forgotten or set aside, not irretrievably lost.

The stages preceding the full formation of the dominant interpretation offer various possibilities for rescuing the other side of the story. Noninterpretative, or unloaded, evidence, whereby an observer records a fact but does not place it in his perception of its context, can be important. In the absolute sense, this concept may be invalid, since it could be argued that one must interpret a fact to perceive and record it. But this is a matter of degree—some recordings of fact are less interpretative than others—and, in practice, the concept is useful. During the New Zealand Wars, the most clear-cut examples were those where an observer recorded a fact vital to the interpretation of an event prior to the event itself. At the siege of Ruapekapeka in 1846, British officers observed many Maoris leaving the *pa* with packs of goods and supplies, and rightly concluded that they were voluntarily evacuating the place. Later, the British occupied the *pa* and the dominant interpretation asserted that they had stormed it, or seized it by a trick while the garrison was out at prayers. The diaries are forgotten, but they are not lost.

The existence of some specific bias, in competition with the general bias which produced the dominant interpretation, is equally important. Self-aggrandisement, self-defence against criticism, personal or political animosity, danger or a sense of crisis—all could produce tendencies which conflicted with those of the dominant interpretation, and had progressively to be absorbed or suppressed by it. In 1860, Taranaki militiaman A. S. Atkinson felt that the achievements of Cracroft's naval brigade at Waireka were being emphasized to the point where the efforts of his fellow settlers were implicitly belittled. He discovered conclusive evidence that Cracroft had stormed a virtually empty *pa*. He could not bring himself publicly to destroy the legend of Waireka, but the means for its destruction are to be found in his journal. To defend themselves against accusations of procrastination in the early part of the Waikato War, Cameron and his staff pointed out that Maori raiding was tying up the bulk of their army in protecting the line of supply. They did not attribute this to a co-ordinated Maori strategy, but, again, we need not follow suit. The animosity of Haultain and Whitmore to McLean and his clients led them to investigate and disprove claims that Te Kooti had suffered enormous casualties at Makaretu—a 'victory' which the McLean faction attributed to their own efforts. Wanganui settlers whose homes and lives were in danger in 1868 were not inclined to understate the threat presented by Titokowaru. This was played down retrospectively, not instantaneously, and the original cries of desperation can still be found.

These types of evidence are produced by conflicts between specific biases and the general bias on which the dominant interpretation is based. But contradictions within the general bias can also be useful. In 1870, colonial officers, concerned to show that Te Kooti had been utterly routed at Te Porere, recorded evidence which indicated that his force had been reduced to 71 men by the battle. But this undercut their subsequent claims that they had defeated large *Ringatu* forces at Tapapa three months later. They tended to exaggerate Maori casualties and Maori numbers, but in this case they could not logically do both.

Occasionally, these types of evidence developed into a fully-fledged minority interpretation—an alternative to the dominant interpretation—which eventually suffered historiographical defeat. Though there were few exceptions to all the rules of the dominant interpretation, few commentators who transcended all the cherished preconceptions of their fellows, there were many exceptions to one rule or another. These were gradually suppressed, or subsumed in the mainstream, but they can be rediscovered. A group of British writers believed that their side had lost the Northern War of 1845-6, although they did not understand how. Their last publication was in 1879, and their view was gradually filtered out, but their books and papers still exist.

Another form of evidence contained in, but separate from, the dominant interpretation can be described as 'embalmed evidence': non-British information, whether interpretative or not, which the British preserved but did not incorporate. In this sense, the situation of one-sided evidence was not absolute. A considerable amount of Maori evidence was received and recorded by the British. It was not taken on board, but dismissed as a romantic curiosity and used to provide anecdotes rather than alternative interpretations. Thus a short history of the Northern War, written by the early settler F. E. Maning but largely based on Maori accounts, has frequently been reprinted and quite widely read. But it is usually dismissed as a fanciful invention of Maning's, and not taken very seriously as a document. Yet on several important issues it is more accurate than the received version. Embalmed evidence is like a package, which is preserved, passed on, and perhaps admired by the historiographically-dominant side, but which remains unopened. We can open it when we choose.

None of these forms of evidence are necessarily reliable in themselves, but taken together, analysed critically, and supplemented by the physical parameters of the possible—configurations of terrain, the performance of contemporary weapons, the capacities of the human body—they present an opportunity for revision. But the opportunity cannot be exploited before one great difficulty is overcome. Historians return to the original chaos of evidence and find it as diverse, contradictory, and confusing as did contemporary interpreters. Like it or not, they must have some criteria of selection around which to organize the morass of material. Often, they will turn to some variant of the received version, the dominant interpretation, and so the problem perpetuates itself. But there is an alternative: to apply knowledge of the way in which contemporary bias worked to the contemporary interpretation, and from this synthesize a model to test against the evidence.

On this basis, perhaps the Victorian interpretation of the New Zealand Wars can form a model for the re-investigation of comparable conflicts, of nineteenth-century British 'small wars' generally. If Americans and European nations interpreted racial conflict in similar ways, then, with appropriate variations, such a model might be of some use in these cases as well. Of course, for some 'small' racial wars, oral evidence or large-scale, undirected empirical research may already have solved the problem. Nor would it do simply to replace one rigid preconceived paradigm with another. The model should be seen as a set of questions to be applied to evidence pre-dating the full formation of the dominant interpretation, and accepted or rejected as appropriate. The dominant interpretation could be right. Allusions to non-European successes and possession of the higher military talents could be absent from the European interpretation for one of two reasons: first, because they did not exist or, second, because they did.

This study has investigated aspects of the interpretation of nineteenth century racial conflict, and its conclusions and hypotheses are restricted to this subject. But this is not to deny that the problem of one-sided evidence, and the phenomenon of the dominant interpretation, may occur in other fields. We rely largely on men for our evidence about women, on conformists for our evidence about deviants, and on élites for our evidence about non-élites. We must confront this historiographical problem, not sneak past it in the cloak of pragmatic empiricism. Our understanding of the ideology of the historiographically-dominant group need not be sympathetic, but it must go beyond the mere detection of bias. How, why, and in what ways did bias work? Precisely how did it effect interpretation, and how can it be used against itself? The study of group ideology, of *mentalité*, is not the opposite of empirical revision, but its necessary partner. The dominant interpretation both camouflages and preserves, and to utilize the latter we must understand the former.

Glossary of Maori Terms

aukati	boundary, line which one does not cross
haka	war dance, dance and accompanying song
hapu	clan, sub-tribe
kainga	(unfortified) village
kareao	supplejack, a climbing plant
kauri	large conifer tree
kawanatanga	Governor's sphere, Governor's authority
kupapa	pro-government Maori (originally passive or neutral)
mana	prestige, influence
manuka	common bushy shrub
mere	short club, sometimes of greenstone (New Zealand jade)
pa	fortress, fortified village, field fortification
Pakeha	foreigner, especially European
pekerangi	light outer fence of a *pa*
rangatira	chief
rangatiratanga	sphere, authority, of the chiefs
rua	pit, anti-artillery bunker
tapu	sacred
taua	war party
taua muru	customary plundering expedition, exacting compensation for an offence, in which blood is seldom shed
taumaihi	tower, part of a *pa*
tupara	double-barrelled gun
whare	house

References

Abbreviations

A.D.	Army Department, New Zealand. Correspondence in N.A.
ADM	Admiralty, Great Britain. Correspondence in PRO
AGG-HB	Agent of the General Government, Hawke's Bay. Correspondence in N.A.
AIM	Auckland Institute and Museum
AJHR	*Appendices to the Journals of the House of Representatives*, New Zealand.
APL	Auckland Public Library
ATL	Alexander Turnbull Library, Wellington
B.L.	British Library, London
CMS	Church Missionary Society, and CMS Archives, London
CN/O	Letters from Missionaries in New Zealand, CMS
C.O.	Colonial Office, Great Britain. Correspondence in PRO
C.S.	Colonial Secretary
DAG	Deputy Adjutant-General
DQMG Journals	Deputy Quartermaster-General Journals. W.O.
G	(New Zealand) Governor, Military Letters. N.A.
JPS	*Journal of the Polynesian Society*
N.A.	National Archives, Wellington
NZJH	*New Zealand Journal of History*
NZPD	*New Zealand Parliamentary Debates*
P.P.	*Parliamentary Papers*, Great Britain
PRO	Public Record Office, London
R-A.P.	*Richmond-Atkinson Papers*
RHL	Rhodes House Library, Oxford
R.M.	Resident Magistrate
S.D.	Select Despatches
TPNZI	*Transactions and Proceedings of the New Zealand Institute*
W.O.	War Office, Great Britain. Correspondence in PRO

Preface

1. Howard, *War in European History*, (Oxford, 1976), p.ix.
2. G. R. Elton, *Political History/Principles and Practice*, New York and London, 1970, p.15; Corelli Barnett, *Britain and Her Army*, London 1970, p.xviii; B. J. Dalton, 'A New Look at the Maori Wars of the Sixties', *Historical Studies, Australia and New Zealand*, XII (1966), pp.230–47, (p.231); Donald C. Gordon, 'Colonial Warfare 1815-1970', in Robin Higham (ed.), *A Guide to the Sources of British Military History*, London 1972, p.301; John Shy, 'The American Military Experience:

History and Learning', *Journal of Interdisciplinary History*, I (1972), pp.207-28; Marvin R. Cain, 'A "Face of Battle" Needed: An Assessment of Motives and Men in Civil War Historiography', *Civil War History*, I (1982), pp.5-27.

3. Mason, *A Matter of Honour: an Account of the Indian Army, its Officers and Men*, London 1974; Fussell, *The Great War and Modern Memory*, Oxford 1975; Keegan, *The Face of Battle*, New York 1976. .

4. Chandler (Letter to Editor), *History Today*, 32, March 1982, p.55.

5. Gordon, 'Colonial Warfare', p.302; Bond (ed.), *Victorian Military Campaigns*, London 1967, p.3 (Introduction); Crowder (ed.), *West African Resistance: The Military Response to Colonial Occupation*, London 1971, p.1. (Introduction). Also see H. L. Wesseling, 'Colonial Wars and Armed Peace, 1870-1914; A Reconnaissance', *Itinerario*, V. (1981), pp.53-69. I am indebted to Professor P. N. Tarling, of Auckland University, for drawing my attention to the last-named article.

Introduction

1. For examples in each of these three categories see Edgar Holt, *The Strangest War*, London 1962; Tom Gibson, *The Maori Wars*, London 1974; Keith Sinclair, *The Origins of the Maori Wars*, Wellington 1957; B. J. Dalton, *War and Politics in New Zealand 1855-1870*, Sydney 1967; Keith Sinclair, *A History of New Zealand*, revised edn, London 1980, pp.79-82, 132-4, 138-41, 144-5; Walter Laqueur, *Guerilla: An Historical and Critical Study*, London 1977, p.77; Philip Mason, *Patterns of Dominance*, London 1970, pp.117, 124; Bernard Porter, *The Lion's Share. A Short History of British Imperialism*, London, New York 1975, pp.50-52.

2. B. J. Dalton, 'A New Look at the Maori Wars of the Sixties', *Historical Studies, Australia and New Zealand*, XII, 1966, pp.230-47.

3. Ian Wards, *The Shadow of the Land. A Study of British Policy and Racial Conflict in New Zealand 1832-1852*, Wellington 1968. Wards rightly downplays the military successes of Governor George Grey, but describes Hone Heke's resistance in the Northern War as 'a hopeless struggle' (p.102). Also see Ward's article 'The Generalship of Governor Grey 1846-52', in Peter Munz ed., *The Feel of Truth: Essays in New Zealand and Pacific History*, Wellington 1969.

4. James Cowan, *Wars*, 2v., Wellington. For the discussion of Parihaka see II, pp.476-91. Some of Cowan's papers are held in ATL. Other of his works relating to the wars are *The Adventures of Kimble Bent*, London 1911, and *Hero Stories of New Zealand*, Wellington 1935.

5. Cowan, *Wars*, I, p.1.

6. Cowan, *Wars*, I, p.394fn.

7. T. L. Buick, *New Zealand's First War*, Wellington 1926; Fortescue, *History of the British Army*, v.XII-III, London 1927-30. Fortescue spent some time in New Zealand and apparently did a little primary research on the wars.

8. A. W. Shrimpton & Alan E. Mulgan, *Maori and Pakeha: A History of New Zealand*, Auckland 1921, p.235.

9. W. P. Reeves, 'New Zealand—History', *Encyclopaedia Britannica*, 14th edn, Cambridge 1926, XVI, p.400; Hight, 'The Maori Wars 1843-1872', *Cambridge History of the British Empire*, 7v., Cambridge 1933, VII, Pt II, p.159; Sinclair, *History of New Zealand*, p.158; Ann Parsonson, 'The Pursuit of Mana', in W. H. Oliver with B. R. Williams, eds, *The Oxford History of New Zealand*, Oxford, Wellington 1981, p.58. For similar opinions see Dalton, *War and Politics*, p.179; Fortescue, *History of the British Army*, XIII, pp.480-1; Tony Simpson, *Te Riri Pakeha—The White Man's Anger*, Martinborough 1979, p.136.

10. Alan Ward, *A Show of Justice. Racial 'Amalgamation' in Nineteenth Century New Zealand*, Auckland 1978, p.10.

11. For recent discussions of early race relations and British annexation see Ward, *Show of Justice*, ch.2-3; J. M. R. Owens, 'New Zealand Before Annexation', *The Oxford History of New Zealand*; Peter Adams, *Fatal Necessity: British Intervention in New Zealand, 1830-1847*, Auckland 1977.

12. R. M. Ross, 'Te Tiriti o Waitangi: Texts and Translations', *NZJH*, 6, 1972, pp.129-57.

13. Perhaps the best published account of the Wairau Affray is contained in Ray Grover's interesting blend of history and fiction, *Cork of War: Ngati Toa and the British Mission; an Historical Narrative*, Dunedin 1982, ch.23-24.

14. Gavin White, 'Firearms in Africa: An Introduction', *Journal of African History*, v.12, 1971, p.180; D. U. Urlich, 'The Introduction and Diffusion of Firearms in New Zealand 1800-1840', *JPS*, LXXIX, 1970, pp.394-410, particularly p.408.

15. Simpson, *Te Riri Pakeha*, p.75.

16. B. Farwell, *For Queen and Country*, London 1981, p.206. Other recent studies of the Victorian Army: Jay Luvaas, *The Education of An Army*. *British Military Thought 1815-1940*, London 1964; G. Harries-Jenkins, *The Army in Victorian Society*, London 1977; A. B. Skelley, *The Victorian Army at Home*, London 1977; Edward M. Spiers, *The Army and Society, 1815-1914*, London 1980.

17. A. P. Vayda, *Maori Warfare*, Wellington 1960, pp.60-63.

18. For examples of open battles during the Musket Wars see S. Percy Smith, *Maori Wars of the Nineteenth Century . . .*, 2nd edn, Christchurch 1910.

19. Aileen Fox, *Prehistoric Maori Fortifications in the North Island of New Zealand*, Auckland 1976, pp.16-18; Andrew Sharp, ed., *Duperry's Visit to New Zealand in 1824*, Wellington 1971, p.93; C. Servant, *Customs and Habits of the New Zealanders, 1838-42*, D. R. Simmons, ed., J. Glasgow, trans., Wellington 1973, p.17; J. S. Polack, *New Zealand . . .*, 2v., London 1838, II, p.64; William Yate, *An Account of New Zealand . . .*, 2nd edn, London 1835, p.122.

20. For example, during the punitive expedition of H.M.S. *Alligator* to Taranaki in 1834. Wards, *Shadow of the Land*, pp.11-12.

21. Lieut. Bennet, 'Report to the Inspector-General of Fortifications on Maori Pahs', War Office Inwards Correspondence, 1/431, Public Record Office, London, and printed in Capt. Collinson, R. E., *Remarks on the Military Operations in New Zealand* [1853], pp.47-52.

1: A Limited War (pages 29-44)

1. Governor Robert FitzRoy to Thomas Beckham (Police Magistrate, Kororareka) 15, 20 June 1845, FitzRoy-Grey Letterbook, 1845-53, APL.

2. FitzRoy to Colonel Hulme, 4 May 1845, FitzRoy to Colonel Despard, 9 June 1845, W.O. 1/433, pp.537-41, 729-31; Governor George Grey to Lord Stanley (Secretary of State for War and the Colonies), 10 Dec. 1845, W.O. 1/433, p.1183.

3. Buick, *New Zealand's First War*, pp.30-54; J. Rutherford, *Hone Heke's Rebellion 1844-46: An Episode in the Establishment of British Rule in New Zealand*, Auckland University College Bulletin 34, 1947, pp.3-32; Wards, *The Shadow of the Land*, pp.95-118.

4. Ward, *Show of Justice*, pp.53-55.

5. Ward, *Show of Justice*, pp.12-60, & 'Law and Law Enforcement on the New Zealand Frontier, 1840-1893', *NZJH*, v.5, 1971, pp.128-49.

6. Hugh Carleton, *The Life of Henry Williams, Archdeacon of Waimate*, 2v. Auckland 1874, II, p.77; *cf. Extracts from a Diary Kept by the Rev. R. Burrows during Heke's War in the North in 1845*, Auckland 1886, p.6.

7. Melville Harcourt, *The Day Before Yesterday: A Short History of the Bay of Islands*, Wellington 1940, p.179.

8. Heke to Gilbert Mair Snr, 16 Oct. 1844 (tr. by Capt. Gilbert Mair Jr.) APL.

9. e.g. *New Zealand Journal*, 18 Jan. 1845; Carleton, *Henry Williams*, I, pp.82-83; Rev. R. Davis to Coleman, 5 Nov. 1844; J. N. Coleman, *A Memoir of the Reverend Richard Davis*, London 1865, p.287.

10. Heke, Proclamation, n.d. [March 1845], C.O., Inwards Correspondence, 209/34, p.76, PRO.

11. J. Cormack, Letter in *New Zealand Journal*, 19 July 1845; also FitzRoy, Speech in Legislative Council, *Southern Cross*, 22 Mar. 1845; Henry Williams to CMS, 26 Mar. 1845, H. Williams Letters 1836-47, CN/O 94(b), CMS (all 'CN/O' references cited hereafter are missionary letter and journal collections from these archives); Robert Burrows to CMS, 14 May 1845, Letters of Mission Secretaries 1842-50, CN/O 8(b); *The New Zealand Journal of John B. Williams*, ed. Robert W. Kenny, Salem 1956, p.7; Mrs Williams to Mrs Heathcote, 5 July 1845, Carleton, *Henry Williams*, I, pp.115-16; Annette Julia Every, 'The War in the North 1844-6', Auckland University College M. A. thesis, 1940, p.20; John Logan Campbell, *Poenamo*, Golden Press edn, 1973, orig. 1881, p.170; F. E. Maning to Archibald Maning, 14 Jan. 1845, Maning Papers, ATL.

12. Williams to CMS, 7 Nov. 1845, CN/O 94(b); R. Burrows, Journal, 3 Mar.-26 Dec. 1845, CN/O

27(b), 25 July 1845, p.61. From this date, Burrows regularly complained about the troops' behaviour.

13. Heke to FitzRoy, 21 May 1845, C.O. 209/35, pp.87-91; W. T. Bainbridge, Diary, 18 Mar. 1845, Buick, *New Zealand's First War*, p.91; *History of the War in the North . . . .Faithfully translated by a 'Pakeha Maori'*, Auckland, n.d., [1862], p.10. This work was compiled and partly written by F. E. Maning, but in the present writer's opinion it incorporated at least one genuine Maori account. It is cited hereafter as *War in the North*, without author.

14. Burrows, Journal, 30 Apr. 1845, p.23.

15. FitzRoy, Speech at meeting with Ngapuhi Chiefs in Sept. 1844, *Southern Cross*, 7 Sept. 1844; Beckham to FitzRoy, 16 Jan. 1845, FitzRoy-Beckham Correspondence, 1845-6, Grey Collection, APL.

16. Heke to FitzRoy, 21 May 1845, C.O. 209/35, pp.87-91. Other examples, Burrows, Journal, 1 Dec. 1845, p.8; Heke to Grey, 2 Dec. 1845, *P.P.*, 1846 (690) XXX, p.12.

17. Williams to Bishop G. A. Selwyn, 12 July 1847, Carleton, *Henry Williams*, II, p.157; Buick, *New Zealand's First War*, pp.52-53; Beckham to FitzRoy, 11 Feb. 1845, FitzRoy-Beckham Correspondence.

18. Williams to Selwyn, 20 Feb. 1845, CN/O 94(b); *cf.* Williams to FitzRoy, 20 Feb. 1845, ibid; Heke, quoted in Burrows, Journal, 1 Dec. 1845, p.8.

19. Speeches in *Southern Cross*, 7 Sept. 1844.

20. e.g. Beckham to FitzRoy, 17 Feb. 1845, FitzRoy-Beckham Correspondence.

21. Burrows, Journal, 3-5 Apr. 1845, pp.13-15.

22. Cowan, *Wars*, I, p.36; *cf.* John Webster, *Reminiscences of an Old Settler in Australia and New Zealand*, Christchurch 1908, pp.259, 270.

23. H. Williams to E. G. Marsh, 18 Apr. 1845, Carleton, *Henry Williams*, II, p.103; R. Burrows, Journal, 3-29 Apr. 1845, pp.15-22; *War in the North*, p.10; *New Zealand Journal*, 8 Nov. 1845.

24. Heke to FitzRoy, 21 May 1845, C.O. 209/35, pp.87-91.

25. George Clarke to C.S., 1 July 1845, C.O. 209/35, p.68.

26. The *Hazard*'s original landing party was 45 strong, but this was later increased to 80 or 90. The number of armed civilians is usually given as 110, but this seems to include only those enrolled as special constables, Williams to Rev. E. G. Marsh, 12 Mar. 1845, Carleton, *Henry Williams*, II, p.100; 'Eyewitness Account', *The Times*, 6 Sept. 1845.

27. Beckham, in J. C. Andersen & G. C. Petersen, *The Mair Family*, Wellington 1956, p.40.

28. *New Zealand Journal*, 19 July 1845; *The Times*, 6 Sept. 1845.

29. FitzRoy to Lord Stanley, 9 Apr. 1845, C.O. 209/34, p.26.

30. Bainbridge, Diary, 21-22 Mar. 1845, Buick, *New Zealand's First War*, pp.92-93; Rev. Lawry to [Bumby?], 16 Apr. 1845, Alfred Barrett, *Life of The Rev. John Hewgill Bumby with a Brief History of the Commencement and Progress of the Wesleyan Mission in New Zealand*, London 1853, p.239; *cf.* John Telford to CMS, [?] Mar. 1845, Telford Letters, CN/O 88.

31. Williams [to CMS], 26 Mar. 1845, CN/O 94(b).

32. e.g. Beckham to FitzRoy, 11 Mar. 1845, *P.P.* 1846 (517-II) XXX, p.16; *New Zealand Journal*, 21 Jan. 1864; *Southern Cross*, 15 Mar. 1845; *The Times*, 6 Sept. 1845; Williams to CMS, 14 Mar. 1845, CN/O 94(b).

33. J. Kemp to FitzRoy, 13 Mar. 1845, C.O. 209/34, p.45; Burrows to CMS, 19 Mar. 1845, CN/O 8(b); [G. A. Selwyn], *New Zealand Part IV: A Letter from the Bishop of New Zealand . . . Containing an Account of the Affray between the Settlers and the Natives of Kororareka*, Church in the Colonies, XII, 1846, p.29; Lloyd's Auckland Agent to Lloyd's London, 28 Mar. 1845, in *New Zealand Journal*, 19 July 1845.

34. [Selwyn] *Affray at Kororareka*, p.29; Kemp to FitzRoy, 13 Mar. 1845, C.O. 209/34, p.45. Heke had only one man wounded in his attack (Burrows to CMS, 19 Mar. 1845, CN/O 8(b)) and the Kapotai lost few men; 100 casualties would have crippled Kawiti's own forces, and subsequent events indicate that this did not happen.

35. The usual figure for British killed is ten to fifteen, but this does not count six settlers killed after the main force evacuated, H. Williams to FitzRoy, 20 Mar. 1845, CN/O 94(b); Buick, *New Zealand's First War*, p.78; Chapman, Diary 1837-63, Mar. 1845, p.44., AIM; *Southern Cross*, 22 Mar. 1845; FitzRoy, in Legislative Council, 15 Mar. 1845, quoted in *Southern Cross*, 22 Mar.

1845; [Selwyn], *Affray at Kororareka*, p.24.

36. Burrows, Journal, 5-8 Mar. 1845, pp.2-3; Burrows to CMS, 19 Mar. 1845, CN/O 8(b); Williams to CMS, 26 Mar. 1845, CN/O 94(b); Captain Gilbert Mair [to James Cowan], 24 June 1919, James Cowan Papers, ATL.

37. Lieut. Barclay to Lieut.-Col. Hulme, 15 Mar. 1845, *P.P.* 1846 (517-II) XXX, p.21; Beckham to FitzRoy, 11, 17 Mar., ibid, pp.16-17; *The Times*, 6 Sept. 1845 ('Eyewitness Account').

38. Philpotts, in H. Williams to FitzRoy, 20 Mar. 1845, CN/O 94(b); FitzRoy to H. Williams, 3 Apr. 1845, ibid; account of Corporal William Free, Cowan Papers, 41D.

39. George Clarke Jr., *Notes on Early Life in New Zealand*, Hobart 1903, p.72; FitzRoy to Stanley, 9 Apr. 1845, C.O. 209/34, p.27.

40. Major Cyprian Bridge, 'Journal of Events on An Expedition to New Zealand commencing on 4 April 1845', 24 May 1845, p.38, ATL.

41. [Selwyn] *Affray at Kororareka*, p.23.

42. Campbell to Hulme, 16 Mar. 1845, *P.P.* 1846 (517-II) XXX, p.23.

43. [Selwyn], *Affray*, p.25.

44. The *Hazard* still had ammunition and there were at least four large bags of powder in the Lower Blockhouse, *Hazard* Captain's Logbook, 11 Mar. 1845, Admiralty, Captains' Logs, 51/5613, PRO; *The Times*, 6 Sept. 1845.

45. Wards, *Shadow of the Land*, p.124.

46. Philpotts to FitzRoy, 11 Mar. 1845, *P.P.* 1846 (517-II) XXX, p.17; *Hazard* Captain's Logbook, 11 Mar. 1845, ADM 51/5613; [Selwyn], *Affray*, p.26; H. Williams to CMS, 14 Mar. 1845, CN/O 94(b).

47. Gibson, *The Maori Wars*, p.33; Cowan, *Wars*, I, p.27; Fortescue, *History of the British Army*, XII, p.401; Holt, *Strangest War*, p.83; also Michael Barthorp, *To Face the Daring Maoris. Soldiers' Impressions of the First Maori War 1845-47*, London 1979, pp.39-40; Buick, *New Zealand's First War*, p.71; Rutherford, *Hone Heke's Rebellion*, p.35; Wards, *Shadow of the Land*, p.124. Wards footnotes Kemp's figure for Maori casualties (p.124, fn 1), but cites the inflated figure in his text.

48. See Hulme to FitzRoy, 1 May 1845, W.O. 1/433, pp.522-7; Bridge, Journal, 29-30 Apr. 1845, pp.6-11; & especially account of J. J. Merrett (Hulme's interpreter) in *Auckland Times*, 17 May 1845.

49. From the morning of 3 May to the evening of 6 May. Hulme to FitzRoy, 7 May 1845, W.O. 1/433, pp.545-54; *cf.* Bridge, Journal, 3-6 May, pp.13-16; Private Alexander Whisker, 'Memorandum Book', Oct. 1844-Feb. 1850, pp.4-5, AIM.

50. Burrows, Journal, 7 May 1845, p.26.

51. Bridge, Journal, 6 May 1845, p.16.

52. *War in the North*, p.19; 'Journal of J. R. Clendon 1839-1872', 8 May 1845, Group C., p.14, APL.

53. FitzRoy to Lord Stanley, 19 May 1845, & FitzRoy to Hulme 18 May 1845, W.O. 1/433, pp.486-93, 609-14; Hulme's Report (9 May 1845), W.O. 1/433, pp.561-70.

54. Hulme to FitzRoy, 9 May 1845, W.O. 1/433; 'Journal of an Officer of the *North Star*', *Sydney Morning Herald*, 13 June 1845; Bridge, Journal, 8 May 1845, pp.17-19; *Auckland Times*, 17 May 1845 ('Our Correspondent at the Front'); Burrows to CMS, 14 May 1845, CN/O 8(b).

55. e.g. Beckham to FitzRoy, 12 May 1845, FitzRoy-Beckham Correspondence; Robert Hattaway, *Reminiscences of the Northern War*, Auckland 1889, p.4.

56. Gibson, *Maori Wars*, pp.40-42; Cowan, *Wars*, I, 42-44; *cf.* Holt, *Strangest War*, p.86; Buick, *New Zealand's First War*, pp.117-21; Fortescue, *History of the British Army*, XII, p.402.

57. 'Journal of an Officer of the *North Star*'; Burrows, Journal, 8 May 1845, pp.28-29.

58. Burrows, Journal, 7 May 1845, p.26. Burrows actually spoke to Kawiti's men on this day.

59. Buick, *New Zealand's First War*, p.117. Many observers noted that the flags were raised and lowered.

60. *War in the North*, p.14.

61. Maning to F. Maning Snr, 18 Sept. 1845, Maning Papers, 1; *War in the North*, p.18; Burrows to CMS, 14 May 1845, CN/O 8 (b); 'Journal of an Officer of the *North Star*'; Bridge, Journal, 11 May 1845. Some of these sources suggest that seven or eight 'chiefs' were killed. Under-estimating the breadth of the chiefly class in Maori society, the British could assume that this reflected dozens of others slain.

2: The Ohaeawai Campaign (pages 45-57)

1. G. Clarke to C.S., 1 July 1845, C.O. 209/35, p.123.
2. FitzRoy to Hulme, 31 May 1845, W.O. 1/433, p.627.
3. *War in the North*, p.25; also Carleton, *Henry Williams*, II, p.110.
4. *War in the North*, pp.25-31.
5. e.g. Wards, *Shadow of the Land*, p.151; Holt, *Strangest War*, p.88.
6. Carleton, *Henry Williams*, II, p.110; Davis to Coleman, 28 June 1845, in Coleman, *Richard Davis*, p.293; *New-Zealander*, 21 June 1845; Burrows, Journal, 13 June 1845, pp.42-43.
7. Burrows, Journal, 13 June 1845, pp.41-42; *War in the North*, pp.25-31. Apart from Heke and Te Kahakaha, Heke's principal lieutenant, Haratua, was also severely wounded. Carleton, *Henry Williams*, II, p.110.
8. Davis to Coleman, 28 June 1845, in Coleman, *Richard Davis*, p.293; Burrows, Journal, 13 June 1845, pp.41-43; *New-Zealander*, 21 June 1845.
9. Quoted in Bridge, Journal, 13 June 1845, pp.46-47; also Despard to FitzRoy, 12 June 1845, W.O.1/433, pp.740-1; Webster, *Reminiscences of an Old Settler*, pp.281-3.
10. Despard to Colonel Bainbrigge, 1 Sept. 1845, W.O.1/527, pp.259-62; also Despard to FitzRoy, 12 and 14 June 1845, W.O.1/433, pp.740-1, 743.
11. For important accounts of Ohaeawai other than those cited below see Despard to FitzRoy, 9 July 1845, to Bainbrigge, 1 Sept. 1845, W.O.1/527, pp.207-9, 225-6; Hattaway, *Reminiscences of the Northern War*, pp.5-10; Clendon, Journal, 26 June-6 July, pp.11-12. For Maori numbers see account of Hohaia Tango, 17 Mar. 1919, Cowan Papers 41D; *War in the North*, p.39; Davis to Coleman, 3 July 1845, in Coleman, *Richard Davis*, p.296. Davis's estimate was probably based on neutral Maori evidence and, though the number seems low, the coincidence of these three accounts on 100 men is convincing.
12. *New Zealand Journal*, 6 Dec. 1845.
13. W. P. Reeves, *The Long White Cloud: Ao Tea Roa*, London 1898, p.210; Holt, *The Strangest War*, p.88; Barthorp, *To Face the Daring Maoris*, pp.85-111.
14. Sgt. Maj. Moir, quoted in John Mitchell, Diary, p.6. AIM.
15. Arthur S. Thomson, *The Story of New Zealand: Past and Present—Savage and Civilized*, 2v., London 1859, II, p.116.
16. Bridge, Journal, 1 July 1845, p.74.
17. See especially Col. Henry Despard, Letterbook 1846-54, Royal Commonwealth Society Library, London; Despard to Grey, 9 Jan. 1846, W.O.1/526, pp.22-26; Brigade-Major C. P. O'Connell (for Despard), General Order, n.d. [Jan. 1846] W.O.1/526., p.102.
18. Account of W. H. Free, Cowan Papers, 41D.
19. R. A. A. Sherrin and J. H. Wallace, *The Early History of New Zealand*, Brett's Historical Series 1890, pp.708-9.
20. Duke of Wellington, Memo, 27 June 1846, W.O.1/527, pp.383-5.
21. O'Connell to W.O., 6 Oct. 1845, W.O.1/527, p.254; *cf.* O'Connell to Military Secretary, 11 Aug. 1845, W.O.1/434, pp.341-3. FitzRoy's attitude, FitzRoy to Despard, 7 July 1845; FitzRoy to the Governor of NSW, 8 July 1845; FitzRoy to Stanley, 9 July 1845; all in W.O.1/433, pp.682, 781, 813.
22. Account of Rihara Kou, 1922, Cowan Papers 41D.
23. *War in the North*, p.31.
24. Despard to FitzRoy, 26 June 1845, W.O.1/433, pp.762-4; also [Despard] 'Narrative of an Expedition into the Interior of New Zealand, During the Months of June and July, 1845', *Colborn's United Service Magazine*, no.213, Aug. 1846, pp.580-81. Despard's 'Narrative' was continued in the three subsequent numbers of this magazine.
25. Burrows, Journal, pp.39, 47.
26. Williams, Journal, 2 July 1845, quoted in Carleton, *Henry Williams*, II, p.113.
27. *War in the North*, pp.31-32. For the effect of the six-pounder, see *New Zealand Journal*, 6 Dec. 1845.
28. Bridge, Journal, 25 June 1845, p.57; *cf.* 29 June 1845, p.64.
29. Davis to Coleman, 3 July 1845, in Coleman, *Richard Davis*, p.295.

30. Frederick Myatt, *The Soldiers Trade: British Military Developments 1660-1914*, London 1974, p.50.
31. Bridge, Journal, pp.56-64.
32. Davis to Coleman, 3 July, in Coleman, *Richard Davis*, p.295.
33. Tawai Kawiti, 'Heke's War in the North', *Te Ao Hou*, no.16, Oct. 1956, p.42. I am indebted to J. M. R. Owens of Massey University for drawing my attention to this article.
34. Account of Rihara Kou, 1922, Cowan Papers, 41D.
35. Davis to Coleman, 3 July 1845, Coleman, *Richard Davis*, p.295; *War in the North*, p.43. Burrows found the Maoris digging six graves in the *pa* after the battle but preferred to believe that their losses were much higher, Journal, 2 July 1845, p.52. The figure of ten Maoris killed in the whole Ohaeawai operation (24 June-11 July) is now generally accepted.
36. Acting Brigade-Major R. B. Dearing (for Despard), Memo of Instructions to assault force, 1 July 1845, W.O.1/433, p.803-7; also Despard, 'Narrative', no. 214, p.33; Despard to FitzRoy, 2, 9 July 1845, W.O.1/433, pp.793-4, 1/527, pp.207-9.
37. Account of W. H. Free, in Cowan, *Wars*, I, p.61.
38. Account of J. P. Dumoulins, quoted in Carleton, *Henry Williams*, I, 111, fn.
39. Mitchell, Diary, p.7.
40. Account of Rawiri te Rura, 17 Mar. 1919, in Cowan, *Wars*, I, p.69.
41. Davis to Coleman, 3 July 1845, in Coleman, *Richard Davis*, pp.294-5.
42. Account of Free in Cowan, *Wars*, I, p.61.
43. Account of Rihara Kou in Cowan, *Wars*, I, p.64.
44. Bridge, Journal, 1 July 1845, p.72.
45. Quoted in Cowan, *Wars*, I, pp.65-66. *War in the North* gives a somewhat different version, p.40.
46. Bridge, Journal, 1 July 1845, p.75.
47. Bridge, Journal, 5 July, pp.81-82; Despard to FitzRoy (Private), 6 July 1845, W.O.1/433, pp.825-7, 831-40.
48. A missionary journal, 7 July 1845, quoted in Carleton, *Henry Williams*, II, p.114 fn.; Bridge, Journal, 8 July 1845, p.84.
49. Burrows, Journal, 7 July, p.54.
50. Despard to FitzRoy, 11 July 1845, W.O.1/433, p.1040; *cf.* Despard to Bainbrigge, 1 Sept. 1845, W.O.1/527, p.264.
51. FitzRoy to Despard, 14 July 1845, W.O.1/527, pp.215-17; FitzRoy to Stanley, 25 Oct. 1845, C.O.209/36, pp.157-8; FitzRoy to Despard, C.O.209/36, p.182.
52. FitzRoy to Despard, W.O.1/433, p.815.
53. Despard to FitzRoy, 11 Sept. 1845, C.O.209/36, p.178; also Burrows, Journal, 12 Aug. 1845, pp.4-5 (new pagination); Burrows to CMS, 30 Oct. 1845, CN/O 8(b).
54. FitzRoy to Despard, C.O.209/36, pp.191-9; also FitzRoy to Despard, 20 Sept. 1845, C.O.209/36, p.180; FitzRoy to Heke, 6 Aug. 1845, 29 Sept. 1845, FitzRoy-Grey Letterbook.
55. Heke to FitzRoy, n.d., C.O.209/35, pp.101-3; Burrows, Journal, 12 Aug. 1845, pp.4-5.
56. Quoted in Despard to O'Connell (Private), 5 Nov. 1845, W.O.1/527, pp.306-7; *cf.* Burrows, Journal, 8 Oct. 1845, pp.14-15; Davis to Coleman, 5 Nov. 1845, in Coleman, *Richard Davis*, p.307.
57. Burrows to [?], 6 Sept. 1845, APL, NZ MSS 308; *cf.* Heke to Williams, 1 Nov. 1845, W.O.1/527, p.308.
58. Burrows, Journal, 10 Oct. 1845, p.18; Grey, Memo., 4 Dec. 1845, *P.P.* 1846 (690) XXX, p.12.
59. Clendon, Journal, 4 Oct. 1845; Burrows, Journal, 1 Aug.-3 Oct. 1845, pp.1-13; Davis to Coleman, 23 Sept. 1845, in Coleman, *Richard Davis*, p.303; G.Clarke Snr. to C.S., 1 July 1845, C.O.209/35, p.62.
60. Despard to FitzRoy, 24 Sept. 1845, C.O.209/36, p.189.
61. Williams to CMS., 28 July 1845, CN/O 94(b); *New-Zealander*, 13 Sept. 1845.

3: The Paper Victory (pages 58-70)

1. *War in the North*, p.25.
2. Grey, Memo. [4 Dec. 1845], *P.P.* 1846 (690) XXX, p.12; Burrows, Journal, 27 Nov. 1845.
3. Despard to Grey, 12 Dec. 1845, W.O.1/433, pp.1193-97; Grey to Stanley, 19 Dec. 1845, W.O.1/433, p.1189; Commander G. Hay to Captain G. Graham R. N., 12 Jan. 1846, W.O.1/526,

pp.89-97.
4. Grey to Stanley, 2 Jan. 1846, W.O.1/526, pp.1-3. The generally accepted figure for Kawiti's Ruapekapeka garrison is 400 men.
5. *War in the North*, p.45; account of Rihara Kou, Cowan Papers, 41D.
6. Grey to Stanley, 2 Jan. 1846, W.O.1/526, p.3; Clendon to Grey, 29 Dec. 1846; Grey Autograph Letters, APL., C22; *War in the North*, p.46.
7. Despard to Grey, 11, 12 Jan. 1846, W.O.1/526, pp.53-54, 66-67; Grey to Stanley, 13 Jan. 1846, W.O.1/526, pp.45-46.
8. Grey to Stanley, 22 Jan. 1846, *P.P.* 1846 (448) XXX, pp.14-15; Andrew Sinclair, C.S. (for Grey), Proclamation, 23 Jan. 1846, *P.P.* 1846 (448) XXX, p.16.
9. Gladstone to Grey, 29 June 1846, W.O.6/96.
10. *Diary of John Newland, 1841-73*, New Plymouth 1959, 11 Jan. 1846.
11. Cowan, *Wars*, I, p.80; Buick, *New Zealand's First War*, p.256.
12. Carleton, *Henry Williams*, II, p.125; for Williams's own opinion see II, p.137 and Williams to CMS., CN/O 94(b); *New-Zealander*, 24 Jan. 1846 (*cf.* 4 Feb. & 4 Apr. issues); Collinson, *Military Operations in New Zealand*, p.70; Telford to CMS., 19 Jan. 1846, CN/O 88.
13. Mrs Williams, Journal, 14 Jan. 1846, quoted in Carleton, *Henry Williams*, II, p.125. Mrs Williams gives nine Maoris killed. Carleton himself subsequently checked with the Maoris and found that twelve had been killed, *Henry Williams*, II, p.125, fn.; also, Henry Williams to CMS, 20 Jan. 1846, CN/O 94(b). British and pro-government Maori casualties were about fourteen killed and thirty-two wounded.
14. Wards, *Shadow of the Land*, p.202.
15. Bridge, Journal, 8 Jan. 1846; Journal of an Officer, quoted in Buick, *New Zealand's First War*, pp.252-3; H. C. Balneavis, Journal, quoted in Carleton, *Henry Williams*, II, p.124 fn.
16. Bridge, Journal, 10 Jan. 1846.
17. *New-Zealander*, 10, 26 Jan. 1846.
18. *War in the North*, p.46.
19. Despard to Grey, 12 Jan. 1846, W.O.1/526, p.66.
20. Evidence of Ruatara Tauramoko, in Cowan, *Wars*, I, p.81.
21. Balneavis, Journal, 11 Jan. 1846, quoted in Carleton, *Henry Williams*, II, p.124 fn.; also, R. Hattaway, *Reminiscences of the Northern War*, p.16; *New-Zealander*, 24 Jan. 1846.
22. *War in the North*, p.47.
23. Collinson, *Military Operations in New Zealand*, p.70.
24. Rutherford, *Sir George Grey*, London 1961, p.91.
25. Rutherford, *Grey*, p.90; paraphrasing Grey to Stanley, 22 Jan. 1845.
26. FitzRoy to Heke, 29 Sept. 1845, FitzRoy-Grey Letterbook.
27. *New-Zealander*, 14 Feb. 1845; Martin Wareumu and Pomare to Grey, 19 Jan. 1846, *P.P.* 1846 (448) XXX, p.16.
28. Alexander Whisker, Memorandum Book, 18-21 Jan. 1846, p.26b; H. F. McKillop, *Reminiscences of Twelve Months' Service in New Zealand*, London 1849, pp.130-31; Kawiti, 'Heke's War in the North', p.45.
29. Davis to Coleman, 22 Jan. 1846, in Coleman, *Richard Davis*, p.309. For speeches at Pomare's *pa*, *New-Zealander*, 14 Feb. 1846.
30. Grey to Stanley, 23 Jan. 1846, *P.P.* 1846 (690) XXX, p.16; Proclamation, 25 Jan. 1846, FitzRoy-Grey Letterbook; Grey to Stanley, 10 Dec. 1845, W.O.1/433; *cf.* Grey to Despard, 17 Nov., 5 Dec. 1845, FitzRoy-Grey Letterbook.
31. *New-Zealander*, 29 Feb. 1846.
32. Grey to Stanley, 19 Sept. 1846, *P.P.* 1847 (763) XXXVIII, p.60.
33. 'E. Meurant's Account of Meeting with Heke', 1-9 Oct. 1846 (copies of speeches enclosed), AIM; *cf.* Edward Meurant, Diaries, 1842-7, 1-9 Oct. 1846, APL.
34. *New-Zealander*, 14 Feb. 1846; also J. Merrett, 'A Visit to Heke and Kawiti', in *New Zealand Journal*, 5 Dec. 1846; Cowan, *Wars*, I, p.83.
35. *War in the North*, p.48.
36. FitzRoy to Hulme, 4 May 1845 and FitzRoy to Despard, 9 June 1845, W.O.1/433, pp.537-41, 729-31; Grey to Despard, 5 Dec. 1845, FitzRoy-Grey Letterbook.

37. Grey to Captain G. Graham, R.N., 21 Sept. 1846, FitzRoy-Grey Letterbook.
38. Grey to O'Connell, 5 May 1846, W.O.1/527, p.372.
39. Commander F. Patten, R. N. & Captain G. Graham, R. N., in Mar., Sept. 1846; Edward Meurant & Sir Godfrey Thomas in Oct., Dec. 1846.
40. See Grey to Captain G. Graham, 21 Sept. 1846, FitzRoy-Grey Letterbook; Grey to Stanley, 19 Sept., Waka Nene to Grey, 10 Sept. 1846, *P.P.* 1847 (763) XXXVIII, pp.60, 60-61.
41. Grey to Stanley, 19 Sept. 1846, *P.P.* 1847 (763) XXXVIII, p.60.
42. F. E. Maning to A. T. Maning, 23 Mar., 24 Nov. 1846, Maning Papers.
43. Williams to CMS, 20 Aug. 1846, CN/O 94(b).
44. Davis to Coleman, 5-8 Jan. 1846, Coleman, *Richard Davis*, pp.323-4.
45. Sir Godfrey Thomas, 'Account of a Visit to the Bay of Islands', Grey Collection, APL.
46. Davis to Coleman, 28 Aug., 19 Oct. 1847, Coleman, *Richard Davis*, pp.314, 317.
47. Carleton, *Henry Williams*, II, p.125; Williams to E. G. Marsh, 28 May 1846, Carleton, *Henry Williams*, II, p.137.

4: A Question of Sovereignty (pages 73-88)

1. Cowan, *Wars*, I, pp.88-144; Wards, *Shadow of the Land*, pp.215-351; Rutherford, *Grey*, pp.99-117; Grover, *Cork of War*, pp.266-303.
2. Sinclair, *Origins of the Maori Wars*.
3. Large areas of government-owned land had not been purchased by settlers, even in the crowded Taranaki province, Dalton, *War and Politics*, pp.85-87; William Martin to the Secretary of State for the Colonies, 1 July 1864, C.O. 209/187, pp.321-6; *Southern Cross*, 9 Nov. 1860 (letter by an 'Old Chum'); B. Wells, *The History of Taranaki*, New Plymouth 1878, p.174.
4. Dalton, *War and Politics*, ch.IV.
5. See below, Ch.15, note 38.
6. Ward, 'The Origins of the Anglo-Maori Wars: A Reconsideration', *NZJH*, 1, 1967, pp.148-70.
7. Ward, 'The Origins . . .', *NZJH*, 1, 1967, pp.148-70.
8. Browne to Newcastle, 27 Apr., 1 Nov. 1860, *P.P.* 1861 (2798) XLI, pp.33, 160.
9. See, for example, the petitions from Auckland, Wellington, Hutt Valley settlers, May, Sept. 1860, *P.P.* 1861 (2798) XLI, pp.66, 150-2. Ward provides further examples in 'The Origins . . .'.
10. Browne to Newcastle, 22 Mar. 1860, *P.P.* 1861 (2798) XLI, p.17.
11. F. D. Bell, F. Whitaker, and T. Gore Browne, *Notes on Sir William Martin's pamphlet entitled The Taranaki Question*, Auckland 1861, p.2; William Martin, *The Taranaki Question*, Auckland 1860, p.1.
12. *Taranaki Herald*, 4 July 1863.
13. Carey, *Narrative of the Late War in New Zealand*, London 1863, pp.118, 66.
14. Sinclair, *History of New Zealand*, p.133; Dalton, *War and Politics*, pp.122-3, 108; Gibson, *Maori Wars*, p.85. Similar opinions, Fortescue, *History of the British Army*, XIII, p.488; Dalton, 'A New Look at the Maori Wars', p.238; W. P. Morrell, *British Colonial Policy in the Mid-Victorian Age*, Oxford 1969, p.261.
15. At least 100 Atiawa supported the British in the war and a local settler convincingly reported the 'rebel' strength at 200, Pratt to Browne, 16 Oct. 1860, *P.P.* 1861 (2798) XLI, pp.164-5; C. Brown to C. W. Richmond, 19 Feb. 1860, G. H. Scholefield, ed., *R-A.P.*, 2v., Wellington 1960, I, pp.522-4.
16. W. W. Turton to C. W. Richmond, 7 Mar. 1860, *P.P.* 1861 (2798) XLI, p.14; F. D. Bell to T. Russell, 15 Mar. 1863, Donald McLean Papers, 14, ATL; *New-Zealander*, 24 June 1863. The warrior strength of these tribes was sometimes put at 1,200, but the facts that their total population in 1860 was 1,800 and that some Taranakis were neutral confirms the lower figure.
17. Gold to Browne, 24 Apr. 1860, *P.P.* 1861 (2798) XLI, p.46.
18. *Taranaki Herald*, 24 Mar. 1860; *New Zealand Examiner*, 10 July 1860; *cf.* A. S. Atkinson, Diary, 1859-60, 18 Mar. 1860, ATL.
19. *Memorials of Sergeant Marjouram . . . Including six years service in New Zealand during the Late Maori War*, ed. William White, London 1863, pp.184-9; H. Ronalds, Diary, 18 Mar. 1860, in *R-A.P.*, I, p.535. For the absence of Maori casualties, Browne to Sir William Denison, 21 Mar.

1860, *P.P.* 1861 (2798) XLI, pp.278-9; *New Zealand Examiner*, 10 July 1860; H. Ronalds to his father, 24 Mar. 1860, Ronalds Letters, TS in Taranaki Museum.

20. *Memorials of Sergeant Marjouram*, pp.74-76, 188; Gold to Browne, 19 Mar. 1860, *P.P.* 1861 (2798) XLI, p.16.

21. Eyewitness accounts on which this summary is based, reports of Murray, Captain P. Cracroft R. N., & Captain C. Brown (militia), 28-30 Mar. 1860, *P.P.* 1861 (2798) XLI, pp.24-28; H. A. Atkinson and A. S. Atkinson to C. W. Richmond, 6, 9 Apr. 1860, *R-A.P.*, I, pp.551-4, 557-60; *The Diary of George Jupp 1851-72*, 3v., New Plymouth n.d., II, 28-31 Mar. 1860, pp.59-60; Rev. Thomas Gilbert, *New Zealand Settlers and Soldiers or the War in Taranaki Being Incidents in The Life of a Settler*, London 1861, pp.94-104; 'A Taranaki Volunteer', in the *Nelson Examiner*, 2 Apr. 1860; Frank Ronalds to his father, 3 Apr. 1860, Ronalds Letters.

22. Only a fraction of Ngati Ruanui were at Waireka. The main body arrived after the battle. B. Wells, *History of Taranaki*, pp.195-6; A. S. Atkinson, Diary, 24 Mar., 1 Apr. 1860.

23. *New Zealand Examiner*, 10 July 1860.

24. *Nelson Examiner*, 2 Apr. 1860; Atkinson to C. W. & Emily Richmond, 6 Apr. 1860 (Atkinson's emphasis), C. W. Richmond to A. S. Atkinson, 3 Apr. 1860, *R-A.P.*, I, pp.553, 550; *New Zealand Examiner*, 10 July 1860; also *Diary of George Jupp*, 28 Mar. 1860, p.59; *Diary of John Newland*, 28 Mar. 1860, p.47.

25. *Nelson Examiner*, 2 Apr. 1860; *New Zealand Examiner*, 10 July 1860; letter of Rev. Samuel Ironside in *Sydney Morning Herald*, 23 Apr. 1860; Commodore Loring to Admiralty, 27 Apr. 1860, C.O.209/58, pp.22-24.

26. Richard Taylor, *The Past and Present of New Zealand with Its Prospects for the Future*, London and Wanganui 1868, pp.125-6; *cf.* T. W. Gudgeon, *Reminiscences of the War in New Zealand*, London 1879, pp.12-13.

27. *New Zealand Examiner*, 10 July 1860; *Nelson Examiner*, 2 Apr. 1860; Diary of H. Ronalds, 29 Mar. 1860, *R-A.P.*, I, p.537; Evidence of A. B. Craven, Cowan, *Wars*, I, p.174.

28. *Spectator*, 14 July 1860.

29. *New Zealand Examiner*, 10 July 1860; *Southern Cross*, 27 Apr. 1860.

30. *New-Zealander*, 28 Apr. 1860; *Southern Cross*, 28 Apr. 1860; Loring to Admiralty, 27 Apr. 1860, C.O.209/158, pp.22-24.

31. Admiralty to C.O., 26 June 1860, *P.P.* 1861 (2798) XLI, p.261. Captains R. N. could only be promoted by seniority. Promotions of the First Lieutenant were therefore frequently used to honour the Captain.

32. *New-Zealander*, 30 Oct. 1860; *cf. New-Zealander*, 1 July 1860.

33. Holt, *The Strangest War*, p.154; Morrell, *British Colonial Policy*, p.244; *cf.* Reeves, *Long White Cloud*, pp.270-2; Cowan, *Wars*, I, p.175; Gibson, *The Maori Wars*, pp.78-79; J. O'C. Ross, *The White Ensign in New Zealand*, Wellington, Auckland, Sydney 1967, p.86; Dalton, *War and Politics*, pp.109-10; J. Rutherford, 'The Maori Wars', A. H. McLintock, ed., *The Encyclopaedia of New Zealand*, 3v., Wellington 1966, II, p.479.

34. Captain C. Brown's report, 29 Mar. 1860, *P.P.* 1861 (2798) XLI, pp.27-28; H. A. Atkinson to C. W. Richmond, 6 Apr. 1860, *R-A.P.*, I, p.553.

35. The column had been reinforced by twenty-six more militia from Omata Stockade and a dozen stragglers from Murray's division.

36. Gilbert, *New Zealand Settlers and Soldiers*, p.103; *Diary of George Jupp*, 31 Mar. 1860, p.59.

37. Quoted in Morgan S. Grace, *A Sketch of the New Zealand War*, London 1899, p.29.

38. Cracroft's Report, 28 Mar. 1860, *P.P.* 1861 (2798) XLI, p.26.

39. Carey, *The Late War in New Zealand*, p.36.

40. Grace, *A Sketch of the New Zealand War*, p.30.

41. Robert Ward, *Life Among the Maoris of New Zealand, Being a Description of Missionary, Colonial and Military Achievements*, eds. Rev. Thomas Lowe & Rev. William Whitby, Toronto 1872, p.361. Maori opinion, Robert Maunsell to C. W. Richmond, 16 Apr. 1860, *R-A.P.*, I, pp.564-5.

42. A. S. Atkinson, Diary, 2 June 1860, *R-A.P.*, I, p.592.

43. Gilbert, *New Zealand Settlers and Soldiers*, pp.94-103.

44. Maunsell to C. W. Richmond, 16 Apr. 1860, *R-A.P.*, I, pp.564-5.

5: The Intervention of the King Movement (pages 89-98)

1. Atkinson, Diary, 19 Apr. 1860, *R-A.P.*, I, p.565; John Morgan to CMS [?] Aug. 1860, CN/O 65(a).

2. Browne to Newcastle, & C. W. Richmond, Memo, both 27 Apr. 1860; Browne to Newcastle, 2 Oct. 1860, all in *P.P.* 1861 (2798) XLI, pp.33, 43, 143.

3. Browne to Newcastle, 26 June, 26 May 1860, *P.P.* 1861 (2798) XLI, pp.67-68, 63-64; F. Whitaker, 3 Sept. 1860, *NZPD*, 1858-60, p.432.

4. e.g. R. Maunsell to CMS, 2 May 1860, CN/O 64(b); R. Burrows to CMS, [16?] Apr. 1860, CN/O 8(c); ch.6, sect.1, below.

5. See Browne to Newcastle, 27 Apr., 27 June, and encl., *P.P.* 1861 (2798) XLI, pp.32-40, 68-73.

6. T. H. Smith, nd., 'Narrative of a visit to Waikato', Rev. T. Buddle to Browne, 25 Apr. 1860 (encl. notes of April meeting speeches), *P.P.* 1862 (2798) XLI, pp.34-39; J. Morgan to C. W. Richmond, 9 May 1860, *R-A.P.*, I, pp.578-9; B. Y. Ashwell to CMS., 30 May 1860, CN/O 19; T. Buddle, *The Maori King Movement . . . with a full report of the Native meetings held at Waikato, April and May, 1860*, Auckland 1860.

7. Wi Tako to the Waikato Chiefs, 10 Apr. 1860, *P.P.* 1861 (2798) XLI, p.39.

8. Seth Tarawhiti to Browne, 16 Apr. 1860, J. Morgan to Browne, 8 May 1860, *P.P.* 1861 (2798) XLI, pp.39-40, 64-65; Wells, *History of Taranaki*, pp.202-5 (evid. of R. Parris); *Taranaki Herald*, 7 July 1860.

9. Maj. T. Nelson to Gold, 7, 8 June 1860, *AJHR*, 1860, E-3C, p.5.

10. Browne to Newcastle, 26 June 1860, before news of the 23 June skirmish arrived in Auckland, *P.P.* 1861 (2798) XLI, p.68; A. S. Atkinson, Diary, 25 June 1860, *R-A.P.*, I, p.598; Bde. Major to Nelson, 26 June 1860, *AJHR*, 1860, E-3C, p.8. This mentions only eighty reinforcements, sent from New Plymouth by steamer, but a further 100 were sent overland. See Lieut. Battiscombe to Senior Naval Officer, 27 June 1860, C.O.209/158, p.40.

11. Grace, *Sketch of the New Zealand War*, pp.33-34; *Sydney Morning Herald*, 21 Sept. 1860.

12. Given to A. S. Atkinson by Maori veterans of the battle whose accounts he considered reliable, Diary, 14 Aug. 1861, *R-A.P.*, I, p.718.

13. Grace, *Sketch of the New Zealand War*, p.76.

14. J. E. Alexander, *Incidents of the Maori War, New Zealand, in 1860-61*, London 1863, p.157; *Sydney Morning Herald*, 11 July 1860; also Nelson to Bde. Major, 28 June 1860, *AJHR*, 1860, E-3C, p.10. The abolition of 'flank' (Grenadier and Light) companies, announced in 1859, did not come into effect in the 40th Regiment until 1862.

15. Gold to Browne, 9 July 1860, *P.P.* 1861 (2798) XLI, p.87; *Memorials of Sergeant Marjouram*, p.217; Marjouram to Nelson, 24 June 1860, *AJHR*, 1860, E-3C, p.7.

16. *Sydney Morning Herald*, 11 July 1860; also Atkinson, Diary, 29 June 1860, *R-A.P.*, I, p.589.

17. *Sydney Morning Herald*, 11 July 1860.

18. A. S. Atkinson, Diary, 29 June 1860, *R-A.P.*, I, p.589.

19. Grace, *Sketch of the New Zealand War*, p.35; also *Memorials of Sergeant Marjouram*, p.219.

20. *Sydney Morning Herald*, 11 July 1860.

21. Lieut. Battiscombe (commanding naval brigade under Seymour), to Senior Naval Officer, 27 June 1860, C.O.209/158, pp.40-42.

22. *Taranaki Herald*, 30 June 1860; also R. Burrows to CMS, 30 July 1860, CN/O 8(c); Wells, *History of Taranaki*, p.207.

23. *Diary of George Jupp*, 27 June 1860, p.61; also Wells, *History of Taranaki*, p.207.

24. Alexander, *Incidents of the Maori War*, pp.157-61; Grace, *Sketch of the New Zealand War*, pp.35-36; *Sydney Morning Herald*, 11 July 1860.

25. Alexander, *Incidents of the Maori War*, p.161; *Taranaki Herald*, 30 June 1860.

26. Account of Peita Kotuku, 23 Feb. 1921, Cowan Papers, 41A.

27. Alexander, *Incidents of the Maori War*, p.161; also Grace, *Sketch of the New Zealand War*, p.36.

28. Nelson to Bde. Major, 27 June 1860, *P.P.* 1861 (2798) XLI, p.81 (hereafter Nelson's report); Proclamation quoted in *Sydney Morning Herald*, 11 July 1860.

29. *Taranaki Herald*, 30 June 1860. Richard Taylor was one of the few who persisted in this opinion, *Past and Present of New Zealand*, p.126.

30. J. C. Richmond to Mary Richmond, [29] June 1860, *R-A.P.*, I, pp.507-8.

31. *Southern Cross*, 6 July 1860.

32. *Sydney Morning Herald*, 11 July 1860; Nelson's Report.

33. Nelson's Report; *Sydney Morning Herald*, 11 July 1860.

34. J. C. Richmond to C. W. Richmond, 2 July 1860, *R-A.P.*, I, p.607.

35. J. C. Richmond to C. W. Richmond, 2 July 1860, *R-A.P.*, I, p.607; A. S. Atkinson, Diary, 14 Aug. 1861, ibid., I, p.798 (from two Maori veterans of the battle, Atkinson commented 'I am afraid it must be true.'); *Taranaki Herald*, 7 July 1860 (two reports); Rev. John Morgan to CMS, [?] Aug. 1860, CN/O 65(a); Statement of Tamati Ngapora, 27 Sept. 1860, *P.P.* 1861 (2798) XLI, p.150 (Ngapora, a reliable source, asserted that no Waikatos were killed); R. Burrows to CMS, 30 July 1860, CN/O 8(c).

36. *Taranaki Herald*, 30 June 1860; *Sydney Morning Herald*, 11 July 1860.

37. *Southern Cross*, 4 July 1860.

38. *Southern Cross*, 6 July 1860.

39. Alexander, *Incidents of the Maori War*, p.162; Nelson's Report.

40. Carey, *The Late War in New Zealand*, pp.40-43; also Grace, *Sketch of the New Zealand War*, p.37.

41. e.g. Capt. R. H. Raymond Smythies, *Historical Records of the 40th (2nd Somersetshire) Regiment . . .*, Devonport 1894, p.390 fn.; Loring to Admiralty, 12 Sept. 1860, C.O.209/158, p.76; *New Zealand Examiner*, 14 Jan. 1861; J.-M. Atkinson, Journal, 11 July 1860, and A. S. Atkinson to C. W. Richmond, 2 July 1860, *R-A.P.*, I, pp.605, 606.

42. Jane-Maria Atkinson to Emily Richmond, 20 May 1860, *R-A.P.*, I, p.584; also Jane-Maria Atkinson, Journal, 11 July 1860, & J. C. Richmond to C. W. Richmond, 2 July 1860, ibid., I, pp.605, 607; *Sydney Morning Herald*, 11 and 12 July; *The Times*, 14 Sept. 1860; Henry Sewell, Journal, v.2, Pt 1, p.71 (typescript), Canterbury Museum. Governor Browne and his wife also attacked Gold's conduct. Browne to Gold, 5 July 1860, *P.P.* 1861 (2798) XLI, p.82; H. L. G. Browne, *Narrative of the Waitara Purchase and the Taranaki War*, ed. W. P. Morrell, Dunedin 1965.

43. Gold to Browne, 9 July 1860, *P.P.* 1861 (2798) XLI, p.87.

44. He left New Plymouth at about 10.00 a.m.—three hours after the battle began, A. S. Atkinson, Journal, 27 June 1860, *R-A.P.*, I, pp.598-9.

45. Bde. Major to Nelson, 26 June 1860, *P.P.* 1861 (2798) XLI, p.81; Grace, *Sketch of the New Zealand War*, p.37; Gold letter, 4 Dec. 1860, to *The Times*, 19 Feb. 1861; also the reply of Nelson's brother, *The Times*, 20 Feb. 1861.

46. Fortescue, *History of the British Army*, XIII, p.478; Gibson, *The Maori Wars*, p.81; also Morrell, *Colonial Policy in the Mid-Victorian Age*, pp.245-6; Holt, *Strangest War*, p.157; Cowan, *Wars*, I, p.78; Dalton, *War and Politics*, p.111.

47. Pasley to his father, 7 Sept. 1860, Letters of Major Charles Pasley R. E., 1853-61, AIM.

48. Lieutenant A. H. W. Battiscombe R. N., Journal kept during the Maori War, 1860-61, 29 Aug. 1860, pp.22-23, ATL.

6: *The Maori Strategy and the British Response (pages 99-116)*

1. Browne to Newcastle, 20 July 1860, *P.P.* 1861 (2798) XLI, pp.87-88; *cf.* Browne to Gold, 10 July 1860, ibid., p.88.

2. Quoted in Browne to Newcastle, 27 Aug. 1860, *P.P.* 1861 (2798) XLI, p.94; Loring to Adm., 12 Sept. 1860, C.O.209/158, p.76; Browne to Pratt, 27 Aug. 1860, *P.P.* 1861 (2798) XLI, p.95.

3. Browne to Pratt, 27 Aug. 1860, *P.P.* 1861 (2798) XLI, p.95.

4. *Memorials of Sergeant Marjouram*, 28 Aug. 1860, p.245; Battiscombe, Journal, 26 Aug. 1860, p.12; also *New-Zealander*, 15 Aug. 1860; Major W. Hutchings to D.A.G., 4 Sept. 1860, 'Selections from Despatches Relative to the Conduct of Military Operations in New Zealand', W.O.33/16, pp.28-29.

5. J. Flight to C. W. Richmond, 6 Aug. 1860, *R-A.P.*, I, pp.624-5; *Memorials of Sergeant Marjouram*, 12 Aug. 1860, pp.238-9.

6. Loring to Admiralty, 11 Sept. 1860, C.O.209/158, pp.71-74; *Sydney Morning Herald*, 21 Sept. 1860; Burrows to CMS, 2 Oct. 1860, CN/O 8(c).

7. *Memorials of Sergeant Marjouram*, 22 Sept. 1860, p.268.

8. Taylor, *New Zealand Past and Present*, p.127; *Diary of George Jupp*, 11 Sept. 1860, p.64; A. S.

Atkinson, Journal, 16 Sept. 1860, *R-A.P.*, I, p.634; H. Ronalds to E. Ronalds, 25 Sept. 1860, Ronalds Letters (H. Ronalds's italics).

9. *New-Zealander*, 3 Oct. 1860.

10. *Auckland Weekly Register*, 15 Oct. 1860, quoted in *New Zealand Examiner*, 17 Dec. 1860.

11. The generally accepted figure is now 150, but survivors stated that only fifty warriors were involved (*Southern Cross*, 4 Dec. 1860). Furthermore, it seems that thirty-seven Maoris were killed or mortally wounded, and several accounts based on Maori evidence refer to there being only a dozen survivors, e.g. *Memorials of Sergeant Marjouram*, 16 Nov. 1860, p.296; A. S. Atkinson, Journal, 23 July 1861, *R-A.P.*, I, p.717; John Gorst, *The Maori King*, ed. Keith Sinclair, London 1959, p.100.

12. Pratt fudged over this fact in his reports, but Carey, his Deputy Adjutant-General, leaves no doubt of it. Pratt to Browne, 6, 10 Nov. 1860, *P.P.* 1860 (2798) XLI, pp.167-8, 256-7; Carey, *The Late War in New Zealand*, pp.121-6.

13. Carey, *The Late War*, p.128; also Pratt's report of 10 Nov. 1860; *Southern Cross*, 9 Nov. 1860.

14. *Sydney Morning Herald*, 21 Nov. 1860; *cf. Taranaki Herald*, 10 Nov. 1860; *New Zealand Gazette*, 7 Nov. 1860; *The Times*, 14 Jan. 1861.

15. *New Zealand Examiner*, 14 Jan. 1861.

16. e.g. Pratt to War Office, 10 Dec. 1860, Select Despatches, pp.39-40; Grace, *Sketch of the New Zealand War*, p.87; *Southern Cross*, 4 Dec. 1860, 5 Apr. 1861; Donald McLean to Pratt, 24 Nov. 1860, McLean Papers, 13, ATL; J. Morgan to CMS, 25 Nov. 1860, CN/O 65(a).

17. Sewell, Journal, v.2, Pt 1, p.108; *New Zealand Examiner*, 17 Dec. 1860; J. C. Richmond to C. W. Richmond, 12 May 1860, *R-A.P.*, I, pp.579-80; *New-Zealander*, 3 Oct. 1860.

18. Gold to D.A.G. Melbourne, 23 June 1860, Pratt to Military Secretary, 10 Dec. 1860, Select Despatches, pp.9, 39-40.

19. Morgan to CMS, 6 Sept. 1860, CN/O 65(a); Morgan to Browne, 1 Jan. 1861, Gore Browne Papers (ts.) National Archives, 1/2d; *New Zealand Examiner*, 17 Dec. 1860, 14 Jan. 1861.

20. Morgan to CMS, [?]Aug. 1860, CN/O 65(a); *Memorials of Sergeant Marjouram*, 1 July 1860, p.223.

21. Alexander, *Incidents of the Maori War*, p.212; *Southern Cross*, 9 Nov., 4 Dec. 1860.

22. Morgan to CMS., 1 Jan. 1861, CN/O 65(a); evidence of Rev. J. A. Wilson in *Southern Cross*, 1 Feb. 1861. Wilson visited the Kingite forces and counted 1,000 warriors, of whom only about 200 could have been Te Atiawa.

23. Morgan to Browne, 8 Feb. 1861, Gore Browne Papers, 1/2d. Other evidence of the flow of warriors to and from Taranaki, Morgan to Browne, 23 Jan. 1861, ibid.; Morgan to Browne, 19 Dec. 1860, *R-A.P.*, I, pp.669-70; Burrows to CMS, 27 Nov. 1860, 3 Jan. 1861, CN/O 8(c); J. A. Wilson to CMS, 3 Dec. 1860, 4 Feb. 1861, CN/O 98; McLean to Pratt, 31 Aug. 1860, *P.P.* 1861 (2798) XLI, pp.126-7; Carey, *The Late War in New Zealand*, pp.70, 118-19, 124.

24. Gorst, *The Maori King*, p.95; *Southern Cross*, 21 Dec. 1860.

25. Burrows to CMS, 4 Mar. 1861, CN/O 8(c).

26. Ware to 'Friend John Robinson', 16 Jan. 1861, 'te kingi' and others to [?], 17 Jan. 1861, McLean Papers, 13. For visiting ships as a source of ammunition see McLean, Memo, 1 July 1861, ibid., 14; Morgan to CMS, 7 Mar. 1861, Gore Browne Papers, 1/2d.

27. Wiremu Nera to Browne, 17 Sept. 1860, *P.P.* 1861 (2798) XLI, p.150; *New Zealand Examiner*, 19 Mar. 1861; Gorst, *Maori King*, p.95.

28. Morgan to CMS, 21 Mar. 1861, CN/O 65(a).

29. e.g. Alexander, *Incidents of the Maori War*, pp.187-8; William Grayling, 'Journal of Events of the War at Taranaki', 22 Mar. 1861, Taranaki Museum.

30. Wells, *History of Taranaki*, p.219.

31. Gold to Browne, 24 July 1860, Pratt to Military Secretary, 4 Aug. 1860, S.D., pp.21, 20.

32. Ward, *Life Among the Maoris*, p.367; Carey, *The Late War in New Zealand*, p.73.

33. A. S. Atkinson, Diary, 4 Aug. 1860, H. R. Richmond to J. C. Richmond, 18 Aug. 1860, *R-A.P.*, I, pp.624, 626-7; Ward, *Life Among the Maoris*, p.369; *Memorials of Sergeant Marjouram*, 24 Aug. 1860, p.245.

34. William Swainson, *New Zealand and the War*, London 1862, p.151.

35. Assistant Commissary-General Strickland to Deputy Commissary-General H. Stanley Jones, 1, 25 Mar. 1865, S.D., pp.336-9, 355.

36. G. Cutfield to Browne, 21 Feb. 1860, *P.P.* 1861 (2798) XLI, p.10.

37. Returns in Carey, *The Late War in New Zealand*, pp.45-46.
38. *Nelson Examiner*, 13 Aug. 1860; *Southern Cross*, 9 Nov. 1860; *cf. Memorials of Sergeant Marjouram*, 9 Aug. 1860, pp.237-8; *New-Zealander*, 15 Aug. 1860; E. L. Humphries to Colonial Secretary, 22 Aug. 1860, 'New Plymouth Provincial Council' Letterbook, Apr.-Nov. 1860, Taranaki Museum.
39. Grayling, Journal, 29 July 1860.
40. Pratt to Browne, 31 Dec. 1861, *P.P.* 1862 (3040) XXXVII, pp.4-5; *New Zealand Examiner*, 19 Mar. 1861; *Southern Cross*, 1, 4 Jan., 1 Feb. 1861.
41. Smythies, *Historical Records of the Fortieth*, p.37. Maori losses were about six killed. See Note 50 below.
42. According to Alexander, several British eyewitnesses thought the *pa* was a trap, *Incidents of the Maori War*, p.229; also *Southern Cross*, 4 Jan. 1861; Mould to Carey, 30 Mar. 1861, S.D., p.48; Battiscombe, Journal, 29, 31 Dec. 1860; Carey, *The Late War in New Zealand*, pp.147-56; Smythies, *Historical Records of the Fortieth*, pp.366-7.
43. J. C. Richmond to Mary Richmond, 23 Jan. 1861, *R-A.P.*, I, pp.681-2; Carey, *The Late War in New Zealand*, p.164. For British reinforcements see Smythies, *Historical Records of the Fortieth*, p.379; Colonel Leslie to Pratt, 23 Jan. 1861, *AJHR* 1861, E-1A, pp.11-13; *Southern Cross*, 1 Feb. 1861.
44. Taylor, *New Zealand Past and Present*, p.127; *Southern Cross*, 25 Jan. 1861.
45. J. C. Richmond to Mary Richmond, 8 Feb. 1860, and Harry Atkinson to A. S. Atkinson, 27 Feb. 1860, *R-A.P.*, I, pp.688, 692.
46. Carey, *The Late War in New Zealand*, pp.17, 2, (*cf.* pp.180, 182-4, 188); Pratt to Military Secretary, 2 Apr. 1861, S.D., pp.46-48 (*cf.* Swainson, *New Zealand and the War*, pp.168-9, quoting a speech made by Pratt after the war); Mould to D.A.G., 30 Mar. 1861, Select Despatches, pp.48-50 (hereafter 'Mould's Report').
47. Carey, *The Late War in New Zealand*, pp.88-89.
48. *Memorials of Sergeant Marjouram*, 3 Jan. 1861, p.309; *Southern Cross*, 4 Jan. 1861; *New Zealand Examiner*, 19 Mar. 1861.
49. e.g. Carey, *The Late War in New Zealand*, pp.152-3; Wells, *History of Taranaki*, pp.217-19, quoting an eyewitness account.
50. Maori reports recorded in Pratt to Browne, 31 Dec. 1860, *AJHR* 1861 E-1A, pp.8-10; Cowan, *Wars*, I, p.197; *Southern Cross*, 1 Feb. 1861; Morgan to Browne, 23 Jan. 1861, Gore Browne Papers, 1/2d.
51. Carey, *The Late War in New Zealand*, p.178; McLean, Memo, 22 Mar. 1861, *P.P.* 1862 (3040) XXXVII, pp.35-37; Gorst, *Maori King*, p.107.
52. Pratt, post-war speech quoted in Swainson, *New Zealand and the War*, pp.168-9; Mould's Report.
53. Alexander, *Incidents of the Maori War*, p.348, based on eyewitness account of Rev. J. A. Wilson.
54. Richmond to Herbert, 9 Feb. 1861, W.O.32/8257.
55. Morgan to CMS, 27 Feb. 1861, CN/O 65(a); Alexander, *Incidents of the Maori War*, p.311; also Notes 22 and 23 above.
56. *Taranaki News*, 7 Feb. 1860, quoted in *New Zealand Examiner*, 19 Mar. 1860.
57. Swainson, *New Zealand and the War*, p.151.
58. Wells, *History of Taranaki*, p.219. For Kingite influence see *Taranaki Herald*, 5 Jan. 1861.
59. Wells, *History of Taranaki*, p.223; E. A. H. Webb, *History of the Twelfth (The Suffolk) Regiment 1685-1913*, London 1914, p.281.
60. Webb, *History of the Twelfth*, p.281; also Carey, *The Late War in New Zealand*, p.171; Alexander, *Incidents of the Maori War*, p.284; Mould's Report.
61. Grayling, Journal, 4 Mar. 1861.
62. Mould's Report.
63. Mould's Report; Wells, *History of Taranaki*, pp.223-4.
64. J. C. Richmond to Mary Richmond, 18 Mar. 1861, *R-A.P.*, I, p.695; *Southern Cross*, 19 Feb. 1861.
65. For Maori casualties see *Southern Cross*, 19 Feb. 1861; Burrows to CMS, 4 Mar. 1861, CN/O 8(c); Colonel Sillery, Memo, 24 Feb. 1861, *AJHR* 1861 E-1A, p.14.
66. J. C. Richmond to Mary Richmond, 18 Mar. 1861, *R-A.P.*, I, p.695.
67. J. C. Richmond to Mary Richmond, 18 Mar. 1861, *R-A.P.*, I, p.695.
68. *Southern Cross*, 19 Mar. 1861, Taranaki Correspondent, 9 Mar.

69. *New Zealand Examiner*, 14 Jan. 1861, Auckland Correspondent, 5 Nov. 1860.

70. *New Zealand Examiner*, 14 Jan. 1861, quoting report by London freight companies & 10 July 1860; also *Southern Cross* & *New-Zealander* monthly summaries for Europe, May 1860 to Feb. 1861. For settler attitudes to the war see W. P. Morrell, *The Provincial System in New Zealand*, 2nd edn, Wellington 1964, pp.117-32; H. G. Wilton, 'The South Island and the Taranaki War, 1860-61', Univ. of Otago M. A. Thesis, 1973.

71. *New Zealand Examiner*, 17 Dec. 1861, Auckland Correspondent, Sept. 1860, 14 Jan. 1861, Wellington Correspondent, 5 Nov. 1860.

72. Browne to G. Gairdner, 3 Sept. 1860, Gore Browne Papers, 2/3; Pratt to Military Secretary, 10 Jan. 1861, *P.P.* 1862 (3040) XXXVII, p.10; Morgan to CMS, 6 Sept. 1860, CN/O 65(a).

73. *AJHR* 1861, E-1B, p.4.

74. e.g. *Diary of John Newland*, 8 Apr. 1861, p.52; C. W. Richmond to Emily Richmond, 12 Apr. 1861, *R-A.P.*, I, p.702; *Southern Cross*, 22 Mar. 1861.

75. Dalton, *War and Politics*, p.126; *AJHR* 1861, E-1B, p.4.

76. A. S. Atkinson, Diary, 21 Mar. 1861, *R-A.P.*, I, pp.695-6; *Taranaki Herald*, 4 May 1861.

77. *Southern Cross*, 26 Mar. 1861; Sara Louise Mathew to [?], 7 Apr. [1861], Mathew Letters, 1858-61, APL. For other examples see Alfred Domett to Grey, 6 June 1861, Grey Autograph Letters, D12; Burrows to CMS, 5 Apr. and 30 May 1861, CN/O 8(c); Mary-Ann Martin to Mrs Owen, 17 Oct. 1861, Owen Correspondence, II, pp.400-03, British Library Addit. MSS. 39954; McLean Memo, 22 Mar. 1861 and to Browne, 1 May 1861, *P.P.* 1862 (3040) XXXVII, pp.35-37, 45; Swainson, *New Zealand and the War*, p.158; *Southern Cross*, 22 Mar. 1861; *Taranaki Herald*, 4 May 1861.

78. e.g. *NZ Herald*, 22 June 1864.

7: The Invasion of Waikato (pages 119-41)

1. Ultimatum, see *P.P.* 1862 (3040) XXXVII, pp.70-71. Confirmation of Browne's intention to invade, Morgan to CMS, 8 July 1861, CN/O 65(a).

2. Maori strength at Katikara, Basil K. Taylor to CMS, 9 July 1863, B. K. Taylor Letters 1861-1878, CN/O 86; Pehi Turoa to Ezekiel & others, 10 June 1863, *AJHR* 1863, E-3, Sect. I, pp.50-51.

3. Ward, *Show of Justice*, p.126; Dalton, *War and Politics*, p.130.

4. Grey to Newcastle, 2 Nov. 1861, C.O.209/164, p.334.

5. W. L. and L. Rees, *The Life and Times of Sir George Grey, K.C.B.*, 2v., London 1892, II, pp.389-91, quoting a letter to *The Times* of 31 Jan 1865, probably from G. S. Whitmore; A. S. Atkinson, Diary, 12 Mar., 30 Apr. 1863, *R-A.P.*, II, pp.30, 37; R. Parris, Memo, 6 May 1863, F. B. Bulkeley, Memo, 7 May 1863, Transcripts from the Department of Maori Affairs Archives, Rhodes House Library, Oxford. Also note the month-long Maori delay in reacting to the occupation of Tataraimaka, and the fact that Grey and General Cameron were so confident that the occupation would not lead to hostilities that they rode about the area unarmed and virtually unaccompanied until the Oakura ambush of 4 May.

6. Col. H. J. Warre's report, 4 Jan. 1864, Governor-Military Letters, 1863-4, N.A., G16/3:10; *cf.* Warre's Reports, 23 July, 8 Nov. 1863, G16/2:4 & G16/2:31A; Warre, *Historical Records of the 57th Regiment*, London 1878, pp.175-80.

7. Grey to Newcastle, 23 Nov. 1862, C.O.209/165, pp.87-88.

8. e.g. Grey to Cameron, 26 June 1862, S.D., p.81.

9. William Fox, *The War in New Zealand*, London 1866, p.73.

10. Newcastle to Grey, 27 Oct. 1861, C.O.209/164, pp.90-91, 22 Sept. 1861, *P.P.* 1862 (3040) XXXVII; Newcastle to Grey, 26 May 1862, *AJHR* 1862, E-1, Sect. III, p.10.

11. Grey to Governor J. Young of NSW, 15 Apr. 1862, C.O.209/168, pp.168-9. Grey used the phrase 'some great disaster' during another example of the same phenomenon, Grey to Newcastle, 29 Jan. 1863, C.O.209/172, pp.18-22.

12. e.g. Grey to Cameron, 19 Dec. 1861, S.D., pp.68-69; Grey to Newcastle, 20 May 1862, C.O.209/168, pp.272-5.

13. Enclosures in Grey to Newcastle, 11 July 1863, C.O.209/172; Dalton, *War and Politics*, pp.176-7. Examples of similar but earlier allegations by Grey, Grey to Newcastle, 7 Dec. 1861, C.O.209/165, p.391 & encl.; 7 June 1862, C.O.209/167, pp.5-16; 7 Mar. 1862, C.O.209/168, pp.42-45; 31 Dec.

1862, C.O.209/170, pp.235-6; 6 Feb. 1863, C.O.209/172, pp.29-32.

14. *AJHR* 1863, B-1, p.11.

15. Correspondence enclosed in Cameron to W.O., 8 June 1863, C.O.209/177, pp.207-8.

16. Grey to Newcastle, 9 May 1863, *P.P.* 1864 (3277) XLI, pp.17-20.

17. Newcastle, Memo, n.d. [Aug. 1863?], C.O.209/177, pp.203-6.

18. Dalton, 'A New Look at the Maori Wars', p.436.

19. A return of 1 Jan. 1864 (S.D., p.478) gives 8,630 regulars. The 68th Regiment, 970 strong, arrived later in January, as did 510 drafts and men from support corps. See W. L. Vane, *The Durham Light Infantry*, London 1914, pp.95-96; J. Featon, *The Waikato War, together with some account of Te Kooti Rikirangi*, rev. edn, Auckland 1923, p.109.

20. Return, 1 May 1864, S.D., p.479. Other returns and estimates of Imperial troops: (1 July 1863) C.O.209/174, pp.217-24; (1 Aug. 1863) ibid., pp.278-85; (1 Oct. 1863) C.O.209/175, pp.159-68; (15 Nov. 1863) ibid., pp.339-46; De Grey to Gladstone, 4 Apr. 1864, Ripon Papers, v. XXIII, pp.119-21, British Library Additional MSS 43513. The most detailed return is in Deputy Quartermaster-General's Original Journals, 30 Oct. 1864, No. 1622, W.O.107/7.

21. For total numbers see colonial returns 5 Sept., 20 Oct., 31 Dec. 1863, 19 May 1864, in Governor-Military Letters 1863-4, N.A., G16/2:8; *AJHR* 1864, A-6, pp.1-4; ibid., E-3, pp.34-36; C.O.209/186, pp.428-32. For Imperial estimates and comments indicating effective strength, Cameron to W.O., 5 Oct. 1863 & returns 1 Jan., 1 May 1864, S. D., pp.141-2, 478-9; 'Journals of the Deputy Quartermaster-General in New Zealand, 1861-5', W.O.33/16, p.66.

22. Brigade-Major J. Paul, Return, W.O.33/12, p.568. Estimates of effective strength by Grey and colonial officials were much higher.

23. *New-Zealander*, 14 June 1864. Similar opinions of Cameron, Alexander, *Incidents of the Maori War*, pp.313-4, *Bush Fighting, Illustrated by Remarkable Actions and Incidents of the Maori War*, London 1873, p.257.

24. M. von Creveld, *Supplying War—Logistics from Wallenstein to Patton*, Cambridge 1979.

25. See Deputy Commissary-General H. Stanley Jones to W.O., 29 Oct. 1863, S.D., p.288; report of Ast. Com.-Gen. Robertson, 7 Sept. 1863, S.D. pp.294-395. This report, with its continuation of 23 Aug. 1864 (pp.460-5) gives a full description of Commissariat operations and difficulties.

26. Robertson Report; *New-Zealander*, 28 Apr. 1864; returns cited in Note 20 above.

27. Stanley Jones to W.O., 29 Oct. 1863, S.D., p.288.

28. J. Rutherford, 'The Maori Wars', *The Encyclopaedia of New Zealand*, II, p.477; Dalton, *War and Politics*, p.179; Simpson, *Te Riri Pakeha*, p.136.

29. Note 67 below; Note 13, Chapter Eight; Note 31, Chapter Nine, Note 75, Chapter Ten. Additional evidence, various letters and enclosures in G16, especially G16/2:30, and G16/3:10, 14, 18, 30, 41 and 45; A. N. Brown to Grey, 2 Jan. 1864, Grey Autograph Letters, B29; R. O. Stewart to Native Minister, 22 Oct. 1863, Grey Collection; Morgan to Browne, 29 Sept. and 23 Oct. 1863, Gore Browne Papers, 1/2d; Burrows to CMS, 31 Aug. 1863, CN/O 8(c); B. Y. Ashwell to CMS, 1 May 1864, CN/O 19; William Williams to CMS, 4 Feb. 1864, CN/O 96(c); Wiremu Tamehana to Rawiri & Tawaha, 28 Feb. 1864, W. G. Mair to Gen. G. J. Carey, 28 Apr. 1864, *AJHR* 1864, E-3, p.40 and E-1, Part II, pp.14-15; W. H. Gifford & H. B. Williams, *A Centennial History of Tauranga*, Dunedin 1940, pp.221-2; Cowan, *Wars*, I, p.308; D. M. Stafford, *Te Arawa: A History of the Arawa People*, Wellington 1967, pp.370-80.

30. Capt. Robert Jenkins, R. N., Log of H.M.S. *Miranda*, 22 Oct. 1863, ATL.

31. Gorst, *The Maori King*, p.180.

32. e.g. Account of Harehare of Ngati Manawa, Cowan Papers, 41; J. Buller to Native Minister, 13 Aug. 1863, C.O.209/174, p.165.

33. e.g. Account of Paitini in Elsdon Best, *Tuhoe, the Children of the Mist*, 2v., New Plymouth 1925, II, pp.566-7.

34. Copy in C.O.209/175, pp.227-9. Examples of recruiting letters and tours, Te Wharepu to Ririhana, n.d., C.O.209/174, p.129. Rewi's visit to the Rangitaiki district in December 1863, Cowan, *Wars*, II, p.359.

35. James Fulloon to Military Secretary, 22 Oct. 1863, Fulloon, 'Correspondence Relative to Native Affairs', Grey Collection; John Rogan to Thomas Smith, 28 Sept. 1861, *AJHR* 1862, E-7, pp.3-7.

36. Leslie G. Kelly, *Tainui, The Story of Hoturoa and His Descendants*, Wellington 1949, pp.370, 432.

37. W. Williams to CMS, 27 Apr. 1864, CN/O 96(c).
38. William Fox, *The War in New Zealand*, pp.70, 74; Cameron to W.O., 30 July, 8 Oct. 1863, W.O.33/12, p.567 & S.D., pp.141-2.
39. Dalton, *War and Politics*, p.179.
40. The most reliable estimate was 1,100, given by an Englishman who had been living with the Maoris. 'Diary of a British Soldier 7 May [1863]-6 March 1867', 27 Aug. 1863, p.15, ATL; also *New-Zealander*, 28 Aug. 1863.
41. Grey to Newcastle, 8 Dec. 1863, C.O.209/175, p.311; DQMG Journals, p.46.
42. Maunsell to CMS, 24 July 1863, CN/O 64(b); *Southern Cross*, 28 July 1863, quoting letter from Princess Sophia [Te Paea] Tiaho to Wiremu Nera, 14 July.
43. Tamehana to Rewiti, [?] July 1863, *AJHR* 1865, E-11, p.15; *Southern Cross*, 27 July 1863, quoting 'Native Account'; statement of Pirimona, n.d., *P.P.* 1864 (3386) XLI, pp.47-48; Petition of 41 Tauranga and Hauraki Chiefs to Queen Victoria, 29 July 1863, C.O.209/187, p.267; *Te Hokioi Flying Away* (a Kingite newspaper), 18 July 1863 (tr. in G16/2:27).
44. Fox, *War in New Zealand*, p.65; report of Captain Ring, 17 July 1863, W.O.33/12, p.564; DQMG Journals, p.47.
45. Tamehana to Rewiti; statement of Pirimona; *Te Hokioi*, 18 July 1863; Cowan, *Wars*, II, p.250; 'Diary of a British Soldier', 17 July 1863, p.4.
46. Featon, *Waikato War*, p.38; report of Ast. Com.-Gen. Robertson, S.D., p.294; DQMG Journals, p.48.
47. Reports of Captain Ring & Colonel Wyatt, both 23 July 1863, W.O.33/12, pp.569-70.
48. *Memoirs of General Sir George Richard Greaves*, London 1924, pp.95-96.
49. Cameron to W.O., 30 July 1863, W.O.33/12, p.567.
50. 'The War in Auckland', *Southern Monthly Magazine*, Mar. 1864, pp.58-59.
51. DQMG Journals, p.54.
52. Cameron to Grey, 9 Aug. 1863, *AJHR* 1863, E-5, p.15; DQMG Journals, pp.53-54; report of Ast. Com.-Gen. Robertson, 7 Sept. 1863, S.D., p.295.
53. e.g. Featon, *Waikato War*, p.63.
54. Ashwell to CMS, 5 Oct. 1863, CN/O 19; Cameron to W.O., 5 Oct. 1863, S.D., pp.141-2; account of Colour Sergeant McKenna in 'Ensign McKenna and the Victoria Cross', British periodical article, c.1864, source unknown, ATL.
55. 'Ensign McKenna and the V.C.'; *cf.*, reports of McKenna, Cameron, Lieutenant Butler, Colonel G. F. Murray, 8-9 Sept. 1863, *AJHR* 1863, E-5, pp.20-27.
56. DQMG Journals, p.57.
57. The Maoris may have lost as many as nine killed (Ashwell to CMS., 14 Sept. 1863, CN/O 19) but most of these probably fell in the two earlier actions. The McKenna incident was the only instance in the whole period for which Cameron acknowledged losing more men than the Maoris, Cameron to W.O., 5 Oct. 1863, S.D., pp.141-2.
58. Report of Ast. Com.-Gen. Robertson, 7 Sept. 1863, S.D., p.295.
59. *The Journal of William Morgan, Pioneer Settler and Maori War Correspondent*, ed. Nona Morris, Auckland 1963, p.100.
60. General Order, 27 Sept. 1863, DQMG Journals, Appendices, p.XI.
61. Report of Ast. Com.-Gen. Robertson, 7 Sept. 1863, S.D., p.293.
62. Cameron to W.O., 28 Oct. 1863, S.D., p.158; [C. G. S. Foljambe], *Three Years on the Australian Station*, (for private circulation 1868), pp.14-22. The troops were 256 of the 1/12th and sailors and marines from the *Curacoa*.
63. Foljambe, *Australian Station*, p.23.
64. Fox, *War in New Zealand*, p.77; *cf. Journal of William Morgan*, p.111; Andrew Dillon Carberry, Journal 1863-6, p.7, AIM; A. Saunders, *History of New Zealand . . .*, 2v., Christchurch 1896-9, II, p.95.
65. Cameron to W.O., 8 July 1863, S.D., p.109.
66. Cameron to W.O., 30 July 1863, W.O.33/12, p.567.
67. Account of Heni Te Kiri-Karamu, Jan. 1920, Cowan Papers 41E, p.4; Tamehana to Rewiti, [?] July 1863, *AJHR* 1865, E-11, p.15; R. O. Stewart to Native Minister, 8 Oct. 1863, Transcripts from Maori Affairs Archives, RHL: Maunsell to CMS, 19 Oct. 1863, CN/O 64(b); Morgan to Browne,

20 July 1863, Gore Browne Papers, 1/2d.

68. Account of Heni Te Kiri-Karamu, p.4; account of Te Huia Raureti, 14 Nov. 1920, in Cowan, *Wars*, II, p.271; Capt. Lloyd to Officer Commanding, Colonial Forces, 6 Sept. 1863, & encl., G16/2:9.

69. J. Fulloon to Military Secretary, 22 Oct. 1863, Fulloon, Letters to Military Officers, Oct. 1863, Grey Collection.

8: Rangiriri (pages 142-57)

1. 'The War in Auckland, No. III', *Southern Monthly Magazine*, June 1864, pp.233-4; account of W. G. Mair in Andersen & Petersen, *The Mair Family*, p.103.

2. According to Cowan, the remains of the line in 1920 were approximately 1,300 yards long (*Wars*, I, p.318). This corresponds with the distance between the two bodies of water today. Heavy rain may have increased the water level, and so reduced the distance, but it could not have done so by much, because the ground slopes upward.

3. Foljambe, *Australian Station*, p.29. Descriptions of the defences other than those cited below, Cameron's Reports, 21, 24 Nov. 1863 (*AJHR* 1863, E-5D, pp.3-4), 26 Nov, S.D., pp.224-6; DQMG Journals, pp.72-73 (incl. sketch by Capt. Brooke R. E.); Alexander, *Bush Fighting*, pp.97-98; Wiseman's Report, 30 Nov. 1863, ADM 1/5817 (L. 124); Arthur Frederick Pickard, Journal, 21 Nov. 1860-26 Nov. 1863, Hawke's Bay Museum, draft letter of 22 Nov. 1863.

4. 'The War in Auckland, No. III', p.235.

5. 'The War in Auckland, No. III', p.236; also *New-Zealander*, 26 Nov. 1863.

6. Report of Lieut. A. F. Pickard, R. A., quoted in Maj. A. H. H. Mercer, *A Great Contrast, Being a Statement of Facts Concerning His Royal Highness The Duke of Cambridge K. G. and his Treatment of Two British Officers*, Blackheath 1893, p.35.

7. Cameron's Report, 26 Nov. 1863; Alexander, *Bush Fighting*, pp.97-98; Carberry, Journal, p.8; 'The War in Auckland, No. III', p.234; *New-Zealander*, 24 Nov. 1863.

8. Wiseman's Report, 30 Nov. 1863, ADM. 1/5817 (L.124).

9. The tribal affiliations of 195 of the Rangiriri garrison are known. The tribal strengths given here are based on the assumption that this sample is roughly representative of the whole. See 'Names of prisoners taken at Rangiriri', and Wiremu Tamehana to Wiremu Te Wheoro, 4 Dec. 1863, *AJHR* E-5D, pp.9-11. Estimates of total Maori numbers, Fox, *War in New Zealand*, p.81, Maunsell to CMS, 30 Nov. 1863, CN/O 64(b). Few reasonable estimates went higher than 600, and 400 to 500 is now generally accepted.

10. 'Rewi Maniapoto', *Encyclopaedia of New Zealand*, II, pp.399-400.

11. e.g. Gustavus Ferdinand Von Tempsky, 'Memoranda of the New Zealand Campaign in 1863-4', p.70, AIM.

12. Cameron's Report, 21 Nov. 1863; Featon, *Waikato War*, p.94.

13. Account of Heni Te Kiri-Karamu, Cowan Papers, 41E; Tamehana to Te Wheoro, & Te Wheoro to Native Minister, both 4 Dec. 1863, *AJHR* 1863, E-5D, pp.10-11, 7-8; Foljambe, *Australian Station*, pp.27, 33; *NZ Herald*, 23 June 1864.

14. Dalton, 'A New Look at the Maori Wars', p.242; Holt, *The Strangest War*, p.196; Rutherford, *Grey*, p.499; also Gibson, *The Maori Wars*, p.111; Cowan, *Wars*, I, p.330; Fortescue, *History of the British Army*, XIII, pp.496-7; Dalton, *War and Politics*, p.183.

15. Sinclair, *History of New Zealand*, p.139; also Simpson, *Te Riri Pakeha*, p.137; Rutherford, *Grey*, p.499. Praise of Cameron, Dalton, 'A New Look at the Maori Wars', pp.242-3, *War and Politics*, p.183.

16. Holt, *Strangest War*, p.197; Gibson, *The Maori Wars*, p.111; Cowan, *Wars*, I, p.330; Fortescue, *History of the British Army*, XIII, p.497.

17. Bond, ed., *Victorian Military Campaigns*, London 1967, p.23 (editor's introduction).

18. DQMG Journals, p.75. Another return (*AJHR* 1863, E-5A, pp.6-10) gives 128 casualties but 132 is the figure confirmed by other sources. All returns and reports agree on the losses of the R. A. & R. N. storming parties.

19. DQMG Journals, p.66; also Wiseman to Admiralty, 5 Nov. 1863, ADM 1/5817 (L.113).

20. Cameron's Report, 26 Nov. 1863.

21. *NZ Herald*, 25 Nov. 1863.

22. The troops' dispositions, Cameron's Reports; DQMG Journals, p.72; Alexander, *Bush Fighting*, pp.96-97; Featon, *Waikato War*, p.92.

23. Cameron's Report, 24 Nov. 1863.

24. DQMG Journals, p.72; Cameron's Reports, 21, 24 Nov. 1863. Cameron's more detailed report of 26 Nov. 1863 implies that there was a check.

25. DQMG Journals, p.72.

26. *NZ Herald*, 25 Nov. 1863; also W. C. S. Mair, 'Reminiscences', in Webb, *History of the 12th*, p.290.

27. 'The War in Auckland, No. III', p.237; Strange's Report, in H. O'Donnell, *Historical Records of the 14th Regiment 1685-1892*, Devonport 1893, p.192; W. C. S. Mair, 'Reminiscences' & Lieut. Boulton, Journal, in Webb, *History of the 12th*, pp.290-1.

28. W. G. Mair, account in Andersen & Petersen, *The Mair Family*, p.102.

29. *New-Zealander*, 21 Nov. (Extra), 24 Nov. 1863; 'Heroes of the Victoria Cross in New Zealand'.

30. W. C. S. Mair, 'Reminiscences'; Boulton, Journal, in Webb, *History of the 12th*, pp.290-1.

31. Boulton in Webb, *History of the 12th*, pp.290-1.

32. It is reasonable to assume that the 12th and 14th suffered the great majority of their total casualties at this point in the battle. The two units lost thirty-nine men at Rangiriri (DQMG Journals, p.75; *AJHR* 1863, E-5A, pp.6-10) to which a few strayed men of the 65th's extreme left should be added.

33. Alexander, *Bush Fighting*, p.98.

34. In addition to parapets and gunsmoke, the ridge running north-south must have obscured their view.

35. *NZ Herald*, 25 Nov. 1863; also Foljambe, *Australian Station*, p.27; Wiseman's Report, 30 Nov. 1863, ADM. 1/5817 (L.124).

36. *NZ Herald*, 25 Nov. 1863.

37. Featon, *Waikato War*, p.92; also 'Heroes of the Victoria Cross in New Zealand'; Alexander, *Bush Fighting*, p.101; *New-Zealander*, 21 Nov. 1863 (Extra), 24 Nov. 1863.

38. 'The War in Auckland, No. III', p.237; Pickard, Journal, draft letter of 22 Nov. 1863; also *New-Zealander*, 24 Nov. 1863.

39. See notes 52-55 below.

40. Featon, *Waikato War*, p.92.

41. Boulton in Webb, *History of the 12th*, p.291.

42. Cowan, *Wars*, I, pp.325-6.

43. Boulton in Webb, *History of the 12th*, p.291; Carberry, Journal, p.9; Bishop Selwyn to his sons, 4 Dec. 1863, in H. W. Tucker, *Memoir of the Life and Episcopate of George Augustus Selwyn*, 2v., London 1879, II, p.190; DQMG Journals, p.73; Alexander, *Bush Fighting*, p.104; Foljambe, *Australian Station*, p.31; R. C. Mainwaring to Native Minister, 25 Nov. 1863, *AJHR* 1863, E-50, p.4.

44. Carberry, Journal, p.8.

45. B. Y. Ashwell to CMS, 26 Nov. 1863, CN/O 19; *New-Zealander*, 26 Nov. 1863.

46. Tamehana to Te Wheoro, 4 Dec. 1863, *AJHR* 1863, E-5D, pp.9-11.

47. *New-Zealander*, 23 June 1864.

48. Mair, account in Andersen and Petersen, *The Mair Family*, p.117; also W. J. Gundry to Native Minister, 22 Nov. 1863, *AJHR* 1863, E-5, p.5; Foljambe, *Australian Station*, p.31; 'The War in Auckland, No. III', p.238.

49. Maunsell to CMS., 2 Jan. 1864, CN/O 64(b) (Maunsell's italics).

50. *New-Zealander*, 26 Nov. 1863.

51. 'Heroes of the Victoria Cross in New Zealand'.

52. Maunsell to CMS., 30 Nov. 1863, CN/O 64(b); *New-Zealander*, 26 Nov. 1863; W. J. Gundry to Native Minister, 22 Nov. 1863, *AJHR*, 1863, E-5D, p.5; Cameron's Reports; Alexander, *Bush Fighting*, p.106. Some of these estimates did not include the non-combatants but Tamehana confirmed that some women were killed, Petition to the General Assembly, 5 Apr. 1865, *AJHR* 1865, G-5, p.2.

53. Gundry to Native Minister, 22 Nov. 1863, *AJHR* 1863, E-5D, p.5; *New-Zealander*, 26 Nov. 1863.

54. Tawhana Tikaokao to Heremia & Wi Tako, 25 Nov. 1863, G16/3:49 (encl.); East Coast Maori report quoted in Bishop William Williams, Memo, *AJHR* 1864, E-3, pp.19-20.

55. Account of Heni Te Kiri-Karamu, Cowan Papers, 41E.

56. *NZ Herald*, 25 Nov. 1863; *New-Zealander*, 28 Nov. 1863.

57. *Army and Navy Gazette*, 30 Apr. 1864 (extract from a private letter); Carberry, Journal, p.11. Examples of huge British estimates of Maori casualties, 'Diary of a British Soldier', p.50, & Foljambe, *Australian Station*, p.32.

58. De Grey to Cameron, 26 Feb. 1864, and Mil. Sec. to W.O., 20 Feb. 1864, S.D., pp.193, 190. Cameron got a K.C.B. for Rangiriri, and his officers got two C.B.s, four promotions and five commendations.

59. *Journal of William Morgan*, p.126 n.; *New-Zealander*, 28 Nov. 1863.

60. *Journal of William Morgan*, p.123.

61. *Journal of William Morgan*, p.122; Maunsell to CMS, 30 Nov. 1863, CN/O 64(b).

62. *NZ Herald*, 2 Dec. 1863; *Journal of William Morgan*, p.128.

63. *The Times*, 14 June 1864.

64. For New Zealand examples of the vituperative criticism of Cameron, Fox, *The War in New Zealand*, pp.86-87, Featon, *The Waikato War*, p.92. English examples, *The United Services Gazette*, 20 Feb. 1864, A. H. H. Mercer, *Captain Henry Mercer: With an Enquiry into the Causes of His Death*, 2nd edn., Toronto 1867, p.21.

65. DQMG Journals, p.73; also De Grey to Cameron, 26 Feb. 1864, S.D., p.193.

9: Paterangi and Orakau (pages 158-76)

1. Grey to Newcastle, 9 Dec. 1863, *AJHR* 1864, E-3, p.3. Examples of similar opinions, DQMG Journals, p.77; *The Times*, 14 Feb. 1864; Williams to CMS, 8 Dec. 1864, CN/O 96(c).

2. e.g. Dalton, *War and Politics*, pp.184-5; Morrell, *British Colonial Policy in the Mid Victorian Age*, p.306; Rutherford, *Grey*, p.501; Harold Miller, *The Invasion of Waikato*, Auckland and Hamilton 1964, p.16.

3. Correspondence in *AJHR* 1863, E-5D and *P.P.* 1864 (3355) XLI, pp.10-11.

4. Tamehana, quoted in 'Account of Wiremu Nera's visit to Maungatautari', [Dec. 1863], *AJHR* 1864, E-3, pp.26-27.

5. Grey to Newcastle, 28 Nov. 1861, C.O. 209/165, p.153.

6. 'The War in Auckland, No. IV', *Southern Monthly Magazine*, July 1864, p.311; *cf.* J. E. Gorst, 'Observations on the Native Inhabitants of Rangiaowhia and Kihikihi', 21 May 1864, C.O. 209/187; account of Te Huia Raureti, 31 Mar. 1920, Cowan Papers 41B.

7. Account of Te Huia Raureti, 31 Mar. 1920, Cowan Papers 41B; Brig. Gen. Waddy to Ast. Mil. Sec., 22 Feb. 1864, *AJHR* 1864, E-3, pp.30-31; Wiseman to Admiralty, 28 Feb. 1864, ADM.1/5868 (L.11); Cameron to W.O., 4 Feb. 1864, S.D., pp.187-9; *New-Zealander*, 20 Jan. 1864. For the existence of more than four *pa* see B. Y. Ashwell to CMS, 1 Feb. 1864, CN/O 19; 'Logbook of HMS *Miranda*', 26 Dec. 1863 (maps).

8. Bishop Selwyn to William Selwyn, 4 Feb. 1864, Tucker, *Life of Selwyn*, II, pp.194-5; *NZ Herald*, 1 Feb 1864; Featon, *Waikato War*, p.110; Ashwell to CMS, 1 Feb. 1864, CN/O 19. For estimate based on Maori evidence see Cowan, *Wars*, I, p.329.

9. e.g. *NZ Herald*, 1 Feb. 1864; *New-Zealander*, 16 Feb. 1864.

10. Report of Ast. Com.-Gen. Robertson, 23 Aug. 1864, S.D., p.460.

11. Featon, *Waikato War*, p.120; also DQMG Journals, pp.93-95; Wiseman to Admiralty, 28 Feb. 1864, ADM1/5868, (L.11); Cameron to W.O., 4 Mar. 1864, S.D., pp.195-9; Wiseman to Grey, 19 Sept. 1866, Grey Autograph Letters, W.52.

12. Alexander, *Bush Fighting*, p.123.

13. Account of W. G. Mair, in Andersen & Petersen, *The Mair Family*, p.108; Von Tempsky, 'Memoranda', p.80; Featon, *Waikato War*, p.110.

14. Cameron to W.O., 4 Feb. 1864, S.D., pp.187-9; Selwyn to William Selwyn, 4 Feb. 1864, in Tucker, *Life of Selwyn*, II, pp.194-5.

15. Grey to Newcastle, 5 Feb. 1864, *P.P.* 1864 (3380) XLI, p.21; *cf.* Cameron to W.O., 4 Feb. 1864, S.D., pp.187-9. Cameron's conduct during the operation confirms that he was seeking decisive battle.

16. *New-Zealander*, 25 Feb. 1864; Cameron's Report, 25 Feb. 1864, *AJHR* 1864, E-3, pp.29-30.

17. Cameron's Report, 25 Feb. 1864, *AJHR* 1864, E-3, pp.29-30; Cameron to W.O., 4 Mar. 1864, S.D., pp.195-9.

18. Cameron to W.O., 4 Mar. 1864, S.D., pp.195-9; Tamehana to Rawiri and Tawaha, 28 Feb. 1864, *AJHR* 1864, E-3, p.40. Other accounts of the action, Col. Weare's report, *AJHR* 1864, E-3, p.31-32; Von Tempsky, 'Memoranda', pp.109-11; DQMG Journals, pp.95-97; account of Te Wairoa Piripi, Cowan Papers, 41B; account of Paora Pipi, *New-Zealander*, 23 June 1864.

19. Cameron's Report, 25 Feb. 1864; account of Paora Pipi; Tamehana to Rawiri and Tawaha; casualty return, *AJHR* 1864, E-3, pp.31-32.

20. Tamehana to Rawiri and Tawaha; account of Paora Pipi.

21. Statement of Te Wairoa Piripi, Cowan Papers, 41B; Wiremu Tamehana, Petition to the General Assembly, 5 Apr. 1865, *AJHR* 1865, G-5; statement of Whitiora Te Kumete, in John Caselberg, ed., *Maori is my Name: Maori Historical Writings in Translation*, Dunedin 1975, p.106.

22. *New-Zealander*, 25 Feb. 1864; Von Tempsky, 'Memoranda', p.111; Cameron to Grey (Private), 30 Mar. 1865, *AJHR* 1865, A-4.

23. Cameron's Report, 25 Feb. 1864, *AJHR* 1864, E-3, pp.29-30.

24. Cowan, *Wars*, I, p.358 (from Maori evidence).

25. Account of Paitini, in Best, *Tuhoe*, II, p.571.

26. Best, *Tuhoe*, II, p.570-1, Cowan, *Wars*, I, pp.359-60 (from Maori evidence); *cf.* account of Peita Kotuku, 23 Feb. 1921, Cowan Papers, 21A; account of 'an Urewera survivor', Cowan, *Wars*, I, p.360.

27. Cowan, *Wars*, I, pp.361, 361fn. (Maori evidence).

28. Evidence of Maori prisoners from Orakau garrison, in W. G. Mair to C.S., 29 Apr. 1864, *AJHR* 1864, E-1, Pt II, p.14; account of W. G. Mair in Andersen & Petersen, *The Mair Family*, p.125.

29. Hitiri Te Paerata, *Description of the Battle of Orakau*, Wellington 1888, p.5.

30. Descriptions of the Orakau defences, Te Paerata, *Battle of Orakau*; account of Paitini in Best, *Tuhoe*, II, pp.571-2; DQMG Journals, p.104; Brig. Gen. G. J. Carey's report, 3 Apr. 1864, *AJHR* 1864, E-3, pp.51-53; Von Tempsky, 'Memoranda', pp.152-4.

31. Accounts of Harehare of Ngati Manawa and Peita Kotuku, Cowan Papers, 41 and 41B; account of Paitini, Best, *Tuhoe*, II, pp.571-2; evidence of Maori prisoners in W. G. Mair to C.S., 29 Apr. 1864, & 'Return of Natives who have surrendered. . .', *AJHR* 1864, E-1, Pt II, pp.13-15 & E-6, p.14; Cowan *Wars*, I, p.364; William Williams to CMS, 29 Apr. 1864, CN/O 96(c); Te Paerata, *Battle of Orakau*, pp.3-4.

32. e.g. Te Paereta, *Battle of Orakau*, p.3; Featon, *Waikato War*, p.129; DQMG Journals, p.105; Cameron to Grey, 7 Apr. 1864, *AJHR* 1864, E-3, pp.50-51.

33. Cowan, *Wars*, I, p.364. Cowan based his figure for the Patu-heuheu and Ngati Whare section of the Tuhoe *taua* on his interview with Harehare (Cowan Papers 41) rather than that with Peita Kotuku (Cowan Papers 41B). Harehare, who was not at the battle, gives fifty people. Kotuku, who was present, gives eight men and three women.

34. In Wiseman to Admiralty, 3 Apr. 1864, ADM. 1/5868; *cf. NZ Herald*, 5 Apr. 1864.

35. *NZ Herald*, 5 Apr. 1864; *New-Zealander*, 6 Apr. 1864.

36. Evidence of Pou-patate of Te Kopua, in Cowan, *Wars*, I, p.361fn.

37. Carey's Report.

38. Carey's Report; DQMG Journals, p.104.

39. Accounts of Te Winitana Tupotahi and Paitini in Cowan, *Wars*, I, p.370, Best, *Tuhoe*, II, p.572.

40. Account of W. G. Mair in Andersen & Petersen, *The Mair Family*, p.116.

41. Von Tempsky, 'Memoranda', p.136.

42. Carey's Report; Greaves, *Memoirs*, p.101.

43. Alexander, *Bush Fighting*, p.164.

44. *NZ Herald*, 4 Apr. 1864.

45. Von Tempsky, 'Memoranda', p.141; Carey's Report.

46. e.g. some Waikato Militia lay within fifty yards of Orakau for five hours before being withdrawn and lost three men without taking part in an assault, *New-Zealander*, 9 Apr. 1864.

47. Account of W. G. Mair (quoting Lieut. Hurst R. E., who directed the sapping) in Andersen & Petersen, *The Mair Family*, p.115.

48. Von Tempsky, 'Memoranda', p.141; also Featon, *Waikato War*, p.129; Lieut. G. E. Hurst's

Report, 14 Apr. 1864, S.D., p.227; account of Paitini in Best, *Tuhoe*, II, p.574.

49. Cartridges were issued from a central armoury run by six men. Best, *Tuhoe*, II, p.573.

50. Von Tempsky, 'Memoranda', p.140; also accounts of Te Huia Raureti and Te Wairoa Piripi, in Cowan, *Wars*, I, p.374 & Cowan Papers 41B.

51. Te Paerata, *Battle of Orakau*, p.13; also Von Tempsky, 'Memoranda', p.137; evidence of Maori prisoners in W. G. Mair to C.S. 29 Apr. 1864, *AJHR* 1864, E-1, Pt II, p.14.

52. Cowan, *Wars*, I, p.376 (Maori evidence).

53. W. G. Mair was Cameron's emissary. For his account, Andersen & Petersen, *The Mair Family*, pp.117-9. Maori accounts, Cowan, *Wars*, I, pp.381-3; account of Te Wairoa Piripi, Cowan Papers 41B.

54. Account of W. G. Mair in Andersen & Petersen, *The Mair Family*, p.117; *cf.* Alexander, *Bush Fighting*, p.168.

55. G. Le M. Gretton, *Campaigns and History of the Royal Irish Regiment 1648-1902*, 1911, p.210.

56. Von Tempsky, 'Memoranda', p.154.

57. Account of Paitini in Best, *Tuhoe*, II, p.575.

58. Account of Rewi Maniapoto in Cowan, *Wars*, I, pp.387-8.

59. DQMG Journals, p.134. Two wounded sappers were not included in this return.

60. e.g. Von Tempsky, 'Memoranda', p.151; Cameron to Grey, 7 Apr. 1864, *AJHR* 1864, E-3, pp.50-51; Cowan, *Wars*, I, p.392.

61. Wiseman to ADM., 3 Apr. 1864, ADM. 1/5868 (L.21); Cameron to Grey, 3 Apr. 1864 (teleg.), *P.P.* 1864 (3380) XLI, p.8; *New-Zealander*, 6 Apr. 1864; *NZ Herald*, 4 Apr. 1864; Rewi Maniapoto, quoted in W. G. Mair to C.S., 29 Apr. 1864, *AJHR* 1864, E-1, Pt II, p.15. R. C. Mainwaring, an official of the Native Department, wrote that 'the native loss may be fairly estimated at 70 killed', Mainwaring to Fox, 2 Apr. 1864, *P.P.* 1864 (3380) XLI, p.9; *cf. NZ Herald*, 5 Apr. 1864, R. A. Logan to Ast. Mil. Sec., 6 May 1864, G16/3:30.

62. *NZ Herald*, 3 May 1864 (quoting *New-Zealander*, n.d.); also account of W. G. Mair, Andersen & Petersen, *The Mair Family*, pp.120-1; Von Tempsky, 'Memoranda', p.152; Featon, *Waikato War*, p.133; Greaves, *Memoirs*, p.102; account of Paitini, Best, *Tuhoe*, II, p.573. Even the official accounts admitted that some women were killed, Carey's Report; DQMG Journals, p.105; Alexander, *Bush Fighting*, p.170.

63. Te Paerata, *Battle of Orakau*, p.10.

64. Von Tempsky, 'Memoranda', p.150.

65. Account of Paitini, Best, *Tuhoe*, II, p.571; evidence of Pou-patate in Cowan, *Wars*, I, p.378.

66. Account of Te Huia Raureti, Cowan, *Wars*, I, p.374.

67. Account of Rewi Maniapoto, Cowan, *Wars*, I, p.388.

68. 'Veritas Vincit' to editor, *New-Zealander*, 23 Apr. 1864. 'Veritas' was particularly offended by a report in the *Southern Cross* of 6 Apr. 1864.

69. Account of W. G. Mair, Andersen & Petersen, *The Mair Family*, p.120.

70. Cameron to Grey, 3 Apr. 1864, *P.P.* 1864 (3380) XLI, pp.9-10; Fox, *The War in New Zealand*, p.103; *Southern Cross*, 6 Apr. 1864.

71. Report of a visit by two envoys to Rewi and Tamehana, May 1864, *AJHR* 1864, E-2, pp.48-50.

72. *AJHR* 1864, E-2, pp.48-50; R. Maunsell to CMS, 26 May 1864, CN/O 64(b); B. Y. Ashwell to CMS, 1 May 1864, CN/O 19; W. G. Mair to Gen. Carey, 28 Apr. 1864, to C.S., 29 Apr. 1864, *AJHR* 1864, E-1, Pt II, pp.14-15; Cowan, *Wars*, I, pp.388-9 (Maori evidence).

73. Cameron to W.O., 28 Mar. 1864, S.D., p.206; also 'Account of Wiremu Nera's Visit to Maungatautari', & 'Reports of a visit by two envoys to Rewi and Tamehana', *AJHR* 1864, E-3, pp.26-27, & E-2, pp.48-50; C. W. Vennell, *Such Things Were—The Story of Cambridge, New Zealand*, Dunedin, Wellington 1939, pp.71-72.

10: The Tauranga Campaign (pages 177-200)

1. Cameron to W.O., 4 Feb. 1864, S.D., pp.187-9; DQMG Journals, p.87.

2. Logbook HMS *Miranda*, 1 Feb. 1864; T. H. Smith to Grey, 22 Jan. 1864, Grey Autograph Letters, S. 33; G. J. Carey (the original commander of the Tauranga expedition) to Grey, 2, 7 Feb. 1864, G16/3:10, 13.

3. Accounts of Hori Ngatai given in 1903, Cowan Papers, 41C; Capt. Gilbert Mair, *The Story of Gate Pa*, Tauranga 1926, pp.21-28; account of Heni Te Kiri-Karamu, Cowan Papers, 41E; Wiremu Patene to Greer, 20 Mar. 1864, quoted in Gifford & Williams, *History of Tauranga*, pp.224-5.

4. Henare Taratoa to Greer, 28 Mar. 1864, DQMG Journals, p.109; also Gifford & Williams, *History of Tauranga*, p.227; note 2 above.

5. Mair, *Story of Gate Pa*, p.119; also Hori Ngatai's accounts; *New-Zealander*, 18 Apr. 1864; Logbook HMS *Miranda*, 16 Apr. 1864.

6. Subsequent colonist writers tended to attribute this Kingite defeat to colonial units which had accompanied the Arawa (e.g. 'Maketu and the Battle of Matata: The attack by the East Coast tribes', *Monthly Review*, 2 (1890), pp.118-30), but the colonist commander reported that his men 'were so fatigued with the march, having far more than the [Arawa] natives to carry, that they were only able to join in the pursuit', George Drummond Hay to Defence Minister, n.d., *AJHR* 1864, E-3, p.68.

7. Accounts of Hori Ngatai & Heni Te Kiri-Karamu.

8. Account of Hori Ngatai.

9. Dalton, 'A New Look at the Maori Wars', p.243. Fortescue called the battle a 'mishap', *History of the British Army*, XIII, p.502; *The Times*, 14 July 1863.

10. Ashwell to CMS, 27 Apr. 1864, CN/O 19; *New-Zealander*, 2 May 1864.

11. 'Samuel Mitchell and the Victoria Cross', periodical article, c.1864, source unknown, ATL; *Melbourne Argus*, n.d. quoted in *New-Zealander*, 28 May 1864; *cf. The Times*, 14 July 1864.

12. 'Samuel Mitchell and the Victoria Cross'.

13. Von Tempsky, 'Memoranda', p.164.

14. 'Samuel Mitchell and the Victoria Cross'.

15. Quoted in Holt, *The Strangest War*, p.211; *cf. The Times*, 7, 14 July 1864; Fox, *The New Zealand War*, p.118; *New-Zealander*, 1 June 1864.

16. Diary of Spencer Percival Nicholls, 15 Oct. 1863-31 Dec. 1864, 15-16 May 1864, p.222, ATL. Grey took the same remarkable course of action.

17. Letter of assault party officer quoted by Von Tempsky, 'Memoranda', p.164; Richard G. A. Levinge, *Historical Records of the Forty-Third*, London 1868, p.285 (*cf.* Letter of 43rd officer, *The Times*, 1 Sept. 1864); statement of John T. Beckett (a Quartermaster of HMS *Esk*), 6 June 1864, in *New-Zealander*, 7 June 1864. Fifty *Esk* seamen 'invaded' the *New-Zealander*'s Auckland offices and forced the editor to publish this statement after the appearance of an article in the issue of 1 June suggesting the Naval Brigade had deserted its officers.

18. 'Samuel Mitchell and the Victoria Cross' (paraphrasing the English press).

19. 'More Words on the War', *Southern Monthly Magazine*, July 1864, p.279; Fox, *War in New Zealand*, p.118; also Mair, *Story of Gate Pa*, p.17.

20. Cameron to Grey, 5 May 1864, *AJHR* 1864, E-3, pp.60-62 (hereafter Cameron's Report); also Alexander, *Bush Fighting*, p.193; DQMG Journals, p.112; Commodore Wiseman to the Admiralty, 3 May 1864; ADM 1/5868 (L.31) (hereafter Wiseman's Report).

21. Statement of John Beckett in *New-Zealander*, 7 June 1864; also Featon, *Waikato War*, p.91; Von Tempsky, 'Memoranda', p.162; Levinge, *Historical Records of the 43rd*, p.285.

22. Dalton, *War and Politics*, pp.187-8; Gibson, *The Maori Wars*, pp.122-3; Holt, *The Strangest War*, pp.208-9; Cowan, *Wars*, I, pp.418-19.

23. Nicholls, Diary, 29 Apr. 1864, p.206.

24. Greer to Deputy Adj.-Gen., 1 May 1864, *AJHR* 1864, E-3, pp.62-63 (Greer's Report); also Cameron's Report; accounts of Hori Ngatai.

25. Logbook HMS *Miranda*, 28 Apr. 1864; also Cameron's, Wiseman's, & Greer's Reports; DQMG Journals, p.111.

26. The two naval cannon were not listed in published accounts of the battle, but see Wiseman's Report. For general descriptions of the British artillery see Wiseman's Report; Cameron's Report; DQMG Journals, p.111; *NZ Herald*, 2 May 1864; Foljambe, *Australian Station*, p.57.

27. Field Marshal Viscount Wolseley, *The Story of a Soldier's Life*, 2v., Westminster 1903, II, p.51.

28. Donald Featherstone, *Colonial Small Wars*, London 1973, pp.89-90.

29. Nicholls, Diary, 27 Apr. 1864, p.200.

30. Nicholls, Diary, 29 Apr. 1864, p.206; Mair, *Story of Gate Pa*, p.14; J. H. Kerry Nicholls, *The King*

Country, or Explorations in New Zealand, London 1884, p.52.

31. Information kindly supplied by Mr Colin Feslier from Radio New Zealand Comnet News, 23 June 1983.

32. Accounts of Heni Te Kiri-Karamu and Hori Ngatai, Cowan Papers, 41E, 41C.

33. Wiseman's Report; Logbook HMS *Miranda*, 29 Apr. 1864.

34. Wiseman's Report.

35. 'Samuel Mitchell and the Victoria Cross'; also Nicholls, Diary, 29 Apr. 1864, pp.205-6; Mair, *Story of Gate Pa*, p.14; Wiseman's Report.

36. Von Tempsky, 'Memoranda', p.161; Greaves, *Memoirs*, p.104; also DQMG Journals, p.112.

37. Statement of John T. Beckett, 6 June 1864, in *New-Zealander*, 7 June 1864.

38. Greer, letter, 1 Oct. 1864, *The Times*, 14 Dec. 1864.

39. Greer's Report; Lieut. Hotham to Wiseman, 30 Apr. 1864, ADM 1/5868, L.40 (encl.); account of Hori Ngatai, Mair, *Story of Gate Pa*, p.25.

40. 'Samuel Mitchell and the Victoria Cross'; also Logbook HMS *Miranda*, 29 Apr. 1864; Foljambe, *Australian Station*, p.59; *The Times*, 14 July 1864; *Sydney Morning Herald*, 11 May 1864.

41. *NZ Herald*, 2 May 1864. Several other accounts note that the breach was entered with little loss, Cameron's Report; Alexander, *Bush Fighting*, p.191; Levinge, *Historical Records of the 43rd*, p.285; Nicholls, Diary, 29 Apr. 1864, p.209.

42. Casualty Return, *AJHR* 1864, E-3, pp.64-67.

43. Logbook HMS *Miranda*, 29 Apr. 1864.

44. *NZ Herald*, 2 May 1864; also account of Hori Ngatai in Mair, *Story of Gate Pa*, p.24; account of Heni Te Kiri-Karamu, Cowan Papers, 41E.

45. Account of Heni Te Kiri-Karamu, Cowan Papers, 41E.

46. Nicholls, Diary, 29 Apr. 1864.

47. 'Samuel Mitchell and the Victoria Cross'.

48. Nicholls, Diary, 30 Apr. 1864, p.216; also Logbook HMS *Miranda*, 29 Apr. 1864.

49. Accounts of Heni Te Kiri-Karamu & Hori Ngatai, Cowan Papers, 41E & Mair, *Story of Gate Pa*, p.24.

50. Account of Heni Te Kiri-Karamu; Foljambe, *Australian Station*, p.58; also DQMG Journals, p.112; Logbook HMS *Miranda*, 29 Apr. 1864.

51. Cowan, *Wars*, II, pp.152-3.

52. Grey to Ormus Biddulph, 7 May 1864, Grey-Biddulph Letters, APL.

53. Dalton, *War and Politics*, p.191 & 'A New Look at the Maori Wars', p.243; also Grey's correspondence with Ministers, *AJHR* 1864, E-2.

54. Featon, *Waikato War*, p.154.

55. *New-Zealander*, 25 May 1864, citing letters to Smith.

56. Wiseman to Admiralty, 6 June 1864, ADM 1/5868 (L.39); also *New-Zealander*, 31 May 1864.

57. Cameron to Grey, 15 May 1864, Grey to Cameron, 19 May 1864, C.O. 209/186, pp.424-6, 428-31; DQMG Journals, p.116.

58. DQMG Journals, p.117.

59. Col. G. J. Carey to Grey, 1 Feb. 1864, G16/3:10.

60. Cameron to Grey, 5 May 1864, *AJHR* 1864, E-3, pp.60-62.

61. DQMG Journals, p.120.

62. Contemporary accounts of Te Ranga, Greer to Cameron, 21, 27 June, with casualty returns, *AJHR* 1864, E-3, pp.74-80 (Greer's Reports); DQMG Journals, pp.121-2; Acting-Capt. Phillimore to Capt. Jenkins [22?] June ADM. 1/5868 (L.63); *NZ Herald*, 22 June 1864; Alexander, *Bush Fighting*, pp.218-24 and *Notes on the Maoris . . .*, London 1865, p.2; Featon, *Waikato War*, pp.156-7; Fox, *The War in New Zealand*, pp.119-20; Von Tempsky, 'Memoranda', pp.172-6; A. Hope Blake, *Sixty Years in New Zealand*, Wellington 1909, pp.59-65; Vane, *The Durham Light Infantry*, p.98 (based on the 68th's Digest of Service); Nicholls, Diary, 22, 25 June 1864, pp.243-6.

63. Greer's Report, 21 June 1864; Levinge, *Historical Records of the 43rd*, p.288; *NZ Herald*, 23 June 1864.

64. Greer's Report, 27 June 1864.

65. Greer's Report, 27 June 1864.

66. DQMG Journals, p.121; Greer's Report, 27 June 1864.

67. *NZ Herald*, 23 June 1864, commenting on Te Ranga.
68. *New-Zealander*, 29 June 1864; Fox, *War in New Zealand*, pp.118-9; DQMG Journals, p.121; Alexander, *Bush Fighting*, pp.223-4; Von Tempsky, 'Memoranda', p.175.
69. *AJHR* 1864, E-6, pp.18-24; Gifford and Williams, *History of Tauranga*, p.252.
70. Von Tempsky, 'Memoranda', pp.174-6.
71. W. B. Baker, Memo, 21 June 1864, *AJHR* 1864, E-3, p.75; Greer's Report, 21 June 1864.
72. Greer, Return of Arms Captured at Te Ranga, DQMG Journals, Appendices, p.XIX.
73. Casualty Return, *AJHR* 1864, E-3, p.80. Two Waikato militia were wounded at Te Ranga but not included in this return, *New-Zealander*, 29 June 1864.
74. Greer, Return of Arms Captured at Te Ranga, n.d., DQMG Journals, Appendices, p.XIX.
75. For the composition of the Maori force, Cowan, *Wars*, I, pp.423, 426-7 (Maori evidence); W. B. Baker, Memo, 21 June 1864, *AJHR* 1864, E-3, p.75; Baker to Greer, 11 June 1864, quoted in Gifford and Williams, *History of Tauranga*, pp.238-9; W. K. Nesbitt to T. H. Smith, 6, 29 June 1864, quoted in Stafford, *Te Arawa*, p.382; various letters encl. in G16/3:59.
76. Cowan, *Wars*, I, p.427; Nesbitt to Smith, 24 June 1864, in Stafford, *Te Arawa*, p.382; Ngati Pikiao and Ngati Porou, the heaviest sufferers, reportedly lost thirty-two and thirty men respectively.
77. DQMG Journals, p.122.
78. Ministerial Memo, 27 June 1864, S.D., pp.267-8.
79. Cameron to Grey, 2 July 1864, S.D., pp.269-70.
80. For accounts of the meetings of 24-25 July and 5-6 August, Greer to DQMG, 25, 26 July 1864, G16/3:66 and 69; Grey, Speeches, 5-6 Aug. 1864, *AJHR* 1867, A-20; correspondence in *AJHR* 1869, A-18; DQMG Journals, pp.126-7, Appendices pp.XVI-XIX.
81. Royal Commission on Confiscated Lands, *AJHR* 1928, G-7.
82. 'Return of Arms Surrendered by the Natives. . .', *AJHR* 1864, E-6, pp.18-24; 'Return of Arms Surrendered [on 24-25 July 1864]', (signed Col. Greer), DQMG Journals, Appendices, p.XVIII.
83. Von Tempsky, 'Memoranda', p.128.
84. Mr Rice (Interpreter), Report, quoted in Gifford & Williams, *History of Tauranga*, p.252; *AJHR* 1865, D-7, p.6 (Contract dated 11 Sept. 1864).
85. See *Sydney Morning Herald*, 20 Aug. 1864; W. B. Baker, Report, 25 July 1864, DQMG Journals, Appendices, pp.XVI-XVII; Greer to DQMG, 25 July 1864, G16/3:66
86. Grey, Speeches, 5-6 Aug. 1864, *AJHR* 1867, A-20; DQMG Journals, pp.125-7.
87. *NZ Herald*, 3 Dec. 1864, and see *N.Z. Herald*, 28 July 1864. The lines are part of an imaginary speech by the Tauranga Maoris. 'The Chief ', of course, is Grey.
88. Brown to Grey, 16 July 1864, Gifford & Williams, *History of Tauranga*, pp.264-7.
89. Isaac Shepherd, Memo, n.d., DQMG Journals, Appendices p.XIX; W. B. Baker, Précis of Proceedings of meeting, 25 July, encl. in G16/3:66.
90. Edward Insley & Takerei, Memos, both 24 July 1864, encl. in G16/3:69; Greer to DQMG, 25 July 1864, G16/3:66; also other encl. in these two despatches, some of which were printed in *AJHR* 1869, A-18.
91. Cowan, *Wars*, I, p.398; Harold Miller, *Race Conflict in New Zealand 1814-1865*, Auckland 1966, p.116. For examples of similar opinions, Dalton, 'A New Look at the Maori Wars', p.239; Simpson, *Te Riri Pakeha*, pp.142-3; Sinclair, *History of New Zealand*, p.140.
92. e.g. B. Y. Ashwell to CMS, 29 Apr. 1864, CN/O 19.
93. *Wellington Independent*, 19 Apr. 1864; *NZ Herald*, 18 June 1864.
94. Morgan to Browne, 24 Oct. 1864, Gore Browne Papers, 1/2d.
95. The implications of this event have been underestimated by historians but see Cameron to W.O., 7 Oct. and 8 Dec. 1864, C.O. 209/186, pp.463-5 and S.D., p.313; *NZ Herald*, 10, 11, 26, 31 Oct. 1864; Captain R. I. Cooper to Grey, 13, 14 Oct. 1864, *AJHR* 1864, E-1, pp.93-94; B. Y. Ashwell to CMS, 26 Sept. 1864, CN/O 19; Foljambe, *Australian Station*, pp.86-88, 112.
96. Burrows to CMS, 25 Oct. 1864, CN/O 8(c); J. L. C. Richardson (Speaker) to C.O., 15 Nov. 1864, C.O. 209/187, p.354 (C.O.'s italics); also Sewell, Journal (ts.), v.2, Pt 2, pp.421-3.
97 Grey to Biddulph, 8 Mar. 1864, Grey-Biddulph Letters; Colonial Ministry, Memo, 25 June 1864, S.D., pp.266-7.
98. A. Domett, Memo, 24 June 1864, S.D., p.267, F. Whitaker, Memo, 22 Sept. 1864, *AJHR* 1864, E-2, p.93; Grey to Cameron, 19 May 1864, C.O. 209/186, pp.428-31; Ministry Memos, 24, 25

June 1864, S.D., pp.267-9; Ministry Memo, 30 Aug. 1864, *AJHR* 1864, E-2, pp.82-83.

99. Letter by Cameron, quoted in Edward Gorton, *Some Home Truths re. the Maori War 1863 to 9*, London 1901, pp.20-23; also Cameron to Grey, 26 May 1865, Duncan Cameron, Letters to Sir George Grey, Grey Collection.

100. Cameron to Grey, 26 May 1865, Grey Collection.

101. *Wellington Independent*, 19 Apr. 1864.

11: A New Kind of War (pages 203-34)

1. J. Belich, 'Titokowaru's War And Its Place In New Zealand History', Victoria Univ. of Wellington M.A. Thesis, 1979, pp.4-6; Ward, *Show of Justice*, pp.224-6; 'Report of Select Committee on Confiscated Lands', *AJHR* 1866, F-2; J. C. Richmond to McLean, 11 Jan. 1868, McLean Papers, 20; W. L. Williams to CMS, 2 Aug. 1869, CN/O 97.

2. Paul Clark, *'Hauhau'/The Pai Marire Search for Maori Identity*, Auckland 1975. Earlier accounts of *Pai Marire*, S. B. Babbage, *Hauhauism. An Episode in the Maori Wars, 1863-6*, Wellington 1937; Robin W. Winks, 'The Doctrine of Hau-Hauism', *JPS* v.62, Sept. 1953, pp.199-236. Contemporary reports, *AJHR* 1865, E-4. Comparative discussions, Michael Adas, *Prophets of Rebellion/Millenarian Protest Movements against the European Colonial Order*, Chapel Hill 1979; John S. Galbraith, 'Appeals to the Supernatural: African and New Zealand Comparisons with the Ghost Dance', *Pacific Historical Review*, v.51, May 1982, pp.115-33.

3. Discussions of the causes of war and responses to *Pai Marire* on the East Coast, Karen Neal, 'Maori Participation in the East Coast Wars 1865-1872', Auckland Univ. M.A. thesis, 1976; W. H. Oliver & Jane M. Thomson, *Challenge and Response: a Study of the Development of the Gisborne-East Coast region*, Gisborne 1971, pp.86-94; K. M. Sanderson, '"These Neglected Tribes"/A Study of the East Coast Maori and Their Missionary, William Williams, 1834-1870', Auckland Univ. M.A. thesis, 1980, pp.168-86.

4. Grey to Newcastle, 26 Apr. 1864, & encl., C.O. 209/179, pp.434-40; 'Statement of Komene's Wife', in Parris to Warre, 23 Apr. 1864, C.O. 209/180, pp.180-81; A. S. Atkinson, Journal, 6-7 Apr. 1864, & Jane-Maria Atkinson to Mary Richmond, 6 Apr. 1864, *R-A.P.*, II, pp.102-4.

5. Account of Te Kahu-pukoro, 30 Aug. 1920, Cowan, *Wars*, II, p.24. For other accounts of Sentry Hill, Warre to DQMG, 1, 3 May 1864, *AJHR* 1864, E-3, pp.72-74; Warre, *Historical Records of the 57th*, pp.184-7.

6. Report of the Superintendent of Wellington (Dr Featherston), *AJHR* 1864, E-3, pp.80-84; account of H. D. Bates, 8 Mar. 1921, Cowan Papers, 41C.

7. Waddy to Cameron, 1 Feb. 1865, S.D., pp.324-5; Cameron to Grey, 28 Jan. 1865, *AJHR* 1865, A-4, pp.6-7.

8. For more information on the Wanganui campaign see *AJHR* 1865, A-4, A-5; S.D., pp.324-59; Cowan, *Wars*, II, ch.5; Dalton, *War and Politics*, pp.218-33.

9. DQMG Journals, p.137; S.D., p.352.

10. Cameron to Grey, 26 May 1865, Cameron-Grey Letters, Grey Collection. The Cameron-Grey controversy as a whole, *AJHR* 1865, A-4, A-5; Rutherford, *Grey*, pp.522-38; Dalton, *War and Politics*, pp.222-34.

11. Dalton, *War and Politics*, pp.232-4 & 'The Military Reputation of Sir George Grey: The Case of Weraroa', *NZJH*, 9, 1975, pp.154-70.

12. Fox, *The War in New Zealand*, p.215. For an over-dramatized account of the 'siege' see Cowan, *Wars*, II, ch.4; also Gudgeon, *Reminiscences*, ch.X.

13. Chute to Grey, 15 Jan. 1866, *AJHR* 1866, A-1, pp.86-88; Warre, *Historical Records of the 57th*, p.198.

14. Alexander, *Bushfighting*, pp.299-300.

15. For Chute's campaign, *A Campaign on the West Coast . . . under the command of Major-General Chute*, Wanganui 1866; O'Donnell, *Historical Records of the 14th Regt.*, pp.194-9; Thos. McDonnell, 'General Chute's Campaign On the West Coast', *Monthly Review*, v.2, 1890, pp.393-404; Gudgeon, *Reminiscences*, ch.XVIII-XX.

16. McDonnell's Report, 4 Oct. 1866, *AJHR* 1867, A-1A, pp.16-18; McDonnell, 'The Survey of the Confiscated Lands. Campaign on the West Coast, 1866-1869', *Monthly Review*, v.2, 1890,

pp.448-62; [McDonnell], *An Explanation of the Principal Causes which Led to the Present War on the West Coast . . .*, Wanganui 1869, pp.5-11; Gudgeon, *Reminiscences*, chs XXI-XXIII.

17. Political aspects of these conflicts, note 3 above. Much remains to be done on the military side, but see Cowan, *Wars*, II, chs 7-14, 16-19; Gudgeon, *Reminiscences*, chs XI-XVI, XXIV-XXVI; Andersen & Petersen, *The Mair Family*, pp.129-66; Tuta Nihoniho, *Narrative of the Fighting on the East Coast with a Monograph on Bush Fighting*, Wellington 1913.

18. Maj. Fraser to Grey, 27 Dec. 1865, *AJHR* 1866, A-1, pp.61-62; correspondence, *AJHR* 1866, A-6.

19. Cowan, *Wars*, II, p.127.

20. Cowan, *Wars*, II, p.139; account of Peita Kotuku, Cowan Papers, 41A; McLean to Stafford, 15 Oct. 1866, & encl., G. S. Cooper to Native Minister, 29 Oct. 1866, *AJHR* 1867, A-1A, pp.68-74, 11-12.

21. Keith Sinclair, ed., *A Soldier's View of Empire/The Reminiscences of James Bodell 1831-92*, London 1982, p.166.

22. J. C. Richmond to Whitmore, 19 Dec. 1868, Whitmore Papers, Hawke's Bay Museum, Box A; Whitmore to Haultain [8 April 1869], Whitmore Collection, ATL, 2.

23. G. S. Whitmore, *The Last Maori War in New Zealand under the Self-Reliant Policy*, London 1902, pp.32-33; Gudgeon, *Reminiscences*, p.197.

24. e.g. A. S. Atkinson, Journal, 21 Aug., 2 Sept., 12 Sept. 1860, Jane-Maria Atkinson to Emily Richmond, 17 July 1860, *R-A.P.*, I, pp.628, 631, 634, 618-9; *New Zealand Examiner*, 10 July 1860; T. Russell to William Jackson, 6 Aug. 1863, Papers Relating to the Forest Rangers, 1863-1886, Grey Collection; 'The Waikato Campaign', 'More Words on the War', *Southern Monthly Magazine*, May, July 1864, pp.151-60, 277-87.

25. *AJHR* 1866, A-14.

26. J. Rutherford, 'Maori Wars', *An Encyclopaedia of New Zealand*, II, p.483; also Holt, *Strangest War*, p.245; A. W. Shrimpton & Alan E. Mulgan, *Maori and Pakeha: A History of New Zealand*, Auckland 1921, pp.235, 257; Ormond Wilson, *War In The Tussock/Te Kooti and the Battle of Te Porere*, Wellington 1961, p.23.

27. The following summary of Te Kooti's early life, imprisonment, and religion is especially indebted to Peter Webster's *Rua and the Maori Millennium*, Wellington 1979, ch.4.

28. Evidence of Michael Mallooly, *AJHR* 1868, A-15, p.6; statement of Hotoma Kahukura, 15 Aug. 1868, Army Department Inwards Letters and Registered Files (hereafter A.D. 1/-) N.A. 2810.

29. G. S. Cooper to J. C. Richmond, 4 Aug. 1868, *AJHR* 1868, A-15, p.12.

30. Statement of Hotoma Kahukura, A.D. 1/2810.

31. *Wellington Independent*, 21 July 1860; cf. F. J. W. Gascoyne, *Soldiering in New Zealand/Being Reminiscences of a Veteran*, London 1916, pp.22-23.

32. Discussions of *Ringatu*, Webster, *Rua*, pp.102-7, 119-21; William Greenwood, *The Upraised Hand. The Spiritual Significance of the Rise of the Ringatu Faith*, Wellington 1942. Te Kooti's code of behaviour, accounts of Te Huare (31 Jan. 1870, *AJHR* 1870, A-8A, p.70) and of another of Te Kooti's followers, in Cowan, *Wars*, II, pp.283-4fn. A slightly different version of the latter is given in Wilson, *War in the Tussock*, pp.4-5, from the *Hawke's Bay Herald* of 12 Oct. 1871.

33. Gudgeon, *Reminiscences* p.332.

34. Memo of speech by Maihi Pohepohe, n.d. [Aug. 1869?], *AJHR* 1870, A-8, p.5.

35. Account of Te Huare, *AJHR* 1870, A-8A; p.70.

36. Memo of speech of Maihi Pohepohe, AJHR 1870, A-8, p.6.

37. Whitmore to Haultain, 27 Oct. 1868, A.D. 1/4182.

38. C. Westrupp to McLean, 29 June 1869, McLean Papers, 630; G. Hamilton-Browne, *With The Lost Legion in New Zealand*, London, n.d., pp.296, 247; H. T. Clarke, quoted in W. T. Parham, *John Roberts, N.Z.C./A Man in His Time/A Life of Lt. Col. John Mackintosh Roberts (1840-1928)*, Whakatane 1983, p.55.

39. Whitmore to Haultain, 30 Oct. 1868, A.D. 1/4182.

40. Whitmore to Haultain, 28 July 1868, A.D. 1/3264.

41. 'Roll of Arms and Ammunition Taken by the Hauhau Prisoners at the Chatham Islands', *AJHR* 1868, A-15, p.8; account of Hotoma Kahukura, 15 Aug. 1868, A.D. 1/2810; account of Peita Kotuku, Cowan Papers, 41A; *Weekly News*, 28 Nov. 1868; *New Zealand Advertiser*, 7 Aug. 1868; Whitmore's Report, 9 Aug. 1868, *AJHR* 1868, A-15C, pp.3-6.

42. Gudgeon, *Reminiscences*, p.213 (evidence of Te Rangitahau); statement of Hotoma Kahukura; Featon, *Waikato War*, p.171; Joseph Angus Mackay, *Historic Poverty Bay and the East Coast*, 2nd ed., Gisborne 1966, pp.238-9; Gudgeon, *Reminiscences*, p.211; *Life in Early Poverty Bay*, Gisborne 1927, p.88. Other accounts of Paparatu, Westrupp to Whitmore, 21 July 1868, *AJHR* 1868, A-15D; Whitmore to Haultain, 21 July 1868, A.D. 1/3264; Arthur Kempthorne, Journal of Events in Poverty Bay, 1868, Hawke's Bay Museum; T. W. R. Porter, *Major Ropata Wahawaha/The Story of His Life and Times*, Gisborne 1897, p.16; Thomas Lambert, *The Story of Old Wairoa*, Dunedin 1925, p.524.

43. Mackay, *Poverty Bay*, p.239; *cf.* Whitmore, *Last Maori War*, p.7.

44. J. Rhodes to Haultain, 26, 31 July 1868, A.D. 1/2522, 2532; Porter, *Ropata*, pp.16-17; Richardson to Rhodes, 29 July 1868, *AJHR* 1868, A-15D; Cowan, *Wars*, II, pp.236-9.

45. Whitmore to Haultain, 27 July, 8 Aug. 1868, A.D. 1/2623, 2707.

46. Whitmore's Report, 9 Aug. 1868, *AJHR* 1868, A-15C, pp.3-6.

47. *New Zealand Advertiser*, 7 Sept. 1868.

48. Whitmore to Haultain, 30 Oct. 1868, A.D. 1/4182; *cf.* Whitmore's Report, 9 Aug. 1868; Whitmore to Haultain, 7 Oct. 1868, A.D. 1/3383.

49. W. G. Mair to Civil Commissioner, Tauranga, 3 Oct. 1868 (reporting Maori accounts), in W. G. Mair Letterbook, 23 Mar. 1868-31 Nov. 1869, Mitchell Library, Sydney (from notes kindly provided by Judith Binney of University of Auckland).

50. R. Biggs to McLean, 18 Aug. 1868, quoted in Mackay, *Poverty Bay*, p.243.

51. Whitmore's Report, 9 Aug. 1868; Westrupp to Rhodes, 21 July 1868, *AJHR* 1868, A-15D; Gudgeon, *Reminiscences*, p.218.

52. 9 Oct. 1868, Army Department Outwards Telegrams (hereafter A.D. 8/1), 178. Other references to Reignier's mission, Whitmore to Haultain, 5 Oct. 1868, A.D. 1/3341; Reignier to O.C., Napier, 17 Oct. 1868, Army Department Register of Inwards Letters, 1868, Entry 3585.

53. Takurangi to Puketapu, 23 Sept. 1868, A.D. 1/4123; *cf.* [Anon.] Memo, 28 Aug. 1868, McLean Papers, 20; Featon, *Waikato War*, p.177.

54. Frederick Helgar to O.C., Napier, 29 Oct. 1868, A.D. 1/4128; Mair to Civil Commissioner, Tauranga, 3, 5 Oct. 1868, W. G. Mair Letterbook.

55. Edward L. Green to McLean, 7 Sept., Hori te Rangi to Te Kooti, 11 Sept., G. Lambert to Haultain, 24 Sept., Whitmore, 'Memo on Defence Generally . . .', 24 Nov. 1868, respectively A.D. 1/3055, 4123, 3224, 4371; G. S. Worgan & S. Deighton to McLean, 22 Aug., 4 Sept. 1868, both McLean Papers, 20; account of Wi Pere, *AJHR* 1868, A-10, pp.29-31; Paora Matuakore to G. Preece, 9 Nov. 1868, in *Weekly News*, 28 Nov. 1868; Sanderson, 'These Neglected Tribes', p.196.

56. Cowan, *Wars*, II, p.236; Webster, *Rua*, p.111.

57. J. D. Ormond to Haultain, 23 Oct. 1868, & encl., *AJHR* 1869, A-4A, pp.5-8; J. C. Richmond & Lambert to Haultain, both 20 Oct. 1868, A.D. 1/3697, 3662.

58. Daniel Pollen to Haultain, 25 Oct. 1868, Lambert to Haultain, 22 Oct. 1868, A.D. 1/3682, 3668; also Lambert to McLean, 6 Nov. 1868, McLean Papers, 383.

59. T. Lambert, *Old Wairoa*, p.543.

60. Gudgeon, *Reminiscences*, p.228.

61 Account of Peita Kotuku, 23 Feb. 1921, Cowan Papers, 41A.

62. Mackay, *Poverty Bay*, pp.271-2; Rhodes to Haultain, 29 Oct. 1868, A.D. 1/3808.

63. In an unnecessary attempt to defend Biggs from posthumous criticism, some writers (e.g. Mackay, *Poverty Bay*, pp.251-4) cast doubt on the existence of these warnings. But it is clear that they were sent and received. W. L. Williams, letter, 23 Dec. 1868, in *Weekly News*, 9 Jan. 1869; Frederick Helgar to O.C., Napier, 29 Oct. 1868, A.D. 1/4128; Mair to Pollen, 7 Dec. 1868, W.G. Mair Letterbook, p.59; Biggs to Whitmore, 26 Oct. 1868, Whitmore Papers, Box A; Gascoyne, *Soldiering in New Zealand*, pp.34-36.

64. First-hand reports, account of Peita Kotuku, 23 Feb. 1921, Cowan Papers, 41A; account of Wi Pere, *AJHR* 1868, A-10, pp.29-31; Maria Morris [or Morete], 'Recollections of the Poverty Bay Campaign', ATL; accounts quoted in Mackay, *Poverty Bay*, pp.256-71; W. L. Williams to CMS, 27 Nov. 1868, CN/O 97, & to McLean, 10, 14, 15 Nov. 1868, McLean Papers, 22; Henare Potae to McLean, 10, 11, 15 Nov. 1868, *AJHR* 1869, A-10, pp.25-26, 28-29; account of John Maynard, in Lambert, *Old Wairoa*, pp.546-8; John G. Gleddy to McLean, 10 Nov. 1868, McLean Papers, 21.

65. Gudgeon, *Reminiscences*, p.233.

66. McLean to J. C. Richmond, 18 Nov. 1868, *AJHR* 1869, A-4A, pp.26-27.

67. The number usually given is thirty to thirty-seven Maoris, as well as thirty-four Europeans, but this does not include all the executions of Maori prisoners, account of Wi Pere, *AJHR* 1868, A-10, pp.29-31; Maria Morris, 'Recollections'; W. L. Williams to McLean, 22 Nov. 1868, McLean Papers, 22; *Hawke's Bay Herald*, 23 Nov. 1868; McLean to J. C. Richmond, 16 Nov. 1868, A.D. 1/4000.

68. Some prisoners, after escaping or being released by Te Kooti during his retreat from Poverty Bay, got lost in the bush and died. See account of Wi Pere, & Maria Morris, 'Reminiscences'. The killings by government troops occurred after the Siege of Ngatapa, in January 1869.

69. Captain Buchanan to Haultain, 22, 23 Oct. 1868, A.D. 1/3676 and 3679.

70. S. Deighton to McLean, 18 Oct. 1868, Tuke to McLean, 22 Oct. 1869, *AJHR* 1869, A-4A, pp.6-7, 8.

71. Gascoyne, *Soldiering in New Zealand*, p.35. Government spying, Lucy Grey to McLean, 17 Sept., 27 Oct. 1869, McLean Papers, 48.

72. For colonist attitudes, *New Zealand Advertiser*, 16 Nov. 1868; [James Hawthorne], *A Dark Chapter from New Zealand History*, Napier 1869, Christchurch 1974.

73. Greenwood, *The Upraised Hand*, pp.25-26; Webster, *Rua*, pp.114-6.

74. Account of Wi Pere, *AJHR* 1868, A-10, pp.29-31; Maria Morris, 'Recollections'. An eyewitness account by one of Te Kooti's warriors is that of Peita Kotuku, 23 Feb 1921, Cowan Papers, 41A.

75. *Weekly News*, 12 Dec. 1868 (evidence of women prisoners escaped from Te Kooti); account of Wi Pere, *AJHR* 1868, A-10, pp.29-31; Westrupp to McLean, 25 Nov. 1868, *AJHR* 1869, A-4A, p.16.

76. Gascoyne, Report to Whitmore, 11 Dec. 1868, *AJHR* 1869, A-[3], pp.14-15, *Soldiering in New Zealand*, pp.45-55, & account in Gudgeon, *The Defenders of New Zealand*, Auckland 1887, pp.296-8; Maria Morris 'Recollections'; account of Wi Pere, *AJHR* 1868, A-10, pp.29-31.

77. Westrupp to McLean, 27 Nov. 1868, McLean Papers, 630. Most British accounts give fifty or sixty, but Westrupp's private letter—as distinct from his official report of the same day—is likely to be the more accurate.

78. Westrupp to McLean (official), 27 Nov. 1868, McLean Papers, 21; *Weekly News*, 12 Dec. 1868; Maria Morris, 'Recollections'; Henare Potae to McLean, 27 Nov. 1868, A.D. 1/4564; Hawthorne, *A Dark Chapter*, pp.30-31; Featon, *Waikato War*, p.190.

79. Correspondence, 21-26 Nov. 1868, *AJHR* 1869, A-4A, pp.14-16.

80. Porter, *Ropata*, p.20.

81. Gascoyne's accounts, note 76 above; *Hawke's Bay Herald*, 5 Dec. 1868; G. Preece to J. C. Richmond, 11 Dec. 1868, *AJHR* 1869, A-4A, pp.16-18; account of Peita Kotuku, Cowan Papers, 41A.

82. W. L. Williams to McLean, 4 Dec. 1868, McLean Papers, 22; McLean & J. C. Richmond to Haultain, 4, 5 Dec. 1868, A.D. 1/4785, 4634; *Hawke's Bay Herald*, 5 Dec. 1868; *Weekly News*, 12 Dec. 1868 (evidence of 'a lad named Pouro', a prisoner escaped from Te Kooti).

83. Haultain to Whitmore, 27 Nov. 1868, Whitmore Papers, A; Whitmore, *Last Maori War*, p.80 (Maori evidence).

84. Gascoyne, *Soldiering in New Zealand*, p.56; also *Weekly News*, 12 Dec. 1868; Porter, *Ropata*, p.20; Gudgeon, *Reminiscences*, p.241.

85. Gascoyne's accounts; *Weekly News*, 19 Dec. 1868; Whitmore to McLean, 6 Dec. 1868, McLean Papers, 635; McLean to Haultain, 5 Dec. 1868, A.D. 1/4635; G. Preece to J. C. Richmond, 11 Dec. 1868, *AJHR* 1869, A-4A, pp.16-18.

86. McLean to Haultain, 4 Dec. 1868, A.D. 1/4785.

87. Gascoyne, *Soldiering in New Zealand*, p.45.

88. Westrupp to McLean & G. S. Cooper, 20, 24 Nov. 1868, McLean Papers, 630.

89. See note 82 above.

90. Gascoyne, account in Gudgeon, *Defenders of New Zealand*, p.297.

91. *Weekly News*, 12 Dec. 1868; J. C. Richmond to Haultain, 5 Dec. 1868, A.D. 1/4634; Westrupp to McLean, 25 Nov. 1868, A.D. 1/4757. Te Kooti's casualties, account of Wi Pere, *AJHR* 1868, A-10, pp.29-31.

92. Westrupp to McLean, 25 Nov. 1868, A.D. 1/4757; *Weekly News*, 12 Dec. 1868; Westrupp to McLean, 27 Nov., W. L. Williams to McLean, 28 Nov. 1868, McLean Papers, 21, 22.

93. G. Preece to J. C. Richmond, 11 Dec. 1868, *AJHR* 1869, A-4A, p.17; W. L. Williams to McLean,

5 Dec. 1868, McLean Papers, 22; Westrupp to McLean, 13, 14 Dec. 1868 (encl. letters from Tuke and Gascoyne), McLean Papers, 630, 22.

94. The *kupapa* lost thirty to thirty-five killed and wounded at the last two Makaretu engagements (Gascoyne's accounts), and at least twelve at Ngatapa (Featon, *Waikato War*, p.191). The *Ringatu* forces had about twenty-six casualties at Makaretu (notes 83 and 91 above) & at least nine at Ngatapa, J. C. Richmond & McLean to Haultain, both 8 Dec. 1868, A.D. 1/4711, 4748.

95. McLean to J. C. Richmond & Haultain, both 5 Dec. 1868, McLean Papers, 22 and A.D. 1/4632; *Weekly News*, 12 Dec. 1868; Westrupp to McLean, 4 Dec. 1868, McLean Papers, 630.

12: Titokowaru and the Brink of Victory (pages 235-57)

1. James Booth (R. M. Patea) to Native Minister, 30 Nov. 1867, *AJHR* 1868, A-8, p.42; also William Newland, 'The Campaign on the West Coast North Island Against Titoko Waru June 1866 to the end of 1869', William Newland Papers, Taranaki Museum; Cowan, *Wars*, II, p.179; R. Parris, 'Report on the Social and Political State of the Natives' (Taranaki), 1 Apr. 1868, *P.P.* 1868-9 (307) XLIV, p.187.

2. Correspondence in *AJHR* 1868, A-8, especially Booth to Native Minister, 11 Apr., 5 May 1868, pp.3, 7, quoting Ngati Ruanui spokesmen. A slightly fuller discussion of the outbreak of war, J. Belich, 'Titokowaru's War', pp.4-7.

3. Pay estimates, 2 Sept. 1868, A.D. 1/3063.

4. Haultain to Adjutant, Dunedin, 18 Dec. 1868, A.D. 8/1:485. Constabulary recruitment in general, the other telegrams in this series for 1868-9.

5. Pay estimates, 2 Sept., 30 Oct. 1868, A.D. 1/3063, 3801.

6. Whitmore to Haultain, 21 Mar. 1869, Whitmore Collection, 2.

7. McDonnell to Haultain, 18 July, 2 Sept. 1868, A.D. 1/2440, 2998; Lieut. Col. E. Gorton to Haultain 18, 29 July 1868, A.D. 1/2395, 2594; *Wanganui Chronicle*, 4 July 1868; *Wellington Independent*, 16 June, 7, 30 July 1868.

8. Haultain, Memo., 3 Sept. 1868, A.D. 1/2957; *Wellington Independent*, 6 June 1868; evidence of Kimble Bent, Tutange Waionui, Whakawhiria, in Cowan, *Kimble Bent*, pp.119, 154, 168.

9. Quoted in Gorton to Haultain, 18 July 1869, A.D. 1/2395.

10. T. McDonnell, 'A Maori History of the Pakeha-Maori Wars in New Zealand', Gudgeon, *Defenders*, p.548. This account was purportedly related to McDonnell by 'Kowhai Ngutu Kaka', but Kowhai was probably an invention of McDonnell's, and it should not be taken too seriously. Its veracity compares very unfavourably with *War in the North*.

11. Quoted in Hone Wiremu to Booth, 25 June 1868, *AJHR* 1868, A-8, p.15.

12. *Wanganui Chronicle*, 18 June 1868; *Wellington Independent*, 4 July 1868; also *New Zealand Advertiser*, 24 Aug. 1868; 'Diary of James Livingston', ed. J. Houston, 9 June to 3 Jan. 1869, 14, 26 June, 9 Aug. 1868, Wanganui Regional Museum; Booth to J. C. Richmond, 16 June 1868, *AJHR* 1868, A-8, p.13.

13. Booth to Haultain, 1 July 1868, *AJHR* 1868, A-8, p.15.

14. McDonnell, *Explanation*, pp.35-38.

15. Cowan, *Hero Stories of New Zealand*, pp.130-41. Analysis of this engagement, Belich, 'Titokowaru's War', pp.13-20.

16. Cowan, *Wars*, II, p.201 (evidence of J. M. Roberts).

17. Belich, 'Titokowaru's War', pp.21-26.

18. McDonnell's Report, 9 Sept. 1868, *AJHR* 1868, A-8, pp.50-51.

19. Newland, 'Campaign on the West Coast'; *Wellington Independent*, 14 Sept. 1868; Takiora [Lucy Grey], M.S. Account of Von Tempsky's Death, Taranaki Museum.

20. Gudgeon, *Reminiscences*, p.183.

21. Cowan, *Kimble Bent*, p.148.

22. Takiora, M.S. Account.

23. Account of Whakawhiria to T. G. Hammond, May 1909, Cowan, *Kimble Bent*, p.170. Maori numbers, *Kimble Bent*, pp.154, 169. Evidence of previously prepared firing-positions, Newland 'Campaign on the West Coast', & McDonnell's Report.

24. Account of Tutange Waionui, Cowan, *Kimble Bent*, pp.166-8.

25. Livingston, Diary, 7 Sept. 1868; Newland, 'Campaign on the West Coast'.

26. Newland, 'Campaign on the West Coast'; McDonnell's Report.

27. McDonnell's Report; account of Tutange Waionui, Cowan, *Kimble Bent*, p.167; accounts of Hirtzell, Scannell, & Shanaghan, Gudgeon, *Defenders*, pp.215-6, 391, 439-40.

28. Accounts of Tutange Waionui & Whakawhiria, Cowan, *Kimble Bent*, pp.154, 169; *New Zealand Advertiser*, 21 Sept. 1868.

29. McDonnell's Report, & Roberts to McDonnell, 9 Sept. 1868, *AJHR* 1868, A-8 pp.50-52; Newland, 'Campaign on the West Coast'; Letter of Men Wounded at Te Ngutu to McDonnell, 19 Sept. 1869, Thomas McDonnell Papers, ATL.

30. *New Zealand Advertiser*, 30 Sept. 1868, states that the *kupapa* chief Rewiti died of wounds received at Te Ngutu.

31. Cowan, *Wars*, II, p.244; *Wanganui Chronicle*, 14 Sept. 1868; Papers on the Mutiny of No. 5 Division, A.D. 32/5011; Whitmore, *Last Maori War*, p.31.

32. *Wellington Independent*, 4 July 1868.

33. Whitmore, letter to editor, *New Zealand Advertiser*, 28 Sept. 1868; N.Z. Correspondent of *The Times*, quoted in A. J. Harrop, *England and the Maori Wars*, London 1937, p.330; McDonnell to Haultain, 30 Sept. 1868, A.D. 1/5285.

34. Haultain, Memo, 3 Sept. 1868, A.D. 1/2957; McDonnell to Haultain, 22 Aug., 5 Sept. 1868, *AJHR* 1868, A-8, p.49 & A.D.1/3107; also McDonnell to Haultain, 12 Aug. 1868, A.D. 1/2791; *Wellington Independent*, 4 July, 25 Aug. 1868; *Wanganui Times* (Extra), 22 Aug. 1868.

35. McDonnell, *Explanation*, p.34; *cf.* McDonnell's Report, 9 Sept. 1868, *AJHR* 1868, pp.50-51; account of J. M. Roberts, in Cowan, *Wars*, II, p.210; D. Munro to Grey, 12 Mar. 1869, Grey Autograph Letters; Whitmore to Haultain, 27 Oct. 1868, A.D. 1/4182; *New Zealand Advertiser*, 2 Nov. 1868; *Wellington Independent*, 15 Sept. 1868.

36. e.g. Cowan, *Wars*, II, p.258 & *Kimble Bent*, p.158; Gibson, *The Maori Wars*, p.207; Holt, *Strangest War*, pp.251, 267.

37. Livingston, Diary, 7 Sept. 1868; also Gudgeon, *Reminiscences*, p.182.

38. Newland, 'Campaign on the West Coast'.

39. Compare strengths in McDonnell's Reports of 22 Aug., 9 Sept. 1868, *AJHR* 1868, A-8, pp.48-51; casualty list, ibid. pp.52-53.

40. Gudgeon, *Reminiscences*, p.186.

41. Gibson, *The Maori Wars*, p.201; Cowan, *Kimble Bent*, p.163.

42. Whitmore, *Last Maori War*, pp.60-61.

43. Titokowaru's numbers at the Battle of Moturoa on 7 Nov. were 100-150 (see note 54 below), but he may not have had his whole force there. Examples of high colonial estimates, Whitmore to Haultain, 27 Oct. 1868, A.D.1/4182; *New Zealand Advertiser*, 28 Oct. 1868.

44. Pay estimates, 23, 30 Oct. 1868, A.D. 1/3646, 3801.

45. *Last Maori War*, p.42.

46. Gorton & Booth to Haultain, 18 Oct. 1868, both in A.D. 1/3524.

47. [?] to Whitmore, 23 Oct. 1868, A.D. 1/3646.

48. Gorton to Whitmore, 1 Nov. 1868, *AJHR* 1869, A-3, p.5; Whitmore, *Last Maori War*, p.36.

49. Calculated from the effective strength of the units involved, making allowance for detachments. Pay estimates, note 44 above; Whitmore's Report, 7 Nov. 1868, *AJHR* 1869, A-3, pp.6-10. Note that No. 6 Division, A.C., 126 strong, arrived on 6 Nov. and is not included in the pay estimates.

50. Whitmore to Gorton, 7 Nov. 1868, A.D. 1/4182. Other quotations in this paragraph are from Whitmore's Report.

51. Whitmore originally claimed that his casualties were far lighter, but see Cowan, *Wars*, II, pp.258-9, particularly the statement of W. E. Gudgeon. Maori estimates of their own casualties, Cowan, *Kimble Bent*, p.209. The more reasonable colonial estimates were not much higher, e.g. *Wanganui Evening Herald*, 9 Nov. 1868.

52. e.g. account of William Wallace, Cowan Papers, 41E; account of J. M. Roberts, quoted in Cowan, *Wars*, II, p.258.

53. Cowan, *Wars*, II, p.258; Holt, *Strangest War*, p.251; also Gibson, *The Maori Wars*, p.207; Parham, *Roberts*, p.45.

54. Whitmore's Report, 7 Nov. 1868; Cowan, *Kimble Bent*, p.203 (Maori evidence).

55. Whitmore to Haultain, 8 Nov. 1868, Whitmore Papers, A; Whitmore to Gorton, 7 Nov. 1868, A.D. 1/4182; Whitmore's Report.
56. Whitmore to Haultain, 23, 25, 31 Oct 1868, A.D. 1/3646, 3708, 3731.
57. Whitmore's Report.
58. Maori descriptions of the fortification, Cowan, *Kimble Bent*, pp.199-203 (evidence of Bent and Tutange Waionui); account of Tu-Patea Te Rongo, Cowan Papers, 41E.
59. Gudgeon, *Reminiscences*, p.200; Newland, 'Campaign on the West Coast'; survivor quoted in Cowan, *Wars*, II, p.251.
60. Cowan, *Kimble Bent*, pp.202-3; account of Tu-Patea Te Rongo, Cowan Papers, 41E.
61. *Wanganui Chronicle*, 12 Nov. 1868; account of William Wallace, Cowan Papers, 41E. Contemporary account of Moturoa not cited above, John Gibson to Charles Edward Gibson, 18 Dec. 1868, John Gibson Letters, 1868, ATL.
62. *New Zealand Advertiser*, 18 Jan. 1869.
63. *Wanganui Times*, 10, 17 Sept. 1868; *Wanganui Evening Herald*, 14 Sept. 1868; *Wanganui Chronicle*, 19 Sept. 1868; *New Zealand Advertiser*, 30 Sept. 1868.
64. Haultain to Capt. Stapp, 18 Nov. 1868, A.D. 1/4054, & Sept.-Dec. series of telegrams in A.D. 8/1; Governor Bowen to the Duke of Buckingham, 7 Jan., 20 Mar. 1869, *P.P.* 1868-9 (307) XLIV, pp.326, 301.
65. *Wanganui Times*, 1 Oct. 1868; Featherston, quoted in *New Zealand Advertiser*, 4 Dec. 1868.
66. *New Zealand Advertiser*, 4 Dec. 1868.
67. Petition in *AJHR*, 1869, A-1, p.21; Bowen to Buckingham, 27 Nov. 1868, *P.P.* 1868-9, (307) XLIV, p.285; letter to *Wanganui Times*, 21 Jan. 1869; also *Weekly News*, 28 Nov. 1868; *New Zealand Advertiser*, 4 Dec. 1869; B. K. Taylor to CMS, 3 Oct. 1868, New Zealand Mission Letterbook, 1868-70, CN/M23, CMS.
68. McLean to Whitmore, 14 Dec. 1868, Whitmore Papers, A; Whitmore to Haultain, 25 Nov. 1868, Whitmore Collection, 2; Stafford to H. R. Russell, 25 Nov. 1868, A.D. 8/1:344; Chas. Stevens, Defence Office Memo., 23 Aug. 1869, McLean Papers, 45.
69. *New Zealand Advertiser*, 16 Nov. 1868.
70. *New Zealand Advertiser*, 28 Oct. 1868; *Weekly News*, 19 Dec. 1869.
71. *Wanganui Evening Herald*, 9 Nov. 1868.
72. Harrop, *England and the Maori Wars*, pp.332, 335.
73. R. Parris, Report, 1 Apr. 1868, *P.P.* 1868-9 (307) XLIV, p.187.
74. Parris to J. C. Richmond, 12 Aug. 1868, *AJHR* 1868, A-8, p.47.
75. *New Zealand Advertiser*, 2 Dec. 1868 (Taupo chief reporting Kingite proclamation, differently translated in McLean Papers, 21); also *New Zealand Advertiser*, 30 Sept., 16, 25, 30 Nov. 1868; St. George, Diary, 1864-9, v.3, 1 Aug. 1868, ATL. Ngati Maniapoto raid, ch.13, sect.II, below.
76. Quoted in *Weekly News*, 28 Nov. 1868 (Supplement).
77. Monro to Grey, 12 Mar. 1869, Grey Autograph Letters, M39A.
78. *New Zealand Advertiser*, 20 Nov. 1868; Bishop W. Williams to CMS, 1, 5 May, 26 July 1869, CN/O 96(c).
79. To CMS, 30 Nov. 1868, CN/O 96(c).
80. Whitmore to Haultain, 25 Nov. 1868, Whitmore Collection, 2; Gudgeon, *Reminiscences*, pp.202-3; Whitmore, *Last Maori War*, p.XXX.
81. Sinclair, *History of New Zealand*; W. H. Oliver, *The Story of New Zealand*, London 1960. Over ninety-five per cent of the first-year New Zealand history students at Victoria University of Wellington in 1983 and 1984 had never heard of Titokowaru.

13: The Turn of the Tide (pages 258-88)

1. Holt, *The Strangest War*, p.245.
2. 'Memorandum on Defence generally . . .', A.D. 1/4371.
3. Whitmore, Memo., 28 Nov. 1868, & to Haultain, 3 Dec. 1868, A.D. 1/4370, 4595; Haultain to Whitmore, 16 Dec. 1868, & to J. C. Richmond, 29 Dec. 1868, A.D. 8/1:472, 530; *New Zealand Advertiser*, 3 Jan. 1869.
4. Haultain to Whitmore, 27 Nov. 1868, Whitmore Papers, A; Haultain to J. C. Richmond, 9, 11

Dec. 1868, A.D. 8/1:430, 457.

5. [Maj. J. H. H. St. John], 'Journal of the seige of Ngatapa', Whitmore Papers, D.

6. Gascoyne, *Soldiering in New Zealand*, p.72.

7. *Weekly News*, 23 Jan. 1869.

8. St. John, 'Journal'; Whitmore, Report, 30 Dec. 1868, *AJHR* 1869, A-3, pp.16–17; J. C. Richmond to Haultain, 25 Dec. 1868, A.D. 1/5217; account of Wi Kingi, *AJHR* 1870, A-8B, pp.26–30. A correspondent with the Field Force wrote: 'In common with the most experienced of the officers, I put down their strength as about 150', *Weekly News*, 9 Jan. 1869.

9. *Weekly News*, 9 Jan. 1869; also Newland, 'Expedition to Turanganui, Poverty Bay', William Newland Papers, Taranaki Museum; Whitmore, reports, 16, 18 Dec. 1868, A.D. 1/5016, *AJHR* 1869, A-3, pp.15–16.

10. Gascoyne, *Soldiering in New Zealand*, pp.62–63; Gascoyne to Whitmore, 11 Dec. 1868, *AJHR* 1869, A-[3], pp.14–15.

11. Whitmore to Haultain, 11 Dec. 1868, A.D. 1/5017; Gudgeon, *Reminiscences*, p.246.

12. Whitmore to Haultain, 16 Dec. 1868, A.D. 1/5015.

13. Mackay, *Poverty Bay*, p.276; William Wells to Whitmore, 9 Jan. 1869, Whitmore Papers, A; Westrupp to McLean, 15 Dec. 1868, McLean Papers, 630.

14. McLean to W. L. Williams, 5 Dec. 1868, McLean Papers, 22, McLean to Haultain, both 28 Nov. 1868, A.D. 1/4438, 4374; McLean to Haultain, 7 Dec. 1868, A.D. 1/4699, & to J. C. Richmond, 12 Dec. 1868, McLean Papers, 22; Captain Buchanan to Haultain, 4 Dec. 1868, A.D. 1/4619.

15. Westrupp to McLean, 9 Dec. 1868, McLean Papers, 630.

16. McLean to J. C. Richmond, 29 Dec. 1868, & Edward L. Green (McLean's Secretary), Journal, 19 Jan. 1869 (paraphrasing Richmond), both McLean Papers, 22.

17. Whitmore to Haultain, 7 Dec. 1868, A.D. 1/4743.

18. McLean's influence, McLean to Whitmore, 14 Dec. 1868, Whitmore Papers, A; *Weekly News*, 9 Jan. 1869; McLean to Haultain, 18 Dec. 1868, to Lambert, 22 Dec. 1868, to Richmond 23 Dec. 1868, & Green, Journal, 19 Dec. 1868–7 Jan. 1869, all in McLean Papers, 22. The government veto, Haultain to McLean, 18 Dec. 1868, ibid. The failure of the Wairoa expedition, Lambert to Haultain, 1, 5 Jan. 1869, A.D. 1/49, 209.

19. W. L. Williams to McLean, 5 Dec. 1869, Whitmore to McLean, 12 Dec. 1868, McLean Papers 22, 635; *NZ Herald*, 24 Dec. 1869; *Weekly News*, 19 Dec. 1868.

20. Richmond to Whitmore, [?] Dec. 1868, Whitmore Papers, A; Westrupp to McLean, 20 Dec. 1868, McLean Papers, 630.

21. Haultain to Richmond, 16 Dec. 1868, A.D. 8/1:477; St. John, 'Return of forces at Ngatapa', Whitmore Papers, B.

22. J. C. Richmond to Whitmore, 19 Dec. 1868, Whitmore Papers, A; Gudgeon, *Reminiscences*, p.248.

23. St. John, 'Journal'; Whitmore's Reports, 30 Dec. 1868, 5 Jan. 1869, *AJHR* 1869, E-3, pp.16–17, 17–19; J. C. Richmond to Whitmore, [?] Dec. 1868, Whitmore Papers, A; Haultain to J. C. Richmond, 29 Dec. 1868, A.D. 1/8:530; *Hawke's Bay Herald*, 9 Jan. 1869, quoted in *Weekly News*, 16 Jan. 1869.

24. Eyewitness accounts of the fighting at Ngatapa, note 23 above; Whitmore's Report, 8 Jan. 1869, *AJHR* 1869, A-3, pp.19–20; *Weekly News*, 9, 16, 23 Jan. 1869; Newland, 'Expedition to Turanganui'; account of Wi Kingi, *AJHR* 1870, A-8B, pp.26–30; statement of Wi Tama, 25 Feb. 1869, McLean Papers, 23; account of Peita Kotuku, Cowan Papers, 41A.

25. Gudgeon, *Reminiscences*, p.252.

26. Richmond to Govt [5 Jan. 1869], *Weekly News*, 16 Jan. 1869; also Gascoyne, *Soldiering in New Zealand*, p.75; Porter, *Ropata*, p.29.

27. Bowen to Granville, 3 Apr. 1869, *P.P.* 1870 (307-1) XLIV, pp.2–3.

28. Whitmore to Haultain, 2 Feb. 1869, A.D. 1/645; *Wanganui Times*, 2, 4 Feb. 1869.

29. Whitmore, *Last Maori War*, p.131; also ibid, pp.123, 128; Booth to J. C. Richmond, 14 Mar. 1869, *AJHR* 1869, A-10, p.37; *Wanganui Times*, 18 Mar. 1869.

30. Cowan, *Wars*, II, pp.300–01.

31. Gascoyne, *Soldiering in New Zealand*, p.94; *cf.* Cowan, *Wars*, II, p.295 (evidence of Tu-Patea Te Rongo); Gudgeon, *Reminiscences*, p.261; *Wanganui Times*, 18 Mar. 1869. Other accounts of Otautu and the pursuit from Tauranga-ika, Whitmore's reports, 3 Feb.–29 Mar. 1869, *AJHR* 1869, A-[3]

(misprinted as A-12), pp.24-34; Whitmore to Haultain, 12 Mar. 1869, A.D. 1/1583; Whitmore to Haultain, 17 Feb.-26 Mar. 1869, Whitmore Collection, 2.

32. Booth to J. C. Richmond, 19 Mar. 1869, *AJHR* 1869, A-10, p.37.

33. Whitmore to Haultain, 26 Mar. 1869, Whitmore Collection, 2. Request for aborigine trackers, Whitmore to Haultain, 11 Mar. 1869, *AJHR* 1869, A-[3], p.30.

34. Parris to J. C. Richmond, 18 Feb. 1869, *AJHR* 1869, A-10, pp.47-48; Cowan, *Wars*, II, pp.304-10, 540-2.

35. Cowan, *Wars*, II, pp.308-9; Gudgeon, *Reminiscences*, p.259; H. R. Richmond to Haultain, 2 Apr. 1869, & encl., *AJHR* 1869, A-3F, pp.7-8.

36. Whitmore to Haultain, 8 [Apr. 1869], Whitmore Collection, 2.

37. Report of Lucy Grey, 20 Jan. 1870, McLean Papers, 48.

38. Distribution of troops, *AJHR* 1869, D-10. Operations, reports of Maj. Noake and Lt. Col. Lyon, 26 Apr.-7 May, 14 June 1869, *AJHR* 1869, A-[3], pp.44-48, A-3A, p.3.

39. Lucy Grey, report, 17 Sept. 1869, McLean Papers, 48; Capt. [?] to McLean, 9 Oct. 1870, ibid; also Lucy Grey, Reports, 27 Oct. 1869, 20 Jan. 1870, ibid.

40. Whitmore's Report, 3 Feb. 1869, *AJHR* 1869, A-[3], pp.22-23. The numbers of Titokowaru's rearguard, Cowan, *Kimble Bent*, p.257.

41. Cowan, *Kimble Bent*, p.256.

42. Gorton, *Some Home Truths*, p.104; *Wanganui Times*, 4 Feb. 1869. Other references to the strength of Tauranga-ika, Kepa to Whitmore, 21 Jan. 1869, A.D. 1/583; Gudgeon, *Reminiscences*, p.259; Cowan, *Kimble Bent*, pp.227-8.

43. Whitmore's Report, 3 Feb. 1869, *AJHR* 1869, A-[3], pp.22-23.

44. *Wanganui Times*, 4 Feb. 1869.

45. Whitmore to Haultain, 2 Dec. 1868, *AJHR* 1869 A-[3], p.13; *Wanganui Times*, 4 Feb. 1869.

46. A. G. Buist, 'The Maori', in K. W. Thomson, ed., *The Legacy of Turi; An Historical Geography of Patea County*, Palmerston North 1976, p.10. But see *Wanganui Times*, 20 Feb., 8 May 1869; Newland 'Campaign on the West Coast'; Whitmore's Report, 3 Feb. 1869.

47. Lucy Grey, report, 17 Sept. 1869, McLean Papers, 48.

48. Cowan, *Kimble Bent*, p.106.

49. Cowan, *Kimble Bent*, p.106.

50. Testimonial to Bent's veracity, T. W. R. Porter, 'The West Coast War', M.S. account in Cowan Papers, 41D.

51. Parris to J. C. Richmond, 4 Mar. 1869, *AJHR* 1869, A-10, p.51.

52. Cowan Papers, 41C.

53. Whitmore to Haultain, 11 Mar. 1869, Booth to J. C. Richmond, 14 Mar. 1869, *AJHR*, 1869, A-[3], p.30, A-10, p.37; also note 29 above; Parris to A. S. Atkinson, 24 June 1869, R-A.P., II, p.288.

54. Cowan, *Kimble Bent*, p.257.

55. *New Zealand Advertiser*, 16 Nov. 1868; *Wellington Independent*, 10 Sept. 1868; *New Zealand Advertiser*, 27 July 1868; E. Maxwell, quoted in Parham, *Roberts*, pp.101-2.

56. 21 Nov. 1868.

57. Cowan, *Kimble Bent*, pp.118, 229-30.

58. This incident was the subject of a celebrated court case in which John Bryce, a volunteer cavalry officer at Handley's Farm and later a cabinet minister, sued the historian G. W. Rusden for defamation. Bryce won, but only because Rusden over-estimated Bryce's personal responsibility for the Handley's Farm affair, and wrongly asserted that women, as well as boys, were among the killed. See [Rusden] *Tragedies in New Zealand in 1868 and 1881 . . .*, London 1888.

59. Livingston, Diary, 15 Dec. 1868.

60. W. Fox to McLean, 13 July 1869, McLean Papers, 278.

61. Fox to McLean, 28 Sept. 1868, McLean Papers, 278; *Wanganui Times*, 11, 23 Feb. 1869.

62. Stafford to Whitmore, 4 Feb. 1869, Whitmore Papers, A; Holt, *Strangest War*, p.254.

63. Gudgeon, *Defenders*, p.362.

64. G. W. Rusden, *Auretanga; Groans of the Maoris*, London 1888, p.55; Gudgeon, *Reminiscences*, p.268; also Frederick J. Moss, *School History of New Zealand*, Auckland 1889, p.237.

65. Westrupp to McLean, 12 Jan., 5 Feb. 1869, McLean Papers, 630.

66. W. G. Mair, Report, 23 Mar. 1869, *P.P.* 1870 (307-1) XLIV, pp.13-15; W. S. Atkinson to G.

Mair, 9 Feb. 1869, McLean Papers, 23.

67. Gudgeon, *Reminiscences*, pp.273-4 (citing Maori evidence).

68. Accounts of the raid, Haultain, Memo., 10 Apr. 1869, W. G. Mair, report, 23 Mar. 1869, *P.P.* 1870 (307-1) XLIV, pp.3-4, 13-15; *Southern Cross*, n.d. extract in *P.P.* 1868-9 (307) XLIV, pp.386-90; Andersen & Petersen, *The Mair Family*, pp.172-7; Featon, *Waikato War*, pp.196-7.

69. Gudgeon, *Reminiscences*, pp.286-9; account of Peita Kotuku, Cowan Papers, 41A; also *Wellington Independent*, 13 Apr. 1869; 'Military Operations at Mohaka', *AJHR* 1869, A-3C.

70. Haultain to Whitmore, 28 May 1869, Whitmore Papers, A; Whitmore to Pollen, 29 Apr. 1869, Whitmore Collection, 3; Gudgeon, *Reminiscences*, pp.270-1, 274-5; Lambert, *Old Wairoa*, p.634.

71. 'Reports by Mr Ormond relative to the Waikare-Moana Expedition', *AJHR* 1869, A-3E.

72. Whitmore, *Last Maori War*, pp.151-76; Gascoyne, *Soldiering in New Zealand*, pp.95-103; account of J. P. Ward, in Lambert, *Old Wairoa*, pp.639-50; Gudgeon, *Reminiscences*, pp.274-84; Featon, *Waikato War*, pp.199-201.

73. Gudgeon, *Reminiscences*, p.274.

74. Whitmore to Haultain, n.d., Whitmore Collection, 3; account of J. P. Ward, in Lambert, *Old Wairoa*, p.650.

75. Whitmore, *Last Maori War*, p.168.

76. Whitmore, *Last Maori War*, p.152; Whitmore to Haultain, 28 Apr. 1869, Whitmore Collection, 3. Taupo invitation to Te Kooti, account of Wi Kingi, *AJHR* 1870, A-8B, pp.26-30.

77. Gudgeon, *Reminiscences*, p.275.

78. Gudgeon, *Reminiscences*, pp.300-01; Cowan, *Wars*, II, pp.362-70; account of George Crosswell, 2 Feb. 1921, Cowan Papers 41D.

79. J. D. Ormond to McDonnell, 6 Sept. 1869, Thomas McDonnell Papers, ATL, 25.

80. Memo of speech by Maihi Pohepohe, *AJHR* 1870, A-8, p.5; also account of Wi Kingi, *AJHR* 1870, A-8B, pp.26-30; W. N. Searancke to McLean, 11 Aug. 1869, McLean Papers, 48; Searancke to Fox, 12 July 1869, *P.P.* 1870 (83) L, p.81; McLean's interview with Kingite chiefs, 9 Nov. 1869, *AJHR* 1870, A-12.

81. Ormond to Bell & to Fox, 6, 22 Oct. 1869, in Agents for the General Government, Hawke's Bay, Papers Relating to Te Kooti 1869-70, N. A. (hereafter AGG-HB7/3); 'Natives on Expedition. . .', *AJHR* 1870, A-8C.

82. J. C. St. George to Clarke, 19 Aug. 1869 (conveying report of spy), *AJHR* 1870, A-8, p.6; W. G. Mair to Civil Commissioner, Auckland, 30 Dec. 1869, *AJHR* 1870, A-8A, pp.19-20; account of Wi Kingi; Ormond to Lt. Col. Herrick, 6 Sept. 1869, AGG-HB7/3.

83. Account of Wi Kingi; Ormond to C.S., 13 Sept. 1869, *AJHR* 1870, A-8, p.11.

84. McDonnell to Ormond, 26 Sept. 1869, R. W. Woon to Native Dept., 6 Oct. 1869, both *AJHR* 1870, A-8, p.17; G. A. Preece, 'Notes for Major Gascoyne', AIM (ts. similar to that published in Gascoyne, *Soldiering in New Zealand*); account of Wi Kingi.

85. Account of Peita Kotuku, Cowan Papers, 41A; Colin D. Smart, 'The Te Porere Earthworks—A Description', in Wilson, *War in the Tussock*, pp.63-69.

86. Ngati Tuwharetoa casualties, W. G. Mair to Civil Comissioner, Auckland, 30 Dec. 1869, *AJHR* 1870, A-8A, pp.19-20. Contemporary accounts of Te Porere, Wilson, *War in the Tussock*, pp.52-60; account of Peita Kotuku, Cowan Papers, 41A; Preece, 'Notes for Major Gascoyne'; Christopher Maling to William Lingard, n.d., Cowan Papers, 41D.

87. *War in the Tussock*.

88. Gudgeon, *Reminiscences*, pp.323-4; also Ormond to McDonnell, 8 Jan. 1870, AGG-HB7/3; McLean to Ormond, 18 Nov. 1869, Ormond to McDonnell, 16 Nov. 1869, Booth to Fox, 10 Dec. 1869, all in *AJHR* 1870 A-8A, pp.5, 9, 16; account of Wi Kingi.

89. Unsigned Memo, 12 Jan. 1870, McLean Papers, 48.

90. McDonnell to McLean, 21 Jan. 1870, Commissioner Brannigan to McLean, 29 Jan. 1870, *AJHR* 1870, A-8A, pp.40, 53.

91. Hitiri Paerata to Te Kopu & Others, 16 Jan. 1870, *AJHR* 1870, A-8A, p.31; Ormond to S. Locke, 15 Jan. 1870, AGG-HB7/3.

92. Ormond to Fox, 19 Jan. 1870, AGG-HB7/3.

93. Account of Wi Kingi, *AJHR* A-8B, pp.24-30; McDonnell to McLean, 25 Jan. 1870, Topia Turoa & Others to Fox, 25-26 Jan. 1870, *AJHR* A-8A, pp.44-45, 46; McDonnell to Ormond, 25 Jan.

1870, AGG-HB7/3. Criticism of McDonnell's performance at Tapapa, McLean to McDonnell, 8 Mar. 1870, McDonnell Papers, 7.

94. Fraser to H. T. Clarke, 3 Feb. 1870, *AJHR* 1870, A-8A, p.52.

95. G. Mair to Clarke, 11 Feb. 1870, *AJHR* 1870, A-8A, pp.68-70; McLean to Ormond, 11 Feb. 1870, AGG-HB7/3; Andersen & Petersen, *The Mair Family*, pp.193-6.

96. Gudgeon, *Reminiscences*, p.334; also McLean to Kepa te Rangihiwinui, 19 Feb. 1870, *AJHR* 1870, A-8B, p.3.

97. Ropata, Memo., 11 Feb. 1870, *AJHR* 1870, A-8B, p.3.

98. Whakatohea chiefs to Clarke, 17 Mar. 1870, Te Kepa Rangipuawhe to McLean, 11 Mar. 1870, *AJHR* 1870, A-8B, pp.21-22, 5.

99. Statement of Tautata, n.d., *AJHR* 1871, F-1, pp.18-19.

100. Kepa to McLean, 30 Mar. 1870, *AJHR* 1870, A-8B, pp.24-25; also Topia Turoa to McLean, ibid., p.25.

101. Accounts of these operations and the other Urewera expeditions of 1870-72, Cowan, *Wars*, II, pp.401-67; Gudgeon, *Reminiscences*, pp.334-67; Reports in *AJHR* 1870, 1871, A-8B, F-1; Preece, 'Notes for Major Gascoyne'.

14: The Maori Achievement (pages 291-310)

1. Ashwell to CMS, 14 Apr. 1862, CN/O 19; Gorst, 'General Report on the State of Upper Waikato, June 1862', *AJHR* 1862, E-9, Sect. III.

2. Cowan, *Wars*, I, p.311; Wiseman to Admiralty, ADM. 1/5817 (L.113).

3. D. R. Headrick, *The Tools of Empire: Technology and European Imperialism in the Nineteenth Century*, New York, Oxford 1981, chap. 4-7; *cf.* Headrick, 'The Tools of Imperialism: Technology and the Expansion of European Colonial Empires in the Nineteenth Century', *Journal of Modern History*, 51, June 1979, pp.231-63.

4. Myatt, *The Soldier's Trade*, p.224.

5. Figures for the Somme calculated from statistics in Keegan, *The Face of Battle*, pp.235-6.

6. Richard Taylor, *Te Ika a Maui, or New Zealand and Its Inhabitants*, London 1855, p.350n.

7. Newman, 'A Study of the Causes Leading to the Extinction of the Maori', *TPNZI*, 14, 1882, p.447; *cf.* Dr Buller, 'The Decrease of the Maori Race', *N.Z. Journal of Science*, 2, 1885, pp.56-57; also R. T. Lange, 'The Revival of a Dying Race: A Study of Maori Health Reform, 1900-1918 and its Ninteeth-Century Background', Auckland Univ. M.A. thesis, 1972, pp.71-76.

8. Edward Tregear, *The Aryan Maori*, Wellington 1885; Smith, *Hawaiki: The Original Home of the Maori*, 2nd edn, Christchurch 1904; Macmillan Brown, *Maori and Polynesian/their Origin, History and Culture*, London 1907. An amusing example of criticism of the theory, A. S. Atkinson, 'The Aryo-Semitic Maori', *TPNZI* 19, 1887, pp.552-76. Modern discussions of the theory, M. P. K. Sorrenson, *Maori Origins and Migrations*, Auckland 1979, ch.1; Michael Belgrave, 'Archipelago of Exiles. A Study of the Imperialism of Ideas: Edward Tregear and John Macmillan Brown', Auckland Univ. M.A. thesis, 1979, esp. ch.2.

9. Tregear, *Aryan Maori*, p.103.

10. Owens, 'New Zealand before Annexation'; Ward, 'The Origins of the Anglo-Maori Wars', & *Show of Justice*; A. Parsonson, 'The Expansion of a Competitive Society: A Study in Nineteenth-Century Maori Social History', *NZJH* 14, 1980, pp.45-60, & 'The Pursuit of Mana'; Williams, *Politics of the New Zealand Maori*, Seattle 1969; Sorrenson, 'Land Purchase Methods and their effect on Maori population, 1865-1901', *JPS*, 14, 1956, pp.183-99, & 'The Maori King Movement', in R. M. Chapman and K. Sinclair, eds, *Studies of a Small Democracy*, pp.33-55. More revisionist work exists in unpublished theses.

11. Wright, *New Zealand 1769-1840: Early Years of Western Contact*, Cambridge, Mass. 1959. Explicit and implicit criticism of Wright, J. M. R. Owens, 'Christianity and the Maoris to 1840', *NZJH* 2, 1968, pp.18-40; Judith Binney, 'Christianity and the Maoris to 1840, a comment', *NZJH* 3, 1969, pp.143-65; Robin Fisher, 'Henry Williams' Leadership of the C.M.S. Mission to New Zealand', *NZJH* 9, 1975, pp.142-53.

12. Ward, *Show of Justice*, p.136.

13. Speech of Reihana, quoted in F. D. Bell to T. Russell, 15 Mar. 1863, McLean Papers, 14.

14. Robinson, 'Non-European Foundations of European Imperialism: Sketch for a Theory of Collaboration', in R. Owen & B. Sutcliffe, eds, *Studies in the Theory of Imperialism*, London 1972.
15. Sorrenson, 'Maori and Pakeha', in *Oxford History of N.Z.*, p.186.
16. Sorrenson, 'The Maori King Movement'.
17. Ann Parsonson, 'King Tawhiao and the New Maori Monarchy, 1878-1882', Paper presented to the Conference of New Zealand Historians, Wellington, May 1972, pp.21-22.
18. B. J. Foster, 'King Country', *Encyclopaedia of N.Z.*, II, pp.233-4.
19. McLean, Memo to Ministry, 4 Mar. 1871, & Tapihana's Speech to McLean at Kawhia, 1873, both quoted in James Cowan, *Sir Donald McLean*, Dunedin, Wellington 1940, pp.115, 117-8.
20. Williams, *Politics of the N.Z. Maori*, pp.91-96.
21. Cowan, *Wars* II, p.485. Details of the Parihaka expedition, Dick Scott, *Ask That Mountain/The Story of Parihaka*, Auckland 1975, esp. chs 6 & 7. One striking example of colonist fear of Titokowaru, Diary of Corporal William Parker, 7 Nov. 1881, quoted in Scott, *Ask That Mountain*, p.120.
22. Sorrenson, 'Maori and Pakeha', pp.192-3.
23. Williams, *Politics of the N.Z. Maori*, pp.41-46.
24. Sorrenson, 'The Maori King Movement', p.55.
25. J. Henderson, *Ratana; The Origins and the Story of the Movement*, Wellington 1963, pp.21-22.
26. Ward, *Show of Justice*, pp.278, 291.
27. Maning to Hugh Lusk, 6 July 1864, Maning Papers, 27.
28. Ward, *Show of Justice*, pp.206-7, 278, 295, 300.
29. Quoted in Williams, *Politics of the N.Z. Maori*, p.62.
30. Ward, *Show of Justice*, pp.208-10.
31. Michael King, 'Between Two Worlds', in *Oxford History of N.Z.*, pp.288-90.
32. Peter Webster, *Rua and the Maori Millenium*, Wellington 1979, pp.243-61.
33. Calculated from unpublished tables compiled by Miles Fairburn & S. J. Haslett, Victoria University of Wellington. Sources: *Annual Statistics of New Zealand* and *New Zealand Official Yearbooks*. Tables and print-outs kindly provided by Miles Fairburn. Also Ward, *Show of Justice*, pp.240, 246; C. Lesley Andrews, 'Aspects of Development, 1870-1890', in I. H. Kawharu, ed. *Conflict and Compromise/Essays on the Maori since Colonisation*, Wellington 1975, p.87.

15: The Victorian Interpretation of Racial Conflict (pages 311-35)

1. 'H', 'On Maori Courage', *Southern Monthly Magazine*, Dec. 1863, p.244.
2. Two interesting exceptions to this rule, Rev. J. Whitely to Grey, 20 May 1863, Grey Autograph Letters, W34; [A. S. Atkinson], 'Diary of a Volunteer', 28 Mar. 1860, R-A.P., I, p.560.
3. *Punch, or the Wellington Charivari*, 17 Aug. 1868.
4. R. Maunsell to CMS, 30 Nov. 1863, CN/O 64(b).
5. *New-Zealander*, 3 Oct. 1860; *N.Z. Journal*, 30 Aug. 1845.
6. *Weekly News*, 5 Dec. 1868; *The Times*, 20 Dec. 1860.
7. Carey, *The Late War in N.Z.*, p.118; *The Times*, 13 Dec. 1860 (Letter from Taranaki); 'Samuel Mitchell and the Victoria Cross'; Greaves, *Memoirs*, p.109.
8. *NZ Herald*, 15 Jan. 1864.
9. Despard to FitzRoy, 12 July 1845, W.O. 1/433, p.1050.
10. e.g. Whisker, 'Memorandum Book', p.121; *Wellington Independent*, 20 Mar. 1860; Robert Ward, *Life Among the Maoris*, p.375; *New-Zealander*, 26 Nov. 1864; G. J. Garland, 'Notes from Memory', 19 Nov. 1937, APL.
11. Warre to Ast. Mil. Sec., 29 April 1864 (Confidential), C.O. 209/180, p.75.
12. e.g. Ware to 'Friend John Robinson', 16 Jan. 1861; 'te Kingi' & others to [?],17 Jan. 1861, McLean Papers, 13; account of Wi Kingi, *AJHR* 1870, A-8B, pp.28-29.
13. *Nelson Examiner*, 11 April 1860; Carey, *The Late War in N.Z.*, p.66; Von Tempsky, 'Memoranda', p.140.
14. Whitmore to Def. Min., 12 Mar. 1864, A.D. 1/1583.
15. Grey, 'Memorandum on the mode in which military operations can most advantageously be carried out in New Zealand', W.O. 1/526, p.137.

16. Harries-Jenkins, *The Army in Victorian Society*, pp.65-66; Alan Sheppard, *Sandhurst: The Royal Military College and its Predecessors*, London 1980, pp.80-81.
17. Greaves, *Memoirs*, p.95, & Haig's Preface, pp.v-vi.
18. Hight, 'The Maori Wars 1843-1872', *Cambridge History of the British Empire*, VII, Pt 2, p.120.
19. DQMG Journals, pp.105, 136.
20. Cowan, *Wars*, I, p.3; *Hero Stories*, p.vii. Hamilton-Browne's works included *Camp Fire Yarns of the Lost Legion*, London n.d., as well as *With the Lost Legion in New Zealand*.
21. *Southern Cross*, n.d.[April 1869], extract in *P.P.* 1868-9 (307) XLIV, pp.386-90.
22. Thomas Carlyle, 'The English', in *Past and Present*, London 1845, p.215.
23. William White, editorial comment, in *Memorials of Sergeant Marjouram*, p.225; *Sydney Morning Herald*, 12 July 1860.
24. S. Bannister, *Humane Policy or Justice to the Aborigines of the New Settlements*, London 1968, orig. 1830, p.15. Bannister cited this as the majority view; he himself disagreed with it.
25. Michael Banton, *The Idea of Race*, London 1977, p.48.
26. e.g. Mr Donnelly, statement in Legislative Council, 13 Mar. 1845, *Southern Cross*, 15 Mar. 1845; T. Gore Browne, quoted in Sinclair, *Origins of the Maori Wars*, p.146; F. Von Hochstetter, *New Zealand*, Stuttgart 1867, German orig. 1863, pp.215, 220; Insp. Gen. J. Mouat, *The New Zealand War of 1863-64-65/Special Report on Wounds and Injuries Received in Battle* [London 1866?], p.54; 'Taranaki', *Saturday Review*, 3 Dec. 1864; 'A Visitor's Impression of New Zealand', *Southern Cross*, 6 Aug. 1863; *Sydney Morning Herald*, 18 Apr. 1860 (editorial); Thomson, *The Story of New Zealand*, II, p.283.
27. Von Tempsky, 'Memoranda', p.176; 'A Volunteer', letter in *Sydney Morning Herald*, 13 July 1860; *Wanganui Chronicle*, 14 July 1868.
28. Farrar, 'Aptitudes of Races', 1867, reprinted in Michael D. Biddiss, ed., *Images of Race*, Leicester, 1979, p.151; also Reginald Horsman, *Race and Manifest Destiny*, Harvard 1981, pp.120, 126, 128, 131; Banton, *Idea of Race*, p.48.
29. A. R. Wallace, 'The Origin of Human Races', 1864, reprinted in Biddiss, ed. *Images of Race*, p.47; also Charles Darwin, *The Descent of Man, and Selection in Relation to Sex*, 2nd edn, London 1888, p.197; J. C. Greene, *Science, Ideology and the World View*, Berkeley 1981, ch.5, esp. pp.100, 103; Herbert Spencer, 'The Comparative Psychology of Man', 1867, reprinted in Biddiss, *Images of Race*, pp.189-204; James G. Kennedy, *Herbert Spencer*, Boston 1978, p.147 fn.24; F. Galton, *Hereditary Genius: an Inquiry into its Causes and Consequences*, 2nd edn, London 1892, p.327.
30. Whately, 'On the Origin of Civilisation', in *Miscellaneous Lectures and Reviews*, London 1856, p.39, cf. pp.38, 45; James Cowles Prichard, *Researches into the Physical History of Man*, ed. George W. Stocking, Chicago, London 1973, esp. Intro., pp.lvi-lvii; Lawrence, quoted in Philip D. Curtin, *The Image of Africa*, London 1965, p.232; Lubbock, *The Origin of Civilisation and the Primitive Condition of Man*, ed. Peter Riviere, Chicago, London 1978, pp.4, 5, 291.
31. Bolt, *Victorian Attitudes to Race*, London, Toronto 1971, p.25.
32. *Otago Witness*, 20 Oct. 1860, quoted in Wilton, 'The South Island and the Taranaki War', p.145; Colenso, 'On the Maori Races of New Zealand', *TPNZI*, 1, 1868, p.339; R. Taylor, *Te Ika a Maui*, p.11; B. K. Taylor to CMS, 8 Mar. 1866, CN/O 86; Thomson, *Story of New Zealand*, I, pp.81-82.
33. Horsman, *Race and Manifest Destiny*, pp.156-7; Curtin, *The Image of Africa*, p.383; Alvar Ellegard, *Darwin and the General Reader; the Reception of Darwin's Theory of Evolution in the British Periodical Press 1859-1872*, Goteborg 1958.
34. Burrow, *Evolution and Society/A Study in Victorian Social Theory*, Cambridge 1966; Poliakov, *The Aryan Myth/A History of Racist and Nationalist Ideas in Europe*, Sussex 1974, orig. 1971; Lorimer, *Colour, Class and the Victorians*, Leicester 1978.
35. William Yate, *Account of New Zealand*, p.294.
36. Charles Hursthouse, *Emigration: Where to Go and Who Should Go*, London 1852, p.42; also William Brown, *New Zealand and its Aborigines*, 2nd edn, London 1851, esp. pp.104-09; John Ward, *Information Relative to New Zealand*, 2nd edn, London 1840, pp.60-95.
37. *Southern Cross*, 7 Aug. 1863.
38. G. A. Selwyn to William Selwyn, 31 Aug. 1863, Tucker, *Life of Selwyn*, II, pp.188-9; William Williams to CMS, 14 Aug. 1863, CN/O 96(c); R. Maunsell to CMS, 1 Jan. 1864, CN/O 64(b); B. Y. Ashwell to CMS, [3?] Sept. 1863, 26 Nov. 1863, CN/O 19; R. Burrows to CMS, 30 June

1864, CN/O 8(c). for confiscation see, R. Burrows to CMS, 30 June 1864, ibid.

39. Mouat, *War in New Zealand*, p.54. Similar example of this view, Von Hochstetter, *New Zealand*, p.215.

40. *New Zealand Examiner*, 15 Apr. 1861; F. E. Maning to A. H. Maning, 7 June 1844, Maning Papers, 1; Swainson, *New Zealand and the War*, p.141.

41. M. P. K. Sorrenson, 'Maori and Pakeha', in *The Oxford History of New Zealand*, p.184; Simpson, *Te Riri Pakeha*, p.141.

42. Von Tempsky, 'Memoranda', p.169; Pickard, Journal, 17 June 1861.

43. White (editorial comment) in *Memorials of Sergeant Marjouram*, p.226. On the use of 'nigger', J. E. Gorst wrote 'This epithet is freely applied to the Natives of New Zealand by colonists and especially by the officers of our regiments', *The Times* [24 Dec. 1863], quoted in *New-Zealander*, 27 Feb. 1864. Also Alexander, *Incidents of the Maori War*, p.125; H. Ronalds, Diary, 13 Mar. 1860, *R-A.P.*, I, p.535; M. S. Grace, *Sketch of the N.Z. War*, pp.114-5. The Imperial soldiers' attitude to non-Europeans in general, Farwell, *For Queen and Country*, pp.90-91, 108-9.

44. Examples of the belief that New Zealand settlers were a cut above those of Australia, Harriet Gore Browne to C. W. Richmond, 8 Jan. 1862, *R-A.P.*, I, p.739; G. A. Henty, *Maori and Settler*, London, Glasgow n.d., pp.26-27. The use of 'infant Hercules', *NZ Journal*, 11 Oct. 1845 and *Southern Cross*, 3 July 1860.

45. William B. Cohen, *The French Encounter with Africans: White Responses to Blacks 1530-1880*, Bloomington 1980; Horsman, *Manifest Destiny*.

46. Ranger, 'Connexions between "Primary Resistance" Movements and Modern Mass Nationalism in East and Central Africa', *Journal of African History*, IX, 3 & 4 (1968).

47. Calwell, *Small Wars; Their Principles and Practice*, 2nd edn, London 1899, pp.50, 62; Falls, *The Art of War: From the Age of Napoleon to the Present Day*, London 1961, pp.83-84; Gann, *Guerillas in History*, Hoover Instit. Press, 1971, p.40.

48. Michael Crowder, ed., *West African Resistance: The Military Response to Colonial Occupation*, London 1971, intro., p.15; Walter Laqueur, *Guerilla: An Historical and Critical Study*, London 1977, p.69. Laqueur seems to place unusual emphasis on Titokowaru (or so a respectful New Zealand reviewer once stated), but in fact he simply confuses him with Te Kooti (p.77).

49. Guy, *The Destruction of the Zulu Kingdom—The Civil War in Zululand 1879-1884*, London 1979, p.xix.

50. e.g. the only evidence Guy cites (*Zulu Kingdom*, p.79) to support his assertion that Zulu casualties were much lower than has been assumed is that of General Garnet Wolseley. Wolseley had his own reasons for presenting Ulundi as something less than a final triumph. The British were 5,300 strong and were armed with breech loaders, but they fired only 35,000 rounds, Donald R. Morris, *The Washing of the Spears*, London 1981, pp.565, 571.

Bibliography

A: PRIMARY SOURCES

1. UNPUBLISHED SOURCES

Alexander Turnbull Library, Wellington

Armstrong, J. H. Letters, 1859-65.

Atkinson, A. S. Diary, 1859-60.

Battiscombe, Lieut. A. H. W. 'Journal kept during the Maori War, 1860-61'.

Bridge, Maj. Cyprian. 'Journal of Events on An Expedition to New Zealand. Commencing on 4 April 1845' (1845-6).

Cowan, James. Papers (including transcripts of interviews with Maori and European veterans).

'Diary of a British Soldier', 7 May [1863]-6 March 1867.

Gibson, John. Letters, 1868.

Jenkins, Capt. Robert. Log of H.M.S. *Miranda*, 1861-3, 1863-5.

McDonnell, Lieut.-Col. Thomas. Papers.

McLean, Donald. Papers.

Mair, Capt. Gilbert. Diaries and Notebooks, 1861-5.

Maning, F. E. Papers.

Morris [Morete], Maria. 'Recollections of the Poverty Bay Campaign'.

Nicholls, Ensign Spencer Percival. Diary, 1863-4.

St. George, Capt. J. C. Diaries, 1864-9.

Warre, Col. H. J. 'Notes and Papers re military Matters'.

Whitmore, Col. George Stoddart. Collection.

Auckland Institute and Museum

Carberry, Surgeon Andrew Dillon. Journal, 1863-6.

Chapman, ?. Diary 1837-63.

Meurant, Edward. 'Account of a Meeting with Heke', 1-9 Oct. 1846.

Mitchell, Sgt. John. Diary of Service, 1845.

Pasley, Maj. Charles. Letters, 1853-61.

Preece, Capt. G. A. 'Notes for Major Gascoyne'.

Von Tempsky, Maj. G. F. 'Memoranda of the New Zealand Campaign in 1863-4'.

Whisker, Pvte. Alexander. 'Memorandum Book', 1844-50.

Auckland Public Library

Burrows, Robert. Letter to ?, 6 Sept. 1845.

Clendon, J. R. Journal, 1839-72.

FitzRoy-Grey Letterbook, 1845-53.

Garland, G. J. 'Notes from Memory', 19 Nov. 1937.

Graham, George. 'Heke's intended attack on Waitemata (1847): copy of notes thereof obtained from Whatarangi of Aki-tai-ui; 1891'.

Grey, George. Letters to Ormus Biddulph, 1862-8.

Heke, Hone Wiremu. Letter to Gilbert Mair, snr, 16 Oct. 1844.

Meurant, Edward. Diaries, 1842-7.

Auckland Public Library — Grey Collection

Cameron, Lieut.-Gen. Duncan. Letters to Sir George Grey.
FitzRoy-Beckham Correspondence, 1845-6.
Fulloon, J. Letters to Military Officers, Oct. 1863.
Grey, George. Autograph Letter Collection.
Grey, George. 'Papers Relating to certain allegations respecting the treatment of native prisoners of war, during the Maori War, 1866'.
McDonnell, Lieut.-Col. Thomas. 'Account of a Reconnaissance of Paparata'.
Papers Relating to the Forest Rangers, 1863-1886.
Stewart, R. O. Letters to the Native Minister, 1863.

British Library, London

Gladstone Papers, Addit. MSS 43512, 44166, 44532, 44535.
Owen, R. Correspondence, Addit. MSS 39954 (Letters from William and Mary-Ann Martin).
Ripon Papers, Vol.XXIII, Addit. MSS 43513.

Canterbury Museum, Christchurch

Sewell, Henry. Journal, 1859-65.

Church Missionary Society Archives, London

Ashwell, B. Y. Letters 1835-80, CN/O 19.
Burrows, Robert. Journal 1845, CN/O 27(b).
Burrows, Robert. Letters of Mission Secretaries 1842-50, CN/O 8(b).
Burrows, Robert. Letters of Mission Secretaries 1851-69, CN/O 8(c).
Hadfield, Octavius. Letters 1838-69, CN/O 57.
Lanfear, Thomas. Letters and Journals 1849-64, CN/O 57.
Maunsell, Robert. Letters 1850-77, CN/O 64(b).
Morgan, John. Letters 1833-65, CN/O 65(a).
New Zealand Mission Letterbook 1868-70, CN/M 23.
Taylor, Basil K. Letters 1861-78, CN/O 86.
Telford, John. Letters 1840-50, CN/O 88.
Williams, Henry. Letters 1836-47, CN/O 94(b).
Williams, William. Letters 1863-76, CN/O 96(c).
Williams, W. L. Letters 1857-80, CN/O 97.
Wilson, John Alexander. Letters 1833-65, CN/O 98.

Hawke's Bay Museum, Napier

Kempthorne, Arthur. Journal of Events in Poverty Bay, 1868.
Pickard, Lieut. Arthur Frederick. Journal, 21 Nov. 1860-26 Nov. 1863.
[St. John, Lieut.-Col. J. H. H.] 'Journal of the Siege of Ngatapa', Whitmore Papers.
Whitmore, Col. G. S. Papers.

Mitchell Library, Sydney

Mair, Maj. W. G. Letterbook, 23 Mar. 1868-31 Nov. 1869 (from notes made by Judith Binney).

National Archives, Wellington

Agent for the General Government, Hawke's Bay. Papers relating to Te Kooti, 1869-70, AGG-HB. 7/3.
Army Department. Inwards Letters and Registered Files, 1868-70, A.D. 1/-.

Army Department. Outwards Telegrams, 1864–8, A.D. 8/-.
Army Department. Registers of Inwards Correspondence, 1868–70.
Browne, T. Gore. Papers (some volumes missing).
Governor. Military Letters 1863–4, G16.
Morgan, John. Letters to Governor Browne, Gore Browne Papers.

Public Record Office, London

Admiralty. Despatches from the Australian Station 1863–4, ADM. 1/5817 and 1/5868.
Admiralty. Captain's Log, H.M.S. *Hazard*, ADM. 52/5613.
Admiralty. Captain's Log, H.M.S. *Eclipse*, ADM. 135/147.
Colonial Office. Despatches to the Secretary of State, including draft outwards despatches, internal minutes, and memoranda:
— (1845–6) C.O. 209/134–6.
— (1860–65) C.O. 209/153–90.
War Office. Despatches to the Secretary of State and the Military Secretary, including internal minutes and memoranda:
— (1845–6) W.O. 1/433–4, 6/96.
— (1860–5) W.O. 33/10, 33/12, 33/17A, 33/8254–85.
War Office. Original Journals of the Deputy Quartermaster-General in New Zealand, 7 Jan. 1862–6 May 1865, W.O. 107/7.
War Office. 'Journals of the Deputy Quartermaster-General in New Zealand from 24 Dec. 1861 to 13 Oct. 1865', W.O. 33/16.
War Office. 'Selections from Despatches and Letters Relative to the Conduct of Military Operations in New Zealand, 1861–5', W.O. 33/16.

Rhodes House Library, Oxford

Burns, David. Letters 1849–53.
Williams, E. T. Transcripts from various New Zealand archives including Native Department minutes and memoranda, 1861–3.

Royal Commonwealth Society Library, London

Despard, Col. Henry. Letterbook, 1846–54.

Taranaki Museum, New Plymouth

Grayling, William. 'Journal of Events of the War at Taranaki'.
New Plymouth Provincial Council. Letterbook, Apr.-Nov. 1860.
Newland, Capt. William. 'The Campaign on the West Coast North Island against Titoko Waru June 1866 to the end of 1869'.
Newland, Capt. William. 'Expedition to Turanganui, Poverty Bay'.
Takiora [Lucy Grey]. Account of Von Tempsky's Death.

Wanganui Museum

Livingston, Sgt. James. Diary, 9 June 1868 to 3 Jan. 1869 (ed. J. Houston).
McDonnell, Capt. William. Papers.

II NEWSPAPERS

Auckland Times, 1845.
(Daily) Southern Cross, 1844–5, 1860–5.
Hawke's Bay Herald, 1868.
Nelson Examiner, 1860.
New-Zealander, 1845–6, 1860, 1863–4.
New Zealand Advertiser, 1868–9.

New Zealand Examiner, 1860-1.
New Zealand Herald, 1863-4, 1869.
New Zealand Journal, 1845.
New Zealand Spectator and Cook's Straits Guardian, 1844-5.
Punch, or the Wellington Charivari, 1868.
Sydney Morning Herald, 1860-1, 1864, 1868.
Taranaki Herald, 1860-1.
Taranaki Punch, 1860.
Wanganui Chronicle, 1868.
Wanganui Evening Herald, 1868.
Wanganui Times, 1868-9.
Weekly News, 1868-9.
Wellington Independent, 1864, 1868-9.
The Times, 1845-6, 1860-1, 1864.

III. PUBLISHED DOCUMENTS AND OFFICIAL PUBLICATIONS

Appendices to the Journals of the House of Representatives, New Zealand, 1860-73.
Journals of the House of Representatives, New Zealand, 1863-4.
McNab, Robert (ed.). *Historical Records of New Zealand*, 2v., Wellington, 1908.
New Zealand Government Gazette, 1860-4.
New Zealand Parliamentary Debates, 1858-69.
Parliamentary Papers, Great Britain. (Papers relating to New Zealand) 1844-70.
Scholefield, G. H. (ed.). *The Richmond-Atkinson Papers*, 2 v., Wellington, 1960.

IV: EARLY PUBLISHED WORKS

Alexander, J. E. *Bush Fighting. Illustrated by Remarkable Actions and Incidents of the Maori War in New Zealand*, London, 1873.
Alexander, J. E. *Incidents of the Maori War, New Zealand, in 1860-1*, London, 1863.
Alexander, J. E. *Notes on the Maoris, with Suggestions for their Pacification and Preservation*, London, 1865.
Atkinson, A. S. 'The Aryo-Semitic Maori', *TPNZI*, v.19 (1887).
Bannister, S. *Humane Policy or Justice to the Aborigines of the New Settlements*, London, 1968 (orig. 1830).
Barrett, Alfred. *Life of the Rev. John Hewgill Bumby with a Brief History of the Commencement and Progress of the Wesleyan Mission in New Zealand*, London, 1853.
Bell, F. D., F. Whitaker, and T. Gore Browne. *Notes on Sir William Martin's Pamphlet Entitled The Taranaki Question*, Auckland, 1861.
Biddiss, Michael D. (ed.). *Images of Race*, Leicester, 1979.
Blake, A. Hope. *Sixty Years in New Zealand*, Wellington, 1909.
Bodell, James. *A Soldier's View of Empire. The Reminiscences of James Bodell*, ed. Keith Sinclair, London, 1982.
Boldrewood, Rolf. *War to the Knife, or Tangata Maori* (novel), London, 1899.
Brown, J. Macmillan. *Maori and Polynesian, their Origin, History and Culture*, London, 1907.
Brown, William. *New Zealand and Its Aborigines*, 2nd ed., London, 1851.
Browne, H. L. G. *Narrative of the Waitara Purchase and The Taranaki War*, ed. W. P. Morrell, Dunedin, 1965.
Buddle, T. *The Maori King Movement . . . with a Full Report of the Native Meetings Held at Waikato, April and May 1860*, Auckland, 1860.
Buller, Dr. W. 'The Decrease of the Maori Race', *New Zealand Journal of Science*, v.2 (1885).
Burrows, R. *Extracts from a Diary Kept by the Rev. R. Burrows During Heke's War in the North in 1845*, Auckland, 1886.
Calwell, C. E. *Small Wars: Their Principles and Practice*, 2nd ed., London, 1899.

A Campaign on the West Coast. . . . under the command of Major-General Chute, Wanganui, 1866.

Campbell, John Logan. *Poenamo,* Golden Press ed., 1973 (orig. 1881).

Carey, Robert. *Narrative of the Late War in New Zealand,* London, 1863.

Carleton, Hugh. *The Life of Henry Williams, Archdeacon of Waimate,* 2v., Auckland, 1874.

Carlyle, Thomas. *Past and Present,* London, 1845.

Clarke, George Jr. *Notes on Early Life in New Zealand,* Hobart, 1903.

Coleman, J. N., *A Memoir of the Reverend Richard Davis,* London, 1865.

Colenso, William. 'On the Maori Races of New Zealand', *TPNZI.* v.1 (1868).

Collinson, T. B. *Remarks on the Military Operations in New Zealand,* [n.p., 1853].

Darwin, Charles. *The Descent of Man, and Selection in Relation to Sex,* 2nd. ed., London, 1888.

Davis, C. O. *The Renowned Kawiti and Other New Zealand Warriors,* Auckland, 1855.

Davis, C. O. *The Life and Times of Patuone, the Celebrated Ngapuhi Chief,* Auckland, 1876.

Despard, Henry. 'Narrative of an Expedition into the Interior of New Zealand', *Colborn's United Services Magazine,* 213-216 (Aug.-Nov. 1846).

Duperry, Louis Isidor. *Duperry's Visit to New Zealand in 1824,* ed. Andrew Sharp, Wellington, 1971.

'Ensign McKenna and the Victoria Cross', British periodical article, c.1864, source unknown, copy in ATL.

Farrar, Frederic William. 'Aptitudes of Races', in Biddiss (ed.) *Images of Race.*

Featon, John. *The Waikato War 1863-4, Together With Some Account of Te Kooti Rikirangi,* Revised ed., Auckland, 1923.

Fenton, F. D. *Observations on the State of the Aboriginal Inhabitants of New Zealand,* Auckland, 1859.

FitzRoy, Robert. *Remarks on New Zealand,* London, 1846.

Foljambe, C. G. S. *Three Years on the Australian Station,* London, 1868.

Fox, William. *The War in New Zealand,* London, 1866.

Fyler, A. E. *The History of the 50th Regiment,* London, 1895.

Galton, F. *Hereditary Genius: an Inquiry into its Causes and Consequences,* 2nd ed., London, 1892.

Gascoyne, F. J. W. *Soldiering in New Zealand, Being the Reminiscences of a Veteran,* London, 1916.

Gilbert, Rev. Thomas. *New Zealand Settlers and Soldiers, or the War in Taranaki, Being Incidents in the Life of a Settler,* London, 1861.

Gorst, John. *The Maori King,* ed. Keith Sinclair, Hamilton and London, 1959 (orig. 1864).

Gorton, Edward, *Some Home Truths Re the Maori War 1863-9,* London, 1901.

Grace, Morgan S. *A Sketch of the New Zealand War,* London, 1899.

Grayling, W. I. *The War in Taranaki During the Years 1860-1861,* New Plymouth, 1862.

Greaves, George. *Memoirs of General Sir George Richard Greaves,* London, 1924.

Gretton, G. Le M. *Campaigns and History of the Royal Irish Regiment 1648-1902,* [n.p., 1911].

Gudgeon, T. W. *The Defenders of New Zealand,* Auckland, 1887.

Gudgeon, T. W. *Reminiscences of the War in New Zealand,* London, 1879.

'H.' 'On Maori Courage', *Southern Monthly Magazine,* Dec. 1863.

Hadfield, Octavius. *One of England's Little Wars. . . ,* London, 1860.

Hadfield, Octavius. *The New Zealand War. The Second Year of One of England's Little Wars,* London, 1861.

Hamilton-Browne, G. *Campfire Yarns of the Lost Legion,* London, n.d.

Hamilton-Browne, G. *With the Lost Legion in New Zealand,* London, n.d.

Hattaway, Robert. *Reminiscences of the Northern War,* Auckland, 1889.

Hawthorne, James. *A Dark Chapter from New Zealand History,* Napier, 1869, Capper Reprint, 1974.

Henderson, G. C. *Sir George Grey. Pioneer of Empire in Southern Lands,* London and New York, 1907.

Henty, G. A. *Maori and Settler; a Story of the New Zealand War* (novel), London and Glasgow, n.d.

'Heroes of the Victoria Cross in New Zealand', British periodical article, c.1864, source unknown, copy in A.T.L.

Hunt, James. 'On the Negro's Place in Nature', *Memoirs Read Before the Anthropological Society of London*, v.1 (1863-4).

Hursthouse, Charles. *Emigration: Where to Go and Who Should Go*, London, 1852.

Jupp, George. *Diary of George Jupp 1861-1872*, 3v., New Plymouth, n.d.

Kerry-Nicholls, J. H. *The King Country, or Explorations in New Zealand*, London, 1884.

'J.H.K.' *Henry Ancrum. A Tale of the Last War in New Zealand* (novel), London, 1872.

Lambert, Thomas. *The Story of Old Wairoa*, Dunedin, 1925.

Levinge, Richard G. A. *Historical Records of the Forty Third Regiment, Monmouthshire Light Infantry*, London, 1868.

Lubbock, John. *The Origin of Civilisation and the Primitive Condition of Man*, ed. Peter Riviere, Chicago and London, 1978.

McDonnell, Thomas. *An Explanation of the Principle Causes Which Led to the Present War on the West Coast . . .*, Wanganui, 1869.

McDonnell, Thomas. 'General Chute's Campaign on the West Coast', *Monthly Review*, v.2 (1890).

McDonnell, Thomas. 'Maketu and the Battle of Matata: the Attack on the East Coast Tribes', *Monthly Review*, v.2 (1890).

McDonnell, Thomas. 'A Maori History of the Pakeha-Maori Wars in New Zealand', in T. W. Gudgeon, *The Defenders of New Zealand*.

McDonnell, Thomas. 'Personal Courage of the Maori', *Monthly Review*, v.1 (1888-9).

McDonnell, Thomas. 'The Survey of the Confiscated Lands. Campaign on the West Coast, 1866-1869', *Monthly Review*, v.2 (1890).

McKillop, H. F. *Reminiscences of Twelve Months Service in New Zealand*, London, 1849.

Mair, Gilbert. *The Story of Gate Pa*, Tauranga, 1926.

[Maning, F. E.] *History of the War in the North of New Zealand Against the Chief Heke. Told by An Old Ngapuhi Chief, Faithfully Translated by a 'Pakeha Maori'*, Auckland, [1862].

Marjouram, Sergeant. *Memorials of Sergeant Marjouram, Royal Artillery, Including Six Years Service in New Zealand During The Late Maori War*, ed. William White, London, 1863.

Marshall, William Barrett. *A Personal Narrative of Two Visits to New Zealand in His Majesty's Ship Alligator, A.D. 1834*, London, 1836.

Mercer, A. H. H. *Captain Henry Mercer. With an Enquiry into the Causes of his Death*, 2nd. ed., Toronto, 1867.

Mercer, A. H. H. *A Great Contrast, Being a Statement of Facts Concerning His Royal Highness the Duke of Cambridge K. G. and His Treatment of Two British Officers*, Blackheath, 1893.

'More Words on the War', *Southern Monthly Magazine*, July 1864.

Morgan, William. *The Journal of William Morgan Pioneer Settler and Maori War Correspondent*, ed. Nona Morris, Auckland, 1963.

Moss, F. J. *School History of New Zealand*, Auckland, 1889.

Mouat, J. *The New Zealand War of 1863-64-65. Special Report on Wounds and Injuries Received in Battle*, [London, 1866?].

Newland, John. *Diary of John Newland 1841-73*, New Plymouth, 1959.

Newman, A. K. 'A Study of the Causes Leading to the Extinction of the Maori', *TPNZI*, v.14 (1882).

Nihoniho, Tuta. *Narrative of the Fighting on the East Coast with a Monograph on Bush Fighting*, Wellington, 1913.

O'Donnell, H. (ed.) *Historical Records of the 14th Regt.*, Devonport, 1894.

Pasley, Charles. 'A Sketch of the War in New Zealand 1860-61', *Journal of the United Services Institute*, v.6 (1862).

Polack, J. S. *New Zealand: Being a Narrative of Travels and Adventures . . . Between the Years 1831 and 1837*, London, 1838.

Polack, J. S. *Manners and Customs of the New Zealanders. . . .*, London, 1840.

Porter, T. W. R. *Major Ropata Wahawaha. The Story of His Life and Times*, Gisborne, 1897.

Prichard, James Cowles. *Researches into the Physical History of Man*, ed. George W. Stocking, Chicago and London, 1973.

Rees, W. L. and L. *The Life and Times of Sir George Grey, K.C.B.*, 2v., London, 1892.

Rusden, G. W. *Auretanga; Groans of the Maoris*, London, 1888.

Rusden, G. W. *History of New Zealand*, 3v., Melbourne, 1889.

Rusden, G. W. *Tragedies in New Zealand in 1868 and 1881, Discussed in England in 1886, and 1887*, London, 1888.

'Samuel Mitchell and the Victoria Cross', British periodical article, 1864, source unknown, copy in A.T.L.

Saunders, A. *History of New Zealand*, 2v., Christchurch, 1896-9.

Selwyn, G. A. 'New Zealand Part IV: a Letter from the Bishop of New Zealand . . . containing an Account of the Affray between the Settlers and the Natives at Kororareka', *Church in the Colonies*, v.12 (1846).

Servant, C. *Customs and Habits of the New Zealanders, 1838-42*, ed. D. R. Simmons, trans. J. Glasgow, Wellington, etc., 1973.

Sherrin, R. A. A. and J. H. Wallace. *The Early History of New Zealand*, Brett's Historical Series, 1890.

Smith, S. Percy. *Hawaiki: The Original Home of the Maori*, 2nd ed., Christchurch, etc., 1904.

Smythies, R. H. Raymond. *Historical Records of the 40th (2nd Somersetshire) Regiment . . . to 1893*, Devonport, 1894.

Spencer, Herbert. 'The Comparative Psychology of Man', in Biddiss (ed.), *Images of Race.*

Stoney, B. *Taranaki: a Tale of the War . . .* (novel), Auckland, 1861.

Swainson, William. *New Zealand and the War*, London, 1862.

Taylor, R. *Te Ika a Maui, or New Zealand and Its Inhabitants*, London, 1855.

Taylor, R. *The Past and Present of New Zealand With Its Prospects for the Future*, London and Wanganui, 1868.

Te Paerata, Hitiri. *Description of the Battle of Orakau*, Wellington, 1888.

Thomson, Arthur S. *The Story of New Zealand — Past, and Present — Savage and Civilized*, 2v., London, 1859.

Tregear, Edward. *The Aryan Maori*, Wellington, 1885.

Tucker, H. W. *Memoir of the Life and Episcopate of George Augustus Selwyn*, 2v., London, 1879.

Vane, W. L. *The Durham Light Infantry*, London, 1914.

Von Hochstetter, F. *New Zealand*, Stuttgart, 1867.

'The Waikato Campaign', *Southern Monthly Magazine*, May 1864.

Wallace, A. R. *Contributions to the Theory of Natural Selection. . . .*, London, 1870.

Wallace, A. R. 'The Origin of Human Races', in Biddiss (ed.), *Images of Race.*

Wallace, J. H. *Manual of New Zealand History*, Wellington, 1886.

'The War in Auckland', nos. I-IV, *Southern Monthly Magazine*, Sept. 1863-July 1864.

Ward, John. *Information Relative to New Zealand*, 2nd. ed. London, 1840.

Ward, Robert. *Life Among the Maoris. Being a Description of Missionary, Colonial, and Military Achievements*, eds. Thomas Lowe and William Whitby, Toronto, 1872.

Warre, H. J. (ed.) *Historical Records of the 57th Regiment*, London, 1878.

Webb, E. A. H. *History of the 12th (The Suffolk) Regt. 1685-1913*, London, 1914.

Webster, John. *Reminiscences of an Old Settler in Australia and New Zealand*, Christchurch, etc., 1908.

Wells, B. *History of Taranaki*, New Plymouth, 1878.

Whately, Richard. *Miscellaneous Lectures and Reviews*, London, 1856.

Whitmore, G. S. *The Last Maori War in New Zealand under the Self-Reliant Policy*, London, 1902.

Whitworth, R. P. *Hine-Ra, or the Maori Scout: a Romance of the New Zealand War* (novel), Melbourne, 1887.

Williams, John B. *The New Zealand Journal of John B. Williams*, ed. Robert W. Kenny, Salem, 1956.
Wolseley, Garnet. *The Story of a Soldier's Life*, 2v., Westminster, 1903.
Yate, William. *An Account of New Zealand and of the Formation and Progress of the Church Missionary Society's Mission in the Northern Island*, 2nd ed., London, 1835.

B. SECONDARY SOURCES

I. BOOKS

Adams, Peter. *Fatal Necessity: British Intervention in New Zealand 1830-1847*, Auckland, 1977.
Adas, Michael. *Prophets of Rebellion. Millenarian Protest Movements against the European Colonial Order*, Chapel Hill, 1979.
Andersen, J. C., and G. C. Petersen. *The Mair Family*, Wellington, 1956.
Babbage, S. B. *Hauhauism. An Episode in the Maori Wars, 1863-6*, Wellington, 1937.
Banton, Michael. *The Idea of Race*, London, 1977.
Banton, Michael. *Race Relations*, London, 1967.
Barnett, Corelli. *Britain and Her Army, 1509-1970*, London, 1970.
Barthorp, Michael. *To Face the Daring Maoris: Soldiers' Impressions of the First Maori War. 1845-47*, London, 1979.
Best, E. *Tuhoe; Children of the Mist*, 2v., Wellington, 1926.
Binney, Judith, Gillian Chaplin, and Craig Wallace. *Mihaia: the Prophet Rua Kenana and His Community at Maungapohatu*, Wellington, 1979.
Bolt, Christine. *Victorian Attitudes to Race*, London and Toronto, 1971.
Bond, Brian (ed.). *Victorian Military Campaigns*, London, 1967.
Buick, T. Lindsay. *New Zealand's First War*, Wellington, 1926.
Burrow, J. W. *Evolution and Society. A Study in Victorian Social Theory*, Cambridge, 1966.
Caselberg, John (ed.) *Maori is My Name: Maori Historical Writings in Translation*, Dunedin, 1975.
Clark, Paul. *Hauhau: The Pai Marire Search for Maori Identity*, Auckland, 1975.
Cohen, William B. *The French Encounter with Africans: White Responses to Blacks 1530-1880*, Bloomington, 1980.
Cowan, James. *The Adventures of Kimble Bent*, Christchurch, etc., 1911.
Cowan, James. *Hero Stories of New Zealand*, Wellington, 1935.
Cowan, James. *The New Zealand Wars and the Pioneering Period*, 2v., Wellington, 1922-3.
Cowan, James. *Sir Donald McLean*, Dunedin and Wellington, 1940.
Cowan, James. *Tales of the Maori Border*, Wellington, 1944.
Crowder, Michael (ed.). *West African Resistance. The Military Response to Colonial Occupation*, London, 1971.
Cunningham, Hugh. *The Volunteer Force. A Social and Political History*, London, 1975.
Curtin, Philip D. *The Image of Africa*, London, 1965.
Dalton, B. J. *War and Politics in New Zealand 1855-1870*, Sydney, 1967.
Dixon, Norman, F. *On the Psychology of Military Incompetence*, London, 1976.
Ellegard, Alvar. *Darwin and the General Reader; the Reception of Darwin's Theory of Evolution in the British Periodical Press 1859-1872*, Goteborg, 1958.
Elton, G. R. *Political History. Principles and Practice*, New York and London, 1970.
Falls, Cyril. *The Art of War. From the Age of Napoleon to the Present Day*, London, 1961.
Farwell, Byron. *Queen Victoria's Little Wars*, London, 1973.
Farwell, Byron. *For Queen and Country. A Social History of the Victorian and Edwardian Army*, London, 1981.
Featherstone, Donald. *Colonial Small Wars*, London, 1973.
Firth, Raymond. *Primitive Economics of the New Zealand Maori*, London, 1927.
Fortescue, J. W. *A History of the British Army*, 13v., London, 1899-1930.
Fox, Aileen. *Prehistoric Maori Fortifications in the North Island of New Zealand*, Auckland, 1976.

Fussell, Paul. *The Great War and Modern Memory*, Oxford, 1975.

Gann, Lewis H. *Guerillas in History*, Hoover Institution Press, 1971.

Gibson, Tom. *The Maori Wars*, London, 1974.

Gifford, W. H., and H. B. Williams. *The Centenary History of Tauranga*, Dunedin and Wellington, 1940.

Greene, J. C. *Science, Ideology and the World View*, Berkeley, etc., 1981.

Greenwood, William, *The Upraised Hand, or the Spiritual Significance of the Ringatu Faith*, Wellington, 1942.

Griffith, Paddy. *Forward into Battle. Fighting Tactics from Waterloo to Vietnam*, Chichester, 1981.

Grover, Ray. *Cork of War: Ngati Toa and the British Mission; an Historical Narrative*, Dunedin, 1982.

Guy, Jeff. *The Destruction of the Zulu Kingdom—the Civil War in Zululand 1879-1884*, London, 1979.

Harcourt, Melville. *The Day Before Yesterday; a Short History of the Bay of Islands*, Wellington, 1940.

Harries-Jenkins, G. *The Army in Victorian Society*, London, 1977.

Harrop, A. J. *England and the Maori Wars*, London, 1937.

Harrop, A. J. *England and New Zealand, from Tasman to the Taranaki War*, London, [1926].

Headrick, Daniel R. *The Tools of Empire: Technology and European Imperialism in the Nineteenth Century*, New York and Oxford, 1981.

Henderson, J. *Ratana; the Origins and Story of the Movement*, Wellington, 1963.

Holt, Edgar. *The Strangest War*, London, 1962.

Horsman, Reginald. *Race and Manifest Destiny*, Cambridge, Massachusetts, 1981.

Houghton, Walter E. *The Victorian Frame of Mind 1830-1870*, New Haven, 1957.

Howard, Michael. *War in European History*, Oxford, 1976.

Howe, K. R., *Race Relations, Australia and New Zealand. A Comparative Survey 1770-1970*, Auckland, 1977.

Keegan, John. *The Face of Battle*, New York, 1976.

Kelly, Leslie G. *Tainui, the Story of Hoturoa and his Descendants*, Wellington, 1949.

Kennedy, James G. *Herbert Spencer*, Boston, 1978.

Kiernan, V. G. *The Lords of Human Kind*, London, 1969.

Laqueur, Walter. *Guerilla: an Historical and Critical Study*, London, 1977.

Life in Early Poverty Bay, Gisborne, 1927.

Lorimer, D. A. *Colour, Class and the Victorians*, Leicester, 1978.

Luvaas, Jay. *The Education of an Army, British Military Thought 1815-1940*, London, 1964.

McLintock, A. H. (ed.). *An Encyclopaedia of New Zealand*, 3v., Wellington, 1966.

Mackay, Joseph Angus. *Historic Poverty Bay and the East Coast*, 2nd ed., Gisborne, 1966.

Mason, Philip. *A Matter of Honour: an Account of the Indian Army, Its Officers and Men*, London, 1974.

Miller, Harold. *The Invasion of Waikato*, Auckland and Hamilton, 1964.

Miller, Harold. *Race Conflict in New Zealand 1814-1865*, Auckland, 1966.

Morrell, W. P. *British Colonial Policy in the Mid-Victorian Age*, Oxford, 1969.

Morrell, W. P. *The Provincial System in New Zealand*, 2nd ed., Wellington, etc., 1964.

Morris, Donald R. *The Washing of the Spears*, Sphere ed., London, 1981.

Myatt, Frederick. *The Soldiers' Trade. British Military Developments, 1660-1914*, London, 1974.

Oliver, W. H., and Jane M. Thomson. *Challenge and Response: a Study of the Gisborne - East Coast Region*, Gisborne, 1971.

Oliver, W. H., with B. R. Williams (eds). *The Oxford History of New Zealand*, Oxford and Wellington, 1981.

Parham, W. T. *John Roberts, N.Z.C. A Man in His Time. A Life of Lt. Col. John Mackintosh Roberts (1840-1928)*, Whakatane, 1983.

Poliakov, Leon. *The Aryan Myth. A History of Racist and Nationalist Ideas in Europe*, London, 1974 (orig. 1971).

Pool, D. Ian. *The Maori Population of New Zealand 1769-1971*, Auckland, 1977.

Porter, Bernard. *The Lion's Share. A Short History of British Imperialism*, London and New York, 1975.
Reeves, William Pember. *The Long White Cloud: Ao Tea Roa*, London, 1898.
Richardson, F. M. *Fighting Spirit—Psychological Factors in War*, London, 1978.
Roads, C. H. *The British Soldier's Firearm, 1850-64*, London, 1964.
Ross, Hugh. *Te Kooti Rikirangi: General and Prophet*, Auckland, 1966.
Ross, J.O'C. *The White Ensign in New Zealand*, Wellington, etc., 1967.
Rutherford, J. *Hone Heke's Rebellion 1845-46. An Episode in the Establishment of British Rule in New Zealand*, Auckland, 1947.
Rutherford, J. *Sir George Grey*, London, 1961.
Scott, Dick. *Ask That Mountain. The Story of Parihaka*, Auckland, 1975.
Sheppard, Alan. *Sandhurst: the Royal Military College and its Predecessors*, London, 1980.
Shrimpton, A. W., and Alan E. Mulgan. *Maori and Pakeha. A History of New Zealand*, Auckland, 1921.
Simpson, Tony. *Te Riri Pakeha. The White Man's Anger*, Martinborough, 1979.
Sinclair, Keith. *The Origins of the Maori Wars*, Wellington, 1957.
Sinclair, Keith. *A History of New Zealand*, rev. ed., London, 1980.
Shelley, A. B. *The Victorian Army at Home*, London, 1977.
Smith, S. Percy. *Maori Wars of the Nineteenth Century . . .* 2nd ed., Christchurch, 1910.
Sorrenson, M. P. K. *Maori Origins and Migrations*, Auckland, 1979.
Spiers, Edward M. *The Army and Society, 1815-1914*, London and New York, 1980.
Stafford, D. M. *Te Arawa. A History of the Arawa People*, Wellington, 1967.
Te Hurunui, Pei. *King Potatau; an Account of the Life of Potatau Te Wherowhero, the First Maori King*, Wellington, 1960.
Van Creveld, Martin. *Supplying War. Logistics from Wallenstein to Patton*, Cambridge, 1979.
Vayda, A. P. *Maori Warfare*, Wellington, 1960.
Vennell, C. W. *Such Things Were—the Story of Cambridge, New Zealand*, Dunedin and Wellington, 1939.
Ward, Alan. *A Show of Justice. Racial 'Amalgamation' in Nineteenth Century New Zealand*, Auckland, 1978.
Wards, Ian McL. *The Shadow of the Land. A Study of British Policy and Racial Conflict in New Zealand 1832-1852*, Wellington, 1968.
Watson, George. *The English Ideology: Studies in the Language of Victorian Politics*, London, 1973.
Webster, Peter. *Rua and the Maori Millennium*, Wellington, 1979.
Williams, John A. *Politics of the New Zealand Maori*, Seattle, 1969.
Wilson, Ormond. *War in the Tussock, Te Kooti and the Battle of Te Porere*, Wellington, 1961.
Wright, H. M. *New Zealand 1769-1840: Early Years of Western Contact*, Cambridge, Massachusetts, 1959.

II: ARTICLES

Andrews, C. Lesley. 'Aspects of Development, 1870-1890', in I. H. Kawharu (ed.), *Conflict and Compromise. Essays on the Maori since Colonization*, Wellington, 1975.
Bailes, Howard. 'Technology and Imperialism: a Case Study of the Victorian Army in Africa', *Victorian Studies*, v.24, no.1 (1980).
Ballara, Angela. 'The Role of Warfare in Maori Society in the Early Contact Period', *JPS*, v.85, no.4 (1976).
Biddiss, M. D. 'The Politics of Anatomy: Dr Robert Knox and Victorian Racism', *Proceedings of the Royal Society of Medicine*, v.69 (April 1976).
Binney, Judith. 'Christianity and the Maoris to 1840, a Comment', *NZJH*, v.3, no.2 (1969).
Buist, A. G. 'The Maori', in K. W. Thomson (ed.), *The Legacy of Turi: An Historical Geography of Patea County*, Palmerston North, 1976.
Burroughs, Peter. 'The Human Cost of Imperial Defence in the Early Victorian Age', *Victorian Studies*, v.34, no.1 (1980).

Cain, Marvin R. 'A "Face of Battle" Needed: an Assessment of Motives and Men in Civil War Historiography', *Civil War History*, v.28, no.2 (1982).

Dalton, B. J. 'The Military Reputation of Sir George Grey: The Case of Weraroa', *NZJH*, v.9, no.2 (1975).

Dalton, B. J. 'A New Look at the Maori Wars of the Sixties', *Historical Studies, Australia and New Zealand*, v.12, no.46 (1966).

Fisher, Robin. 'Henry Williams' Leadership of the C.M.S. Mission to New Zealand' *NZJH*, v.9, no.2 (1975).

Galbraith, John S. 'Appeals to the Supernatural: African and New Zealand Comparisons with the Ghost Dance', *Pacific Historical Review*, v.51, no.2 (1982).

Gordon, Donald C. 'Colonial Warfare 1815-1970', in Robin Higham (ed.), *A Guide to the Sources of British Military History*, London, 1972.

Headrick, Daniel R. 'The Tools of Imperialism: Technology and the Expansion of European Colonial Empires in the Nineteenth Century', *Journal of Modern History*, v.51, no.2 (1979).

Hight, James. 'The Maori Wars 1843-1972', in J. Holland Rose, A. P. Newton, and E. A. Benians (eds) *The Cambridge History of the British Empire*, 7v., Cambridge, 1933.

Kawiti, Tawai. 'Heke's War in the North', *Te Ao Hou*, no.16 (Oct. 1956).

King, Michael. 'Between Two Worlds', in Oliver and Williams (eds), *The Oxford History of New Zealand*.

Kirk-Greene, Anthony H. M. '"Damnosa Hereditas": Ethnic Ranking and the Martial Races Imperative in Africa', *Ethnic and Racial Studies*, v.3, no.4 (1980).

Marks, Shula, and Anthony Atmore. 'Firearms in Southern Africa: a Survey', *Journal of African History*, v.13, no.4 (1971).

Owens, J. M. R. 'Christianity and the Maoris to 1840', *NZJH*, v.2, no.2 (1968).

Owens, J. M. R. 'New Zealand Before Annexation', in Oliver and Williams (eds), *The Oxford History of New Zealand*.

Parsonson, Ann. 'The Expansion of a Competitive Society: a Study in Nineteenth Century Maori Social History', *NZJH*, v.14, no.1 (1980).

Parsonson, Ann. 'King Tawhiao and the New Maori Monarchy, 1878-1882', paper presented to the conference of New Zealand historians, Wellington, May 1972.

Parsonson, Ann. 'The Pursuit of Mana', in Oliver and Williams (eds), *The Oxford History of New Zealand*.

Ranger, T. O. 'Connexions Between "Primary Resistance" Movements and Modern Mass Nationalism in East and Central Africa', *Journal of African History*, v.9, nos. 3 & 4 (1968).

Robinson, R. E. 'Non-European Foundations of European Imperialism: Sketch for a Theory of Collaboration', in R. Owen and B. Sutcliffe (eds), *Studies in the Theory of Imperialism*, London, 1972.

Ross, Ruth. 'Te Tiriti O Waitangi: Texts and Translations', *NZJH*, v.6, no.2 (1972).

Rutherford, J. 'The Maori Wars', in A. H. McLintock (ed.), *An Encyclopaedia of New Zealand*.

Shy, John. 'The American Military Experience: History and Learning', *Journal of Interdisciplinary History*, v.1, no.2 (1971).

Sinclair, Keith. 'Why are Race Relations in New Zealand better than in South Africa, South Australia, or South Dakota?', *NZJH*, v.5, no.2 (1971).

Sorrenson, M. P. K. 'How to Civilize Savages: Some "Answers" from Nineteenth Century New Zealand', *NZJH*, v.9, no.2 (1975).

Sorrenson, M. P. K. 'Land Purchase Methods and Their Effect on Maori Population, 1865-1901', *JPS*, v.65, no.3 (1956).

Sorrenson, M. P. K. 'The Maori King Movement', in R. M. Chapman and K. Sinclair (eds), *Studies of A Small Democracy: Essays in Honour of Willis Airey*, Auckland, 1963.

Urlich, D. U. 'The Introduction and Diffusion of Firearms in New Zealand 1809-1840', *JPS*, v.79, no.4 (1970).

Ward, Alan. 'Law and Law Enforcement on the New Zealand Frontier 1840-1893', *NZJH*, v.5, no.2 (1971).

Ward, Alan. 'Law and Law Enforcement on the New Zealand Frontier 1840-1893', *NZJH*, v.5, no.2 (1971).

Ward, Alan. 'The Origins of the Anglo-Maori Wars: a Reconsideration', *NZJH*, v.1, no.2 (1967).

Wards, Ian McL. 'The Generalship of Governor Grey 1846-52', in Peter Munz (ed.), *The Feel of Truth. Essays in New Zealand and Pacific History*, Wellington, etc., 1969.

Wesseling, H. L. 'Colonial Wars and Armed Peace, 1870-1914: a Reconnaissance', *Itinerario*, v.5, no.2 (1981).

White, Gavin. 'Firearms in Africa: an Introduction', *Journal of African History*, v.12, no.2 (1971).

Williams, David Owen. 'Racial Ideas in Early Victorian England', *Ethnic and Racial Studies*, v.5, no.2 (1982).

Winks, Robin W. 'The Doctrine of Hau-hauism', *JPS*, v.62, no.3 (1953).

III. THESES

Belgrave, Michael. 'Archipelago of Exiles. A Study of the Imperialism of Ideas: Edward Tregear and John Macmillan Brown', University of Auckland M.A., 1979.

Belich, James. 'Titokowaru's War and Its Place in New Zealand History', Victoria University of Wellington M.A., 1979.

Belich, James. 'The New Zealand Wars 1845-70. An Analysis of Their History and Interpretation', Oxford University D. Phil., 1982.

Every, Annette Julia. 'The War in the North 1844-6', University of N.Z. (Auckland) M.A., 1940.

Hensley, Gerald C. 'The Crisis Over the Withdrawal of the British Troops from New Zealand 1864-1870', University of N.Z. (Canterbury) M.A., 1957.

Howe, K. R. 'Missionaries, Maoris and "Civilization" in the Upper Waikato 1833-63. A Study in Culture Contact, with Special Reference to the Attitudes and Activities of the Rev. John Morgan of Otawhao', University of Auckland M.A., 1970.

Lange, R. T. 'The Revival of a Dying Race: a Study of Maori Health Reform 1900-1918 and its Nineteenth Century Background', University of Auckland M.A., 1972.

Neal, Karen S. 'Maori Participation in the East Coast Wars 1865-72', University of Auckland M.A., 1976.

Salmond, Mary Anne. 'Hui—a Study of Maori Ceremonial Gatherings', University of Pennsylvania Ph.D., 1972.

Sanderson, K. M. '"These Neglected Tribes": A Study of the East Coast Maoris and Their Missionary, William Williams', University of Auckland M.A., 1980.

Sinclair, Karen Phyllis. 'Maramatanga: Ideology and Social Process Among the Maoris of New Zealand', Brown University Ph.D., 1976.

Wilton, H. G. 'The South Island and the Taranaki War, 1860-1861', University of Otago M.A., 1973.

Index

Note: *passim* = scattered throughout the pages indicated.
et passim = explanatory first reference or references on pages indicated, and scattered throughout the pages thereafter.

Afghan resistance, 291
Ahikereru, 277
Ahitana, 273
Aitanga-a-Mahaki, 210, 217
Alexander, Col. J. E., 192
American Civil War, 294-5, 297
American War of Independence, 131
Andrews, W. P., 328
Arawa, in Waikato War, 126, 128, 168, 178, 194; campaigns of 1864-8, 208, 210-12; in Te Kooti's War, 220, 264-6, 276, 278-86; in Titokowaru's War, 269, post-war, 308
Arawa Flying Column, 285-6
Armed Constabulary, 214 *et passim*; assessments, 238-9, 280
Armitage, James, 136
Armstrong guns, 17, 170, 182-3, 189, 295, 322
'Aryan Maori' theory, 300, 310
Ashanti resistance, 294
Ashwell, B. Y., 292, 328
Atkinson, A. S., 87, 333
Atkinson, Capt. H. A. (Harry), 85-86, 109
Auckland, 20, 219, 249, 279, 329; during Northern War, 30, 36, 37, 41, 55, 65; during Taranaki War, 86, 114; during Waikato War, 119, 122, 125, 133, 135, 161, 170, 176, 178, 188-9, 198; alleged Maori threats to, 90, 104, 119, 124; Maori trade with, 129, 103-4; Militia and Volunteers, 126; Province, 76, 103, 125
Auckland *Punch*, 273
Aukati, 175, 203
Austen, Lieut-Col. C. W., 148-9
Australia, 58, 254, 269, 299; New Zealand trade, 30, 114, 127; press attitude to wars, 77, 180; as source of troops, 36, 41, 66, 99, 123, 126, 139, 253. *See also* Sydney
Avon, s.s., 135, 139, 161-2

Baker, Capt., 169
Balneavis, Lieut. H. C., 61
Barclay, Lieut. E., 39-40, 83
Barthorp, Michael, 47

Bay of Islands, 29-70 *passim*
Bay of Plenty, 203, 216, 219, 275
Beckham, Thomas, 30, 33-34, 37, 39-40
Bell Block, 106
Belmont, 295
Bennet, Lieut. G., 25
Bent, Kimble, 272-3
Biggs, Maj. R. N., 214, 222, 227-9
Boers, 291, 294
Bolt, Christine, 325
Bond, Brian, 12, 146
Booth, Lieut-Col. H. G., 183
Booth, James, 240
Bowdler, Capt. John, 93-94
Bowen, G. F., 211, 240, 253-4
Brassey, Maj. W., 207
Bridge, Maj. Cyprian, 51-53
'Britain of the South', 330
Brooke, Lieut. C. F., 95
Brown, A. N., 195
Brown, H. H., 87
Brown, J. Macmillan, 300
Browne, Thomas Gore, 76-116 *passim*, 119, 123
Bryce, John, 307
Buck, Capt. George, 320
Buck, Peter, 309
'Buck's Bravos', 320. *See also* 'Wellington Rifles'
Buick, T. Lindsay, 16
Bulwer Lytton, E. G. E. (compared with Grey), 125
Burrow, J. W., 327
Burrows, Robert, 50-51, 55-56, 58, 103, 198, 328
'Bush-scouring' theory, 213-15

Calwell, C. E., 331
Cameron, Lieut-Gen. Duncan Alexander, 119, 124-5, 220, 292-3, 306, 319, 329, 333: Waikato War, 133-200 *passim*; Wanganui campaign, 206-8, 215; assessment, 127, 165, 190-1, 317-18
Camerontown, 136-7, 141
Campbell, Gen. Colin (opinion of Cameron), 127

Campbell, Ensign J., 39-40, 58
Carberry, Andrew Dillon, 156
Carey, Brig.-Gen. G. J., 168-71, 176
Carey, Lieut.-Col. Robert, 81, 87, 96, 105, 109-10, 115-16, 127, 316
Carleton, Hugh, 60, 70
Carlyle, Thomas, 155, 322, 328
Carroll, James, 309
Cawnpore Massacre (compared with Poverty Bay), 229
Chad, 294
Chandler, D. G., 11
Chatham Islands, 216-19, 222, 225-6, 230, 262, 275-6, 287
Church Missionary Society, 328
Chute, Maj.-Gen. W. C. T., 207-8, 214, 236, 251
Clark, Paul, 204-5
Clyde, Lord, see Campbell, Gen. Colin
Colenso, William, 326
Collinson, Capt. T. B., 61, 64
Colonial Defence Force, 126, 163
Colonial Office (British), 119-20, 123-4, 198. See also Imperial government
Commissariat Transport Corps, 124, 126-7, 138-9
Confiscation, 126, 194, 198, 200, 203
Cook, James, 19
Cowan, James, 16, 53, 153, 166, 168, 241, 272, 320-1
Cracroft, Capt. Peter, 84-88, 313, 333
Creveld, Martin Van, 127
Crimean War, 22, 23, 47, 53, 127, 313
Crowder, Michael, 12
'Crow's Nest', 260, 265
Curacoa, H.M.S., 139

Dalton, B. J., 15, 77, 115, 124-5, 133, 188, 207
Darwin and Darwinism, 299, 323, 325
Davis, Capt., 214
Davis, Richard, 65, 69
De Surville, Jean, 19
Defence Office (colonial), 225, 280
Despard, Col. Henry, 45-64 passim, 315
Drury, 124, 134, 136, 139

East Cape, 132, 177, 216
'East Coast Expedition', 208
'East Coast War', 208
East India Company (forces in New Zealand), 59
Edwards, James (Himi Manuao), 162-3, 165
Egmont, Mount (Mount Taranaki), 207-8, 236, 253, 269
El-Kadr, Abd, 291, 294
Enfield rifle, 22, 146, 194, 214
English Civil War, 77
Epiha Tokohihi, 91-92, 99, 102
Esk, H.M.S., 184
Ethiopian resistance, 291

Falls, Cyril, 331

Farrar, Frederic William, 325
Farwell, Byron, 23
'Fatal Impact' theory, 299-301, 323-4, 326
Featherston, Isaac, 253-4
Featon, John, 319
'Fighting Mac', 281, 320. See also McDonnell, Thomas
Firth, J. C., 256, 283
FitzRoy, Robert, 21, 29-58 passim, 65-68, 70, 119, 304
Flank companies, 52, 92
Forest Rangers, 126, 138, 172-3, 214, 238
Fort Arawa, 264-5
Fort Fraser, 264
Fort Richmond, 264
Fort St. John, 264
Fortescue, J. W., 16, 97
Fox, William, 133, 174, 192, 207, 280-1, 319
Foxton, 254
Fraser, Maj. James, 214, 222-3, 265-6, 284
Fussell, Paul, 11

Gabion, 108, 113
Galton, Francis, 325
Gamble, Lieut-Col. D. J., 127, 192, 194, 319
Gann, Lewis H., 331
Gascoyne, Lieut. F. J. W., 229-30, 233, 262
Gate Pa (or Pukehinahina), 178-96, 199, 247, 295-7, 314
Gilbert, Thomas, 87-88
Gold, Col. C. E., 81-86, 92, 96-97, 99, 101, 104-5
Gordon, Donald C., 12
Goring, Capt. F. Y. 214, 239
Gorst, John, 129, 292
Grace, Morgan S., 87, 97
Grant, Capt. W. E., 53
Graspan, 295
Great South Road, 122, 124, 134-5, 138
Greaves, Capt. G. R., 127, 184, 317-18
Green, Ensign, 148-9
Greer, Lieut.-Col. H. H., 176-8, 181, 188-91, 196
Grey, George, 29, 56-70 passim, 73-77, 90, 116, 119-211 passim, 303, 317; assessment,* 58, 120-1, 211
Gudgeon, T. W., 224, 257, 285, 320-1
Guy, Jeff, 331-2

Hadfield, Octavius, 79, 180
Haig, Field-Marshal Douglas, 318
Hairini, 163-5
Hakaraia, 204, 210, 219, 280, 283-4, 286
Hamilton-Browne, G., 320-1
Hamlin, F. E., 231
Hamuora Tairoa, 230
Handley's Farm, 274
Hangatiki, 122, 129, 160, 164, 175
Haowhenua, 239, 241
Hapurona, 92, 98, 177
Harington, Lieut.-Col. Philip, 280

Haughton, C. E., 253
'Hauhau', 'Hauhauism', see Pai Marire
Haultain, T. M. (Defence Minister), 220, 225, 253, 258, 260, 269, 280, 333
Hawke's Bay, 167, 210, 219-20, 232
Hay, Commander George, 183
Hazard, H.M.S., 36-38, 40
Headrick, Daniel R., 293
Heke, Hone, 29-70 *passim*, 74, 79, 104, 198, 267, 304-5
Herrick, Lieut.-Col. J. L., 224, 277-8, 282
Hight, James, 17, 318-19
Hikurangi, 55, 59
Hiruhama, 276-7
Hobson, William, 21
Hokianga, 34
Holt, Edgar, 47, 146
Horotiu River, 164
Hotene Porourangi, 265
Howard, Michael, 11
Huirangi, 100, 107-9, 111-12
Hulme, Lieut.-Col. William, 41-43, 45, 47
Hunter, Maj. W. M., 239, 241, 243, 250, 251
Hunua Ranges, 135
Hutt Valley, 254

Ihaia Te Kirikumara, 76, 93
Ihaka Whanga, 210, 277
Imperial government, 123-5, 199. *See also* Colonial Office
Isandlawhna, 332

Jackson, Lieut., 94
Jamaica Rebellion, 229, 328
James, Mrs, 228
Jones, H. Stanley, 127

Kahuroa, Petera, 219
Kaihihi, 101, 107
Kai-iwi Stream, 236, 260
Kaikohe, 56, 67
Kapotai *hapu*, 37-38, 67
Katene Tu-whakaruru, 239, 243
Katikara, 119-20, 190-2
Kauhanganui, 307
Kawakawa River, 58
Kawanatanga, 21
Kawau Island, 197-9
Kawhia, 103, 144
Kawiti, 29-70 *passim*, 79, 104, 188, 198, 267, 297, 304-5
Keegan, John, 11
Kemp, James, 38, 40
Kepa te Rangihiwinui, 212, 238, 241-3, 245, 248, 250, 252, 269, 281-2, 284-6, 308
Ketemarae, 236
Kihikihi, 166
King Country, 280, 283, 286, 306
King Movement, 75-80, 203, 301, 303, 322; in Taranaki War, 83, 89-91, 102-4, 116; in Waikato War, 119-200 *passim*, 211, 267, 305;

during conflicts of 1864-8, 205, 210, 215; involvement with Te Kooti and Titokowaru, 225, 255-6, 258, 269-70, 277, 279-81, 283, 286; post-war, 305-7, 309-10; military forces, 82, 99, 101-3, 109, 128-32, 144-5, 157, 292-3
Kingi, Wiremu, 76, 79-80, 82, 90-92, 96, 102, 104-5, 116, 191
Kirikiri, 135
Knox, Robert, 323, 325
Koheroa, 133-4, 175, 190-2
Koheroa, s.s., 161, 163
Kopu Parapara, 210
Kororareka, 29-30, 33-34, 36-41, 43, 50, 56, 66, 69-70, 304, 314
Kotahitanga, 309
Kotuku, Peita, 277
Kukutai, Paora, 87
Kukutai, Waata, 136
Kupapa, 207, 211-13 *et passim*

Lambert, Maj. Charles, 227
Last, Maj. E., 74
Lawrence, William, 325, 328
Leach, Capt., 208
Leslie, Lieut.-Col. Arthur, 100, 147-8, 150, 174
Lewis, Lieut. A. H., 151
Lord (Kororareka settler), 66
Lorimer, D. A., 327
Loring, Commodore William, 86, 99-100, 105
L-Pa, 82-83, 98, 191
Lubbock, John, 325
Lyon, Lieut.-Col. W. C., 268

McDonnell brothers, 214
McDonnell, Lieut.-Col. Thomas, 208, 214, 220-1, 236, 239-48, 250, 268, 281-4
McKenna, Colour-Serg. E., 137
McLean, Donald, 109-10, 220-1, 231-3, 262-4, 280-1, 285, 306-7, 333
McLean, Edward Baker, see Makarini, Eru Peka
Mackay, James, 196
Mahoetahi, 101, 109, 119, 190-2
Maiki Hill, Kororareka, 33, 36
Mair, Gilbert (senior), 37
Mair, Lieut. Gilbert, 285-6, 320
Mair, W. G., 149, 154, 276, 320
Makaretu, 230-3, 333
Makarini, Eru Peka, 219, 222, 231, 233, 278, 284-5
Maketu (Ngapuhi chief), 30
Maketu (locality), 178
Manawatu, 74, 128, 168, 254, 257, 305
Manawatu River, 74
Manga-pukatea, 160
Mangakawa Ranges, 175
Mangatawhiri Stream, 133
Mangotahi Stream, 242
Maning, F. E., 43, 69, 308, 329, 334
Mantelet, see sap-roller
Manuao, Himi, see Edwards, James

Maori artillery, 292-3
Maori members of Parliament, 309
Maoritanga, 306, 309
Maraetahi, 286
Martin, William, 79
Martin's Farm, 134-6
Mason, Philip, 11
Mataitawa, 92, 112
Matamata, 122, 160, 164, 198, 283
Matarikoriko, 108, 110, 112
Matata, 178, 277
'Matavia Pass', 36, 39
Matawhero, 228-9
Maungapohatu, 277
Maungatautari, 129, 158, 164, 166-8, 171, 175
Maunsell, Robert, 154, 156, 328
Mayne, Commander H. G., 152
Mercer, Capt. H. A., 152
Meremere, 129-30, 133-5, 139-42, 145, 147-8,
    160-1, 165, 191, 292-3
Messenger, Capt., 93-96, 98
Messenger, Edward, 87
Meurant, Edward, 66
Middleton, Gen. Frederick, 317
Military Settlers, *see* Waikato Militia
Military Train (battalion of, in New Zealand),
    126
Milner, Alfred (compared with Grey), 125
Minie bullet, 22
Modder River, 295
Mohaka, 276-7, 279, 287
Mokau, 269
Monro, David, 256
Morgan, John, 102-3, 114, 197
Morgan, William, 156
Morrison, Capt. H. C., 239
Moturoa, 248-55, 258, 260, 267, 271, 296
Mouat, James, 127, 329
Mould, Col. T. R., 109-11, 116
Moule, Lieut.-Col., 284
Moutoa, 205, 212
'Moveable Column', 138, 184
Muaupoko, 73
Murphy, Lieut., 148-9
Murray, Lieut.-Col. G. F., 84-86, 105
Musket Wars, 20, 21, 46, 49-50, 73, 131, 296

Nama, 219, 226
Napier, 210, 212, 220-4, 227, 231, 254, 263
Native Land Court, 305, 308
Nelson, 20, 21, 238
Nelson Examiner, 316
Nelson, Horatio, 314
Nelson, Maj. Thomas, 92-98, 177
Nera, Wiremu, 158
'New Institutions', 119-20, 303
New Plymouth, 20, 79-116 *passim*, 207, 238,
    255, 269, 277, 303; disease among towns-
    people of, 100, 105, 112
New Zealand Company, 20, 21, 73
New Zealand Herald, 197

New-Zealander, 57, 61, 65, 69, 154, 314
Newcastle, Duke of (Secretary of State for the
    Colonies), 123-5, 158, 163
Newman, Alfred K., 299
Ngai-Tama, 211
Ngai-te-Rangi, 128, 140, 176-8, 185-9, 192-6,
    247
Ngapora, Tamati, 280
Ngapuhi, 29-70 *passim*, 87, 128, 198, 308
Ngarauru, 128, 236, 239, 248, 253, 270
Ngaruahine, 235-48 *passim*, 268
Ngaruawahia, 158, 160-2
Ngatai, Hori, 187
Ngatapa, 212, 220-1, 227, 231-3, 258, 260-8,
    275, 279, 283, 287, 320
Ngati Apa, 73
Ngati Apakura, 145
Ngati Awa, 128, 194, 275
Ngati Haua, 101, 128, 140, 144-5, 158, 164, 168,
    171, 175, 198, 306
Ngati Hinetu, 167. *See also* 'Waikato proper'
Ngati Hineuru *hapu*, 210, 217, 219, 222
Ngati Kahungunu, in Waikato War, 128, 167;
    in conflicts of 1864-8, 205, 210, 212; in Te
    Kooti's War, 219-20, 222, 224-6, 230-3,
    263-4, 276-7, 281-2, 285; post-war, 308-9
Ngati Koheriki *hapu*, 178, 187
Ngati Kowhatu *hapu*, 222, 225
Ngati Mahanga, 167. *See also* 'Waikato proper'
Ngati Mahuta, 144, 167. *See also* 'Waikato proper'
Ngati Manawa, 168, 276
Ngati Maniapoto, in Taranaki War, 91, 94; in
    Waikato War, 128, 136, 140, 145, 158, 164,
    166-8, 170, 175, 198; intervention in Tito-
    kowaru's War, 256, 269; relations with Te
    Kooti, 280; post-war, 306
Ngati Maru, 128
Ngati Mihi *hapu*, 226
Ngati Pahauwera *hapu*, 276-7
Ngati Paoa, 128, 134, 140, 144-5
Ngati Pikiao, 194
Ngati Porou, in Waikato War, 126, 128, 167, 194;
    in conflicts of 1864-8, 205, 208, 210, 212;
    in Te Kooti's War, 220, 227, 231-3, 263-6,
    286; in Titokowaru's War, 269; post-war,
    308
Ngati Pukeko, 276
Ngati Rangitahi *hapu*, 73
Ngati Rangiwewehi, 194
Ngati Raukawa, of Manawatu, 73, 128; of North
    Taupo, 128, 140, 164, 166-7, 170-1, 173,
    175, 283, 306
Ngati Ruanui, 119, 203, 206, 303; in Taranaki
    War, 76, 82, 84, 96, 104, 115; in Waikato
    War, 128, 177; in Titokowaru's War, 235-
    57 *passim*, 270, 287
Ngati Tamaoho, 153
Ngati te Kohera *hapu*, 167
Ngati Toa, 21, 73
Ngati Tuwharetoa, 128, 145, 167, 171, 210,
    219, 279, 281-3, 306

Ngati Whatua, 128
Ngati Whauroa *hapu*, 126, 136
Ngatihine, 144. *See also* 'Waikato proper'
Ngatiteata, 144. *See also* 'Waikato proper'
Nicholl, Ensign Spencer Perceval, 181
Niger, H.M.S., 84, 86
'Nigger' (British use of), 329
Nikora, 219, 222
Nikora te Tuhi, 286
Nixon, Lieut.-Col. M., 163
Nopera Panakaraeo, 58
Northcroft, Capt. H. W., 239
Northern War, 21, 22, 29-70, 73, 75, 81, 83, 95,
    98, 211, 215, 267, 304-5, 313, 324, 331, 334
Nott, J. C., 323, 325
Nukumaru, 206-7, 215, 253
Number Three Redoubt, 109, 111, 215

Oakura, 119-20, 124, 205
Ohaeawai, 45-57, 61, 63, 65, 67, 245, 292, 295-7,
    315
Ohiwa, 276
Okotuku, 251
Omapere, Lake, 41, 67
Omaramutu, 286
Omaranui, 210, 217, 219
Omata, 84, 106
Onehunga, 136
Onewhero Bay, 41
Onukukaitara, 92-94, 98
Opepe, 279
Opotiki, 204, 208, 210, 225, 276-7
Orakau, 16, 130, 160, 164-75, 181, 186, 191,
    197, 199-200, 210, 266-7, 296, 300, 314, 319,
    329
Orangakiwa, 278
Ormond, J. D., 281, 284
Otago, 126, 198, 274
Otago Witness, 254, 325
Otapawa, 207
Otautu, 269, 275
Otoia, 248-9
Owens, J. M. R., 300
Oweta, 262

Pai Marire, 204-5 *et passim*
Paihia, 34
Pakakohe, 236, 239, 248, 252, 270
Panapa, 210
Paparata, 130, 133, 135, 137-8, 140
Paparatu, 221-2, 224, 226
Parihaka, 16, 235, 270, 306-7
Parris, Robert Reid, 87, 273
Parsonson, Ann, 300-1
Patea, 236, 238, 244, 248-50, 253, 255, 260
Patea Field Force, 238, 241, 243
Patea Rangers, 214
Paterangi, 129-30, 133, 160-6, 175, 292
Patuone, 29
Patupou, 144. *See also* 'Waikato proper'
Patutahi, 227-8, 230-1

Pauatahanui, 74
Pekerangi, 49-50, 167
Pene Taka, 188
Pennefather, Lieut. George, 154-5
Peria, 160, 164
Phelps, Capt., 148-9
Philpotts, Lieut. G., 39-40, 53
Pihareinga, 52
Pikopiko (or Puketoke), 160, 162
Pioneer, s.s., 139, 161, 293
Pipiriki, 207
Piri Rakau, 192, 210
Pokeno Ranges, 135
Polack's Stockade, 36-37, 40
Poliakov, Leon, 327
Polygenism, 323, 325
Pomare, 41, 56, 59, 65, 74
Potae, Henare, 227
Potatau Te Wherowhero, King, 75-76, 91, 132,
    200
Poutu, Camp, 281
Poverty Bay, 216-19, 221-9, 240, 253-4, 256-8,
    260-5, 277, 287
Poverty Bay Campaign, 227-34, 258, 263
Pratt, Maj.-Gen. T. S., 81, 97, 99-101, 105,
    107-16
Preece, Lieut. G. A., 214, 281, 285-6
Prichard, J. C., 325, 328
Pukearuhe, 269-70, 306
Pukehinahina, *see* Gate Pa
Pukekawa, 130, 133, 135-7, 140
Pukekohe East, 137
Puketakauere, 82, 89-107 *passim*, 157, 168, 177,
    247, 295-6, 314
Puketapu, 221-7
Puketutu, 35, 41-45, 50, 63, 67, 104, 313
Puniu River, 164, 166-8, 175

'Queenites', 125-6 *et passim*
Queen's Redoubt, 134-6, 139, 141

Raglan, 141
Rangatiratanga, 21
Ranger, T. O., 331
Rangiaowhia, 122, 160-5, 197
Rangiatea, 160
Rangiriri, 130, 133, 142-60, 164, 175, 181, 187,
    190, 197-9, 296, 320
Rangitane, 73
Rangitikei, 254
Rarawa, 58, 128
Ratana, T. W. (and Ratana Movement), 308-9
Raupora, 276
Rawiri Puhirake, 177-8, 185-90, 193
Reeves, W. P., 17, 47
Regiments: 12th (1st battalion), 148-51; 14th
    (2nd battalion), 148-51, 153; 18th, 253; 40th,
    92-93, 147, 172, 174, 314, 329; 43rd, 178,
    180-1, 183-4, 186, 189, 192, 314; 50th, 163;
    58th, 41, 52, 317; 65th, 148-51, 153, 155;
    68th, 181-2, 184, 186, 189; 96th, 36, 314;

99th, 52
Regnier, Euloge, 225
Rere, 227
Rewi Maniapoto, 76, 131, 140, 160, 164, 166-75, 266, 280, 282, 287
Rewi's Last Stand, 166
Rice, H. E., 196
Richardson, Capt. W. A., 222-3
Richmond, J. C., 95, 109, 111, 113, 220, 262-6, 277-8
Riemenschneider, J. F., 87
Rifleman, 217-18, 221
Ring, Capt. James T., 169
Ringatu, 218-19 *et passim*
Roberts, Field-Marshal Frederick (compared with Cameron), 127
Roberts, Maj. J. M., 239, 241, 243, 265
Robertson, Commander David, 37-39
Robinson, Ronald, 303
'Romantic Anglo-Saxonism', 326
Rongowhakaata, 128, 203, 210, 212, 217, 220, 225, 230, 233
Ropata Wahawaha, 208, 212, 220, 231-2, 263-6, 285
Rorke's Drift (compared with Turuturu-Mokai), 241
Ross, Ruth, 21
Rotoaira, Lake, 282
Rotorua, 102, 210, 284-5
Rua Kenana, 307, 309
Ruakituri, 221-4, 226
Ruapekapeka, 52, 58-66, 292, 316, 333
Ruaruru, 242
Ruatahuna, 277-9
Russo-Japanese War, 297
Russo-Turkish War of 1877-8, 294, 297
Rutherford, James, 65, 146
Ryan, Maj., 184

St. George, Capt. J. C., 281
St. Hill, Lieut. W. H., 127, 149, 151
St. John, Lieut.-Col. J. H. H., 214, 268, 277-9
Sandhurst, 317
Sap-roller, 108, 113
Selwyn, George Augustus, 38, 77, 162, 164, 328
Senegal, 294
Sentry Hill, 205
Seymour, Capt. Beauchamp, 92
Shaka, 291
Shamil, 291, 294
Sikh Wars, 24, 58, 294
Sinclair, Keith, 17, 77
Sitting Bull, 291
Smith, S. P., 300
Smith, T. H., 188
Sokoto, 294
Somme, The, 295
Sorrenson, M. P. K., 301, 306
South African War (Second), 291, 294-5, 320, 322
Southern Cross, 115, 174
Spencer, Herbert, 323, 325-6

Stafford, E. W., 114, 220, 253-4, 278, 280
Strange, Capt., 148
Sturt, s.s., 262
Sudanese resistance, 291, 297
Swainson, William, 329
Swindley, Capt. F., 239
Sydney, 22, 161

Tainui tribes, 75, 103. *See also* Waikato tribes
Takapau, 139
Taku Forts (effect of Armstrong guns on), 182
Tamaikowha, Eru, 211, 276
Tamehana, Wiremu, 76, 109, 131-2, 140, 144, 153, 158, 163-4, 166-8, 171, 175
Tangahoe, 236, 239, 248, 270
Tapapa, 283-4, 334
Taranaki, during Taranaki War, 79-116 *passim*, 122, 129, 236, 294-5, 305; so-called 'Second Taranaki War', 119-20, 176; conflicts of 1864-8, 203-4, 208, 213; Titokowaru's War, 235, 269-70; North Taranaki, 208, 256, 269, 281; South Taranaki, 105, 206-7, 216, 235-6, 239-40, 271, 273, 306-7
Taranaki Herald, 95
Taranaki tribe, 76, 82, 84, 96, 104, 115, 119, 128, 140, 204-5, 253
Taranaki War, 76-116, 119, 123, 130-1, 140, 154, 211, 213-15, 297, 303, 315, 324, 328; 'Second Taranaki War', 120
Tareha te Moananui, 210, 230-2
Tasman, Abel, 19
Tatahoata, 278
Tataraimaka, 106, 115-16, 119-20
Taua muru, 35, 66
Tauaroa, 276-7
Taumarunui, 283
Taupo, 102, 131, 145, 216, 225, 279-81, 284, 287
Tauranga, 102, 128, 131, 176-97 *passim*, 199, 210, 264
Tauranga Campaign, 128, 130, 133, 177-96, 324, 332
Tauranga Harbour, 176-9
Tauranga-ika, 247, 253, 255, 267-75, 287
Tauranga-Taupo, 282
Tawhai, Mohi, 29, 61
Tawhiao Te Wherowhero, King, 76, 132, 144, 153, 204-5, 256, 280, 283, 306-7
Taylor, B. K., 326
Taylor, Richard, 326
Telford, John, 61
Te Ahuahu, 29, 35, 45-46, 57, 63
Te Arei, 108-10, 112-13, 130, 295, 297
Te Atiawa, 73, 76, 82-83, 91-93, 104, 109, 112, 115, 128, 253
Te Awamutu, 162-3, 164, 168
Te Hapua, 286
Te Heuheu, Piripi, 166
Te Heuheu Horonuku, 145, 171, 281-2
Te Kahakaha, 45
Te Kiri-Karamu, Heni (Heni Pore), 186-7
Te Kohia, *see* L-Pa

Te Koneke, 221-4, 226
Te Kooti Rikirangi Te Turuki, 203-4, 210-35 *passim*, 240, 252-67 *passim*, 270, 274-88, 292, 305, 320, 322, 333-4
Te Kooti's War, 216-34, 260-7, 275-88
Te Mamaku, Topine, 73-74, 283
Te Ngaere, 269
Te Ngaio, 206-7, 215
Te Ngutu o te Manu, 225-6, 236, 240-8, 250, 252-4, 271, 296
Te Paerata, 166
Te Papa, Camp, 176, 178, 188-9
Te Pononga, 282
Te Porere, 282-3, 287, 334
Te Porunu, 276
Te Puea Herangi, 307
Te Puke, 284
Te Ranga, 189-97
Te Rangihaeata, 21, 73-74, 76
Te Rangitahau, 219, 222, 279, 281
Te Rauparaha, 21, 74, 304
Te Rore, 161
Te Taonui, Makoare, 29, 45, 59, 63
Te Tiki o te Ihingarangi, 175-6
Te Ua Haumene, 204-5
Te Waru Tamatea, 210, 219, 226, 276, 285
Te Wharepu, 144, 148, 153, 157-8
Te Whenua-nui, 166
Te Wheoro, Wiremu, 136
Te Wherowhero, *see* Potatau Te Wherowhero
Te Whiti o Rongomai, 204, 235, 270, 306-8
Te Winitana Tupotahi, 170
Teira, 76, 79
Terry and Calisher carbine, 214
Thames, 129, 135, 141
'The Bluff' (Te Ia), 139
The Times, 226, 314
Thomas, Capt. W. E., 218
Thomson, A. S., 326
Tikaokao, 131, 140, 280, 282
Tikitiki, 208
Tioriori, 144
Titokowaru, Riwha, 64, 177, 203-4, 212-13, 216, 225, 235-308 *passim*, 317-18, 320, 330, 333
Titokowaru's War, 204, 215-16, 235-57, 267-75, 324
Toi Whakataka, 239
Tokaanu, 280-2, 284
Tokangamutu, 280
Tolaga Bay, 286
Tomoana, Henare, 224, 230, 281-2
Topia Turoa, 283-4
Totara, 269-70
Traverse, 49-50, 108
Tregear, Edward, 300
Tuakau, 136-7
Tuhi-Karamea, 161-2
Tuhoe, 128, 166-7, 170-2, 210, 225-6, 261, 275-8, 285-6, 307, 309
Tuhua, 283
Tuke, Arthur, 233

Turanganui, 210, 221, 227-8, 230-3
Turuturu-Mokai, 241

Ulundi, 331-2
Urewera, 216, 221, 225, 275-9, 284-5, 306-7, 309, 320

Victoria Cross, 86
Victoria, Queen, 133
Volkner, C. S., 204-5, 208
Von Tempsky, Gustavus, 173, 180, 192-3, 214, 239, 241-4, 316, 324, 329

Waddy, Brig.-Gen. R., 206
Waerenga-a-Hika, 210, 217, 219
Waihi (Camp Waihi), 236, 241-4, 246
Waikare, Lake, 143, 145, 147, 152
Waikaremoana, Lake, 221, 276-8, 285
Waikato, 75, 206, 210, 256, 283, 306; in Taranaki War, 90-91, 102-3, 109, 112, 115; in Waikato War, 126-200 *passim*, 294-5; British plans for invasion of, 116, 119-20, 122-5; Upper Waikato, 122; Central Waikato, 176, 200, 284; Lower Waikato, 133, 136, 139-41
Waikato Heads, 136-8
Waikato Lines, 133, 142-3, 175, 199. *See also* Meremere, Rangiriri, Paterangi
Waikato Militia (or 'Military Settlers'), 126-7, 139, 189, 198, 214
'Waikato proper' tribe, 126, 128, 144-5, 158, 167, 197, 200
Waikato River, 122, 130, 133, 135, 139, 143, 147
Waikato tribes, 205, 256, 280; in Taranaki War, 88-90, 96, 104, 111, 114-15; in Waikato War, 129, 132, 144, 197, 199. *See also* Tainui tribes, King Movement, 'Waikato proper' tribe, Ngati Maniapoto, Ngati Haua, Ngati Raukawa
Waikato War, 24, 76-81, 103-4, 119-200, 203-4, 207, 211, 215, 220, 255-6, 291-2, 297, 305, 315, 324, 328, 333
Waimate, 46
Waingongoro River, 206, 236, 240-3, 248, 270
Waipa (river and district), 158, 161. *See also* Waikato (Upper Waikato)
Waipaoa, 286
Wairau Affray, 21, 73, 304
Waireka, 82, 84-88, 92, 105-7, 313, 333
Wairoa (Auckland Province), 135
Wairoa (Hawke's Bay), 210, 221-3, 226-8, 231, 263, 276-8; Upper Wairoa, 219, 226, 285; Lower Wairoa, 226
Wairoa (South Taranaki), 236, 249-50, 253, 255
Waitangi, Chatham Islands, 217
Waitangi, Treaty of, 19, 20-21, 34-35, 55, 78, 80, 302
Waitara, 76, 79-80, 82, 90-91, 109, 113, 116, 119-20; Block, 79, 115, 119; Camp, 91-94, 97, 105, 107; Upper Waitara, 269
Waitara River, 92, 108, 112

Waitotara purchase, 206
Waitotara River, 207, 236, 240, 249
Waiuku, 103-4
Waka Nene, Tamati, 29-30, 33-36, 45-46, 54, 59-61, 63, 65-67, 69-70
Wakefield, Edward Gibbon, 20
Wallace, A. R., 323, 325
Wallace, William, 252
Wanganui, 20, 305, 313, 333; 1847 conflict in, 73-75; conflicts of 1864-8, 199, 203-7, 212; Titokowaru's War, 216, 236-68 passim
Wanganui Rangers, 214
Wanganui River, 308
Wanganui tribes, 73-74, 128, 208, 212, 238, 248-51, 256, 260, 281-6, 306-8; Upper Wanganui, 205, 207; Lower Wanganui, 205, 212
Ward, Alan, 77-78, 300-1, 303
Ward, Robert, 105
Wards, Ian, 15, 61, 73
Warea, 87, 107, 270
Warre, Col. H. J., 316
Weber, C. H., 214
Wellington, 20, 76, 114, 124, 128, 236, 245, 253-5, 257, 262, 305; 1846 conflict in, 73-75; Province, 216, 260
Wellington, Duke of, 48, 314
Wellington Independent, 200
'Wellington Rangers', 238, 244, 246
'Wellington Rifles', 238, 244, 246
Weraroa, 206-7
Western Front (in First World War), 295, 297, 318. See also World War, First
Westrupp, Capt. Charles, 222, 232-3, 263-4
Whakamaru, 284
Whakatane, 275-9, 287
Whakatane River, 277, 279

Whakatohea, 128, 167, 194, 208, 275, 285
Whanau-a-Apanui, 128, 167, 194
Whangaroa mission, 302
Wharekauri, 217
Wharekopae Stream, 230
Whareongaonga, 218, 221-2
Wharepapa, 166
Whatawhata, 161
Whately, Richard, 325
White, Serg. William, 329
Whitecliffs, 269
Whitely, J., 269
Whitmore, Col. G. S., 210, 214, 317, 333; in Titokowaru's War, 238-60 passim, 267-72, 274; in Te Kooti's War, 222-4, 226, 260-6, 277-80; assessment, 220-1, 239, 258
Williams, John A., 301
Williams, Henry, 34-36, 39, 46, 50-51, 55-57, 58, 60-61, 69-70
Williams, W. L. 233
Williams, William, 77, 132, 256-7, 328
Wilson, Lieut. J., 222
Wilson, Ormond, 283
Wiseman, Commodore William, 183, 188-9
Wolseley, Field-Marshal Garnet, 127, 182, 317
World War, First, 187, 320. See also Western Front
Wright, H. M., 301
Wyatt, Lieut.-Col. Alfred, 148

'Young Brigade' (No. 6 Division, Armed Constabulary), 320
'Young Maori Party', 300, 309
Ypres Salient, 297

Zulu resistance, 291, 331-2